Criminal Law

Third Edition

Criminal Law

Sue Titus Reid, J.D., Ph.D.

Florida State University

PRENTICE HALL
Englewood Cliffs, New Jersey 07632

Library of Congress Cataloging-in-Publication Data

Reid, Sue Titus.
    Criminal law / Sue Titus Reid. —3rd ed.
      p. cm.
    Includes indexes.
    ISBN 0-02-399211-5
      1. Criminal law—United States—Cases. I. Title.
KF9218.R38 1995   94-12638
345.73—dc20   CIP
[347.305]

Editor: Christine Cardone
Production Supervisor: WordCrafters Editorial Services, Inc.
Production Manager: Mary Carnis
Cover Designer: Blake Logan
Photo Researcher: Diane Kraut
Illustrations: Carlisle Communications

This book was typeset in New Aster by Carlisle Communications and was printed at von Hoffman Press, Inc. The cover was printed by Lehigh Press.

©1995 by Prentice-Hall, Inc.
A Paramount Communications Company
Englewood Cliffs, New Jersey 07632

Photo Credits: p. 5: AP/Wide World Photos; p. 16: © Catherine Allport/The Image Works; p. 24: © Bob Daemmrich/Stock, Boston; p. 38: UPI/Bettmann; p. 42: © Michael Schwarz/The Image Works; p. 74: Reuters/Bettmann; p. 77: © Michael Siluk/The Image Works; p. 90: © Jeffrey Markowitz/SYGMA; p. 106: © Pickerell/The Image Works; p. 117: Phil Ramey/SYGMA; p. 121: Reuters/Bettmann; p. 147: © L.A. Daily News/SYGMA; p. 148: AP/Wide World Photos; p. 150: © Matthieu Polak/SYGMA; p. 172: Jean-Louis Atlan/SYGMA; p. 196: © Jeffrey Markowitz/SYGMA; p. 225: © Argus Courier/SYGMA; p. 227: AP/Wide World Photos; p. 250: © James Shaffer, PhotoEdit; p. 254: Reuters/Bettmann; p. 272: Bill Nation/SYGMA; p. 283: Sue Titus Reid; p. 288: © Patrick Forestier/SYGMA; p. 302: Les Stone, SYGMA; p. 328: AP/Wide World Photos; p. 350: © M. Stone, Boston Herald/SYGMA; p. 369: Reuters/Bettmann; p. 379: David Bergman/Miami Herald; p. 411: Reuters/Bettmann; p. 416: UPI/Bettmann; p. 473: © Wojnarowicz/The Image Works; p. 478: Courtesy BI Incorporated, Boulder, CO; p. 483: Sue Titus Reid; p. 493: Courtesy American Correctional Association; p. 495: AP/Wide World Photos

Printed in the United States of America
10   9   8   7   6   5   4   3   2

ISBN 0-02-399211-5

Prentice-Hall International (UK) Limited, *London*
Prentice-Hall of Australia Pty. Limited, *Sydney*
Prentice-Hall Canada Inc., *Toronto*
Prentice-Hall Hispanoamericana, S.A., *Mexico*
Prentice-Hall of India Private Limited, *New Delhi*
Prentice-Hall of Japan, Inc., *Tokyo*
Simon & Schuster Asia Pte. Ltd., *Singapore*
Editora Prentice-Hall do Brasil, Ltda., *Rio de Janeiro*

To Roy Black and Mark D. Seiden, attorneys

With my admiration for your contributions
to the legal profession
and your recognition of
the importance of the social sciences to that profession

With gratitude and affection for you and your families

Brief Contents

Contents

Preface

In the preface to my first text, *Crime and Criminology,* published in 1976, I stated that "during my eleven years of teaching . . . undergraduates, I was impressed with their eagerness to learn how law related to traditional topics covered in the [criminology] course, even to the point of enjoying reading judicial opinions." The utilization of a modified case approach to teaching has been very successful, for that text is in its seventh edition.

In the study of criminal law, I believe it is even more important for students to be exposed to fact patterns of actual cases and to appellate judicial opinions of those cases. Yet, it is unrealistic in an undergraduate course to cover the amount of material included in a law school course.

This text uses a modified case approach. The facts of cases and the reproduction of appellate opinions are included to *illustrate* points of law rather than to *extract* points of law. This approach gives undergraduates a sample of the traditional case method utilized in many law courses without burdening the course with the massive amounts of material covered in an introductory criminal law course in law school.

It is important, however, for undergraduates to understand that principles of criminal law vary from state to state and between states and the federal system. Although it is not reasonable to survey all jurisdictions, a sampling of federal and state statutes and cases is utilized to convey the divergence (and in some cases, the agreement) within criminal law.

In recent years many jurisdictions have modified their criminal statutes; some have revised their criminal codes in their entirety. The Model Penal Code, drafted by the American Law Institute and first published in 1962, has influenced many of these revisions. Sections of that code are utilized throughout the text, and Appendix C contains a listing of the sections cited. The English common law, which has been a strong influence on the development of criminal law in the United States, is referred to as well.

The cases in this text are excerpted carefully to exclude complicated criminal procedure issues that are not necessary for an understanding of criminal law. Despite the focus on substantive criminal law rather than criminal procedure, however, it is necessary to discuss some constitutional principles that relate directly to criminal law, and that is done where applicable.

Statutes and case excerpts are included within rather than at the end of the text to facilitate their integration into the discussion of principles. "Focus" boxes are utilized to highlight some statutes, Model Penal Code provisions, and a few cases, but these inserts are designed primarily to supplement the text discussion. Many of these inserts include current events, charts, or summaries that illustrate the principles discussed in the text and are designed to stimulate discussion in light of the current events. International as well as national examples are used. Pictures are used to highlight recent events.

To facilitate the reader's study, each chapter begins with a brief outline of the chapter's contents and a list of Key Terms. Key Terms are boldfaced within the chapters and are included in the Glossary at the end of the text. Each chapter has a detailed summary designed to give the reader an overview of that chapter's material.

Each chapter concludes with Study Questions, which are designed to facilitate the combined purposes of (1) learning substantive criminal law and (2) thinking about criminal law and the problems and issues that it raises. Pictures are used to enhance the reader's interest while relating general principles and laws to current events.

The chapter outline follows that of the third edition, but new topics are added within most of the chapters. All reasonable efforts have been made to have the text current to the time of publication; thus, each legal case citation was checked as late as possible in the production process. But because most of the cases are recent, some will be granted appeals after this text is published. Many areas of criminal law have been changing rapidly, and it is reasonable to expect this trend to continue.

The text begins with a chapter introducing criminal law, raising the issue of which acts should be covered by the criminal law and how society should react to them. Comparisons are made between criminal and civil law, with illustrations such as the Pan Am Flight 103 crash and the Jeffrey Dahmer case. Both involve criminal acts for which individuals may be punished within the criminal law as well as civil actions that provide damages to the crime victims. In addition, Chapter 1 discusses the sources of criminal law as well as the limitations placed on criminal law by the federal and state constitutions. The nature of the adversary system is discussed.

Chapter 2 analyzes the elements of criminal liability, including the criminal act (as well as the failure to act), the criminal state of mind, and the attendant circumstances that must accompany acts for them to be considered criminal. Chapters 3 and 4 cover defenses to criminal acts. Chapter 3 discusses the nature of defenses and covers the more traditional defenses, such as entrapment, defense of persons and property, insanity, and so on. The recent Supreme Court case on entrapment (involving child pornography) is excerpted, and a new section covers *outrageous government conduct*. The recent protests at abortion clinics are utilized to illustrate the attempt to incorporate these behaviors into the traditional necessity defense. The discussion of self-defense is expanded to include its use by police (illustrated by the case of William Lozano) and private citizens as in the killing of a Japanese exchange student in Louisiana.

Chapter 4 covers some of the more recently recognized defenses, such as stress disorders and domestic violence, as well as recent developments in more traditional defenses, such as substance abuse. Featured in particular is the growing area of the *battered person syndrome,* including battered women who kill their husbands and other significant others as well as children who kill their abusive parents. In addition, this chapter includes brief discussions of attempts to raise new defenses, such as the rough sex or the urban psychosis defenses.

Chapter 5's discussion of manslaughter is expanded, including a discussion of involuntary manslaughter, along with recent manslaughter cases such as that of Miami police officer William Lozano and the New York subway crash case. The discussion of euthanasia has been expanded, too, along with the chapter's discussion of the rights of fetuses and how those rights relate to criminal law. Doctor-assisted suicide is discussed, with particular reference to the Michigan case of Dr. Jack Kevorkian.

The organization of Chapter 6, "Crimes against the Person: Part II," has been changed. The chapter begins with a discussion of assault and battery, including a new section on reckless assault and battery. The chapter's discussion of mayhem is illustrated by the recent trials of the Bobbitts, including charges of marital abuse against the husband and malicious wounding by the wife, who cut off her husband's penis. The kidnapping discussion is illustrated with such recent cases as the Exxon case, while statutory rape is illustrated by such notorious cases as that of Amy Fisher. New sections on the following topics have been added: rape trauma and rape victims, continuous child sexual abuse, terrorism and related crimes (including hate crimes, stalking, and highway violence). Particular attention is given to violence against tourists.

Chapter 7, "Property Crimes," has been reorganized, now including three primary sections: serious property offenses, less serious property offenses, and hybrid offenses. The latter includes discussions of robbery, extortion, and a new one, carjacking. A new section on motor vehicle theft is included.

Revisions in Chapter 8 illustrate the rapidly changing nature of the American legal system. For example, the relatively recent New York harassment statutes included in the second edition of this text have been revised significantly, and those changes are reflected in this edition. Likewise, some cases cited in the previous edition of this text, such as that of the New York Transit Authority, were altered on appeal and those changes are reflected. The most recent events, such as the arrest of Heidi Fleiss on prostitution charges, have been included, along with recent changes in regulations concerning carrying weapons. Sodomy statutes are changing rapidly, too, and some of those are discussed.

Chapter 9's discussion of crimes against the government includes such recent events as the arrest, plea, and sentencing of Katherine Ann Power for her 1970 crimes, numerous recent bribery cases, and the police brutality cases associated with the arrest and subsequent treatment of Rodney King by Los Angeles police officers. A discussion of the arrest and pretrial hearings of former football star O. J. Simpson in connection with the murders of his ex-wife and her friend are discussed. The trial was scheduled to begin in late September 1994, after this text was in press. Chapter 10 includes a new section on AIDS and features discussions of how that disease may be related to criminal activity. Chapter 11 includes an analysis of the war on drugs as well as the most recent arrests and convictions in the world of organized crime and new developments in business crimes.

Chapter 12 has been revised extensively. With the continued increase in violence in the United States, sentencing, the focus of Chapter 12, is a hot topic. The chapter discusses recent trends in sentencing, as well as the recent rise in the popularity of sentencing alternatives, such as boot camps. The long and controversial efforts of the U. S. Congress to revise the federal criminal code resulted in the passage of sentencing reform in late August 1994. The Violent Crime Control and Law Enforcement Act of 1994 was signed by President Clinton in September after this text was in press. Although it was too late to incorporate that statute into the text, Appendix D was added to include an overall view of the new statute. Appendix D lists the Table of Contents of the statute. Those headings give an indication of the breadth of topics covered by the statute and provide section number references for those who wish to consult the statute.

Acknowledgments

The revision of a criminal law text is a major effort, for criminal law changes rapidly. Cases and statutes must be checked numerous times from the beginning to the completion of the manuscript. This work is tedious and time consuming, and I am grateful to two research assistants for help with that work. Alisa M. Smith, a graduate student in criminology and a full-time lawyer with the Florida Bar, worked on the project during her "spare time," while Natalya ("Natasha") Zakharova Trogen spent part of her graduate research assistance position in the School of Public Administration and Policy working on this manuscript. Natasha, who came to the United States from Russia only two years ago, learned the American legal system quickly and with a dedication and enthusiasm that were refreshing. Both Alisa and Natasha provided me with encouragement and humor when I felt buried in work. Both illustrate the real meaning of a work ethic, and I am having difficulty coping with the fact that both have left Tallahassee. I wish them well in their respective careers and am grateful for the time they shared with me in work as well as in friendship.

Florida State University Dean of Faculties and Deputy Provost Steve Edwards, who has been a friend as well as a colleague during my tenure at FSU, provided his usual encouragement for my scholarly activities. Steve, I thank you for your continued support. Faye Brown and Ann Shuford assisted with word processing. My colleague Dr. Carlene Thornton assisted me with the indexes and provided encouragement throughout all stages of the writing and production of this manuscript.

My family and friends continue to provide me with needed support for such projects, and to my sister, Jill Pickett, and her family, I am grateful for love, understanding, and uncompromising support. Our beloved mother passed away during the early stages of this text's production, but she will be remembered for the love and care she gave to us, along with the example of professionalism she demonstrated during her long and distinguished teaching career. Dr. Marlyn Mather, my former colleague and friend for over twenty-five years, provided encouragement as she has throughout the long periods of work on all of my books.

My friends and professional colleagues, attorneys Roy Black and Mark D. Seiden, provided me with opportunities to become involved in the "real world" of law. These excellent defense attorneys added a challenging and exciting dimension to my career in criminal justice. I am grateful to them for these opportunities as well as for their friendship. To them this edition is dedicated.

The revision of a text can be a very difficult process, especially during the production stages, but my work was aided significantly by my editors and dear friends, D. Anthony English, Editor-in-Chief, and Chris Cardone, Senior Editor of the College Division of Macmillan/Prentice Hall, as well as by Robin Baliszewski, Senior Editor at Prentice Hall. They were assisted by Linda Zuk of WordCrafters Editorial Services.

Many of my professional colleagues have assisted us with this revision, but special thanks go to the reviewers for the excellent suggestions they provided.

An Instructor's Manual, prepared by Diane Daane, is available to professors who adopt the text.

Criminal Law

Chapter 1

An Introduction to Criminal Law

Outline

Key Terms

administrative law	discretion	norms
adversary system	due process	plaintiff
bill of attainder	equal protection	procedural law
case law	*ex post facto* law	prosecutor or prose-
civil law	felony	cuting attorney
common law	incapacitation	rehabilitation
crime	inquisitorial system	retribution
criminal law	jurisdiction	revenge
cruel and unusual	just deserts	social control
punishment	*mala in se*	sodomy
defendant	*mala prohibita*	statutory law
defense attorney	misdemeanor	strict liability
deterrence	Model Penal Code	substantive law
		tort

Introduction

For centuries people have been fascinated by law, particularly by criminal law. Scholars and philosophers have written volumes in the attempt to explain the history and evolution of criminal law, and citizens have made the topic one of great political focus. Americans have called for stricter criminal laws and punishments, while expressing increasing fears of becoming crime victims.[1]

The purpose of this text is to explore the dimensions of criminal law. Chapter 1 introduces the subject by looking at the emergence of criminal law and covering the traditional reasons for imposing criminal penalties on those who violate society's rules. This introduction includes a discussion of the extent to which the criminal law should be used to regulate behavior. Specific attention is given to the inclusion in the criminal law of behavior that some people consider private.

The chapter explains the sources and characteristics of criminal law before distinguishing criminal law and torts. Criminal laws are classified in several ways. These are defined and illustrated. Limitations placed on criminal law in the United States are analyzed, and brief attention is given to proving a criminal case. The chapter concludes with a brief summary of the establishment of guilt within the adversary system.

Emergence of Law

Why is law necessary? In small groups, particularly in primitive societies, formal laws are not necessary. Human behavior is regulated through informal methods of **social control**. As soon as children are old enough to learn, they are taught proper behavior by their families and other social institutions, such as churches and schools. Penalties exist for violating society's **norms**, but those penalties are informal. They range from a disapproving glance to social ostracism or physical expulsion from the community. In most cases the threat of being banished from the community is sufficient to ensure proper behavior. The key to the success of such informal social controls is that these small groups or societies are cohesive. Most members accept and follow the norms; those who do not are detected easily and can be punished swiftly and effectively without formal criminal laws.

As societies become more complex these informal social controls are less effective. With increasing numbers of people comes a decrease in the power of major social institutions to control human behavior. More conflicts arise among members and between groups, and a more formal, rationally thought-out method of social control is necessary. Although there is disagreement over the nature of the evolution of laws, it is clear that at some point civil and criminal law emerged as formal methods by which conflicts are resolved and behavior is controlled.

Both **civil law** and **criminal law** are designed to control behavior to protect the interests of society and of individuals. Both may prohibit or require specific actions. Both permit the government to impose penalties. Both may impose financial penalties. Both may result in social stigma. The basic difference between civil and criminal law lies primarily in the *degree* to which people condemn those who have violated the law. Normally society's moral condemnation is greater against those who violate the criminal rather than the civil law, but there are exceptions. Usually the possibility of a jail or prison sentence for conviction of a criminal law is viewed as a more severe penalty than those imposed in civil law.

Civil laws are designed for the protection of a variety of interests, such as preserving the family (for example, divorce law), protecting business relationships (for example, contract law), preserving property rights, and many interests covered under tort law, an important body of law that is distinguishable from criminal law.

Torts and Crimes Distinguished

Tort law is a large body of civil law that includes such acts as libel, slander, false imprisonment, assault and battery, negligently or intentionally causing physical or emotional injury or wrongful death, products liability, trespassing, and other acts. Tort law grew out of criminal law. Although today some acts are covered by both criminal and tort law, the distinction between the two is important.

Torts are civil wrongs in which the law assumes that the injured parties, called **plaintiffs** in the subsequent legal actions, should be compensated for their losses. The plaintiff sues the **defendant** in a civil action. Different procedural rules apply in torts and criminal cases. Defendants who lose in torts actions may be ordered to pay damages to plaintiffs. Although these actions may be seen as having a deterrent effect, in most cases the primary purpose is to compensate plaintiffs.

Torts may be *negligent* or *intentional*; both involve a fault concept, but the defendant is not looked upon with the social condemnation reserved for those who violate the criminal law. Criminal penalties such as imprisonment are not imposed, although punitive damages may be assessed. *Punitive damages* are damages in excess of compensatory or actual damages, and they are imposed as a punishment and a deterrent. Tort law is imposed also on the basis of **strict liability**, which means liability without fault. For example, if an airplane falls out of the sky onto your property, you may recover for the property damages even if no negligence or intentional actions were involved.

The distinctions between torts and crimes are not easy, however, for some acts constitute both a tort and a crime. Focus 1.1 provides an illustration. As discussion of the Richard Grimshaw case indicates, a successful tort claim may be far more beneficial to a victim than a successful criminal action. But even an unsuccessful criminal action may indicate to other potential wrongdoers that the law does not tolerate such actions. On the other hand, the stiff punitive damages awarded in this tort case may have a greater deterrent effect than criminal prosecution. In addition, a civil case is easier to prove because of different standards and burdens of proof in civil and criminal cases.

Compensatory damages (for loss of income, loss of companionship, hospital, funeral, or medical expenses, and so on) and punitive damages have been awarded in numerous other recent cases involving crimes and torts. In 1992 a judge approved the first judgment against the family of Jeffrey L. Dahmer, convicted of multiple murders of young men whose bodies he mutilated. A $10.2 million claim was approved for the mother of one of the victims. Although there is little chance of collecting the money, the victim's family sued to claim any money Dahmer might collect from movie, television, or publication rights to his story.[2] In 1993, however, a federal judge dismissed a claim from the family of a Dahmer victim. The family claimed that the police violated their son's civil rights when they returned him to Dahmer after questioning. The judge held that under the facts of that case the police had no constitutional duty to protect the boy as they could not be expected to realize the threat Dahmer posed to the young Laotian man.[3] And, in 1992 a court found General Motors Corporation liable for negligence in not installing a combination lap-shoulder belt in a car. The cost would have been only $12 per car. A Chinese student who was paralyzed from an accident while riding in the car was awarded $3.7 million, which included nearly $1 million for his spouse.

On the other hand, in 1994 a Georgia appellate court reversed and remanded for another trial a case in which a family had been awarded $105 million for the death of a teen killed when his General Motors pickup burst into flames when struck by another vehicle. And a national survey of torts cases indicates a downward trend in the number and amount of jury awards to plaintiffs.[4]

An example of international note occurred in 1992 when Pan Am was found negligent and thus subject to liability for civil damages relating to Pan Am's flight 103, which crashed in Lockerbie, Scotland in 1988, killing 270 persons, including eleven on the ground. The crash resulted from a bomb placed on the aircraft, but the court ruled that Pan Am was negligent in not detecting that bomb. The first jury award in that case was a $9.23 million judgment for the family of a Pepsico attorney who earned $160,000 yearly and had millions of dollars of stock options with the company.[5] In 1991 the U.S. Supreme Court upheld the discretion of juries to award punitive damages.[6]

FOCUS 1.1 *Tort or Crime? The Case of Richard Grimshaw and the Ford Pinto*

Richard Grimshaw, a thirteen-year-old passenger in the Ford Pinto operated by Lilly Gray, was burned severely over 90 percent of his body; Gray was killed when the car was rear-ended while stalled on a California freeway in 1972. By the time his case went to trial, Grimshaw had undergone fifty operations and was expected to have many more over the next ten years. He had lost portions of several fingers on one hand and portions of his left ear. After a six-month trial, the jury awarded Grimshaw $2,516,000 in compensatory damages and $125 million in punitive damages. The punitive damages were reduced by the trial judge to

$3.5 million as a condition of denying Ford's motion for a new trial. Ford appealed the judgment, but the appellate court upheld the $3.5 million punitive judgment award, stating that the award was well within reason considering the degree of reprehensibility of Ford's conduct, the corporation's wealth, the amount of compensatory damages, and the amount of damages needed to deter other corporate executives from engaging in the same conduct.

Grimshaw had sued Ford Motor Company for the tort of strict liability for defective design in the location of the Ford Pinto's gas tank. Evidence at trial indicated that Ford engineers knew that the design did not meet proposed federal standards and that the cost of changing the design to meet those standards was minor. But, in a rush to get the new compact on the market, Ford officials ignored the advice of their own engineers and proceeded with the allegedly defective design. The appellate court concluded that punitive damages remain "as the most effective remedy for consumer protection against defectively designed mass produced articles."[1]

Some people do not agree, however, that stringent, punitive damages, in addition to compensatory damages that theoretically reimburse the plaintiff for all damages actually suffered (including damages for pain and suffering), are sufficient to deter such reprehensible conduct. This is where criminal law and tort law are similar. Under the facts of this case, it was argued that Ford Motor Company's callous disregard for human safety constituted recklessness sufficient to substantiate the elements of criminal homicide. The company was prosecuted criminally under Indiana law. Although the state did not get a conviction, the case illustrates the similarities between torts and crimes. In addition, the case raises the issue of whether criminal law is the best approach for deterring the actions of Ford Motor Company, which put the Pinto on the market despite warnings concerning the safety of the product.

1. Grimshaw v. Ford Motor Co., 119 Cal.App.3d 757, 810 (Cal.App. 1981).

Nature and Purpose of Criminal Law

Criminal law is the most serious approach used by society to control human behavior. Although punishments differ from society to society and from one time period to the next within a society, criminal law has been used extensively in an effort to protect the welfare of the people whom it governs. The nature and explanation of punishments have varied over time.

Historical Development

Development of criminal law is extensive, going back to the first known written legal document, the Code of Hammurabi, dated to various times, approximately around 1900 B.C. This document codified Babylonia's rules and customs. It incorporated religious habits and emphasized the importance of religious beliefs. The code reflected the economic problems of Babylonian society. The "eye for an eye, tooth for a tooth," philosophy was ingrained in the code. This emphasis on retribution and religion is seen also in the early codes of many countries, including the United States.

Of greatest influence on the development of U.S. criminal law were some developments in the eighteenth and nineteenth centuries in Europe. Criminal law reformers were rebelling against an arbitrary and corrupt legal system in which judges held almost tyrannical power over those who came before them. Most laws were vague, and liberal judicial interpretations led to a lack of consistency and impartiality. In many cases accusations were secret and trials a farce. Confessions were obtained by hideous tortures, and the death penalty was used for many offenses. For example, English law provided the death penalty for over 200 offenses, including petty theft and sex offenses such as **sodomy**. Many cases involved extreme corporal punishment, which at times resulted in death.[7]

In France writers such as Montesquieu, Rousseau, and Voltaire fought for criminal law reform. Philosopher Jeremy Bentham, a prolific writer, attacked the criminal laws of his time, "fearlessly challenging the assumptions of criminal law."[8] Criminal codes of Bentham's time have been described as "a mass of incongruities, absurdities, contradictions and barbarities."[9] Bentham emphasized *utilitarianism*, which assumes that virtue is based on utility and that conduct should be directed toward promoting

FOCUS 1.2 Punishment Philosophies

Retribution or Revenge

In earlier times crime victims were permitted (and expected) to take direct action against criminal offenders, and private revenge took such extreme forms as murder. Revenge was viewed in the "eye for an eye, tooth for a tooth" philosophy that permitted one to inflict on criminals the same acts they inflicted on victims. But private revenge can and does get out of hand, creating other problems for the society, as illustrated by the California mother who entered the courtroom with a weapon and shot the man who was accused of molesting her son. She pleaded insanity, but a jury found that she was sane when she fired the gun and found her guilty of voluntary manslaughter, the least serious of the crimes for which she could have been convicted.[1] She was sentenced to ten years in prison.

In time official private revenge gave way to public revenge or retribution. Both are based on the assumption that the criminal deserves to be punished.

Retribution is referred to by some as *legal revenge* because this punishment philosophy permits the society's governing body to impose punishment on criminal offenders. Retribution is based on the belief that offenders should be given the punishment they deserve. In a 1972 landmark capital punishment case, *Furman* v. *Georgia,*, the U.S. Supreme Court recognized retribution as an appropriate reason for punishment even though all the justices did not agree.[2] Later the Court said that retribution is neither "a forbidden objective nor one inconsistent with our respect for the dignity of men."[3] The modern retributive concept of "just deserts" emphasizes that people should

be punished only because they have committed a criminal act for which the state has provided punishment. They *deserve* punishment. This approach considers it improper to punish people for any other reason, such as to improve the offender or to prevent other people from committing criminal acts.[4]

Incapacitation

Historically incapacitation was employed literally in some societies. The hands of a thief were cut off to prevent further thefts. Sex offenders were castrated. Although such practices are not commonly endorsed today, it has been suggested that sexual castration might be offered as an alternative to jail or prison for sexual offenders. Most courts have not accepted this sentence even when it is "voluntary." The same goes for the use of chemicals to effect chemical castration. In 1992 a Texas judge agreed to the punishment of castration for an African-American defendant convicted of rape. The judge removed himself from the case when he was accused of racist behavior in assessing this penalty, but he did publish articles on the issue.[5]

Today in most cases incapacitation takes the form of incarceration in a prison or jail, thus theoretically making it impossible for the offender to prey on society. But the fact that inmates may prey on other inmates or prison officials leads some to advocate capital punishment, the extreme form of incapacitation.

Deterrence

Deterrence is based on the assumption that behavior is rational and that criminal behavior can be prevented if people are afraid of the penalties. Punishment of a specific offender, or specific deterrence, may involve physical restraint or incapacitation, such as incarceration or capital punishment. But deterrence assumes also that people may be prevented from choosing to engage in criminal acts; thus, it is not necessary to amputate their hands to prevent theft. In addition, such punishments should deter others (general deterrence) from committing the same or similar criminal acts.

Deterrence is difficult to prove or disprove. Many of its supporters argue from intuition and emotion rather than from scientific data. Some empirical studies fail to distinguish between general and specific deterrence or to measure the perceived swiftness and probability of being punished. Some potential criminals may not be deterred from crime despite harsh penalties if they perceive that the laws will not be enforced or that they will not be apprehended.[6]

Reformation or Rehabilitation

Retribution and deterrence focus on crime; reformation or rehabilitation focus on criminals, emphasizing the possibility of change. Criminals can become noncriminals with proper treatment. Rehabilitation was the dominant focus of U.S. criminal justice systems during the late 1960s and 1970s, following the classic statement of law professor Francis Allen, who coined the phrase *rehabilitative ideal* in 1959. In the late 1970s and 1980s, however, the trend shifted. When the public demanded harsher punishments, statutes were changed, as exemplified in the federal system. In 1984, after hearing testimony that rehabilitation had failed and was an outmoded concept on which to base sentences, Congress enacted a comprehensive federal sentencing statute and rejected rehabilitation as the primary basis for determining sentence length.[7]

Although rehabilitation is still in vogue in some states, the philosophy has been replaced by an emphasis on deterrence and retribution in most jurisdictions. By 1981 even Allen acknowledged the demise of the rehabilitative ideal.[8]

[1] "Mother Is Found Sane in Killing Accused Molester," *New York Times* (30 September 1993), p. 14.

[2] Furman v. Georgia, 408 U.S. 238 (1972).

[3] Gregg v. Georgia, 428 U.S. 153, 183 (1976).

[4] For a discussion, see David Fogel, *We Are the Living Proof: The Justice Model for Corrections*, 2d ed. (Cincinnati: W. H. Anderson, 1979).

[5] Michael T. McSpadden, "Castration Will Work," *Houston Chronicle* (22 February 1993), p. 13. See also "Court Abandons Castration Plan In a Rape Case," *New York Times* (17 March 1992), p. 6.

[6] See Jack P. Gibbs, *Crime, Punishment and Deterrence* (New York: Elsevier North-Holland, 1975) and John Hagen, ed., *Deterrence Reconsidered: Methodological Innovations* (Berkeley, Calif.: Sage, 1982). For general research on deterrence, see the following articles: Steven Klepper and Daniel Nagin, "The Deterrent Effect of Perceived Certainty and Severity of Punishment Revisited," *Criminology* 27 (November 1989): 721–746; and Jack P. Gibbs and Glenn Firebaugh, "The Artifact Issue in Deterrence Research," Criminology 28 (May 1990): 347–365.

[7] See the Sentence Reform Act of 1984, U.S. Code., Title 18, Section 3551 *et seq.*, and U.S. Code, Title 28, Sections 991–998, 1994). For more information on the federal sentencing reform act, see the symposium, "Federal Sentencing Guidelines," *Criminal Law Bulletin* 26 (January-February 1990).

[8] Compare Francis A. Allen, "Criminal Justice, Legal Values and the Rehabilitative Ideal," *Journal of Criminal Law, Criminology, and Police Science* 50 (September–October, 1959): 226–232, with Francis A. Allen, *The Decline of the Rehabiliatative Ideal: Penal Policy and Social Purpose* (New Haven, Conn.: Yale University Press, 1981).

the greatest good for the greatest number of people. Bentham, along with his contemporary, Cesare Beccaria, an Italian, believed in *free will*, which assumes that human behavior is purposive and based on *hedonism*, the pleasure-pain principle. People choose those actions that give pleasure and avoid those that bring pain. Therefore punishment should be assigned to each crime in a degree that would result in more pain than pleasure for those who commit the forbidden act.

Beccaria incorporated the doctrines of free will and utilitarianism into his punishment philosophy, which forms the basis of current criminal law reform in the United States: "Let the punishment fit the crime." If crimes are committed because people think they will get more pleasure than pain from the acts, and this decision is based on free will, such acts may be deterred only if punishments are just a little more painful than the pleasure of committing those crimes.[10]

Beccaria advocated that laws should be written clearly and not open to judicial interpretation. Laws should apply equally to all people; no defenses to criminal acts should be permitted. The issue at trial was whether a person committed the act; if so, a particular penalty prescribed by law for that act should be imposed. Judges were viewed as instruments of the law, allowed to determine only innocence or guilt and prescribe the set punishment. The law became rigid, structured, and impartial.

Beccaria should be recognized for his contribution to making law impartial, and many scholars have done so. During the 1980s he was called a *prophet* by one scholar who, with others, celebrated the 250th anniversary of Becarria's birth while attending a conference in Milan, Italy.[11] Others have criticized Beccaria's work, with one noted scholar calling him a "pampered intellectual who had no first hand knowledge of the criminal justice system."[12]

Some philosophers and other law reformers found the classical approach of Bentham and Beccaria too harsh. During the neoclassical period revisions were made in some criminal codes to permit judicial discretion, including deciding sentence lengths within legislatively mandated limits. Age, gender, and mental condition were to be considered in the application of criminal law; thus legal defenses were introduced. No longer would young children accused of crimes be processed in the judicial system in the same manner as adults, and the same penalties would not apply. Mental disease was viewed as another sufficient cause to limit or remove criminal liability.

This brief summary of the reform efforts of the classical and neoclassical writers provides a basis for analyzing the punishment philosophies that have provided historical justification for criminal law. Although the emphasis on each has varied over time, there has been some consistency in the philosophies advanced to support criminal law.

Punishment Philosophies

Punishing individuals through criminal law is a serious act and should be based on reasonable philosophies that are presumed to assist society to meet worthy goals such as the maintenance of social solidarity and the protection of citizens. Throughout history the basic goals have been **retribution** (or **revenge** or **just deserts**), **incapacitation**, **deterrence**, and **rehabilitation** (or reformation). Focus 1.2 defines each of these terms.

In an old but frequently cited case, *Commonwealth* v. *Ritter*, the judge explains how punishment philosophies influenced his sentencing decision. Do you agree with the judge, or would you have applied the punishment philosophies differently?[13]

Commonwealth v. *Ritter*

Generally speaking, there have been advanced four theories as the basis upon which society should act in imposing penalties upon those who violate its laws. These are: (1) To bring about the reformation of the evil-doer; (2) to effect retribution or revenge upon him; (3) to restrain him physically, so as to make it impossible for him to commit further crimes; and (4) to deter others from similarly violating the law.... [The judge discussed each philosophy].

In the present case, the nature of the crime and the psychology of the criminal are clear. For several years the defendant, although a man of mature age, long married and the father of five children, had been embroiled in a love passion for a woman who was not his wife. She, of approximately the same age, and the mother of three children, apparently entered with him upon an illicit relationship. Having, by his business ability, succeeded in achieving a fair degree of material prosperity, he squandered large sums of money upon the woman who had thus come into his life. He developed an extreme jealousy in regard to her and what seems to have been a constant terror that she would desert him, especially when he had arrived at the end of his financial means. He took more and more to drinking and enfeebled his health and mentality to a point where he was obliged to go to a medical institution on two successive occasions a year apart. Finally, he reached so low a depth in the matter of his finances that in order to obtain the very pistol with which he committed the murder he was obliged to pawn his overcoat. He continually haunted the woman, besieging her with visits and telephone calls at her place of employment. For the few days immediately preceding the murder he was in a condition of tremendous excitement and agitation, even to the extent of doing without food. Immediately after the shooting he tried to commit suicide, firing two bullets into vital parts of his body, and it seems miraculous that although one of the bullets caused four perforations in his liver, his attempt to destroy himself was unsuccessful. Although he shot with the intention of killing his victim, and expressed the hope that he had done so, in the same breath he was solicitous about her photograph, for which he had a sentimental affection, and he expressed himself to the effect that, she being gone, he cared nothing about himself and was not concerned about his fate. The very afternoon of the murder he had told the proprietress of his lodging house that he loved the woman better than his life. In short, the case was plainly one of a frenzied and jealous passion on his part, working on a man destroyed by drink and desperate by reason of the fact that he had come to the end of his resources. For the reasons already stated, it is not believed that the death penalty in a case such as this would have any effect of deterrence on persons who might commit similar crimes, because offenses of this nature are not the result of calm and thoughtful planning or of rationalized deliberation. In conclusion, it may be said that, perhaps, after all, the penalty of life imprisonment is not so much a substitute of capital punishment as a slower method of inflicting it.

The court, therefore, adjudges the defendant to be guilty of murder of the first degree, and imposes upon him the penalty of imprisonment for and during the term of his natural life.

Deciding how to apply punishment philosophies in the preceding case or in any other case may be difficult, but deciding which acts to include within the criminal law is an issue of controversy as well.

Criminal Law and Morality

The debate over whether certain acts (such as gambling, the abuse of alcohol and other drugs, and prostitution and other sexual acts that are consensual and committed in private between adults) should be included within the purview of the criminal law has gone on for some time. The distinction is made between acts that are **mala in se** and those that are **mala prohibita**.

Mala in se crimes, such as murder, forcible rape, robbery, aggravated assault, and arson—crimes that endanger human life or property directly— are acts considered to be evil in themselves. They are acts that most, if not all, people consider criminal. *Mala prohibita* crimes are acts considered crimes only because statutes have defined them as such. They are not regarded universally as criminal; they may not be regarded as criminal by most people. Examples might be private sexual acts between consenting adults, abuse of alcohol and other drugs, or carrying a concealed weapon. Enforcement of *mala prohibita* crimes may be more difficult because of the lack of agreement over whether these acts should be criminalized.

Historical analyses of criminal law indicate the influence of religion and morality in decisions concerning which acts should be criminalized. The literal meaning of the word *crime* in some languages illustrates this phenomenon. In Hungarian, crime means a sinful act or evil fault as well as a legally prohibited act. In Roman law, the word *crime* comes from the word *crimen*, which means "fault, sinning, an act against morality the fundamentals of which were common to all."[14] Many of the early laws in the United States were taken verbatim from the Bible. The influence of the Bible is seen in some modern criminal statutes, too.[15]

The current controversy over which acts should be included within the criminal law may be analyzed historically. In the nineteenth century, John Stuart Mill argued that the only part of an individual's behavior over which society should have control is behavior that concerns others. But "over himself, over his own body and mind, the individual is sovereign."[16] Norval Morris and Gordon Hawkins, American scholars who have written extensively about criminal law, contend that "for the criminal law at least, man has an inalienable right to go to hell in his own fashion, provided he does not directly injure the person or property of another on the way. The criminal law is an inefficient instrument for imposing the good life on others."[17]

Morris and Hawkins claim that, with the possible exception of John Calvin's sixteenth-century Geneva, the United States has the most moralistic criminal law in history. They refer to laws governing sexual offenses as designed "to provide an enormous legislative chastity belt encompassing the whole population and proscribing everything but solitary and joyless masturbation and 'normal coitus' inside wedlock."[18]

Later chapters detail some of the crimes that might be classified as private morality that perhaps should not be included in criminal law. But when deciding whether such acts should be covered by the criminal law, we must consider to what extent those acts involve areas that are of legitimate concern to the public, such as the spread of disease or the commission of other, more serious crimes. It is important also to consider whether the criminal law is an effective way for controlling such behaviors.

Sources of Criminal Law

Administrative Law and Constitutions

Law is derived from four sources: administrative regulations, constitutions, judicial decisions, and statutes. The latter two are the most important in criminal law, but the first two should be noted. **Administrative law** refers to a body of regulations and rules that come from administrative agencies (such as the Internal Revenue Service) to which Congress or state legislatures have delegated rule-making power. Generally regulations and decisions of administrative agencies are civil, not criminal matters, but even in those cases, violations may constitute offenses that can be enforced through the criminal courts. Because thousands of state and federal agencies exist in this country, enacting and enforcing administrative rules that affect our daily lives in many ways, administrative law is an important method for controlling our activities.

To a limited extent, criminal laws are contained in state constitutions. The U.S. Constitution deals primarily with procedural criminal law, but it does define *treason* as a crime.[19]

Common Law

Analyzing statutes and judicial decisions as sources of law requires a brief look at **common law**, which refers to laws that derive from long custom and usage or from judicial decisions, in contrast to laws passed by legislatures or Congress. Historically common law refers to England's ancient laws that developed through judicial decisions on a case-by-case basis (leading to the term **case law**) and that have influenced the development of English and American case and statutory law.[20]

Statutory Criminal Law

Today most states have codified their criminal laws, and they do not recognize an act as criminal unless it is included within the **statutory law**. The federal system does not recognize common law crimes if they are not codified. But even when statutory law is required to establish an act as criminal, the common law may be (and often is) used to interpret the statute. Likewise, if a criminal statute uses the wording of a common law crime but does not define that crime, the common law may be used to define the crime.[21]

Each state's criminal statutes define the crimes and penalties applicable in that state. These laws are published in state statute books. This text makes some references to them. Although the names and citations vary, the sources are referred to as the *Criminal Code* or *Penal Code*, preceded by the name of the state. For example, Cal. Penal Code refers to the California Penal Code. Congress is responsible for passing statutes that define federal crimes. These are recorded in the United States Code or U.S. Code.

A study of criminal law should distinguish between procedural and substantive law. **Substantive law** defines the elements, rights, and responsibilities of law, whereas **procedural law** defines the methods by which the law may be enforced. This text is concerned primarily with substantive criminal law.

The Model Penal Code and Criminal Law Reform

In recent years many states (as well as Congress) have attempted a complete revision of their criminal statutes. They have been assisted in this process by the American Law Institute (ALI), an organization of lawyers, judges, and legal scholars. The ALI, founded in 1923, considered a proposal for a model penal code in 1931 but did not receive adequate funding for the project until 1950 when it received a large grant from the Rockefeller Foundation. In 1962 the Proposed Official Draft of the **Model Penal Code** was submitted. Subsequent volumes have been published, setting out the proposed model statutes and commentary on each. Although it was never expected that the M.P.C. would be adopted without modification by any state, many states follow the M.P.C., at least in part. Because of its extensive influence on state criminal code revisions, frequent references to the M.P.C. are made in this text to illustrate definitions of crimes.

Classification of Crimes and Related Offenses

Before looking at the various classifications of crimes and related offenses, we must define *crime*. Scholars have debated its meaning. Some definitions are concise, whereas others attempt to include every element. The next chapter discusses the elements of crime, so no attempt is made here to define the word to include every element. Simply stated, a **crime** is the commission of an act prohibited by criminal law or the failure to act as required by criminal law. Implicit in this definition is the power of the government to impose penalties.

Two basic principles of U.S. systems of criminal justice are important to an understanding of the definition of crime. The first is *nulla poena sine lege*, or "no punishment without law." The second is *nullum crimen sine poena*, which means "no crime without punishment." For example, the Model Penal Code provides that "No conduct constitutes an offense unless it is a crime or violation under this Code or another statute of this State."[22] These principles do not preclude permitting the state to decline to prosecute or to refuse to punish even upon a defendant's conviction or guilty plea. Rather, it means that unless the state has defined an act or omission as a crime and provided punishment, punishment may not be inflicted just because the act is considered to be harmful socially.

Discretion and Criminal Law

Whether or not the state takes action when a criminal act is thought to have occurred depends on many factors. As Focus 1.3 indicates, criminal justice systems permit considerable **discretion**, leaving public officials and others the freedom to make independent judgments concerning the disposition of cases. This discretion has been the subject of extensive debate, which usually has focused on judicial sentencing and police discretion.[23]

Often overlooked but of particular significance to an understanding of criminal law is prosecutorial discretion. The **prosecutor** is an attorney who represents the state (or federal government; he or she is called a U.S. Attorney) in a criminal case, in contrast to the **defense attorney**, who represents the accused. After police arrest a suspect, the prosecutor makes the initial decision whether to pursue the case. Even after the decision has been made to prosecute a case and the judge has found sufficient reason for doing so, in most instances it is the prosecutor who decides whether to drop the case.[24]

The decision not to prosecute is a powerful one for which there are few checks within the criminal justice system. A few states have statutes that permit private persons to challenge prosecutorial decisions not to prosecute, but most states and the federal government have no such provisions.[25] Most cases brought to the attention of prosecutors are not prosecuted. In many cases in which prosecution does occur, the prosecutor has discretion in deciding the offense with which to charge the accused. Thus, a person arrested for rape might be charged with aggravated assault and battery or a lesser sexual offense. The prosecutor may make this decision for legitimate reasons, such as insufficient evidence or evidence that is not admissable at trial, refusal of witnesses or victims to cooperate, lack of credibility of victims and witnesses, insufficient resources within the system to devote to a long trial, societal interests, welfare of the accused, and many other reasons. The decision may be made for extralegal reasons as well, such as

---

FOCUS 1.3   Discretion and Criminal Law

These criminal justice officials ...	... must often decide whether or not or how to—
Police	Enforce specific laws
	Investigate specific crimes
	Search people, vicinities, buildings
	Arrest or detain people
Prosecutors	File charges or petitions for adjudication
	Seek indictments
	Drop cases
	Reduce charges
Judges or magistrates	Set bail or conditions for release
	Accept pleas
	Determine delinquency
	Dismiss charges
	Impose sentences
	Revoke probation
Correctional officials	Assign to type of correctional facility
	Award privileges
	Punish for disciplinary infractions
Paroling authority	Determine date and conditions of parole
	Revoke parole

SOURCE: Bureau of Justice Statistics, *Report to the Nation on Crime and Justice: The Data*, 2d ed. (Washington, D.C.: U.S. Government Printing Office, 1988), p. 59.

---

race or gender.[26] There is evidence, too, that some prosecutors make their decisions for political reasons, such as the effect the decision might have on their careers.[27]

The control of prosecutorial discretion is important, and courts have made some efforts in this direction. It is clear that prosecutors may prosecute selectively, but the U.S. Supreme Court has held that prosecutors may not increase charges against a defendant in retaliation for the defendant's assertion of a statutory right.[28] Additionally, it is common and acceptable for prosecutors to target high-rate dangerous offenders for priority prosecution.[29] But prosecutors are not permitted to prosecute suspects for vindictive reasons. Courts have held, however, that some prosecutorial decisions do not lend themselves to review by courts, making prosecutorial vindictiveness difficult to detect and prove. A brief excerpt from *United States v. Richardson* illustrates this point. Richardson was accused of receiving videocassettes involving the sexual exploitation of minors. Four others arrested the same day were not prosecuted but instead were permitted to participate in a pretrial diversion program. The defendant alleged that he was discriminated against by the prosecutor because he exercised one of his constitutional rights. The court disagreed.[30]

United States v. Richardson

A defendant has no right to be placed in pretrial diversion. The decision of whether a particular defendant will be allowed the opportunity to participate in the program is one entrusted to the United States Attorney. Like other prosecutorial decisions, the government has broad discretion in determining which defendants are best suited for pretrial diversion. These decisions are "particularly ill-suited to judicial review" and we are "properly hesitant to examine the decision whether to prosecute." However, prosecutorial discretion is not totally unfettered. The government may not selectively prosecute a defendant based upon arbitrary classifications such as race or religion, or the exercise of constitutional rights....

In order to establish selective prosecution a defendant must show that the government was motivated by a discriminatory purpose with a resulting discriminatory effect. The defendant must establish not only that he has been singled out while others similarly situated have not been prosecuted but also that the decision to prosecute was based on impermissible considerations. A defendant challenging the government's pretrial diversion decision must set forth specific facts supporting his selective prosecution contention and may not rest on bald assertions of constitutional violations.

Police have wide discretion in deciding whether to make arrests. Mass arrests may occur when police perceive that large numbers of people are breaking the law.

Discretion exists also in the classification of crimes. Scholars use discretion in deciding which classifications to use and how to categorize those classifications.

Classification by Grade of Offense

Crimes may be classified in several ways. The most common classification is by the degree of seriousness of the offense. Although the common law classified crimes as treason, felony, and misdemeanor, most modern statutes divide crimes into serious offenses—**felonies**—and less serious offenses—**misdemeanors**.

Under the English common law most felonies were punishable by death; thus, the distinction between felony and misdemeanor was very important. Misdemeanor included any crime that was not a felony. Today felonies and misdemeanors are distinguished primarily by the sentences that may be imposed. Generally, felonies are crimes for which the offender may be sentenced to death or imprisoned for a long period, whereas misdemeanors are less serious offenses punishable by fines, work, probation, community service, or short-term incarceration, usually in a jail rather than a state or federal prison. Some statutes do not specify whether a particular crime is a felony or a misdemeanor. The determination is made by the punishment specified for that crime. Some statutes add a third category—*petty misdemeanors*, also called *petty offenses* in some codes. Some statutes use the terms *violation* or *infraction* to refer to less serious crimes, such as *traffic infractions*.[31]

In addition to punishment, the distinction between felony and misdemeanor (and petty offenses, where they are classified separately) may determine in which court the case may be heard. The distinction may have a bearing also on the procedures that must be followed in the criminal proceedings. Arrest rules may vary, and civil penalties that follow convictions may differ. For example, a defendant might lose the right to vote upon conviction of a felony, but not upon conviction of a misdemeanor.

Classification with Reference to Moral Turpitude

Crimes may be classified in terms of moral turpitude. In law, *moral turpitude* refers to acts that are base, vile, and immoral. They are considered inherently wrong, or *mala in se* crimes in contrast to those that are *mala prohibita*, or wrong because they are illegal. A crime of moral turpitude is an act or behavior "that gravely violates moral sentiment or accepted moral standards of the community and is a morally culpable quality held to be present in some criminal offenses as distinguished from others."[32]

The distinction between crimes that do and those that do not involve moral turpitude is important. For example, conviction for a crime of moral turpitude may result in a lawyer's disbarment, the revocation of a doctor's license, or the deportation of an alien. It may result in enhanced penalties as well. In many instances, however, it is difficult to define what is and what is not a crime of moral turpitude. Generally, moral turpitude involves acts that demonstrate dishonesty, disrepute, corruption, and baseness—acts that violate good morals and good judgment.

Other Classifications

Crimes may be classified in other ways as well. Some codes distinguish between crimes that are *infamous* and those that are not. Included are acts that are considered shameful or disgraceful, without fame or good report. This classification was used in common law to exclude persons from testifying in court on the belief that anyone who would commit such crimes was so depraved that he or she would not tell the truth. Included were treason, most felonies, and crimes involving dishonesty such as embezzlement, false pretense, criminal fraud, and perjury.

Other special categories may involve behaviors that technically are not criminal, such as acts committed by juveniles and processed through the juvenile court. Likewise, violations of local ordinances technically are not criminal acts, although they may resemble crimes. State legislatures delegate to municipal authorities the power to pass ordinances to regulate health, welfare, and safety. Some of these ordinances provide penalties such as short jail terms or fines, but violations of these ordinances may be considered civil, not criminal.

Limitations on Criminal Law

Congress and state legislatures are limited in what they may do to define acts as criminal; courts are limited in their enforcement of criminal law. Many of the limitations are matters of criminal procedure, but a few are necessary for an adequate understanding of criminal law.

Jurisdiction

Jurisdiction refers to the lawful right of the legislative, executive, or judicial branch to exercise official authority. For example, city, county, and state police officers may be limited by statute to law enforcement duties within specified geographical areas.

Courts may not decide cases for which they do not have jurisdiction. For example, some courts may hear and decide misdemeanor cases only; others may decide felony cases exclusively. Some courts are empowered to decide certain types of cases, such as criminal or civil, domestic or probate (wills and estates). Special courts that decide juvenile cases normally do not have jurisdiction to hear other types of cases. Some courts are trial courts exclusively; others hear cases on appeal only. State courts may not decide federal court cases and vice versa. State court decisions are not appealed to federal courts and vice versa, although a state court decision may be appealed to the U.S. Supreme Court if a federal constitutional or statutory issue is involved.

Void-for-Vagueness and Overbreadth

Interpretations of the U.S. Constitution require that a criminal statute must be declared void-for-vagueness when it is so vague that "men of common intelligence must necessarily guess at its meaning and differ as to its application."[33] In 1983 the U.S. Supreme Court held a California statute unconstitutionally vague. *Kolender* v. *Lawson* involved a tall, muscular, black man with long hair who walked frequently in an all-white neighborhood. Lawson was stopped by police about fifteen times between 1975 and 1977; each time Lawson refused to identify himself.

Lawson was arrested five times, convicted once, and served several weeks in jail. The statute under which he was arrested defined the misdemeanor of *disorderly conduct* as the actions of one who

> loiters or wanders on the streets from place to place without apparent reason or business and who refuses to identify himself and to account for his presence when requested by any peace officer to do so, if the surrounding circumstances are such as to indicate to a reasonable man that the public safety demands such identification.[34]

The Supreme Court held that the statute was vague because it did not establish a standard for what a suspect must do to provide a "credible and reliable" identification. The result was that police had "virtually complete discretion…to determine whether the suspect has satisfied the statute." The statute permitted people to walk the streets without interference from police "only at the whim of any police officer." The Court ruled that the statute was unconstitutional because its vagueness failed to give adequate notice.[35]

It is not always easy to determine whether a statute is void-for-vagueness. Laws cannot specify everything that is prohibited. But to avoid the void-for-vagueness problem, statutes must have three characteristics: (1) they must give fair notice or warning to those subject to them, (2) they must guard against arbitrary and discriminatory enforcement, and (3) they must not unreasonably deny people their First Amendment rights, such as the right to free speech (see Appendix A).

Consider the following fact pattern. A municipal ordinance provides that it is illegal for a person to sleep in a car that is parked on a public street. You are sleeping in your car parked on a public street, and you are arrested. You retain an attorney and challenge the constitutionality of the ordinance. What would you argue? Are there any circumstances under which you should be permitted to sleep in your car on a public street? Are there reasons for having an ordinance of this nature? Does *Kolender* v. *Lawson* apply to your case?

The Alabama Court of Criminal Appeals considered these questions in a decision it rendered in May 1993, with a majority of the court holding the Montgomery ordinance unconstitutional under *Kolender* v. *Lawson*. Consider this brief excerpt from the majority opinion, along with the excerpt from the dissent. Which do you think is the best reasoning?[36]

Horn v. City of Montgomery

Majority Opinion

...Numerous situations could arise that would be essentially inno-cent—such as a driver pulling over to the curb and parking because he was too sleepy, too ill, or too tired to drive. The arresting officer rec-ognized this possibility and admitted that he and other officers believed that they were free to decide whether to enforce the ordi-nance in those cases. The vagueness of the ordinance encourages arbi-trary and discriminatory enforcement....

Dissenting Opinion

[The dissent argued that the discretion permitted by the statute was constitutional in that it permitted officers to distinguish between dri-vers who were too tired to drive and those who were too drunk to drive but might do so and become a menace to society.]
...That kind of measured discretion, guided by easily ascertained cri-teria, simply does not constitute the 'standardless sweep [that] allows policemen, prosecutors and juries to pursue their personal predilec-tions' condemned in *Kolender*....

It is unconstitutional for statutes to be too broad or vague. Statutes must be written so that reasonable people know what they mean, and they must be specific regarding the conduct prohibited. The statute may not reach beyond conduct that may be prohibited constitutionally and include con-duct that is protected constitutionally. These issues arise most frequently in cases involving *free speech*. Although the First Amendment (see Appendix A) states that Congress shall pass "no law" inhibiting free speech, the inter-pretation has been that some speech and some actions that convey speech are not covered, but those exceptions are limited. A statute should be draft-ed so that it focuses on the specific behavior to be restricted. It should not "sweep within its ambit other activities that constitute an exercise" of pro-tected expressive or associational rights.[37]

Ex Post Facto Laws and Bills of Attainder

The U.S. Constitution provides that "no bill of attainder or *ex post facto* law shall be passed."[38] In a 1990 decision, the U.S. Supreme Court defined an *ex post facto law* as one that "retroactively alter[s] the definition of crimes or increase[s] the punishment for criminal acts."[39]

In an 1867 case the Supreme Court defined a **bill of attainder** as a "leg-islative act which inflicts punishment without a judicial trial." Originally, the term referred only to the death penalty, and a bill of attainder involving lesser penalties was called a *bill of pains and penalties*.[40] Today the concept is defined more broadly as "legislative acts, no matter what their form, that apply either to named individuals or to easily ascertainable members of a group in such a way as to inflict punishment on them without a judicial trial."[41] A statute that prohibited from practicing law individuals who refused to take an oath that they had not opposed the United States in the Civil War was held unconstitutional. The practice of law may be regulated, but the Court held that this particular requirement bore no relationship to the fitness to practice law.[42] On the other hand, a statute providing for governmental custody of the late President Richard Nixon's presidential papers was permissible. The statute was not punitive in nature but instead dealt with the preservation of presidential papers. Although Nixon was named as a party of one and was easily identifiable, the statute did not constitute a bill of attainder.[43]

Repeal or Amendment of a Statute

If a statute is repealed or amended after the accused committed the act but before he or she is tried, may the suspect be tried for the offense specified in that statute? Under the common law the answer was no unless the repeal or amendment had a "saving" provision that indicated legislative intent not to eliminate prosecutions of previous offenses. The rule applied to cases in which prosecutions had begun but had not been completed and to cases not yet begun. Prosecutions could continue or start, however, if the new statute or amendment contained a provision that had essentially all of the elements of the former statute. For example, a new sexual assault statute that required the same elements for first-degree sexual assault as those required for a prior rape statute would not preclude prosecution of a defendant charged under the prior rape statute.[44]

Cruel and Unusual Punishment

The criminal law may not inflict **cruel and unusual punishment** as prohibited by the Eighth Amendment of the U.S. Constitution (see Appendix A). There is little agreement, however, on the meaning of this phrase. The Supreme Court has interpreted the phrase in numerous cases, particularly those involving capital punishment. Although some justices disagree, the Court as a whole has not declared capital punishment per se to be cruel and unusual. Some ancient methods of punishment, such as the rack and the screw, have been considered unconstitutional. When faced with the issue, the Court has upheld all modern methods of capital punishment.[45] However, capital punishment may be cruel and unusual for other reasons. If the penalty is not proportional to the crime for which it is imposed, it is cruel and unusual. According to the Court, capital punishment for the rape of an adult woman falls within this category.[46]

Punishment may be considered disproportional because it is too severe in light of the offense for which it was imposed.[47] This issue may arise when additional penalties are provided by statute for offenders with prior convictions, but these situations must be analyzed carefully.[48] The case might be different, however, for persons convicted of *violent* felonies.[49] The Court has held also that disproportionality does not necessarily mean that defendants convicted of a particular crime in one jurisdiction may not be assessed more severe punishments than defendants convicted of that crime in another jurisdiction. Nor is a court required to conduct a review prior to sentencing (called a *proportionality review*) to determine the sentences that have been imposed on defendants in other jurisdictions. Like many other issues in sentencing, proportionality is raised frequently in cases involving capital punishment.[50]

Due Process and Equal Protection

The U.S. Constitution prohibits the federal government (in the Fifth Amendment) and the states (in the Fourteenth Amendment) from depriving persons of life, liberty, or property without **due process** and **equal protection** of the law (see Appendix A). The meaning of these important concepts is debatable. Many cases have been decided by lower courts and by the Supreme Court in attempts to define them. That body of case law cannot be reviewed here, but a definition and brief interpretation of each term are important. As with statutes, the concepts of due process and equal protection refer to *substantive* and *procedural* matters.

Due process means that statutes may not be defined or enforced in an unreasonable, capricious, or arbitrary manner. People charged with crimes have a right to be notified, to be heard, and to defend against the charges. Due process refers also to other constitutional guarantees throughout and after a criminal trial. The particulars of due process may vary from case to case, as the brief excerpt from *Burton* v. *Livingston* illustrates.[51]

Burton v. *Livingston*

Due process of law has been said to encompass a "guarantee of respect for those personal immunities which are 'so rooted in the traditions and conscience of our people as to be ranked as fundamental.'" The guarantee of due process draws a line between the power of the government, on the one hand, and the security of the individual, on the other. This line is not a fixed one like a property boundary. Its location must be surveyed anew by the court in each case through an examination of the benchmarks disclosed by the circumstances surrounding the case. Among these landmarks are the nature of the individual right, the relationship between the individual and the government, and the justification offered by the government for its conduct.

The *equal protection clause* means that no person or class of persons may be denied the same protection of laws that is provided to other persons or classes of persons. The litigation in this area is extensive, too. The Supreme Court has defined some areas while leaving states considerable room to establish others.

Other Constitutional Limitations

Criminal law must operate within the framework of constitutional rights, such as freedom of religion, freedom of speech and the press, the right to assemble peacefully, the right to petition the government for redress, freedom from unreasonable searches and seizures, freedom from compulsory self-incrimination, and the right to privacy. Although any or all of these freedoms and others may become important in passing and enforcing a criminal statute, the right of privacy deserves particular attention. In later discussions of specific crimes, such as sexual acts between consenting adults, the privacy issue arises. Should the government be permitted to legislate in these areas? If so, how is the government to obtain evidence without violating individual rights? The issue concerns the circumstances under which the right of privacy should be subordinated to the need to protect society.

Some jurisdictions have recognized the right to privacy in their state constitutions and have interpreted the right to exclude criminalizing acts such as the possession of marijuana in a private home. For example, the Alaska Supreme Court held that its constitutional provision—"The right of the people to privacy is recognized and shall not be infringed"—gives citizens a basic right to privacy in their homes. "This right to privacy would encompass the possession and ingestion of substances such as marijuana in a purely personal, non-commercial context in the home unless the state can meet its substantial burden and show that proscription of possession of marijuana is supportable by achievement of a legitimate state interest."[52] Other states have rejected this extension of the right of privacy.[53] Nor would the Alaska Supreme Court include personal possession of cocaine within the privacy right. According to the Alaska court, scientific evidence indicates that cocaine is more dangerous than marijuana because cocaine can cause death.[54]

The Establishment of Guilt

Although much of the law applying to the establishment of guilt in a criminal case is procedural and thus not the subject matter of this text, some points must be covered for an adequate understanding of criminal law. The adversary nature of the U.S. system of criminal law, in contrast to the inquisitorial system of some other countries, is very important and relates to the critical issue of the burden of proof in a criminal case.

The Adversary System

In the **inquisitorial system** the defendant is presumed guilty and must prove his or her innocence. In the **adversary system**, the prosecutor (representing the state and the victim) and the defense counsel (representing the defendant) oppose each other in a trial if they are unable or unwilling to dispose of the case prior to a trial, and the defendant is presumed innocent. The state must prove guilt.[55]

In the adversary system a trial may be held to determine questions of fact.
Evidence may be presented through the testimony of witnesses.

Many scholars criticize the U.S. adversary system, with its extensive use of the lay jury in which ordinary citizens are selected to determine ultimate facts in a trial, such as the guilt or innocence of the defendant. One legal scholar, noting that the United States has almost all of the civil jury trials and approximately 90 percent of the world's criminal jury trials, argues for drastic changes in the adversary system. He encourages us to analyze the criminal justice systems of European countries, many of which utilize professional jurors (such as judges) rather than lay jurors. In addition, the jury system is not used as extensively.[56]

The Burden of Proof

In each trial one party has the burden of proof on certain issues. In a civil or torts case, the plaintiff, the party initiating the suit, must prove his or her allegations by a *preponderance of the evidence*. That means that the evidence must be sufficient to lead a jury or a judge to conclude that it is more probable than not that the allegations are correct. In a criminal trial, the prosecution must prove its allegations *beyond a reasonable doubt*, a much higher standard than that of a preponderance of the evidence.

For a long time courts recognized that the prosecutor in an adult criminal trial must prove guilt beyond a reasonable doubt; but the standard was not recognized so clearly in juvenile cases, nor had it been interpreted as required by the Constitution. In 1970, in *In re Winship*, the Supreme Court held that this burden is a federal constitutional requirement in juvenile cases. The case has been interpreted as applying as well to the trials of adult defendants. The Court cited its reasons as follows, in this brief excerpt from the case.[57]

In re Winship

The reasonable-doubt standard plays a vital role in the American scheme of criminal procedure. It is a prime instrument for reducing the risk of convictions resting on factual error. The standard provides concrete substance for the presumption of innocence—that bedrock "axiomatic and elementary" principle whose "enforcement lies at the foundation of the administration of our criminal law." As the dissenters in the New York Court of Appeals [below] observed, and we agree, "a person accused of crime ... would be at a severe disadvantage, a disadvantage amounting to a lack of fundamental fairness, if he could be adjudged guilty and imprisoned for years on the strength of the same evidence as would suffice in a civil case."

The requirement of proof beyond a reasonable doubt has this vital role in our criminal procedure for cogent reasons. The accused during a criminal prosecution has at stake interest of immense importance, both because of the possibility that he may lose his liberty upon conviction and because of the certainty that he would be stigmatized by the conviction. Accordingly, a society that values the good name and freedom of every individual should not condemn a man for commission of a crime when there is reasonable doubt about his guilt.

Moreover, use of the reasonable-doubt standard is indispensable to command the respect and confidence of the community in application of the criminal law. It is critical that the moral force of the criminal law not be diluted by a standard of proof that leaves people in doubt whether innocent men are being condemned. It is also important in our free society that every individual going about his ordinary affairs have confidence that his government cannot adjudge him guilty of a criminal offense without convincing a proper factfinder of his guilt with utmost certainty.

There have been some problems in interpreting the meaning and extent of the beyond-a-reasonable-doubt requirement, but those problems are beyond the scope of this text. It is clear, however, that a phrase such as *beyond a reasonable doubt*, which appears at first glance to be easily understandable, may lead to extensive disagreement and debate among lawyers and judges.[58]

In 1994 the U.S. Supreme Court discussed the problems of defining *beyond a reasonable doubt*. In two cases consolidated for argument and decision because of their similarities, the Court upheld the jury instructions concerning the concept. However, the justices expressed their dissatisfactions with the instructions, which were similar in these cases. In particular, the justices were concerned about a reference to the uncertainty of all matters "depending on moral evidence," as well as the statement that a reasonable doubt exists when a juror lacks an "abiding conviction, to a moral certainty, of the truth of the charge." These and other concerns with the problems of defining *beyond a reasonable doubt* have led some appellate courts to rule that an instruction on the concept should not be given to the jury.[59]

In some instances the defendant may have a burden of proof, even in a criminal case. Some defenses are defined as to require the defendant to prove their existence. Even here there may be exceptions, and the case law is extensive and complicated.[60] Generally when the defendant has a burden of proof in a criminal case, the standard of proof will be by a preponderance of the evidence rather than the more stringent standard of beyond a reasonable doubt.

SUMMARY

This chapter provides a brief overview of criminal law, beginning with a discussion of historical reasons for law and comparing its emergence with other, less formal methods of social control. In earlier times, when societies were less complex and everyone knew everyone else, human behavior could be reasonably controlled by informal means. Even the criminal law permitted people to engage in private revenge, which usually was a successful method for apprehending and punishing those who did not behave within the norms. As societies grew and became more complex, informal controls were replaced with a formal system of state action; in criminal law, private revenge was replaced by what some have called *public revenge*.

A brief general distinction between civil and criminal law is followed by a more intensive analysis of the differences between torts and crimes. Some acts constitute both a tort and a crime. Tort remedies are intended primarily to compensate victims; criminal laws are intended primarily to punish offenders, who are viewed as a threat to all, not just to the immediate victims. But at times there is a punitive element to torts, as illustrated by the assessment of punitive damages. The examples given in this chapter demonstrate the difficulties of distinguishing torts and crimes and illustrate the types of behavior that may be processed as either or both.

The chapter discusses the nature and purpose of criminal law, tracing the law historically with an emphasis on the classical school and the contributions of Beccaria and Bentham. Because their "let the punishment fit the crime rather than the criminal" approach was considered too harsh by some, defenses such as those based on mental illness and age were introduced. The influence of the classical writers is seen in modern law.

Because punishment for crimes is a serious intrusion into private lives, the state needs reasonable justifications for its imposition. The punishment philosophies of retribution (or revenge), incapacitation, deterrence, and rehabilitation (or reformation) are considered historically and viewed in the context of a court case in which a judge wrestled with why and how to punish.

In modern times, retribution, or just deserts, has replaced revenge as a primary reason for criminal punishment. Another primary purpose of punishment is deterrence, both general and specific. Until recently a primary purpose of criminal law was to rehabilitate offenders. This purpose lost favor in the 1970s and 1980s, but with the increased prison populations of the 1980s and 1990s, there is a slight return to an emphasis on treatment and rehabilitation in some jurisdictions.

Regardless of which of these philosophies serves as the basis for criminal law, we have to face the difficult question of which acts to include as crimes. The issue of whether acts such as private sexual behavior between consenting adults, the use and abuse of alcohol and other drugs, and some other types of behavior should be criminal continues to be debated. This chapter looks at the historical basis for the inclusion of morality within the criminal law and raises the general question of how extensive the criminal law should be. Subsequent discussions look in more detail at particular areas of concern, such as sexual behavior and the use of alcohol and other drugs.

Law comes from several sources. Administrative law, which is civil and not criminal, is an important source of law for analyzing criminal law. The enforcement of some administrative decisions may require the criminal law, and administrative law permeates much of our lives. In many instances, it is more effective than criminal law in controlling behavior.

An understanding of criminal law must involve a look at English common law, for that body of law continues to have a strong influence on the evolution of criminal law in the various states and in the federal system of the United States. Whether a current law is stated in the legislative enactments of Congress or state legislatures, in the federal or a state constitution, or whether it comes from judicial decisions, it may reflect the English common law. It is important to understand that judicial decisions, or case law, may be as binding as statutory law.

Because the processing of criminal law involves wide discretion, the chapter discusses the extent and nature of prosecutorial discretion. It cannot and should not be eliminated, but more attention should be given to judicial review of prosecutorial discretion.

Classification of crimes is important, too. Crimes are classified in several ways; the distinctions are not always agreed upon, but they are important for several reasons. The categories of felony or misdemeanor, *mala in se* or *mala prohibita*, crimes of moral turpitude or infamous crimes, and acts that are processed in separate hearings (such as juvenile delinquency), are important in determining procedures that must be followed and in assessing punishment. The category may determine whether civil penalties, such as loss of the right to vote, accompany conviction for the crime. Discretion plays an important role in determining which crimes are defined within each category and which actions are filed by the prosecutor.

An important discussion in this chapter focuses on some of the limitations on criminal law in the United States. Courts may hear and decide cases only when they have jurisdiction to do so. Statutes that are vague may not be used against the accused. Suspects may not be convicted for acts that were not defined as crimes when they were committed. Nor is it permissible to pass statutes aimed at *criminal punishment* for particular categories of persons to the exclusion of others. Categories such as race, ethnicity, and gender are examples. In addition, attention must be paid to statutes that have been repealed or amended and the circumstances under which people may be prosecuted in these instances.

Criminal statutes may not impose cruel and unusual punishment or punishment disproportional to the crime for which it is imposed. In both substantive and procedural criminal law, due process and equal protection of the laws must be observed. Other constitutional rights, such as the right to privacy, the right to free speech, and freedom of religion, may give way to criminal prosecutions in instances that endanger the public welfare.

The establishment of guilt in an adversary system is a crucial process. In U.S. criminal justice systems, the prosecution is required to prove all elements of a crime beyond a reasonable doubt. Unless that is done, the defendant should not be convicted. If that strong burden of proof is met by the prosecution, the defendant may be entitled to an acquittal or the prosecution may be limited to a conviction on a charge of a lesser crime if the defendant provides proof by a preponderance of the evidence that he or she had an adequate defense in the commission of the alleged crime.

Elements of a crime, defenses, and other issues are discussed in more detail in subsequent chapters, but this introductory chapter provides a basis for those more detailed discussions. The next three chapters are relevant to this overview as they discuss general principles of criminal liability and defenses to that liability.

STUDY QUESTIONS

1. Why do we have a *formal* system of criminal law, and what are its advantages and disadvantages when compared with an informal system?
2. Distinguish *civil law* from *criminal law*. What are torts, and why are they important? How should we decide whether a forbidden act should be covered by tort law, criminal law, or both? Relate your answers to the Ford Pinto case of Richard Grimshaw and more recent examples.
3. Who were Bentham and Beccaria, and why were they important?
4. Has the criminal justice system progressed or regressed by deemphasizing reformation or rehabilitation? Why or why not? Is retribution a reasonable justification for imposing the criminal law? If not, why not? If so, how far would you carry the concept?
5. Distinguish *mala in se* and *mala prohibita* crimes. Discuss the pros and cons of using the criminal law to control the use of drugs or alcohol. What about the prohibition of private sexual behavior between consenting adults?
6. What is *administrative law*, and why is it important to a study of criminal law?
7. Explain the meaning and importance of *common law*, *case law*, *statutory law*, and *procedural law*.
8. What is the Model Penal Code, and why is it important?
9. Articulate a plan for curbing prosecutorial discretion, and explain why your plan is a good one.
10. Why is it important to classify crimes, and in what ways may that be done?

11. Explain why a court may decide only cases over which it has jurisdiction.
12. Why do U.S. criminal justice systems provide that a statute is void if it is vague or too broad? How does the California case of *Kolender* illustrate these principles? What are the problems of applying *Kolender* to other fact patterns? Illustrate.
13. Distinguish between *ex post facto* laws and *bills of attainder*, *due process* and *equal protection*.
14. Do you think capital punishment is cruel and unusual punishment? Would your answer differ if you were comparing adults and juveniles?
15. Distinguish between *beyond a reasonable doubt* and *preponderance of the evidence*.

ENDNOTES

1. For a discussion of public attitudes toward punishing criminals, see Richard C. McCorkle, "Research Note: Punish and Rehabilitate? Public Attitudes Toward Six Common Crimes," *Crime & Delinquency* 39 (April 1993): 240-252. For a discussion of the impact of fear about crime on business, see Bonnie Fisher, "A Neighborhood Business Area Is Hurting: Crime, Fear of Crime, and Disorders Take Their Toll," *Crime & Delinquency* 37 (July 1991): 363-373.
2. "Family of Dahmer Victim Wins Claim," *St. Petersburg Times* (29 July 1992), p. 4. Numerous other lawsuits were filed in an effort to keep Dahmer from making any money on publications about the case. By 31 March 1994 one attorney had secured $80 million in civil judgments for his clients. To raise money to help pay these claims, the attorney proposed to have an auction of various articles owned by Dahmer, who objected to the auction. See "Trading on Gore: A Killer Garage Sale," *Plain Dealer* (31 March 1994), p.1B.
3. "Dahmer Victim's Family Loses Claim Against Police," *Orlando Sentinel* (26 November 1993), p. 20.
4. National Briefs, *Houston Chronicle* (15 November 1992), p. 7; "$105 Million Liability Award Against G.M. Is Struck Down," *New York Times* (14 June 1994), p. 8; "U.S. Juries Grow Tougher on Plaintiffs in Lawsuits," *New York Times* (17 June 1994), p. 1.
5. "Jury Awards $9.23 Million in Pan Am Bombing," *Miami Herald* (23 July 1992), p. 12. The jury decided against awarding additional damages for pain and suffering for the deaths of the attorney and another victim, whose family was awarded $9 million in actual damages. Attorneys for the estates of the two victims argued unsuccessfully that the victims had survived the midair explosion and were not killed until the plane hit the ground. Thus, they endured pain and suffering before they died. The jury disagreed. See "Today's News Update," *New York Law Journal* (28 August 1992), p. 1.
6. Pacific Mutual Life Ins. Co. v. Haslip, 499 U.S. 1 (1991). For a discussion of punitive damages, with reference to this case, see Jonathan Kagan, "Toward A Uniform Application of Punishment: Using the Federal Sentencing Guidelines As A Model for Punitive Damage Reform," *University of California Law Review* 40 (February 1993): 753-796.
7. For more detail, see the following sources: Max Grunhut, *Penal Reform: A Comparative Study* (Oxford: Clarendon Press, 1948); and William Blackstone, *Commentaries on the Laws of England (1763-1769)*, vol. 4 (reprinted Chicago: University of Chicago Press, 1979).

8. Gilbert Geis, "Jeremy Bentham," in Herman Mannheim, ed., *Pioneers in Criminology,* 2d ed. enlarged (Montclair, N.J.: Patterson Smith, 1972), p. 53.

9. Coleman Phillipson, *Three Criminal Law Reformers: Beccaria, Bentham, Romilly (1923)* (reprinted, Montclair, N.J.: Patterson Smith, 1970), pp. 166-168.

10. Beccaria's significant scholarly contribution, *On Crimes and Punishments,* was published in Italy in 1764 and in England in 1767. Cesare Beccaria, *On Crimes and Punishments,* trans. Henry Paolucci (Indianapolis: Bobbs-Merrill, l963).

11. Gerhard Mueller, "Cesare Beccaria and the Social Significance of his Concept of Criminal Policy." Paper presented at the International Congress on Cesare Beccaria and Modern Criminal Policy (Milan, Italy, 1988), referred to in Graeme Newman and Pietro Marongiu, "Penological Reform and the Myth of Beccaria," *Criminology* 28 (May 1990): 325-346; reference is on p. 325.

12. Graeme Newman, *Just and Painful: A Case for the Corporal Punishment of Criminals* (New York: Free Press, 1983), p. 71.

13. Commonwealth v. Ritter, Court of Oyer and Terminer, Philadelphia, 13 D. & C. 285 (1930).

14. Stephen Schafer, *Theories of Criminology* (New York: Random House, 1969), p. 72.

15. For a discussion see Harold Grasmick et al., "Protestant Fundamentalism and the Retributive Doctrine of Punishment," *Criminology* 30 (February 1992): 21-46.

16. John Stuart Mill, quoted in John Kaplan, *Criminal Justice: Introductory Cases and Materials* (Mineola, N.Y.: Foundation Press, 1973).

17. Norval Morris and Gordon Hawkins, *The Honest Politician's Guide to Crime Control* (Chicago: University of Chicago Press, 1969), p. 2. See also Patrick Devlin, *The Enforcement of Morals* (New York: Oxford University Press, 1965); and Jeffrey Reiman, *Justice and Modern Moral Philosophy* (New Haven, Conn.: Yale University Press, 1990).

18. Morris and Hawkins, ibid., p. 15.

19. U.S. Constitution, Article III, Section 3.

20. See William Blackstone, *Commentaries on the Laws of England 1765-1769,* 4 vols. (reprinted Chicago: University of Chicago Press, 1979).

21. See Hite v. United States, 168 F.2d 973 (10th Cir. 1948); and Boone v. United States, 235 F.2d 939 (4th Cir. 1956).

22. American Law Institute, *Model Penal Code and Commentaries,* Section 1.05 (1985).

23. For a general discussion of discretion, see Michael R. Gottfredson and Don M. Gottfredson, *Decision Making in Criminal Justice: Toward the Rational Exercise of Discretion* (Cambridge, Mass.: Ballinger, 1980). For a discussion of police discretion see Kenneth Culp Davis, *Police Discretion* (St. Paul, Minn.: West, 1975). Discretion in sentencing is discussed in Chapter 12 of this text.

24. For a journalistic account of prosecutors and their work based on interviews with famous prosecutors, see James Stewart, *The Prosecutors* (New York: Simon and Schuster, 1987), reviewed and criticized by law professor and trial attorney Alan M. Dershowitz of Harvard, in the *American Bar Association Journal* (1 October 1987): 144-146.

25. For a discussion, see Stuart P. Green, "Private Challenges to Prosecutorial Inaction: A Model Declaratory Judgment Statute," *Yale Law Journal* 97 (February 1988): 488-507; and Kenneth L. Wainstein, "Judicially Initiated Prosecution: A Means of Preventing Continuing Victimization in the Event of Prosecutorial Inaction," *California Law Review* 76 (May 1988): 727-778.

26. See, for example, Cassia Spohn et al., "The Impact of the Ethnicity and Gender of Defendants on the Decision to Reject or Dismiss Felony Charges," *Criminology* 25 (February 1987): 175-191; "Selective Prosecution: Critics See Racism Behind Indictment of Federal Judge," *American Bar Association Journal*

77 (May 1991): 15; Stewart J. D'Alessio and Lisa Stolzenberg, "Socioeconomic Status and the Sentencing of the Traditional Offender," *Journal of Criminal Justice* 21 (1993): 61-77; and Darrell Steffensmeier et al., "Gender and Imprisonment Decisions," *Criminology* 31 (August 1993): 411-446.

27. See Celesta A. Albonetti, "Criminality, Prosecutorial Screening, and Uncertainty: Toward a Theory of Discretionary Decision Making in Felony Case Processings," *Criminology* 24 (November 1986): 623-644.

28. Blackledge v. Perry, 417 U.S. 21 (1974), *overruled on other grounds,* Bordenkircher v. Hayes, 434 U.S. 357 (1978), *reh'g. denied,* 435 U.S. 918 (1978). See also United States v. Burt, 619 F.2d 831 (9th Cir. 1980); and Adamson v. Rickette, 865 F.2d 1011 (9th Cir. 1988), *cert. denied,* 497 U.S. 1031 (1990), *and stay denied,* 955 F.2d 614 (9th Cir. 1992).

29. For a discussion, see Marcia R. Chaiken and Jan M. Chaiken, *Priority Prosecution of High-Rate Dangerous Offenders* (Washington, D.C.: National Institute of Justice, March 1991).

30. United States v. Richardson, 856 F.2d 644 (4th Cir. 1988), case citations omitted.

31. See New York Penal Code, Title E, Article 55, Section 55.10 (1994).

32. Lee v. Wisconsin State Board of Dental Examiners, 139 N.W.2d 61, 65 (Wis. 1966).

33. Connally v. General Construction Co., 269 U.S. 385 (1926).

34. Cal. Penal Code, Section 647(e) (1994).

35. Kolender v. Lawson 461 U.S. 352 (1983).

36. Horn v. City of Montgomery, Ala., 619 So.2d 949 (Ala.Crim.App. 1993), cases and citations omitted.

37. Thornhill v. Alabama, 310 U.S. 88, 97 (1940).

38. U.S. Constitution, Article I, Section 9(3).

39. Collins v. Youngblood, 497 U.S. 37 (1990), *remanded,* 909 F.2d 803 (5th Cir. 1990).

40. Cummings v. Missouri, 71 U.S. (4 Wall.) 277 (1867). See this case for a history of the concept.

41. United States v. Lovett, 328 U.S. 303 (1946).

42. *Ex parte* Garland, 71 U.S. (4 Wall.) 333 (1866).

43. See Nixon v. Administrator of General Services, 433 U.S. 425 (1977).

44. See State v. Babbitt, 457 A.2d 1049 (R.I. 1983).

45. For a discussion of the concept of cruel and unusual punishment in relationship to methods of capital punishment, see Chapter 12 of this text.

46. See Coker v. Georgia, 433 U.S. 584 (1977). For discussions of the Court's holdings on capital punishment in general, see the earlier cases of Furman v. Georgia, 408 U.S. 238 (1972); Gregg v. Georgia, 428 U.S. 153 (1976); Proffitt v. Florida, 428 U.S. 242 (1976); Jurek v. Texas, 428 U.S. 262 (1976); Woodson v. North Carolina, 428 U.S. 280 (1976); and Roberts v. Louisiana, 428 U.S. 325 (1976).

47. See Weems v. United States, 217 U.S. 349 (1910). See also Chapter 12 of this text.

48. See Chapter 12 for a discussion of Rummel v. Estelle, 445 U.S. 263 (1980).

49. See Seritt v. Alabama, 731 F.2d 728 (11th Cir. 1984), *cert. denied,* 469 U.S. 1062 (1984).

50. See, for example, Pulley v. Harris, 465 U.S. 37 (1984).

51. Burton v. Livingston, 791 F.2d 97, 99-100. (8th Cir. 1986), citations omitted.

52. Ravin v. State, 537 P.2d 494, 504 (Alaska 1975).

53. See State v. Murphy, 570 P.2d 1070 (Ariz. 1977); and State v. Smith, 610 P.2d 869 (Wash. 1980), *cert. denied,* 449 U.S. 873 (1980).

54. State v. Erickson, 574 P.2d 1 (Alaska 1978).

55. For a brief discussion of the adversary system and a comparison with the inquisitory system, see Mirjan Damaska, "Adversary System," in Sanford H. Kadish, ed., *Encyclopedia of Crime and Justice*, vol. 1 (New York: Free Press, 1983), pp. 24-30. See also Gordon Van Kessel, "Adversary Excesses in the American Criminal Trial," *Notre Dame Law Review* 67 (1992): 403-543.

56. Gordon Van Kessel, "Adversary Excesses in the American Criminal Trial," *Notre Dame Law Review* 67 (1992): 403-543. See also the classic study of juries by Harry Kalven and Hans Zeisel, *The American Jury* (Boston: Little Brown, 1966). For more recent analyses see Lawrence S. Wrightsman, *In The Jury Box: Controversies in the Courtroom* (Beverly Hills, Calif.: Sage, 1987); and Valerie P. Hans and Neil Vidmar, *Judging the Jury* (New York: Plenum, 1986).

57. *In re* Winship, 397 U.S. 358, 363-364 (1970), case names and citations omitted.

58. See Mullaney v. Wilbur, 421 U.S. 684 (1975); and Patterson v. New York, 432 U.S. 197 (1977).

59. Victor v. Nebraska, 114 S.Ct. 1239 (1994), *reh'g denied,* 114 S. Ct. 1872 (1994) For a discussion, see David O. Stewart, "Uncertainty about Reasonable Doubt," *American Bar Association Journal* 80 (June 1994): 38. For an interpretation and application, see State v. Smith, 637 So. 2d 398 (La. 1994).

60. See Martin v. Ohio, 480 U.S. 228 (1987), *reh'g. denied*, 481 U.S. 1024 (1987), holding in an assault case that the burden of proof on self-defense could be shifted to the defendant if the absence of self-defense is not an element of murder or assault in the statute in question.

Chapter 2

Elements of Criminal Liability

Outline

Key Terms

actus reus
attendant
    circumstances
causation
circumstantial
    evidence

culpability
elements of a crime
enterprise liability
euthanasia
intent
mens rea

mistrial
motive
negligence
proximate cause
strict liability
vicarious liability

Introduction

This chapter discusses the **elements of a crime**, those generally applicable to crimes in U.S. criminal justice systems. Subsequent chapters consider the elements of specific crimes. Although it is possible to explain and illustrate these general elements, interpretations may differ considerably from jurisdiction to jurisdiction. Thus, in the actual practice of criminal law, it is important to analyze the case law of a specific jurisdiction.

Also important to U.S. criminal law is the concept that only the guilty party is punished. This principle is an ancient one and can be illustrated by some of the punishments in the Bible. Chapter 22 of Deuteronomy stipulates the following punishments for illicit sexual relations. If a man has relations with a betrothed virgin whom he finds in the city, both will be stoned to death—she, because she did not cry for help, being in the city where she could get help, and he for "humbling her." But if a man finds a betrothed virgin in the field and forces her into sexual relations, only he will die. Because she cried and there was no one to help her, she was an unwilling party and therefore not guilty. Chapter 24 includes this statement: "The fathers shall not be put to death for the children, neither shall the children be put to death for the fathers: every man shall be put to death for his own sin."

Chapter 10 discusses the meaning of *guilty party*, for a person may be guilty of a crime by assisting another person to commit the act. This chapter focuses on the elements of criminal liability (listed in Focus 2.1) that apply to all crimes.

The Criminal Act

Although it might seem simplistic to state that a crime involves a criminal act, the matter is complex. The term *criminal act*, or **actus reus**, is open to interpretation. Technically the term means a wrongful deed that, if combined with the other elements of a crime, may result in the legal arrest, trial, and conviction of the accused. This definition eliminates the possibility of criminal punishment for one's thoughts. Although assisting, conspiring with, or hiring another to commit a crime may be a crime (as discussed in Chapter 10), one may not be punished for criminal thoughts alone.

Reasons for Requiring a Criminal Act

There are many reasons for not punishing thoughts. Administering a system that did so would be difficult, if not impossible, because we cannot punish acts about which we have no knowledge. Personal privacy, very important in our system, would be invaded; life would be intolerable. We cherish the freedom to daydream and to fantasize even when those thoughts and fantasies concern unacceptable, perhaps illegal behavior.

Under the principles of U.S. criminal laws, generally it is a violation to punish a person for a particular *status* (with the possible exception of the status of being a multiple felon), such as the status of being a drug addict.

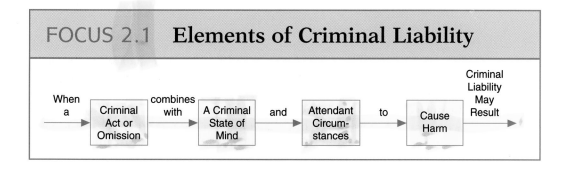

FOCUS 2.1 Elements of Criminal Liability

In the 1962 landmark case of *Robinson* v. *California*, the U.S. Supreme Court invalidated a state statute that made it a misdemeanor for a person to "be addicted to the use of narcotics." The penalty for conviction of this crime was a mandatory jail term of not less than ninety days. The Court emphasized that the length of that jail term was not cruel and unusual punishment per se, but it was cruel and unusual to make the status of being an addict a crime for which one could be "continuously guilty . . . whether or not he has ever used or possessed any narcotics within the State, and whether or not he has been guilty of an antisocial behavior there." According to the Court, this would be the same as making it a crime "for a person to be mentally ill, or a leper, or to be afflicted with a venereal disease."[1]

Nature and Meaning of the Criminal Act Requirement

Given the requirement of a criminal act, we must decide what constitutes an act, a controversial subject. Some scholars include involuntary acts; others omit them. The Model Penal Code (M.P.C.) requires a voluntary act and excludes the following as involuntary:

1. a reflex or convulsion;
2. a bodily movement during unconsciousness or sleep;
3. conduct during hypnosis or resulting from hypnotic suggestion;
4. a bodily movement that otherwise is not a product of the effort or determination of the actor, either conscious or habitual.[2]

Exclusion of Involuntary Conduct

The comments to the M.P.C. note that involuntary actions might endanger society's health and welfare but that the criminal law is not the appropriate way to handle such problems. Assume that while driving your car you have an unexpected stroke, lose control of the car, run into another car, and cause a death. This is not a voluntary act; you will not be responsible for the tort of wrongful death or for a criminal act. You might be held responsible in both tort and criminal law, however, if you *knew* you were subject to such attacks because of previous attacks and circumstances that would indicate probable future attacks. This issue arises frequently in cases involving epileptics, exemplified in *People* v. *Decina*.[3]

People v. *Decina*

[The defendant drove his car on a public highway, had an epileptic seizure, lost control of his car, and killed four people. He was charged with violation of a criminal statute that provided, "A person who operates or drives any vehicle of any kind in a reckless or culpably negligent manner, whereby a human being is killed is guilty of criminal negligence in the operation of a vehicle resulting in death." In upholding the conviction, the court said:]

[T]his defendant knew he was subject to epileptic attacks and seizures that might strike at any time. He also knew that a moving vehicle uncontrolled on a public highway is a highly dangerous instrumentality capable of unrestrained destruction. With this *knowledge*, and without anyone accompanying him, he deliberately took a chance. . . . How can we say as a matter of law that this did not amount to culpable negligence . . . ?

To hold otherwise would be to say that a man may freely indulge himself in liquor in the same hope that it will not affect his driving, and if it later develops that ensuing intoxication causes dangerous and reckless driving resulting in death, his unconsciousness or involuntariness at that time would relieve him from prosecution under the statute. His awareness of a condition which he knows may produce such consequences as here, and his disregard of the consequences, renders him liable for culpable negligence, as the courts below have properly held. To have a sudden sleeping spell, an unexpected heart or other disabling attack, without any prior knowledge or warning thereof, is an altogether different situation.

The court's last sentence raises interesting legal questions, for example, in the reference to sleeping. Although committing a crime during your sleep may not subject you to the criminal law, it is not necessarily true that falling asleep at the wheel will relieve you of criminal liability for wrongful death or injury that results when the car crashes. The facts of each case must be examined carefully before criminal liability is determined. That is what makes law exciting and challenging but also difficult.

Contrast these two cases. In one, decided in 1879, the defendant fell asleep in the public room of a hotel. A porter, in an effort to awaken the defendant and get him to leave, shook him whereupon the defendant pulled a gun and killed the porter. The court said that if the defendant fired the gun without gaining consciousness, he could not be held liable for the murder. Under these facts, the issue would be one of deciding whether or not the defendant acted while unconscious. If he did, he may have had an adequate defense.[4] (Defenses are discussed in the next two chapters.)

In the second case, the defendant fell asleep while driving, and his car ran over a pedestrian. The court found criminal liability and said, "While one cannot be liable for what he does during the unconsciousness of sleep, he is responsible for allowing himself to go to sleep to get into a condition where the accident could happen without his being aware of it."[5] Criminal liability may be found also when injuries and deaths are caused by those who operate vehicles under the influence of alcohol or other drugs. Focus 2.2 discusses two nationally publicized cases that illustrate this point.

On the other hand, a Texas soft-drink delivery truck driver was acquitted of all twenty-one counts of criminally negligent homicide arising from the deaths of school children who died when his truck crashed with the bus in which they were riding. The bus plunged into a roadside gravel pit on 21 September 1989, resulting in the worst school bus accident in Texas history. The jury heard two-and one-half weeks of testimony in the case of Ruben Perez before deliberating and deciding that the cause of the accident was defective brakes on the truck. The victims' families have received over $150 million in civil damages from the owner and the designer of the tractor-trailer driven by Mr. Perez. Mr. Perez has filed civil claims against the owner of the vehicle, claiming that he is emotionally scarred and brain damaged as a result of the accident, which was caused by their negligence in not maintaining the brakes in proper condition.[6]

PROOF OF AN ACT

Although involuntary conduct may be excluded from the act requirement of a crime, it is not always easy to determine the difference between a voluntary act and an involuntary act. If a person engages in conduct under orders or duress, is the conduct voluntary or involuntary? The federal criminal code provides that whoever within a federal prison "conveys . . . from place to place any weapon . . . designed to kill, injure or disable any officer, agent, employee or inmate thereof" may be charged with an offense and, if convicted, incarcerated for not more than ten years.[7]

How would you interpret the following facts under that statute? Greschner and Logan were inmates in a federal penitentiary. While Logan was cutting Greschner's hair, a fight between the two developed. Greschner, who swung at Logan, was seen holding a weapon at some point during the fight. A correctional officer intervened, stopped the fight, and ordered Greschner, who was not harmed, to return to his cell after surrendering his homemade knife to the officer.

Did Greschner "convey" a weapon in terms of the statute under which he was charged? Although the appellate court upheld Greschner's assault conviction, it reversed the conveying charge for lack of sufficient evidence. The court emphasized that although the defendant possessed and used the weapon, there was no evidence that he transported it from place to place within the institution, as required by the statute. Although it is possible that Greschner did convey the weapon, the government did not offer evidence of that element at trial. To the contrary, the evidence suggested that another inmate gave Greschner the weapon after he was attacked by Logan.[8]

The same court that reversed Greschner's conveyance conviction upheld that of another inmate in whose case there was evidence that he transported the weapon within the prison before being apprehended.[9] Thus, the facts of each case must be considered carefully. There must be sufficient evidence to support each element of the crime. As noted in Chapter 1, the

FOCUS 2.2 Criminal Liability for the Results of Vehicular Accidents

Most cases of legal liability for injuries or deaths caused by the negligence of vehicle drivers fall within tort law, but there are exceptions, as these cases illustrate.

1. Engineer Sentenced in Conrail Crash

Rick Gates, an ex-Conrail engineer, was sentenced to five years in prison and a $1,000 fine after his attorney negotiated a plea bargain shortly before his trial was scheduled to begin in March 1988. Gates entered a plea of guilty to one misdemeanor manslaughter count, although sixteen people were killed and 175 were injured when Gates drove three linked Conrail locomotives into the path of an Amtrak passenger train, creating the worst accident in Amtrak history. Gates admitted that he had used marijuana, but the prosecution accepted a plea bargain because of the difficulty or impossibility of positive proof after the federal circuit court in the Maryland jurisdiction ruled against postcrash drug testing.

Judge Joseph Murphy, who accepted the plea and sentenced Gates, said, "I don't think any fair analysis can really result in the conclusion that he was stoned on marijuana at the time...But what he did in terms of failure to follow procedures was to show us that he didn't give a damn. He just didn't care." In other court action, Gates entered a guilty plea to a federal charge of conspiring to obstruct an investigation of the wreck.

2. Driver Sentenced to Sixteen-Year Prison Term After Twenty-Seven Died in a Bus-Pickup Collision

The jury acquitted him of murder in late 1989 but convicted thirty-six-year-old Larry Mahoney of manslaughter, assault, and wanton endangerment after twenty-seven people died and thirty-nine were injured (twelve of whom were badly burned) when he drove his pick-up into a school bus. Most of the dead died of smoke inhalation when the bus caught fire after impact. Mahoney, who said he had spent most of the day prior to the crash drinking with his friends, caused the worst drunk-driving accident in history. He is serving his sentence in the Kentucky State Penitentiary.

Rick Gates

Two couples whose daughters were killed in the wreck filed civil suits against Mahoney and the Ford Motor Company, seeking over $38.5 million in specific damages and $20 billion in punitive damages. These lawsuits and sixty-four others were dismissed in 1992. Several cases were settled out of court.

Summarized by the author from media sources.

prosecution has the burden of proving "beyond a reasonable doubt every element of the charged offense."[10]

Possession As an Act

An act might include *possession* of illegal goods, such as narcotics, alcohol, or stolen property. Possession is considered the act. As with other acts, however, possession alone may not be sufficient for a successful criminal prosecution. Generally when a criminal statute includes possession as a crime, it is interpreted to mean conscious possession. Attempts and solicitations may be considered acts, too; they are discussed in Chapter 10.

Criminal Failure to Act

Omission or failure to act may constitute an act for purposes of criminal liability but only when there is a legal duty to act, such as the legal duty imposed on parents to come to the aid of their children or any duty imposed by a contract, such as marriage, employment, or custody. This principle is controversial in both tort and criminal law. Many situations in which there is no duty to act appear to call for human action to prevent harm to others.

A highly publicized criminal act watched by people who did not intervene is featured in Focus 2.3. The moral outrage at hearing that some people not only watched but cheered during a gang rape in New Bedford, Massachusetts led some states to consider legislation to criminalize the failure to act to help prevent a crime. After this case Rhode Island enacted a statute providing for a $500 fine and/or up to one year in jail for people convicted of the misdemeanor of failing to report to police a sexual assault or attempted sexual assault that takes place in their presence.[11]

Similar results occurred in Chicago after one month in which bystanders, in four separate incidents, ignored victims' pleas for help in the city's transit system. Their refusal to become involved in two murders, one rape, and one slashing led to a citizen outcry for more security and greater police protection and for legislation to require bystanders to take affirmative action when they witness alleged criminal acts. According to a University of Chicago sociologist, "People are afraid, they are angry, but no one can tell them how they should respond . . . . And the police are no help on this."[12]

Despite the moral outrage one might have in reading the facts of these cases, it is important to consider why the law is reluctant to legislate affir-

FOCUS 2.3 Should Failure to Report or Stop a Crime Be a Crime?

In the spring of 1983, four men raped a young woman repeatedly in a New Bedford, Massachusetts, bar. They were indicted along with two men who were arrested for encouraging them while holding the woman down on the bar table where the acts occurred. Numerous witnesses observed the gang rape without calling the police, some reportedly yelling, "Go for it."

Public outrage at these acts led to attempts to enact statutes to require bystanders, under penalty of civil or criminal law, to come to the aid of crime victims. It was argued that at a minimum the law should require witnesses to call the police. Some have argued that the law should require affirmative action to intervene when alleged criminal acts are observed.

The incident and subsequent trial received considerable media attention. The trial resulted in two acquittals and two convictions. The case stirred up debate on the ancient theory of imitation as a cause of crime. In April 1984, a twelve-year-old boy was charged with the sexual assault of a ten-year-old girl. He forced the girl to engage in oral sex and then forced her onto a pool table, further assaulting her while other children watched. Officials claimed that he might have gotten the idea for these alleged crimes by watching television accounts of the New Bedford rape trial.[1]

The refusal of bystanders to come to the aid of the New Bedford rape victim was reminiscent of the widely publicized 1967 case of Kitty Genovese whose New York neighbors refused to come to her aid while she was stabbed repeatedly. In discussing these and other cases in 1993, criminologist Gilbert Geis stated, "It's becoming a much more anonymous society, a much more uncaring society." Many bystanders do not want to become involved in any way in alleged criminal activity. Even as a witness they may be threatened; it is easier to avoid involvement. On the other hand, some bystanders have taken affirmative, dangerous action to save the lives of victims, as illustrated by those who came to the aid of the truck driver who was beaten in Los Angeles during the riots following the acquittal in state court of four white police officers accused of using excessive force in apprehending Rodney King in 1992.[2]

Legally the issue is not whether bystanders should go to the aid of others but whether the law should *require* them to do so.

[1.] Summarized by the author from media accounts.
[2.] "Silent Crime: Bystanders Who Say, Do Nothing," *Orlando Sentinel* (11 May 1993), p. 5.

mative action to aid others. Even in tort law generally there is no legal duty to come to the aid of another unless there is a special relationship, such as that of husband and wife or parent and child or a contractual relationship (such as exists between the officials of a day-care center and a parent).

Problems with Requiring Affirmative Action

Requiring people to take affirmative action to aid others, whether through a civil or criminal statute, creates problems. How much action should be required? What if the bystander might be injured or killed by taking affirmative action? Consider the case that occurred on a New York subway. A forty-five-year-old mentally disabled man was shot and killed when he said "Leave him alone" to an armed robber whom he observed trying to rob another subway passenger.[13] This good samaritan had no legal duty to take affirmative action to try to prevent the crime. Had he had a legal duty and died as a result of performing that duty, do you believe the law should provide any compensation for his survivors?

If you believe the law should require all of us to attempt to prevent alleged crimes, what would you require bystanders to do in a situation like the facts of the New Bedford rape case? It is one thing to require people to call the police but quite another to require them to try to stop the offender. This is true particularly in light of potential violence and increasing evidence that in crowded cities like New York, amateur pickpockets, working in teams, victimize people who go to the aid of a team member pretending to be in trouble. According to a ten-year veteran of New York City's Transit Authority Police Department's pickpocket squad, "That's a very common ruse . . . .Sometimes they fake epileptic seizures or sickness....All they need is a fraction of a second, and they've got your wallet."[14]

Some cases are easier in terms of requirements but raise the issue of whether civil or criminal law should be used. The line between civil and criminal actions may be drawn in terms of the degree of seriousness of the violation. The civil responsibility of landlords to tenants who are injured because of the landlord's failure to keep the premises in repair might be placed within the criminal law when the failures indicate *gross* negligence. An example of gross negligence might be the landlord's failure to repair broken door locks, which facilitates the criminal assault and battery or murder of a tenant, particularly after the landlord was notified that the locks were broken and that there had been violent crimes in the area. Another might be the failure to provide fire escapes, the lack of which results in the burning death of a tenant.

A legal duty might exist also when a person takes affirmative action that creates a situation of danger to one to whom no duty is owed otherwise. A California appellate court upheld the conviction of a defendant who met her victim at a bar. The two went to her home where he appeared to be drugged. When he asked the defendant for a spoon, she gave him one, knowing that he wanted it for using drugs. Subsequently the guest passed out, and the defendant returned to the bar, leaving him at her home. When the defendant returned to her home, the guest was unconscious. The court held that the defendant had a civil (tort) duty to exercise some care when she became aware that the victim needed medical attention. Her act of leaving him alone rather than seeking adequate medical help constituted criminal negligence that was sufficient to sustain her criminal conviction after his death.[15]

Failure to attempt to rescue a person in danger may be a crime, but only if there is a legal duty to act.

One final point should be mentioned in this discussion. Failure to act where there is a legal duty to act is not a crime unless that failure *caused* the harm, injury, or death. A discussion of causation occurs later in this chapter.

The Criminal State of Mind

An act requires a criminal mind or criminal intent. The term ***mens rea*** is used even in popular writing; yet it is one of the most debated and frequently litigated terms in criminal law. The word, literally meaning "a guilty mind," refers to the **intent** requirement of criminal law. The statement that *mens rea* is a required element of a crime, however, is misleading if taken literally. As we discuss later in this chapter, some acts involving *fault* but unaccompanied by a guilty mind may constitute crimes.

The Common Law Approach

The common law defines three qualities of criminal mind: *general intent, specific intent,* and *criminal negligence.* Criminal negligence is discussed later with the Model Penal Code approach. General intent and specific intent are difficult to distinguish. Simply stated, *general intent* refers to the willful commission or omission of the criminal act, and *specific intent* requires more. The difference may be illustrated by the common law crime of larceny-theft. To establish that the defendant committed this crime, the prosecution must prove that the accused meant to take the property of another and carry it away, which indicates a general intent to commit the forbidden act. An additional element of larceny-theft is a specific intent, usually stated as *the intent to steal* the property. That is, the prosecution must prove that the defendant intended to deprive the owner of the property permanently or for an unreasonable length of time, not just that the property was taken away intentionally. Theoretically a person could intend to take property away from its lawful owner without having an intent to steal that property.

If one compares the numerous cases in which courts have tried to differentiate the terms, the distinction between general and specific intent is so confusing that some scholars have suggested that the terms be abandoned and that we refer only to the *intent* requirement. One legal scholar has noted that terms like specific and general intent "contribute far more to confusion than to clarity." In particular, "general intent is an extraordinarily esoteric concept."[16]

The drafters of the Model Penal Code offered a solution to the confusion between the general and specific intent requirements by suggesting a differentiation of the *levels* of intent. Their approach has been followed so widely that it deserves special attention.

The Model Penal Code Approach

As indicated in Focus 2.4, the Model Penal Code's four levels of criminal **culpability**, or criminal blameworthiness, are *purposely, knowingly, recklessly,* and *negligently.* The Explanatory Note of the M.P.C. indicates that these elements apply to all crimes except those involving *strict liability,* discussed later in this chapter. These levels of culpability apply also to each *material element* of a crime. We have seen that the elements of most crimes involve an act and a criminal state of mind that concur to produce a harmful result. All of these are *material elements* of the crime.

The applicable level of culpability that applies to each element of a specific crime may be defined by a general provision within that state's criminal code or by the statute that defines that crime. But the language of the statute may not be clear and thus may require interpretation by the courts.

PROBLEMS OF INTERPRETATION: AN EXAMPLE

An example of a criminal statute that led to interpretation problems is found in the Texas Penal Code, which at the time of the case discussed below defined injury to a child as follows: "(a) A person commits an offense if he intentionally, knowingly, recklessly or with criminal negligence engages in conduct that causes serious bodily injury...to a child who is 14 years of age or younger."[17]

A defendant charged with intentionally and knowingly causing serious bodily injury to her child by placing him in a tub of hot water was convicted under this statute. On appeal she argued that the trial judge was in error when he charged the jury that a person acts *intentionally, or with intent* when it is that person's *"conscious objective or desire to engage in the conduct or cause the result."* In other words, for a conviction under this statute, the prosecution must prove only that the defendant knowingly or intentionally put the child in hot water.

The defense argued that the statute requires the prosecution to prove that the defendant had a "conscious objective or desire to cause serious bodily

FOCUS 2.4 General Requirements of Culpability

Model Penal Code, Section 2.02

(1) *Minimum Requirements of Culpability.* Except as provided in Section 2.05, a person is not guilty of an offense unless he acted purposely, knowingly, recklessly or negligently, as the law may require, with respect to each material element of the offense.

(2) *Kinds of Culpability Defined.*

(a) *Purposely.*

A person acts purposely with respect to a material element of an offense when:

(i) if the element involves the nature of his conduct or a result thereof, it is his conscious object to engage in conduct of that nature or to cause such a result; and

(ii) if the element involves the attendant circumstances, he is aware of the existence of such circumstances or he believes or hopes that they exist.

(b) *Knowingly.*

A person acts knowingly with respect to a material element of an offense when:

(i) if the element involves the nature of his conduct or the attendant circumstances, he is aware that his conduct is of that nature or that such circumstances exist; and

(ii) if the element involves the result of his conduct, he is aware that it is practically certain that his conduct will cause such a result.

(c) *Recklessly.*

A person acts recklessly with respect to a material element of an offense when he consciously disregards a substantial and unjustifiable risk that the material element exists or will result from his conduct. The risk must be of such a nature and degree that, considering the nature and purpose of the actor's conduct and the circumstances known to him, its disregard involves a gross deviation from the standard of conduct that a law-abiding person would observe in the actor's situation.

(d) *Negligently.*

A person acts negligently with respect to a material element of an offense when he should be aware of a substantial and unjustifiable risk that the material element exists or will result from his conduct. The risk must be of such a nature and degree that the actor's failure to perceive it, considering the nature and purpose of his conduct and the circumstances known to him, involves a gross deviation from the standard of care that a reasonable person would observe in the actor's situation.

SOURCE: *Model Penal Code*, Copyright 1985 by The American Law Institute. Reprinted with the permission of the American Law Institute.

injury to the child or that she was aware that putting the child in the water was reasonably certain to cause serious bodily injury to the child."[18]

The confusion arose over whether the statute meant that the required level of culpability applied only to the criminal act or also to the *result* of that act. The appellate court held that the prosecution had to prove that in addition to having the mental culpability required for the commission of the act, the defendant intended or knew that serious bodily injury would result from that act.

Because such interpretation problems are extensive in case law, it is important to understand the impossibility of stating what is meant by *the law of intent* in criminal law. Rather, it is necessary to analyze carefully the prior interpretations of a statute before concluding how that statute might apply to the facts of a new case. It is necessary also to consider the intent requirement in terms of state and federal constitutional law. For example, the Ninth Circuit has held that the First Amendment right to free speech (see Appendix A) requires that a federal statute prohibiting the distribution, shipping, or receipt of child pornography requires knowledge that the material involved minority performers.

In *United States* v. *X-Citement Video, Inc.*, the defendant was convicted of violating the federal Protection of Children Against Sexual Exploitation Act by purchasing videotapes (and having some of those tapes shipped through interstate commerce) featuring Traci Lords, whose performance in pornographic films while she was an adolescent produced considerable litigation. The case involved a number of issues on appeal, but for our purposes here, only one phase of the holding is important. In 1992 a federal appeals court concluded that "the constitutional minimum requirement of scienter [intent] for the Act's proscription of transporting or receiving child pornography is knowledge that at least one of the performers is under age 18." In March 1994, the U.S. Supreme Court agreed to hear the case and decide whether in prosecuting a case under the statute in question the government must prove that the defendant who distributed or received sexually explicit films or photographs involving minors knew that those performers were not adults.[19]

LEVELS OF CULPABILITY DEFINED

In categorizing levels of culpability, the Model Penal Code distinguishes between *purposely* and *knowingly*. Both involve knowledge, but *purposely* is a stronger, more culpable intent because the defendant *consciously* intended to engage in the criminal act or to bring about a particular result, as distinct from having been "practically certain" that particular results would follow the act.

Both *purposely* and *knowingly* are to be distinguished from *recklessness*, which involves serious risks and which, according to the M.P.C. comments, "resembles acting knowingly in that a state of awareness is involved, but the awareness is of risk, that is of a probability less than substantial certainty; the matter is contingent from the actor's point of view."

To constitute recklessness, the risk must be substantial *and* unjustified. The substantial risk taken by a surgeon who knows that an operation *may* be fatal but who knows also that the patient will die without the operation does not constitute reckless behavior under this code. The M.P.C. comments indicate that there is no way to make the definition of recklessness more specific; the jury must analyze the facts of each case in determining whether behavior was reckless.

There is some disagreement over the inclusion within the criminal law of acts that involve negligence, the fourth level of culpability in the M.P.C. **Negligence** refers to acts that a reasonable person would not do or the failure to do something that a reasonable person would do under the same or similar circumstances. It does not require a criminal intent.

It may be argued that none of the purposes of criminal punishment discussed in Chapter 1 are furthered by including negligent acts within the criminal law. But in defense of including negligence as a basis for criminal culpability, we should note that the Model Penal Code refers to conduct that is *grossly* negligent, which is conduct that is more culpable than ordinary negligence. Ordinary negligence is sufficient to establish a legal *civil* cause of action in torts but not in criminal law.

Proving Criminal Intent

Proving that a defendant intended to commit a crime is not always an easy task, but the law does permit inferences of intent from relevant facts. If defendant A fires a loaded pistol at B, intending to kill B, but instead kills C, the law will permit an inference of intent sufficient to charge A with the murder of C. But how may one prove that A intended to kill B, particularly as it is unlikely that A will admit that intent when questioned? Suppose A intended only to wound or scare B? These are factual issues that must be determined by the jury or by the judge if the case is not tried by a jury. If sufficient **circumstantial evidence** is presented, the jury may be permitted to infer intent from that evidence. Consider the facts in the tragic incident described in Focus 2.5 and conclude how you would decide the case.

One law student found out the meaning of this statement when he tried unsuccessfully to convince the court that he was speeding because he spilled hot coffee on himself inadvertently. The defendant argued that he had no intention of violating the speeding ordinance. The judge agreed that if he could not control his speeding (for example, the brakes failed and he had no prior warning that they might be defective) he would not be legally liable for driving 40 MPH in a 30 MPH zone. But the court noted that the defendant chose to take the hot coffee into the car and drink it while driving. He thus "set in motion the sequence of events leading to a violation of the statute."[20]

Intent Distinguished from Motive

In criminal law, intent and motive must be distinguished. **Motive** refers to the *why* of a defendant's actions. Hungry parents who steal bread from the local store may do so to feed their families, but that motive does not negate the crime. The state does not have to prove a bad motive to get a convic-

---

FOCUS 2.5 Little League's First Homicide Victim

In May 1993 the town of Castro Valley, California, thirty miles from San Francisco, was the scene of the first homicide in the fifty-four-year history of Little League baseball. It was alleged that during the game a member of the Castro Valley Black Socks, a predominantly white team, was not playing at the time he yelled racial epithets at the opponents, the Ashland American Indians, a team composed primarily of African Americans and Hispanics. Other verbal exchanges occurred, but apparently no one expected violence. After the game the players shook hands, but before they left the field a fight began.

According to police, the Ashland catcher, Antonio John Messina, swung a bat at the Castro player who yelled the racial epithet. That player ducked, and Joseph Matteucci, who was behind the targeted victim, was struck in the head. Matteucci never regained consciousness; he died three days later. A Castro player threw a stone at Messina, allegedly to prevent him from leaving, resulting in a head injury to Messina. Messina was charged with murder. The player who threw the rock was arrested but released. According to the district attorney, that player "used reasonable force against a fleeing murderer."[1]

The fact that the catcher hit a person he did not intend to hit will not eliminate the required intent element of the crime.

[1.] Summarized from "Town Asks, 'Why?' After a Little-League Killing," *New York Times* (23 May 1993), p. 10; and "Trash-talking Ends in Death on a Little League Field: Words to Die By," *Time* (7 June 1993), p. 83.

---

tion. Motive arises frequently in cases of **euthanasia**, which literally means "easy death." The term is used most frequently to refer to a person who ends the life of another, allegedly for the purpose of benefiting the deceased who was terminally ill and in considerable pain. Often the testimony indicates that the deceased begged for euthanasia. However, such motives do not negate the elements of murder, although evidence of good motive may influence a jury to return a not-guilty verdict. Euthanasia is to be distinguished from the legal recognition of the right of a patient (or of a family when the patient is unconscious) to refuse life-sustaining treatment.[21]

The issue of murder arose in the physician-assisted suicides in which Dr. Jack Kevorkian engaged. Kevorkian was charged with murder for his role in assisting with two suicides, but those charges were dropped after a judge noted that Michigan, where the suicides were committed, had no law against physician-assisted suicides. According to the judge, Kevorkian's acts of hooking patients up to a "suicide machine" did not meet the elements of first-degree murder.[22]

In 1992 Michigan enacted a statute that prohibits physician-assisted suicide, providing for a penalty of four years in prison and a $2,000 fine upon conviction. In 1992 Dr. Kevorkian was arrested and jailed for violating this statute. In November 1993, just two weeks after he was released from jail, Kevorkian was present at the suicide of Dr. Ali Khalili, the first fellow-physician whom Kevorkian had aided since he began physician-assisted suicides in 1990. It was suggested that Dr. Khalili, who suffered from bone cancer and was in severe and constant pain, was making a statement to society when he took his own life in the presence of Kevorkian rather than doing so alone. Kevorkian was arrested again on charges of violating the physician-assisted suicide law. He was jailed and immediately began a hunger strike, raising the legal issue of whether authorities had the right to force-feed him. On 18 December 1993, Kevorkian was released from jail and placed under house arrest with electronic surveillance. A condition of his release was that he not assist other suicides until the issue of the constitutionality of Michigan's ban on physician-assisted suicides is resolved. Judges disagreed on the constitutionality of the statute, but in January 1994 one judge ruled the law unconstitutional, dismissed two of the three remaining charges against Kevorkian, and released him from house arrest.[23]

In March 1994 Michigan's Commission on Death and Dying narrowly backed physician-assisted suicide, and in April Kevorkian was tried and acquitted of violating the physician-assisted suicide statute. In May 1994 the Michigan Court of Appeals declared the Michigan physician-assisted suicide statute unconstitutional but reinstated the two charges of murder for suicides Kevorkian committed prior to the passage of the physician-assisted statute. Kevorkian replied, "Isn't this the dumbest ruling you ever heard of? Any rationality on the part of the judiciary surprises me." His attorney is appealing that ruling. In June 1994 the Michigan Supreme Court issued an order that temporarily reinstated the ban on suicide aid, but that court did not address the decisions by three county judges who had ruled the law unconstitutional. Michigan's highest court has agreed to hear various appeals regarding the statute, and those appeals were scheduled for October 1994.[24] Kevorkian's California medical license has been revoked, and his Michigan license has been suspended.

Attendant Circumstances

Some crimes have an additional element that must accompany the criminal act and the criminal mind. **Attendant circumstances** are facts surrounding an event. In criminal law this means that a criminal act may not be prosecuted as a crime even if the guilty mind is present unless the specified circumstances coexist with the act and guilty mind. For example, under the common law a man could not be prosecuted for raping his wife. Rape statutes excluded marital sexual relations even when they involved force. Thus, to prove rape, it was necessary to prove (in addition to other elements of the crime) that the defendant raped someone who was not his wife. This common law approach to rape has been changed in many U.S. jurisdictions and is discussed in a later chapter. Other examples of statutes that require attendant circumstances are listed in Focus 2.6.

FOCUS 2.6 Examples of Statutory Requirements of Attendant Circumstances

Texas Penal Code, Title 8, Section 37.02 (1994). Perjury

(a) A person commits an offense if, with intent to deceive and with knowledge of the statement's meaning:

(1) he makes a false statement under oath or swears to the truth of a false statement previously made; and

(2) the statement is required or authorized by law to be made under oath.

Attendant Circumstance — actor must be under oath.

Texas Penal Code, Title 6, Section 25.01 (1994). Bigamy

(a) An individual commits an offense if:

(1) he is legally married and he:

(A) purports to marry or does marry a person other than his spouse ... under circumstances that would, but for the actor's prior marriage, constitute a marriage; or

(B) lives with a person other than his spouse in this state under the appearance of being married; ...

Attendant Circumstance—requires proof of actor's prior marriage.

Model Penal Code, Section 213.3. Corruption of Minors and Seduction[1]

(1) **Offense Defined**. A male who has sexual intercourse with a female not his wife, or any person who engages in deviate sexual intercourse or causes another to engage in deviate sexual intercourse, is guilty of an offense if:

(a) the other person is less than [16] years old and the actor is at least [4] years older than the other person; or ...

Attendant Circumstances—requires proof that female is under sixteen and the defendant is at least four years older and that the woman is not the defendant's wife.

[1] *Model Penal Code*, Copyright 1985 by The American Law Institute. Reprinted with the permission of the American Law Institute.

Concurrence of Criminal Act and Criminal State of Mind

It is a general principle of American law that the criminal state of mind, or *mens rea*, and the criminal act, *actus reus*, must coincide. This principle is illustrated by the California Penal Code: "To constitute crime there must be unity of act and intent. In every crime or public offense there must exist a union, or joint operation of act and intent, or criminal negligence."[25] In addition, there must be evidence that the criminal act is attributable to the *mens rea*. If A intends to kill B, buys a gun, fires at B, misses, decides not to make another attempt to kill B but later does so accidentally, A has not committed murder. The criminal state of mind required for murder did not coincide with the act that caused B's death.

It is not required, however, that the final result of the criminal act occur at the time of the criminal state of mind. This principle may be illustrated by the common law *year-and-a-day* rule. If a person with the requisite criminal mind struck a victim on the head with the intent to kill but death did not result until later, that person could be charged with murder (assuming sufficient evidence of all other elements of murder) as long as the victim died within one year and a day. This rule was intended to prevent murder charges from being brought long after the criminal attack, the assumption being that medical science was not advanced sufficiently to determine the cause of remote death. The longer the time period, the more likely it was that the victim died of other causes. With advances in medical science, many jurisdictions have altered or abolished this rule.

Liability without Fault

Under the common law and in modern law criminal liability is imposed in some situations even though no fault or evil intent can be shown on the part of the accused. Historically the typical criminal acts covered by no-fault statutes were those involving narcotics, pure food and drugs, and traffic laws. In later years sexual acts with minors who consent, such as statutory rape, were added. In all of these circumstances it is assumed that someone needs protection. The consumer cannot inspect canned foods prior to purchase; the child is too young to consent to sex, and so on. Protection of society in general may be a reason, too, such as criminalizing the attempt to board an airplane while carrying a weapon. It is not necessary to show that a person who engages in this act has any intention of using the weapon for illegal purposes.[26]

There are three categories of liability without fault: **strict liability**, **vicarious liability**, and **enterprise liability**. These categories of liability are justified on the grounds that in most cases in which they are applied only minor penalties are assessed; proof of intent is difficult if not impossible to obtain; and criminal liability is needed for deterrence.

Strict Liability

Strict liability is an important concept in tort law, applying, for example, to manufacturers who put defective and unreasonably dangerous products on the market. Even though at the time the products were manufactured and sold the manufacturers (and retailers) had no knowledge (or even a way to obtain such knowledge) of the defects, they may be held liable for harm caused by those products. Strict liability in torts is based on the belief that consumers, injured through no fault of their own, should be compensated by those who made money on the products.

The deterrence principle plays a role in strict liability, too. It is assumed that if manufacturers and others are held liable in torts for the injury to people or damage to property caused by their defective products, they will be more careful in testing their products before putting them on the market.

Strict liability is utilized also in criminal law. For example, in most jurisdictions selling alcoholic beverages to a minor is a strict liability crime. It is not necessary to intend to sell to a minor. Proof that the liquor was sold to the minor is sufficient.

Statutory rape is a strict liability offense in most jurisdictions. Historically it made no difference that the minor victim appeared to be of age or that she initiated the activity. The crime of statutory rape was intended for the protection of girls considered to be too young to consent to sex.[27] Over the years this rationale has been questioned, and today some exceptions are made to the strict liability approach to statutory rape prosecutions, with a few courts allowing the defense that a reasonable person would have thought the alleged victim was of age.[28] Some jurisdictions have included boys as well as girls in the definition of *victim* of statutory rape. Because prison sentences for statutory rape may be quite long, the use of the strict liability approach in this crime is an exception to the rationale that strict liability crimes involve only minor penalties.

Vicarious Liability

Vicarious liability, "in contrast to strict liability, dispenses with the requirement of the *actus reus* and imputes the criminal act of one person to another."[29] Vicarious liability is another tort concept that may be applied to criminal law as well. In torts a person might be held responsible for the negligent acts of employees, a concept called *respondeat superior*. Thus, a person injured in an automobile accident caused by a poor, uninsured, drunken minor might bring a successful torts action against the owner of the bar where the minor purchased the liquor. This suit might succeed even though the owner did not sell the liquor and was not present when it was sold. The owner may be held liable for the bartender's actions. This does not preclude a suit by the plaintiff against the bartender, but if the bartender has little money, this action would not be a satisfactory alternative for the plaintiff. The law permits the injured party to seek compensation from the owner-employer, who is viewed in tort law as the primary person who could have prevented the illegal acts and who therefore should be responsible for compensating the victim.

Although there are some exceptions,[30] most jurisdictions do not permit imprisonment for vicarious liability. The excerpt from a classic case, *Commonwealth* v. *Koczwara*, indicates why. Koczwara, a tavern owner, was fined $500 and sentenced to three months in prison for vicarious liability when one of his employees sold liquor to a minor. Koczwara had not authorized his employees to violate the Pennsylvania statute prohibiting the sale of liquor to minors, nor did he know the violation had occurred. On appeal, the court upheld the fine but not the prison term.[31]

Commonwealth v. *Koczwara*

The distinction between respondeat superior in tort law and its application to the criminal law is obvious. In tort law, the doctrine is employed for the purpose of settling the incidence of loss upon the party who can best bear such loss. But the criminal law is supported by totally different concepts. We impose penal treatment upon those who injure or menace social interest, partly in order to reform, partly to prevent the continuation of the anti-social activity and partly to deter others. If a defendant has personally lived up to the social standards of the criminal law and has not menaced or injured anyone, why impose penal treatment?...

The Courts of the Commonwealth have already strained to permit the legislature to carry over the civil doctrine of respondeat superior as a means of enforcing the regulatory scheme that covers the liquor trade. We have done so on the theory that the Code established petty misdemeanors involving only light monetary fines. It would be unthinkable to impose vicarious criminal responsibility in cases involving true crimes.... Liability for all true crimes, wherein an offense carries with it a jail sentence, must be based exclusively upon personal causation.... A man's liberty cannot rest on so frail a reed as whether his employee will commit a mistake in judgment.

The more recent case of *United States* v. *Park* emphasizes the reasons for vicarious liability. In *Park*, the president of Acme Markets, a major supermarket chain, and the corporation were charged with violations of the Federal Food, Drug and Cosmetic Act. Due to the presence of rats in the warehouse, food packaged and shipped by this company was contaminated. The Supreme Court rejected the defendant's argument that he should not be found guilty because he did not consciously do any wrong. According to the Court, the only defense permitted in such cases is for the defendant to produce evidence that he was powerless to correct or prevent the violation. This brief excerpt explains the Court's reasoning.[32]

United States v. Park

[Cases] reveal that in providing sanctions which reach and touch the individuals who execute the corporate mission—and this is by no means necessarily confined to a single corporate agent or employee—the Act imposes not only a positive duty to seek out and remedy violations when they occur but also, and primarily, a duty to implement measures that will ensure that violations will not occur. The requirements of foresight and vigilance imposed on responsible corporate agents are beyond question demanding, and perhaps onerous, but they are no more stringent than the public has a right to expect of those who voluntarily assume positions of authority in business enterprises whose services and products affect the health and well-being of the public that supports them....

> The duty imposed by Congress on responsible corporate agents is, we emphasize, one that requires the highest standard of foresight and vigilance; but the Act, in its criminal aspect, does not require that which is objectively impossible. The theory upon which responsible corporate agents are held criminally accountable for "causing" violations of the Act permits a claim that a defendant was "powerless" to prevent or correct the violation.

Enterprise Liability

Under the common law, corporations could not be charged with crimes. This position rested on the argument that corporations had no mind (thus there could be no intent) and had no bodies (thus there could be no imprisonment). As the criminal law broke away from that position, the first impositions of criminal liability on corporations or other business enterprises were criminal fines (which could be levied on them). The charges were limited to social welfare situations, such as the mislabeling of drugs or the packing and distribution of adulterated products. Today it is held widely that corporations or business enterprises may be held criminally liable for the criminal acts (or omissions) of their agents who are acting on behalf of the enterprise.[33]

The U.S. Supreme Court has upheld the constitutionality of criminal laws that impute the agents' acts to the corporation, holding the latter responsible. In *New York Central and Hudson River Railroad* v. *United States*, the Court said, "The act of agent, while exercising the authority delegated to him...may be controlled, in the interest of public policy, by imputing his act to his employer and imposing penalties upon the corporation for which he is acting."[34] This case has been read to mean that the mental state as well as the act of the agent may be imputed to the corporation.

There are limitations to enterprise liability. Corporations are held liable for the criminal acts of their agents only when those agents are acting within the scope of the corporate employment. Further, if the statute in question provides only the punishments of death or imprisonment, corporations cannot be held liable, as those punishments would not be applicable. Some courts have held that crimes that may be considered inherently personal or human, such as perjury, rape, murder, or bigamy, are not included within enterprise liability.

Chapter 1 examines the Ford Pinto case, which involved both civil and criminal litigation. Although Ford Motor Company was acquitted of criminal charges, the court recognized the validity of such charges when the defectively designed Pinto caused the fiery death of several people. The previously successful argument by corporations that they should be liable only for property crimes was refuted by one court in an opinion that noted the potential harm to society of personal crimes committed by corporate agents. In *Granite Construction Co.* v. *Superior Court*, the court emphasized the economic benefit that corporations might enjoy if they were not responsible for damage and personal injury caused by their defective products.

"To get these economic benefits, corporate management may shortcut expensive safety precautions, respond forcibly to strikes, or engage in criminal anticompetitive behavior."[35]

In 1973, by refusing to hear a case appealed from a lower federal court, the Supreme Court let stand the principle of enterprise liability even when the corporate officials are acting "contrary to general corporate policy and express instructions." Even though the corporate officials are acting within the scope of their employment with the intent to benefit the corporation, they may be held criminally liable for crimes they commit.[36]

With the increasing number of serious injuries and deaths caused by defectively designed products, we can expect to see more prosecutions under the enterprise theory of criminal liability. The arguments against criminal liability, however, are strong. In addition to giving serious consideration to the policy aspect of enterprise criminal liability, we should consider empirical research on whether criminal liability is a deterrent in these cases.

Causation

Even if all of the elements discussed so far are proven beyond a reasonable doubt, defendants may not be held liable criminally unless it can be shown that their acts *caused* the injury, death, or property damage to the victims. **Causation** is a complicated term, for it has different meanings, depending on the circumstances and the type of law involved. In criminal law the search for cause is not easy, but generally what we are looking for is the *legal* or **proximate cause** of the harm, which technically means the act that is nearest in the order of causation. This does not necessarily mean the act occurs closest to the result. For example, a criminal act committed against a victim who dies later may be followed by other noncriminal acts that contribute to the victim's death. But if the crime is the substantial factor contributing to that death, it may be judged the proximate cause.

On the other hand, the intervening act may be judged the proximate cause or at least a contributing cause of the death. This, too, can be complicated. For example, a person with the *mens rea* for murder who fires a gun at the victim, misses the heart (for which the bullet was aimed), and hits the arm is not liable for murder when that victim dies of cancer in two weeks. The actor may be liable for *attempted murder*. (Attempt crimes are discussed in Chapter 10.) He or she had the requisite intent and committed the criminal act, but that act did not *cause* the victim's death. On the other hand, if the actor fires the nonfatal shot and the victim's death is caused by medical malpractice, the actor may be held liable for murder unless the doctor's actions are grossly negligent or intentional. In the latter case, the doctor's acts may be considered an *independent, intervening cause*, relieving the original actor of criminal liability, although again the actor may be liable for attempted murder.

In *People* v. *Stewart*, the defendant was charged with criminal homicide after stabbing a victim. While operating on the victim's wound, a surgeon discovered a hernia and decided to correct that problem. During the hernia operation, the victim had a heart attack and died. There was evidence that the anesthesiologist's failure to provide sufficient oxygen caused the heart attack. The jury's guilty verdict was reversed on appeal, the appellate court finding that the anesthesiologist's negligence was a sufficient independent intervening cause to relieve the defendant of criminal liability.[37]

The defendant's criminal liability may be reduced or eliminated also if the victim engages in actions that could contribute to increased injuries or death. Consider the case of a robbery and stabbing victim whose injuries required surgery. After surgery, the patient-victim was disoriented and resisted treatment. On four occasions the patient removed the tube that had been inserted into his stomach; subsequently he died. Was this death *caused* by the robbery and stabbing or by the patient's acts? A Pennsylvania appellate court upheld the murder conviction, stating:

> The fact that the victim, while in weakened physical condition and disoriented mental state, pulled out the tubes and created the immediate situation, which resulted in his death, is not such an intervening and independent act sufficient to break the chain of causation of events between the stabbing and the death.[38]

The case might have been decided differently if the deceased had not been disoriented and it could have been shown that he was in full control of his actions and, in effect, committed suicide.

It is possible also that an act not caused by the defendant may combine with the defendant's act to produce the harmful result. The other causes may be the result of the negligence or criminal activities of other parties or of natural causes such as a storm. When multiple causes occur, it may be difficult to determine whether the defendant should be held liable criminally for the harmful results. The case of *People* v. *Arzon* illustrates this problem. The defendant in this case was indicted for second-degree murder and third-degree arson after he allegedly set fire to a couch, causing a serious fire on the fifth and sixth floors of an abandoned building. When fire fighters found it impossible to bring the fire under control, they left the building. Another fire on the second floor (also thought to be arson but not connected with the defendant) combined with the smoke from the fifth and sixth floors, making evacuation dangerous. One fire fighter died.[39]

People v. *Arzon*

Accordingly, the defendant was accused of murder in the second degree for having, "under circumstances evincing a depraved indifference to human life, recklessly engaged in conduct which created a grave risk of death to another person," thereby causing the death of Martin Celic, and with felony murder....

[See Chapter 5 of this text for a discussion of felony murder. In this case the defendant argued that his alleged arson did not cause the fire fighter's death.]

There is remarkably little authority on precisely what sort of behavior constitutes "depraved indifference to human life." In the leading case on the subject, the Court of Appeals affirmed the conviction of defendants who had abandoned their helplessly intoxicated robbery victim by the side of a dark road in subfreezing temperature, one-half mile from the nearest structure, without shoes or eyeglasses, with his trousers at his ankles, his shirt pulled up and his outer clothing removed. The court held that while the deceased was actually killed by a passing truck, the defendants' conduct was a sufficiently direct cause of the ensuing death to warrant criminal liability and that "it is not necessary that the ultimate harm be intended by the actor. It will suffice if it can be said beyond a reasonable doubt...that the ultimate harm is something which should have been foreseen as being reasonably related to the acts of the accused."

Clearly, an obscure or merely probable connection between the defendant's conduct and another person's death is not enough to support a charge of homicide...

[T]he defendant's conduct need not be the sole and exclusive factor in the victim's death... [but] an individual is criminally liable if his conduct was a sufficiently direct cause of the death, and the ultimate harm is something which should have been foreseen as being reasonably related to his acts. It is irrelevant that, in this instance the fire which had erupted on the second floor intervened, thus contributing to the conditions that culminated in the death of Fireman Celic.... Certainly it was foreseeable that firemen would respond to the situation, thus exposing them, along with the persons already present in the vicinity, to a life-threatening danger. The fire set by the defendant was an indispensable link in the chain of events that resulted in the death. It continued to burn out of control, greatly adding to the problem of evacuating the building by blocking off one of the access routes. At the very least, the defendant's act...placed the deceased in a position where he was particularly vulnerable to the separate and independent force, in this instance, the fire on the second floor.

Determining Criminal Liability: The Judge and Jury

Chapter 1 points out that in a criminal case, for *all elements* of the crime, the prosecution must offer evidence sufficient to lead a reasonable person to find beyond a reasonable doubt that those elements exist. Whether the defendant is guilty is a question of fact to be determined by the jury (or by the judge if the case is not tried by a jury).

Chapter 1 stated also that considerable discretion exists within criminal justice systems. The roles of the trial judge and the jury illustrate this discretion. If the trial judge believes that the prosecution has not proved every element beyond a reasonable doubt, he or she may grant a defense motion for a directed verdict of acquittal. The judge has wide discretion in this and other decisions at the trial stage. In addition the judge may dismiss the case for lack of evidence during the proceeding or after all evidence is presented.

If certain procedural rules are violated, the judge may declare a **mistrial**, which is an incomplete trial. A mistrial may be declared if certain problems exist with the jury, such as the death, illness, or misbehavior of a juror. After a mistrial, a case may be tried again before another jury. A subsequent trial may be held also if the jury cannot reach a verdict, a situation referred to as a *hung jury*.

Even if there are no procedural problems and the evidence indicates beyond a reasonable doubt that the defendant is guilty, the jury may refuse to return a guilty verdict. In U.S. criminal justice systems juries have wide discretion. Juries represent the community's voice in the criminal justice process, and it is understood and accepted that there are some cases in which a guilty verdict may not be returned despite the evidence. Most of those cases are not tried because the prosecutor refuses to charge the defendant, the charges are reduced, or the judge dismisses the case.

For public pressure or other reasons, some controversial cases are tried, and the jury may refuse to convict. Examples are mercy killings or cases in which there is considerable sympathy for the defendants, such as those in which spouses or children kill spouses or parents who were abusing them sexually or otherwise over long periods of time, as illustrated by the widely publicized case of Lyle and Erik Menendez. Lyle and Erik killed their wealthy parents. Mistrials were declared in the first trials of each defendant after their respective juries were unable to reach verdicts on any counts. The brothers alleged that their parents abused them for years. When charges are filed in such cases, defendants might have one or more defenses, the focus of the next two chapters.

SUMMARY

This chapter focuses on the general elements of criminal liability. Some specific crimes that may have additional elements are discussed in later chapters, but the purpose of this chapter is to establish the foundation for an understanding of the general elements of criminal liability. Although interpretations vary from jurisdiction to jurisdiction and from time to time, some general statements may be made about criminal liability.

All crimes must involve a criminal act or a failure to act where there is a legal duty to act. We may not be prosecuted for our criminal thoughts, but criminal liability may exist once we take a substantial step toward a criminal act. Involuntary reflexes or convulsions, bodily movements during sleep or unconsciousness, or conduct during hypnosis are not considered voluntary acts. They do not occur with the volition of the actor. Some voluntary acts may be criminal but may not result in criminal liability because of recognized defenses, which are discussed in the next two chapters. But critical here is the understanding that the act (or failure to act) must have occurred through the volition of the actor.

The failure to act does not constitute an act for purposes of criminal liability unless there is a legal duty to act. The criminal law has moved cautiously in requiring affirmative acts to aid others. An act should not result in criminal liability unless the requisite *mens rea*, or criminal intent, is present. Despite the general acceptance of a requirement of criminal intent (with the exception of cases involving strict liability, vicarious liability, and enterprise liability), there is little agreement on the meaning of that term. Attempts to distinguish *specific* from *general* intent have led to more confusion than clarity.

The Model Penal Code's approach, which is followed widely, is to establish levels of culpability or intent. These levels may be distinguished analytically, although not all agree on their definitions. There is disagreement, too, over the application of these levels in particular cases, but for analytical purposes the terms may be distinguished most easily by looking at the relationship of the level of culpability and the result of the criminal act.

The highest level of culpability—*purposely*—exists when the actor consciously desires to cause the result that occurs. The second-highest level — *knowledge*—refers to a *practical certainty* that a result will occur. Although *recklessly* requires a *conscious awareness* of a great risk that harm will result if the act is committed, *negligently* requires only that the great risk be one that a *reasonable person* would recognize. In both of these last two levels of culpability, the risk must be a great, not a slight, one. This distinguishes criminal liability from lesser degrees of risk that may establish liability in civil or tort cases.

Although a criminal act and a criminal intent may be sufficient to establish liability for some crimes, others require proof of attendant circumstances. Normally these circumstances are specified by the statute establishing the crime, and they may not always require the same level of criminal intent as that required to prove the act and the state of mind.

One final matter is required before the criminal liability of a defendant is established. The prosecution must offer sufficient evidence that the act of the defendant *caused* the injury or damage in question. This is one of the most difficult areas of proof, often because we do not know enough about the problem, we cannot get sufficient evidence, or there may be more than one actual cause.

Despite sufficient proof on all of the elements of a crime, U.S. systems of criminal justice in any given case permit a jury (or a judge if the case is not tried before a jury) to decide against criminal liability. In addition, by presenting an adequate defense, it is possible to avoid (or reduce the level of) criminal liability, despite the prosecution's successful presentation of sufficient evidence on all elements of the crime. Defenses in criminal law are so important that the next two chapters are devoted to that subject.

STUDY QUESTIONS

1. Explain the meaning of the terms *actus reus* and *mens rea*.
2. When is a behavior not an *act* in the criminal law? Explain.
3. Distinguish between *failure to act* (or *omission*) and *act*. Under what circumstances do you think *failure to act* should be a crime? A violation of tort law only? Neither a tort nor a crime? Relate your answers to cases discussed in the text.

4. List the four levels of intent or culpability in the Model Penal Code, and define each.
5. What are the difficulties with trying to prove criminal intent? Illustrate.
6. What is meant by this quote from the U.S. Supreme Court: "The law presumes that a person intends the ordinary consequences of his voluntary acts?"
7. How does *motive* differ from *intent* in criminal law?
8. What is meant by *attendant circumstances*, and how do you know when they exist?
9. Distinguish *strict liability*, *vicarious liability*, and *enterprise liability*. Would you exclude any of these from the criminal law? Why or why not?
10. What is meant by *causation* in criminal law?
11. How does the concept of *intervening causes* influence legal causation? How does *multiple causation* affect criminal liability?
12. What position, if any, do you think the criminal law should take toward physician-assisted suicide? Relate your answer to the case of Dr. Kevorkian.
13. What is the role of the jury in determining criminal liability? Should that be changed?

ENDNOTES

1. Robinson v. California, 370 U.S. 660 (1962), *reh'g. denied,* 371 U.S. 905 (1962).
2. Model Penal Code, Section 2.01(2) (Proposed Official Draft, 1985.)
3. People v. Decina, 138 N.E.2d 799 (N.Y. 1956).
4. See Fain v. Commonwealth, 78 Ky. 183 (1879).
5. State v. Olsen, 160 P.2d 427 (Utah 1945).
6. "Driver Acquitted of Homicide in School Bus Crash in Texas," *New York Times* (7 May 1993), p. 10.
7. U.S. Code, Title 18, Section 1792 (1994).
8. United States v. Greschner, 647 F.2d 740 (7th Cir. 1981).
9. United States v. Fountain, 642 F.2d 1083 (7th Cir. 1981), *cert. denied,* 451 U.S. 993 (1981).
10. *In re* Winship, 397 U.S. 358, 364 (1970).
11. R.I. Gen. Laws., Section 11-37-3.3 (1994).
12. Richard Taub, quoted in "Chicago Crimes Raise Question of What Bystanders Should Do," *St. Petersburg Times* (16 October 1988), p. 1.
13. "Good Samaritan Killed," *Tallahassee Democrat* (19 May 1990), p. 3.
14. "Pickpockets in New York City Are Taking up New Tactics," *New York Times* (6 September 1983), p. 17.
15. People v. Oliver, 258 Cal.Rptr. 138 (Cal.App.1st Dist. 1989), *later proceeding* (Cal.App.1st Dist. 1989), and *review denied* (Cal. 1989).
16. Arnold H. Loewy, *Criminal Law,* 2d ed. (St. Paul, Minn.: West, 1987), p. 119.
17. Tex. Penal Code, Title 5, Section 22.04 (1985). Subsequently this statute was amended as follows: "(a) A person commits an offense if he intentionally, knowingly, recklessly or with criminal negligence by act or intentionally, knowingly, or recklessly by omission, causes to a child, elderly individual, or invalid individual: (1) serious bodily injury; (2) serious physical or mental deficiency or impairment; (3) disfigurement or deformity; or (4) bodily injury... The act applies to an actor who has "a legal or statutory duty to act" or one who has

"assumed care, custody, or control of a child, elderly individual, or invalid individual." A child is defined as "a person 14 years of age or younger." Texas Penal Code, Title 5, Section 22.04 (1994).

18. Alvarado v. State, 704 S.W.2d 36 (Tex.Crim.App. 1985), *reh'g. denied* (26 February 1986).

19. United States v. X-Citement Video, Inc., 982 F.2d 1285, 1291 (9th Cir. 1992), *cert. granted*, 114 S. Ct. 1186 (1994).

20. State v. Miller, 395 N.W.2d 431 (Minn.App. 1986).

21. See *In the Matter of* Quinlan, 355 A.2d 647 (N.J. 1976), *cert. denied sub. nom.*, 429 U.S. 922 (1976), in which the court granted permission for doctors to remove the life-support systems from Karen Ann Quinlan, who was in a vegetative state. Quinlan lived without those supports until 1985. In 1990, the Supreme Court affirmed the Missouri supreme court decision that without "clear and convincing evidence of [the unconscious daughter's] desire to have life-sustaining treatment withdrawn, the parents lacked authority to effectuate such a request." Cruzan v. Director, Missouri Department of Health, 497 U.S. 261 (1990). The Court remanded the case to Missouri to determine whether such evidence existed. The judge ruled that it did; the tubes were removed, and Cruzan died.

22. "Suicide Doctor Wins Dismissal," *American Bar Association Journal* 77 (February 1991): 22.

23. "Kevorkian Is Charged Again with Aiding Suicide," *New York Times* (30 November 1993), p. 8; "While Out on Bail, Kevorkian Attends A Doctor's Suicide," *New York Times* (23 November 1993), p.1; "Kevorkian Is Freed After Pledging To Refrain From Aiding Suicides," *New York Times* (18 December 1993), p. 7; "Kevorkian Victory: 3d Judge Says Suicide Law Is Unconstitutional," *New York Times* (28 January 1994), p. 9; and "Michigan Panel Narrowly Backs Suicide Aid," *New York Times* (6 March 1994), p. 11. See also Julia Pugliese, "Don't Ask—Don't Tell: The Secret Practice of Physician-Assisted Suicide," *Hastings Law Journal* 44 (1993): 1291–1330.

24. "Law Barring Suicide Aid By Doctors Is Thrown Out," *Wall Street Journal* (21 May 1993); "Clarifying Ruling, Michigan Judge Voids All of Assisted Suicide Law," *New York Times* (15 December 1993), p. 13; "Judge Throws Out State Law Banning Assisted Suicide," *Miami Herald* (5 May 1994), p. 8; "Michigan Court Invalidates Law Banning Aid for Suicide," *New York Times* (11 May 1994), p. 10; "Michigan Court Reinstates Ban on Suicide Aid, for Now," *New York Times* (8 June 1994), p. 16. The May decision is Hobbins v. Attorney General, 205 Mich.App. 194 (Mich.App. 1994). The case regarding the murder statute is People v. Kevorkian, 205 Mich.App. 180 (Mich.App 1994). Subsequently the Michigan Supreme Court held that the appellate court's decision shall not be effective until the supreme court disposes of two cases already docketed or issues further orders. People v. Kevorkian, 445 Mich. 917 (Mich. 1994).

In May 1994 a federal court in Seattle, Washington, became the first federal court to rule that a state's law banning assisted suicide was unconstitutional, constituting an infringement of civil liberties. The case is Compassion in Dying v. Washington, 850 F.Supp. 1454 (W.D.Wash. 1994).

25. Cal. Penal Code, Section 20 (1994).

26. See, for example, United States v. Flum, 518 F.2d 39 (8th Cir. 1975), *cert. denied*, 423 U.S. 1018 (1975).

27. For the historical view see Commonwealth v. Murphy, 42 N.E. 504 (Mass. 1895).

28. See People v. Hernandez, 393 P.2d 673 (Cal. 1964), and discussion in Chapter 6 of this text.
29. State v. Beaudry, 365 N.W.2d 593 (Wis. 1985).
30. See, for example, *In re* Marley, 175 P.2d 832 (Cal. 1946).
31. Commonwealth v. Koczwara, 155 A.2d 825 (1959), *cert. denied*, 363 U.S. 848 (1960). See also State v. Beaudry, 365 N.W.2d 593 (Wis. 1985).
32. United States v. Park, 421 U.S. 658 (1975).
33. See Commonwealth v. Beneficial Finance Co., 275 N.E.2d 33 (1971), *cert. denied*, 407 U.S. 910 (1972).
34. New York Central & Hudson River Railroad Co. v. United States, 212 U.S. 481 (1909).
35. Granite Construction Co. v. Superior Court, 149 Cal.App.3d 465 (5th Dist. 1983).
36. United States v. Hilton Hotel Corp., 467 F.2d 1000 (9th Cir. 1972), *cert. denied*, 409 U.S. 1125 (1973).
37. People v. Stewart, 40 N.Y.2d 692 (1976).
38. Commonwealth v. Cheeks, 223 A.2d 291 (Pa. 1966).
39. People v. Arzon, 401 N.Y.S.2d 156 (1978), citations omitted.

Chapter 3

Defenses to Criminal Liability: Part I

Outline

Key Terms

affirmative defense	entrapment	mistake
A.L.I. rule	expert testimony	M'Naghten rule
automatism	fleeing felon	necessity
deadly force	insanity	presumption
defense	irresistible impulse	substantial capacity
duress	test	test
Durham rule		

Introduction

In U.S. criminal justice systems, the prosecution is required to prove beyond a reasonable doubt that the defendant is guilty of the crime (or crimes) charged. All elements of the crime in question must be proved. The prosecution must prove that a particular defendant committed a specified criminal act, that any attendant circumstances required by the statute were present, and that the act was the legal cause of the harm in question. It is possible, however, that proof on all of these elements is not sufficient for a conviction.

In criminal law, a successful defense may result in a reduced charge or an acquittal. Defenses are very important, but they are not understood easily. Because of the possible confusion between a *defense* and an *element* of a crime, it is necessary to analyze the issues involved in distinguishing these terms and allocating the burden of proof between the prosecution and the defense.

This discussion is important not only in distinguishing issues and defenses, but also in illustrating the importance of analyzing the facts of each criminal case. It is not possible to make categorical statements that may be memorized and applied. Each case requires an analysis of general legal principles to determine whether they are or are not applicable in that case. This uncertainty makes the law difficult but challenging.

Issues Concerning Defenses

Specific defenses are covered in this and the following chapter, but some definitions and issues are common to all.

Definitions

A **defense** is a response made by a defendant in a civil or a criminal case. That response may be a denial of the factual allegations raised by the prosecution (in a criminal case) or by the plaintiff (in a civil case). In a civil case, the response states why the plaintiff's request should not be granted. In a criminal case it states why the defendant should not be held responsible for the alleged acts or why the charge should be reduced.

In some cases the defense is not a response to facts alleged by the prosecution but instead is an introduction of new factual allegations that, if true, constitute a defense to the *charge* in a criminal case or to the *complaint* in a civil case. These are called **affirmative defenses**. In a criminal case, they may include the defenses of intoxication, insanity, battered person syndrome, duress, coercion, automatism, self-defense, and others.

Defenses may be *partial* or *complete*, meaning that they serve to reduce or to defeat the charge. A partial defense to the charge of murder might result in a manslaughter conviction because it defeats one of the elements of murder. A successful complete defense, such as insanity, may lead to a verdict of not guilty. As with most concepts in criminal law, the distinction between partial and complete defenses may be difficult to ascertain.

The defense may elect not to present a defense. In the nationally publicized 1993 trial of Officer William Lozano (discussed later in this chapter) the defense rested without presenting a case. Although the defense introduced some evidence during its cross-examination of the prosecution's witnesses, after the prosecution rested its case, noted defense attorney Roy Black addressed the court with these words. "Due to the lack of credible evidence in this case, we rest." As our subsequent discussion indicates, that was a successful strategy in that case.

Burden of Proof and Presumptions

Chapter 2 discusses the *elements* of a crime, noting that the term refers to what the prosecution must prove to sustain a conviction. Included are an act and a criminal state of mind that concur to produce a harmful result. In addition, some crimes require proof of attendant circumstances. Chapter 1 emphasizes that the prosecution must prove these elements beyond a reasonable doubt. In addition, Chapter 1 points out that even in a criminal case the defendant has the burden of proof in some instances. When that occurs, the usual standard is a preponderance of the evidence, a lower standard than the prosecution's beyond a reasonable doubt burden. As with most areas of law, there may be exceptions to these rules.

Although it is tempting to make statements such as "the prosecution must prove all elements of a crime beyond a reasonable doubt" and "the defense must prove all defenses by a preponderance of the evidence," in reality the issues are far more complicated. In addition to the exceptions to these general declarations are the problems of interpreting or defining *element* and *defense* and determining how each is affected by presumptions.

A **presumption** is an assumption of a fact that is based on other facts. It is not a fact but an inference from a fact. A presumption may be *conclusive*, in which case it is accepted by law, or *rebuttable*, in which case the opposing party may offer evidence to refute the presumption.

Some of the problems that arise in allocating the burden of proof may be illustrated by a look at the *presumption of innocence*. According to this crucial principle, in U.S. systems of criminal justice everyone charged with a crime faces the judicial system as an innocent person. The prosecution has the difficult burden of proving beyond a reasonable doubt all the required elements of the crime charged as well as the allegation that the defendant committed the crime. To ease that prosecutorial burden, the legislature could draft a statute that would shift the burden of proof on an element of the crime from the prosecution to the defendant. That is not permitted constitutionally, but the problem arises when a statute does that by the use of presumptions or by the method of defining defenses.

RECENT DEVELOPMENTS: SUPREME COURT DECISIONS

In recent years the U.S. Supreme Court has decided several key cases involving presumptions, defenses, elements of a crime, and the allocation of the burden of proof in criminal cases. Five of these cases, along with one from a lower federal court, are summarized briefly in Focus 3.1; but as this discussion indicates, it is important to view such summaries in light of the facts of each case.

In *Mullaney* v. *Wilbur*, decided in 1975, the defendant, Wilbur, was charged under a Maine statute that recognized two categories of homicide, murder and manslaughter, both of which required that the prosecution prove the elements of an unlawful, intentional killing. Murder involved the additional element of malice aforethought, but the statute provided that malice aforethought could be presumed if the state proved an intentional, unlawful killing.[1]

In addition, Maine provided a *heat of passion* defense to a murder charge. The defendant had the burden of proving that defense by a preponderance of the evidence. Wilbur was accused of killing the victim following homosexual advances. He argued that permitting the prosecution to presume malice aforethought on sufficient proof of an unlawful, intentional killing and therefore permitting a murder conviction unless the defense proved that the homosexual advances constituted a heat of passion defense in effect shifted to the defense the burden of proving an *element* of murder—malice aforethought. The Supreme Court agreed.

Against the argument that the prosecution had to prove only those elements that would require an acquittal if not proved, the Court held that the beyond-a-reasonable-doubt standard required of the prosecution means that the prosecution must meet that standard in *all elements* of a particular crime. The Court held that the Maine approach shifted the burden of proof to the defendant and thus increased "the likelihood of an erroneous murder conviction."[2]

Mullaney established that the prosecution must prove *all* elements of a crime beyond a reasonable doubt and that the state could not shift that burden by the way in which it defined and established the burden of proof for a defense. But the Court did not answer the question of whether it would be permissible constitutionally to place on the defendant the burden of proving *all* affirmative defenses. Would that always involve shifting from the prosecution the burden of proving an essential *element* of the crime?

The burden of proof issue received further attention in *Patterson* v. *New York*, decided by the Supreme Court in 1977. Patterson was charged with second-degree murder after allegedly shooting and killing the man with whom he saw his partially clothed estranged wife. Patterson confessed to

FOCUS 3.1 Defenses, Elements, and the Burden of Proof in a Criminal Case: A Summary of Cases

The discussion in this chapter indicates some of the problems of allocating the burden of proof in a criminal case. This focus lists the major cases, along with a brief statement of the importance of the case.

In re Winship[1]
The prosecution in a criminal case must prove its case by the *beyond a reasonable doubt* standard.

Mullaney v. Wilbur[2]
The beyond a reasonable doubt standard established by *Winship* refers to *all elements* of the crime.

Patterson v. New York[3]
The New York murder statute did not involve shifting the burden of proof on an *element* of second-degree murder from the prosecution to the defense when it required the defendant to prove the defense of being "under the influence of extreme emotional disturbance."

Sandstrom v. Montana[4]
Instructing the jury that the law "presumes that a person intends the ordinary consequences of his voluntary acts" is unconstitutional because it might lead a juror to think the defendant rather than the prosecution has the burden of proof on the issue of criminal intent.

Francis v. Franklin[5]
A jury instruction that the defendant, found in possession of stolen property, was presumed to have stolen that property unless a satisfactory explanation had been offered for its possession was held unconstitutional because it shifted the burden of proof and denied the presumption of innocence.

Martin v. Ohio[6]
It is permissible to place on the defendant the burden of proving the affirmative defense of self-defense.

United States v. Byrd[7]
The Insanity Defense Reform Act in the federal system does not shift to the defendant the burden of proof on the intent element of a crime when it requires the defendant to prove the insanity defense by clear and convincing evidence.

[1] *In re* Winship, 397 U.S. 358 (1970).
[2] Mullaney v. Wilbur, 421 U.S. 684 (1975).
[3] Patterson v. New York, 432 U.S. 197 (1977).
[4] Sandstrom v. Montana, 442 U.S. 510 (1979), *remanded*, 603 P.2d 244 (Mont. 1979).
[5] Francis v. Franklin, 471 U.S. 307 (1985).
[6] Martin v. Ohio, 480 U.S. 228 (1985), *reh'g.*, *denied*, 481 U.S. 1024 (1987).
[7] United States v. Byrd, 834 F.2d 145 (8th Cir. 1987).

the killing but argued that he was "under the influence of extreme emotional disturbance," which constituted a defense under New York law. He argued that the charge should have been manslaughter, not second-degree murder.

Proof of second-degree murder under New York law required the prosecution to prove two elements: "intent to cause the death of another person" and "causing the death of such person or of a third person." Malice aforethought was not an element, as it was in the Maine statute involved in the *Mullaney* case.

The Supreme Court upheld Patterson's conviction, distinguishing the case from *Mullaney* by the fact that the Maine statute required malice aforethought as an *element* of murder; the New York statute did not have that requirement. The Court viewed the New York affirmative defense of *extreme* emotional disturbance as "a substantially expanded version of the older heat-of-passion concept." The Court concluded that the New York statute in *Patterson* did not involve a "shifting of the burden to the defendant to disprove any fact essential to the offense charged since the New York affirmative defense of extreme emotional disturbance bears no direct relationship to any element of murder." In this brief excerpt from the case, the Court indicates that there are some limits to its holding concerning the beyond-a-reasonable-doubt standard and the allocation of the burden of proof on elements and defenses in a criminal case.[3]

Patterson v. *New York*

The requirement of proof beyond a reasonable doubt in a criminal case is "bottomed on a fundamental value determination of our society that it is far worse to convict an innocent man than to let a guilty man go free." The social cost of placing the burden on the prosecution to prove guilt beyond a reasonable doubt is thus an increased risk that the guilty will go free. While it is clear that our society has willingly chosen to bear a substantial burden in order to protect the innocent, it is equally clear that the risk it must bear is not without limits; ... Due process does not require that every conceivable step be taken, at whatever cost, to eliminate the possibility of convicting an innocent person....

We ... decline to adopt as a constitutional imperative, operative countrywide, that a State must disprove beyond a reasonable doubt every fact constituting any and all affirmative defenses related to the culpability of an accused. Traditionally, due process has required that only the most basic procedural safeguards be observed; more subtle balancing of society's interests against those of the accused have been left to the legislative branch. We therefore will not disturb the balance struck in previous cases holding that the Due Process Clause requires the prosecution to prove beyond a reasonable doubt all of the elements included in the definition of the offense of which the defendant is charged. Proof of the nonexistence of all affirmative defenses has never been constitutionally required; and we perceive no reason to fashion such a rule in this case and apply it to the statutory defense at issue here.

Mullaney and *Patterson* indicate some of the problems involved in allocating the burden of proof on defenses in a criminal case. Clearly, before the burden of proof may be placed on the defendant, a defense must be a real defense and not a shifting of the burden of proof for an element of the crime. The problem arises in determining when the state has defined a statute (or a judge instructed a jury) in such a way that the defendant's burden of proof involves an element of the crime. The required element of *mens rea* provides the framework in which to analyze this possibility.

THE PRESUMPTION OF INTENT

Criminal intent, or *mens rea*, is an element of a crime and therefore must be proved beyond a reasonable doubt by the prosecution. Thus, it appears that a presumption of intent is unconstitutional. In *Sandstrom* v. *Montana*, the Supreme Court overturned a murder conviction because the trial court had instructed the jury that "the law presumes that a person intends the ordinary consequences of his voluntary acts." This instruction is unconstitutional because it could lead a jury to conclude that once the prosecution proved the defendant had committed the killing voluntarily, the jury should convict even if the prosecution had not proved the element of criminal intent.[4] The result would be to compromise or nullify the presumption of innocence.

In *Francis* v. *Franklin*, the Supreme Court considered the issue of a jury instruction that could lead a juror to conclude that the defendant had the burden of proof on intent. The jury had been instructed that "a person of sound mind and discretion is presumed to intend the natural and probable consequences of his acts, but the presumption may be rebutted." The Court held that this instruction was unconstitutional. Referring to the requirement that the prosecution must prove all elements of a crime beyond a reasonable doubt, the Court said:

> This "bedrock, 'axiomatic and elementary' [constitutional] principle," prohibits the State from using evidentiary presumptions in a jury charge that have the effect of relieving the State of its burden of persuasion beyond a reasonable doubt of every essential element of a crime.[5]

Citing *Francis*, the Utah Supreme Court held unconstitutional a jury instruction that possession of recently stolen property "when no satisfactory explanation of such possession is made, shall be deemed prima facie [at first sight; on the face of it; presumed to be true unless proven otherwise] evidence that the person in possession stole the property." The Utah court held that this instruction shifts to defendants the burden of proving that they did not steal the property. This shift makes defendants "guilty until proven innocent, thus violating their constitutional right to be presumed innocent until proven guilty."[6]

BURDEN OF PROOF AND SELF-DEFENSE

Distinguishing elements of a crime from affirmative defenses has occurred in self-defense cases. In *Martin* v. *Ohio* the Supreme Court upheld an Ohio statute that required the defendant to sustain the burden of proof on self-defense. Under Ohio law, self-defense is an affirmative defense. The case involved a defendant who was charged with aggravated murder, defined as "purposely, and with prior calculation and design, causing the death of another." The defendant testified that she shot and killed her husband after he struck her.[7]

In analyzing the facts and issues in *Martin*, the Supreme Court said that the Ohio statute did not shift to the defendant any of the required elements of aggravated murder. The prosecution had the burden of proving these elements beyond a reasonable doubt:

1. that the defendant killed her husband, and
2. that she had the specific purpose and intent to cause his death or that she had done so with prior calculation and design.

According to the Court, requiring the defendant to sustain the burden of proof on self-defense did not shift to the defendant the burden of proof on either of the elements of aggravated murder.

BURDEN OF PROOF AND THE INSANITY DEFENSE

Allocation of the burden of proof in some insanity cases raises the issue of whether proof of insanity is an affirmative defense to be proved by the defendant or whether it negates intent, a required element that the prosecution must prove. The Supreme Court views insanity as an affirmative defense.[8]

In a Pennsylvania case the defendant argued unsuccessfully that her murder conviction should be reversed because the state did not prove her sanity. The court refused, noting that sanity is the normal human condition and that requiring the state to prove sanity beyond a reasonable doubt puts an undue burden on the prosecution. The court ruled that insanity is an affirmative defense and must be proved by the defense.[9]

The issue of whether insanity is an affirmative defense or a negation of *mens rea* is important particularly in the federal system because the Insanity Defense Reform Act of the federal code places on the defendant the burden of proving insanity by *clear and convincing evidence*, a standard that is stricter than a preponderance of the evidence but not as strict as beyond a reasonable doubt.[10]

In some courts there may be a problem in defining these terms. One trial judge instructed the jury that the standard *clear and convincing evidence* means uncertain and unambiguous but is not as strict as *beyond a reasonable doubt*. The appellate court held that the clear-and-convincing standard was correct but that the definition was erroneous in that it was too strict, placing too great a burden on the defense. Further, the trial judge should have defined *beyond a reasonable doubt* for the jurors so they would have a basis for distinguishing that standard from *clear and convincing*. This case represents the problems of trying to define words that we think we understand![11]

Prior to the passage of the Insanity Defense Reform Act, the defendant had the burden of introducing the insanity defense, after which the prosecution had the burden of proving beyond a reasonable doubt that the defendant was sane when the crime was committed. The case of John Hinckley, discussed in Focus 3.2, was tried prior to the passage of this act. The government could not prove beyond a reasonable doubt that Hinckley was sane when he attempted to assassinate President Reagan; thus, Hinckley's insanity defense was successful.

The federal standard of requiring the defense to prove insanity by clear and convincing evidence was challenged in a federal court in 1987. The Eighth Circuit Court of Appeals held in the case of *United States* v. *Byrd* that requiring a defendant to prove insanity by clear and convincing evidence did not require him to prove the *element* of intent, or willfullness, for robbery.[12]

Types of Defenses

A quick look at scholarly writings in criminal law, along with various state codes, indicates little agreement on how to classify or categorize defenses. A review of the various approaches contributes confusion and adds little in a positive way, other than to permit dividing discussions into sections or chapters. Thus, no attempt is made to classify or categorize types of defenses; nor are all defenses discussed.

In studying defenses, it is important to recall what we have learned about the meaning and purpose of criminal law. The moral or blameworthy element of punishment through the criminal law is critical to the topic of defenses, for by recognizing types of defenses we are saying that some criminal acts will not be punished or that punishment may be reduced because of such a defense. As with most criminal law, the lines are hard to draw in particular cases. Only a few examples may be considered in an introductory text. Likewise, jurisdictions differ in their statutory definitions and interpretations of defenses.

Ignorance or Mistake

For the statement, "I did not know it was a crime," frequently we hear the response that "ignorance of the law is no excuse." If people could get by with the excuse of ignorance, law enforcement would be difficult if not impossible. Under some circumstances, however, ignorance of the law, mistake of fact, and mistake of law are recognized defenses to criminal liability.

In criminal law, the defense of **mistake** refers to a situation in which actors commit criminal acts that they would not have committed had they had knowledge of the law or the facts. The mistake may be a *mistake of law* or a *mistake of fact*. The difference between the two categories has been stated as follows.

> Mistake and ignorance of *fact* involve perceptions of the world and empirical judgments derived from those perceptions. Mistake and ignorance of *law* involve assessment of whether, given a certain set of acts, the actor would or would not be violating the law.[13]

FOCUS 3.2 John Hinckley: Not Guilty by Reason of Insanity

On 30 March 1981, John Warnock Hinckley, Jr., stepped from behind a crowd of onlookers watching President Ronald Reagan leave a Washington hotel. He leveled a handgun at President Reagan and in one last, desperate attempt tried to blast his way into the heart of actress Jodie Foster. Hinckley shot and wounded President Reagan; Reagan's press secretary, James Brady; a Secret Service agent; and a District of Columbia police officer.

An estimated 100 million Americans watched as newscasts replayed the scene of the boyish-looking, twenty-five-year-old Hinckley firing shots at the presidential party and of Secret Service agents wrestling the gun from Hinckley's hands while Reagan was rushed from the scene. The public thought this case would be an easy one for the prosecutor to win; there was little doubt about Hinckley's guilt.

As Hinckley's trial began, however, his attorneys announced that their client would plead not guilty by reason of insanity. As the trial progressed, the defense pieced together evidence from psychiatric examinations to show that Hinckley was legally insane at the time of the shootings. The most sensational evidence, and the cornerstone of Hinckley's defense, was the revelation of his obsession with the 1976 movie *Taxi Driver*. Jurors watched as TV monitors replayed *Taxi Driver*, in which Foster plays the part of a twelve-year-old prostitute. The lead character is a lonely taxi driver who becomes so obsessed with the prostitute that he stalks a United States senator with a gun to gain publicity and the attention of the character played by Foster. At the end of the movie, the taxi driver kills the prostitute's pimp and becomes a hero.

After watching *Taxi Driver* several times, Hinckley became obsessed with the plot and with Foster, whom he had never met. The defense argued that Hinckley plotted to kill the president, thinking that it was the only way to get Foster to notice him. Other less drastic attempts to win her attention had failed. The defense presented evidence that attempted to show that Hinckley was psychotic and depressed and that he suffered delusions. A federal jury deliberated for over four days before finding Hinckley not guilty by reason of insanity. Hinckley is confined in St. Elizabeth's Psychiatric Hospital in Washington, D.C.

The average stay at St. Elizabeth's is five years. With assassins or attempted assassins the rule appears to be different. Perhaps Hinckley's fate will be no different than that of other would-be presidential assassins. The man who attempted to assassinate President Andrew Jackson used the insanity defense successfully but spent the rest of his life in an asylum. An attempted assassin of Theodore Roosevelt, who claimed that he had been operating under the instructions of the ghost of President William McKinley, spent the last thirty-one years of his life in a mental ward. No attempted presidential assassin who has used the insanity defense successfully has left custody alive.[1]

[1] See James W. Clarke, American Assassins: The Darker Side of Politics (Princeton, N.J.:

Princeton University Press, 1982), for an examination of the assassinations and attempted
assassinations of presidents in our nation's history. For a detailed discussion of Hinckley's

trial, see Peter W. Low et al., *The Trial of John
W. Hinckley, Jr.: A Case Study in the Insanity
Defense* (Mineola, N.Y.: Foundation Press,
1987).

The mistake defense may be used to negate a mental element of the crime, such as the knowledge or belief requirement. "Under the proper circumstances . . . a good faith misunderstanding of the law may negate willfulness." For example, a good-faith belief with regard to an income tax deduction may negate the federal statute's requirement of *willful* as an element of income tax evasion.[14]

The mistake defense may be applied in two situations. In the first, individuals do not know the law exists. Normally this is not an excuse, although it may be in rare cases, as illustrated by *Lambert* v. *California*, a landmark case decided by the Supreme Court in 1957. In *Lambert*, the Court invalidated a Los Angeles municipal ordinance that forbade any convicted person to be or remain in the city for more than five days without registering. The Court emphasized that although "ignorance of the law will not excuse," the law requires reasonable notice. Because most people would not expect this ordinance to exist, actual knowledge of the duty to register and meet other requirements of the ordinance would be required for the ordinance to be constitutional. "Were it otherwise, the evil would be as great as it is when the law is written in print too fine to read or in a language foreign to the community."[15]

The second type of mistake occurs when individuals are mistaken about some collateral element, such as the legality of previous divorces, which causes them to misunderstand the legal significance of their conduct; for example, remarrying. The crime of bigamy has been committed; and although usually bigamy is a strict liability crime, some jurisdictions recognize an honest and reasonable mistake as a *partial* or *complete* defense. The same is true of statutory rape cases in which the defendant has a reasonable belief that the alleged victim is of legal age to consent to sexual intercourse and the jurisdiction recognizes a reasonable belief as a defense.

The application of the mistake defense as a partial rather than a complete defense is illustrated in a Washington statutory rape case in which a twenty-year-old defendant had sexual intercourse with a thirteen-year-old. The defendant proved that he had a reasonable belief that the alleged victim was between fourteen and sixteen years of age. The state statute defines *statutory rape in the second degree* as sexual intercourse committed by one who is over sixteen with a person who is eleven or older but less than fourteen. The reasonable mistake is not a complete defense; thus, the defendant is not entitled to an acquittal but may be convicted of a lesser offense. The Washington Court of Appeals upheld the conviction of *statutory rape in the third degree,* a less serious offense, which includes sexual intercourse of a person over eighteen with one under fourteen but less than sixteen.[16]

Duress or Necessity

Defendants may succeed in defending their criminal acts if they can show that they acted under **duress** or **necessity** or that they were following the lesser of a choice of evils. To succeed on duress, defendants must prove that when they committed the crimes they were threatened by unlawful force. Not many defendants attempt this defense; thus, the case law is limited. Most cases hold that the force must be such that would cause serious bodily injury or death, and the threat of harm must be imminent. Most states require that the threat be to the defendant rather than to a third party, although a few permit the defense in the case of a threat to a close relative of the defendant.[17] The defendant must have acted reasonably to assert the duress defense. "If there was a reasonable, legal alternative to violating the law, the defense of necessity will fail."[18] Normally the defense is not available for murder.

An example of an unsuccessful use of the defense occurred in a prison escape case. The defendant inmate argued that the refusal of prison officials to treat him for extremely painful kidney stones threatened him with substantial bodily harm and that further requests for treatment would have been futile; so he had to escape. The court disagreed, stating that to show that he acted under duress when he escaped, he would have to show (1) that he was faced with a specific threat of death or substantial bodily harm in the immediate future and (2) that there was no time for complaints to authorities or (3) that there was a history of futile complaints, thus indicating that complaints would not result in a solution to the problem. Finally, the prisoner must prove that he had intended to report immediately to proper authorities after the escape.[19]

Likewise, the defendant who argued that he should have been permitted the defense of duress when he escaped from prison, broke into a home, terrorized the occupants, raped the wife, kidnapped the eleven-year-old daughter and assaulted her sexually found no sympathy from the court despite his argument that he had to commit all of these acts subsequent to his escape because the governor had issued a "shoot-to-kill" order against him. The court emphasized that aside from the fact that defendant offered no proof for the alleged shoot-to-kill order, even proof of such an order would not be adequate to permit him to introduce the duress defense.

> [The defendant] had other reasonable opportunities to avoid the danger; he could have contacted law enforcement authorities to arrange for a safe surrender. No imaginable set of circumstances could possibly justify kidnapping the Blades family in a neighboring state, some two or three weeks after the governor's alleged order.[20]

The Model Penal Code provides that the duress defense is not available when defendants recklessly place themselves in positions in which it is probable that they will be subjected to duress. It is unavailable for those who negligently place themselves in such circumstances if negligence is the basis for culpability for the crime in question. The Model Penal Code abolishes the common law presumption that a married woman acts on the command of her husband.[21]

The defense of necessity is similar to that of duress with the exception that in most cases the coercive forces in this defense are forces of nature rather than human forces. In actual cases, however, the distinction is not always clear. Like duress, the necessity defense is based on the assumption that a person ought to be free to commit some crimes in order to prevent greater harm. Thus, breaking into the home of another to secure shelter or food or to telephone the police during an emergency may constitute a defense to breaking and entering.

Unlike duress, a successful necessity defense need not be based on avoiding injury or death to humans; avoiding property damage may be acceptable. In rare cases, it includes serious crimes, such as intentional homicide, when that is necessary to avoid a greater harm, such as killing one person to avoid the deaths of two others. The actor must have the intent to avoid a greater harm. The decision regarding whether a greater or lesser harm was avoided is left to the court, not to defendants. Some people may think that killing a neighbor to save their own pets is engaging in a lesser harm to prevent a greater harm. The choice between pets and humans may be easy, but as Focus 3.3 indicates, deciding who should be sacrificed and saved among humans may be difficult.

The defendant is not permitted the defense of necessity if another alter-

In reacting to disasters, it is permissible to take some actions that otherwise might be criminal but that are necessary to preserve life and property.

FOCUS 3.3   Should Single Men Be Sacrificed First in a Crisis?

If you were the captain of a ship that was in danger of sinking and the only way to save anyone was to reduce the weight on the ship, what would you do if unloading cargo was not a sufficient weight reduction? If it were necessary for people to get off the ship and there were not enough volunteers, how would you decide who should go overboard?

This situation arose in 1841 when the American ship *William Brown* was sinking in the Atlantic Ocean after hitting an iceberg. The prosecution in this case arose over the decisions that were made regarding the people on the overloaded "long boat," which held thirty-two passengers, eight seamen, and the first mate, Holmes. Holmes ordered the crew to throw overboard all the male passengers except two whose wives were present. Fourteen single men were thrown overboard after Holmes repeated the order; two single men who hid were found and thrown overboard the next day. Shortly thereafter the ship was spotted, and all remaining passengers and crew were saved.

If you were the prosecutor, what would you do? Would you file any criminal charges against Holmes? If so, would you file first-degree murder charges? The prosecutor in this case refused to file murder charges but did charge Holmes with manslaughter. He was convicted, sentenced to six months at hard labor (in addition to the eight-months' prison term he already had served pending trial). The president refused to pardon Holmes. In his charge to the jury after the evidence was presented at trial, the judge emphasized that in these situations passengers are to be favored over seamen, although sufficient crew must be maintained to preserve the boat and passengers. After that, the decision of who is to die must be made by drawing lots.[1]

In discussing this case, two scholars said, "There was no suggestion ... that in shipwreck cases women and children should be assigned a higher value than men—and indeed it would be hard to prove that there is a greater intrinsic value in the life of woman over that of a man!"[2]

[1.] United States v. Holmes, 26 F.Cas. 360 (No. 15, 383) (C.C.E.D.Pa. 1842).
[2.] Wayne R. LaFave and Austin W. Scott, Jr., *Criminal Law*, 2d ed. (St. Paul, Minn.: West Publishing Co., 1986), p. 447, n. 46.

native is available that would avoid the greater harm and still be legal. It is not permissible to steal clothes for needy children if clothing may be secured from local institutions that provide such services. The defense is not available to defendants who created the necessity to choose between two evils, but it may be available to prevent a greater evil. The difficulty arises in deciding what is a greater evil, as this discussion of protests at abortion clinics illustrates.

ABORTION CLINIC PROTESTS

It is not uncommon for political protestors to attempt to use the necessity defense when they are charged with criminal trespass.[22] In recent years the issue has arisen frequently in cases involving abortion clinic protestors. It is argued by the protestors that the only way they can prevent a greater harm (death of a fetus) is to protest at abortion clinics by attempting to prevent pregnant women (or doctors) from entering the clinics. The extreme case involves killing the woman or the physician. The latter occurred in Florida on 10 March 1993 when Dr. David Gunn was shot in the back and killed when he arrived at an abortion clinic in Pensacola.

Michael F. Griffin, a thirty-one-year-old former chemical plant worker, was charged with the crime and faced the death penalty if convicted. Griffin was convicted and sentenced to life in prison. He must serve twenty-five years before he is eligible for parole.[23] In 1994 another doctor and his security escort were killed as they arrived at a Pensacola, Florida, abortion clinic. The security escort's wife was injured. Paul J. Hill was arrested and charged with these crimes.

One month after Dr. Gunn was killed, a bill designed to curb violence outside abortion clinics in Florida failed to become law.[24] In April 1993 a Florida judge issued an order providing that abortion protestors must stay at least thirty-six feet away from the front door of the abortion clinic in Melbourne. If they did not do so, they would face fines of up to $500. Many people were arrested for violating this order. After several hearings and decisions in lower federal appellate courts, this order was upheld by the U.S. Supreme Court on the last day of its 1993-94 term. Chief Justice William Rehnquist wrote the opinion for the majority and stated:

> The 36-foot buffer zone protecting the entrances to the clinic and the parking lot is a means of protecting unfettered ingress to and egress from the clinic and ensuring that petitioners do not block traffic on Dixie Way. The state court seems to have had few other options to protect access given the narrow confines around the clinic.[25]

In May 1994 President Clinton signed a bill that prohibits bombings, arson, and blockades at abortion clinics, along with shootings and threats of violence against doctors, nurses, and others who work at abortion clinics. Under the statute, blocking access to abortion clinics is a federal crime, with violent offenders facing $100,000 fines and a year in prison for a first conviction and $250,000 fines and three years in prison for subsequent convictions. Lesser penalties are provided for nonviolent offenders. The statute was in effect only two weeks before its first test. Six demonstrators who attempted to block access to a Milwaukee, Wisconsin, abortion clinic were arrested in early June 1994.[26]

In most cases, however, serious personal injury and death do not result from protests at abortion clinics. Rather, the protestors are charged with criminal trespass, and in many cases their attempts to use the necessity defense are unsuccessful. For example, the Alaska Court of Appeals affirmed the trespass convictions of twenty-one defendants who refused to leave the front door of the Alaska Women's Health Services building when requested to do so. The trial judge denied the defendants' request to have the jury instructed on the necessity defense. In upholding that decision, the appellate court noted that to establish the necessity defense, defendants must show the following:

1. the act charged was done to prevent a significant evil;
2. there was no adequate alternative;
3. the harm caused was not disproportionate to the harm avoided.[27]

Citing a case decided by the Alaska Supreme Court, the appellate court ruled that the necessity defense is not applicable in abortion cases even though defendants claim to have acted with a reasonable belief that their crimes were necessary to avoid abortions. The defense is available in Alaska only "where the alleged harm sought to be avoided arose either from the physical forces of nature or from unlawful acts. Since abortion is not unlawful in this state, the necessity defense would not be available to those who break the law in an effort to prevent abortions."[28]

Because abortion is a highly controversial act, we may expect more cases in which those who protest for the purpose of preventing abortions attempt to use the necessity defense in their subsequent criminal trials. Some trial courts allow the defense, but generally appellate courts hold that as a matter of law the necessity defense is not permissible as a defense to criminal trespass in protests at abortion clinics.[29]

Another area in which necessity has not been a successful defense is illustrated in Focus 3.4.

Protests at abortion clinics are common but controversial.

FOCUS 3.4 Medical Necessity is Not a Defense to Cultivating Marihuana

Some researchers and scholars take the position that the use of marihuana is beneficial for some health problems. A few persons have been given the legal right to smoke marihuana, but courts have not smiled on a defendant who attempts to use necessity as a defense to growing marihuana. When a court analyzes the necessity argument, it must decide whether the alleged conduct outweighs the reasons for the statute prohibiting that conduct.

In *Commonwealth* v. *Hutchins* the Massachusetts Supreme Judicial Court held that "the alleviation of the defendant's medical symptoms... would not clearly and significantly outweigh the potential harm to the public were we to declare that the defendant's cultivation of marihuana and its use for its medicinal purposes may not be punishable."[1]

Commonwealth v. *Hutchins* involved a forty-seven-year-old defendant who suffered from the chronic disease called *scleroderma*, a progressive systemic sclerosis that causes the build-up of scar tissues throughout the body. Joseph T. Hutchins cultivated marihuana to use to treat his disease, which has such side effects as suicidal depression, reduced mobility, severe constriction of the esophagus, painful joints, hypertension, vomiting, fatigue, nausea, and diarrhea. Doctors disagree on whether marijuana is a reasonable treatment for these side effects, and Hutchins had been unsuccessful in his attempts to get a legal prescription for marihuana.

The court recognized the serious nature of Hutchins' medical problems but concluded that there was not sufficient evidence to support the necessity defense. In this brief excerpt the court states its reasons.[1]

Commonwealth v. Hutchins

[From the majority opinion]

In our view, the alleviation of the defendant's medical symptoms, the importance to the defendant of which we do not underestimate, would not clearly and significantly outweigh the potential harm to the public were we to declare that the defendant's cultivation of marihuana and its use for its medicinal purposes may not be punishable. We cannot dismiss the reasonably possible negative impact of such a judicial declaration on the enforcement of our drug laws, including but not limited to those dealing with marihuana, nor can we ignore the government's overriding interest in the regulation for such substances.

[From the dissenting opinion]

The superseding value in a case such as the present one is the humanitarian and compassionate value in allowing an individual to seek relief from agonizing symptoms caused by a progressive and incurable illness in circumstances which risk no harm to any other individual. In my view, the harm to an individual in having to endure such symptoms may well outweigh society's generalized interest in prohibiting him or her from using the marihuana in such circumstances. On a proper offer of proof, I would recognize the availability of a necessity defense when marihuana is used for medical purposes. [The dissent argued that the jury, not the judge, should decide whether growing marihuana constitutes a medical necessity in a particular case.]

[1] Commonwealth v. Hutchins, 575 N.E.2d 741 (Mass.Sup. 1991).

Infancy

Under common law, children under seven could not be convicted of a crime because of a conclusive presumption that they were not capable of forming the requisite criminal intent. A rebuttable presumption of incapacity governed children who were between the ages of seven and fourteen, with the exception that boys under fourteen were conclusively presumed incapable of rape. A rebuttal presumption of criminal intent existed for children fourteen and over, and they could be charged as adults.

Although most U.S. jurisdictions retain some of these distinctions, they are less important now than under the common law because of the prevalence of the juvenile court, which has jurisdiction over children of specified ages. However, most jurisdictions provide for waivers of juvenile court jurisdiction when children commit serious crimes that are "heinous or of an aggravated character."[30] Jurisdiction may be waived also when doing so appears to be in the best interest of society; the children appear to be beyond rehabilitation, or they have committed several serious crimes. In such cases, juveniles may be tried as adults.[31] Some states specify by statute that serious juvenile crimes may be tried in criminal courts without going through the waiver procedures.[32]

Insanity

The **insanity** defense is a controversial defense despite the fact that it is not a common defense. The defense is raised in less than 1 percent of all felony cases, and the success rate averages about 26 percent. One study indicates that approximately 15 percent of defendants judged insane did not raise the defense. They pleaded not guilty but were judged not guilty on the basis of insanity. Twenty-eight percent of defendants who raised the insanity defense and were found guilty were not sent to prison "but were released after their conviction." A comparison of success and failure in the use of the insanity defense indicated that the successful defendants were more likely to be "older, female, better educated, and single." They were more likely to have been hospitalized for mental illness and to have been judged not guilty by reason of insanity by a judge rather than a jury or plea bargaining negotiations.[33]

Technically, insanity is a social and legal term, but usually it is assumed to be a medical term, often used synonymously with mental illness. In criminal law, *insanity* refers to a mental condition that negates defendants' responsibilities for their actions. When used successfully, this defense results in acquittal. But unlike the successful use of other defenses, in most cases the defendant who is found not guilty by reason of insanity is not released but is confined to a mental hospital for treatment, as illustrated by the case of John Hinckley, Jr., discussed earlier in Focus 3.2.[34]

A Florida case illustrates the successful use of the insanity defense that did not result in confinement. A nineteen-year-old college student charged with murder was found not guilty by reason of insanity in the death of her newborn, whom she left to die in a toilet. It had been fourteen years since anyone charged with murder in that South Florida county had been successful in the insanity defense. And, it was rare that the defendant did not serve time. According to the defense attorneys, the jury did not see a "deranged and dangerous individual" who should never walk the streets again but a very disturbed young college student who posed no threat to society. The judge agreed. He did not order hospitalization for the defendant although he did order that she continue seeing her psychiatrist. "Otherwise, she's free."[35] One year later the young woman was released from psychiatric care.

PURPOSE OF THE INSANITY DEFENSE

The concept of mental competency is used in contexts other than defenses within criminal law. For example, a defendant may be sane at the time the alleged offense was committed but incompetent at the time of trial. The defendant must be competent to stand trial. "A defendant's mental competence to stand trial is a fundamental prerequisite to participation in our adversarial system of criminal justice."[36] The primary concern in this chapter, however, is the insanity defense as it is used in the determination of criminal liability.[37] The purpose of this highly controversial defense must be related to the general purposes of punishment (discussed in Chapter 1). The critical question is whether punishment of insane offenders achieves incapacitation, just deserts, rehabilitation, retribution or revenge, or general or specific deterrence. In addition, there is the issue of fairness and humaneness. Do we want to punish insane people? Finally, is the requisite *mens rea* present when an insane person commits a criminal act?

INSANITY TESTS

Over the years several tests have been developed to define and measure insanity. The elements of these tests are stated briefly in Focus 3.5.

The M'Naghten Rule The traditional, most frequently used test of insanity comes from an English case. It has become known as the **M'Naghten rule**, or the "right-versus-wrong" test. Under this rule a defendant may be found not guilty by reason of insanity if, as a result of a defect of reason from disease of the mind, it can be shown that the defendant (1) did not know the nature and quality of the act committed or (2) did not know that the act was wrong.[38]

In the English case, defendant M'Naghten was found not guilty by reason of insanity after he argued successfully that the criminal act of which he was accused was caused by his delusions. Daniel M'Naghten was accused of shooting and killing the British Prime Minister's secretary, thinking he was the Prime Minister, whom M'Naghten believed was heading a conspiracy to take his life.

The main problems with the M'Naghten rule have centered around definitions. There is little case law on the meaning of the phrase *disease of the mind*. However, most courts have not seemed too concerned about that problem and, without defining that term, tell the jury that they must find that the defendant suffered from a mental disease. The meaning of the word *know* is a more serious problem. Does the word mean that the defendant has cognitive knowledge or that he or she has a moral understanding

---

FOCUS 3.5 Insanity Tests

M'Naghten Rule—Right v. Wrong Test

A defendant may be found not guilty by reason of insanity if, as the result of a defect of reason from disease of the mind, the defendant

1. did not know the nature and quality of the act committed, or
2. did not know that the act was wrong.

The Irresistible Impulse Test

The defendant's state of mind is such that he or she may know the nature and quality of an act and that it is wrong but cannot forbear from committing the act.

The Durham Rule— Product Test

If the unlawful act was the product of mental disease or defect, the accused is not criminally responsible for his or her conduct.

The A.L.I. Test of the Model Penal Code—Substantial Capacity Test

Section 4.01. Mental Disease or Defect Excluding Responsibility

1) A person is not responsible for criminal conduct if at the time of such conduct as a result of mental disease or defect he lacks substantial capacity to appreciate the criminality of his conduct or to conform his conduct to the requirements of law.

---

of the nature and quality of the act? Again, most courts do not decide; the M'Naghten rule is stated without a definition of this important word.

The M'Naghten rule has other words that may present interpretation problems, such as the phrase *nature and quality of the act* and *wrong*. Does the former mean that the defendant understands both the physical nature and the physical consequences of an act, for example, that putting a match to kerosene will cause a fire that will burn a building and kill people sleeping inside? Does *wrong* mean knowing that an act is legally wrong, morally wrong, or both? For these and other reasons, the rule is criticized frequently.

Some argue that the M'Naghten rule emphasizes the cognitive part of the personality to the exclusion of the emotional elements, that the ability to control one's behavior is not determined solely by cognition. It is argued also that the M'Naghten rule presents psychiatrists with impossible questions that must be answered when they testify as expert witnesses at trial and that the test is not an adequate way to identify defendants who should not be subjected to criminal punishments.[39]

The Irresistible Impulse Test Some jurisdictions that use the M'Naghten rule have adopted the **irresistible impulse test** either by statute or court decision. The first statment of this test in the United States was in an 1834 case in which the jury charge was as follows:

> If [the defendant's] mind was such that he retained the power of discriminating, or to leave him conscious he was doing wrong, a state of mind in which at the time of the deed he was free to forbear, or to do the act, he is responsible as a sane man.[40]

The definition of *irresistible impulse* varies from case to case, with one case indicating that it means a defendant would commit a crime even if there were a "policeman at [his] elbow."[41] Some argue that this is too restrictive. Some people might be able to exercise self-control in the presence of a police officer but be unable to control their behavior in other circumstances.

The Durham Rule The **Durham rule**, which was patterned after a rule applied in an 1869 New Hampshire case, comes from a 1954 District of Columbia case, *Durham v. United States*. In *Durham*, the late Judge David L. Bazelon, who wrote many opinions in which he attempted to integrate law and the social sciences, saw the insanity defense as an opportunity for psychiatrists to offer their insights into mental disease to assist in determining insanity. Judge Bazelon argued that the right-wrong test did not take "sufficient account of psychic realities and scientific knowledge" and that "it is based upon one symptom and so cannot validly be applied in all circumstances." A broader test was needed, articulated as follows: "An accused is not criminally responsible if his unlawful act was the product of mental disease or mental defect."[42] The Durham rule became known as the *product rule*.

Judge Bazelon distinguished *disease* and *defect*: the former is "capable of either improving or deteriorating," whereas the latter is a "condition which is not considered capable of either improving or deteriorating and which may be either congenital, or the result of injury, or the residual effect of a physical or mental disease." He emphasized that this rule would assist in eliminating from criminal liability those people who are not punishable in U.S. criminal justice systems because they lack moral blame.

As articulated by Judge Bazelon, the Durham rule was not precise enough to convince many states to adopt it. Critics argued that the test left too much influence to expert witnesses and too much discretion to the jury. In addition, no standards were set by the court. In 1972 the *Durham* case was overruled in the District of Columbia, where it originated. The court adopted a modified version of the Model Penal Code test of insanity.[43]

The A.L.I. Test of the Model Penal Code The scholars of the American Law Institute, who drafted the Model Penal Code, rejected the Durham rule and drafted a modified version of the M'Naghten and irresistible impulse tests. This test is called the **substantial capacity test**, or the **A.L.I. rule**, and provides as follows:

> *Section 4.01. Mental Disease or Defect Excluding Responsibility*
> (1) A person is not responsible for criminal conduct if at the time of such

conduct as a result of mental disease or defect he lacks substantial capacity to appreciate the criminality [wrongfulness] of his conduct or to conform his conduct to the requirements of law.

(2) As used in this Article, the terms "mental disease or defect" do not include an abnormality manifested only by repeated criminal or otherwise anti-social conduct.

The A.L.I. (or substantial capacity) test is broader than the M'Naghten rule in its substitution of *appreciate* for *know*. Thus, under the A.L.I. test, a defendant who knows the difference between right and wrong but who does not appreciate that difference may be successful with the insanity defense. It is appropriate to introduce **expert testimony,** such as that provided by psychiatrists and psychologists, to provide evidence of the defendant's emotional and intellectual capacity. In establishing a substantial capacity test, the A.L.I. test appears to be a compromise between what has been interpreted as the total impairment requirement of the M'Naghten and irresistible impulse tests and the apparent requirement of only slight impairment in the Durham rule.

The second paragraph of the A.L.I. test was written to exclude *sociopathic* or *psychopathic* personalities because of disagreement among authorities over whether or not sociopaths or psychopaths are sufficiently different from other people that they suffer from a mental disease. This paragraph is controversial and has been rejected by some jurisdictions. But it has been adopted by most jurisdictions that utilize the A.L.I. test.

REACTIONS TO THE INSANITY DEFENSE

The jury verdict of not guilty by reason of insanity in the trial of John W. Hinckley, Jr., who was charged with attempting to assassinate President Reagan and others on 30 March 1981 (this case is discussed in Focus 3.2), led to strong public support for changes in the insanity defense.[44] Some states follow the Michigan plan, discussion follows; others argue for the abolition of the insanity defense.

Guilty but Mentally Ill Since 1975 a defendant who raises the insanity defense in Michigan, in addition to being found guilty, not guilty, or not guilty by reason of insanity, may be found guilty but mentally ill. The Michigan statute distinguishes insanity and mental illness and provides for a finding of guilty but mentally ill if the jury is convinced beyond a reasonable doubt of *all* of the following:

1. that the defendant is guilty of an offense;
2. that the defendant was mentally ill at the time of the commission of that offense;
3. that the defendant was not legally insane at the time of the commission of that offense.[45]

Under the Michigan statute, a defendant who pleads guilty or who is found after a trial to be mentally ill may receive the sentence that could be imposed under a guilty plea alone. The difference is that a verdict of guilty but mentally ill obligates the Department of Mental Health to provide psychiatric treatment while the defendant is on probation or in prison.

The Michigan Supreme Court has upheld this statute, stating that the major purpose of the guilty but mentally ill verdict is "to limit the number of persons who . . . were *improperly* being relieved of all criminal responsibility by way of the insanity verdict."[46]

Calls for Abolition Some states have abolished the insanity defense. The Idaho Code states: "Mental condition shall not be a defense to any charge of criminal conduct." The code does permit the admission of expert testimony to negate the *mens rea* required for the charged offense. Thus, evidence of mental illness may be used only to show that the defendant did not have the requisite *mens rea*.[47] Some states permit evidence of mental illness to be admitted only for the purpose of determining the appropriate sentence.

Support for abolishing the insanity defense is related in some cases to the unrealistic assumption that all or most persons found not guilty by reason of insanity are released back into society. As noted in the discussion of Hinckley, some defendants are confined to mental institutions or hospitals. There are legal limitations on this practice. In 1983 the Supreme Court upheld a District of Columbia statute that provides for the indefinite commitment to a mental hospital of a criminal defendant found not guilty by reason of insanity. Within fifty days of this commitment, the individual is entitled to a judicial hearing to determine release eligibility. The patient must prove by a preponderance of the evidence that he or she is ready for release. Failure to do so results in continued commitment. In *Jones* v. *United States*, the Court said, "A verdict of not guilty by reason of insanity is sufficiently probative of mental illness and dangerousness to justify commitment of the acquittee for the purposes of treatment and the protection of society." The Court held that this is true even if the commitment is longer than would have been the case had the individual been found guilty and sentenced under the applicable statute.[48]

By a 5–4 vote the Supreme Court limited indefinite commitment of persons found not guilty by reason of insanity. In its 1992 decision in *Foucha* v. *Louisiana* the majority invalidated the Louisiana statute that permitted the state to continue confining insanity acquittees even if they are no longer mentally ill as long as they are judged by a court to be dangerous to themselves or others.[49] To be released, the insanity acquittee must prove that he or she is not dangerous.

Foucha was found to be dangerous based on the testimony that he had an antisocial personality, a condition that is not treatable and is not a mental disease. The Court emphasized that in order to detain Foucha when he no longer had a mental disease, the state would have to go through civil commitment proceedings and prove current mental illness and dangerousness.[50] The state had not done that. Although the state may punish, even imprison criminals for reasons of deterrence, Louisiana may not do so in the case of Foucha who has not been convicted of a crime. The Court distinguished *Foucha* from a pretrial detention case in which the Court permitted preventive detention of persons accused of crimes. In *United States* v. *Salerno* the Court upheld the pretrial detention of dangerous persons who were awaiting trials, but the circumstances were narrowly limited and a full adversary hearing was required. In *Salerno* the Court said, "In our society liberty is the norm, and detention prior to trial or without trial is the carefully limited exception."[51]

Diminished Capacity or Partial Responsibility

Some defendants who are not insane may establish the defense of diminished capacity or partial responsibility. This defense is available when it can be established that the mental illness of the defendant, though not sufficient to establish insanity, caused such sufficient lack of capacity that the defendant could not have achieved the requisite intent at the time of the crime. The defense may be used to show that the defendant charged with first-degree murder did not have the requisite intent, although that person might be convicted of manslaughter, a lesser crime.[52]

The Model Penal Code states that evidence "that the defendant suffered from a mental disease or defect is admissible whenever it is relevant to prove that the defendant did or did not have a state of mind which is an element of the offense." The Code states also that in cases in which capital punishment or imprisonment might be the defendant's punishment, "evidence that the capacity of the defendant to appreciate the criminality [wrongfulness] of his conduct or to conform his conduct to the requirements of law was impaired as a result of mental disease or defect is admissible in favor of sentence of imprisonment."[53]

Automatism

Similar to the insanity defense is the **automatism** defense, which may be raised by defendants who have evidence that they were unconscious or semiconscious when the alleged crimes were committed. For example, a physical problem such as epilepsy, a concussion, or an unexplained blackout while driving, any one of which results in an accident that kills someone, might support a complete defense for the driver charged with manslaughter.[54] If the driver knew or should have known that such physical problems existed, probably the defense would not be applicable.

Emotional trauma might be another acceptable basis for the automatism defense, but brainwashing is not a sufficient basis for asserting the defense. Nor is unconsciousness caused by voluntary intoxication sufficient, as is noted in the next chapter.

From the defendant's point of view, automatism as a defense is to be preferred over that of insanity, because, unlike insanity, acquittal is complete and the defendant is released, although civil commitment proceedings might follow.

Entrapment

The **entrapment** defense applies only to actions by government agents or their employees. A successful defense requires proof of two elements: (1) a government agent induced the defendant to commit the crime, and (2) the defendant was not otherwise predisposed to commit the crime. Both elements are required.[55]

It is obvious that one of the best ways for police to gather evidence against offenders is to be present when the crimes are committed or to hire informers. Both practices are acceptable as long as government agents do not go too far in their activities. As the Supreme Court indicated in 1932 in *Sorrells* v. *United States*, "Society is at war with the criminal classes, and courts have uniformly held that in waging this warfare the forces of prevention and detection may use traps, decoys, and deception to obtain evidence of crime."[56]

In a later case, *Hampton* v. *United States*, the Court said "It is clear that the government may supply drugs to a suspect in a drug investigation."[57] But there are limits to what the government may do without committing entrapment. To keep the government from going too far, two requirements constitute the entrapment defense. As the Supreme Court said in *Sherman* v. *United States*, "To determine whether entrapment has been established a line must be drawn between the trap for the unwary innocent and the trap for the unwary criminal."[58]

The entrapment defense is raised frequently in cases involving alleged illegal drug sales or prostitution. Two Montana cases illustrate these uses. In the first, the defense was successful in the case of a defendant with whom a government informant became a friend over a period of six months. The informant requested several times that the defendant help him to procure illegal drugs. Eventually the defendant succumbed. The court held that the defendant "was not predisposed to commit this offense."[59]

In *State* v. *Kim*, decided in Montana in 1989, the entrapment defense did not result in an acquittal. In Missoula, Montana, the defendant, Ms. Kim, operated a massage business named the Crossroads Sauna. After numerous citizen complaints, the county attorney's office began an investigation of the business. Two detectives, posing as truck drivers, went to the sauna where they were shown around the facilities and were told by a female employee that the business offered $40, $60, and $100 massages. When asked what the latter involved, they were told "everything."[60]

The detectives left but returned later and talked with Ms. Kim, who told them that only the $100 massage was available. They refused, and she then said they could have a $40 massage, which consisted of a sauna, a shower, and a back rub by Ms. Kim and another employee. They agreed and signed a form acknowledging that they would not give anything of value for any sexual conduct. During that same visit, the detectives inquired about having a bachelor party at the Crossroads Sauna. Ms. Kim agreed, indicating, however, that each guest would have to agree to the $100 massage, which on questioning, she said "included everything." Allegedly she said also that she would teach the groom how to make love to his wife.

At a later date six deputies and a deputy county attorney arrived for the purported bachelor party. On the way, each consumed a beer so they would appear to be in a partying mood, and they carried beer with them to the business. They were escorted to a back room, where the groom was given a bottle of champagne. Two employees sat on his lap and began unbuttoning his shirt and taking off his belt. Two of the men began talking to Ms. Kim outside the room. There was conflicting testimony over who initiated discussions of sexual relations, but the officers testified that the conversation took place in a very quiet and businesslike manner and included a discussion of protection. Ms. Kim said condoms were available. She was arrested and handcuffed, along with the two employees. On request, she consented to a search of the premises and showed the officers where the condoms were kept in the freezer. A later count indicated there were 334 condoms.

If you had been presented these facts as a juror, would you have decided for or against the entrapment defense? Do you think Ms. Kim and her employees would have committed a crime had the law enforcement officers not been there? Keep in mind that the bachelor party was their idea. Prior to their arrival for that event, despite their participation in massages, they had not seen any illegal activities taking place. Nor had they been offered sex. An investigation of Ms. Kim's prior activities did not turn up any criminal charges or even suspicion of criminal charges.

This case is a difficult one, as are many that raise the entrapment defense. The owner was convicted of prostitution and promoting prostitution. That conviction was upheld on appeal. A dissenting judge argued that the entrapment defense was appropriate; "this was entrapment pure and simple." The officers, not Ms. Kim, originated the design to *solicit* sexual activity. They did more than offer her an opportunity; they "first committed the offense themselves." They set up the situation by "ingratiating themselves with her even though they found no evidence of any criminal activity in connection with her business." The dissent concluded, "The whole mess is a dirty business, but it originated in the Sheriff's Department."[61]

An example of the successful use of the entrapment defense is presented in Focus 3.6.

Outrageous Government Conduct

Theoretically a defense of outrageous government conduct exists, although it is not well defined. The defense is based on the assumption that some behavior is so offensive and so outrageous that when committed by a government agent it cannot be the basis for collecting evidence to convict a suspect. The Supreme Court first raised the prospect of this defense in *United States* v. *Russell*, in which the Court stated:

> [W]e may some day be presented with a situation in which the conduct of law enforcement agents is so outrageous that due process principles would absolutely bar the government from invoking judicial processes to obtain a conviction.[62]

In the outrageous government conduct defense, the emphasis is on the behavior of the government rather than the mind of the defendant, as in the entrapment defense. "When the government's conduct...is sufficiently outrageous, the courts will not allow the government to prosecute offenses developed through that conduct."[63] In making that statement in 1992, the

FOCUS 3.6 U.S. Supreme Court Rebukes Government Action: Nebraska Farmer Wins on Entrapment Defense

In *Jacobson* v. *United States*, the U.S. Supreme Court reversed a Nebraska farmer's conviction for violation of the Child Pornography Act of 1984, which criminalizes the knowing receipt through the mails of a "visual depiction [that] involves the use of a minor engaging in sexually explicit conduct...." The following excerpt outlines the basic facts and conclusions of law of this recent case.[1]

Jacobson v. *United States*

In February 1984, petitioner, a 56-year-old veteran-turned-farmer who supported his elderly father in Nebraska, ordered two magazines and a brochure from a California adult bookstore. The magazines, entitled Bare Boys I and Bare Boys II, contained photographs of nude preteen and teenage boys. The contents of the magazines startled petitioner, who testified that he had expected to receive photographs of "young men 18 years or older."... The young men depicted in the magazines were not engaged in sexual activity, and petitioner's receipt of the magazine was legal under both federal and Nebraska law. Within three months, the law with respect to child pornography changed; Congress passed the Act illegalizing the receipt through the mails of sexually explicit depictions of children. In the very month that the new provision became law, postal inspectors found petitioner's name on the mailing list of the California bookstore that had mailed him Bare Boys I and II. There followed over the next 2 1/2 years, repeated efforts by two Government agencies, through five fictitious organizations and a bogus pen pal, to explore petitioner's willingness to break the law by ordering sexually explicit photographs of children through the mail....

[The Court described the government's actions in detail]

There can be no dispute about the evils of child pornography or the difficulties that laws and law enforcement have encountered in eliminating it. Likewise, there can be no dispute that the Government may use undercover agents to enforce the law....

In their zeal to enforce the law, however, Government agents may not originate a criminal design, implant in an innocent person's mind the disposition to commit a criminal act, and then induce commission of the crime so that the Government may prosecute. . . .

By the time the petitioner finally placed his order, he had already been the target of 26 months of repeated mailings and communications from Government agents and fictitious organizations. Therefore, although he had become predisposed to break the law by May 1987, it is our view that the Government did not prove that this predisposition was independent and not the product of the attention that the Government had directed at petitioner since January 1985.

[1] Jacobson v. United States, 112 S.Ct. 1535 (1992), citations omitted. For a discussion see Eulis Simien, Jr., "Criminal Law and Procedure: 1991–92 in Review," *Louisiana Law Review* 53 (1993): 771–774; and Lori G. Rhodes, "Criminal Procedure—Entrapment—Defendant Has Been Entrapped as a Matter of Law when the Government's Protracted and Insistent Efforts Create in Defendant a Predisposition to Engage in Unlawful Conduct," *Seton Hall Law Review* 23 (1993): 459–509.

Tenth Circuit noted that outrageous government conduct is a viable defense that may be raised even when the accused may not succeed on the entrapment defense because of a predisposition to commit the defense. The "thrust of [the defense as articulated in other cases] is that the challenged conduct must be shocking, outrageous, and clearly intolerable." The federal court went on to note that cases

> make it clear that this is an extraordinary defense reserved for only the most egregious circumstances. It is not to be invoked each time the government acts deceptively or participates in a crime that it is investigating. Nor is it intended merely as a device to circumvent the predisposition test in the entrapment defense.[64]

The outrageous conduct defense rarely is successful, although it has been held that the government's behavior was outrageous when a government agent supplied the knowledge, most of the supplies (including indispensable ingredients) and established the lab in which methamphetamine was manufactured.[65] Another federal court has held that the government engaged in outrageous conduct when its agents assisted in establishing and sustaining a bootlegging operation in which the government was the only customer as well as a partial supplier.[66]

In 1993 the Tenth Circuit held that the outrageous conduct prohibition would not preclude a government agent from supplying some drugs to addicts while working undercover, but

> At a certain threshold, the government's conduct would violate due process. For instance, we speculate that if a government agent entered a drug rehabilitation treatment center and sold heroin to a recovering addict, and the addict was subsequently prosecuted for possession of a controlled substance, the outrageous government conduct defense might properly be invoked.[67]

Defense of Persons and Property

The law permits people to defend themselves, other people, and property under certain circumstances. This is one of the most controversial defenses today, as more and more people are buying guns and using them for defense. In some instances these guns are used by young children, resulting in death or serious injury to themselves or others. Recent media articles indicate that it costs more than $14,000 to treat each U.S. child hit by gunfire, with over 5,000 children losing their lives to gunfire in any given year.[68] Some guns are used by spouses and children to kill those who batter them, an issue discussed in subsequent chapters.[69] Although all ages, races, and both genders are victims of gunfire in the United States, the most likely victims are young, African-American males ages sixteen to twenty-four.[70]

Earlier newswriters referred to some urban areas as "Dead Zones" or "Urban War Zones," areas that "are being written off as anarchic badlands, places where cops fear to go and acknowledge: 'This is Beirut, U.S.A.' "[71] They allege that some of America's streets have "become free-fire zones as police, criminals and terrified citizens wield more and ever deadlier guns."[72]

More recently, President Clinton told his weekly radio audience that anti-crime legislation is his top priority. In late November 1993, the president said, "We have to be concerned that in both our cities and our rural areas, the value of life has been cheapened." Further, "Too many children are killing children with weapons of destruction."[73] The crime bill passed in August 1994 (see Appendix D).

The danger that may occur when private citizens arm themselves with guns to protect lives and property was dramatized in the tragic death of a sixteen-year-old Japanese exchange student in Baton Rouge, Louisiana. The student was looking for a Halloween party to which he had been invited. He approached the home of Rodney Peairs, which was the wrong house. Peairs, a thirty-one-year-old butcher, thought he was an assailant and yelled, "Freeze." The Japanese student, who did not understand the word, did not stop. Peairs, who shot and killed the victim, testified at his manslaughter trial in 1993 that he was "scared to death that this person was not going to stop. He was going to do harm to me."[74]

Peairs' was acquitted, leading one writer to note that the verdict was "reverberating from radio talk shows to newspaper editorial pages, raising difficult issues of law, justice and race in a nation with more than 200 million guns and where 4.2 million new guns are sold each year."[75]

A 1993 report indicated that for the two previous years more Texans died from gunshot wounds than from auto accidents. In 1991 more Texans were

President Clinton signs the Brady Handgun Violence Prevention Act, while Jim Brady (seated), Vice President Gore, Attorney General Janet Reno, and Sara Brady (Brady's wife) look on.

killed by guns "than were killed in the entire Vietnam War."[76] In South Florida, the location of numerous violent acts against Floridians as well as tourists, gun sales have soared as citizens rush to buy weapons to protect themselves.[77]

In North Florida the arrests of four teenagers accused of murdering a British tourist and injuring his companion at an Interstate 10 rest stop in 1993, along with other incidents of teen violence, led lawmakers to enact a statute aimed at preventing the unsupervised possession of guns by teenagers. The new statute may be used to penalize parents as well as their children who are in possession of guns without appropriate supervision. Dealers may be punished, too, and the penalties range from community service to incarceration. The law permits police to seize guns from juveniles even if they are not suspected of having used those guns for committing crimes.[78]

The use of guns has become a serious problem even in other countries historically known for strict gun control. In the last five years gun crimes have doubled in Great Britain, where officials reported in 1993 that "the number of serious shootings has soared to more than two a day."[79] In the United States gun-related cases are causing much of the clogging of courts, especially in those jurisdictions in which penalties may be enhanced for crimes committed with the use of a dangerous weapon. "Federal judges...are alarmed that their dockets are increasingly filled by cases involving drugs and guns, while important constitutional issues like civil rights and antitrust actions await hearings for months or years."[80] This situation could be exacerbated by the recent enactment of a federal gun law, known as the Brady Handgun Violence Prevention Act, named for the former press secretary who was shot and injured when Hinckley fired shots at President Reagan (see Focus 3.2). In signing the bill, President Clinton indicated that Americans realize that their constitutional right to bear arms must be regulated because that right has become "an instrument of maintaining madness." The Brady Bill requires handgun purchasers to wait five days before taking possession of the weapon. During that waiting period local law enforcement authorities are to check the person's background for evidence of criminality or mental instability.[81]

Defense of self or others or of property may not be separated in all cases; some instances involve all of these types of defense. To the extent that they are separable, the rules differ with regard to acts that are permitted legally.

Self-Defense

The general rule on self-defense is that a person is permitted to use as much force as is reasonably necessary for protection when threatened with unlawful force that would cause immediate harm. The word *reasonably* is important, for it establishes an objective rather than a subjective test, meaning that the accused acted as reasonable people would have acted under the circumstances. If the belief were a reasonable one, it would not matter that it was inaccurate. That is, if it can be shown that most people would reasonably believe they were in danger of immediate physical harm, use of force is justified. The threatened harm must be imminent and unlawful.

In some jurisdictions the rules are different when a police officer claims self-defense. For example, Florida uses the *subjective test* for police officers. If the officer believes that his or her life (or the lives of others) is in danger, force is permitted and a resulting death does not constitute manslaughter. The issue was raised in the case of Officer William Lozano, a Miami police officer who shot and killed a motorcyclist in January 1989. A passenger on the cycle died as a result of the crash that followed the shooting. In his first trial on manslaughter charges, Lozano testified that the cycle was coming toward him and that he feared for his life. Witnesses testified that the cycle was in the other lane and that Lozano's life was not in danger.

Three days of rioting in Miami following this incident became local, national, and world news. Lozano's motion for a change of venue out of Miami was denied. He was tried in Miami, convicted of two counts of manslaughter, and sentenced to seven years in prison. His conviction was reversed and remanded for a new trial by an appellate court, which held that the change of venue should have been granted. Lozano succeeded in his argument that he could not get a fair trial in Miami.[82]

The venue of Lozano's second trial was changed several times.[83] The trial was held in Orlando. After the prosecution rested its case, defense attorney Roy Black shocked many court observers and perhaps some of the participants when, instead of calling witnesses, he stated, "Based on the lack of credible evidence in this case, we rest." During the cross-examination of prosecution witnesses, however, Mr. Black and his partner, attorney Mark Seiden, a former police officer, introduced evidence to support their argument that their client acted in self-defense. Apparently the jury agreed. Lozano was acquitted of both charges of manslaughter.

The right to use force does not always mean the right to use **deadly force**—force intended to inflict great bodily harm or death. Deadly force may be used only when the actor faces an *imminent* threat of death or serious bodily harm. The Model Penal Code permits the use of deadly force when "the actor believes that such force is necessary to protect himself against death, serious bodily injury, kidnapping or sexual intercourse compelled by force or threat." The code does not permit the use of deadly force as a defense if, in the same encounter, the actor provoked the incident that led to the threat of harm or death.[84]

Some jurisdictions require a person to retreat before using deadly force. The Model Penal Code requires retreating if it can be done with "complete safety," although, with a few exceptions, the code does not require actors to retreat within their own homes.[85] This is know as the *Castle Doctrine*, and according to the Rhode Island Supreme Court, a "majority of American jurisdictions recognize [this doctrine] pursuant to which a person attacked in his dwelling is not required to retreat before using fatal force to repel the attack." The Rhode Island court extended the Castle Doctrine in a 1992 case involving a social guest who had been asked to leave. "We now hold that one who is attacked in his dwelling by one who initially entered as a social guest but who has become a trespasser by remaining after being ordered to leave is similarly absolved from the duty to retreat."[86]

The following year, the same Rhode Island court decided a case involving a woman who stabbed her husband in their home. He died shortly thereafter, and the wife was charged with murder. The defendant claimed that her husband had beaten her for years and that on this occasion, he was threatening her life. She was convicted of manslaughter, and she appealed on several issues, one of which was the court's instruction that there is a duty to retreat even in your own home if you are being threatened by a co-occupant. The appellate court upheld that instruction.[87]

One final point on self-defense involves the use of force to resist arrest. Jurisdictions differ with regard to whether force may be used to resist arrest. The traditional position is that a person may use force to resist an *unlawful* arrest. The Model Penal Code rejects that approach. Even if the actor is the subject of an unlawful arrest, he or she may not use force to resist that arrest by a *known* police officer.[88] This rule was drafted to prevent citizens from making their own judgments about the legality of the arrest. In addition, the rule is designed to prevent force from escalating. When a suspect resists an arrest, the officer can be expected to use more force, and the result may be injury to the suspect, the officer, or others.

DEFENSE OF OTHERS

The rules governing the use of force to protect others are similar to those for self-defense. The actor is justified in using force to protect others if conditions exist that would justify the use of force for self-defense for the actor and for the threatened person and if the actor believes it is necessary to use force to protect the other person. According to the Model Penal Code, "retreat, surrender of possession and compliance with demands are not required of the actor unless he knows that he can thereby secure the complete safety of the other person." When retreat is required, actors must try to convince the potential victim to retreat.[89] Although under English common law a special relationship between the parties was required before the use of force was justified to protect another, the modern view has no such requirement.

DEFENSE OF PROPERTY

Even though defense of property is permitted legally, the rules are more stringent than those for self-defense or for the defense of others. Some of these rules differ among the jurisdictions, though it is well accepted that unless property occupiers need to protect themselves, they are not privileged to use deadly force to protect property. Otherwise, if it is reasonably necessary to use force to protect property from the immediate criminal acts of others, such force is permitted. The force is limited to the amount needed to prevent the criminal acts; it is not reasonable to use any force if the acts can be prevented by asking the intruder to stop. The property owner is not privileged to use force against a trespasser who would be placed in substantial danger of serious bodily injury upon exclusion.[90]

In most instances the use of devices that are not designed to cause serious bodily injury or death is justified for the protection of property. Devices that are not designed to cause serious bodily injury or death may be used if they are reasonable under the circumstances and if those devices are used customarily or reasonable care is taken to inform potential intruders of the presence of the device.[91]

Law Enforcement

Conduct that is criminal under most circumstances may be justified and therefore not criminal when committed by a law enforcement officer or by a private citizen attempting to enforce the law. New York's is a typical statute. It provides that conduct is not criminal when "Such conduct is required or authorized by law or by a judicial decree, or is performed by a public servant in the reasonable exercise of his official powers, duties, or functions."[92] Thus, a police officer may possess narcotics for the purpose of law enforcement, as long as the officer does not engage in acts that might be classified as *outrageous*, as discussed earlier in this chapter.

There is a reasonable limit to the crimes that may be committed to gain evidence of other crimes. The highly controversial practice of police officers getting involved in morality offenses is an example, as illustrated by the earlier discussion of *State* v. *Kim*. Some offenses are permitted (depending on how far the officers go in the activities), but it would not be permissible for an officer to commit an armed robbery or to hire someone to commit a murder.

Force, including deadly force, may be used by private citizens as well as by police officers in certain circumstances without creating criminal liability. Police officers and people aiding them may use force to effect an arrest. Under some circumstances an arrest warrant is necessary for a legal arrest; the exceptions are matters of criminal procedure and are not discussed here. Authorities may use force to prevent an arrested person from escaping or to protect officers and other people. The most critical issues arise over the use of deadly force.

Under the common law, police were permitted to shoot any **fleeing felon**—a person who had committed a felony and was eluding arrest. This rule developed over a period of time when all felonies were capital offenses and apprehending criminals was difficult. Felons were likely to get away if not apprehended quickly. Many states codified the common law rule, although some limited the shooting to fleeing felons who were accused of more serious felonies, such as murder or forcible rape. This was changed as a result of a 1985 Supreme Court decision.

In *Tennessee* v. *Garner*, police dispatched to a "prowler inside call" were told by a neighbor that she heard a glass break in the house next door. An officer went to the back of the house, heard a door slam, and saw a man running toward the fence. With the aid of his flashlight, the officer saw the man's face and hands and said the person was about seventeen or eighteen and about 5'5" or 5'7" tall. The suspect was actually fifteen, weighed about 100 or 110 pounds, and was 5'4" tall. The officer yelled, "Police, halt," but the suspect did not stop. The officer testified that although apparently the suspect was not armed, he thought that if the suspect got over the fence, he would elude police officers. The officer fired, hit the suspect in the back of the head, and killed him. Under the Tennessee statute, the officer was permitted to fire after giving warning. After acknowledging the importance of crime prevention, the Court ruled that the Tennessee statute was unconstitutional and gave reasons and guidelines for the use of deadly force when police are attempting to arrest a suspect.[93]

Tennessee v. *Garner*

Without in any way disparaging the importance of these [law enforcement] goals, we are not convinced that the use of deadly force is a sufficiently productive means of accomplishing them to justify the killing of nonviolent suspects. The use of deadly force is a self-defeating way of apprehending a suspect and of setting the criminal justice mechanism in motion. If successful, it guarantees that that mechanism will not be set in motion. While the meaningful threat of deadly force might be thought to lead to the arrest of more live suspects by discouraging escape attempts, the presently available evidence does not support this thesis....

The use of deadly force to prevent the escape of all felony suspects, whatever the circumstances, is constitutionally unreasonable. It is not better that all felony suspects die than that they escape. Where the suspect poses no immediate threat to the officer and no threat to others, the harm resulting from failing to apprehend him does not justify the use of deadly force to do so.... A police officer may not seize an unarmed, nondangerous suspect by shooting him dead....

[The Court noted that the statute, although unconstitutional as applied to the facts of this case, is not unconstitutional on its face, which means it would be upheld under some circumstances.]

Where the officer has probable cause to believe that the suspect poses a threat of serious physical harm, either to the officer or to others, it is not constitutionally unreasonable to prevent escape by using deadly force. Thus, if the suspect threatens the officer with a weapon or there is probable cause to believe that he has committed a crime involving the infliction or threatened infliction of serious physical harm, deadly force may be used when necessary to prevent escape and when some warning has been given where feasible. Applied in such circumstances, the Tennessee statute would pass constitutional muster.

Under restricted conditions (usually a requirement that the suspect committed a *dangerous* felony, such as murder), a private person may use deadly force to effect an arrest. Under the Model Penal Code this may occur without liability only when the person believes that he or she is assisting the police to make an arrest.[94] Most statutes permit people who are not assisting peace officers to use deadly force only when they are protecting themselves or others.

SUMMARY

This chapter begins a discussion of the major defenses that may be raised to negate a crime or some element of a crime. The next chapter completes that discussion. These defenses are very important, but they are complicated. The chapter gives definitions and a few examples; but the case law on defenses is immense, and new challenges continue to arise in the interpretations of long-used defenses.

The introduction, which sets the stage for discussing individual defenses, presents material of extreme importance. Legislatures have considerable discretion in drafting criminal codes. As subsequent discussions indicate, a crime, such as rape, murder, robbery, or burglary, may have different elements in different jurisdictions. In addition, legislatures have considerable discretion in establishing defenses to crimes and in allocating the burden of proof on those defenses. This chapter illustrates that it is not easy to distinguish some defenses from elements of a crime and that the allocation of the burden of proof is not a simple matter.

Although it is not possible to write a simple statement or draft a list of what can and cannot be done on these issues, it is possible to make general statements. It must be understood, however, that these general statements may lead to different results, depending on a particular fact pattern.

With these limitations in mind, we may state that generally the prosecution must prove all elements of a crime beyond a reasonable doubt and that the defense must prove all affirmative defenses by a preponderance of the evidence. Defenses must be defined so that they do not shift from the prosecution to the defendant the burden of proof on *any element* of a crime. A defense that shifts to defendants the burden of proving that they were innocent may be viewed as relieving the prosecutor of the burden of proving guilt. This is unconstitutional in U.S. criminal justice systems.

The discussion of types of defenses begins with a discussion of ignorance or mistake. Despite the commonly held belief that "ignorance of the law is no excuse," the law recognizes some circumstances of mistake and ignorance. In addition, the law recognizes that some otherwise criminal acts are committed under duress, in which cases actors are not criminally liable. In other circumstances someone may need to commit an otherwise criminal act to prevent a greater harm; the defense of necessity is permitted. It is not agreed, however, whether this defense applies to such activities as criminal trespass to protect legal abortions.

Age is another factor in determining criminal liability. Statutes differ on how they define *juvenile* and *adult*. All states have a juvenile court system that differs significantly from the adult criminal court. More and more states are changing their statutes to permit the prosecution to try juveniles in criminal courts when they are charged with serious felonies, such as murder.

The *insanity* defense, although used infrequently, is one of the most controversial defenses, particularly because the defense of not guilty by reason of insanity was successful in the trial of John Hinckley, Jr., who attempted to assassinate President Reagan. The insanity defense raises the problems of defining the term *insanity* and, once the defense is introduced, deciding whether the prosecution must prove that the defendant was sane at the time of the alleged act or whether the defense has the burden of proving insanity. Because the Supreme Court has held that insanity is an affirmative defense, it is permissible to place the burden of proof on the defendant. When this occurs, generally the standard of proof required is the civil standard of a preponderance of the evidence. The federal criminal code, however, requires proof by clear and convincing evidence, which is a higher standard than the civil one.

Several tests are used to define insanity. The one used most frequently, the *M'Naghten rule*, is referred to as the *right or wrong rule*. It permits finding a defendant not guilty by reason of insanity if it can be shown that, at the time the crime was committed and as the result of a defect of reason caused by a disease of the mind, the defendant did not know the nature and quality of the act or did not know that the act was wrong.

There was dissatisfaction with the M'Naghten rule because it did not apply to defendants who knew the nature, quality, and illegality of their acts but could not control themselves and keep from committing the crimes. Some jurisdictions combined the M'Naghten rule with the *irresistible impulse test*, which was drafted to include this situation.

Dissatisfaction with both of these rules led the District of Columbia to draft the *Durham rule*, which is called the *product rule*. The test of insanity under the Durham rule is whether the defendant's act is the product of mental disease or mental defect. The difficulty of defining *product*, *mental disease*, and *mental defect* led the District of Columbia courts to abolish the Durham rule.

The Model Penal Code's *substantial capacity test* has been adopted widely. This test permits the insanity defense in cases in which mental disease or defect results in the lack of a substantial capacity to appreciate the criminality of an act or to conform to the law. This test, in substituting *appreciate* for *know* in the M'Naghten rule, is broader. The M.P.C. excludes sociopathic or psychopathic personalities from its definition of insanity.

Dissatisfaction with the insanity defense has led a few states to legislate a provision for *guilty but mentally ill*. Michigan led the way with this provision, which applies to a person who is guilty of an offense and mentally ill when the offense is committed but who is not legally insane at that time. A defendant found guilty but mentally ill may receive the same sentence as a defendent found guilty. However, for the guilty but mentally ill defendant, the state would be obligated to provide psychiatric treatment. The Michigan Supreme Court has upheld this statute. Others have argued that the insanity defense should be abolished.

The *diminished capacity* or *partial responsibility* defense is similar to the insanity defense and may be used by defendants who are not insane but who suffer from such mental impairment that they cannot form the required criminal intent for a particular crime. The defense of *automatism* is available to defendants who are not in control of their actions either because of unconsciousness or semiconsciousness.

One of the most litigated defenses is *entrapment*. Despite numerous attempts to define the term, case law indicates that it remains unclear when the defense is applicable. In general, the defense may be used by defendants who can prove that their criminal acts were the result of inducement by a government official or employee and that they were not otherwise predisposed to commit the crimes. This defense is used frequently in cases involving drugs or sex.

Individuals are permitted to defend themselves, their property, and other persons, but *self-defense* is another frequently litigated defense that raises considerable controversy. Although the defense must be analyzed in light of the facts of a particular situation, usually it is available when a person is threatened with unlawful force that would cause immediate harm. However, the person may use only as much force as is reasonably necessary for protection. Defense of property permits less use of force than defense of persons, and usually the use of deadly force is permissible only when people are threatened with death or serious bodily injury.

Police officers are permitted to use deadly force in some instances without incurring criminal liability. The common law rule that permitted police to shoot and kill a fleeing felon was changed by ordinances and statutes in some jurisdictions prior to the U.S. Supreme Court's ruling in *Tennessee* v. *Garner*. Today police and private persons may not use deadly force except under restricted conditions (usually those involving a dangerous felony).

One of the fascinating and challenging aspects of the law is that it changes so much. One might say there are fads and fashions in criminal law and in criminology just as there are in clothing and other areas of life. Defenses that are used frequently today may not be as popular in the future. Furthermore, the specific uses of any given defense may change, and the laws regarding those uses continue to develop and grow. It is important in the practice or enforcement of law to be aware of the latest changes in one's jurisdiction. The next chapter discusses some defenses that are relatively new or that have been expanded in recent years.

STUDY QUESTIONS

1. Why is it necessary to distinguish *elements* of a crime from *defenses* to a crime?
2. How does the standard of proof required by the prosecution differ from that required of the defense?
3. How might a *presumption* affect the burden of proof?
4. How did the Supreme Court distinguish *Mullaney* v. *Wilbur* from *Patterson* v. *New York*? Do you find this distinction meaningful? If so, why? If not, why not?
5. What is wrong with telling the jury in a murder case that the "law presumes that a person intends the ordinary consequences of his or her voluntary act"? Discuss applicable case law.
6. Who has the burden of proof in self-defense and why? In the insanity defense?
7. When would ignorance or mistake be a defense? Should a reasonable mistake be a defense to statutory rape?
8. Distinguish the defense of automatism from that of duress or necessity.

9. If you were drafting a statute on capital punishment, would you exclude juveniles who commit murder? Should age have any bearing on our reaction to serious crimes?

10. Define and compare the major tests of insanity and contrast the insanity defense and the irresistible impulse defense. Do you think either of these defenses should be abolished? Is *guilty but mentally ill* an improvement over the traditional defenses involving mental illness?

11. What are the key elements of an entrapment defense? Should law enforcement officers engage in activities illustrated in *State v. Kim*? Did they entrap? Do you agree with the Court's decision in *Jacobson v. United States*?

12. Distinguish the *outrageous government conduct defense* from the *entrapment defense*.

13. Under what circumstances may one defend person or property, and how much force may be used?

14. Briefly describe the implication of the *Lozano* case to the issue of self-defense.

15. Compare the position taken by the Supreme Court in *Tennessee v. Garner* to the traditional common law approach to the use of deadly force by police officers.

ENDNOTES

1. Mullaney v. Wilbur, 421 U.S. 684 (1975).
2. Mullaney v. Wilbur, 421 U.S. 684, 701 (1975).
3. Patterson v. New York, 432 U.S. 197 (1977), cases and citations omitted.
4. Sandstrom v. Montana, 442 U.S. 510 (1979), *remanded*, 603 P.2d 244 (Mont. 1979).
5. Francis v. Franklin, 471 U.S. 307 (1985).
6. State v. Chambers, 709 P.2d 321 (Utah 1985).
7. Martin v. Ohio, 480 U.S. 228 (1987), *reh'g. denied*, 481 U.S. 1024 (1987).
8. See Rivera v. Delaware, 429 U.S. 877 (1976). See also Medina v. California, 112 S.Ct. 2572 (1992), *reh'g. denied*, 113 S.Ct. 19 (1992), indicating that requiring the defendant to sustain the burden of proof on incompetence to stand trial does not violate due process.
9. Commonwealth v. Reilly, 549 A.2d 503 (Pa. 1988).
10. See U.S. Code, Title 18, Section 17(b) (1994), formerly at Section 20.
11. State v. King, 763 P.2d 239 (Ariz. 1988). See Chapter 1 concerning problems of defining *beyond a reasonable doubt*.
12. United States v. Byrd, 834 F.2d 145 (8th Cir. 1987). See also Herrara v. State, 594 So.2d 275 (Fla. 1992), holding that requiring a defendant to prove the affirmative defense of entrapment beyond a reasonable doubt does not violate the U.S. or the Florida constitutions as long as that shifting does not lessen the state's burden of proving all elements of the charged offense.
13. Kenneth W. Simons, "Mistake and Impossibility, Law and Fact, and Culpability: A Speculative Essay," *Journal of Criminal Law & Criminology* 81 (Fall 1990): 469.
14. United States v. Cheek, 882 F.2d 1263, 1267 (7th Cir. 1989), *cert. granted*, 493 U.S. 1068 (1990), *vacated and remanded*, 498 U.S. 192 (1991). See also Model Penal Code, Section 204(1)(a) and the discussion in Simons, ibid., pp. 447-517.

15. Lambert v. California, 355 U.S. 225 (1957), *reh'g. denied*, 355 U.S. 937 (1958).

16. State v. Dodd, 765 P.2d 1337 (Wash.App. 1989).

17. See State v. Milum, 516 P.2d 984 (Kan. 1973).

18. United States v. Bailey, 444 U.S. 394 (1980), *remanded*, 675 F.2d 1292 (D.C.App. 1982), *cert. denied sub. nom.*, 459 U.S. 853 (1982). See also United States v. Polanco-Gomez, 841 F.2d 235 (8th Cir. 1988).

19. United States v. Bifield, 702 F.2d 342 (2d Cir. 1983), *cert. denied*, 461 U.S. 931 (1983).

20. United States v. Kinslow, 860 F.2d 963, 966 (9th Cir. 1988), *cert. denied*, 493 U.S. 829 (1989).

21. Model Penal Code, Section 2.09(3).

22. See Matthew Lippman, "The Necessity Defense and Political Protest," *Criminal Law Bulletin* 26 (July–August 1990): 317-356.

23. "Anti-Abortion Protester to Represent Self in Trial," *Tallahassee Democrat* (7 July 1993), p. 2B; "Trial Delayed in Abortion Doctor's Slaying," *Miami Herald* (1 December 1993), p. 2B; "Life Term for Killing Abortionist," *Miami Herald* (6 March 1994), p. 1.

24. See "Florida Bill to Protect Abortion Clinics Dies," *New York Times* (4 April 1993), p. 14.

25. Madsen v. Women's Health Center, 114 S. Ct. 2516 (1994).

26. "Law on Abortion Protesters Gets First Test," *New York Times* (7 June 1994), p. 8. The Bill is the Freedom of Access to Clinic Entrances Act of 1994, P.L. 103-259 (1994), amending U.S. Code, Title 18, Section 248.

27. Bird v. Anchorage, 787 P.2d 119 (Alas.App. 1990).

28. Bird v. Anchorage, 787 P.2d 119, 121 (Alas.App. 1990), referring to Cleveland v. Anchorage, 631 P.2d 1073 (Alas. 1981).

29. For a discussion see Commentary: "The Use of the Necessity Defense by Abortion Clinic Protestors," *Journal of Criminal Law & Criminology* 81 (Fall 1990): 677-712. For a recent case holding that the defense is not allowed, see State v. Cozzens, 490 N.W.2d 184 (Neb. 1992). For a discussion of the history of abortion in the United States, see Kathryn Ann Farr, "Shaping Policy Through Litigation: Abortion Law in the United States," *Crime & Delinquency* 39 (April 1992): 167-183. The controversial U.S. Supreme Court that recognized the right of a woman to an abortion is Roe v. Wade, 410 U.S. 113 (1973). The right was confirmed (although some restrictions of a Pennsylvania statute were held) in Planned Parenthood of Southeastern Pennsylvania v. Casey, 112 S.Ct. 2791 (1992), *remanded*, 978 F.2d 74 (3d Cir. 1992), *remanded*, 812 F.Supp. 541 (E.D.Pa. 1993), *on remand, motion granted*, 822 F.Supp. 227 (E.D.Pa. 1993), *on remand, motion granted*, 822 F.Supp. 227 (E.D.Pa. 1993), *rev'd., remanded*, 14 F.3d 848 (3d Cir. 1994), *and stay denied*, 114 S.Ct. 909 (1994).

30. See Summers v. State, 230 N.E.2d 320 (Ind. 1967).

31. See "More Courts Are Treating Violent Youths as Adults," *New York Times* (3 December 1993), p. 1.

32. See Kent v. United States, 383 U.S. 541 (1966), for constitutional requirements of waiver.

33. "Insanity Defense Used in One Percent of All Felony Cases, Report Says," *NCJA Justice Research* (March/April 1992), p. 3.

34. For a discussion of the legal issues regarding the conditional release of defendants acquitted on the grounds of insanity, see David B. Wexler, "Health Care Compliance Principles and the Insanity Acquittee Conditional Release Process," *Criminal Law Bulletin* 27 (January–February 1991): 18-41.

35. "Woman Acquitted in Death of Infant: Jurors Decide Moritt Is Not Guilty by Reason of Insanity," *St. Petersburg Times* (8 April 1990), p. 1.

36. Benjamin James Vernia, "The Burden of Proving Competence to Stand Trial: Due Process at the Limits of Adversarial Justice," *Vanderbilt Law Review* 45 (January 1992): 199-240, quotation is on p. 199. See this article for a discussion of some of the issues regarding competency to stand trial. See also State v. Williamson, 853 P.2d 56 (Kan. 1993).

37. For an earlier but classic discussion of many of the issues surrounding the insanity defense, see Abraham S. Goldstein, *The Insanity Defense* (New Haven, Conn.: Yale University Press, 1967).

38. M'Naghten's case, 8 Eng. Rep. 718, 722 (H.L. 1843). For an analysis of the M'Naghten rule, see R. D. Mackay, "McNaghten Rules OK? The Need for Revision of the Automatism and Insanity Defenses in English Criminal Law," *Dickinson Journal of International Law* 5 (Spring 1987): 167-192.

39. For a discussion of these and other issues, see Wayne R. LaFave and Austin W. Scott, Jr., *Criminal Law*, 2d ed. (St. Paul, Minn.: West, 1986), pp. 312-320. For a recent case that explores many of the issues involved in the M'Naghten rule, see People v. Serravo, 823 P.2d 128 (Colo. 1992).

40. State v. Thompson, Wright's Ohio Rep. 617 (1834). The rule was developed further in Parsons v. State, 2 So. 854 (Ala. 1887).

41. United States v. Kunak, 5 U.S.C.M.A. 346 (1954).

42. Durham v. United States, 214 F.2d 862 (D.C.Cir. 1954), *overruled* by United States v. Brawner, 471 F.2d 969 (D.C.Cir. 1972).

43. United States v. Brawner, 471 F.2d 969 (D.C.Cir. 1972).

44. For an overview of changes in the insanity defense, see Rita J. Simon and David E. Aaronson, *The Insanity Defense: A Critical Assessment of Law and Policy in the Post-Hinckley Era* (Westport, Conn.: Greenwood Press, 1988); and Norman J. Finkel, *Insanity on Trial* (New York: Plenum, 1988).

45. Mich. Comp. Laws, Section 768.36 (1994).

46. People v. Ramsey, 375 N.W.2d 297 (Mich. 1985). The New Mexico statute is virtually the same as that of Michigan and was upheld in State v. Neely, 819 P.2d 249 (N.M. 1991). For a recent case upholding the guilty but mentally ill statute in Utah, see State v. Young, 853 P.2d 327 (Utah 1993).

47. Idaho Code, Section 18-207 (1994). See also Mont. Code Ann. 46-14-102 (1994); and Utah Code Ann. Section 76-2-305 (1994). The Montana supreme court upheld that state's abolition of the insanity defense. The U.S. Supreme Court refused to review the case, thus permitting the Montana decision to stand and paving the way for other states to abolish the insanity defense. Montana v. Cowan, 861 P.2d 884 (Mont. 1993), *cert. denied*, 114 S. Ct. 1371 (1994).

48. Jones v. United States, 463 U.S. 354 (1983).

49. Foucha v. Louisiana, 112 S.Ct. 1780 (1992), *later proceeding*, 604 So.2d 951 (La. 1992).

50. See Addington v. Texas, 441 U.S. 418 (1979), holding that in an involuntary civil commitment of a person to a mental institution due process requires the state to prove by clear and convincing evidence that the person is mentally ill and requires hospitalization to protect himself and others.

51. United States v. Salerno, 481 U.S. 739, 755 (1987).

52. See Peter Arenella, "Diminished Capacity and Diminished Responsibility Defenses: Two Children of a Doomed Marriage," *Columbia Law Review* 77 (1987): 827-865.

53. Model Penal Code, Section 4.02.

54. See Government of the Virgin Islands v. Smith, 278 F.2d 169 (3d Cir. 1960); and People v. Freeman, 142 P.2d 435 (Cal. 1943), both involving unconsciousness caused by epilepsy.

55. See United States v. West, 898 F.2d 1493 (11th Cir. 1990), *cert. denied*, 498 U.S. 1030 (1991).

56. Sorrells v. United States, 287 U.S. 435, 453-54 (1932).
57. Hampton v. United States, 425 U.S. 484 (1976).
58. Sherman v. United States, 356 U.S. 369 (1958).
59. State v. Grenfell, 564 P.2d 171 (Mont. 1977). See also State v. Kamrud, 611 P.2d 188 (Mont. 1980).
60. State v. Kim, 779 P.2d 512 (Mont. 1989).
61. State v. Kim, 779 P.2d 512, 519 (Mont. 1989). See also United States v. West, 898 F.2d 1493 (11th Cir. 1990), *cert. denied* 498 U.S. 1030 (1991).
62. United States v. Russell, 411 U.S. 423, 431-432 (1973). See also Hampton v. United States, 425 U.S. 484 (1976).
63. United States v. Mosley, 965 F.2d 906, 909 (10th Cir. 1992).
64. United States v. Mosley, 965 F.2d 906 (10th Cir. 1992).
65. See United States v. Twigg, 588 F.2d 373, 380-381 (3d Cir. 1978).
66. See Greene v. United States, 454 F.2d 783 (9th Cir. 1971).
67. United States v. Harris, 997 F.2d 812, 818 (10th Cir. 1993).
68. "Hail of Bullets, Reign of Violence Cost $14,000 a Child, Study Finds," *Orlando Sentinel* (26 November 1993), p. 8.
69. See Jennifer L. Layton, "When the Abused Child Fatally Says, 'No More!': Can Parricide be Self-Defense in Ohio?" *University of Dayton Law Review* 18 (1993): 447-474.
70. Michael R. Rand, *Handgun Crime Victims*, Bureau of Justice Statistics *Special Report* (Washington, D.C.: U.S. Department of Justice, July 1990): 1.
71. "Dead Zones," *U.S. News & World Report* (10 April 1989), p. 20.
72. "The Other Arms Race," *Time* (6 February 1989), p. 20.
73. "Clinton Calls Anti-Crime Legislation His Top Priority," *St. Petersburg Times* (28 November 1993), p. 4.
74. "Defendant: 'I Had No Other Choice,' " *Orlando Sentinel* (23 May 1993), p. 13.
75. "Verdict in Louisiana Killing Reverberates Across Nation," *New York Times* (26 May 1993), p. 7. For a discussion of guns and violence and gun control, see Gary Kleck, *Point Blank: Guns and Violence in America* (Hawthorne, N.Y.: Aldine de Gruyter, 1991). See also Liz Marie Marciniak and Colin Loftin, "Measuring Protective Handgun Ownership," *Criminology* 29 (August 1991): 531-540.
76. "More Texans Still Die by Guns," *Orlando Sentinel* (7 May 1993), p. 3.
77. "Up in Arms: Gun Sales Are Soaring Among Nervous South Floridians," *Miami Herald* (17 October 1993), p. 1.
78. "Florida Enacts Firearms Law Curbing Possession by Young," *New York Times* (26 November 1993), p. 7; 1993 Fl. ALS 416.
79. "Gun Crimes Double in Law Five Years," *Sunday Times* (6 June 1993), p. 1.
80. "Gun-Related Cases on Federal Courts," *New York Times* (17 May 1991), p. 1.
81. Brady Handgun Violence Prevention Act, U.S. Code, Title 18, Section 922 (1994). See also "Clinton Signs Handgun Bill, Calling it Victory for Public," *New York Times* (1 December 1993), p. 14.
82. Lozano v. Florida, 584 So.2d 19 (Fla.Dist.Ct.App.3d Dist. 1991); *review denied*, 595 So.2d 558 (Fla. 1992); *mandamus granted, remanded, sub. nom.*, 609 So.2d 1291 (Fla. 1992), *and petition granted sub. nom.*, 616 So.2d 73 (Fla.Dist.Ct.App.1st Dist. 1993), *review denied sub. nom.*, 618 So.2d 758 (Fla.Dist.Ct.App.5th Dist. 1993), *and related proceeding sub. nom.*, 618 So.2d 758 (Fla.Dist.Ct.App.5th Dist. 1993).
83. For a discussion, see Florida v. Lozano, 616 So.2d 73 (Fla.Dist.Ct.App.1st Dist. 1993), *review denied sub. nom.*, 1993 Fla. LEXIS 708 (Fla. Apr. 23, 1993), *and related proceeding sub. nom.*, 618 So.2d 758 (Fla.Dist.Ct.App. 5th Dist. 1993).
84. Model Penal Code, Section 3.04(2)(b).

85. Model Penal Code, Section 3.04(2)(b)(ii)(A).
86. State v. Richard Walton, 615 A.2d 469 (R.I. 1992).
87. State v. Ordway, 619 A.2d 819 (R.I. 1992).
88. Model Penal Code, Section 3.04(2)(a)(i).
89. Model Penal Code, Section 3.05, Explanatory Note.
90. See Model Penal Code, Section 3.06.
91. See Model Penal Code, Section 3.06.
92. New York Penal Law, Section 35.05(1) (1994).
93. Tennessee v. Garner, 471 U.S. 1, 9, 10 (1985), citations and footnotes omitted. See also Sam Walker and Lorie A. Fridell, "Forces of Change in Police Policy: The Impact of *Tennessee v. Garner*," *American Journal of Police* 11, no. 3 (1993): 97-112; Geoffrey P. Alpert and Lorie A. Fridell, *Police Vehicles and Firearms: Instruments of Deadly Force* (Prospect Heights, Ill.: Waveland, 1992); and Jerry R. Sparger and David J. Giacopassi, "Memphis Revisited: A Reexamination of Police Shootings After the Garner Decision," *Justice Quarterly* 9 (June 1992): 211-225.
94. Model Penal Code, Section 3.07(2)(b)(ii).

Chapter 4

Defenses to Criminal Liability: Part II

Outline

Key Terms

battered person
    syndrome
clemency
condonation
date rape
euthanasia

involuntary intoxica-
    tion
pardon
posttraumatic stress
    disorder (PTSD)

premenstrual syn-
    drome (PMS)
rape trauma syndrome
urban psychosis
voluntary intoxication

Introduction

Previous chapters state that in a criminal case the prosecution must prove all *elements* of the crime beyond a reasonable doubt and that this burden of proof may not be shifted to the defendant. The previous chapter points out that even if the prosecution sustains this burden of proof, a defendant may not be criminally liable for the crime if an affirmative defense is proved. That chapter looks at the more traditional defenses, some of which are not very successful (such as entrapment and insanity) in contrast to others that are more likely to be successful, such as law enforcement and self-defense.

This chapter continues the discussion on affirmative defenses in criminal law by looking at some additional traditional defenses, such as intoxication, which have received more attention recently. It focuses as well on defenses that have emerged and developed recently and that are still in the formative stages of acceptance by the courts, such as rape trauma syndrome. As with previous chapters, it is crucial to understand that the law changes rapidly in these areas and that although all cases are checked for accuracy at the point of publication of the text, they could be changed or overruled shortly thereafter.

Intoxication

Intoxication has been recognized as a defense in criminal law under some circumstances, and the term includes alcohol and other drugs. The Model Penal Code defines *intoxication* as "a disturbance of mental or physical capacities resulting from the introduction of substances into the body."[1] The defense is not recognized in situations in which intoxication is an element of the crime, as for example, in the case of driving while intoxicated. The defense is permitted in some instances in which there is evidence that intoxication created a state of mind similar to that of an insane person and thus the defendant could not form the requisite intent required for criminal liability. In jurisdictions recognizing the irresistible impulse test, the intoxication defense may be utilized when defendants offer evidence that as a result of intoxication they were unable to control themselves and thus engaged in criminal behavior although they knew that behavior was wrong.

The law has long recognized that there is a difference between utilizing alcohol and other drugs voluntarily and doing so because one has no control—as for example, being forced to use drugs. Recently, however, attention has focused on whether the extensive use of alcohol or other drugs is a voluntary act that may be considered a moral problem and thus create criminal liability or the result of a disease over which the individual has no control.

Substance Abuse: Disease or Moral Problem?

Some authorities have argued that alcoholism and drug addiction are diseases, not moral problems, and that they should be treated as such in the criminal law.[2] In 1990, scientists at the University of California at Los Angeles and the University of Texas Health Science Center in San Antonio reported that they had identified a gene that puts people at risk for becoming alcoholics.[3] Researchers have found some evidence that the protective enzyme alcohol dehydrogenase that breaks down alcohol in the stomach may be the reason that many men can drink more than women without becoming intoxicated.[4]

The resolution of this issue is important to a discussion of the intoxication defense and may be expected to influence changes in legislation and court decisions on the defense. The U.S. Supreme Court has considered a related issue. In *Traynor* v. *Turnage*, the Court decided a case involving the Veteran's Administration and the benefits that are provided by law to eligible veterans. Most of the facts are not important to this discussion. What is important is the issue of whether alcoholism constitutes *willful misconduct*. After analyzing the history of congressional statutes concerning the use of the term *willful misconduct*, particularly with regard to Veteran's Administration legislation, the Court held that alcoholism does constitute willful misconduct. The Court emphasized, however, that it was not deciding the disease issue. "This litigation does not require the Court to decide whether alcoholism is a disease whose course its victims cannot control. It is not our role to resolve this medical issue on which the authorities remain sharply divided." But the Court did agree with the Veteran's Administration legislation that primary alcoholism (alcoholism that is not "secondary to and a manifestation of an acquired psychiatric disorder") is the result of the veteran's "own willful misconduct."[5]

Some authorities take the position that extensive use of alcohol or other drugs constitutes a disease and should be treated accordingly in criminal law.

Intoxication As a Legal Defense

The intoxication defense includes drugs and alcohol and is divided into two types: involuntary and voluntary. **Involuntary intoxication**, a seldom-used defense, is appropriate when a defendant has acted under intoxication that was compelled or coerced by another or when a defendant became intoxicated as the result of deception, mistake, or ignorance. The latter category might involve a defendant who is unaware of the side effects of a prescription drug.[6]

Involuntary intoxication might include pathological intoxication, too. According to the Model Penal Code, *pathological intoxication* is "intoxication grossly excessive in degree, given the amount of the intoxicant, to which the actor does not know he is susceptible." The code permits pathological intoxication and intoxication that is not self-induced to serve as affirmative defenses "if by reason of such intoxication the actor at the time of his conduct lacks substantial capacity either to appreciate its criminality [wrongfulness] or to conform his conduct to the requirements of law."[7]

In most cases, **voluntary intoxication**, which is self-induced, is not a defense unless it negates an element of the offense. Voluntary intoxication is at best a partial defense, meaning that intoxication cannot negate general intent but may negate specific intent. Even though intoxication releases some inhibitions and may cause a person to behave in a way he or she would not have done in a nonintoxicated state, that is not a defense. However, the law may recognize intoxication as a defense to the specific intent required for a crime such as first-degree murder, in which case the defendant might be convicted of second-degree murder.[8] For example, Kansas law provides:

> An act committed while in a state of voluntary intoxication is not less criminal by reason thereof, but when a particular intent or other state of mind is a necessary element to constitute a particular crime, the fact of intoxication may be taken into consideration in determining such intent or state of mind.[9]

In the federal system involuntary intoxication may negate a specific but not a general intent.[10]

In most jurisdictions voluntary intoxication cannot negate recklessness or negligence when those elements, rather than purpose or knowledge, are required for the crime.[11] Some jurisdictions do not recognize voluntary intoxication even as a partial defense. According to the Texas code, "Voluntary intoxication does not constitute a defense to the commission of a crime." That code does permit evidence of temporary insanity caused by intoxication as a mitigating circumstance for sentencing.[12]

Focus 4.1 discusses some recent uses of attempts to explain improper and illegal behavior in terms of intoxication. The excerpt from *People* v. *Tocco* illustrates the use of the intoxication defense and gives an overview of the issue of whether alcoholism is a disease.[13]

People v. *Tocco*

The defendant here is charged with arson in the second degree and reckless endangerment in the first degree. More specifically, he is alleged to have set fire to the apartment in which he resided with his ex-wife and children....

The defense admits the act. It contends that the defendant, who testified that he did not remember his arrest on the occasion for which he was being tried by reason of his intoxicated state, was incapable of formulating the requisite intent necessary to subject him to liability for the crime of arson in the second degree....

Alcoholism is generally defined as the chronic, pathological use of alcohol. There is a 30 year consensus in the medical profession that such pathological use of alcohol is a disease....

Even were our courts inclined to accept the disease thesis advanced by the medical profession, ignorance largely prevails as to its etiology....

At common law, intoxication was never a defense to criminal misconduct. Instead, it was viewed as an aggravating circumstance which heightened moral culpability. "The common law courts viewed the decision to drink to excess with its attendant risks to self and others, as an independent culpable act." Later cases allowed evidence of intoxication to be introduced for limited purposes, such as to negative proof that the defendant possessed the physical capacity to commit the crime.

Under the present state of the law, voluntary intoxication is not a defense to a criminal charge; however, in crimes that have specific intent as an essential element, voluntary intoxication has been found to negative such intent, thereby rendering the defendant not guilty of the crime charged....

And while intoxication may negative the *mens rea* in a crime requiring specific intent, it may not negative the lower culpable mental state required in crimes of recklessness....

Involuntary intoxication is a defense if it deprives the intoxicated person of understanding the nature and quality of his act or the knowingness that the act is wrong....

[T]here is a recognition among physicians that alcoholism is a disease characterized by loss of control over the consumption of alcoholic beverages. Can then an alcoholic's inebriated state(s) ever be considered truly voluntary? This question and a related one dealing with narcotic addiction have been dealt with by some courts. [The court discusses *Robinson* v. *California* and *Powell* v. *Texas*]....

Some commentators have speculated that courts will be required, some time in the future, to meet the argument that the intoxication of a chronic alcoholic, is...involuntary. If such were the case, the chronic alcoholic could never be held liable for crimes that he committed while in a severely intoxicated state. As of yet, no court has extended the defense to preclude prosecution of an alcoholic for non-alcohol related crimes committed while in an intoxicated state. And, presently, alcoholism is not a defense even to alcohol related crimes that punish more than mere status....

[I]t would appear that any change in the law would find basis only in conclusive medical evidence spurred by growing social concern, rather than constitutional pivots. Yet, if alcoholism is a disease characterized by an inability to control the consumption of alcoholic beverages, then the imposition of criminal liability for acts performed while drunk would at first blush defy logic.

Separating the physical act of drinking from the causative condition, alcoholism, is the distinguishing factor to which we must pay heed. Alcoholics should be held responsible for their conduct; they should not be penalized for their condition. An enlightened society cannot otherwise justify itself.

If an alcoholic knows that he is prone to commit criminal acts while drunk and that the consumption of even one drink will destroy his ability to resist further drinking, to the point of intoxication, as in the instant case, it must follow that his voluntarily imbibing of the first drink is the very initiation of a reckless act—and the concomitant disregard of the substantial and unjustifiable risk attendant thereto. If so, under our law the consumption of said drink by such alcoholic raises the act to the level of recklessness per se, subjecting him to strict accountability for crimes such as reckless arson and/or reckless endangerment now before the Court. No case has been uncovered imposing liability at this early threshold.

Arguendo, if we accept alcoholism as a disease, the hypothesis suggests that some (though probably not all) alcoholics lack the ability to control the taking of even the first drink....

[U]pon the evidence adduced at the trial of this action, this Court finds the defendant not guilty of arson in the second degree, which is defined as "intentionally damag[ing] a building...by starting a fire" as he lacked the specific intent to damage a building. However, the Court finds the defendant guilty of the lesser included offense of arson in the fourth degree, which is defined as "recklessly damag[ing] a building...by intentionally starting a fire."

Further, and likewise, the Court finds the defendant guilty of reckless endangerment in the first degree. Here, the defendant voluntarily commenced a reckless course of action (i.e., the act of his taking an alcoholic beverage), a risk in itself, the natural consequences of which, the unjustifiable endangerment of the lives of others thus being intended.

People v. *Tocco* raises a number of important issues. Note the references to *Powell* and *Robinson*, Supreme Court decisions that relate to the issue of punishing people for an act versus a status. "Powell was convicted not of being a chronic alcoholic, but for being drunk in a public place on a particular occasion. Thus, he was being punished for the performance of an act, rather than for mere status." Further, the Supreme Court said that when Powell took a drink while sober, he was exercising free will. What if scientific evidence indicates that is not the case, and that to the contrary, people

FOCUS 4.1 Should Intoxication Be a Legal Defense to Illegal Behavior?

In recent years a number of allegations that antisocial or illegal behavior is caused by intoxication have captured national attention. Some cases involve allegations that substance abuse caused the behavior, resulting in civil legal actions; other cases utilize the intoxication defense in criminal cases. Although the civil cases involve a different standard of proof, they are important in establishing the willingness of courts to accept intoxication as a legally acceptable explanation for the cause of behavior.

In 1992 a Dallas jury awarded $1.8 million in damages to the family of William Freeman, former assistant police chief of Fort Stockton, Texas, who claimed he killed his best friend because of the influence of the drug Halcion. Freeman and his family sued; the jury awarded damages only to the family. The jury determined that Upjohn, the manufacturers of Halcion, was 20 percent responsible for the murder, along with Freeman, who committed the act and was found to be 50 percent responsible, and his physician, who prescribed the drug and was assessed 30 percent liability. No damages were awarded to Freeman, who claimed that the sleeping pill, prescribed in the mid-1980s when he was having trouble sleeping after back surgery, altered his personality. It was argued that Freeman experienced paranoia, psychosis, and amnesia while taking the drug and that after he stopped taking the drug his personality returned to normal.[1]

Freeman is serving a life sentence for the 1987 killing of his friend. Freeman did not raise the Halcion defense at trial, claiming at first that he killed in self-defense and then that the killing was an accident. The success of this civil suit against Upjohn, however, raises the possibility that the influence of Halcion (or similar drugs) might be used successfully in the future as at least a partial defense to criminal acts. A state district judge reduced the damage award by $700,000. The remaining award includes $200,000 in punitive damages. This case was the first of its kind against Halcion, formerly the most widely prescribed sleeping pill in the world.[2]

In 1993 a Michigan defendant was found not guilty by reason of insanity after he claimed that he shot his estranged wife because of the influence of Halcion. In his first trial in 1990, the defendant, John Caulley, was convicted of first-degree murder and sentenced to life in prison. He was granted a retrial after an appellate court ruled that the jury should have been permitted to consider the effect of Halcion on the defendant's behavior.[3]

In a 1992 Florida trial, defendant Kevin Callahan argued that he was under the influence of Prozac, the most prescribed antidepressant drug in the United States, when he stabbed and almost killed his wife. A doctor who testified for Callahan at his trial said the doctor who treated Callahan had mixed drugs "to the point where you had a stew that was out of control," and that was the cause of the crime.[4] Callahan was convicted of attempted murder. On the last day of his trial he faked suicide and wrote a note alleging that the makers of Prozac, Eli Lilly and Company, had bribed court officials and that they would "burn in hell" for their actions. The judge sentenced Callahan to twenty-five years in prison despite the recommendation from Department of Corrections officials that the term be only twelve years. The prosecution had sought a life term.[5]

Dade County (Miami) Florida's largest judicial corruption scandal resulted in charges against numerous court officials. In the spring of 1993, after a nine-month trial, two judges were convicted in the so-called Operation Court Broom investigation. One of the defendants, circuit judge Phillip Davis, testified that he did not want to take the $20,000 bribe, which he gave to another judge who "demanded the money as payment for past favors." Davis said, "I didn't want to be involved. There was something in me that said I had to do it." Davis testified that drug abuse and paranoia caused him to lose control of his life and become involved in the scandal. He admitted that he took Demerol and drank alcohol in his chambers; later he used cocaine, which he called the "everything drug."[6]

In 1992 numerous women and former employees of Senator Robert Packwood of Oregon claimed that the senator had made unwelcome sexual advances toward them. Packwood, one of the most senior members of the U.S. Senate, has been a long-time backer of women's rights issues. He opposed the nomination of Clarence Thomas to the Supreme Court after Thomas was accused of sexual harassment by law professor Anita Hill. Some of Packwood's accusers said he appeared to be under the influence of alcohol during the incidents in question. Packwood said, "Whether alcohol was a factor in these incidents, I do not know. In any event, alcohol at best can only be a partial explanation, not an excuse." He acknowledged a drinking problem and said he would seek help.[7]

The extent to which Packwood will use the alcohol defense if charges are filed is not known. By the fall of 1994 Packwood remained in office despite rumors that he would resign after the Senate voted overwhelmingly to enforce the ethics committee's subpoena for Packwood's personal diaries. The charges against Packwood occurred before the enactment of sexual harassment laws pertaining to Congress.[8]

[1.] "Halcion Maker Assessed Part of Blame in Death," *Dallas Morning News* (13 November 1992), p. 1; "Jury Partly Blames Sleeping Pill in a Murder," *New York Times* (13 November 1992), p. 10.
[2.] "Judge Cuts Award in Suit Over Halcion," *Houston Chronicle* (8 December 1992), p. 24; "Suit Verdict May Keep Halcion Reeling," *Los Angeles Times* (16 November 1992), p. 2D.
[3.] "Man Who Killed His Wife Found Insane: Had Blamed Sleep Aid," *Phoenix Gazette* (21 October 1993), p. 10.
[4.] "Prosecution Challenges Prozac Defense," *St. Petersburg Times* (24 January 1992), p. 3B.
[5.] "Twenty-Five Years for Man who Faked Suicide," *St. Petersburg Times* (21 March 1992), p. 3B.
[6.] "Drugs, Alcohol Brought Him Down, Davis Testifies," *Miami Herald* (22 January 1993), p. 1B; "Two Judges Guilty," *American Bar Association Journal* 79 (July 1993): 20. In March 1994, five attorneys were sentenced to prison for their respective roles in the Operation Court Broom Scandal. See "Court Broom Lawyers Get Prison Time," *Miami Herald* (18 March 1994), p. 1B.
[7.] "Drinking Might Have Prompted Sexual Advances, Senator Says," *New York Times* (30 November 1992), p. 8. See also "The Blame-it-on-Booze Defense: Alcohol Explanation Becomes D.C.'s 'Equivalent of the Insanity Plea,'" *Miami Herald* (30 November 1992), p. 6. "
[8.] "The Culture of the Long Goodbye," *Newsweek* (15 November 1993), p. 31.

who have certain genes do not control their actions with regard to drinking (or taking drugs)? Should that evidence change our practices regarding intoxication as a defense to criminal acts? Should it change any of the results in the cases discussed in Focus 4.1? If so, to what extent? Should intoxication be a complete defense to a criminal act? These are crucial questions that courts continue to face in the light of new scientific evidence. "Analyzing the way in which scientific findings are brought to bear on legal questions is an issue that we are only beginning to grapple with today."[14]

Earlier decisions showed some unwillingness to integrate research findings into legal issues. In his dissenting opinion in *Powell*, Justice Abe Fortas, joined by three other justices, emphasized that one important issue is to distinguish between a criminal act and a condition. *Powell* did not involve a criminal act but rather, "the mere *condition* of being intoxicated in public. The opinion continued as follows.[15]

Powell v. *Texas*

[From the dissenting opinion]

The questions for this Court are not settled by reference to medicine or penology. Our task is to determine whether the principles embodied in the Constitution of the United States place any limitations upon the circumstances under which punishment may be inflicted....

[The justice distinguished *Robinson* and *Powell*.]

Robinson stands upon a principle which, despite its subtlety, must be simply stated and respectfully applied because it is the foundation of individual liberty and the cornerstone of the relations between a civilized state and its citizens. Criminal penalties may not be inflicted upon a person for being in a condition he is powerless to change. In all probability, Robinson at some time before his conviction elected to take narcotics. But the crime as defined did not punish this conduct. The statute imposed a penalty for the offense of "addiction"—a condition which Robinson could not control. Once Robinson had become an addict, he was utterly powerless to avoid criminal guilt. He was powerless to choose not to violate the law.

In the present case, appellant is charged with a crime composed of two elements—being intoxicated and being found in a public place while in that condition. The crime, so defined, differs from that in *Robinson*. The statute covers more than mere status. But the essential constitutional defect here is the same as in *Robinson*, for in both cases the particular defendant was accused of being in a condition which he had no capacity to change or avoid....

[The opinion states the trial court judge's findings regarding Powell's drinking and continues:] I read these findings to mean that appellant was powerless to avoid drinking: that having taken his first drink, he had "an uncontrollable compulsion to drink" to the point of intoxication; and that once intoxicated, he could not prevent himself from appearing in public places.

It is important to distinguish the general acceptance of intoxication as a defense from its exclusion in a particular case in which the judge may rule that there is insufficient evidence to sustain the defense. An example of an unsuccessful attempt to use the alcoholism defense occurred in the trial of Michael K. Deaver, a former aide to President Reagan. Deaver's attorney wanted to introduce evidence that his client was an alcoholic, that he was intoxicated frequently during the period of time in question, and that as a result of his intoxication he was unable to remember details asked him by a federal grand jury and by a congressional subcommittee. Both were investigating transactions concerning Deaver's highly paid career as a lobbyist in Washington, a job he took after leaving his position at the White House.

Deaver's attorneys argued that their client's memory was clouded by excessive drinking and that he was a former alcoholic. In Deaver's case, the judge refused to permit evidence of alcoholism to be admitted at the trial, although he would have permitted evidence of other variables that might have caused a lapse of memory. The trial judge in the Deaver case ruled that the evidence that the defense wanted to introduce at the trial was not sufficient to support an alcoholism defense. Deaver was convicted of perjury and given a suspended three-year sentence and a $100,000 fine. This judicial decision is to be distinguished from a refusal to recognize and admit evidence to be introduced on the alcoholism defense.

Two additional points about the alcoholism defense should be noted. First, intoxication may be grounds for mitigating a sentence. For example, Texas provides that "Evidence of temporary insanity caused by intoxication may be introduced by the actor in mitigation of the penalty attached to the offense for which he is being tried."[16] Second, in crimes such as public drunkenness, for which intoxication is an element of the crime, generally the intoxication defense is not recognized unless the defendant can prove involuntary intoxication.[17]

Domestic Violence Defenses

Historically domestic violence was considered a personal or family matter, not a social problem or even a crime. Parents were the legal guardians of their children, and most forms of physical and psychological discipline were considered appropriate. Women were the property of their fathers and, after marriage, of their husbands, who had unlimited sexual access to them legally. Rape laws precluded prosecution of a man for raping his wife (unless he assisted another man to do so). Few instances of spouse battering were called to the attention of police, and, when this did occur, the reaction was counseling, not arrest, although according to some sources the most frequent calls to police are calls concerning domestic violence cases.[18] Much of this has changed, however, as domestic violence has become a serious problem in the United States as well as in other countries, although the extent of such violence is not known.[19]

The issue here, however, is whether continued abuse in a domestic relationship constitutes a defense to a criminal act against the abuser. Although some jurisdictions permit the defenses discussed in this section, many do not, although the law is changing rapidly in this area. Definitions of domestic violence differ from jurisdiction to jurisdiction, but in general domestic violence includes violence of adults against children and of children against adults, as well as violence of adults against adults, the most commonly reported form of which is violence of husbands against their wives.

Battered Person Syndrome Defense

The **battered person syndrome** is a recently recognized condition used in some jurisdictions as a defense against crime analogous to the use of self-defense. The difference is that evidence of the battered person syndrome is permitted in some courts as a defense to criminal acts even though the element of imminent danger, required of self-defense, is not present. Indeed, in some cases in which the evidence has been permitted, the assailant, usually a woman, injured or murdered her lover or spouse in a situation in which he was not a threat, as, for example, a sleeping spouse.[20]

Most commonly the term *battered wife syndrome* is used, but the extension of the concept to a defense by children who murder their parents after years of alleged physical and sexual abuse has led to the use of the more neutral term, *battered person syndrome*, although at times the term *battered child syndrome* is used to describe the evidence presented for the defense of a child who murders a parent after years of alleged abuse. In this discussion the neutral term *battered person syndrome* is used to include all cases in which evidence of long-term battering is introduced in defense of a criminal act, in mitigation of a sentence for a conviction, or as evidence that a convicted person should receive clemency.

It is important to distinguish between a court's agreement that evidence on the battered person syndrome should be permitted and a court's decision that the evidence in a particular case should not be permitted for whatever reason. For example, one court did not find the defense applicable in the case before the court but did imply that in some cases the defense might be applicable. "The use of 'abused spouse syndrome' as a defense to a forcible felony is a recent occurrence. States which have considered this issue are divided on whether the syndrome in fact exists and, if so, whether it should be allowed as a defense to a homicide charge."[21]

Recent studies indicate that an increasing number of women are killing their husbands and other intimates and that in many of these cases the women allege that they have been abused physically or sexually over a long period.[22] More recently, some women who allege years of abuse by their husbands have maimed them, as in the case of Lorena L. and John Wayne Bobbitt. Lorena admitted that she cut off her husband's penis with a butcher knife while he was sleeping. She claimed he had raped her and fallen asleep just prior to her act but that he had abused her for years. John was tried for marital sexual assault. Lorena testified at the trial. John was acquitted. Lorena was tried for malicious wounding. She was found not guilty by reason of insanity.[23] She was ordered to spend forty-five days in a psychiatric hospital for tests and evaluations, and was released in March 1994.

Recent studies indicate that an increasing number of children are killing their parents after alleged physical abuse, especially sexual abuse. Some of these recent cases are discussed in Focus 4.2.[24]

NATURE AND USE OF THE BATTERED PERSON SYNDROME AS A DEFENSE

Dr. Lenore Walker, who testifies frequently about the battered woman syndrome, defines the battered woman as one who is

> repeatedly subjected to any forceful or psychological behavior by a man in order to coerce her to do something he wants her to do without concern for her rights.... Furthermore...the couple must go through the battering cycle at least twice.... [And if] she remains in the situation, she is defined as a battered woman.[25]

This definition of the battered woman has been adopted by some courts.[26] It has been extended as well to children who batter their parents. In what is said to be the first case of that extension, a Washington appellate court reversed the second-degree murder conviction of a youth who shot his stepfather who he claimed had abused him for years. The court ruled that the trial court erred in refusing to admit evidence of the battered child syndrome, holding that sufficient evidence exists to extend the battered woman syndrome to "analogous situations affecting children." According to the court, the battered child fears reprisal of the battering parent, feels helpless, has low self-esteem, believes it is futile to resist, and believes in the omnipotence of the parent. The court did note, however, that evidence of battering was not sufficient. The child offender had to show a "perceived imminence of danger, based on the appearance of some threatening behavior."[27]

On appeal, the Washington Supreme Court held that evidence on the battered child syndrome is admissible

> to help prove self-defense whenever such a defense is relevant. The underlying principles of the battered child syndrome are generally accepted in the scientific community and satisfy the [evidence] requirements by helping the trier of fact to understand a little-known psychological problem.[28]

The court went further, however, and ruled that evidence of battered child syndrome alone is not sufficient to ensure that the defendant had the reasonable belief that he or she was in imminent danger, an element of the defense of self-defense. The court remanded the case to the trial court to reconsider the impact of evidence of child abuse syndrome on its decision to deny a self-defense instruction.[29]

It is the perceived threat of imminent danger that is a crucial element in the battered person syndrome defense, and it is this element that requires expert testimony to assist the jury in understanding why the abused person remains in the relationship. Especially in the case of adults, the argument is that the abused person should leave the relationship rather than murder the abuser.

FOCUS 4.2 Abused Children who Kill Their Parents

Should children be justified in killing parents who abuse them? If not, why not? If so, under what circumstances? A number of cases have occurred in recent years. In many of these cases self-defense is not an appropriate defense.

In 1992 in Cheyenne, Wyoming, a sixteen-year-old shot and killed his father when his parents came home one night. The son and father had argued before the parents left; when they returned, the son and daughter were prepared to kill them. Both testified that the father had physically abused them and their mother over a period of years. The son was tried for first-degree murder. In his defense, his attorney argued that "for fourteen years this man murdered his son inch by inch.... That's the crime, the slow, day-by-day, week-by-week torture."[1] The son was convicted of the lesser crime of manslaughter and sentenced to five to fifteen years. That term was commuted to three years by the governor. The daughter was placed on probation for one year.

After a six-week trial, Sociz "Johnny" Junatanov, nineteen, was acquitted of trying to have his father killed. The defendant admitted the charge but insisted that his father had beaten him since childhood, chained and handcuffed him, and raped him. In another case a jury asked the judge for leniency for an eighteen-year-old they found guilty of manslaughter for killing his legal guardian. Evidence indicated that the youth was abused sexually by his guardian four or five times a week for four years. The judge placed the youth on probation for three years.[2]

In a 1989 precedent-setting case in Florida, Diana Goodykootz, fifteen, used the battered child syndrome defense successfully. Goodykootz was acquitted of second-degree murder for shooting her abusive father with his own gun. The defense attorney argued successfully that the alleged abuse caused the daughter to have a reasonable belief that she was in *imminent* danger of harm.[3]

National attention was focused on the television-covered trials of Erik and Lyle Menendez, accused of murdering their wealthy parents in their $4 million California home in 1989. For the four years prior to the first trial the brothers claimed to be innocent. Shortly before the trial began in July 1993 the defense announced that the boys shot their parents after years of mental and physical abuse, including sexual abuse. The prosecution claimed that greed over their inheritance led the brothers to kill their parents. The brothers were charged with two counts of murder and one of conspiracy in a trial that lasted five months, resulting in mistrials for both defendants when their respective juries could not reach verdicts. The prosecutor announced plans to retry both defendants.

[1] "Jury Gets Case of Boy Who Says He Shot Father Because of Abuse," *New York Times* (20 February 1993), p. 23.
[2] Nancy Blodgett, "Self-Defense," *American Bar Association Journal* 73 (June 1987): 36.
[3] "Girl Acquitted in Father's Death," *Tampa Tribune* (1 January 1989), p. 1B.

Lyle (22) and Erik (19) Menendez confessed to killing their wealthy parents but argued they did so only after years of physical and mental abuse, including sexual abuse. A mistrial was declared in the first trial; the prosecutor decided to retry both defendants.

Expert witnesses may be called to testify at trial that battered persons may develop the belief that they are threatened with serious bodily harm and death when in fact they are not so threatened. They act based on these beliefs—reasonable beliefs in light of their experiences—and they kill the people who batter them. Because it is so difficult for most people to understand why people remain in a relationship in which they are battered, expert testimony is used to explain the sociological and psychological aspects of the battered person syndrome. Expert testimony is used when lay jurors need information to understand the issues. Although not all courts faced with the issue have permitted expert witnesses to testify about the battered person syndrome, an increasing number are doing so. Such evidence was first held admissible in the 1979 case of *Ibn-Tamas* v. *United States*.[30]

In 1990 the Ohio Supreme Court held that evidence of the battered woman's syndrome should be admitted to assist the jury (or judge if there is no jury) to decide whether the defendant had reasonable grounds for committing the crime in defense of self. The following excerpts from *State* v. *Koss* may represent a modern trend toward acceptance of expert testimony on the battered woman syndrome and possibly even an expansion of the self-defense argument. Note that the case overrules one of its 1981 decisions concerning some of these issues. Note also that the case emphasizes the *subjective* perception of the battered woman in determining whether there was a threat of *imminent* great bodily harm or death. The case emphasizes also the nature and extent of testimony on the battered woman syndrome.

In *State* v. *Koss*, the defendant, who had been abused physically by her husband on many occasions, testified that on the day her husband was killed she went to their bedroom where he was in bed sleeping. As she undressed, he "hauled off and hit her." The next thing she remembered was "a noise or something." She grabbed a holster that she saw on the floor, left the house, picked up her son at her daughter's house, and drove to her mother's home in another city. When asked if she shot her husband while he slept, she replied, "No." A patrolman responding to a "man shot" call discovered the deceased in the couple's bedroom, dressed in his Coast Guard uniform, with his head lying over one edge of the bed and his feet lying over the other edge. The cause of death was one gunshot wound to his head.[31]

State v. *Koss*

We shall first address whether the trial court erred in refusing to admit evidence of the battered woman syndrome. The trial court excluded the testimony based on the earlier decision of this court in *State* v. *Thomas*. In *Thomas*, the defendant alleged that she killed her common-law husband in self-defense. The trial court did not allow the defendant to introduce expert testimony on the battered woman syndrome in support of her defense. This court held that expert testimony on the battered woman syndrome was

> inadmissible in evidence where (1) it is irrelevant and immaterial to the issue of whether defendant acted in self-defense at the time of the shooting; (2) the subject of the expert testimony is within the understanding of the jury; (3) the "battered wife syndrome" is not sufficiently developed, as a matter of commonly accepted scientific knowledge, to warrant testimony under the guise of expertise; and (4) its prejudicial impact outweighs its probative value.

In the case before us, appellant urges this court to overrule *Thomas* and hold that the trial court incorrectly excluded expert testimony as to the battered woman syndrome.

In *Thomas*, we stated that "such expert testimony is inadmissible because it is not distinctly related to some science, profession or occupation so as to be beyond the ken of the average lay person. Furthermore, no general acceptance of the expert's particular methodology has been established." However, since 1981, several books and articles have been written on this subject. In jurisdictions which have been confronted with this issue, most have allowed expert testimony on the battered woman syndrome....

Ohio has adopted a subjective test in determining whether a particular defendant properly acted in self-defense. The defendant's state of mind is crucial to this defense.

The trial court in the instant case properly instructed the jury that it must put itself in the position of the appellant in determining whether she acted in self-defense....

Expert testimony regarding the battered woman syndrome can be admitted to help the jury not only to understand the battered woman syndrome but also to determine whether the defendant had reasonable grounds for an honest belief that she was in imminent danger when considering the issue of self-defense.

> Expert testimony on the battered woman syndrome would help dispel the ordinary lay person's perception that a woman in a battering relationship is free to leave at any time. The expert evidence would counter any "common sense" conclusions by the jury that if the beatings were really that bad the woman would have left her husband much earlier. Popular misconceptions about battered women would be put to rest, including the beliefs that the women are masochistic and enjoy the beatings and that they intentionally provoke their husbands into fits of rage....
>
> A history of physical abuse alone does not justify the killing of the abuser. Having been physically assaulted by the abuser in the past is pertinent to such cases only as it contributes to the defendant's state of mind at the time the killing occurred; e.g., in that it formed the basis for the woman's perception of being in imminent danger of severe bodily harm or death at the hands of her partner.

We believe that the battered woman syndrome has gained substantial scientific acceptance to warrant admissibility....

According, we overrule *State* v. *Thomas* to the extent that it holds that expert testimony concerning the battered woman syndrome may not be admitted to support the affirmative defense of self-defense. Where the evidence establishes that a woman is a battered woman, and when the expert is qualified to testify about the battered woman syndrome, expert testimony concerning the syndrome may be admitted to assist the trier of fact [the judge or jury] in determining whether the defendant acted in self-defense.

EXTENT OF THE DEFENSE

Courts that have admitted evidence on the battered woman's syndrome, thereby permitting the jury to use that evidence in deciding whether the killing was justified, continue to face many questions about the use of the defense. One issue is how far the defense should be extended. An Illinois case involving domestic violence presented an unusual question. The defendant-wife used the self-defense argument *after* she murdered her husband. According to the defendant, her husband came home one night with a male prostitute, placed heavy barbells across her legs so that she could not move, and forced her to watch the two men engage in homosexual sexual intercourse. Then each attacked her sexually. Later her husband attacked her again and tried to drown her by holding her head in the toilet. He tried to choke her. She pushed him back in self-defense, and he fell to the floor dead. She dismembered his body. She wanted to introduce evidence on the battered woman syndrome to justify the dismemberment. The trial court refused, holding that such evidence is admissible only on the question of why the killing was committed and therefore is not relevant to acts that occurred later.[32]

The prosecution used the dismemberment evidence to prove the defendant's *consciousness* of guilt. The appellate court held that the defendant was entitled to introduce evidence of the battered woman syndrome to refute that inference. The expert witness would have testified that the syndrome is relevant to conduct *after* as well as *at* the time of the killing.

In some cases in which evidence of the battered person syndrome was excluded by the trial court, appellate courts have reversed and remanded the case for a new trial with the evidence admitted. In 1992 a California court ruled that a woman who was convicted of killing her live-in boyfriend received ineffective assistance of counsel because her attorney did not introduce evidence of the battered woman syndrome.[33]

In 1993 a Florida judge extended the use of the battered person syndrome to a case involving murder-for-hire. In the case that came to be known as the *Lobster Boy* case (because of the claw-like hands and legs like stumps of the deceased), the judge ruled that the defendants (wife and stepson), accused of hiring a hit man to murder Grady Stiles, Jr., were entitled to introduce evidence that she was a battered wife and he was a battered child. They claimed self-defense in the case in which a third defendant, a neighbor, allegedly was paid $1,500 to kill Stiles, who was shot in the back. Stiles, who appeared in carnivals, was confined to a wheelchair, but his family claimed his condition did not prevent him from abusing them.[34] Mary Stiles was convicted of manslaughter and received a 12-year sentence. The stepson was convicted of first-degree murder and murder conspiracy, which carries a mandatory life sentence.[35] The hit man was convicted and sentenced to twenty-seven years in prison.

Another issue, raised in the discussion in Focus 4.3, is whether the battered person syndrome should be permitted only in cases of physical abuse or whether psychological abuse is sufficient.

One final point on the extent of the use of the battered woman syndrome is very important. Even when the defense fails or the court refuses to allow evidence of the defense, juries may refuse to convict or judges may assess light penalties for defendants convicted of murdering spouses, parents, or close friends after a history of battering. In one case, for example, the judge sentenced a woman to probation after her conviction for shooting and killing her husband. The defendant pleaded guilty to first-degree manslaughter after indicating that her husband had abused her for twenty-five years. In assessing the light penalty, which included a $2,000 fine and a $500 payment to the state victims' compensation fund, the judge responded to requests for leniency from the defendant's children and her late husband's sisters. Said the judge, "Unusual facts often bring unusual sentences."[36] In 1990 a California judge imposed probation on a woman who shot and killed her husband while he slept. The judge said he was not send-

FOCUS 4.3 Psychological Battering As a Defense

In a widely publicized murder trial in San Diego, Elizabeth "Betty" Broderick argued that she shot and killed her ex-husband and his second wife because Mr. Broderick battered her psychologically to such an extent that violence was her only recourse. She claimed that the highly successful lawyer used his legal connections to deprive her of a fair divorce and drove her children away from her. Broderick's attorney argued that she was provoked to kill. She "was the victim of a covert, methodical and discreet assault." Her first trial ended in a mistrial; ten jurors wanted to convict her of murder, while two favored manslaughter. Broderick has drawn wide-spread support for her argument that she was the victim of domestic psychological abuse. She was held in jail while awaiting trial. Of that period she said, "I live a lot happier

than I did when I had all that money...I have my self-respect back. I feel like I can make it."[1]

At her second trial in December 1991, Broderick was convicted of two counts of second-degree murder. She was sentenced to thirty-two years in prison and could be paroled in seventeen years. She appealed her conviction on the grounds that the trial court erred in excluding key testimony and other evidence. Specifically, the defense claimed that some of the excluded witnesses would have testified that on two occasions Daniel Broderick discussed the idea of hiring someone to kill Betty Broderick and of driving her insane. It was argued that this testimony, along with the testimony of other witnesses and Betty Broderick's diaries, which were excluded also, would have shown her state of mind and supported her insanity defense.[2] The appeal was heard in March 1994, but a decision was not rendered by press time.

The Broderick case has produced widespread reaction and been the focus of articles, television talk shows, and made-for TV movies. In November 1992, the attorney who prosecuted Broderick commented that she had heard enough of Elizabeth Broderick. "She was not a battered woman. She was getting $16,000 a month alimony. She had a million-dollar La Jolla house, a car, a boyfriend. I see abused women every day with broken bones and smashed faces. Give me a break." In March 1993 three of her four children sued Broderick for the wrongful death of their father. They asked for over $20 million each.[3]

1. "Marriage Gone Bad, Double Slaying and a Hung Jury Leave a City Divided," *New York Times* (20 September 1991), p. 10. On the issue of psychological battering as a basis for self defense, see Charles Patrick Ewing, "Psychological Self-Defense: A Proposed Justification for Battered Women Who Kill," *Law and Human Behavior* 14 (1990): 569/594.
2. "Broderick Convictions Appeal Says Key Testimony Excluded," *San Diego Union-Tribune* (3 April 1993), p. 4B; "Jurists Hear Betty Broderick's Bid for a New Trial," *San Diego Union-Tribune*. (10 March 1994), p. 7, Section B-3.
3. Cathy Scott, "A Final Chapter in the Broderick Case," *San Diego Union-Tribune* (17 March 1993), p. 7B. See also Betty Stumbo's book account of the case, *Until the Twelfth of Never: The Deadly Divorce of Dan and Betty Broderick*, reviewed in the 25 July 1993 edition of the *San Francisco Chronicle*, p. Sunday Review Section, p. 1.

ing a message to anyone but that he could not "in good conscience send her to jail." The defendant testified that her husband abused her physically for twenty-five years.[37]

Mitigation of sentences based on evidence of the battered woman syndrome is recognized in the federal system. In a 1992 case a federal court ruled that even though the defendant's evidence did not convince the jury that she killed in self-defense, the evidence should have been used in mitigation of her sentence. Use of evidence of the syndrome for the purpose of mitigating the sentence does not require the same proof as the standard required for establishing self-defense.[38]

CLEMENCY AFTER CONVICTION

In an increasing number of cases in which defendants have been convicted of murder or other personal offenses after a history of abuse, **clemency**, or leniency, has been granted. Generally this procedure is invoked by the governor after a consideration of the evidence or even a hearing. In 1989 the governor of Washington granted a release from prison to a woman who had served only two years of her ten-year, three-month sentence for hiring a gunman to murder her husband who she alleged had abused her for seventeen years. In granting clemency, the governor said the woman and her children had suffered enough and that society would not be harmed by her release. He hoped his act would alert society to the need for more shelters and counselors to provide for abused women alternatives other than staying with their husbands and being abused or engaging in criminal acts.[39]

Also in 1989 the governor of Illinois commuted to the time already served the sentences of two women who had hired gunmen to murder their husbands. One of the women had served nine years of a forty-year sentence; the other had served six years of a twenty-year sentence. In commuting these sentences, the governor indicated that although the husbands' violence did not excuse the murders, it did explain the motives. In New Hampshire, a conditional **pardon** was granted by the New Hampshire governor in a similar circumstance. After the defendant served a year, she could work outside the prison for fifteen months, at which time she would be released on parole. In 1993, for the first time in the state's history, a Massachusetts governor recommended the release of a convicted killer based on evidence that she was a victim of battering. Eugenia Moore, who was incarcerated after her conviction for killing her boyfriend who abused her physically, spoke at the Harvard Law School in December 1993. Moore, thirty-five, was released after serving seven and one-half years in prison. The keynote address at the criminal justice conference at which Moore spoke was given by Jean Harris, seventy, who spent twelve years in prison after killing her lover, Dr. Herman Tarnower, who was responsible for the Scarsdale Diet.[40]

Other governors have released female offenders who were serving time for murdering the men who battered them. Opponents of these actions emphasize that because the killings are planned they constitute murder and the women should be punished.[41]

Not all states have followed this procedure, however, and after much consideration and lobbying, in 1993 California's governor denied clemency to fourteen women who killed after allegedly suffering years of abuse. He commuted the sentence of another woman because of her age and poor health, "but he rejected her claim that spousal abuse was an extenuating circumstance in the killing of her husband."[42]

LEGISLATION

Several state legislatures have considered bills to permit admitting evidence of the battered woman (or person) syndrome in court in cases involving murder or assault after years of abuse. Ohio's statute is an example of recent legislation in this area. The statute states the reasons for permitting evidence of the battered woman syndrome in appropriate cases:

1) That the syndrome currently is a matter of commonly accepted scientific knowledge;
2) That the subject matter and details of the syndrome are not within the general understanding or experience of a person who is a member of the general populace and are not within the field of common knowledge.[43]

In the federal system, the Battered Women's Testimony Act of 1992 provides for the establishment of a state justice institute as follows:

The State Justice Institute shall
(1) collect nationwide and analyze information regarding
  (A) the admissibility and quality of expert testimony on the experiences of battered women offered as part of the defense in criminal cases under State law, and
  (B) sources of, and methods to obtain, funds to pay costs incurred to provide such testimony, particularly in cases involving indigent women defendants,
(2) develop training materials to assist
  (A) battered women, operators of domestic violence shelters, battered women's advocates, and attorneys to use such expert testimony in appropriate cases, particularly appropriate cases involving indigent women defendants, and

(B) individuals with expertise in the experience of battered women to develop skills appropriate to providing such expert testimony, and

(3) disseminate such information and such training materials, and provide related technical assistance, to battered women, such operators, such advocates, such attorneys, and such individuals.[44]

Domestic Authority

Under some ancient laws, husbands had the legal right to discipline their wives with a "whip or rattan no bigger than [my] thumb, in order to inforce the salutary restraints of domestic discipline."[45] This position has been questioned. It is not legal in modern common law, but the law recognizes the right of parents to discipline their children. Under some circumstances, those acting in the place of parents may do likewise. Additionally, teachers may administer discipline to their pupils. "By law as well as immemorial usage, a schoolmaster is regarded as standing in loco parentis [in the place of parents], and, like the parent, has the authority to moderately chastise pupils under his care."[46] Discipline under the domestic authority provision must be reasonable, however, or it will constitute assault and battery or violation of civil rights.[47]

Domestic authority exists in other situations, such as the right of persons in charge of trains, theaters, boats, airplanes, and other similar places to eject persons who are disruptive. The force used must be reasonable and moderate. Prison officials may discipline inmates, but they may not inflict punishment that violates the Eighth Amendment's prohibition against cruel and unusual punishment (see Appendix A). Ship captains, service officers, and others may discipline those who serve under them. In all of these situations the discipline must be *reasonable*. If unreasonable force is used, the actors may be subject to criminal prosecution (if the unreasonable behavior constitutes a crime) or civil liability in tort. Numerous recent federal court cases involve suits by inmates against prison officials alleging that unreasonable force has been used against them.

There are numerous cases interpreting what *reasonable* means regarding punishment in these and other contexts, particularly punishment inflicted on prison inmates. Recently there have been numerous cases of alleged child abuse by parents and those acting in the role of parents. Concern here is with whether the inflicted punishment falls within the domestic authority defense when a criminal charge is brought against the person inflicting that publishment. That question cannot be answered unless we can determine which punishments are reasonable. With children, the Model Penal Code stipulates that the force a parent may use on a child is limited to force that "is not designed to cause or known to create a substantial risk of causing death, serious bodily injury, disfigurement, extreme pain or mental distress or gross degradation." In addition, the parental force must be used for the purpose "of safeguarding or promoting the welfare of the minor, including the prevention or punishment of his misconduct."[48] Of course, each of those terms must be interpreted.

The Supreme Court has ruled that discipline of schoolchildren may include paddling. According to the Court, the Eighth Amendment prohibition against cruel and unusual punishment applies to criminals, not to school students. The Court emphasized, however, that any punishment that goes beyond that which is reasonably necessary to maintain discipline in the classroom may result in both civil and criminal liability.[49]

How far should the domestic authority defense go to protect parents from criminal liability in disciplining their children? In an Illinois case, a father was charged with aggravated battery and cruelty to children after he whipped his two sons, ages twelve and nine, with an electrical extension cord. The mother-wife testified that she did not realize the extent of the injuries until she examined the sons the next morning. When she found red marks on their backs, she took them to the hospital. Do you think the discipline was reasonable? The children had stolen money from their mother's purse.

The father appealed his conviction for cruelty to children on the one count that involved the son who did not sustain permanent injuries. The appellate court refused to reverse that conviction, holding that the force used fell within the statutory provisions that prohibited a person from willfully and unnecessarily injuring a child under his legal control.[50]

Consent, Condonation, or Victim's Conduct

Usually a victim's consent to a crime, negligence in bringing about that crime, or forgiveness of that act is not a defense. The issue of consent arises frequently in cases of **euthanasia**, in which a person kills a relative (often a spouse) after allegedly being begged by that person to end his or her pain and misery with death. The law does not permit such cooperation and agreement to negate the criminal act, just as the law does not permit a patient to agree to malpractice or a sports star to agree to bribery. The acts are crimes despite the consent. However, it is not uncommon in cases of euthanasia that prosecutors refuse to bring charges; grand juries refuse to indict; or juries refuse to convict.

Consent may negate an element of the crime, however. By definition *forcible rape* is sexual intercourse without the victim's consent. If the victim consents, the act is not forcible rape, but if the victim is under the legal age of consent, the act may constitute another crime, that of *statutory rape*. Consent does not negate statutory rape, since the statute for that crime was enacted to protect young people sexually. These crimes are discussed in more detail in Chapter 6.

Consent may be a defense to less serious acts, such as those that might occur in a lawful sports activity, in which a person might be hurt by the nature of the game. An act that might constitute a criminal assault and battery under other circumstances might not be considered criminal during a sporting event. In any case in which consent is a defense to the crime, that consent must be given voluntarily (not the product of force, duress, or deception) and knowingly by a person legally competent to consent.[51]

Condonation—forgiveness of the crime—is not a defense either. Victims may forgive; but that forgiveness does not eliminate criminal liability, for crimes are considered offenses against society as well as against individual victims. Under some circumstances, victims of less serious crimes are permitted to negotiate a settlement with their defendants, after which the court may dismiss the criminal charges.

Stress Disorders

A number of disorders associated with stress are being recognized by courts as a defense or a partial defense to criminal acts.

Extreme Emotional Disturbance

Oregon statutes provide that extreme emotional disturbance may constitute a partial defense to intentional murder but not to aggravated murder.[52] That statute was the focus of *State* v. *Hessel*, in which the defendant appealed his convictions on several grounds, including his argument that the trial court erred in instructing the jury that extreme emotional disturbance is a partial defense to intentional but not to aggravated murder.[53]

State v. Hessel

[After stating the grounds of appeal, the court states the facts of the case.]

In October, 1989, the victim drove to Portland from her home in Albany with plans to spend the night there. She met her ex-boyfriend, Amell, at a mutual friend's houseboat on Hayden Island. She and Amell went out to dinner. While in the parking lot of a lounge at about 1:30 or 2:00 a.m., they had a fight, during which Amell threw her against a wall and put his hands around her neck. She returned to the houseboat and collected her belongings. When she left the houseboat, she told a friend that she and Amell had quarrelled and that someone was waiting for her in the parking lot. The victim then met defendant and drove to Portland, bought some cocaine and went to his house to smoke it. He asked her to spend the night, but she declined. As he was driving the victim back to her car, he turned right instead of left, which would have taken them to her car. He then stopped his car and asked her to "give him some head." She complied but, when she tried to raise her head, he pushed it back down and she then bit his penis. He hit her on the head and then pulled her out of the car and into bushes, where he killed her by strangling her with his belt and hitting her repeatedly with a rock.

The next day defendant told a friend that he had killed the "girl at Hayden Island." The friend contacted the police and had another conversation with defendant while wearing a body wire. Defendant told the friend that he had hit the victim after becoming angry that she had

> bit him and that he had panicked because he believed that she had bitten off his penis. He also said that he had killed her to cover up his actions.
>
> Defendant was charged with eight counts of aggravated murder. In the jury trial, he was convicted on six counts of the lesser included crime of intentional murder and on two counts of aggravated murder. The two counts of aggravated murder on which he was convicted were under ORS 163.095(2)(d) for personally and intentionally committing a homicide in the course and furtherance of a felony and under ORS 163.095(2)(e) for committing a murder in an effort to conceal the identity of the perpetrator of a crime.

After analyzing the applicable statutes and case law, the appellate court concluded that the trial court's instruction was correct. The legislature did not intend for extreme emotional disturbance to be a partial defense to aggravated murder; consequently, the instruction was correct. Do you think the partial defense should be available for aggravated murder as well as for intentional murder and that the legislature simply forgot to include the defense for both when it was added in 1981? The court indicated that it was "not at liberty to fill in perceived legislative omissions....Moreover, the inclusion of a specific matter suggests a legislative intent to exclude related matters that are not mentioned."[54]

Posttraumatic Stress Disorders (PTSD)

A variety of relatively recently developed defenses may fall under the category of **posttraumatic stress disorders (PTSD)**. Some argue that those who suffer from PTSD are not able to control their behavior and therefore should not be legally responsible for their criminal acts.

Posttraumatic stress disorders may be manifested in nightmares, flashbacks, severe guilt, and a loss of orientation. During World War I, the syndrome was called *shell shock*. Other terms have been used, such as operational fatigue, combat fatigue, and war neurosis. Whatever the term, the earlier reaction to the syndrome (particularly by officers in the military) was that those who manifested it were cowardly. Treatment was not provided, but by 1952 the American Psychiatric Association recognized the need to provide diagnosis and treatment for war-related stress.[55]

The Vietnam War and its aftermath raised again the problems of reactions to combat. Such problems were magnified by new types of warfare that killed or maimed quickly. Advances in medical technology saved many who would have died in previous wars. Multiple amputees, paraplegics, and soldiers with other problems returned home. There was a greater understanding of stress syndromes during and after the Vietnam War, and treatment was available.[56] Some examples of PTSD involving Vietnam War veterans and criminal acts are discussed in Focus 4.4

FOCUS 4.4   The Vietnam Stress Syndrome as a Defense

The stress of combat has been recognized for years, but it was the Vietnam War that gave impetus to a renewed recognition of the impact war stresses can have on young people. The average age of those who served in Vietnam was only nineteen, younger than in previous years, "and while combat in other wars was often intense but relatively brief, in Vietnam the threat of attack or ambush was nearly constant for many soldiers." The strong antiwar feelings of many U.S. citizens made the impact of the war stresses even more significant.[1]

In 1988 the first person in Louisiana to use his Vietnam service as a basis for a criminal insanity plea was electrocuted for murdering a policeman who was taking him to jail for drunkenness. In Chicago a gunman who killed two people in an auto-parts store and fatally wounded a police officer and a custodian before he was shot to death by police was described by a friend as full of anger since his tour of duty in Vietnam.[2]

In Florida in 1993 considerable sympathy was expressed for a Vietnam vet-

eran condemned to die for killing a gas station attendant fourteen years previously. Governor Lawton Chiles blocked the execution of Larry Joe Johnson in early 1993, but after a study of the case, a new execution date was set. The Florida Supreme Court turned down Johnson's appeal, with three justices agreeing reluctantly on the basis of procedures in effect at the time of the original sentencing. Justice Gerald Kogan, writing for those three justices, said, "When this death warrant is executed, Florida will electrocute a man injured and most probably maimed psychologically while serving in his nation's military in Vietnam and elsewhere." The U.S. Supreme Court refused to review the case, and Johnson was executed.[3]

[1] "Sympathy for Killer Claiming Post-Vietnam Stress," *New York Times* (14 February 1993), p. 16.
[2] "Five Die in Chicago Shootings," *Tallahassee Democrat* (23 September 1988), p. 1.
[3] "Court: Justice Not Served by Execution," *Miami Herald* (30 April 1993), p. 5B. See Johnson v. Singletary, 618 So. 2d 731 (Fla. 1993), *cert. denied*, 113 S.Ct. 2049 (1993).

For many veterans, problems arose when they returned home and confronted protestors who argued that the war was immoral. Some suffered stress syndromes that became known as the *Vietnam stress syndrome*. Marital problems, poor job performance, and general adjustment problems were typical reactions to stress. Many men suffered sudden feelings of combat, startle responses, sleep disturbances, survival guilt, catastrophic dreams, intrusive memories, anger, isolation, and alienation.

In 1980 the American Psychiatric Association defined these reactions as posttraumatic stress disorder, a trauma that "is generally outside the range of...common experiences" and "that would evoke significant symptoms of distress in most people." Such traumas included combat, some natural disasters, bombing, torture, and death camps but excluded simple bereavement, marital conflicts, or business losses.[57]

Some courts have admitted expert testimony on PTSD. Frequently the evidence is used to show that the defendant was in a dissociative state and has entered a plea of insanity or diminished capacity.[58] Although the court upheld the convictions of a recent defendant who was unable to show that he was in a dissociative state caused by PTSD at the time he committed the crimes of kidnapping, aggravated assault, aggravated burglary, and criminal damage to property, portions of the case are reprinted here to show the Kansas Supreme Court's review of PTSD and its importance. In *State* v. *DeMoss*, the defendant's use of expert testimony on PTSD was weakened by testimony that voluntary intoxication, not PTSD, caused him to engage in the criminal acts in question. But the use of the syndrome as a defense is growing, and there is reason to believe that as medical researchers discover more evidence of the impact of PTSD and attorneys gain greater understanding of the syndrome, expert testimony on PTSD will become even more important in the criminal courtroom.[59]

State v. *DeMoss*

[A] brief discussion of the nature of P.T.S.D is required. The American Psychiatric Association classifies P.T.S.D. as an anxiety disorder. This disorder is one which may be suffered following a traumatic event which is outside the normal realm of human experiences. These events, known as "stressors," include both natural disasters and deliberate man-made disasters such as military combat, rape, assault, torture, bombing, and death camps. Stressors of human origin, such as war and military combat, produce more severe and longer lasting disorders than do natural disasters.

Perhaps the best known symptom of P.T.S.D. is the reexperiencing of the traumatic event, which can occur either through recollections of the event, recurrent dreams of the event, or a sudden acting out or feeling that the traumatic event is actually occurring at the moment. This last possibility is known as a "dissociative state" and is the rarest symptom of P.T.S.D., occurring only in extreme cases. Dreams and recollections are far more common.

Additional symptoms include numbing of responsiveness to, or involvement in, the outside world; hyperalertness or exaggerated startle response; sleep disturbances; guilt about the person's own survival or about the tactics which the person used in order to survive; memory impairment and difficulty concentrating; and avoidance of activities which may cause the person to recall the stressful event. Any and all symptoms may also be intensified by exposure to events which resemble the stressor. This becomes particularly important in terms of the dissociative state and criminal behavior. Other problems associated with P.T.S.D. which become significant when viewed in the context of criminal behavior are the person's tendency toward increased irritability, impulsive behavior, and unpredictable explosions of aggression with little or no provocation.

RAPE TRAUMA SYNDROME

A form of PTSD is **rape trauma syndrome**. In many rape cases the prosecution's most difficult element to prove is lack of consent. In recent cases the prosecution has relied on the rape trauma syndrome, which is a type of PTSD that follows forced sex. The term was coined by Ann Wolbert Burgess and Lynda Lytle Holmstrom in their study of women who claimed to be rape victims.[60]

Evidence of rape trauma syndrome may be introduced at trial to support the victim's credibility. Evidence of the syndrome may be sufficient to convince the jury that victims are telling the truth when they claim that they submitted to sexual intercourse only to avoid more serious injuries or death. This is important because many people do not understand rape; they may not believe that a woman was raped unless she shows evidence of a serious fight. Expert psychiatric testimony on the rape trauma syndrome may assist the jury in its attempt to decide whether alleged rape victims are telling the truth.

Some courts permit evidence of the rape trauma syndrome in cases involving delayed reporting of the alleged crime. If the victim waits a long time to report the crime, the defense attorney may argue that the significant delay indicates that the victim was not raped. The defense attorney may contend that the alleged victim participated in the act willingly but later became angry at the defendant or was embarrassed that the act occurred.

The Colorado Supreme Court has held that expert testimony on the rape trauma syndrome was admissible on the issue of why the alleged victim did not report the rape for eighty-nine days. The prosecution wanted to introduce expert testimony to the effect that victims who are raped by acquaintances are less likely to report the incidents than are victims who are raped by strangers.

The Colorado Supreme Court held that the evidence was admissible because the average juror does not understand why rape victims might wait several days or even longer to report the alleged crime. However, the case of *Colorado* v. *Hampton*, like all cases, must be read carefully. As one of the justices noted in his concurring opinion, "The majority does not approve the admission of rape trauma syndrome evidence generally, to prove that the victim was raped, or to corroborate the victim's truthfulness, but only to provide an explanation for the victim's reporting delay."[61]

In 1990 the New York Court of Appeals approved the admission of expert testimony on rape trauma syndrome, indicating that the testimony could be admitted to assist the jury in understanding the alleged victim's behavior after the rape but not as evidence that a rape did in fact occur. The court held that the testimony was helpful in dispelling certain myths that the average person has about rape and postrape behavior. In *New York* v. *Taylor* the court was deciding two cases: thus the reference to *Taylor* and to *Banks* within this excerpt. The court permitted the evidence in the former but not in the latter case. Do you agree with the court's position that the evidence should not be admitted solely on the issue of whether a rape occurred?[62]

New York v. Taylor

We realize that rape trauma syndrome encompasses a broad range of symptoms and varied patterns of recovery. Some women are better able to cope with the aftermath of sexual assault than other women. There is no single typical profile of a rape victim, and different victims express themselves and come to terms with the experience of rape in different ways. We are satisfied, however, that the relevant scientific community has generally accepted that rape is a highly traumatic event that will in many women trigger the onset of certain identifiable symptoms....

We are aware that rape trauma syndrome is a therapeutic and not a legal concept. Physicians and rape counselors who treat victims of sexual assault are not charged with the responsibility of ascertaining whether the victim is telling the truth when she says that a rape occurred. We do not believe, however, that the therapeutic origin of the syndrome renders it unreliable for trial purposes. Thus, although we acknowledge that evidence of rape trauma syndrome does not by itself prove that the complainant was raped, we believe that this should not preclude its admissibility into evidence at trial when relevance to a particular disputed issue has been demonstrated.

Because cultural myths still affect common understanding of rape and rape victims and because experts have been studying the effects of rape upon its victims only since the 1970s, we believe that patterns of response among rape victims are not within the ordinary understanding of the lay juror. For that reason, we conclude that introduction of expert testimony describing rape trauma syndrome may under certain circumstances assist a lay jury in deciding issues in a rape trial.

The Kansas Supreme Court has ruled that when the defendant claims the alleged victim consented to the sexual act, expert testimony on rape trauma syndrome may be admitted to support the contention that consent was not given.[63] All of these cases are illustrative of ways in which states have handled the rape trauma syndrome defense. Some courts have excluded evidence on the defense; some have admitted evidence of rape trauma syndrome for all purposes for which it is relevant; others have limited the purposes for which it may be admitted. Cases differ according to their individual facts; thus, each one must be analyzed carefully. The fact that it is not yet possible to generalize the law in this area illustrates the importance of reading a case carefully to see exactly how far the court went in deciding an issue.

The Indiana Supreme Court has held that if evidence of rape trauma syndrome is admitted by the prosecution it may be introduced by the defense as well. In *Henson* v. *State* the lower court had refused the defense's request to introduce evidence of the syndrome after he had presented evidence that the night after the alleged rape the alleged victim was seen dancing and drinking at the same bar in which he had first met her. The defense wanted the evidence to show that the behavior of the complainant was inconsistent with that of one who had been raped the night before. The court agreed that the evidence was relevant to that point and ruled that it should have been admitted. The court noted that in other cases it had permitted the use of evidence on rape trauma syndrome to be introduced by the prosecution and concluded that it would be unfair not to permit the defense to do likewise.[64]

Finally, it has been held that if the prosecution is permitted to introduce evidence of rape trauma syndrome after having the complainant examined by an expert, the defense should be permitted to have that complainant examined by its expert. The complainant may refuse this examination but if so the court should permit the prosecution to introduce evidence about rape trauma syndrome only from witnesses who did not examine the complainant.[65]

URBAN PSYCHOSIS

Evidence of the posttraumatic stress syndrome has been used recently by defense attorneys to argue that their clients who have been brought up in dangerous and violent urban settings suffer from **urban psychosis**, which should be recognized as a defense to their criminal acts. The defense was raised in the case of Felicia Morgan, who was raped at age twelve, grew up in a violent neighborhood, and by the age of seventeen had lost several of her young friends to violent deaths. On 26 October 1991 Morgan, age seventeen, shot and killed another teenager during her attempt to steal that teen's leather coat. Morgan was convicted of first-degree murder and armed robbery.

Morgan's insanity defense was rejected by the jury, but the defense attorney believes that it was evidence of Morgan's PTSD and two other psychiatric conditions that led the judge to make Morgan eligible for parole in thirteen years and four months. The prosecution had asked for a sixty-year minimum for parole eligibility. According to the defense attorney, "When Morgan found herself in a highly stressful situation, the three disorders in combination rendered Morgan unable to function rationally....If you live on that edge, you essentially slip into a psychotic state." The defense appealed the case on the grounds that the trial court erred in refusing to admit evidence of Morgan's mental state during the determination of guilt, evidence that the defense claims would have led the jury to render a verdict of a lesser crime than first-degree murder.[66]

The urban psychosis or culture defense was raised in the case of Ronald Ray Howard, nineteen, who killed a Texas state trooper. Howard has been sentenced to die for the murder, but his defense argued that his client's behavior was the result of living a difficult life in the inner city and listening to hard-core rap music. Howard said he learned to hate police from listening to the music with violent antipolice themes. CBS News' "Eye on America" carried a story on the case. According to the newscast, "The fight over Ronald Ray Howard's life reveals a great deal about the divisions in our own." With reference to the defense, the commentator said, "They have come to court like witnesses from another world." The defendant "saw himself as a soldier between the police and young black men. Everything he did in his life came from the rap songs." In a later Texas case, however, a jury deadlocked after hearing the defense attorney argue that his client killed because of the "urban survival syndrome," which made him afraid that he would be hurt if he did not kill. The attorney defined this syndrome as "the fear that black people have of other black people that's pivotal in the case." After the jury deadlock, the judge declared a mistrial in the case of Damion Osby, 18, charged with two murder counts.[67]

In September 1993 an attorney indicated that he was considering a "suburban psychosis" defense for his client, a nineteen-year-old woman accused (with six other youths) of first-degree murder and conspiracy in the death of a twenty-year-old youth and friend of the accused. The deceased was lured into a rock pit, "where they allegedly stabbed him and battered him with a baseball bat." According to the attorney, "If you are constantly subjected to violence, you develop sort of a psychosis toward it and you feel violence is the only way to stop violence....That may be appropriate in this case." In responding to the urban psychosis defense, one law professor questioned where the line would be drawn. Would he be able to defend, "The city made me do it?" He concluded that "terminal boredom is not a defense."[68]

In 1993 sixteen-year-old Victor Brancaccio was charged with the death of a seventy-eight-year-old woman who complained about his rap music. The woman was bludgeoned to death with a cassette player; an attempt was made to burn her body to remove fingerprints (but only her shorts and part of her leg were burned); her body was spray-painted with a metallic red to remove any additional fingerprints.[69]

Premenstrual Syndrome (PMS)

Considerable attention has been given recently in the medical community to the existence and effects of **premenstrual syndrome (PMS)**. The term refers to the physiological changes that occur in some women between ovulation and menstruation, primarily during the four days preceding menstruation. Over 150 symptoms of PMS have been identified, but most are not thought to be associated with criminal behavior. The most prevalent symptoms that might be associated with criminal behavior are depression, irritability, and temporary psychosis. In severe cases, medical treatment is required and consists mainly of hormone therapy.[70]

Many physicians believe that PMS is related to behavior; one has concluded that it should be a recognized legal defense.

> It is unfortunate that many PMS sufferers may have been imprisoned because the law does not recognize PMS as a valid defense. This injustice must be corrected. Premenstrual syndrome is real. Its effects on many women can be catastrophic and must be taken into account by the criminal justice system. It is grossly improper to make moral judgments about a condition which may have such devastating effects on individuals and society.[71]

It has been reported that PMS is a worldwide phenomenon,[72] and evidence of PMS has been used successfully in other countries in mitigation of sentences.[73] Evidence of PMS has not been very successful in U.S. courts. In an unreported case in New York, the trial judge permitted the introduction of expert testimony on the defense, but the expert witness testified that the defendant, who was charged with physically abusing her child, was not suffering from PMS at the time of the alleged acts.[74] In a reported case the PMS defense was used successfully. A Virginia state trooper reported that when he arrested orthopedic surgeon Geraldine Richter for drunk driving in November 1990 she responded as follows:

> You son of a [expletive]; you [expletive] can't do this to me; I'm a doctor. I hope you [expletive] get shot and come into my hospital so I can refuse to treat you, or if any other trooper gets shot, I will also refuse to treat them.[75]

Richter argued that her erratic behavior, which allegedly included kicking the trooper, was the result of PMS, not drunkenness. In March 1993 Dr. Richter's ex-husband and attorney sued the Virginia Board of Medicine for $73 million on behalf of his client, arguing that the Board's hearings resulting in a public reprimand of Dr. Richter consisted of "a kangaroo court proceeding of the worst kind." A federal judge dismissed the suit on the grounds that the defendants had reason for the investigation, were fulfilling their governmental functions when the investigation was conducted, and therefore were immune from civil suit.[76]

Other Defenses

Numerous other offenses are recognized in various jurisdictions; some of these have been raised in U.S. courts and rejected, although they have been successful in other countries. Others are being used more frequently or more successfully.

Public Duty, Patriotism, Superior Orders

If they are executing a court order, performing public duties required for their offices, or engaging in certain military duties, public officers are justified in taking certain actions that would not be permitted otherwise. In general, statutes specify the situations in which the law may be violated by public officials or military officers. The defense issue arises when it is not clear that the action taken falls within the public duty defense exception.

The *patriotism defense* was raised by Lieutenant Colonel Oliver L. North, a former national security aide against whom criminal charges were made in connection with the Iran-Contra affair. Iran-Contra involved numerous allegations of illegal sales of arms to Iran in exchange for release of U.S. hostages as well as the shifting of some of the profits from those sales to buy arms for the anti-Communist "Contra" rebels in Nicaragua. North testified, "I can tell you this. Everything that I did was done in the best interests of the United States of America." Prior to North's case, the patriotism

defense was used extensively in the Watergate scandals of the Nixon administration. Most of the men charged in that situation were convicted and
served prison terms. But some lawyers argued that the Iran-Contra case is
different because so many of those involved had outstanding military and
public service records.[77]

North was found guilty of aiding and abetting in the obstruction of
Congress; altering, concealing, and destroying National Security Council
documents; and receiving an illegal gratuity. He was acquitted on charges
of obstructing and lying to Congress, obstructing a congressional inquiry,
obstructing a presidential inquiry, improperly converting traveler's checks,
and conspiring to defraud the United States and the Internal Revenue
Service. He was given a suspended prison term, fined $150,000, placed on
probation, and ordered to perform 1,200 hours of community service.
Three counts were vacated and remanded for retrial, and one count of his
convictions (destroying official documents) was reversed on appeal, after
which the prosecutor announced that he would drop all charges against
North.[78] North became an effective fundraiser and a popular speaker.[79.] He
tested the political waters in 1994 by running for the U.S. Senate.

Several others who were convicted in the Iran-Contra scandal also
escaped prison sentences; but the man who said, "The buck stops here,"
retired Navy Admiral John Poindexter, was not so fortunate initially.
North's boss was convicted of all five criminal charges for his role in the
scandal: one count of conspiracy, two counts of obstructing congressional
inquiries, and two counts of lying to Congress, all felonies. His conviction
was reversed on appeal.[80] Other Iran-Contra defendants were pardoned by
President George Bush shortly before he left office. Independent prosecutor Lawrence Walsh was furious about those pardons, arguing that the trials of those defendants was the last chance we had to determine whether
President Reagan and then–Vice President Bush played any role in the
Iran-Contra scandal.[81]

The Rough Sex Defense

Earlier we discussed conduct of the victim as a defense to criminal acts. In
previous days, "she asked for it" was a common defense to rape, and in
many cases it was a successful defense. Defense counsel attempted this
defense in the recent case of a seventeen-year-old mildly retarded New
Jersey woman who was sexually assauted by four friends. The young woman
testified that the men used a stick, a bat, and a broom in their assault but
that they are her friends and she still likes them. The defense argued that
she consented to the acts, that the defendants were not criminals but
teenage boys who responded to a sexually agressive woman and their own
hormones. Psychiatrists testified that she was not capable of consent. The
defendants were convicted; three were sentenced to up to fifteen years in
youth detention; the fourth was placed on probation and ordered to perform community service.[82]

The New Jersey case was complicated by the fact that the alleged victim
was mildly retarded, which raised the issue of whether she could consent

to sex. In most cases this is not an issue, but recently enacted statutes in many jurisdictions make it more difficult or impossible to introduce evidence of the alleged victim's prior sexual experience in an effort to justify the "she asked for it" defense. However, a new defense has evolved—the *rough sex defense*. According to Harvard Law professor and defense attorney Alan Dershowitz, "The she-asked-for-it defense doesn't exist anymore....So now we're hearing she demanded it."[83] One expert witness testified that the practice of rough sex is much more frequent than is commonly thought.[84]

The rough sex defense, used primarily in murder or attempted murder cases, is based on the use of rough physical action during sex. It is assumed that such actions heighten sexual pleasure. Thus, in his murder trial for the 1986 death of Kathleen Holland, Joseph Porto testified that Holland asked him to tie a rope around her neck and pull; he became very excited, pulled too hard, and she died. The prosecutor called it the "oops" defense, but the jury may have been impressed. The defendant was convicted of criminally negligent homicide, a lesser charge, punishable by no more than four years in prison.[85]

The rough sex defense gained national publicity in the "Preppie Murder Trial" of Robert Chambers for the death of his girlfriend, Jennifer Levin. Both the defendant and the victim were from affluent families; they had dated only casually. Chambers testified that he and Levin left a bar on 26 August 1986 and went to New York's Central Park for a walk, that they became sexually involved, and that during an act of "rough sex," she died. Chambers was able to plea bargain a reduced sentence after pleading guilty to Levin's murder.

The rough sex defense was used in a Missouri case in which a husband bound his wife to a chair with adhesive tape during what he called a sexual episode in which she participated willingly. The defendant admitted that he torched the house later, but he testified that the deceased died from accidental choking during their sexual encounter, not from the fire. He was charged with murder and faced the death penalty, but he was convicted of the lesser charge of manslaughter and sentenced to only seven years in prison.

In 1993, in her trial for first-degree murder for killing her boyfriend, Sandra Pettus argued to a Florida court that the deceased was a Satanic cult leader and that she strangled him accidentally during sex. His nude body was found handcuffed and bound with straps in the back yard of an apartment the couple shared. The defendant advanced three arguments for her defense: (1) the death resulted from an accident during deviant sexual behavior; (2) the defendant acted in self-defense because the decedent abused her and her children; and (3) the defendant acted in self-defense because the decedent threatened to sacrifice one of her children.[86]

These cases raise the issue of the victim's consent. On the one hand it can be argued that bodily harm resulting from "rough sex" should not be considered criminal if the alleged victim agreed to the act. On the other hand, it is reasonable to argue that an individual cannot consent to serious bodily harm or death through a sex act or any other act; the result is murder or aggravated assault. However, evidence of consent does raise the issue of whether the defendant had the requisite intent element necessary to support a charge of first-degree murder.

Religious Beliefs

Religious beliefs have been raised as a defense in some cases. For example, when a child dies as the result of the parents' refusal to obtain medical care, the parents may be prosecuted for murder or manslaughter. In April 1989 William and Christine Hermanson, who are Christian Scientists, were convicted of third-degree murder and felony child abuse when their seven-year-old daughter died after they refused to obtain medical care for her. The religion defense was not successful in this case, but the case was "the first case in the United States in twenty-two years in which Christian Scientists have been held criminally responsible for the death of a child after relying solely on prayer to cure an illness." The Hermansons were sentenced to fifteen years probation and ordered to secure medical care when needed for their other two children. On appeal, the case was reversed by the Florida Supreme Court.[87]

In 1989 David and Ginger Twitchell were sentenced to probation for their manslaughter convictions in failing to seek medical care for their two-year-old son, who died of a bowel obstruction in 1986. One of the terms of probation was that the parents take the other children for regular pediatric check-ups. In 1993 the Massachusetts Supreme Judicial Court overturned the conviction on technical grounds. The court noted that although the religious beliefs would not shield parents from prosecution for manslaughter, the Twitchells should have been permitted to introduce evidence that they believed that to be the case. The prosecutor decided not to retry the couple.[88]

The Devil's Defense

The opposite type of defense from religion is that of "the devil made me do it." This defense was raised in the highly publicized case of one of the most racially charged trials in recent New York history in which eight white men were charged with the murder of an innocent black teenager in the Bensonhurst section of Brooklyn, New York. Only one of the defendants, the alleged triggerman, Joseph Fama, nineteen, was convicted of murder. Three were acquitted of all charges; the rest were convicted of lesser charges. Fama was sentenced to a prison term of thirty-two years and eight months to life.

The "she made me do it" defense in the Bensonhurst murder case was based on evidence that Gina Feliciano, "the tart-tongued eighteen-year-old who invited black and Hispanic friends to the mostly white Brooklyn neighborhood the night Jusuf K. Hawkins, a sixteen-year-old black youth, was killed." Feliciano was a former girlfriend of Keith Mondello, a gang member. It was alleged that when Mondello heard she had invited these minority people to her birthday party, he vowed to attack them. He organized a group of about thirty white gang members who were armed with baseball bats. Apparently he thought Hawkins and his three teenage friends, all of whom were black, were the expected outsiders threatening the white youths' turf. Mondellos' gang surrounded the four blacks. Four shots were fired; three hit Hawkins, who died as a result. Feliciano was called to testify regarding the emotionally charged evening and the extreme hostility that her former boyfriend had toward her and her friends.[89]

These and other defenses may be expected to gain even more attention in the future as we continue to explore human behavior and its causes.

SUMMARY

This chapter continues the previous chapter's discussion of defenses to criminal acts. Chapter 3 includes the more traditional defenses; this chapter focuses on some traditional defenses, such as intoxication, that may gain greater acceptance with increased understanding of the human body, or lesser acceptance as a result of the "get tough" theme in criminal justice today. This chapter includes some new defenses that are gaining in acceptance.

Recent scientific studies question the belief that substance abuse, at least in the case of alcohol, is a moral problem. Rather, it may be the result of genetics; if that is true and if individuals cannot control the abuse, the intoxication defense must take on a greater role in criminal law. It would mean that the distinction the Supreme Court has made between *status* and *a voluntary act* is meaningless in the area of substance abuse. Furthermore it would constitute "cruel and unusual punishment" to punish one for the status of being intoxicated if intoxication were not subject to individual control.

Despite the reluctance of the Supreme Court and other courts to view alcoholism and other substance abuse as illnesses or conditions rather than the result of free will, intoxication is recognized as a partial defense in some situations, particularly when it negates a specific intent required to prove the crime in question.

Domestic violence defenses stem from increased recognition of the problem of domestic violence as well as the difficulty of utilizing self-defense as a defense in most of these cases. The injury or killing does not occur when the perpetrator is being threatened with *imminent* harm but rather after a long period of abuse and during a period in which the threatened harm is not imminent. In an increasing number of cases, defense attorneys are successful in their arguments that a person who has suffered abuse over a long period of time may reasonably believe he or she is in danger of imminent harm or death in situations in which that is not the case. Because this is not a matter of common knowledge, courts that recognize the battered person defense permit the admission of expert testimony to inform the jury of how a person reacts to the battered person syndrome.

The battered person syndrome may be a complete or a partial defense. It is used also in mitigation of sentences. The defense has been extended beyond spouses or lovers to include children who kill their parents who have allegedly abused them for years. In some jurisdictions, when the battered person defense is not recognized and the defendants are convicted, governors issue pardons or commute prison terms. The passage of the Battered Women's Testimony Act of 1992 indicates that the primary emphasis in the battered person syndrome area remains on the battered woman. This statute indicates also the increased importance being placed on the effects of years of battering.

Acts that would be criminal in other circumstances may not be so when committed under domestic authority, such as a parent disciplining a child or a teacher disciplining a pupil. This area is highly controversial, and the laws and rules are not clear, leaving room for interpretation.

In some cases, consent, conduct, or the victim's condonation may provide a defense to criminal acts. Euthanasia is cited as an example. Technically one cannot consent to be killed, but when that happens in cases of terminally ill patients, charges may not be brought. If they are, juries may not convict. Consent may negate an element of a crime, as for example in the case of rape, one element of which is lack of consent.

A variety of stress disorders are being advanced as defenses today. Extreme emotional disturbance is one example. The chapter features a case involving a statute in which this stress syndrome may be a defense to intentional but not to aggravated murder.

The return of many Vietnam War veterans with psychological and emotional problems led to a greater awareness of posttraumatic stress disorders; consequently, courts have been more receptive to admitting expert testimony on the posttraumatic stress syndrome, and the use of the PTSD is expected to expand, especially with the return of men and women who experienced violence and death during the Persian Gulf War.

Another form of PTSD defense is that of rape trauma syndrome. Although courts do not recognize the defense to prove that rape occurred, expert testimony on the condition is recognized in an increasing number of jurisdictions to explain the delay in reporting the rape as well as the alleged victim's general behavior after the rape. Testimony on rape trauma may be permitted in support of the defendant's case as well.

A new defense discussed in this edition is that of urban psychosis, which occurs when young people are brought up in dangerous and violent urban settings. The defense did not succeed in the highly publicized Texas case involving the defendant who shot and killed a state trooper, but with the increased attention to racial problems, more people are willing to consider the merits of this approach. The analogous argument that the lyrics of rap music cause violence is gaining some support as well.

PMS, or premenstrual syndrome, was used successfully by one female defendant against charges of driving while intoxicated, but the defense has not been successful in most cases, although it is gaining more credibility as a viable explanation of behavior and may be used in mitigating sentences.

The Iran-Contra scandal focused on the *patriotism* defense—"I did it for my country." Although the conviction rate was high, the sentences were mild, so perhaps this defense did impress juries in these cases. Apparently it impressed former President Bush in his exercise of pardons.

It may seem silly to mention the rough sex defense, but a look at the cases in which it has been raised in recent years indicates that the defense may result in conviction of a lesser crime and receiving a lighter sentence. This may occur more frequently in future cases as more courts admit expert testimony on the issue of the frequency of rough sex.

Finally, generally religious beliefs are not a defense to a crime resulting from a refusal to obtain medical aid for a child (although some juries are hesitant to convict of murder in these situations), and it is unlikely that "the devil made me do it" defense will result in acquittals.

STUDY QUESTIONS

1. What is meant by *substance abuse*?
2. Do you think substance abuse (or any type of substance abuse) is a disease or a moral problem? Explain your answer.
3. Discuss the nature and extent of the intoxication defense and indicate whether you agree with the current general legal position of this defense.
4. Explain how several recent cases have utilized the intoxication defense.
5. Discuss the meaning of the *battered person syndrome* along with the extent to which you think it should or should not constitute a defense to a criminal act, such as murdering a spouse, lover, child, friend, or parent. Do you think the law should distinguish any categories of battered persons? Should the defense extend to psychological battering? If so, where would you draw the line?
6. What is the relationship between the battered person defense and self-defense?
7. How do *pardons* and *clemency* affect the battered person syndrome defense?
8. Under what circumstances, if any, should *condonation* and *consent* be defenses to criminal behavior?
9. Should *exteme emotional disorder* be a defense? Discuss.
10. What is PTSD, and how does it relate to the Vietnam War?
11. Discuss the use of *rape trauma syndrome* as a defense. How far should this defense be extended?
12. What is meant by *urban psychosis*, and what attempts have been made to use the condition as a defense? Evaluate.
13. What is PMS, and what is the general position of American courts on this defense?
14. Should *rough sex* ever be a defense?
15. Under what, if any, circumstances would you advocate use of the *patriotism* defense as a complete defense?
16. Should religious beliefs constitute an affirmative defense to criminal activity?

ENDNOTES

1. Model Penal Code, Section 2.08(5)(a).
2. See Steven S. Nemerson, "Alcoholism, Intoxication, and the Criminal Law," *Cardozo Law Review* 10 (1988): 393–473.

3. "Scientists Say a Specific Gene May Foreshadow Alcoholism," *New York Times* (18 April 1990), p. 1. See also "Study Ties Genes to Alcoholism in Women," *New York Times* (14 October 1992), p. 9B; and "A Population-Based Twin Study of Alcoholism in Women," *Journal of the American Medical Association* 268 (14 October 1992): 1877–1882.

4. See "Why Men Can Outdrink Women," *Time* (22 January 1990), p. 61.

5. Traynor v. Turnage, 485 U.S. 535 (1988). For a discussion see Andrea Neal, "Is Alcoholism a Disease?" *American Bar Association Journal* 74 (1 February 1988): 58–62.

6. See Minneapolis v. Altimus, 238 N.W.2d 851 (Minn. 1976).

7. Model Penal Code, Section 2.08(4).

8. See Hopt v. People, 104 U.S. 631 (1881).

9. Kan. Statutes Ann., Section 21-3208(2) (1994), as quoted in State v. Gadelkarim, 802 P.2d 507 (Kan. 1990). See also State v. Montano, 855 P.2d 979 (Kan.App. 1993), and United States v. Reed, 991 F.2d 399 (7th Cir. 1993).

10. See United States v. Sneezer, 900 F.2d 177 (9th Cir. 1990).

11. See Model Penal Code, Section 2.08(2) and the earlier discussion of intent in this text.

12. Texas Penal Code, Title 2, Section 8.04(a)(b) (1994).

13. People v. Tocco, 525 N.Y.S.2d 137 (N.Y. 1988), footnotes and citations omitted.

14. Rochelle Cooper Dreyfuss and Dorothy Nelkin, "The Jurisprudence of Genetics," *Vanderbilt Law Review* 45 (March 1992): 313–348; quotation is on p. 348.

15. Powell v. Texas, 392 U.S. 514 (1967), dissenting opinion.

16. Texas Penal Code, Title 2, Section 8.04(b) (1994).

17. See City of Seattle v. Hill, 435 P.2d 692 (Wash. 1967), *cert. denied*, 393 U.S. 872 (1968).

18. See, for example, Joan Zorza, "The Criminal Law of Misdemeanor Domestic Violence, 1970–1990," *Journal of Criminal Law & Criminology* 83 (Spring 1992): 46–77. See also Michael Steinman, ed., *Woman Battering: Policy Responses* (Cincinnati, Ohio: Anderson, 1991).

19. For a review of research on family violence, see Lloyd Ohlin and Michael Tonry, eds., *Family Violence* (Chicago: University of Chicago Press, 1989); and Richard J. Gelles and Claire Pedrick Cornell, *Intimate Violence in Families*, 2d ed. (Newbury Park, Calif.: Sage, 1990). For a discussion of domestic violence in other countries, see David Levinson, *Family Violence in Cross Cultural Perspective* (Beverly Hills, Calif.: Sage, 1989). For a short piece on the view that domestic violence is a crime rather than a domestic problem, see Joseph R. Biden, "Domestic Violence: A Crime, Not A Quarrel," *Trial* 29 (June 1993): 56–62.

20. See "Criminal Law—Battered Women and Self-Defense," *Temple Law Review* 63 (1990): 375–384, concerning the case of Commonwealth v. Stonehouse, 555 A.2d 772 (Pa. 1989). See also Cynthia K. Gillespie, *Justifiable Homicide: Battered Women, Self-Defense, and the Law* (Columbus: Ohio State University Press, 1989); Richard A. Rosen, "On Self-Defense, Imminence, and Women who Kill their Batterers," *North Carolina Law Review* 71 (January 1993): 371–417; and "Developments in the Law—Legal Responses to Domestic Violence Against Battered Women Who Kill Their Abusers," *Harvard Law Review* 106 (May 1993): 1574–1601. For an extensive discussion of the constitutional issues of the defense, see Erich D. Andersen and Anne Read-Andersen, "Constitutional Dimensions of the Battered Woman Syndrome," *Ohio State Law Journal* 53 (Spring 1992): 363–411.

21. State v. Dannels, 734 P.2d 188, 192 (Mont. 1987).

22. See Murray Straus, Richard Gelles, and Susanne Steinmetz, *Behind Closed Doors: Violence in the American Family* (New York: Doubleday/Anchor, 1979); Richard Gelles, *Family Violence* (Beverly Hills, Cal.: Sage Publications, 1979); Leonore Walker, *The Battered Woman Syndrome* (New York: Springer Publishing Co., 1984); Leonore Walker, *Terrifying Love: Why Battered Women Kill and How Society Responds* (New York: Harper and Row, 1989); A. Browne, *When Battered Women Kill* (New York: Macmillan Publishing Co., 1987); and Charles Patrick Ewing, *Battered Women Who Kill* (Lexington, Mass.: Lexington Books, 1987).

23. "Lorena Bobbitt Acquitted in Mutilation of Husband," *New York Times* (22 January 1994), p. 1.

24. For more information on children who kill their abusers, see the following articles, all published in *Journal of Interpersonal Violence* 8 (June 1993): Lucy Berliner, "When Should Children Be Allowed to Kill Abusers?," pp. 296–297; Paul Mones, "When the Innocent Strike Back: Abused Children Who Kill Their Parents," pp. 297–298; and Seth Aaron Fine, "Do Not Blur Self-Defense and Revenge," pp. 299–301. For a discussion of legal issues, see Susan C. Smith, "Abused Children Who Kill Abusive Parents: Moving Toward an Appropriate Legal Response," *Catholic University Law Review* 42 (1992): 141–178.

25. Quoted in State v. Kelly, 478 A.2d 364, 371 (N.J. 1984).

26. See, for example, State v. Kelley, 478 A.2d 364, 371 (N.J. 1984).

27. State v. Janes, 822 P.2d 1238 (Wash.App. 1992), *remanded.*, 850 P.2d 495 (Wash. 1993). See also Estelle v. McGuire 502 U.S. 62 (1991), in which the U.S. Supreme Court held that admission of evidence of the battered child syndrome in cases in which a child is killed by a parent does not violate the defendant's constitutional rights. This evidence supports the argument that the child did not die by accidental means.

28. State v. Janes, 850 P.2d 495 (Wash. 1993).

29. State v. Janes, 850 P.2d 495 (Wash. 1993).

30. Ibn-Tamas v. United States, 407 A.2d 626 (D.C. 1979), *appeal after remand*, 455 A.2d 893 (D.C.App. 1983). For a discussion of the history of the defense and an analysis of the legal issues, see Victoria MiKesell Mather, "The Skeleton in the Closet: The Battered Woman Syndrome, Self-Defense, and Expert Testimony," *Mercer Law Review* 39 (Winter 1988): 545–589. See also Richard A. Rosen, "On Self-Defense, Imminence, and Women Who Kill Their Batterers," *North Carolina Law Review* 74 (January 1993): 371–417.

31. State v. Koss, 551 N.E.2d 970 (Ohio 1990), footnotes and citations omitted.

32. People v. Minnis, 455 N.E.2d 209, 214–215 (4th Dist. Ill. 1983). See State v. Dannels, 734 P.2d 188 (Mont. 1987) for a case upholding the trial court's decision to disallow public expenditures for an expert witness to testify on the battered woman's syndrome to buttress the credibility of the victim in her attempt to explain why she lied to officers about the cause of her bruises.

33. People v. Day, 2 Cal.Rptr. 2d 916 (Cal.App.5th Dist. 1992).

34. "Killing of Sideshow Performer Takes Center Stage at Trial," *St. Petersburg Times* (20 July 1993), p. 1B; "Self-Defense Argued in Hired Killing Case," *St. Petersburg Times* (4 June 1993), p. 1B.

35. "Stepson Convicted in Murder-for-Hire of 'Lobster Boy,'" *Los Angeles Times* (10 August 1994), p. 25.

36. "Woman Gets Probation After Fatally Shooting Abusive Spouse," *Dallas Morning News* (30 May 1987), p. 37. For a discussion of the legal and social issues in the battered woman syndrome defense, see Sara Lee Johann and Frank Osanka, *Representing...Battered Women Who Kill* (Springfield, Ill.: Charles C. Thomas, 1989).

37. "Abused Wife Gets Break in Slaying of Husband," *Miami Herald* (14 June 1990), p. 2.
38. See United States v. Whitetail, 956 F.2d 857 (8th Cir. 1992). See also United States v. Cheape, 889 F.2d 477 (3d Cir. 1989).
39. "Battered Woman Granted Clemency," *Tallahassee Democrat* (26 October 1989), p. 8.
40. "Mass. Governor: Commute Battered Woman's Sentence," *St. Petersburg Times* (21 January 1993), p. 8; "Freed Abuse Victim Says Life Is Good Again," *Boston Globe* (4 December 1993), p. 17.
41. "View of Abused Women is Changing, Some Say," *New York Times* (30 January 1989), p. 7.
42. "California Denies Clemency Pleas of Fourteen Women Who Killed Spouses," *New York Times* (30 May 1993), p. 4. For a brief discussion of some of the controversy over clemency in these cases, see "License to Kill?" *American Bar Association Journal* 79 (April 1993): 37.
43. Ohio Revised Code, Section 2901.06 (1994).
44. Battered Women's Testimony Act of 1992, Public Law 102-527 (U.S. Code, Title 42, Section 10702 (1994), Section 2. Authority of State Justice Institute.
45. Bradley v. State, Walker 156, 157 (Miss. 1824).
46. Floyd v. State, 116 So. 318 (Ala.App. 1928), *cert. denied*, 116 So. 320 (Ala. 1928).
47. See Garcia v. Miera, 817 F.2d 650 (10th Cir. 1987), *cert. denied*, 485 U.S. 959 (1988).
48. Model Penal Code, Section 3.08(1)(a)(b).
49. Ingraham v. Wright, 430 U.S. 651 (1977).
50. People v. Johnson, 479 N.E.2d 481 (Ill.App. 1985).
51. See Model Penal Code, Section 2.11.
52. Ore. Rev. Statute 163.135 (1994).
53. State v. Hessel, 844 P.2d 209 (Or.App. 1992), *review denied*, 862 P.2d 1305 (Ore. 1993).
54. State v. Hessel, 844 P.2d 209, 211 (Or.App. 1992), *review denied*, 862 P.2d 1305 (Ore. 1993).
55. See American Psychiatric Association, *Diagnosis and Statistical Manual of Mental Disorders* (Washington, D.C.: American Psychiatric Association, 1952).
56. See P. G. Bourne, *Men, Stress, and Vietnam* (Boston: Little, Brown, 1981).
57. American Psychiatric Association, *Diagnostic and Statistical Manual of Mental Disorders*, 3d ed. rev. (Washington, D.C.: American Psychiatric Association, 1987), Section 309.89. See also Ari Kiev, "Post-Traumatic Stress Disorder: The Unrecognized Syndrome," *Trial* 24 (May 1988): 62, 64–65.
58. See, for example, State v. Felde, 422 So.2d 370 (La. 1982) (defendant claimed he believed he was in North Vietnam when he shot a police officer); and Miller v. State, 338 N.W.2d 673 (S.D. 1983) (defendant escapee from prison work farm testified he believed he was in Vietnam and believed he was running back home).
59. State v. DeMoss, 770 P.2d 441, 444 (Kan. 1989), cases and citations omitted. For a recent case in which the court held that evidence of PTSD was excluded improperly in the trial of a Vietnam veteran, see Shepard v. State, 847 P.2d 75 (Alas.App. 1993).
60. Ann Wolbert Burgess and Lynda Lytle Holmstrom, "Rape Trauma Syndrome," *American Journal of Psychiatry* 131 (1974): 981.
61. People v. Hampton, 746 P.2d 947 (Colo. 1987).
62. People v. Taylor, 552 N.E.2d 131 (N.Y. 1990).
63. State v. Marks, 647 P.2d 1292 (Kan. 1982).

64. Henson v. State, 535 N.E.2d 1189 (Ind. 1989).

65. See People v. Wheeler, 602 N.E.2d 826 (Ill. 1992). For a discussion of some of the legal implications of rape trauma syndrome evidence, see "Defense Expert Testimony on Rape Trauma Syndrome: Implications for the Stoic Victim," *Hastings Law Journal* 42 (April 1991): 1143–1173.

66. "Criminal Lawyers Develop Urban Psychosis Defense," *Trial* 29 (August 1993), 12–13.

67. "CBS News: Eye on America," (1 July 1993); "Man Who Blamed Rap Music Is Convicted of Killing Officer," *New York Times* (10 June 1993), p. 10; "Trooper's Killer is Condemned," *Miami Herald* (15 July 1993), p. 9. See also Jill Leslie Rosenbaum and Lorraine Prinsky, "The Presumption of Influence: Recent Responses to Popular Music Subcultures," *Crime & Delinquency* 37 (October 1991): 528–535; "Mistrial Declared in 'Urban Survival' Case," *New York Times* (21 April 1994), p. 9.

68. "'Suburban Psychosis' May be Killing Defense," *St. Petersburg Times* (2 September 1993), p. 4B.

69. "Woman Killed After She Complains About Music," *St. Petersburg Times* (16 June 1993), p. 4B.

70. For more details on the physical and medical aspects of PMS, see Katharina Dalton, "PreMenstrual Syndrome," *Hamline Law Review* 9 (February 1986): 143–154; and, in the same volume, an article by William R. Keye, Jr., and Eric Trunnell, "Premenstrual Syndrome: A Medical Perspective," pp. 165–182. See also Deborah V. Denno, "Human Biology and Criminal Responsibility: Free Will or Free ride?" *University of Pennsylvania Law Review* 137 (December 1988): 615–667.

71. Thomas L. Riley, "Premenstrual Syndrome as a Legal Defense," *Hamline Law Review* 9 (February 1986): 193–202; quote is on 201–202.

72. "Health Watch: PMS Is A Worldwide Phenomenon," *New York Times* (11 November 1992), p. 8B.

73. *National Law Journal* 15 (February 1982): 12.

74. People v. Santos, unreported New York case No. 1 KO4622 (Crim.Ct. N.Y. Nov. 3, 1982), discussed in Richard T. Oakes, "PMS: A Plea Bargain in Brooklyn Does Not a Rule of Law Make," *Hamline Law Review* 9 (February 1986): 203–217.

75. Quoted in "Overheard," *Newsweek* (17 June 1991), p. 17.

76. "PMS Physician Sues State Medical Board," *Washington Times* (7 March 1993), p. 11. See also "Mothers Who Kill: Postpartum Disorders and Criminal Infanticide," *UCLA Law Review* 38 (February 1991): 699–760; "Judge Dismisses Doctor's Suit," *Washington Times* (9 April 1993), p. 2B.

77. "The Patriotism Defense: Sometimes It Works, Sometimes It Doesn't," *New York Times* (29 May 1987), p. 8.

78. United States v. North, 910 F.2d 843 (D.C.App. 1990), *cert. denied*, 500 U.S. 941 (1991).

79. "Oliver North Is On A Quest for Redemption," *Miami Herald* (30 May 1993), p. 27.

80. United States v. Poindexter, 951 F.2d 369 (D.C.App. 1991), *cert. denied*, 113 S.Ct. 656 (1992).

81. "Independent Counsel's Statement on the Pardons," *New York Times* (25 December 1992), p. 10. For an overview of Walsh's role, see Henry J. Reske, "Walsh Winds Up Probe," *American Bar Association Journal* 79 (January 1993): 14, 16.

82. See "Defense in Abuse Case Call Woman Aggressor," *New York Times* (16 October 1992), p. 5; "Woman Gives an Account of Sex Abuse," *New York Times* (10 December 1992), p. 16; and "Glen Ridge Rapists Get Light Sentences," *St. Petersburg Times* (24 April 1993), p. 1.

83. "The Rough-Sex Defense: When Killers Blame Erotic Impulses, Does Rough Justice Result?" *Time* (23 May 1988), p. 55.

84. For a discussion of this defense, see "Comment: The 'Rough Sex' Defense," *The Journal of Criminal Law and Criminology* 80 (Summer 1989): 557–584.

85. "The Rough Sex Defense." The following examples in the text are from the same source unless otherwise indicated.

86. "New Claim Interrupts Murder Trial," *Orlando Sentinel* (23 June 1993), p. 1B. See also "Cult Talk Continues," *Orlando Sentinel* (3 July 1993), p. 1B.

87. "Religion Is Rejected as Murder Defense," *New York Times* (20 April 1989), p. 12; "Beliefs Tested by Girl's Death," *St. Petersburg Times* (1 December 1991), p. 1. The case is Hermanson v. State, 604 So.2d 775 (Fla. 1992).

88. "Christian Scientists Get Probation in Death of Son," *New York Times* (7 July 1990), p. 1C; "Weld Bid on Law Faulted; Critics Hit Stance on 'Religious' Statute," *Boston Globe* (11 December 1993), p. 15 Metro/Region. The case is Commonwealth v. Twitchell, 617 N.E.2d 609 (Mass. 1993).

89. "One Defendant Is Found Guilty in Racial Slaying in Bensonhurst," *New York Times* (18 May 1990), p. 1; "'Blame the Woman' Defense Tried," *New York Times* (23 April 1990), p. 17; and "Bensonhurst Case Ends, Leaving Few Satisfied," *New York Times* (14 March 1991), p. 13.

Chapter 5

Crimes against the Person: Part I

Outline

Key Terms

corpus delicti	involuntary	manslaughter
corroborating	manslaughter	murder
evidence	lesser included	negligent homicide
felony murder	offense	premeditation
homicide	malice	voluntary
infanticide	aforethought	manslaughter

Introduction

He stopped his 1992 red Lexus on a small North Carolina utility road and rested after midnight on 23 July 1993 after leaving a friend's home in Wilmington. He was never seen alive again. On August 3 a fisherman discovered his badly decomposed body. It was taken to the morgue; dental imprints were made; and the body was cremated on August 6. It was almost a week later before the victim's remains were identified by the dental imprints. Allegedly two eighteen-year-olds abducted and killed the victim and drove around for a couple of hours before dumping his body in a creek just over the South Carolina border.

A few days after Jordan's remains were identified authorities charged Daniel Andre Green and Larry Demery with first-degree murder in the death of James Jordan, father of Michael Jordan, basketball superstar who

James Jordan, father of Michael Jordan, was found dead in his car in what was presumed to be the result of random violence.

led the Chicago Bulls to three consecutive national titles before his retirement from basketball in 1993. Police did not believe the crime was related to the fame of Jordan's son or of the business dealings of either Jordan, as some had feared originally. The director of the State Bureau of Investigation said, "As this matter unfolds, you will find that what happened to Mr. Jordan was the kind of random violence that all the public are concerned and afraid of."[1]

In 1990, shortly before this chapter was written for this text's previous edition, the brutal deaths of five university students in Gainesville, Florida shocked the small town and the nation. The trial of Danny Harold Rolling, scheduled for 1 September 1993, was postponed until January 1994 to permit the defense more time to prepare for trial. Rolling entered guilty pleas. A jury recommended the death penalty. The judge followed that recommendation.

The possibility of a death sentence raised serious questions, however, when popular former football star O. J. Simpson was accused of murdering his ex-wife, Nicole Brown Simpson, and her friend, Ronald Goldman. The nation and the world watched in disbelief as the story unfolded and Simpson became the prime (and only) suspect in the brutal knifings of the two victims, found dead outside Nicole's luxury California condo while the two children of Nicole and O. J. slept inside. As police prepared to arrest Simpson, he fled from the home in which he was supposedly meeting with his attorney and his physicians. With his long-time friend, Al Cowlings, at the wheel, O. J. clutched two photos of his family and held a gun to his own head while asking to be taken to see his mother. Police followed the slow-

Danny Rolling, who entered guilty pleas to brutal murders and mutilations of five young people in Gainesville, Florida, was sentenced to die in Florida's electric chair.

moving car down California freeways while bystanders cheered O. J in a procession that ended with the return of Simpson and Cowlings to O. J.'s Brentwood, California, home, where both surrendered peacefully to Los Angeles police after some negotiations. Simpson entered a plea of not guilty, while legal commentators began their analyses of what might happen in the forthcoming trial, with many noting the improbability that the death penalty would ever be imposed on such a popular person as O. J. Simpson.

These deaths and others discussed in Focus 5.1 illustrate several points about homicide. The randomness of some victims creates fear in many people that they too might be found in the wrong place at the wrong time and lose their lives. Second, many of today's homicides are committed by young people. Third, some of the homicides involve torture and other atrocities. Finally, as alleged in the case of O. J. Simpson, domestic violence may play a role in some murders.

All of the deaths discussed here and in Focus 5.1 were homicides, but the circumstances surrounding these tragedies and the characteristics of those who committed the atrocities could distinguish the different homicides. The previous two chapters discuss defenses to criminal acts; it is possible that the accused in these trials could have successful defenses (such as insanity). It is possible also that in any of these cases the prosecution could not prove all elements of the crimes beyond a reasonable doubt. Thus, homicide may not be murder or manslaughter in these cases.

Jurisdictions differ in how they define homicide and how they categorize the act of killing. This chapter explores these issues and looks at the elements that are required for a homicide to be murder or manslaughter.

Homicide: An Introduction

Homicide is an inclusive term that refers to all cases in which human beings kill other human beings by their own acts, omissions, or procurements. The phrase *other human being* excludes suicide. This modern definition differs from earlier ones that included suicide by referring to *a human being* rather than *other human being*. As the discussion indicates, historically a fetus was excluded, but that area of law is changing in some jurisdictions.

Common Law Homicide: An Overview

Under early English common law, all homicides were punishable by death, as were many other offenses; so categories were not necessary. Later, *justifiable* and *excusable* homicides were distinguished from *criminal homicides*. Justifiable and excusable homicides were ones for which actors would not be responsible; criminal homicides were ones for which they were responsible. Some states have retained these categories.

Justifiable homicides are those for which no fault is involved because the law permits the homicide. It is permissible for a designated person to perform whatever tasks are necessary to carry out the death penalty. That is a

FOCUS 5.1 The Rise of Violence and Homicides Among the Young

"Is this going to take long? I've got someplace to go tonight," said an eight-year-old boy as detectives questioned him about using a semiautomatic handgun to shoot a girl in the spine.[1]

In what police called another case of random violence, four California youths, ages eleven, thirteen, fourteen, and sixteen were arrested in the slaying of the father of two, who went to his car because he was not feeling well during his daughter's band concert. It was alleged that the youngest was the assailant who used the knife to stab Thomas Weinhofer to death.[2]

Okiki, a thirteen-year-old honor student, and her friend Marlena, twelve, plotted to kill one of their teachers with a twelve-inch fillet knife that Okiki carried to school in her book bag. Over $200 was wagered by other students who bet the girls would not carry out their plan. An assistant principal found one of the girls crying and was referred to others, one of whom told her of the plot, which was intercepted prior to the planned homicide. When the assistant principal went into the classroom, some of the students whispered, "Get her now," although others said, "You better not." Okiki said the teacher "got in her face" the previous day, which made her very angry and to her friends she said, "I'm going to kill her." The bets began, and she planned the crime. According to the investigator, when the girls were taken to the police department, "they were giggling."[3]

In June 1993 Jesse Lloyd Misskelley, seventeen; Michael Wayne Echols, eighteen; and Charles Janson Baldwin, sixteen, were charged with capital murder for allegedly killing three second-grade boys in West Memphis, Arkansas and leaving their bodies in a drainage ditch.[4]

In August 1993 Eric Smith, thirteen, admitted that he battered and killed a four-year-old. Eric is being tried as an adult; no motive for the killing is known; it is suspected that the victim, Derrick Robie, was a random victim.[5]

Teen violence in recent years has not been limited to the United States. In 1993 two ten-year-old boys were charged with kidnapping, battering, and murdering James Bulger, a two-

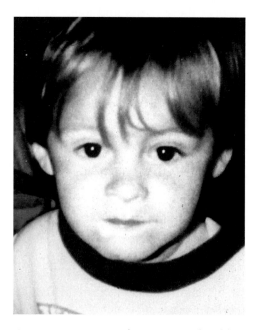

At age two, James Bulger was murdered by two eleven-year-olds who abducted him from his mother in an English shopping center.

year-old toddler, in England. At age eleven the defendants became the youngest persons convicted of murder in England in 250 years. They were sentenced to indefinite custody, and Bulger's uncle vowed that if the murderers were released "we will kill them." A few weeks after the Bulger abduction and murder, two seventeen-year-old English girls were charged with torturing and murdering an elderly woman.[6]

FBI crime data indicate that violence among juveniles is on the rise, with arrest rates up dramatically among African-American males. "Specifically, between 1980 and 1990, the arrest rate for this group increased 145 percent, while the rate for whites rose 48 percent and for other races, declined 45 percent." Between 1965 and 1990 the overall murder rate for juveniles increased 332 percent.[7] Criminologist James Alan Fox, co-author of a report on juvenile violence, says, "What is so dangerous about this is that a fifteen-year-old with a gun in his hand is a much more volatile individual than a forty-year-old or even an eighteen-year-old."[8]

In Florida alone a juvenile murders someone on the average of every other day.[9] The covers of two national news magazines published during the first week of August 1993 focused on kids and guns. The articles described the torture and murder of numerous victims by gangs armed with knives and guns.[10] The previous month *Newsweek* ran an article entitled, "Life Means

Nothing," in which the murders of two girls by six Houston, Texas teenagers was detailed. The nude bodies of the victims, who had been beaten, raped repeatedly, and strangled, were found four days later in the woods they used as a short cut on their way home from a party. The suspects showed little remorse but "seemed to glory in their 15 minutes of fame."[11]

[1.] Quoted in "Overheard," *Newsweek* (23 March 1992), p. 21.

[2.] "Man Slain—Suspects Are Eleven, Thirteen, Fourteen, Sixteen," *Orlando Sentinel* (22 October 1992), p. 21.

[3.] "The Knife in the Book Bag," *Time* (8 February 1993), p. 37.

[4.] "Three Teen-Agers Are Held in Slayings of Boys," *New York Times* (5 June 1993), p. 9; "Killing Rocks Nation Once Again," *Tallahassee Democrat* (11 March 1993), p. 8.

[5.] "Town Tries to Make Sense of Murder," *Tallahassee Democrat* (15 August 1993), p. 12.

[6.] "Boys Plead Not Guilty in Toddler's Murder," *New York Times* (15 May 1993), p. 5. "Killed Boy's Family Vows Revenge," *St. Petersburg Times* (26 November 1993), p. 1.

[7.] Federal Bureau of Investigation, *Crime in the United States, Uniform Crime Reports 1991* (Washington, D.C.: U.S. Government Printing Office, 1992), p. 279.

[8.] "Seeds of Murder Epidemic: Teen-Age Boys with Guns," *New York Times* (15 October 1992), p. 8.

[9.] "Killed by Kids," *St. Petersburg Times* (28 February 1993), p. 1.

[10.] See "Teen Violence: Wild in the Streets," *Newsweek* (2 August 1993), front cover; and "Big Shots: An Inside Look at the Deadly Love Affair Between America's Kids and their Guns," *Time* (2 August 1993), front cover.

[11.] "Life Means Nothing," *Newsweek* (19 July 1993), p. 16.

planned, well-thought-out killing, but it is not criminal homicide. Likewise, under some circumstances police may kill in the line of duty and citizens may kill in self-defense, without incurring criminal liability.

Excusable homicides involve some fault but not enough that the law considers the act worthy of criminal liability. In many cases it is difficult to distinguish excusable from justifiable homicide. Persons threatened with immediate great bodily harm or death are permitted to use reasonable means to prevent that harm. If the threatened person has legal cause to kill in self-defense and does so intentionally, the result is *justifiable homicide*. If the actor does not intend to kill but does cause the death of another while engaging in self-defense legally, the result is *excusable homicide*. However, if the actor is sufficiently negligent, the killing may be considered *negligent homicide*, for which he or she could be criminally liable.

Initially the common law divided culpable or criminal homicides into murder—the most serious offense—and manslaughter. Later, each of those categories was divided into grades of offenses. The common law definitions of these terms are noted in subsequent discussions. The common law of homicide was developed by judges over centuries. The results are inconsistent and confusing. Nevertheless, many jurisdictions follow at least part of the common law approach to homicide; so it cannot be ignored. Others follow the Model Penal Code approach.

The Model Penal Code Approach: An Overview

Because of the problems of distinguishing justifiable and excusable homicides, the drafters of the Model Penal Code did not use those terms. Rather, they used the term *criminal homicide* to refer to killings to which criminal liability may be attached. Criminal homicide in the M.P.C. is defined as purposely, knowingly, recklessly, or negligently (defined in Focus 2.4, Chapter 2) causing the death of another human being. Under the M.P.C. there are four types of criminal homicide: murder, manslaughter, negligent homicide, and causing or aiding suicide.[2]

General Definitional Problems

Some terms in the Model Penal Code's definition of criminal homicide have presented definitional problems. These terms are used in many state statutes, and they require closer scrutiny. An example is the term *human being*. The M.P.C. defines *human being* as "a person who has been born and is alive."[3]

THE LIVING HUMAN BEING REQUIREMENT

The requirement of a *living human being* becomes an issue in the cases of fetuses who are killed as the result of a crime. Under the common law, the killing of a fetus did not constitute homicide; the fetus had to be born alive before a homicide could occur. Most state statutes followed the common law rule.

But what does it mean to be born alive? Some states require that the fetus be expelled from the mother's body and be breathing on its own; others require that the baby cry; others require that the umbilical cord be severed. Some courts, such as the California Supreme Court, have held that if the birth process has started and the fetus is viable, the baby is considered to have been born alive.[4]

The born-alive requirement may affect other crimes, such as **infanticide**, which refers to killing a child soon after birth. Historically, i fanticide was acceptable in some countries in which parents were per.nitted to kill deformed children, and in some cases, female children, as male children were preferred. Where it has been a crime, it has not been considered as serious as murder.

Decriminalizing abortion has resulted in a problem in that the act of abortion is legal. But what happens if the fetus is born alive? To cover this situation some states, such as Pennsylvania, have enacted statutes requiring health care professionals to do what they can to save the life of the fetus when that occurs. Thus, in 1989 a Pennsylvania physician was convicted of infanticide when he failed to take positive steps to preserve the life of a fetus born alive after he conducted an abortion. The baby survived for about ninety minutes after the abortion. The physician, who could have been sentenced to three-and-a-half to seven years in prison, was placed on three years' probation and ordered to perform 300 hours of community service. In sentencing him, the judge said she did not wish to make an example of him, that prison and a heavy fine would serve no purpose, and that he had made a "criminal mistake."[5]

The decision regarding the status of a fetus has religious, moral, and ethical as well as legal implications.[6] Some states have made statutory changes in the common law requirement of being born alive and include the fetus within their murder statutes. (Others define killing a fetus as manslaughter, discussed later in the chapter). California is an example, but the change was made after a judicial decision that was unpopular. In a 1970 case, in which an estranged husband announced his intention to kill his wife's baby and kicked his wife in the abdomen, causing the fetus to be stillborn, the California Supreme Court followed the common law exclusion of a fetus from homicide statutes and ruled that in that case prosecution for murder was improper.[7] Subsequently the California legislature amended the state statute, which had stated, "Murder is the unlawful killing of a human being, with malice aforethought," to provide that, "Murder is the unlawful killing of a human being, or a fetus, with malice aforethought." There are exclusions for such acts as legal abortions. In 1994 the California Supreme Court held that in an assault upon a pregnant woman who subsequently loses a baby, the assailant may be prosecuted for murder even if the fetus was not viable at the time of the assault.[8]

The Minnesota statute was changed in 1986 to substitute the words *unborn child* for *human being* and *person* in its murder statutes for both first- and second-degree murder.[9] The change has been tested in the courts, as explained in Focus 5.2. Within recent years, a number of other states have enacted legislation that includes the killing of a fetus (apart from abortion) as homicide. Some of those statutes limit the homicide to cases involving a viable fetus, generally considered to be a fetus at twenty-eight weeks of development.[10]

Such statutory changes may result in criminal charges against pregnant women who take cocaine or some other substance that results in fetal death, but prosecutors and grand juries may be reluctant to bring these charges. In Illinois a grand jury refused to indict a young mother whose infant died shortly after birth and whose death was linked to the mother's

FOCUS 5.2   Should Killing a Fetus Constitute Murder?

The Minnesota Supreme Court held that the state statute defining the crime of *murder of an unborn child* is constitutional and the state therefore could proceed with its prosecution of Sean Merrill for murder of the twenty-seven or twenty-eight day old embryo of Gail Anderson, as well as for the murder of Anderson. It is unclear whether the defendant knew that Anderson was pregnant and that the embryo was not viable.

In *State* v. *Merrill*, the court held that the phrase *causes the death of an unborn child* is not vague and that the use of the word *living* in the statute presented no problem, in that *living* is nothing more than the property of growing or becoming, a property of all living things. The dissent argued that the use of the phrase *causes the death of an unborn child* is not well defined. The statute is vague and leads to arbitrary and discriminatory interpretation; therefore, it is unconstitutional.

The Minnesota statute was enacted by the legislature after the Minnesota Supreme Court ruled in a 1985 case that the state's homicide statutes did not apply to the death of a viable fetus.[1] Merrill claimed unsuccessfully that the statute is vague because it does not define when life begins or when death occurs. In reaction to that argument, the court said:

The difficulty with this argument, however, is that the statutes do not raise the issue of when life as a human person begins or ends. The state must prove only that the implanted embryo or the fetus in the mother's womb was living, that it had life, and that it has life no longer. To have life, as that term is commonly understood, means to have the property of all living things to grow, to become. It is not necessary to prove, nor does the statute require, that the living organism in the womb in its embryonic or fetal state be considered a person or a human being. People are free to differ or abstain on the profound philosophical and moral questions of whether an embryo is a human being, or on whether or at what stage the embryo or fetus is ensouled or acquires "personhood." These questions are entirely irrelevant to criminal liability under the statute. Criminal liability here requires only that the genetically human embryo be a living organism that is growing into a human being. Death occurs when the embryo is no longer living, when it ceases to have the properties of life.[2]

In the Merrill case, the Minnesota Civil Liberties Union argued that the state statute conflicted with the U.S. Supreme Court's approval of abortion in the controversial *Roe* v. *Wade* decision.[3]

In July 1993 two charges of first-degree murder and two charges of second-degree murder were filed against Chao Yang, accused in the stabbing deaths of a twenty-nine-year-old Rochester, Minnesota woman and her eight-month-old fetus. Yang was arrested in October 1993.[4]

In June 1993 two counts of second-degree murder were filed against Barren Lawrence Netland, alleged to have stabbed his pregnant girlfriend while she was sleeping. She and her fetus died.[5]

[1] State v. Soto, 378 N.W.2d 625 (Minn. 1985).
[2] State v. Merrill, 450 N.W.2d 318, 323 (Minn. 1990), *cert. denied*, 496 U.S. 931 (1990).

3. See Roe v. Wade, 410 U.S. 113 (1973). See also Planned Parenthood v. Casey, 112 U.S. 2791 (1992), in which the Court upheld a woman's basic right to an abortion while upholding most of the restrictive requirements of the Pennsylvania abortion law. For a recent scholarly discussion of abortion laws, see Kathryn Ann Farr, "Shaping Policy Through Litigation: Abortion Law in the United States," *Crime & Delinquency* 39 (April 1993): 167–183.

4. "Man Charged in Stabbing Death of Rochester Woman, Her Fetus," *Star Tribune, Metro Edition* (3 July 1993), p. 5B; "Suspect in Rochester Slaying Is Arrested," *Star Tribune Metro Edition* (9 October 1993), p. 1B.
5. "Pregnant Woman Slain, Man Seriously Injured in Stabbing," *Star Tribune* (19 June 1993), p. 1B. For a brief discussion of other similar cases, see "Law Unclear on Killing Fetus," *Washington Times* (20 February 1993), p. 6.

use of cocaine. The prosecutor's earlier announcement of his intention to bring charges brought serious criticism on the grounds that such action might deter other pregnant women who used drugs from seeking prenatal care. The practice was objected to on the privacy issue as well. Said one attorney, "If the state can create prenatal patrols for cocaine use, then where would they draw the line?"[11]

Would the case be an easier one if the death of the newborn was caused by the mother's failure to get adequate medical attention prior to the baby's birth? On 25 September 1986 Pamela Rae Stewart Monson was arrested and charged with violating a California statute that requires parents to provide food, shelter, clothing, and medical attention for a child or fetus. During her pregnancy, Monson's doctor, who diagnosed a condition in which the placenta separates from the uterine wall before birth, told her to stay off her feet, stop taking drugs, and get immediate medical attention if she started hemorrhaging. She was instructed not to have sexual intercourse if hemorrhaging occurred. She did not obey those orders; the baby was born with massive brain damage and died a month later.

A toxicological report indicated that the baby had amphetamines in his body at the time of death; authorities were notified, and Monson was arrested. Her case was dismissed by a San Diego judge, who ruled that it was the intent of the legislature in enacting the statute in question that it applied to fathers who refused to make adequate provisions for their children; specifically, fathers who were delinquent in child support payments. The judge ruled that the statute did not cover fetal abuse as it existed in this case. However, the judge did say in dicta (thus, these comments are not a part of the court's ruling) that the legislature could enact a statute to criminalize harmful conduct toward a fetus, and if properly worded, that statute would be constitutional.[12]

More likely than homicide charges against mothers whose fetuses die as a result of the mother's substance abuse are charges against women whose children suffer birth defects as a result of such abuse. Some have been charged with child abuse, fetal abuse, delivering a controlled substance, and other crimes. In 1992 two state supreme courts overruled such punitive treatment. The Florida Supreme Court ruled that the state's statute prohibiting delivering drugs to minors was not applicable in the case of a woman who ingested illegal drugs while pregnant and gave birth to a drug-addicted baby.[13] The Connecticut Supreme Court overruled a lower court holding that a pregnant woman's cocaine injections shortly before she gave birth did not constitute child neglect in the case of her child, which was born suffering from cocaine withdrawal. The court held that the statute did not cover a pregnant woman's prenatal conduct.[14]

THE DEFINITION OF DEATH

Death is another term that is difficult to define. Historically the term was not defined legally. As the Model Penal Code points out, generally the definition of death was not an issue because most people agreed that death meant the cessation of breathing and heartbeat.[15] Today the term *death* has become a critical issue in many homicide cases, however, because of the developments of modern science that enable doctors to keep patients functioning with the aid of life-support systems when those patients could not function without that assistance. Second, organ transplantation has created problems of defining when death occurs. For some organs to be viable for successful transplants, they must be removed before all body functions have ceased, and they must be preserved carefully until quick transplantation occurs.

The issue of when death occurs arose in a recent Florida case involving an anencephalic (congenital absence of all or part of the brain) child who was born with a functioning brain stem and whose heart was beating and who was breathing. The child's parents wanted her declared dead so that her functioning organs could be transplanted to other children. The Florida Supreme Court ruled that donation of the child's organs would not be legal under these circumstances. The court noted that there was no agreement on the utility of such transplants; the ethical issues had not been resolved; and the legal and constitutional issues had not been resolved.[16]

Today many jurisdictions follow the Uniform Determination of Death Act, which states:

> An individual who has sustained either (1) irreversible cessation of circulatory and respiratory functions or (2) irreversible cessation of all functions of the entire brain, including the brain stem, is dead. A determination of death must be made in accordance with accepted medical standards.[17]

The Model Penal Code does not define death. The commentators cite two reasons. First, the modern scientific information that has raised serious questions about the time of death was not available when the code was drafted. Second, the commentators stated that "this delicate interplay between the criminal law and the advances of medical science is yet too uncertain to reduce to statutory formulation."[18]

The problem of when death occurs is complicated further by the growing requests of individuals for living wills. These wills are formal, written statements made by individuals when they are legally competent to make a decision about what they want to be done to them regarding life-support systems or organ transplants. Some states now recognize living wills, but problems still arise.[19] These statutes vary, and definitions are a problem, but the general conclusion that can be drawn is that when properly executed, termination of life-support systems, resulting in the death of a patient, will not constitute murder when a proper living will is available. The resolution of these issues regarding the definition of death and the right to terminate life are critical not only for religious and ethical reasons but also for legal reasons, particularly regarding the causation element of homicide.[20]

Causation in Homicide Cases

Another important element that the prosecution must prove in homicide cases is that the alleged crime and not some other act *caused* the victim's death. Because of the difficulties in determining cause of death, the common law utilized a *year-and-a-day rule*, meaning that if the death of the victim did not occur within that time period, the alleged offender could not be convicted of criminal homicide. Some state legislatures have incorporated that rule into their homicide statutes. Other legislatures, in moving from the common law to legislative law, have not mentioned the year-and-a-day rule. Failure to include the rule in a statute has been interpreted as an abandonment of the rule.[21]

The year-and-a-day rule has come under close scrutiny in, among others, cases involving child abuse. In a Georgia case a father was indicted for homicide in the death of his child, based on an alleged incident of child abuse in August 1987. David Lebron Cross admitted that he shook his daughter but said he did so because she was choking on her bottle. Prosecutors claimed successfully that the defendant inflicted such injury that the child sustained brain damage and became comatose. In December 1988, a judge ruled that the child could be taken off life support; she was, and she died within a few weeks. This occurred seventeen months after the alleged child abuse. The father had fought the mother's request to have the life-support systems removed. A Georgia judge granted the defense motion to dismiss, based on the argument that death did not occur within a year-and-a-day after the alleged criminal abuse. The prosecutor appealed that ruling to the Georgia Supreme Court, which invalidated the state's year-and-a-day rule and ordered the father to stand trial on murder charges. According to the court, that rule was eliminated when the legislature rewrote the criminal code in 1968 and did not include the common law rule.[22]

In 1991 the North Carolina Supreme Court said that the year-and-a-day rule was "anachronistic today." The court noted that it was following the modern trend and that in North Carolina "the rule is no longer part of the common law . . .for any purpose."[23] In 1992 the New Mexico Court of Appeals indicated that the rule should be abolished in that state as well.[24] Although the rule has not been the subject of recent litigation in U.S. federal courts, "the rule remains a viable doctrine in contemporary federal jurisprudence and . . . courts should not overlook the rule in federal murder prosecutions."[25]

California has retained the theory of the year-and-a-day rule but expanded the time period. According to the California Penal Code, "To make the killing either murder or manslaughter, it is requisite that the party die within three years and a day after the stroke received or the cause of death administered. In the computation of such time, the whole of the day on which the act was done shall be reckoned the first."[26]

The year-and-a-day rule does not always solve the causation problem, because a victim may die within that time period but may have been subjected to more than one cause of death. For instance, assume that a person who is injured severely by a criminal act is taken to the hospital, where a surgeon performs surgery required by the injury. The doctor's surgery constitutes medical malpractice. The patient dies two days after being stabbed. Who is responsible for the death?

Usually a negligent act by a third party occurring after a criminal act does not relieve the original wrongdoer of criminal liability if the first act was a *substantial factor* in causing the death. An Arizona case states: "Medical malpractice will break the chain of causation and constitute a defense only if death is attributable solely to the medical malpractice and not induced at all by the original wound."[27] This case involved a victim of a criminal stab wound. The attending physician who conducted exploratory surgery to determine the extent of the wound unknowingly perforated the lower intestine and did not discover his mistake. The patient developed peritonitis, which led to his death. The court upheld the defendant's conviction.

In a similar case, a New York appellate court reversed a criminal homicide conviction. While the physician was operating on the stab wound caused by the defendant, he discovered that the patient had a hernia. The patient went into cardiac arrest and died during the hernia operation. There was evidence that the heart attack was caused by the negligence of the anesthesiologist. Thus, it could be concluded that the doctor's act, not the defendant's, was the *cause* of death.[28]

Causation also presents problems when two or more parties commit acts, not one of which would have been sufficient to cause the victim's death. In those cases many courts look carefully at the *intent* of the individuals who committed the acts. If the prosecution can prove that a defendant *intended* to cause death, most courts find that intention sufficient for a conviction for homicide unless the second act clearly broke the chain of causation between the defendant's act and the victim's death. For example, in an 1840 case in England, a mother who wanted to kill her nine-month-old son gave her son's nurse a bottle of poison and told the nurse it was medicine to be given to the child every night. The nurse did not think the child needed medication. She did not give the baby the bottle but placed it on the mantle. Several days later, while the nurse was out, her five-year-old boy picked up the bottle and fed the baby, who died. The mother was convicted of murder. That conviction was upheld even though the mother's intention was not executed as she had planned and a third party had intervened.[29]

Many state statutes do not define causation for criminal homicide cases and rely instead on court interpretations of the word *cause*. Yet, it is not uncommon for courts to neglect to define *cause* other than to say that the defendant's act must have caused the victim's death. It is assumed that we all know the meaning of the word *cause*. Not so, said the U.S. Court of Appeals for the Second Circuit, in the following fact pattern.

Kibbe and his codefendant, Krall, met their victim, Stafford, at a bar. Stafford was drunk. The bartender refused to serve him further although Stafford flashed a $100 bill, which Kibbe and Krall saw. When Stafford began soliciting a ride from patrons, Kibbe and Krall offered. They drove to another bar, which refused to serve drinks to Stafford, and then to a third bar, where drinks were served. After leaving that bar, they demanded Stafford's money, received it, and then forced him to lower his pants and remove his boots to prove that he did not have more money. They abandoned Stafford by the side of the road, placing his boots and jacket on the shoulder of the road.

Shortly thereafter Blake, a college student, while speeding down the rural road, saw Stafford sitting in the middle of the road with his hands in the air. Blake testified that he did not have time to react; thus he did not try to avoid hitting Stafford, who died shortly after the collision. The autopsy showed that Stafford had a high alcohol concentration of 0.25 percent in his blood. The medical examiner testified that he died of wounds suffered from the impact of Blake's car. Should Kibbe and Krall have been convicted of murder? The jury convicted them of second-degree murder, second-degree robbery, and third-degree grand larceny.

In the excerpt below, the federal appellate court explains why it reversed the conviction for second-degree murder. The issue hinged on the state's requirement to prove beyond a reasonable doubt all of the elements of the crime: that the defendants exhibited a depraved indifference to Stafford's life; that they recklessly engaged in conduct that created a grave risk of death to him; and that their actions caused his death. The appellate court noted that the trial court did not instruct the jury on the meaning of causation, and continued as follows:[30]

Kibbe v. Henderson

The omission of any definition of causation, however, permitted the jury to conclude that the issue was not before them or that causation could be inferred merely from the fact that Stafford's death succeeded his abandonment by Kibbe and Krall.

Even if the jury were aware of the need to determine causation, the court's instruction did not provide the tools necessary to that task. The possibility that jurors, as laymen, may misconstrue the evidence before them makes mandatory in every case instruction as to the legal standards they must apply . . . It has been held that where death is produced by an intervening force, such as Blake's operation of his truck, the liability of one who put an antecedent force into action will depend on the difficult determination of whether the intervening force was a sufficiently independent or supervening cause of death. The few cases that provide similar factual circumstances suggest that the controlling questions are whether the ultimate result was foreseeable to the original actor and whether the victim failed to do something easily within his grasp that would have extricated him from danger.

If you had been on that jury, do you think you would have concluded that the defendants should have foreseen that Stafford would not take action to protect himself and that approximately one-half hour after they abandoned him he would be hit and killed by a speeding truck? On appeal, the Supreme Court reversed the lower appellate court, holding that no evidence had been presented that the lack of an instruction on causation prejudiced the defendants. Thus, the conviction of second-degree murder was reinstated. According to the Court, "A person who is 'aware of and consciously disregards' a substantial risk must also foresee the ultimate harm that the risk entails. Thus, the jury's determination that the respondent acted recklessly necessarily included a determination that the ultimate harm was foreseeable to him."[31]

The case is included here to show how difficult it may be to deal with the issue of causation in a homicide case. Can you distinguish the conclusion of this case from that of the New York case cited earlier? The defendant's criminal homicide conviction was reversed when the patient whom he had stabbed went into cardiac arrest during surgery because of the negligence of the anesthesiologist. These two cases present the challenge—both fun and frustration—of the criminal law, especially in the area of causation.

Corpus Delicti

A final legal concept that is important to all crimes but especially to homicides is *corpus delicti* (which means the body of the crime). **Corpus delicti** refers to the body or other material substance of a crime that constitutes the foundation of that particular crime. A burned house might be the *corpus delicti* in an arson case. In homicide, *corpus delicti* includes much more than the body of the deceased, although to prosecute a defendant for any category of homicide, theoretically the prosecutor has to produce the dead body or evidence that a dead body exists.

The *corpus delicti* is required as **corroborating evidence** that the crime occurred. Even if the accused confesses to a murder, if the body cannot be found or there is no evidence of a dead body, that confession is not sufficient for a conviction. Thus, in many cases the prosecutor will not file charges until the body is found. There are some exceptions to the *corpus delicti* requirement. The federal courts and some state courts have abandoned this requirement because in some cases it is difficult if not impossible to get a tangible *corpus delicti*. Examples would be attempted crimes, conspiracy, and income tax evasion.

The *corpus delicti* rule does not require that the actual body be produced. For example, as noted earlier, in the recent death of James Jordan, father of basketball superstar Michael Jordan, the body of the victim of the alleged homicide is not available as evidence. The body was cremated, but the fingers and dental plate were preserved, thus enabling authorities to identify the body as that of James Jordan. That evidence should be sufficient to establish that a death occurred.

Murder

Although a commonly recognized crime, **murder** may be the most difficult to define.[32] The common law and the Model Penal Code definitions are the most frequently used today. But regardless of the definition, the crime of *murder* generally has the same elements, which are as follows:

1. There must be an unlawful act (or omission) committed by a human being.
2. The act must be accompanied by the requisite *mens rea*. *intent*
3. The act must be the legal cause of the victim's death.
4. The victim must be a living human being (some jurisdictions now include a fetus).
5. Death must occur within a reasonable period (usually specified, such as a year-and-a-day under the common law; now extended under some modern statutes).

Most of these elements are discussed in general in Chapter 2. Some, for example, the year-and-a-day rule, are discussed earlier in this chapter. Others, such as the definition of the *mens rea* requirement, need further elaboration, and that is done in the context of the common law development of the crime of murder.

Common Law Murder

Under the common law, the crime of murder developed over several centuries, and so much confusion exists over the meaning of the literal definition (an unlawful killing of another human being with malice aforethought)[33] that some commentators have suggested that, rather than dwell on the common law definition, the emphasis should be on *categories* or *types* of murder, which is the approach taken in this chapter. Some states follow the common law definition. Others have modified the common law definition (as, for example, to include the killing of a fetus) or adopted the Model Penal Code approach.

Under the common law and many modern statutes, murder requires **malice aforethought**. However, these terms are not used literally. "At first the judges in fact did require for murder that the defendant actually have a previously thought-out (i.e., premeditated) intent to kill, though probably the spite, etc. was never actually necessary."[34]

Over the centuries, the malice aforethought requirement was eroded. Common law judges interpreted *malice aforethought* so differently that in many cases it bore no resemblance to the ordinary meaning of the term. "Whatever the original meaning of that phrase, it became over time an 'arbitrary symbol' used by judges to signify any of a number of mental states deemed sufficient to support liability for murder."[35] In addition, common law judges developed types of murder that did not involve malice aforethought.

Where the term *malice aforethought* is still used, it necessitates definition. A typical traditional murder statute, such as California's, requires malice aforethought. Malice may be expressed or implied, which may be distinguished as follows:

> It is expressed when there is manifested a deliberate intention unlawfully to take away the life of a fellow creature. It is implied, when no considerable provocation appears, or when the circumstances attending the killing show an abandoned and malignant heart.[36]

Defendants who claim that, because they had no malice toward anyone in the area, they should not be charged with murder when they fired into a crowd at a shopping center will find judges are unsympathetic to their claims. Malice may be inferred from these facts. More specifically, "Malice aforethought may be inferred from the intentional use of a deadly weapon in a deadly and dangerous manner."[37]

Some jurisdictions have abandoned the malice aforethought requirement in favor of using categories to define the various types of murder in terms of the type of mental element or intent involved. They may use the term *malice aforethought,* however, to distinguish between first- and second-degree murder. Other jurisdictions avoid the use of this confusing terminology and pattern their definitions after the Model Penal Code.

The Model Penal Code Definition of Murder

Under the Model Penal Code, criminal homicide is *murder,* a first-degree felony, when

1. it is committed purposely or knowingly; or
2. it is committed recklessly under circumstances manifesting extreme indifference to the value of human life. Such recklessness and indifference are presumed if the actor is engaged or is an accomplice in the commission of, or an attempt to commit, or flight after committing or attempting to commit robbery, rape or deviate sexual intercourse by force or threat of force, arson, burglary, kidnapping, or felonious escape.[38]

Types of Murder

Jurisdictions may vary significantly in the ways in which murder is categorized. A few categories are distinguished here.

Intent to Kill

The most common murders involve the intent to kill. If there are no mitigating circumstances to reduce the charge to manslaughter and if the killing is not excusable or justifiable, the defendant may be convicted of murder. Intent-to-kill murders do not require acts; omissions are sufficient, provided there is a legal duty to act. The intent to kill may be shown when the killing takes place under circumstances that would likely result in a death, as well as in those rare cases in which the defendant articulates an intent to kill.

The intentional (as contrasted to negligent) use of a deadly weapon may be used as evidence from which an inference of intent to kill may be made, although the defendant may refute that inference. The intent to kill must be shown. It is possible that a person might intend to shoot at another person with the intention of scaring, not killing. The real intent, of course, may not be known. The jury must infer intent or lack of intent from all of the facts presented as evidence.

Although historically the intent to kill had to be premeditated, premeditation is no longer required. It is sufficient for this type of murder to show an unpremeditated intent to kill.

INTENT TO INFLICT GREAT BODILY HARM

Death that results from serious bodily injuries may be murder when it can be shown that the defendant intended to inflict serious bodily injury, even though the defendant did not intend to inflict death. Of course, in addition to proving intent, the prosecutor must prove an intent to inflict *great bodily harm*. That phrase means harm greater than plain bodily injury (which must be interpreted) but less than death to prevent murder convictions when death occurs from simple injury. In the language of an early American case, "Every assault involves bodily harm. But any doctrine which would hold every assailant as a murderer where death follows his act would be barbarous and unreasonable."[39] In this case, however, a manslaughter charge might be appropriate.

DEPRAVED HEART

Depraved heart murders are killings resulting from the extremely reckless conduct of the defendant. This type of murder is said to be the result of a depraved mind, an abandoned and malignant heart, or wickedness. The Model Penal Code definition categorizes as murder a killing that is committed recklessly or "under circumstances manifesting extreme indifference to the value of human life." The code presumes that such recklessness and indifference exist when a killing results from the commission of another felony. But other facts could provide sufficient evidence from which a jury could find the requisite *mens rea*.

For depraved heart murder, the defendant must create the risk, but courts differ in their holdings concerning whether the defendant must be aware of the risk (the subjective test) or whether it is sufficient that a reasonable person would have been aware of the risk (the objective test). The risk must be greater than that required in negligence cases, but drawing the line between a great risk sufficient for murder and one that permits only negligence is a matter of degree.

The Model Penal Code requires "circumstances manifesting extreme indifference to the value of human life." The firing of a loaded gun into an occupied automobile that results in death to one or more persons is an example of creating a risk that exhibits extreme indifference to the value of human life.[40]

Intent to Commit a Felony

Felony murder refers to an unintended death resulting from the commission of a felony. Under the English common law, such deaths were considered murders; but over the years the felony murder doctrine developed by statute, and it differs among the jurisdictions. Some limit felony murder to deaths resulting from the more serious felonies—armed robbery, rape, or arson—or they state that the doctrine is limited to "inherently dangerous felonies." Others limit the time period involved; some are more restrictive on legal cause. Others require that the killing be independent of the felony. Focus 5.3 gives examples of felony murders.

There is considerable debate on the felony murder rule.[41] The doctrine may have made sense under the common law, when all felonies were punishable by death. Then it made little difference whether the defendant was convicted of murder or of another felony. Today, because capital punishment may be imposed only in murder cases and because some states consider felony murder a capital offense, it is argued that it is unconstitutional to impose the death penalty for those who were involved in the felony but did not commit the killing.

The Supreme Court appeared to agree with this position in 1982. The Court held that it was unconstitutional to impose the death penalty on a defendant who drove the getaway car in an armed robbery in which his cohorts killed the robbery victims. In *Enmund* v. *Florida,* the Court ruled that it would be cruel and unusual punishment to impose the death penalty on one "who aids and abets a felony in the course of which a murder is committed by others but who does not himself kill, attempt to kill, or intend that a killing take place or that lethal force will be employed."[42] But in 1987, in *Tison* v. *Arizona,* the Court held that under some circumstances it is permissible to impose the death penalty in felony murder cases. The details of that case are included in Focus 5.3.[43]

Causation may be difficult in felony murder cases as in this instance. A defendant raped and severely beat an eighty-five-year-old woman, who was moved to a nursing home after the attack. She was so depressed that she would not eat. She could not be fed through a nasal tube because of her facial injuries. When nurses were trying to feed her, she died of asphyxiation because, due to a broken rib that limited lung capacity, she was unable to expel food aspirated into her trachea. The defendant was convicted of murder. Would you uphold that conviction?

If the woman had died during the raping and beating, the defendant could be charged with murder. But was her death by asphyxiation a reasonably foreseeable result of his criminal act? The court said yes, that even though an intervening event may relieve a defendant of murder after the commission of another felony, in this case the defendant's criminal acts set in motion a series of events that caused the victim's death. Thus, his murder conviction was proper.[44]

Several recent felony murder cases are illustrative of the developments in the law of felony murder. In 1990, the New Mexico Supreme Court held that kidnapping is an inherently dangerous crime on which felony murder may be based.[45] In 1989, the California Supreme Court held that supplying

FOCUS 5.3   Felony Murder Cases

One spring morning in 1977, William Henry Jackson and James Wells, Jr., set out to rob a jewelry store in Baltimore, Maryland. Apparently the plan was to take as much jewelry as possible and to get away; there were to be no killings.

Acting on a tip, police surrounded Jackson and Wells in the store. In a desperate attempt to escape, the two robbers took the owners hostage. Using them as shields, Jackson and Wells escaped temporarily when they commandeered a police car. A lengthy car chase ended in a hail of gunfire at a police roadblock. During the shoot-out one of the owners was killed accidentally by police gunfire.

Jackson and Wells were convicted of first-degree murder under the Maryland felony murder statute. The Court of Appeals of Maryland, in affirming the conviction, found that the acts of Jackson and Wells "established such a causal relationship with respect to the death as to make them criminally liable therefor."[1]

This case contrasts with the decision reached by the California Supreme Court in *People* v. *Phillips*. In *Phillips*, the defendant, a chiropractor, persuaded parents to remove their daughter from a hospital where she was scheduled to undergo cancer surgery. He assured them he could cure her without surgery. After the daughter died, the state charged the chiropractor, who had received $500 in compensation, with felony grand theft and felony murder. The California Supreme Court struck down the defendant's conviction for second-degree murder, holding that grand theft was not an inherently dan-gerous crime and therefore could not support a conviction for felony murder.[2]

In *Tison* v. *Arizona*, a felony murder case decided by the U.S. Supreme Court, two brothers helped free their father and another convict from prison. When the car broke down, one of the brothers stopped another car. Both brothers watched and did nothing to stop their father from killing the four passengers, all of one family. All were convicted of capital murder and sentenced to the death penalty. The Tison brothers appealed to the U.S. Supreme Court, claiming that their participation in the murders was so minor that the imposition of the death penalty would not serve its purposes of retribution and deterrence. The Supreme Court responded that the brothers' participation was "anything but minor" but that even if a defendant's participation in a crime is minor and his mental state is one of "reckless indifference," the death penalty is not precluded.[3]

In *Enmund* v. *Florida*, the Supreme Court considered a case with facts similar to those in *Tison*. In *Enmund*, the petitioner received the death sentence despite the fact that he had done nothing more than drive a getaway car. The lower court held that it was irrelevant to this case that when the killings took place the petitioner was not present; nor did he anticipate or intend the killings. The Supreme Court reversed the lower court, holding that the death penalty should be imposed only in situations where the defendant "intended, contemplated or anticipated that lethal force would or might be used or that life would or might be taken in accomplishing the underlying felony."[4]

The differences in *Tison* and *Enmund* may be explained by a closer examination of the facts in the two cases. In *Tison*, the defendant looked on while his father murdered the victims, whereas in *Enmund*, the defendant sat in a car alongside the road unaware that the victims were being executed. In *Enmund*, the defendant's involvement in the murder was too remote.

In 1993 a Florida man was found guilty of felony murder after an elderly victim died three weeks after he grabbed her purse. Jonathan Parker faced life in prison with no chance of parole for twenty-five years for the murder charge and up to thirty years on the robbery charge. Experts testified that the seventy-year-old woman died of a brain hemorrhage resulting from a burst aneurysm that could have been the result of increased blood pressure due to the robbery.[5]

The parents of a two-year-old boy who was shot to death during the rob-

bery of a drug dealer were charged with second-degree felony murder under Florida law. The parents robbed a drug dealer of crack cocaine. As they sped away friends of the drug dealer fired shots at their car. The child was killed when a bullet that ricocheted from a taillight through a hole in the boy's car seat and struck him in the head as he slept. The couple fabricated a story for police, but later the father confessed to the facts. He told detectives, "I have a conscience . . . . I know what happened was wrong . . . . I don't want to live a lie."[6]

[1] Jackson v. State, 408 A.2d 711 (Md. 1979).
[2] People v. Phillips, 414 P.2d 353 (Cal. 1966).
[3] Tison v. Arizona, 481 U.S. 137 (1987), *reh'g. denied*, 482 U. S. 921 (1987).
[4] Enmund v. Florida, 458 U.S. 782 (1982).
[5] "Man Found Guilty in Death After Purse Snatching," *Tallahassee Democrat* (3 April 1993), p. 14B.
[6] "Parents Charged After Son's Death During Robbery," *Tallahassee Democrat* (10 December 1992), p. 3B. The Florida statute is found in Fla. Stat., Section 782.04 (1994).

cocaine to a user who dies after it is ingested may constitute the predicate crime for felony murder but only if the drug has a "high probability" of resulting in death. This position goes further in interpreting the "inherently dangerous to human life" approach which, in many jurisdictions, has looked only to the inherent nature of the predicate crime—thus, rape and kidnapping are inherently dangerous crimes. Supplying cocaine may not always be inherently dangerous, but under some circumstances, it may fall within this traditional category.[46]

Degrees of Murder

Although the common law had no degrees of murder, most modern statutes divide murder into at least two categories in order to assess different penalties. For instance, capital punishment (where legally available) is limited to the most heinous murders. *First-degree murder* includes deliberate, premeditated, intent-to-kill murders as well as felony murders committed during the commission of enumerated felonies such as rape, arson, robbery, or kidnapping. The enumerated felonies differ from jurisdiction to jurisdiction.

Some states include as first-degree murder those committed by use of poison, lying in wait, or bombing. More recently, some have included murders that involve torture. For example, California defines first-degree murder as "all murder which is perpetrated by means of a destructive device or explosive, knowing use of ammunition designed primarily to penetrate metal or armor, poison, lying in wait, torture, or by any other kind of willful, deliberate, and premeditated killing . . . ."[47]

One of the key elements of first-degree murder is **premeditation,** or thought about in advance. The time required for premeditation may be short, and courts differ on their interpretation of this requirement. This brief excerpt from a recent Arizona case illustrates the issue. Defendant Guerra was convicted of premeditated first-degree murder. The jury instruction included in this excerpt gives one approach to defining *premeditation.*[48]

State v. *Guerra*

According to Guerra's own testimony, he went to the alley armed with a mace and a hunting knife, dressed in camouflage clothing, and planning to do some "pranks." While there, he overheard and witnessed the confrontation between McMahon and Cox. Aware of the volatile situation [based on previous confrontations about which Guerra had knowledge], Guerra, carrying his "perpetrator" and knife, walked a considerable distance down the alley to confront McMahon. [Guerra stabbed McMahon to death.] We believe this provides substantial evidence to support a guilty verdict on premeditated murder. A reasonable mind could find that Guerra, even if he did not premeditate a murder before he went to the alley, had sufficient time to reflect and premeditate a murder after McMahon confronted Cox.

Premeditation requires a length of time to permit reflection. The trial judge instructed the jury as follows:

Premeditation means that the defendant's intention or knowledge existed before the killing long enough to permit reflection.

The time for reflection need not be prolonged and there need be no appreciable space of time between the intention to kill unlawfully and the act of killing.

It may be as instantaneous as the successive thoughts of the human mind, however it must be longer than the time required to form the intent or knowledge that such conduct will cause death.

An act is not done with premeditation if it is the instant effect of a sudden quarrel or heat of passion.

Generally *second-degree murder* is defined as all murders not included in first-degree murder, which includes intent-to-kill murders that are not deliberate or premeditated, felony murders that are not considered first-degree murders (such as killings committed during larceny-theft), depraved heart murders, and intent-to-inflict-serious-bodily-harm murders, whether or not those are premeditated and deliberate.

The difficulty of distinguishing between first- and second-degree murder is illustrated by the excerpt from *State* v. *Bingham,* in which the court discusses the concept of premeditation.[49]

State v. Bingham

We are asked to decide whether the time to effect death by manual strangulation is alone sufficient to support a finding of premeditation in the absence of any other evidence supporting such a finding . . . .

[The victim, a retarded adult, was last seen with the defendant. Her body was found three days later. She had been raped and strangled. The defendant was convicted of aggravated first-degree murder, with rape considered the aggravating circumstance. The defendant agreed that a murder conviction was appropriate but argued on appeal that it should have been second-degree, not first-degree, murder, since he lacked premeditation. The appellate court agreed and reversed the first-degree murder conviction and remanded the case for appropriate sentencing for second-degree murder.]

Premeditation is a separate and distinct element of first-degree murder. It involves the mental process of thinking over beforehand, deliberation, reflection, weighing or reasoning for a period of time, however short, after which the intent to kill is formed. The time required for manual strangulation [3 to 5 minutes in this case] is sufficient to permit deliberation. However, time alone is not enough. The evidence must be sufficient to support the inference that the defendant not only had the time to deliberate but that he actually did so. To require anything less would permit a jury to focus on the method of killing to the exclusion of the mental process involved in the separate element of premeditation . . . .

Unless evidence of both time for and fact of deliberation are required, premeditation could be inferred in any case where the means of effecting death requires more than a moment in time. For all practical purposes it would merge with intent; proof of intent would become proof of premeditation. However, the two elements are separate. Premeditation cannot be inferred from intent.

Premeditation can be proved by direct evidence [evidence offered by an eyewitness who testifies to what he or she saw, heard, tasted, smelled, or touched; any other evidence that directly shows the existence of a disputed fact and therefore requires no inferences], or it can be proved by circumstantial evidence [evidence that may be inferred from a fact or a series of facts] where the inferences drawn by the jury are reasonable and the evidence supporting the jury's findings is substantial. There was no such evidence here, either direct or circumstantial.

Lesser Included Offenses

The court in *State* v. *Bingham* held that the defendant could be sentenced for second-degree murder even though his conviction for first-degree murder was overturned. This was because the jury had been instructed on **lesser included offenses**—offenses that have some though not all of the elements of the offense charged. All of the elements of the lesser offense are required for the charged offense. All of the elements required for conviction of second-degree murder are included within those of first-degree; but premeditation is not required for second-degree murder. Thus, the lack of evidence for that element, although precluding a conviction for first-degree murder, does not preclude a finding of second-degree murder.

When defendants are charged with murder, it is possible to convict them of the lesser included offense of manslaughter, provided the jury has been instructed properly on that issue. The controversial Howard Beach trial in New York City is an example, as indicated in Focus 5.4. Manslaughter is discussed later in this chapter.

Mercy Killing—An Exception or Murder?

In 1987, CBS aired the movie *Mercy or Murder?*, about Roswell Gilbert, who killed his ailing wife on 4 March 1985. Gilbert's wife of fifty-one years, who was suffering from Alzheimer's disease and osteoporosis, had begged him to take her life. Gilbert was convicted of first-degree murder and given a life sentence. His conviction was upheld by the Florida Supreme Court. In 1990, Florida's governor commuted that sentence after a plea from many to release Gilbert, who was very ill. Upon his release, Gilbert admitted that his act was wrong and that he was sorry. "I tried to help her as much as I could. The best word to use is desperation." In late 1993, as Gilbert was losing weight and strength to cancer, he stated, "I have no regrets. I wouldn't have done anything differently." He reflected on the half-century he and his wife shared together, not on her death.[50] Gilbert died in September 1994.

In 1988, also in Florida, Dr. Peter Rosier was acquitted of murder after he injected his wife with morphine. Mrs. Rosier had terminal cancer and had failed in an attempted suicide. Her stepfather testified under immunity from prosecution that he also smothered her. The Rosier case may be distinguished from the Gilbert case in that Rosier's wife had attempted suicide. Should that make a difference in whether the defendant-spouse is convicted of murder or a lesser charge or acquitted?

Another Florida case involves a father who, after drinking heavily, killed his brain-damaged and hospitalized two-and-one-half-year-old daughter. Charles Griffith is serving a twenty-five-year-to-life sentence for murder. He says that what he considers a mercy killing will haunt him the rest of his life. His daughter was normal until a freak accident that cut off oxygen to her brain. She had climbed on a recliner chair while visiting her grandmother and the recliner clamped onto her neck. In his words, she was "the joy of my life." Griffith applied for clemency in 1992 but withdrew his application in 1993 after his ex-wife testified against him, bashing his character and claiming that he had not been rehabilitated.[51]

FOCUS 5.4 Murder or Manslaughter: The Howard Beach Case

The Howard Beach murder trial involved white teenage defendants from Howard Beach, a predominantly white neighborhood in Queens, New York, who were charged with murder in the death of an African-American youth killed by a car after the four defendants and eight other white youths chased him out of their neighborhood. The jury refused to convict the defendants of murder but did return manslaughter and assault verdicts for three defendants. One defendant was acquitted.

One of the defendants was sentenced to the maximum term, ten to thirty years in prison, for his role in the death of one victim and the vicious beating of another. The trial judge denounced Jon Lester's actions as "savage," the result of a racial attack. The judge criticized the 1,500 people who wrote letters urging leniency in the Howard Beach case. He received only two letters asking that he not be lenient. One was from the mayor, who urged the maximum penalty, as did the prosecutor.[1] A second defendant, Scott Kern, was sentenced to six to eighteen years, while a third, Jason Ladone, was sentenced to five to fifteen years in prison. Ladone received the lightest sentence because he was repentant, apologizing in court to the dead victim's mother. Ladone and Kern were free on bail for two years while their cases were appealed. In April 1990, after their convictions were affirmed, they surrendered to begin their prison sentences.[2]

The Howard Beach incident began when Michael Griffith, an African American, and two of his African-American friends wandered into the Howard Beach neighborhood after their car broke down. They were confronted by about a dozen white youths who shouted racial epithets and waved a baseball bat and tree limbs. When Griffith, twenty-three, ran from his attackers he was killed by a car. The defense argued that his death was an accident.

When the not-guilty verdict in the case of one defendant was read, spectators in the courtroom shouted, "Murderers! Murderers!" A New York state appeals court upheld the convictions of the other three and refused a request to reduce the prison terms, describing as "vicious and wanton" the threats and beatings that resulted in the death of one and the "savage beating" of another. The court rejected the defense argument that Griffith's death did not constitute manslaughter because the defendants could not foresee that he would flee from the beatings and be struck by a car. On appeal to New York's highest court, the decision on the lower appellate court was affirmed.[3]

In December 1992 a parole was granted to Ladone despite the fact that he had served less than three years of his five-year maximum sentence. Although Ladone was sentenced in 1988, he was free on bail pending his appeal and did not begin serving time until April 1990.[4]

[1.] "Defendant Gets Maximum Term in Racial Attack," *New York Times* (23 January 1988), p. 1.

2. "Three in Howard Beach Attack Are Guilty of Manslaughter," *New York Times* (22 December 1987), p. 1; "Howard Beach Sentence Is Five to Fifteen Years," *New York Times* (12 February 1988), p. 15.
3. People v. Kern, 554 N.E.2d 1235 (N.Y.App. 1990). The facts and the trial in this case are

discussed in Charles J. Hynes and Bob Drugy, *Incident at Howard Beach: The Case for Murder* (New York: G.P. Putnam's Sons, 1990).
4. "State to Study Parole Decree In Racial Case," *New York Times* (12 December 1992), p. 11.

These three cases, all from one state, illustrate some ways in which mercy killing may be processed: life sentence; long prison term; or acquittal. Another approach is to convict but assess a light penalty. For example, a sixty-nine-year-old Texan who said he killed his terminally ill older brother as an act of compassion was given a ten-year sentence consisting of probation and ten hours a week of work at a home for the elderly. He could have been sentenced to life in prison.[52]

Another approach is for grand juries to refuse to return indictments or for prosecutors to refuse to prosecute. In June 1993 Chicago prosecutors announced that they would drop the murder charge against Walter Fick, seventy-eight, who used a hammer to kill his cancer-stricken wife of fifty years. Fick said he could no longer stand to see his wife suffer from brain cancer.[53]

LEGALIZATION OF EUTHANASIA: DOCTOR-ASSISTED SUICIDE

It is obvious that society does not agree on how mercy killings should be handled despite the fact that, in most cases, the state can prove the elements required for a first-degree murder conviction. One solution is to legalize euthanasia at least in some form. Doctor-assisted suicide is the most acceptable form. A 1991 survey indicated that two out of three Americans favored doctor-assisted suicide and euthanasia for terminally ill patients who requested it.[54] But that same year voters in Washington state rejected legal euthanasia.[55]

In 1993 the Netherlands became the first country in the Western world to enact legislation providing for doctor-assisted suicides. The legislation retains criminal penalties for euthanasia but exempts doctors who follow a narrowly defined set of guidelines. Doctors are exempt only if their patients are terminally ill, have made many requests to die, can think for themselves, and are in intolerable pain. Doctors who take the lives of mentally ill persons and severely deformed babies remain subject to prosecution. In April 1993, Dutch officials brought charges against a psychiatrist who had prescribed lethal drugs for a woman who said she wanted to die because her marriage had failed and her two children had died traumatic deaths. In all probability this case would not meet the requirements of the new statute even if it had been in effect at the time. The psychiatrist faces a maximum of three years in prison if convicted.[56]

Doctor-assisted suicide has gained national attention in recent years in the United States primarily because of the actions of Michigan's Dr. Jack Kevorkian, who has assisted several terminally ill patients to terminate their lives. Focus 5.5 contains a discussion of Dr. Kevorkian. In late 1992,

Dr. Jack Kevorkian, who assisted numerous people with suicide, was acquitted of violating the statute Michigan legislators enacted to prevent his conducting physician-assisted suicides.

shortly after California voters rejected a provision that would have provided legal protection to doctors who assist terminally ill patients to die, three physicians urged a new public policy to permit such actions. One of those doctors, Dr. Timothy E. Quill, admitted that he prescribed a lethal dose of barbiturates to a cancer patient who had "rejected the arduous treatment that would have given her a one-in-four chance of survival." Dr. Quill had known the patient for years; she was mentally alert; she wished to die. If convicted, the doctor could have been sentenced to from five to fifteen years in prison. The grand jury refused to indict.[57] Society continues to wrestle with the issue of whether doctor-assisted suicide is murder, some other serious crime, or an act of mercy.

Manslaughter

A second category of homicide is **manslaughter,** which traditionally has been defined as an unlawful killing without malice aforethought. Manslaughter has been described as constituting "a sort of catch-all category which includes homicides which are not bad enough to be murder but which are too bad to be no crime whatever."[58] Under the common law, manslaughter was divided into two types, involuntary and voluntary, for the purpose of distinguishing different kinds of conduct but not for the purposes of differential punishment. Some jurisdictions utilize these categories; others define manslaughter in terms of degrees. Other jurdisictions follow the modern trend and the Model Penal Code approach of only one category: manslaughter, which the M.P.C. defines as a homicide that otherwise would be murder except for the fact that it was "committed under

FOCUS 5.5 Doctor-Assisted Suicide: Mercy or Murder?

In recent years national and international attention has been focused on Michigan doctor Dr. Jack Kevorkian (also known as Dr. Death), a retired pathologist who has assisted several terminally ill patients to commit suicide. In August 1993, after assisting his seventeenth patient, Dr. Kevorkian was charged with violating Michigan's new statute that prohibits physicians from assisting in suicides.

Michigan has tried for several years to stop Dr. Kevorkian. When he first began assisting people to end their lives, the state did not have a statute that covered his actions. He was charged with murder in several cases; those charges were dismissed after a judge ruled that the prosecution could not prove that the doctor tripped the machine that released the lethal doses that killed the two women for whose murders he was being charged. At best they could show that he assisted the women to commit suicide.[1]

A temporary Michigan provision prohibiting physician-assisted suicides for fifteen months while the issue is being studied, became law in March 1993. Conviction of the new measure may result in a four-year prison term. Dr. Kevorkian was the first person charged under the statute when he was charged in August 1993 with helping a man with Lou Gehrig's disease to commit suicide. According to Dr. Kevorkian's attorney, "This [the criminal charge] is what we asked for. When a law mandates suffering, such as this law, it must be disobeyed." The prosecutor who filed the charges is in sympathy with the practice but says the law must be upheld.[2]

Kevorkian was arrested and jailed; he refused to post bond, but an anonymous donor did so for him. Later he was arrested and jailed again for assisting another suicide. He went on a hunger strike, refusing to eat solid food. In December 1993 he was taken to the emergency room after suffering chest pains. Doctors said he might have suffered a mild heart attack but that the sixty-five-year-old Kevorkian was not in imminent danger. The doctor was returned to jail, but he was released shortly thereafter. Kevorkian had vowed to remain on his hunger strike until the Michigan law banning doctor-assisted suicide was declared unconstitutional. On 13 December 1993 that law was ruled unconstitutional by Judge Richard Kaufman of the Wayne County Circuit Court.[3]

In subsequent actions, two other judges declared the Michigan statute unconstitutional. In late January 1994 a Michigan judge who so ruled dropped two of the three charges against Dr. Kevorkian and freed him from house arrest. In February another judge, stating that he was not bound by the rulings of other judges that the state's physician-assisted law is unconstitutional, refused to drop the third charge and set a trial date for 19 April 1994. Kevorkian's response was that a trial would be a farce. "Nobody's going to trample my rights . . . . This trial is a touch of the Inquisition."[4]

In March 1994 Kevorkian indicated that he would break his promise that was a condition of release from jail: that he would not assist in any more suicides. He announced that if no other doctor would assist a patient whom he had counseled for two years and who was in severe pain and wished to die, he would assist her with her suicide. Later that month several doctors indicated that they would help ease the woman's severe pain.[5] Subsequently Kevorkian was acquitted, and Michigan courts continue to argue about the constitutionality of the state's ban on physician-assisted suicide. Details of those events are discussed in Chapter 2.

In 1991 a California man who traveled to Michigan to help his terminally ill wife take her own life, with the assistance of Dr. Kevorkian, was charged with murder for his role in his wife's death. Her daughter who accompanied them was not charged.

The attorney for Bertram Harper told the jury, "This is no crime of violence . . . . This is an act of love." After two hours of deliberation the jury acquitted the defendant.[6]

[1] "Murder Charges Against Kevorkian Are Dismissed," *New York Times* (22 July 1992), p. 6.
[2] "As He Hoped, Kevorkian Is Charged in a Suicide," *New York Times* (18 August 1993), p. 7.
[3] "Kevorkian Is Taken To Emergency Room with Pains in Chest," *New York Times* (13 December 1993), p. 11C.
[4] "Judge Orders Kevorkian To Be Tried In Assisted Suicide," *Los Angeles Times* (19 February 1994), p. 16.
[5] "Pain-Racked Patient Appeals for an 'Out,'" *Houston Chronicle* (29 March 1994), p. 4; "Doctors Offer to Aid Kevorkian Patient," *St. Petersburg Times* (30 March 1994), p. 10.
[6] "Man Cleared of Murder In Aiding Wife's Suicide," *New York Times* (11 May 1991), p. 8.

the influence of extreme mental or emotional disturbance for which there is reasonable explanation or excuse" or is committed recklessly.[59] The types of manslaughter are examined more closely.

Voluntary Manslaughter

An unlawful killing that does not involve malice aforethought but that occurs after adequate provocation may be classified as **voluntary manslaughter**. The facts must be examined carefully to determine whether they constitute a type of *murder* (such as depraved heart murder) or *voluntary manslaughter*. To constitute voluntary manslaughter, the killing must occur after such provocation by the victim that even reasonable people could be expected to react violently. It is required also that the particular defendant was in fact provoked. Further, it must be shown that a reasonable person would not have cooled off between the time of the provocation and the killing, and that the defendant in fact did not cool off.

Heat-of-Passion Manslaughter

A homicide of this type may be called a *heat-of-passion-homicide* or *heat-of-passion-voluntary manslaughter*. *Heat of passion* was the term used under the common law (and followed by some states) to describe this type of voluntary manslaughter. The Model Penal Code's use of "extreme mental or emotional disturbance" is utilized as well. A Utah case, *State v. Standiford*, illustrates a modern reaction to these concepts. Standiford was convicted of second-degree murder after he killed the victim who he "claimed came after him with a gun, screaming in Japanese, and grabbed him. He [Standiford] seized the closest weapon, a kitchen knife, intending only to scare her, and since the threat of the knife did not stop her, he just started swinging the knife." Standiford appealed on several issues, including his argument that the trial court erred in refusing to give his requested heat-of-passion manslaughter instruction. In the full opinion, the appellate court criticizes the common law term *malice aforethought*, which it describes as "a confusing carry-over from prior law [that] . . . can lead to confusion, if not error [and that] should no longer be used." Other mental-state requirements should be used, and the excerpt here begins with a listing of the requirements for second-degree murder, indicating why these are preferable to the term *malice aforethought*. The court explains the concept of *heat-of-passion manslaughter* before upholding the trial court on its refusal to give a jury instruction on the latter.[60]

State v. Standiford

[T]he culpable mental states included in the second degree murder statute are (1) an intent to kill, (2) an intent to inflict serious bodily harm, (3) conduct knowingly engaged in and evidencing a depraved indifference to human life, and (4) intent to commit a felony other than murder.

These terms are comparable to the old malice aforethought, but are much more precise and less confusing. The statute treats these forms of homicide as having similar culpability. Second degree murder is based on a very high degree of moral culpability. That culpability arises either from an actual intent to kill or from a mental state that is essentially equivalent thereto—such as intending grievous bodily injury and knowingly creating a very high risk of death. The risk of death in the latter two instances must be so great as to evidence such an indifference to life as to be tantamount to that evidenced by an intent to kill. In contrast, the felony-murder provision of the second-degree murder statute is something of an exception to the above principle, as it does not require an intent to kill or any similar mental state . . . .

Defendant also challenges the trial court's refusal to give his requested heat-of-passion manslaughter instruction. The common law, and our previous law, defined manslaughter, *inter alia*, as a killing committed without malice, and the term *without malice* meant a homicide committed either (1) in the "heat of passion" for which there was an adequate provocation, or (2) by an unduly dangerous or otherwise unlawful act. Instead of incorporating the "heat of passion" standard, the current criminal code redefined that type of manslaughter to describe the conduct of one who "causes the death of another under the influence of extreme emotional disturbance for which there is a reasonable explanation or excuse.". . . This definition reformulates and enlarges the heat-of-passion standard to include any extreme emotional disturbance based on a reasonable excuse or explanation that mitigates the blameworthiness of the homicide.

[The court held that Standiford's contention that this killing fell within the "extreme emotional disturbance" category was "without merit."]

MANSLAUGHTER IN DOMESTIC RELATIONS

The difficulty of drawing the line between murder and voluntary manslaughter is illustrated by the approach taken by the common law and many modern statutes to a killing by a husband who caught his wife engaged in the act of adultery. It was assumed that seeing his wife in such a compromising situation was sufficient provocation for killing the lover or the wife.[61] Some, but fewer, jurisdictions extended this rule to women who caught their husbands in the act of adultery and killed the husband or his lover.[62] Thus, most jurisdictions considered it murder if a woman killed her husband or his lover caught in the act of adultery, as compared to men who killed under similar circumstances. Given the way the law differented between women and men, this is not surprising. A few jurisdictions considered it permissible for a man who caught his wife committing adultery to kill her or her lover and not be considered criminally liable at all. The killing was understandable and excusable. This is no longer the case, but the changes have been recent, as noted by a 1977 decision stating that "any idea that a spouse is ever justified in taking the life of another—adulterous spouse or illicit lover—to prevent adultery is uncivilized."[63]

Some jurisdictions that treated such homicides as manslaughter rather than murder (or justifiable homicide) required that the exception was appropriate only when the offended spouse caught the spouse and his or her lover in the adulterous act and the killing followed immediately. Other jurisdictions extended the concept of voluntary manslaughter to spousal killings that followed being told of adultery, even if that report were erroneous but reasonable.[64] In 1989 the Illinois Supreme Court held that a confession of adultery is not sufficient to reduce a killing from murder to manslaughter. In *People* v. *Chevalier*, the court refused to reverse the convictions in two cases in which a spouse killed an adulterous spouse. In one case, the defendant killed his wife after she jeered at his sexual abilities and confessed that she had committed adultery; in the other, the defendant killed his wife after she confessed to having committed adultery in their bed. The court was unwilling to extend homicide from murder to manslaughter under these facts.[65]

Despite the demise of adultery as a condition for reducing murder to manslaughter, other circumstances may warrant a manslaughter rather than a murder charge. The California code defines *voluntary manslaughter* as manslaughter (an "unlawful killing of a human being without malice . . .)

committed "upon a sudden quarrel or heat of passion."[66] Words, fights, and other circumstances that would lead a reasonable person to kill may suffice, depending on the jurisdiction's statutes and case law. It is important to understand that the law is not saying that it is permissible to kill under any of these circumstances as it is permissible to kill in self-defense, to protect the life of another, and under other circumstances. Manslaughter statutes recognized that it is reasonable to be provoked to kill under circumstances that do not warrant justifiable or excusable homicide. The person who kills is criminally liable but not to the extent of murder. The concept of reasonableness is crucial in deciding whether a killing constitutes murder or manslaughter.

THE REASONABLE PERSON STANDARD

The reasonable person standard, or objective standard, common to tort law, is critical in deciding whether a homicide constitutes voluntary manslaughter or murder. Two English cases illustrate the point. In the first case an impotent defendant who killed a prostitute when she laughed at his unsuccessful attempts to have sexual intercourse with her argued unsuccessfully that his behavior should be measured by what a reasonable impotent man would do. The House of Lords held that the behavior of a reasonable person, not a reasonable person with the peculiar characteristics of the defendant, is the test. It upheld the jury's verdict for murder, despite the defendant's argument that, had the jurors been instructed that the standard is how a reasonable impotent man would react to such provocation, they might have returned a verdict of manslaughter.[67]

In 1978, however, the House of Lords reversed itself in a case involving a fifteen-year-old who killed the older man who sexually molested and then mocked him. The jury was instructed to view the defendant's behavior in terms of how a *reasonable adult* would act under the same or similar circumstances. The House of Lords ruled that the jury should have been instructed to consider how a *reasonable person of the same age* would have acted under the same or similar circumstances.[68]

The two English cases raise the issue of whether the reasonable person standard in a criminal case should be interpreted to mean that defendants should be viewed in terms of the reasonable person endowed with *all* of the defendant's characteristics. In tort cases, where the reasonable person standard is utilized most frequently, most courts do not interpret the standard in that manner, although age may be an included characteristic in the standard.

The reasonable person standard is important in manslaughter cases because the rationale behind the manslaughter (as opposed to murder) charge is that reasonable people, when sufficiently provoked, will react without thinking. If they kill, they should be responsible for the death, but not to the extent of murder.

In some manslaughter cases courts have held that provocation resulting from battery, adultery, mutual combat, assault, injury to third parties, illegal arrest, and fighting words constitutes adequate provocation to reduce murder charges to manslaughter. Various courts interpret these categories differently. Attempts have been made to define the relevant terms in the statutes. Two examples are noted. Do they make it clear to you which facts would fall within these definitions?

> *Heat of passion* . . . means that at the time of the act the reason is disturbed or obscured by passion to an extent which might [make] ordinary men of fair, average disposition liable to act irrationally without due deliberation or reflection, and from passion rather than judgment.
>
> [*Sudden provocation* was defined as:]
>
> [H]eat of passion will not avail unless upon sudden provocation. Sudden means happening without previous notice or with very brief notice; coming unexpectedly, precipitated, or unlooked for . . . . It is not every provocation, it is not every rage of passion that will reduce a killing from murder to manslaughter. The provocation must be of such a character and so close upon the act of killing, that for a moment a person could be considered as not being the master of his own understanding.[69]

Some jurisdictions have extended voluntary manslaughter beyond the heat-of-passion or extreme emotional problem situations. Most of these extensions have occurred by statute rather than by case law. Examples are situations in which defendants advance such defenses as self-defense, the right to prevent a felony, or acting under coercion or duress, but cannot prove all of the elements of the defense. In such cases, murder may be reduced to manslaughter.[70]

Involuntary Manslaughter

Although the Model Penal Code does not use the term ***involuntary manslaughter,*** its category of manslaughter as a killing that is committed recklessly coincides with the general category of involuntary manslaughter. The killing is not intended; generally it applies when a defendant is engaged in a criminal act that is not a felony. For example, a California man was found guilty of involuntary manslaughter and of owning a mischievous animal, cultivating marijuana, and keeping a fighting dog after one of his pit bulls killed a two-year-old boy.[71]

The California Penal Code defines *involuntary manslaughter* as "the unlawful killing of a human being without malice . . . in the commission of an unlawful act, not amounting to felony, or in the commission of a lawful act which might produce death, in an unlawful manner, or without due caution and circumspection." The provision excludes "acts committed in the driving of a vehicle," which is a separate type of manslaughter.[72]

MISDEMEANOR OR NEGLIGENT MANSLAUGHTER

In some jurisdictions involuntary manslaughter is called *misdemeanor manslaughter.* Involuntary manslaughter also may include deaths that occur as the result of criminal negligence. In the "Twilight Zone" case in which a movie director and four other people were charged with involuntary manslaughter for the deaths of actor Vic Morrow and two children during the filming of a movie, the jury acquitted the defendants. The jury decided that the deaths were accidents; they did not believe that the prosecution's evidence supported the wanton and reckless conduct that was required to support a conviction for involuntary manslaughter based on criminal negligence.

Likewise, in the 1993 retrial of Miami police officer William Lozano, the jury acquitted the defendant of two charges of manslaughter, finding that the officer acted reasonably in a situation that he believed was threatening to his life. An abbreviated statement of the facts in that case is reported in the following excerpt from the decision of the Court of Appeals of the First District of Florida upon granting a change of venue motion.[73]

State v. *Lozano*

This case serves to remind us that under our constitution, we are governed by rules that ensure a fair trial. The State of Florida petitions this court for a writ of certiorari to review a non-final order of the Circuit Court for Leon County which denied the defendant's motion for change of venue, a motion in which the State had joined. We grant the petition.

William Lozano is Hispanic and of Columbian descent. While on duty as a City of Miami police officer, he shot and killed the Black driver of a motorcycle who was attempting to avoid a stop for a traffic infraction. A passenger on the motorcycle, also a Black male, died from injuries from the resulting crash of the motorcycle. Serious civil disturbances immediately followed in Dade County.

Subsequently, Lozano was tried and convicted of two counts of manslaughter. On appeal, the District Court of Appeal for the Third District found that the trial court had committed reversible error when it denied the defendant's motion for change of venue. The defense had sought the change on the theory that jurors would be reluctant to vote for acquittal for fear of causing further violence in the community. The court reversed and remanded for a new trial in another venue.

[The court describes the series of changes of venue in this case, which took the trial from Miami to Orlando to Tallahassee to Orlando to Tallahassee. Some of the issues were technical procedural issues; the main issue involved race and ethnicity, with the trial judge having moved the trial from Orlando to Tallahassee on his own motion after the Los Angeles riots (following the state trial acquittal of four white police officers accused of beating Rodney King). In a subsequent federal trial two of the officers were found guilty of violating King's civil rights; they were sentenced to prison.] The Florida trial judge moved the Lozano trial to Tallahassee for the stated purpose of getting more blacks on the jury. On its appeal of that decision, the defense argued that it was inappropriate to consider the race of the victim without any consideration of the ethnicity of the defendant. Leon County, in which Tallahassee is located, has an Hispanic population of 2.4 percent, compared to 49.22 percent in Orange County, in which Orlando is located.] . . .

> We grant certiorari and quash the trial court's order of March 5, 1993, which denied the motion for change of venue. We find that the effect of this disposition is to void the order of May 6, 1992, which moved the trial from Orlando to Tallahassee, and to reinstate the April 2, 1992, order which set the trial in Orlando.

At his May 1993 retrial in Orlando, Lozano was acquitted of two charges of manslaughter. The State tried to convince the jury that Lozano had acted with a reckless disregard for human life when he shot the motorcyclist. After hearing the evidence presented by the prosecution, Lozano's lead attorney, Roy Black, rose and said, "Based on the lack of credible evidence in this case, we rest." The jury was not convinced beyond a reasonable doubt that Lozano's actions constituted manslaughter. Lozano had been sentenced to seven years in prison after his first trial, which resulted in two manslaughter convictions.

The Lozano case illustrates the difference between an accidental killing or a killing in self-defense, which does not result in criminal liability, and a killing resulting from a sincere but unreasonable act that resulted in death. The jury accepted the defense argument that Lozano acted in the belief that his life was in danger. Obviously not everyone agreed with that position, and that is typical in many killings, especially those in which a police officer is involved. It is important, however, to make the legal distinction between a killing that results in criminal liability and one that does not. Another example is the controversial Louisiana case, also decided in 1993.

In June 1993 a Louisiana homeowner was acquitted of manslaughter charges in the shooting death of a Japanese exchange student who came to his home the previous fall looking for a Halloween party. Rodney Peairs thought the young man was a burglar, and when the stranger failed to comply with his order to "freeze," Peairs fired a .44 Magnum and killed the suspect, who had not understood the order. He was at a wrong address, clearly in the wrong place at the wrong time.[74]

Vehicular and DUI Manslaughter

Another type of manslaughter is *vehicular manslaughter.* In California this category encompasses numerous types of vehicular homicides, including those caused by gross negligence.[75] Some states include within this category a killing that results from an accident while the driver is intoxicated. Some states, such as California, have a separate statutory provision for the crime of *gross vehicular manslaughter while intoxicated*, a felony punishable by imprisonment in the state prison for four, six, or ten years.[76]

Deaths that result from accidents occurring while defendants are under the influence of alcohol or drugs may be prosecuted as involuntary or vehicular manslaughter. Ricky Gates, the engineer of the Conrail locomotive that collided with an Amtrak passenger train on 4 January 1987, faced sixteen counts of manslaughter by locomotive, a misdemeanor. Gates pleaded guilty to one count of manslaughter in Amtrak's deadliest crash in history. The state agreed to drop the other fifteen charges, but the names of all the deceased were included in the one charge. The negotiated plea was finalized as jury selection was beginning for Gates' trial.

In 1992 Robert E. Ray was convicted of manslaughter in the deaths of five people who died as the result of a New York subway crash caused when Ray fell asleep at the controls. Ray had been drinking prior to the accident. The prosecutor argued for a conviction on second-degree murder, alleging that Ray's actions showed "depraved indifference" to the lives and welfare of others. The jury convicted him of second-degree manslaughter, with two jurors reporting to the press that they found his behavior showed a reckless disregard for others but did not reach the depraved indifference standard required for a second-degree murder conviction.[77]

FAILURE-TO-ACT MANSLAUGHTER

Manslaughter charges may be brought when failure to act is the crime. In 1989, the California Court of Appeals for the First District upheld a manslaughter conviction for a defendant who did not summon help for an obviously intoxicated guest in her home. This guest had been permitted to inject himself with heroin in the defendant's presence. The court ruled that under these circumstances, the hostess owed a duty to the guest; that duty was breached; and a manslaughter conviction was permissible. The defendant had met the victim at a bar, invited him to her home, given him a spoon, and let him use her bathroom for the injection. She knew that he intended to inject himself with the drug. After the victim emerged from the bathroom and collapsed on the floor and the defendant tried unsuccessfully to rouse him, she conferred with the bartender by phone and then returned to the bar.

The defendant's daughter returned home later that afternoon, found the unconscious guest, called the bar, and was told by her mother to drag him outside and hide him behind the shed so neighbors could not see him. The daughter and two friends did so. They checked on him that night and found that he still had a pulse and was snoring, but by the next morning he was dead. An autopsy indicated that the cause of death was morphine poisoning, resulting from the heroin he had injected. The defendant's argument that she did not cause the death because she did not cause his condition was unsuccessful. The court noted that the deceased was extremely drunk when the defendant took him from a public place to her home, a private place, in which only she could provide assistance. Thus, she owed him a legal duty and having breached that duty, was criminally liable for his death.[78]

ABOLITION OF INVOLUNTARY MANSLAUGHTER

In 1990 the Massachusetts Supreme Judicial Court abolished the common law crime of *involuntary act manslaughter* in a case involving the indictment of a defendant who sold heroin to a person who died after injecting herself with the heroin. The defendant knew that the victim could not handle the amount of heroin that he sold to her, that he had assisted her from overdosing on previous occasions, and that another person whom he knew had died under similar circumstances. The court argued that involuntary act manslaughter criminalizes without any reference to moral culpability and that to attempt to redefine the term would be even more confusing; thus, it should be abolished. The court concluded that henceforth, a person may be prosecuted for involuntary manslaughter only when causing an intentional death while engaging in wanton or reckless conduct or while committing a battery.[79]

Negligent Homicide

A third and final category of criminal homicide, as defined by the Model Penal Code, is negligent homicide. According to the Code, **negligent homicide** occurs when a criminal homicide is the result of negligence.[80] Negligent homicide, a third-degree felony, is less serious than manslaughter, although in some cases it is difficult to draw the line between the two categories. Jurisdictions do not agree on what is required.

In jurisdictions that do not have a vehicular manslaughter statute, deaths caused by negligent drivers might be prosecuted under a negligent homicide statute. If, however, the behavior of the driver is found to be reckless rather than merely negligent, the driver might be prosecuted under an involuntary manslaughter statute.

Other forms of negligence that lead to serious injury or death may be prosecuted as negligent homicides. For example, a Tennessee owner of two pit bulls that killed a woman was sentenced to two years in prison after his conviction for criminally negligent homicide.[81]

In cases involving negligent drivers, it is important to recall earlier discussions of *discretion* in the criminal justice system. Prosecutors have wide discretion in deciding whether to prosecute these cases. They may and frequently do decline to prosecute drivers whose negligence causes death to others when the drivers were neither speeding excessively nor driving under the influence of alcohol or drugs.

SUMMARY

Although the probability of victimization by violent crimes is less than the probability of victimization by property crimes, the fear of violent personal crimes leads many people to change their lifestyles, move to other locations, and remain locked in their homes at night. This chapter focuses on the violent acts of murder and manslaughter, two types of homicide.

Homicide is a general term, referring to killings that are justifiable or excusable, such as killings by police officers under some circumstances and killings by anyone when the use of deadly force is necessary for self-defense or the defense of others. The term applies also to killings that are not legally acceptable and thus may result in criminal liability.

Confusion over distinguishing among justifiable, excusable, and criminal homicides, the three categories of the common law, has led some jurisdictions to abandon those categories. The Model Penal Code divides homicides into three categories: murder, manslaughter, and negligent homicide. Some states follow this model; others retain the common law distinctions; some have a mixture of both or yet another version individually drafted.

Still, in such cases confusion may arise over deciding what is meant by *born alive* and what is meant by *death*, for criminal homicide must involve a person who was alive at the time the alleged criminal act occurred. These issues are particularly confusing with the advent of modern medicine, which prolongs life; the desire of some to be able to terminate (or have terminated) their lives; and the legalization of abortion.

Frequently causation is a difficult problem in homicide cases, especially when two or more acts may contribute to the victim's death. Some courts look to the *intent* of the offender; evidence of a criminal intent may be sufficient to establish criminal liability when actual causation is mixed. Some states require that the defendant's act must have been a *substantial factor* in the victim's death.

The difficulties of determining cause of death led the common law to adopt a *year-and-a-day* rule, meaning that no defendant could be held criminally liable for a death occurring after that time period. Modern science gives us greater accuracy and speed in determining the cause of death; thus, some states have abandoned the common law rule. Others, such as California, have retained the rule but extend it to a longer time period.

Distinguishing between murder and manslaughter may present problems in homicide prosecutions. Usually murder requires premeditation and malice aforethought, which may be expressed or implied from other facts. Manslaughter is an unlawful killing without malice. But the word *malice* is confusing too, because it does not necessarily mean hatred or ill will, but, rather, an evil motive. The Model Penal Code has abandoned this requirement and instead defines all homicides in terms of its four categories of culpability: purposely, knowingly, recklessly, or negligently.

Even in those states that have abolished the requirement of malice aforethought, the concept may be used to distinguish first-degree murder from lesser degrees of murder. In general, first-degree murder includes deliberate, premeditated, intent-to-kill murders as well as felony murders.

Second-degree murder may be defined in terms of "murder that is not first-degree." Included might be deaths that occur while an offender is engaged in another criminal act that is not included in the felony-murder category. Also included might be intent-to-kill murders that are not deliberate or premeditated, depraved heart murders, and-intent-to-inflict-serious-bodily-harm murders.

Second-degree murders may be difficult to distinguish from manslaughter, which may be divided into two categories. Voluntary manslaughter is a killing that would be murder except that it is committed under circumstances of extreme mental or emotional disturbance (or heat of passion); involuntary manslaughter is a criminal killing that is committed recklessly but unintentionally, usually during the commission of an unlawful act, such as driving while intoxicated. In addition, acts that do not reach the level of voluntary manslaughter may be called *misdemeanor manslaughter* or *vehicular manslaughter.*

The third category of criminal homicide, *negligent homicide,* includes deaths that result from negligence, although generally more than simple or ordinary negligence (running a stop sign by slowing down considerably but not completely stopping) is required.

This chapter focuses on only two of the most violent types of crime: murder and manslaughter, both homicides. It is not meant to be exhaustive in its discussion of those crimes. Both involve many legal fine points that are beyond the scope of this text. Nor is it meant to suggest that these crimes are more important or create more fear than other violent crimes. In many cases the emotional and psychological scars may be far greater for victims of less violent or even nonviolent crimes.

The next chapter focuses on assault and battery, rape, and other violent crimes, as well as less violent crimes, such as sex-related offenses, some of which involve consent and are considered by many people to be private matters that should be beyond the reach of the criminal law. Others involve the exploitation of others and engender little dispute when they are defined as crimes, especially when the victims are children.

STUDY QUESTIONS

1. Define *homicide* and distinguish *justifiable* and *excusable* from *criminal* homicide.
2. What are the three types of *criminal homicide?*
3. What is *infanticide,* and how is it related to modern criminal law? What is the meaning of *born alive?* How has its meaning changed in recent years?
4. What is the meaning of *person* in homicide statutes?
5. Define *death.*
6. What causation problems does homicide present?
7. What is the year-and-a-day rule? Why was it originally adopted? Why have some states abandoned it?
8. What is *corpus delicti?* How important is that concept today compared to the common law?
9. Distinguish between *murder* and *manslaughter.*
10. List and define the basic elements of murder.
11. What is meant by *malice aforethought?*
12. Explain what is meant by these types of murder: intent to kill, intent to inflict great bodily harm, and depraved heart.
13. What is felony murder?
14. Distinguish between first- and second-degree murder.
15. What is meant by *lesser included offense?* How does that concept apply to murder?
16. Should mercy killing be considered murder?

17. Name and define the types of manslaughter.
18. Explain the application of the *reasonable person* concept to manslaughter cases.
19. What is *negligent homicide?*

ENDNOTES

1. "Two Teens Held in Slaying of Jordan's Dad," *Miami Herald* (16 August 1993), p. 1.
2. See Model Penal Code, Sections 210.1–210.5.
3. Model Penal Code, Section 210.0(1).
4. See People v. Chavez, 176 P.2d 92 (Cal. 1947).
5. "Doctor Sentenced in Infant's Death," *New York Times* (20 December 1989), p. 14. The case is Brokans v. Melnick, 569 A.2d 1373 (Pa.Super. 1989), *appeal denied,* 584 A.2d 310 (Pa. 1990).
6. For a discussion, see Stephen C. Hicks, "The Right to Life in Law: The Embryo and Fetus, The Body and Soul, The Family and Society," *Florida State Law Review* 19 (Winter 1992): 805–851.
7. See Keeler v. Superior Court, 470 P.2d 617 (Cal. 1970), *superseded by statute/rule* as stated in People v. Carlson, 37 Cal.App.3d 349 (1st Dist. 1974).
8. People v. Davis, 872 P.2d 591 (Cal. Sup. 1994). The revised statute is Cal. Penal Code, Section 187 (a) (b) (1994).
9. See Minn. Stat. Sections 609.2661 (first-degree murder) and 609.2662 (second-degree murder) (1993).
10. The statutes are discussed by the Minnesota Supreme Court in State v. Merrill, 450 N.W.2d 318 (Minn. 1990), *cert. denied,* 496 U.S. 931 (1990). See also "Trial Adds Facet to the Abortion Debate," *New York Times* (15 June 1990), p. 5B and discussion in Focus 5.2.
11. "Here Come the Pregnancy Police," *Time* (22 May 1989), p. 104. See also: "Note: Maternal Rights and Fetal Wrongs: The Case Against the Criminalization of 'Fetal Abuse,'" *Harvard Law Review* 101 (March 1988): 994–1012; Michele Oberman, "Substance Use During Pregnancy: Legal and Social Responses:Sex, Drugs, Pregnancy, and the Law: Rethinking the Problems of Pregnant Women Who Use Drugs," *Hastings Law Journal* 43 (March 1992): 505–567; and Jeffrey A. Parness, "Arming the Pregnancy Police: More Outlandish Concoctions?" *Louisiana Law Review* 53 (November 1992): 427–448.
12. People v. Pamela R. Stewart, M.508 197 (San Diego Municipal Ct. 1987). The California statute in question is codified in Cal. Penal Code, Title 9, Chapter 2, Section 270 (1994).
13. Johnson v. State, 578 So.2d 419 (Fla.App. 1991), *certified question answered, quashed,* 602 So.2d 1288 (Fla. 1992). For a discussion of this and similar cases, see "Courts Side With Moms in Drug Cases," *American Bar Association Journal* 78 (November 1992): 18.
14. *In re* Valerie D., 613 A.2d 748 (Conn. 1992).
15. See Commentary to Model Penal Code, Section 210.1, and Smith v. Smith, 317 S.W.2d 275 (1958).
16. *In re* T.A.C.P., 609 So.2d 588 (Fla. 1992).
17. Uniform Determination of Death Act, Uniform Law Ann., Chapter 12 (1981 Supp.), p. 187.
18. Model Penal Code, Section 210.1, Commentary, p. 11.

19. See California Natural Death Act, Cal. Health & Safety Code, Section 7186 *et seq.* (1994). The living will is to be distinguished from problems that arise in civil actions when legal guardians wish to remove life support systems from loved ones who do not have a chance of recovering and who have not made living wills. The courts have permitted some of these wishes, but these cases involve civil, not criminal issues. See, for example, Cruzan v. Director, Missouri Department of Health, 497 U.S. 261 (1990), in which the U.S. Supreme Court affirmed the principle of a right-to-die but refused to permit the parents of Nancy Cruzan, a car-accident victim who had been in a comatose state for seven years, to have life-support equipment withdrawn from their daughter. The Court ruled that for such support to be withdrawn, it must be shown by clear and convincing evidence that the person from whom the support is withdrawn would have wanted such action to be taken. The Court remanded the case to Missouri; the parents offered evidence that their daughter would not have wanted to remain alive in a vegetative state. The judge ruled that the evidence was sufficient and ordered that the life-support systems could be removed. Nancy Cruzan died shortly thereafter. See also *In re* Estate of Greenspan, 558 N.E.2d 1194 (Ill. 1990).
20. For a discussion of the right to die, see JoAnna Weinberg, "Whose Right Is It Anyway? Individualism, Community, and the Right to Die: A Commentary on the New Jersey Experience," *Hastings Law Journal* 40 (November 1988): 119–167; Note: "Cruzan v. Director, Missouri Department of Health: A Clear and Convincing Call for Comprehensive Legislation to Protect Incompetent Patients' Rights," *American University Law Review* 49 (Summer 1991): 1477–1519; and Sanford H. Kadish, "Letting Patients Die: Legal and Moral Reflections," *California Law Review* 80 (July 1992): 857–888.
21. See State v. Hudson, 642 P.2d 331 (Ore. App. 1982), *review denied,* 651 P.2d 143 (Ore. 1982).
22. "Avoiding Prosecution: Common Law Rule May Shield Georgia Man from Murder Charges," *American Bar Association Journal* 76 (October 1990): 18; "Year-And-A-Day Case," *American Bar Association Journal* 77 (June 1991): 31. The case is State v. Cross, 401 S.E.2d 510 (Ga. 1991).
23. State v. Vance, 403 S.E.2d 495 (N.C. 1991).
24. State v. Gabehart, 836 P.2d 102 (N.M.App. 1992).
25. Donald E. Walther, "Taming A Phoenix: The Year-and-a-Day Rule in Federal Prosecutions for Murder," *University of Chicago Law Review* 59 (Summer 1992): 1337–1362.
26. Cal. Penal Code, Section 194 (1994).
27. State v. Hills, 605 P.2d 893, 894 (Ariz. 1980).
28. People v. Stewart, 358 N.E.2d 487 (N.Y.App. 1976).
29. Regina v. Michael, 2 Moody 120, 169 Eng. Rep. 48 (1840).
30. Kibbe v. Henderson, 534 F.2d 493 (2d Cir. 1976), footnotes and citations omitted, *reversed,* Henderson v. Kibbe, 431 U.S. 145 (1977).
31. Henderson v. Kibbe, 431 U.S. 145 (1977).
32. For a discussion of murder, including references to bizarre murders such as serial and mass murders, see the recently published treatise by Ronald M. Holmes and Stephen T. Holmes, *Murder in America* (Newbury Park, Calif.: Sage, 1993).
33. See Pinder v. State, 8 So. 837 (Fla. 1891).
34. Wayne R. LaFave and Austin W. Scott, Jr., *Criminal Law,* 2d ed. (St. Paul, Minn.: West, 1986), p. 605.
35. Model Penal Code, Section 210.2, comment 1, pp. 13–15.
36. Cal. Penal Code, Section 188 (1994).

37. Keys v. State, 766 P.2d 270 (Nev. 1988), quoting Moser v. State, 544 P.2d 424, 426 (Nev. 1975).

38. Model Penal Code, Section 210.2.

39. Willar v. People, 30 Mich. 16 (1874).

40. Model Penal Code, Section 210.2, Comment 1, pp. 13–15.

41. See for example, David Crump and Susan Waite Crump, "In Defense of the Felony Murder Doctrine," *Harvard Journal of Law and Public Policy* 8 (Spring 1985): 359–398, citing scholarly opposition to the rule and support for the rule.

42. Enmund v. Florida, 458 U.S. 782 (1982).

43. Tison v. Arizona, 481 U.S. 137 (1987), *reh'g. denied,* 482 U.S. 921 (1987).

44. People v. Brackett, 510 N.E.2d 877 (Ill. 1987).

45. State v. Pierce, 788 P.2d 352 (N.M. 1990).

46. People v. Patterson, 778 P.2d 549 (Cal. 1989), *reh'g. denied,* (8 November 1989).

47. Cal. Penal Code, Section 189 (1994).

48. State v. Guerra, 778 P.2d 1185, 1189–90 (Ariz. 1989), emphasis not in the original jury instruction but added by the appellate court in this opinion.

49. State v. Bingham, 699 P.2d 262, 265 (Wash.App. 1985), *aff'd.,* 719 P.2d 109 (Wash. 1986).

50. "Freed Gilbert Says He was Wrong," *Tallahassee Democrat* (3 August 1990), p. 3C; "Mercy-Killer Remembers Death, Life of Wife He Loved," *Miami Herald* (28 November 1993), p. 3B.

51. "Girl's Mercy Killing to Haunt Dad Forever," *Miami Herald* (3 May 1990), p. 1B; "Killer's Plea Runs into an Obstacle—An Ex-Wife," *Orlando Sentinel* (12 May 1993), p. 5B; and "Man Withdraws Clemency Bid," *St. Petersburg Times* (12 May 1993), p. 5B.

52. "Texan Given Probation in Brother's Mercy Death," *New York Times* (5 March 1982), p. 9.

53. "Man Won't Be Prosecuted in Mercy Killing of Wife," *Orlando Sentinel* (13 June 1993), p. 22.

54. "Euthanasia Favored in Poll," *New York Times* (4 November 1991), p. 9.

55. "Voters Turn Down Legal Euthanasia," *New York Times* (7 November 1991), p. 10. See also James Podgers, "Matters of Life and Death: Debate Grows Over Euthanasia," *American Bar Association Journal* 78 (May 1992): 60–63; and Yale Kamisar, "Active v. Passive Euthanasia: Why Keep the Distinction?" *Trial* 29 (March 1993): 32–37.

56. "Netherlands Allows Euthanasia," *Miami Herald* (10 February 1993), p. 15; "Dutch Psychiatrist to be Tried in Euthanasia," *New York Times* (6 April 1993), p. 3.

57. "Jury Declines to Indict a Doctor Who Said He Aided in a Suicide," *New York Times* (27 July 1991), p. 1; "Doctors Urge Policies Allowing Doctors to Aid in Patients' Suicides," *New York Times* (5 November 1992), p. 8.

58. LaFave and Scott, *Criminal Law,* p. 652.

59. Model Penal Code, Section 210.3.

60. State v. Standiford, 769 P.2d 254, 259, 268 (Utah 1988), citations omitted.

61. See Rowland v. State, 35 So. 826 (Miss. 1904).

62. See Scroggs v. State, 93 S.E.2d 583 (Ga.App. 1956).

63. See, for example, Burger v. State, 231 S.E.2d 769 (Ga. 1977).

64. See, for example, State v. Yanz, 50 A.37 (Conn. 1901).

65. People v. Chevalier, 544 N.E.2d 942 (Ill. 1989).

66. Cal. Penal Code, Section 192(a) (1994).

67. Bedder v. Director of Public Prosecutions, 2 All E.R. 801 (House of Lords, 1954).

68. Director of Public Prosecutions v. Camplin, 2 All E.R. 168 (House of Lords 1978).

69. Maine trial court's instructions as quoted by the Supreme Court in *Mullaney* v. *Wilbur,* 421 U.S. 684 (1973).

70. For a discussion, see LaFave and Scott, *Criminal Law,* pp. 665–668.

71. "Pit Bull Owner Convicted in Death of Two-Year-Old Boy," *Miami Herald* (24 December 1989), p. 9.

72. Cal. Penal Code, Section 192(b)(1994).

73. State v. Lozano, 616 So.2d 73 (Fla.App.1st Dist. 1993), cases and citations omitted.

74. "After Gunman's Acquittal, Japan Struggles to Understand America," *New York Times* (25 May 1993), p. 1.

75. Cal. Penal Code, Section 192(c) (1994).

76. Cal. Penal Code, Section 191.5(a)(c) (1994).

77. "Subway Driver Is Convicted In Fatal Manhattan Crash," *New York Times* (16 October 1992), p. 15.

78. People v. Oliver, 258 Cal. Rptr. 138 (Cal.App.1st Dist. 1989), *later proceeding,* Cal.App.1st Dist., 1989, *review denied,* CAL LEXIS 4188 (1989).

79. Commonwealth v. Catalina, 556 N.E.2d 973 (Mass. 1990).

80. Model Penal Code, Section 210.4.

81. "Owner of Killer Dogs Gets Prison Sentence," *New York Times* (23 June 1991), p. 11.

Chapter 6

Crimes against the Person: Part II

Outline

Key Terms

assault
battery
date rape
corroborating
    evidence
child abuse
false imprisonment

hate crime
incest
kidnapping
marital rape
mayhem
rape
rape shield statutes

rape trauma
    syndrome
sexual abuse
sodomy
statutory rape
terrorism

Introduction

Discrete, easily differentiated definitions of crimes are impossible. Perhaps this fact is illustrated most clearly by some of the crimes that are discussed in this chapter, for there is overlap between such crimes as rape and focible sodomy and the crimes of assault and battery. Crimes such as rape and aggravated assault and battery may lead to murder. Some of the crimes discussed in this chapter, such as aggravated sexual assault, may be indistinguishable from aggravated assault except that the crimes focus on sex.

This chapter includes a variety of crimes against the person, some violent, some consensual but which occur in situations in which the law does not permit consent, such as sex with minors or others considered by law to be incapable of granting consent. Sex crimes against adults and children have become issues of national concern in recent years. These offenses may not have increased, as the data infer, but they may be reported more frequently today as the result of increased sensitivity to the crimes and their victims. Nevertheless, crimes that previously were considered improper for discussion (such as sex with children) or issues of domestic concern and not violence (such as date and marital rape) increasingly are viewed as serious crimes against the person.

Nonsexual crimes discussed in this chapter, such as aggravated assault and battery, kidnapping, and imprisonment, have been considered crimes historically, while others, such as hate crimes and stalking, are relatively recent additions to our growing list of crimes against the person. Some of these crimes, along with violent acts against tourists and others, have captured national and international attention in recent months. In addition to discussing the historical approach to violent crimes against the person, this chapter focuses on some of the recent changes in legislation and case law in these areas. Although this text focuses on criminal law and not criminal procedure, some of those procedural changes are substantial and provide the basis for the criminal law prosecution. Where that occurs, procedural changes are noted.

The emphasis in this chapter is on crimes against the person, excluding homicide, which is discussed in Chapter 5. It is important to understand that these actions are *crimes;* they are not merely *problems.* Thus, a person who rapes his or her date or spouse engages in the commission of a violent crime, not merely a domestic problem or dispute. A parent or other adult who engages in sexual activities with a child commits a crime even if the sexual activities are not violent. The discussion in this chapter, however, excludes sex-related crimes that involve consenting adults. Those crimes are discussed in Chapter 8, since it may be argued that such offenses are not crimes against the person because those persons, as adults, have consented to the sexual acts.

The discussion begins with assault and battery, crimes against the person that provide a basis for the modern-day approach to some of the subsequent crimes analyzed in this chapter.

Assault and Battery

Frequently the terms *assault* and *battery* are used together or interchangeably, but historically they were different crimes. Each could occur without the other. **Assault** referred to the unlawful attempt or threat to inflict immediate harm or death, whereas **battery** referred to an unauthorized harmful or offensive touching. Under this approach, it is incorrect to say that A assaulted B when describing a physical attack by A on B. That is the battery, although it is quite possible that the battery was preceded by an assault; that is, A threatened to inflict an immediate battery and did inflict that battery. Under the common law assault and battery were misdemeanors, although we might categorize rape, robbery, and mayhem (all discussed subsequently) as aggravated assaults and batteries under the common law. Under most modern statutes, assault and battery are categorized by degrees or types, and in most cases, the two crimes are merged into one. For example, the Model Penal Code defines *assault* to include both assault and battery, and the code takes *mens rea* as well as the harm intended by the actor into account in its definitions. In analyzing the Model Penal Code definitions below, it would be helpful to refer back to Focus 2.4 in Chapter 2 for the Model Penal Code's inclusion and definitions of the words involving intent: purposely, knowingly, intentionally, or recklessly.

Two additional points regarding definitions are important to this discussion. First, some jurisdictions require that for an act to be an assault there must be a threat of *immediate* harm. An intent to frighten will not be sufficient. Some jurisdictions require also that the defendant have the *present ability to succeed* in carrying out the threat. Second, in those jurisdictions in which assault and battery are defined as distinct crimes, in practice they may be treated as one. Generally assault is categorized as *simple* or *aggravated*, each of which may be subdivided.

Simple Assault and Battery

Under the Model Penal Code, a person is guilty of *simple assault* "if he: (a) attempts to cause bodily injury to another; or (b) attempts by physical menace to put another in fear of imminent serious bodily harm." The code provides that a simple assault is a misdemeanor "unless committed in a fight or scuffle entered into by mutual consent, in which case the assault is a petty misdemeanor."[1]

Simple assault and battery includes acts that do not include aggravation. The law recognizes that some unauthorized touchings are offensive even if they are not dangerous. As one court noted,

> It has long been established, both in tort and criminal law, that 'the least touching' may constitute a battery. In other words, *force* against the person is enough, it need not be violent or severe, it need not cause bodily harm or even pain, and it need not leave any mark.[2]

Historically, it was a battery for a male to kiss an unwilling female. In some jurisdictions this battery was extended to females kissing unwilling males. It has long been considered a battery to spit in the face of another. But not every offensive touching constitutes a battery. As with most areas of law, the difficulty is in drawing the line, particularly when the law permits the use of force to control people in some circumstances.

The case of *Government of Virgin Islands* v. *Stull* is illustrative. This case involves a man who was disruptive in a bar described by its owner's attorney as "a waterfront saloon and poolroom which cannot be expected to attract clientele always likely to maintain the highest degree of order." The man had been told on previous occasions to leave because he was disruptive. On the occasion in question, when the customer refused to leave, Stull grabbed him by the arm and led him to the door. The customer claimed he was kicked. That claim was in dispute, but the trial court found Stull guilty of simple assault and battery. The appellate court vacated that decision with instructions to enter a verdict of not guilty. The appellate court stated:[3]

Government of Virgin Islands v. *Stull*

The Municipal Court apparently recognized, as this court does, that the owner of a bar or other public or semi-public place has the right to eject unwanted or disorderly persons from the premises. Indeed, the law is rather clear on this point:

> The owner, occupant, or person in charge of any public or semipublic place of business may request the departure of a person who does not rightfully belong there or who by his conduct has forfeited his right to be there, and may treat him as a trespasser, using reasonable force to eject him from the premises . . . .

Under the circumstances of the present case, the Court cannot see how appellant could have used any lesser degree of force in removing Matthew from the premises, an act which he had the right to do. Matthew, in Stull's view, was causing a disturbance. He was told to leave. He objected. Whereupon Stull took him by the arm and led him out. It was not incumbent upon Stull to argue or plead with Matthew. His license to remain on the premises had been terminated, and reasonably so, as the court views the facts. His failure to leave when requested to do so authorized Stull to exercise a reasonable degree of force. Had Stull kicked Matthew, as Matthew alleged, this would be a

> different case, but the taking of Matthew by the arm and pushing, pulling, or leading him to the door was, in the Court's opinion, entirely reasonable and in fact the minimal amount of force employable under the circumstances.

Aggravated Assault and Battery

Aggravated assault and battery involves acts committed with the intention of committing another crime or acts accompanied by particularly outrageous or atrocious circumstances. This may include assault and battery with a dangerous weapon. Rape and other offensive sexual touchings may be considered batteries, with rape viewed as an aggravated battery and some other sexual touchings (not resulting in physical injuries) as simple batteries. The modern approach, however, is to limit batteries to offensive touchings that cause physical injury and to cover other offensive touchings, such as sexual contacts, under a separate crime category.

The Model Penal Code provides that "a person is guilty of aggravated assault if he:"

> (a) attempts to cause serious bodily injury to another, or causes such injury purposely, knowingly or recklessly under circumstances manifesting extreme indifference to the value of human life; or
>
> (b) attempts to cause or purposely or knowingly causes bodily injury to another with a deadly weapon.
>
> An assault under Category (a) is a second-degree felony; one under Category (b) is a third-degree felony.[4]

Aggravated assault (defined as the "unlawful attack by one person upon another for the purpose of inflicting severe or aggravated bodily injury") is the most frequently committed of the four violent crimes categorized by the FBI as Part I Index, or serious offenses. For example, in 1992, aggravated assault constituted 58 percent of all violent crimes known to the police, for a total of 1,126,974 offenses, up 3.1 percent from the previous year. Of those offenses, 31 percent were committed with blunt objects or other dangerous weapons; 26 percent by hands, feet, and fists; and 25 percent by firearms. It is important to note that the FBI includes attempted crimes in the aggravated assault category. (Attempt crimes are discussed in Chapter 10.)[5]

On the other hand, data on aggravated assault would be significantly higher if all cases of domestic violence were included. With the current attention paid to domestic violence against spouses, lovers, parents or other older relatives, and children, some jurisdictions have established separate statutes to cover these problems. Thus, an aggravated battery against a child may be prosecuted as child abuse; aggravated battery against a spouse may be prosecuted as spouse abuse; and aggravated battery against an elderly person prosecuted as elder abuse or some similar name. Such statutes, as for example in the case of child abuse, may cover criminal acts beyond those covered in general assault and battery statutes.[6] Furthermore, violence within the home is not reported by many victims and is considered by some people, including some police, to be a domestic problem, not a problem of violent crime. This position is changing but only slowly, and many crimes remain unreported, but it is important to understand that domestic violence cases constitute either simple or aggravated battery no matter how they are handled by the police or by victims. To view them as domestic problems rather than crimes of violence is to ignore the nature of the problem.[7]

In some cases aggravated battery charges are brought in conjunction with attempt crimes, such as aggravated battery with the attempt to commit rape, in which an assailant beats a victim brutally but does not complete the attempted rape. The degree of assault and subsequent penalty may be greater when the attempt to commit another felony is involved. This is true particularly when a dangerous weapon is involved in the commission of an assault.

The use of a weapon to define an act as an aggravated battery, however, means that the court must define what is meant by a deadly weapon. A recent Florida case illustrates the problem. Defendant/appellant was charged with attempted murder but convicted of the lesser included charge of aggravated battery. He appealed, arguing that the use of his hands did not meet the statutory definition of a deadly weapon. The case excerpted below is based on the Florida statute, which provides that a person commits aggravated battery if he or she

1. Intentionally or knowingly causes great bodily harm, permanent disability, or permanent disfigurement; or
2. Uses a deadly weapon[8]

The case, *Dixon* v. *State*, was decided by a three-judge appellate panel, which affirmed the conviction, upholding the jury instruction that hands may constitute a deadly weapon. The defendant requested a hearing before the full court. That was granted, and the conviction was reversed and remanded. The complaining witness, Juanita Dixon, testified at trial that she "had separated from appellant, her husband of twenty-two years, for a few years before May 1990, when she lived with him for a few days. She stated that on 18 August 1990 at approximately 4:30 in the afternoon appellant arrived with her daughter. They talked for a while, and she asked appellant whether he was going to stay or leave with her daughter. He said he would stay, and she told him to leave. They argued about that, and eventually Dixon said, "Well, the heck with it . . . . Just stay because I don't feel like arguing." The daughter left, and according to Dixon, appellant said to her, "I'm going to kill you." Dixon testified that she thought he "was jiving" as they were watching television when the statement was made.

Dixon testified that appellant went to the kitchen; when he returned he grabbed her by placing his hands around her neck, at which point she decided, "Oh my gosh he is for real." He hit her several times in the jaw and ribs. She testified that she passed out for about ten minutes as a result of the choking and that when she came to appellant was going through her purse. She ran to a neighbor's house and called 911.

Defense counsel argued that no aggravated assault occurred as the injuries described in Section 1. of the statute were not met; nor was there a deadly weapon; so Section 2 was not met. The three-judge panel reviewed Florida case law as well as the case law of other jurisdictions and concluded that "circumstances surrounding the actual use of the hands must be taken into consideration on a case-by-case basis, and that where there are facts sufficient upon which a jury could reasonably find an object, such as a person's hand, to be a deadly weapon based upon the manner in which it was used, the jury should be so instructed." The court noted that the "fact that the object, such as a hand, is not a conventional deadly weapon, such as a firearm, does not mean that the object was used in a manner that could not be considered deadly . . . . Where an individual uses his hands to strangle a person, the use of his hands in such a manner turns his hands into a deadly weapon." The full court disagreed, as this excerpt indicates.[9]

State v. Dixon

We are reluctant to overturn Dixon's conviction for aggravated battery, since proof that he brutally attacked his wife was clear. However, it is axiomatic in our legal system that a defendant cannot be convicted of a crime unless the state proves all the necessary elements of the crime, and that crime must be properly charged.

The trial court reasoned that depending on how they are used, fists and hands can be considered to be deadly weapons. If the circumstances are such that bare hands inflict deadly force, this issue is one which should be resolved by the jury. Although there is some out-of-state authority for this view, we have found no Florida appellate case that so holds.

We think that view is contrary to good public policy, the law in this district, and the law in most other jurisdictions . . . .

We conclude that, in general, bare hands (like bare feet) are not deadly weapons for purposes of alleging or proving the crime of aggravated battery. The issue of whether the bare hands or feet of a person specially skilled or trained in martial arts to kill or inflict deadly force with them can be deemed "deadly weapons" is reserved for future consideration. But, in this case, there was no allegation or proof Dixon had any such skills or training.

Accordingly, we reverse Dixon's conviction for aggravated battery and we direct that it be reduced to simple battery. We remand to the lower court for resentencing on simple battery.

Reckless Assault and Battery

One final category of assault in the Model Penal Code is a misdemeanor involving reckless behavior and is defined as follows:

> A person commits a misdemeanor if he recklessly engaged in conduct which places or may place another person in danger of death or serious bodily injury. Recklessness and danger shall be presumed where a person knowingly points a firearm at or in the direction of another, whether or not the actor believed the firearm to be loaded.[10]

Mayhem

Some statutes include within assault and battery the common law offense of **mayhem**, which referred to rendering a person less able to fight. Mayhem could occur by dismemberment or disablement. Later the crime was extended to include disfigurement that did not disable the victim.

Today some jurisdictions retain the crime (although without reference to the ability to fight), including disfigurement, which refers to batteries that change the appearance of a person. The injury must be permanent, but that is open to interpretation. One court approved the following definition:

> To be permanently disfigured means that the person is appreciably less attractive or that a part of his body is to some appreciable degree less useful or functional than it was before the injury.[11]

Analyze the facts of Focus 6.1 and determine whether you think the defendant should have been convicted of malicious wounding, a crime similar to mayhem.

Some statutes require the prosecution to prove that the defendant accused of mayhem had the intent to injure. Some statutes require an intent to disable or disfigure. Some list the body parts that are included.

Under early common law, mayhem was a felony punishable by causing the perpetrator to lose the same body part that the victim lost, but that punishment gave way to imprisonment (or in some cases, capital punishment). Under most modern statutes mayhem is a felony, but the punishment is not as severe as it was under the common law. Some states do not specify mayhem in their criminal codes, but, like the Model Penal Code, include the crime within another category, such as aggravated assault.[12]

Lorena Bobbitt, acquitted of malicious wounding after severing her husband's penis, argued that she was the victim of years of sexual abuse. Her husband, John, was acquitted of charges of marital rape.

FOCUS 6.1   Domestic Dispute Leads to Violence

Newsweek began its story on this case with the following: "This is the story of a man, a woman, a fillet knife and a penis." It is the case of a Virginia couple, John Wayne Bobbitt and Lorena Bobbitt. She claims he came home drunk on the night of 23 June 1993 and that he raped her and then fell asleep.

After the alleged rape, Lorena went to the kitchen, secured a twelve-inch blade, returned to the bedroom, pulled back the sheets, and sliced off two-thirds of her husband's penis. She admits these acts but says that she did so in self-defense as the result of the alleged rape, which she claims had happened before. Further, she added this comment, "He always has an orgasm and doesn't wait for me . . . . It's unfair." Then she panicked and drove away, discarding the penis on the way.

John Bobbitt got to an emergency room, where doctors reattached his penis, which had been recovered by police after Lorena notified them of its location. She had thrown the organ from the window of her car after she left the house. The nine-and-one-half hour operation was considered a success. The physician said it "looks excellent . . . . These aren't the kind of scars he can show off in public, obviously, but he's doing very well."

John Bobbitt was indicted for marital sexual assault, a charge he denied. He could have received up to twenty years in prison upon conviction, but he was acquitted. Lorena Bobbitt was charged with malicious wounding. If convicted, she could have received up to twenty years in prison. She was found not guilty by reason of insanity, ordered confined for forty-five days of psychiatric testing and evaluation, and released after that period.

The media have shown great interest in the Bobbitt case, and both John and Lorena secured agents as well as attorneys. The couple filed for a divorce.

SOURCE: Summarized from media reports. Quotations are from "The Unkindest Cut," *Newsweek* (18 August 1993), p. 56.

Forcible Rape and Sodomy

Forcible **rape** and forcible **sodomy** could be included within the crime of assault and battery, for they constitute offensive, unauthorized applications of force to the person of another, usually preceded by an assault or threat. Both are considered so serious that traditionally they have been defined as separate crimes. Some characteristics of forcible rape offenders and their victims are contained in Focus 6.2.

A point of caution is in order. Although official data on most of the crimes of sexual force discussed in this chapter involve female victims, boys

FOCUS 6.2 The Crime of Forcible Rape

[The following information is based on an analysis of data from the National Crime Survey for a ten-year period, 1973–1982, and is the first in-depth study of these data. The study indicates that only about one-half of rape victims report the crimes to police. The data in this survey come from rape victims.]

The Setting

Two-thirds of all rapes and rape attempts occur at night, with the largest proportion occurring between 6 P.M. and midnight. The patterns for rape and rape attempts are slightly different. Rape attempts were about twice as likely as rapes to occur during the daytime and only half as likely to occur between midnight and 6 A.M.

The sites of rapes and rape attempts also vary. A third of the completed rapes occurred in the home. Nearly half the rest occurred on the street or in a park, field, playground, parking lot, or parking garage. Only one-fourth of the attempted rapes occurred in the home; well over half the rest occurred on the street or in a park, field, playground, parking lot, or parking garage.

The Victim

Rape victims are young. The ages with the highest victimization rates for rape and attempted rape were sixteen- to twenty-four-year-olds. Young women in these age groups were two to three times more likely to be victims of rape or attempted rape than the adult female population as a whole. The age profile for whites is similar to that for blacks.

Most victims of rape or attempted rape are white, reflecting the racial composition of the general population. However, the likelihood of being a rape victim is significantly higher for black women than for white women.

The marital status of rape and attempted rape victims strongly reflects their age distribution. More than half of all victims had never been married, while widows accounted for only 3 percent of all rape or attempted rape victims. One in five victims was married; about the same proportion was separated or divorced.

Rape victims are usually members of low-income families. About half of all victims from 1973 to 1982 reported family incomes of less than $10,000 a year and less than 10 percent reported yearly family incomes of $25,000 or more. About three-fourths of all black victims had incomes of less than $10,000 and about one-third had incomes of less than $3,000. Because income figures were collected over a ten-year period of rising prices and have not been adjusted for inflation, the absolute income levels are understated in current dollars.

The Offender

The most frightening form of rape, an assault by a total stranger, is also the most common. A woman is twice as likely to be attacked by a stranger as by someone she knows. There was little difference in the percentage of rapes committed by strangers for blacks, whites, or victims of other races.

It has been suggested that a victim may be less likely to report a rape—

either to the police or to a survey interviewer—when she knows her assailant than when he is a stranger. The victim may feel a greater sense of embarrassment under these circumstances. She may feel that she should have been able to prevent the attack. She may wish to protect the identity of an assailant who is a friend or family member. She may even fear reprisals or worry that her account of the attack will not be believed. There is some support in the statistics for this line of reasoning. According to the victims, somewhat more than half of the rapes or rape attempts involving strangers were reported to the police; somewhat less than half of the rapes and rape attempts involving assailants known to the victim were reported.

More than three-fourths of all rapes involve one victim and one offender . . . . Most offenders are unarmed. Weapons were used in only 25 percent of the rapes and rape attempts. The victim was not sure whether or not a weapon had been used in about 11 percent of the cases. Not surprisingly, weapons were used more often in completed rapes than in attempted rapes. Knives were used in about 12 percent of all rapes and rape attempts and guns in 10 percent. Other weapons were used in 4 percent of the incidents.

The Outcome

Most victims offered some form of resistance. Most individuals using self-protection were victims of attempted rape, while most not using self-protection were victims of completed rapes. The most common responses to the situation were to try to get help; to resist physically; to threaten, argue, or reason with the offender; or to resist without force, for example, by running away or hiding. Victims rarely used weapons against their assailants.

Some of the victims of attempted rape were exposed to verbal threats or weapons, but were not physically attacked. Those who were physically attacked received injuries in addition to the rape or attempted rape more than half the time. In cases where the victim used some form of resistance, injury was somewhat more likely (57 percent) than in cases where she did not (47 percent).

The most common injuries in addition to the rape itself were bruises, black eyes, and cuts (31 percent), but the nature or severity of these injuries is not known. An extremely small proportion of the victims sustained gunshot or weapon wounds or broken bones.

SOURCE: Bureau of Justice Statistics, *The Crime of Rape* (Washington, D.C.: U.S. Department of Justice, March 1985), p. 14, footnotes omitted.

and men are victimized by sex-related crimes as well. However, data on sex crimes involving male victims are less accurate than data on female victims. Sex crimes are very sensitive. Many victims do not want to report the crimes, and many, especially male victims, refuse to report. Forced sodomy or homosexual rape by males against males may not occur often outside of prison, where it is reported to occur with some frequency, but is not likely to be reported by victims, many of whom fear retaliation or embarrassment. Thus, the chapter focuses on the criminal law aspects of these crimes, but the reader should understand that enforcing that criminal law is another matter.

Common Law Definitions

Under the common law, *rape* was defined as the unlawful carnal knowledge of a female without her consent. The term *unlawful* meant that the act was not authorized by law. For centuries that definition was interpreted to preclude applying the law to a husband who had forced sexual intercourse with his wife (although he could be convicted of rape if he assisted someone else in raping his wife). *Carnal knowledge* is synonymous with sexual intercourse, but under the common law the term was limited to acts involving the penis and the vagina. The crime required *penetration*, which was defined as the insertion of the penis into the vagina to any extent; emission did not have to occur for the crime to be complete.

Common law rape applied only to female victims; forcing a male to engage in sex was not considered rape. The final element of the common law definition of rape is that intercourse occurred without the consent of the victim. Proving the lack of consent was a factual problem, which led to many interesting statutory and case law rules about evidence in rape cases. Only within recent years have these been changed in some jurisdictions, and that trend applies also to sodomy.

Sodomy is a more difficult term to define. It was not a common law crime in England (it was later defined by statute); it was an American common law crime, later defined by statute, and generally included both the ancient and religious crimes (punishable by ecclesiastical courts) of *bestiality* (sex with a beast) and *buggery* (sexual intercourse *per anum*, or per anus), later defined to include sex *per os*, or oral sex. The sex acts involved in these offenses was considered to be "unnatural." A few current statutes retain the definition of sodomy in terms of "that abominable crime against nature." In earlier cases when defendants complained that they did not know what the term *sodomy* meant, usually they were told that everyone knows what it means, but polite people do not talk about it even in court.

Until recently, all states had sodomy statutes; some still do. For example, Idaho prohibits "the infamous crimes against nature, committed with mankind or with any animal."[13] This brief excerpt from a modern Idaho case illustrates the crime of sodomy as well as rape, kidnapping (discussed later in this chapter), and assault. Note the problems of proof (discussed later in this chapter) and the court's reaction in upholding the conviction for all of the crimes.[14]

State v. Burnham

The state presented the following evidence. Burnham's victim testified that Burnham forced her into his car, threatened her with a steel crowbar, struck her, coerced her to perform fellatio upon him, and then raped her. Pictures taken of the victim shortly after the incident show substantial bruises and abrasions. A number of the victim's possessions were later found in Burnham's car. Burnham denied forcing the victim into his car or striking her. He testified that the victim willingly performed fellatio upon him and consented to sexual intercourse. He denied any use of force.

The conflicting testimony of Burnham and the victim set up a credibility issue for the jury to resolve. The jury was entitled to believe the victim. This is especially so since her testimony was corroborated by photographs. We hold that there was substantial evidence to find the essential elements of each crime charged.

As *State* v. *Burnham* indicates, some jurisdictions include *fellatio*, oral stimulation of the penis, either within sodomy statutes or within the interpretation of those statutes. Oral sexual stimulation of a woman is included by some but not all courts that have interpreted similar statutes.[15]

Modern Sexual Offense Statutes

Some jurisdictions have enlarged their judicial interpretations of rape and sodomy, but the major changes in the legal definitions of sexual offenses have come from the legislatures. The legislatures of several states have undertaken a complete revision of their criminal sexual offense statutes, while numerous courts have expanded the traditional definitions of rape and sodomy or abandoned those terms and used others. The 1986 revision of the federal code is an example.

The federal criminal code revised rape and **sexual abuse** laws to apply equally to men and women and removed immunities from prosecution for marital rape, thus making forced sexual intercourse within marriage a crime in the federal system. The code refers to *aggravated sexual abuse*, which includes sexual acts by force or threat, in any of the following situations: (1) with persons who are dead, kidnapped, or seriously injured; or (2) with those who have been made unconscious or drugged to the extent that their ability to control their own conduct is impaired; or (3) sexual acts with children (defined as persons under the age of twelve). The penalty for these crimes is a fine and/or a prison term of specified years or a life sentence.[16]

Lesser penalties are provided for *sexual abuse*, which includes knowingly causing another to engage in a sexual act when that person is incapable of understanding the nature of the conduct or physically incapable of declining participation. The term includes persons placed in fear (less than the fear included under *aggravated sexual abuse*). The code includes a provision for lesser crimes that prohibits *sexual abuse of a minor or ward* and *abusive sexual contact*.[17]

The federal code defines *sexual act* as follows:

> (A) contact between the penis and the vulva or the penis and the anus, and for purposes of this subparagraph contact involving the penis occurs upon penetration, however slight;

(B) contact between the mouth and the penis, the mouth and the vulva, or the mouth and the anus; or

(C) the penetration, however slight, of the anal or genital opening of another by a hand or finger or by any object, with an intent to abuse, humiliate, harass, degrade, or arouse or gratify the sexual desire of any person.

The term *sexual contact* means: "the intentional touching, either directly or through the clothing, of the genitalia, anus, groin, breast, inner thigh, or buttocks of any person with an intent to abuse, humiliate, harass, degrade, or arouse or gratify the sexual desire of any person."[18]

Yet another method of categorizing sexual offenses in recent criminal law revisions is illustrated by the Michigan code, which establishes four degrees of criminal sexual conduct, with declining penalties. To complicate matters further, some jurisdictions retain the term *rape* and add another, such as *criminal sexual assault or battery*, but define the latter as a separate and serious crime, not a lesser offense within rape. This position was taken by the Kansas Supreme Court in *State* v. *Gibson*.[19]

In *Gibson*, the defendant was convicted of rape after he entered the complainant's apartment through an unlocked window, threatened to choke her, and forced her to engage in sexual intercourse. He alleged that the trial court erred in not giving the jury his requested instruction on *aggravated sexual battery* as a lesser included offense within rape. The Kansas Code defines *aggravated sexual battery* as: "The unlawful, intentional application of force to the person of another who is not the spouse of the offender and who does not consent thereto, with the intent to arouse or satisfy the sexual desires of the offender or another."[20]

These statutes illustrate the impossibility of generalizing sexual offense statutes. They differ from jurisdiction to jurisdiction and may be called *rape, sodomy, sexual abuse, sexual battery*, or other terms. The terms *aggravated* or *forced* may be added to all but rape (which by definition involves force). Thus, consensual sodomy may be a crime, but generally it carries a lesser penalty than forced sodomy or aggravated sodomy and, in fact, is rarely prosecuted.

Elements of Forcible Rape and Sodomy

Despite the problems of definition and of interpreting the elements of forced sexual acts, there are some general elements of these offenses.

GENDER OF THE ACTOR AND OF THE VICTIM

The common law limitation of rape to male perpetrators and female victims is retained in some modern statutes. The Model Penal Code's definition of forcible rape refers to "a male who has sexual intercourse with a female."[21] As noted earlier, in recent years, some states have adopted gender-neutral language for both perpetrators and victims. For example, California's former requirement that "rape is an act of sexual intercourse, accomplished with a female" has been changed to substitute the word *person* for *female*.[22] The revised Michigan statute, which uses the term *crimi-*

nal sexual conduct rather than *rape*, provides that "a person is guilty of criminal sexual conduct in the first degree if he or she . . ."[23]

Some modern statutes specify that males may be rape victims. The Michigan statute defines *victim* as "the person alleging to have been subjected to criminal sexual conduct."[24] On the other hand, the Model Penal Code specifies a female victim, while the revised federal code, referred to as the Sexual Abuse Act of 1986, applies equally to men and women by using *whoever* to refer to the actor and *another person* to refer to the victim.[25]

THE REQUIREMENT OF PENETRATION

Under the common law, generally penetration was interpreted to mean *any* penetration. This interpretation is followed by most courts today.[26] Some statutes no longer require penetration of the vagina by a penis. For example, Michigan defines *sexual penetration* as "sexual intercourse, cunnilingus, fellatio, anal intercourse, or any other intrusion, however slight, of any part of a person's body or of any object into the genital or anal openings of another person's body, but emission of semen is not required."[27] The inclusion of the word *object* criminalizes *rape by instrumentation*. Unlike common law rape, rape by instrumentation may be committed by a female and by an impotent male.

The penetration requirement has been one of the most difficult and frequently litigated elements of rape and sodomy. In a Kansas case in which the defendant who committed oral sex on his daughter was convicted of aggravated criminal sodomy (among other offenses), the appellate court reversed his conviction for sodomy (but upheld his conviction for *indecent liberties with child*, a less serious crime, carrying a much shorter prison term than aggravated criminal sodomy) because there was no evidence of penetration or oral copulation. The court said that "cunnilingus is not an act of 'sodomy' as that term is defined by statute." The state statute was revised subsequently, and today the Kansas statute defines *sodomy* to include "oral contact or oral penetration of the female genitalia or oral contact of the male genitalia . . . ."[28]

In contrast, a federal court in Arkansas upheld the rape conviction of a defendant who argued that no evidence of penetration was presented by the young victim who testified that he made her put her mouth "on" his penis and made her "lick his penis." The appellate court said, "We agree with the district court that a rational juror could reasonably have concluded that putting the mouth on the penis constitutes penetration."[29]

LACK OF CONSENT

A conviction for forcible rape or sodomy requires that the victim did not consent to the sexual act. Lack of consent is another element that is difficult to prove, because in most cases there are no witnesses. Consent is not legal if obtained by duress, threats of harm if one refuses, fraud, or if it is given by a person who cannot consent legally (for example, mentally incompetent or underage persons). Recent cases illustrating some of these conditions are featured in Focus 6.3.

FOCUS 6.3 Rape or Consent: Unusual Cases Test the Law

1. Multiple Personalities

He claimed she consented to sexual intercourse; the prosecution claimed that she could not consent legally because she suffered from multiple personality disorder and the defendant knew that. The alleged victim testified regarding her various personalities, demonstrating some of them for the jury. The jury convicted Mark Peterson, a twenty-nine-year-old married grocery store worker, of second-degree sexual assault under the Wisconsin statutes that criminalize sex with a mentally retarded person if that person is unable to understand the consequences of the behavior and if the other person knows of that mental illness.

This widely publicized case, which was tried in 1990, raised the critical issue of legal consent to sexual intercourse in an unusual fact pattern. After the trial the victim alleged that she had sexual relations with one of the trial witnesses, Gerald Reeves, her neighbor. This revelation could have resulted in another charge of sexual assault and might have provided evidence that would assist Peterson in his appeal. But the prosecutor did not file charges because there had not been a complaining victim in this case. In further developments, Peterson was granted a new trial because the trial judge refused to permit a defense psychiatrist to examine the alleged victim prior to the trial. The district attorney decided not to retry the case because he believed the alleged victim's condition would deteriorate if she had to go through another trial.

2. Glen Ridge, New Jersey

Less than two months after the 1989 brutal beating and gang rape of a New York woman who was jogging in Central Park, the nearby affluent community of Glen Ridge, New Jersey (population 7,700) was shocked by allegations that several high school students had engaged in sexual relations, including performing sexual acts with a broomstick and a miniature baseball bat, with a mildly retarded seventeen-year-old whom they invited to the home of one of the defendants. The young woman engaged in some sexual acts voluntarily, and defense attorneys argued that she was an aggressive temptress. Prosecutors argued that she could not give legal consent due to her retardation.

Three youths were convicted of first-degree sexual assault in the 1993 trial of this case, and the decision to let them remain free pending appeals outraged many. Although the judge said he did not think the defendants had grounds for a reversal, he said, "What if I am wrong about that? If it should turn out that I am wrong . . ., then defendants will have spent, by the time that determination is made, a substantial amount of time incarcerated, possibly unjustly."[1]

3. Gouverneur, New York

After drinking excessively, a twenty-four-year-old hospital technician passed out in the restroom of a bar on 26 October 1991. Five men in their twenties, all acquaintances of the woman, carried her to a dining room booth, removed her clothing, and four had sexual intercourse with her while she was unconscious. Each man was fined $750 and ordered to pay $90 in court costs after a plea bargain resulted in the reduction of first-degree rape charges to misdemeanor sexual misconduct charges. Angry citizens called for the resignation of District Attorney Richard V. Manning, who approved the plea bargaining.[2]

In late March 1994 the state attorney argued that the plea bargains were invalid due to a series of procedural errors and asked the court to reinstate the first-degree rape indictments. A hearing was set for 15 April 1994. The complainant in the case said she had been hoping for this action. She had filed civil suits against the five men and the restaurant owner, who is the father of one of the men. Governor Mario M. Cuomo appointed a special prosecutor in this case after public outrage at the plea bargains.[3]

A state judge reinstated the rape charges, thus nullifing the guilty pleas. The alleged victim said she felt vindicated even though the trial would not be held for months. "I can finally see the light of day now that I'll finally get my day in court. . . . This will be fair now instead of some backroom deal," said Krista Absalon, a twenty-six-year-old hospital technician.[4]

4. Austin, Texas

In 1992 a Texas grand jury refused to indict Joel Rene Valdez, accused of confronting a woman with a knife and demanding sex. The complainant indicated that she asked her assailant to wear a condom to protect her from pregnancy and disease. When he said he did not have one, she supplied one for him. Grand jury proceedings are secret; so it is not known why the first grand jury refused to indict although it might be speculated that the jurors interpreted the complainant's actions as constituting consent.

The refusal to indict created an outpouring of reaction, mostly of outrage. A second grand jury indicted Valdez, who was tried and convicted by a jury that deliberated for only two hours before reaching its decision. Valdez was sentenced to forty years in prison.

SOURCE: Summarized from media sources.
[1] "Justice Turns Blind Eye to Violence Against Women," *New Jersey Law Journal* (14 June 1993), p. 20.
[2] "Rape Case In Small Town Stirs Cries of Injustice," *New York Times* (12 June 1993), p. 6.
[3] "Reinstatement of Charges Is Sought in a Rape Case," *New York Times* (22 March 1994), p. 5B.
[4] "Rape Charges Reinstated Against Five," *New York Times* (27 April 1994), p.1B.

Because of the difficulty of proving consent or lack of consent, evidence of a struggle was a common requirement in the past. Today in many jurisdictions it is not necessary that victims indicate that they struggled. It is not necessary for a potential victim to risk great bodily injury or death in order to show resistance. Generally the requirement is that the resistance was reasonable in light of the victim's age, strength, the surrounding facts, and all attendant circumstances,[30] or that no resistance need be shown. The issue is whether or not consent was given.

A 1980 amendment to the California rape statute deleted all references to the requirement to show resistance. The California Supreme Court has held that a victim's failure to show resistance does not invalidate a defendant's conviction. The victim testified that she feared that if she resisted, the defendant would become physically violent. The court referred to research indicating that although some victims react to rape with resistance, others may be quite passive or even initiate acts while being in a state of terror. Thus, the victim's lack of resistance is not evidence of consent. In fact, there is some evidence that resistance increases the chances of serious injury or death.[31]

In 1994 the Pennsylvania Supreme Court decided a controversial rape case, *Commonwealth* v. *Berkowitz*, a decision that alarmed and dismayed victims' rights advocates. The case involved a sexual relationship between a man and a woman in the man's dormitory room. The woman had stopped by his room to leave a message for his roommate. When she saw someone on the bed with a pillow over his head, she walked over to the bed and removed the pillow, later testifying that she thought the person was her friend. The woman had consumed a mixed drink previously in her room, to "relax a little" before she met her boyfriend with whom she had had an argument. Her boyfriend was not in his room; so she decided to visit her other friend nearby.

According to the female student, the male student initiated sexual intercourse by shoving her to the bed (not a big shove but not a romantic one either) and getting on top of her. She did not resist physically because he was on top of her, but she did say, "no." The male student testified that the woman came to his room and awakened him and consented willingly to sexual intercourse. She said, "No," but in "a moaning way," which he took to communicate consent. He testified that on previous occasions they had discussed sex, in particular the size of his penis, and that she had asked him to show it to her. The Pennsylvania Supreme Court held that under the facts of the case, sufficient physical force as required by the state statute was not shown. The court noted that the statutory requirement of "forcible compulsion" or "by threat of forcible compulsion that would prevent resistance by a person of reasonable resolution" did not require physical force. The phrase includes "moral, psychological or intellectual force used to compel a person to engage in sexual intercourse against that person's will." The court found no evidence of such coercion and discharged the rape conviction while reversing and remanding on the charge of indecent exposure.[32]

Where resistance is required to show lack of consent, proof of resistance may be offered by showing evidence of torn clothing, physical bruises or cuts, broken bones, and so forth. Such evidence is called **corroborating evidence**, which is additional or supplementary evidence to prove an element of the crime. For example, physical evidence of sexual intercourse taken from the victim within a reasonable period of time after the alleged crime might be used to show evidence of intercourse; sperm samples found on the victim's body may be compared with sperm samples taken from the defendant. Clothing or bed linens might provide corroborating evidence as well.

The modern trend is that the victim's testimony is sufficient on the consent issue; corroborating evidence is not required. In *State* v. *Gibson*, the Kansas Supreme Court took this position by stating:

We have consistently held that a conviction of rape may be upheld based sole-ly upon the testimony of the victim without any corroboration. Here there was sufficient credible evidence. While the defendant contended the sexual activi-ty was consensual, the victim testified to the contrary. Unfortunately for the defendant, the jury believed the victim.[33]

Another common practice for showing consent has been to permit the defense to introduce evidence of the victim's prior sexual experiences, the assumption being that someone who previously had engaged in sexual acts would be more likely to have consented. Such evidence might be consid-ered important particularly if, on a prior occasion, the complainant had sex with the defendant. But such evidence is highly prejudicial as well as embarrassing to victims, who may refuse to report rapes rather than sub-mit to such questioning. The evidence may have no relevance to the case. As one court noted, "Just as it is possible for a very wicked man to be mur-dered, so it is possible for a prostitute to be raped."[34]

Rape Shield Provisions

In jurisdictions in which the alleged victim's prior sexual experiences are admissible in rape trials, the evidence may be limited to the complainant's general reputation and not to specific sexual acts. Some jurisdictions have passed **rape shield statutes**, which protect the alleged rape victim from evidence of past sexual experiences that would not be relevant to the case and that are highly prejudicial. For example, a Vermont statute prohibits the introduction of opinion or other evidence about the complaining wit-ness's prior sexual conduct. Evidence of prior sexual conduct with the defendant may be admitted under some circumstances; likewise, evidence of "specific instances of the complaining witness' sexual conduct showing the source or origin of semen, pregnancy or disease" may be admitted.[35]

Virginia's rape shield statute provides that evidence of prior sexual expe-rience with the defendant may be admitted if it is relevant on the issue of consent and it occurred within a time period "reasonably proximate" to the current offense. That statute was tested in a case in which the complainant agreed that she had sex with the defendant eight or nine months prior to the alleged rape. At the trial the defendant tried to introduce evidence that at that time the complainant offered to have sex with him in the future for $50 and that on the day of the alleged rape she had invited him to her home. She told him she had financial problems and reminded him of the previous agreement regarding sex for pay. The trial judge found that evi-dence too remote to be relevant, and it was excluded from the trial. The appellate court ruled that the evidence was not too remote and that it was relevant to the issue of consent and therefore should have been admitted.[36]

Another case, involving an eleven-year-old who claimed that her mother's boyfriend raped her, held that the rape shield statute does not prevent introduction of evidence relevant to the issue of prior, allegedly false, accu-sations of sexual abuse. But before that evidence is admitted, the court must have evidence of a reasonable probability that the alleged victim had falsely accused others of sexual abuse.[37]

These cases are illustrative of statutory or judicial changes that have occurred concerning evidence that may be admitted regarding the consent element to rape, sodomy, or other sexual crimes. As with other areas of the law, the rules differ from jurisdiction to jurisdiction. In this particular area, because most of the statutes are relatively recent, judicial interpretations are particularly relevant. It is important to keep in mind that the purpose of the rape shield statutes is to focus the trial on the issue of consent without introducing prejudicial evidence that may not be related to that issue. Discerning the truth in rape cases is extremely difficult; conviction on the basis of perjury does occur, as Focus 6.4 indicates.

Protecting defendants' rights is a concern in rape cases as well. Thus, to enable defendants to present their full defenses, some exceptions may be permitted to the rape shield protections. For example, a California appellate court held that a defendant in a rape case should have been permitted to introduce evidence of his comment about the complainant's sexual experiences. She alleged that he forcibly tried to have sexual intercourse with her. He responded that she agreed to intercourse but that she became angry when he commented on their position, saying, "Don't you like this? Tim Hall said you did." The defendant argued that this comment made the complainant angry, and she told him to stop, which he did. He alleged that her anger at his remark led her to fabricate her story regarding her consent. The court agreed with the defendant/appellant.

> Stephens has the right to present his entire version of the incident to the jury. The jury should have been allowed to hear Stephens' unabridged account of the incident in order to properly balance the credibility and believability of both Stephens' and Wilburn's testimony.[38]

Rape Trauma and Rape Victims

There are many other evidentiary problems in rape prosecutions, but brief attention to the use of **rape trauma syndrome** evidence is appropriate in light of our earlier discussion of rape trauma as a *defense* when victims commit violent acts against their offenders. Admission of expert testimony on the rape trauma syndrome is more likely to be permitted as evidence of the victim's reaction to the rape than as evidence that the victim did not consent to sexual intercourse. The difference is that consent is an *element* of the crime and therefore requires a higher standard of proof (beyond a reasonable doubt) compared to the defendant's burden of proving a defense by a preponderance of the evidence.

The Minnesota Supreme Court has held that expert testimony on the rape trauma syndrome is not permissible as evidence that the victim did not consent.[39] However, it may be admitted as "profile" evidence in cases involving the intrafamilial sexual abuse of young children when the expert's knowledge would assist the jury in evaluating the testimony of the child. The reason for permitting the evidence in an incest case is that the average juror does not have the experience and knowledge to evaluate and assess the credibility of young children who are incest victims and who testify against defendants in this type of case.[40]

FOCUS 6.4   From Convicted Rapist to a Free Person: Gary Dotson's Story

In 1977, Cathleen Crowell Webb claimed that she was raped by Gary Dotson. He claimed that he had never had a sexual relationship with Webb. It was his word against hers; the jury believed her. Dotson was sentenced to twenty-five to fifty years in prison. He served six years, continuing to maintain his innocence, before Webb confessed that she fabricated the rape charge because she was concerned that she had been impregnated by her boyfriend. After a religious conversion, she decided to tell the truth.

Many people, including the judge, rejected Webb's recantation, and Dotson remained in prison while attorneys and private citizens sought his release. Over 70,000 people signed a petition asking the Illinois governor to extend executive clemency and free Dotson after new scientific tests indicated that it was not Dotson's semen but rather that of her boyfriend that was found on Webb's clothing on that July day in 1977. The governor refused to grant a pardon because he said he did not believe Webb's recantation.

Dotson's motion for a new trial was granted, and in 1989 all charges against him were dismissed. Dotson, who subsequently married and fathered one child, was living in an alcohol and drug treatment center as one of the terms of his parole from prison after serving a term for subsequent minor but recurring problems.

In 1989, one month after he was cleared of rape and kidnapping charges in the Webb case, he was arrested for criminal trespassing resulting from a dispute with his estranged wife. They were attempting a reconciliation, and she gave him a key to her apartment. Later problems led her to ask him to return the key. He refused, and while she was out of town, he entered the apartment and refused to leave as requested by her upon her return.

Webb and Dotson appeared together on a nationally televised talk show in 1985, and he stated that he had forgiven her and that he had more ill will against the criminal justice system than against Webb.

SOURCE: Summarized by the author from media sources.

These and other changes in the prosecution of rape cases have been made to ease the trauma that rape inflicts upon victims and to make it more reasonable for these victims to participate in the criminal justice proceedings.[41] Despite these changes, many alleged rape victims say they are victimized by the criminal justice system in addition to the victimization they suffer as rape victims.[42] Additional changes are proposed, including a bill introduced by U.S. Senator Joseph R. Biden, the Violence Against Women Act of 1993, which would increase the penalties for rape and increase aid to sexual assault victims.[43] On the other hand, some recent changes are perceived as harmful to sexual assault victims. For example, the eighty-two-year-old Florida statute that prohibits the media from publishing the names of complainants in sexual assault cases has been held unconstitutional as a violation of free speech and other constitutional protections.[44]

Date Rape

The consent issue is the critical element in proving **date rape**, a term used to describe forced sexual intercourse (or other sexual acts included in the jurisdiction's rape statute) that occurs after an individual has agreed to accompany the alleged offender on a social occasion. Because the complainant has agreed to some social activity, some people assume that she must have agreed to a sexual relationship. Susan Estrich has written a book about what she refers to as *simple rape* in contrast to *real rape*. The thesis of the book is that some people do not believe a woman is raped unless the encounter occurred with a stranger and the woman showed evidence of a struggle.[45] But the issue is not whether the two people knew each other but whether the complainant consented to sexual relations. There is no such concept as *real rape* versus *simple rape*. If the elements of forcible rape are present, the crime is *rape*, whether the parties are strangers, acquaintances, casual dates, or steady lovers. Problems of proof, of course, are an issue.

The difficulty in distinguishing rape from consensual sexual intercourse in a social setting has been illustrated by several cases in recent years. In particular, an allegation of rape made by a social acquaintance against William Kennedy Smith, nephew of Senator Ted Kennedy, the late John F. Kennedy, and Robert Kennedy, gained international media attention. Smith was acquitted of charges that he raped Patricia Bowman at the Kennedy family estate in Palm Beach, Florida. Another well-known case involved boxing champion Mike Tyson, who is serving a prison term after having been convicted of rape charges involving Desiree Washington.

A court's struggle to separate consensual sexual relations from those involving force is illustrated by the facts in the excerpt from *People v. Evans*. While reading the excerpt, consider whether Ms. P. engaged in these sexual acts because of fear, fraud, deception, or trickery, which would negate her consent. There was evidence that the defendant had said, "I could kill you. I could rape you." Did those words constitute a threat that could reasonably put Ms. P. in fear of bodily harm or death if she did not consent? The court said that if he was saying Ms. P. was helpless and had better do what he said or be hurt, that would be a threat to induce fear.[46]

People v. Evans

The defendant, a bachelor of approximately thirty-seven years of age, aptly described in the testimony as "glib," on July 15, 1974, met an incoming plane at LaGuardia Airport, from which disembarked L. E.

P., of Charlotte, North Carolina, a twenty-year-old petite, attractive second-year student at Wellesley College, an unworldly girl, evidently unacquainted with New York City and the sophisticated city ways, a girl who proved to be, as indicated by the testimony, incredibly gullible, trusting and naive.

The testimony indicates that the defendant struck up a conversation with her, posing as a psychologist doing a magazine article and using a name that was not his, inducing Miss P. to answer questions for an interview.

The evidence further shows that the defendant invited Miss P. to accompany him by automobile to Manhattan, her destination being Grand Central Station . . . Then the evidence indicates that this defendant and a girl named Bridget took Miss P. to an establishment called Maxwell's Plum, which the defendant explained was for the purpose of conducting a sociological experiment in which he would observe her reactions and the reactions of males towards her in the setting of a singles bar. After several hours there . . . she was induced to come up to an apartment . . . which the defendant explained was used as one of his five offices or apartments throughout the city.

She had been there for one to two hours when the defendant made his move and pulled her on to the opened sofa-bed in the living room of that apartment and attempted to disrobe her. She resisted that, and she claims that as articles of clothing were attempted to be removed she would pull them back on and ultimately she was able to ward off these advances and to get herself dressed again. At that point, the defendant's tactics, according to her testimony, appeared to have changed.

[The defendant informed her that he was disappointed that she had failed the test, that he was really running a psychological experiment on her to reach her innermost consciousness. He then tried to cause fear and doubt in her mind by asking her whether she realized that he could be a murderer or a rapist. Miss P. became frightened. The defendant then changed his tactics and tried to play on her sympathy by telling her how she reminded him of a lost love who had committed suicide.]

Obviously, Miss P.'s sympathy was engaged, and at that time acting instinctively, she took a step forward and reached out for him and put her hand on his shoulders, and then he grabbed her and said, "You're mine, you are mine." Thereupon followed an act of sexual intercourse, an act of oral-genital contact; a half-hour later a second act of sexual intercourse, and then, before she left, about seven o-clock that morning, an additional act . . . .

The testimony indicates that during these various sexual acts Miss P., in fact, offered little resistance. She said that she was pinned down by the defendant's body weight, but in some manner all her clothing was removed, all his clothing was removed, and the acts took place. There was no torn clothing, there were no scratches, there were no bruises.

The court noted that the defendant's words could be taken to mean that she was a foolish girl who had permitted herself to be placed in a vulnerable and defenseless position and that some other man might take advantage of that situation.

The important element distinguishing a crime from a tort is the criminal intent of the perpetrator. In this case the court found that, although Ms. P. might have construed the defendant's words as a threat, they were not so intended. However, the court concluded that the defendant was a con man, "The Abominable Snowman," whose behavior was reprehensible but did not show a criminal intent beyond a reasonable doubt.

The court in *People* v. *Evans* did not find that the facts supported rape. The state's seduction statute had been repealed; so the court did not have the option of instructing the jury on that crime.

Do you find the case an easy one, or do you believe the facts support a rape charge? How would you analyze the case if Ms. P. had offered resistance immediately prior to the sexual acts? How does this case compare to the 1994 Pennsylvania case mentioned earlier? How much resistance do you think should be required to constitute a lack of consent? These are the unanswered questions that exist in rape prosecutions. Therefore, each case must be decided on the basis of its unique facts.

The prevalence of acquaintance or date rape is not known, with some authorities reporting that as many as 90 percent of date or acquaintance rapes are not reported. The lack of reporting is attributed to several factors, such as embarrassment or a fear that no one will believe a person was raped by an acquaintance or date.[47]

Acquaintance or date rapes have been reported on college and university campuses in recent years, with some of the incidents involving gang rape. According to Michael Clay Smith, an expert on campus crime,

> More than 50 instances of campus-related gang rapes have been reported in a study by the Project on the Status and Education of Women of the Association of American Colleges. The great majority of those cases occurred at fraternity parties, and about 20 percent involved student athletes. The study said that victims of such rapes typically drop out of school, while the men are generally unaware they have committed rape and view their actions as "normal party behavior."[48]

Some scholars are finding in their research evidence of increased violence in dating relationships, and in some cases that violence leads to rape.[49]

Marital Rape

As prosecutions for marital rape have increased, courts and legislatures have had to reevaluate the common law position that a husband cannot legally rape his wife, with the exception of his aiding another person to have intercourse with her.

Historically, husbands had unlimited legal sexual access to their wives. Implicit in the marriage contract was a willingness on the part of the wife to participate in sexual intercourse at her husband's desire. Most rape statutes excluded the wife as a rape victim.

Some states have revised their rape statutes to include marital rape victims. Others, such as California, have passed specific statutes that permit either husbands or wives as victims. The California statute is titled *Rape of Spouse*. It begins,

> Rape of a person who is the spouse of a perpetrator is an act of sexual intercourse accomplished against the will of the spouse by means of force or fear of immediate and unlawful bodily injury on the spouse or another, or where the act is accomplished against the victim's will by threatening to retaliate in the future against the victim or any other person, and there is a reasonable possibility that the perpetrator will execute the threat.

Rape of a spouse is punishable by imprisonment in the county jail for not more than one year or in the state prison for three, six, or eight years.[50]

In some jurisdictions, statutes that did not specify the marital rape exception by defining rape victims as "other than spouse" have been interpreted not to preclude spouses. The Georgia statute that defines rape as "carnal knowledge of a female forcibly and against her will" was interpreted by the Georgia Supreme Court to include marital rape. The Georgia court held that, when a woman says "I do," she does not mean "I always will" as far as sexual intercourse is concerned. In *Warren* v. *State*, decided in 1985, the court upheld the conviction of a man accused of raping and sodomizing his wife while they were living together. "Certainly no normal woman who falls in love and wishes to marry . . . would knowingly include an irrevocable term to her revocable marriage contract that would allow her husband to rape her."[51]

In other jurisdictions that have by statute excluded the spouse as a victim of rape by the other spouse, some interesting interpretations of marriage have occurred to permit this exclusion. The case of *Liberta* v. *Kelly* illustrates this point. This case holds also that it is not a violation of equal protection to have rape and sodomy statutes that define only the male as perpetrator of a female victim and that define *female* as "any female person who is not married to the actor." Finally, the case illustrates a jurisdiction that treats forcible sodomy and rape in the same manner.[52]

Liberta v. *Kelly*

A jury . . . convicted Mario R. Liberta of forcibly raping and sodomizing his estranged wife. The rape statute provided that only men could be convicted of rape. In addition, although both the rape and sodomy statutes exempted from criminal liability individuals committing forcible sexual acts upon their spouses, Liberta was considered unmarried under the statutes because he had been ordered by a family court to live apart from his wife. . . . [The court gives background information on the couple.]

Mario Liberta and Denise Liberta were married on March 19, 1978. Soon after the birth of their only child, Michael, Mario began to beat Denise. Consequently, after about one year of marriage, Denise obtained a judicial order ordering Mario to stay away from her. The couple continued to live together sporadically, although Denise obtained at least two other protective orders from a family court. The second of these protective orders...again required Mario to live apart from Denise but allowed him to visit Michael on weekends. After missing his visit on the previous Saturday, Mario persuaded Denise to allow him to visit Michael on Tuesday, March 24, 1981, by promising her that a friend of his would attend. Mario and his friend Joe Meli then brought Denise and Michael to the Mohawk Motor Inn, where Mario was living. Meli left the motel, however, while Mario, Denise and Michael went to Mario's room. Denise testified that once they entered the room, Mario forced Denise to perform oral sex upon him as their son watched. Mario then raped Denise . . . .

Liberta thus contends that, assuming the constitutionality of the marital exemption, no rational basis exists for excluding from such an exemption married men who are living apart from their wives pursuant to valid protective orders. This contention is without merit. A state is certainly entitled to conclude that a husband already ordered by a court to live apart from his wife, as the result of his physically or sexually abusive conduct, represents a far greater threat to her safety than does a husband not subject to a protective order. Accordingly, New York might reasonably have concluded that the law should pose a greater deterrent to marital rape or sodomy for husbands who are subject to such protective orders. Since the goal of deterring forcible rape and sodomy is unquestionably a valid legislative objective, the New York Penal Law's distinction between married men who are subject to protective orders and those who are not "rationally furthers a legitimate state purpose." [The court discusses Liberta's argument that the limitation of the statute's prohibition of rape to males violates the equal protection clause.]

Accordingly, a statute containing a gender-based classification must be upheld "where the gender classification is not invidious, but rather realistically reflects the fact that the sexes are not similarly situated in certain circumstances . . . .

Certainly the Constitution does not require legislatures to anticipate virtually nonexistent or purely hypothetical events in drafting penal statutes. Indeed, we find it inconceivable that males who rape should go free solely because the legislature focused on a real problem, rape of women by men, with verified attendant physical and psyhological trauma, and failed to act on a hypothetical problem, rape of men by women....

Women and men thus are not similarly situated with regard to rape. Rape is unquestionably a crime that requires male participation as a practical matter, and only male rape of a female can impose an unwanted pregnancy. These facts, in our view, provide an "exceedingly persuasive justification," for a statute that provides heightened sanctions for rapes committed by men. Moreover, it cannot be contended that a rape statute punishing only men "demean[s] the ability or social status" of either men or women, particularly in the context of a penal code that prohibits coercive sexual conduct by women. The exclusion of women from the scope of [the statute] therefore, does not deny men equal protection of the laws.

In 1991 the House of Lords, Britian's highest court, overturned 250 years of common law when it held that rape may occur within a marriage. The court upheld the conviction and sentencing of a man who assaulted and attempted to rape his estranged wife at the home of her parents.[53]

Even when the law recognizes marital rape, convictions are difficult, as illustrated by the 1992 South Carolina case involving a woman who was tied up, with her eyes and mouth taped, and videotaped while her husband assaulted her. The tape was shown to the jury, but the husband testified that his wife liked rough sex and that the cries they heard on the tape when he slapped her were cries of joy, part of a sex game. He was acquitted.[54]

Sexual Abuse of Children

Child abuse may involve the violent personal crimes discussed previously, in which case the crimes may be included within those categories or within separate child abuse statutes. Child abuse also may include child stealing or parental kidnapping, in which the noncustodial parent takes the child against the wishes of the custodial parent. Often, however, child abuse includes sexual assault by family members or others, with the child's compliance. Because children are not legally capable of consenting, these acts are criminal. Although we do not know the extent of child sexual abuse, the crime is gaining more attention nationally, with the Los Angeles day care center case highlighting that attention in recent years. That case and others are discussed in Focus 6.5.

Statutory Rape

Unlike forcible rape, **statutory rape** was not a common law crime, although later it became a crime by statute, thus originating the term *statutory rape*, which historically referred to sexual intercourse with an underage girl. Some recent statutes include male minors as victims, too. The minor's consent is not a factor. The philosophy behind these statutes is that minors may be taken advantage of sexually. In order to protect minors, sexual intercourse with them is defined as a crime. The age under which minors may not give legal consent to sexual relations (and thus the acts constitute statutory rape) varies throughout the jurisdictions. The federal criminal code defines a minor as a person under eighteen years of age; some states set sixteen or younger as the minimum age for legal consent to sex.

In most jurisdictions statutory rape is a strict liablilty crime, meaning that the perpetrator does not have to be aware of the minor's age. In a few jurisdictions a reasonable mistake of the minor's age may constitute a defense.[55]

In 1981, a male defendant challenged the historical view of statutory rape laws, but was not successful. The U.S. Supreme Court upheld the constitutionality of the California statute that defined statutory rape as "unlawful sexual intercourse accomplished with a female not the wife of the perpetrator, where the female is under the age of eighteen years," thus refusing to reverse the conviction of the seventeen-and-one-half-year-old male. In the brief excerpt from the case of *Michael M.*, the Court gives its reasons for upholding the statute.[56]

Michael M. v. Superior Court of Sonoma County

We are satisfied not only that the prevention of illegitimate pregnancy is at least one of the "purposes" of the statute, but also that the State has a strong interest in preventing such pregnancy. At the risk of stating the obvious, teenage pregnancies, which have increased dramatically over the last two decades, have significant social, medical, and economic consequences for both the mother and her child, and the State. Of particular concern to the State is that approximately half of all teenage pregnancies end in abortion. And of those children who are born, their illegitimacy makes them likely candidates to become wards of the State.

We need not be medical doctors to discern that young men and young women are not similarly situated with respect to the problems and the risks of sexual intercourse. Only women may become pregnant, and they suffer disproportionately the profound physical, emotional and psychological consequences of sexual activity. The statute at issue here protects women from sexual intercourse at an age when those consequences are particularly severe.

The question thus boils down to whether a State may attack the problem of sexual intercourse and teenage pregnancy directly by prohibiting a male from having sexual intercourse with a minor female. We hold that such a statute is sufficiently related to the State's objectives to pass constitutional muster.

Because virtually all of the significant harmful and inescapably identifiable consequences of teenage pregnancy fall on the young female, a legislature acts well within its authority when it elects to punish only the participant who, by nature, suffers few of the consequences of his conduct. It is hardly unreasonable for a legislature acting to protect minor females to exclude them from punishment. Moreover, the risk of pregnancy itself constitutes a substantial deterrence to young females. No similar natural sanctions deter males. A criminal sanction imposed solely on males thus serves to roughly "equalize" the deterrents on the sexes.

Legal, moral, and ethical questions remain concerning statutory rape laws. Do they violate a youth's right to privacy? If so, where is the line drawn? Does a sixteen-year-old have a right to privacy that gives him or her the legal right to consent to sex but an eight-year-old does not have that right? Should statutory rape laws be limited to female victims? Despite an expanding recognition of children's rights, statutory rape laws remain in effect in most jurisdictions. For example, in 1994 the Florida Court of Appeals, Fifth District, upheld the state's statutory rape law.[57]

It is reasonable to expect that some jurisdictions will reexamine statutory rape laws in light of recent cases, such as that of Amy Fisher. Fisher is serving a five-to-fifteen-year sentence in prison for shooting and wounding

FOCUS 6.5 Allegations of Sexual Abuse of Children: Recent Cases

Los Angeles, California

The nation's most shocking child abuse case erupted in 1983 when a two-and-one-half-year-old child apparently told his mother of alleged incidents of sexual abuse that occurred at the McMartin Preschool in a Los Angeles suburb. Seven administrators and teachers from the prestigious preschool were indicted on 208 counts of sexual molestation.

The case became more and more shocking as the district attorney's office attempted to gather evidence to bring the case to trial. Throughout an eighteen-month preliminary hearing, the longest in California's history, children testified about rape, sodomy, satanic rituals, and the mutilation of animals. However, while an enraged public cried out for a vigorous prosecution, the case showed signs of unraveling. Prosecutors, saying that they had insufficient evidence, dropped charges against five of the seven defendants.

Attorneys for the two remaining defendants, Peggy McMartin Buckey and her son, Raymond Buckey, claimed that the children who testified had responded to leading questions and created elaborate tales of molestation. The defense alleged that the district attorney's office engaged in discriminatory prosecution in dropping the charges against five of the defendants while continuing to prosecute the remaining two.

The prosecutor's woes continued when evidence indicated that the district attorney's office may have suppressed crucial evidence that related to the woman making the initial allegations. The defense contended that the district attorney's office concealed conversations in which the child's mother claimed the child had scissors stuck in his eyes, saw a goat climb stairs at the school, and saw the head of a baby chopped off. The child claimed he was forced to drink the baby's blood. While hearings were being held to consider these allegations, the mother of the child was found dead in her home. There were no indications of foul play.

A former assistant district attorney, who was fired after leaks to the press, claimed that the whole case was nothing more than sensational headlines motivated by political considerations; all seven of the initial defendants, he said, were innocent. The prosecution maintained that the two remaining defendants, Buckey and her son Raymond, were guilty and should face the charges in court.

As the case headed for trial after nearly four years, questions remained: Who were the victims? Were the victims children who were sexually abused by adults, as the initial headlines and evidence appeared to indicate? Or were the victims the administrators and teachers who were caught in a crossfire from the imaginations of children and the paranoia of adults?

In January 1990, the longest trial in U.S. history, a trial that had already cost over $15 million, ended with acquittals on fifty-two counts of molesting young children. The jury deadlocked on one count of conspiracy against both defendants and twelve molestation charges against defendant

Raymond Buckey. He was retried; the trial began in April 1990, and was expected to continue into 1991, but it ended in July, 1990, with a mistrial.

Edenton, North Carolina

In the longest criminal trial to occur in North Carolina, Robert Fulton Kelly, Jr. was convicted in 1991 of ninety-nine of one hundred counts of sexually abusing children in the Little Rascal's Day Care Center. Fulton was sentenced to twelve consecutive life sentences, one for each of the children who testified against him. Kathryn Dawn Wilson, the cook, was sentenced to one life term.

A 1993 documentary raises questions about the 1991 trial, reporting that three of the jurors said they believed Kelly was innocent. The documentary, which was aired on national television, questions the reliability of the twelve children who testified. They were two and three years of age when the alleged abuse occurred, five and six when they testified. They told horror stories of sexual and other violent acts and of threats to kill their parents if the children revealed what happened at the day care center. The jury believed the children; others claim the case was the result of mass hysteria and that Kelly is innocent.[1]

In January 1994 Kelly's wife, Elizabeth Kelly, accepted a plea bargain in the case. She proclaimed that she is innocent but too tired to continue the legal battles. She agreed to a seven-year prison term in exchange for the prosecutor's agreement to drop eighteen of the child sexual abuse charges against her. Conviction on all of those charges could have resulted in a life sentence for Kelly, who entered a formal plea of no contest to thirty less-er charges, including having sex with her husband in the presence of children, photographing her husband as he molested a two-year-old girl, forcing a boy to have oral sex with her, concealing her husband's rape and abuse of two girls, and conspiracy. Kelly told the court the following:[2]

When I began this journal almost five years ago, I was a very strong, very optimistic, very believing and very innocent person. . . . As I stand here today, I have become very tired, very disillusioned, very unbelieving, but very much the innocent woman I was. . . . I have come to realize that although prison is some place I do not want to return to, there are many worse prisons to endure out in the free world.

Kelly's attorney called this plea agreement an "act of heroism" on the part of his client, who did not want to put the children through the suffering of a trial.

In June 1994 a fourth person entered a plea negotiation in the North Carolina case. Willard Scott Privott pleaded no contest to thirty-seven charges involving abuse of sixteen children. Privott had served over three and a half years in jail before he posted bond in 1993. He had faced a maximum sentence of 363 years; he was placed on probation for five years after the judge gave him credit for his time served. He was ordered to pay for counseling and for his court-appointed attorney.[3]

Nationwide Abuse

In other cases throughout the United States, charges of sexual abuse of children by the clergy,[4] by their own parents (as illustrated by the allegations of sexual abuse of one of their children by actress Mia Farrow against her longtime companion, actor Woody Allen), and by well-known persons (as illustrated by the fall 1993 allegations of child sexual abuse against pop star Michael Jackson) grip the nation and the world. Attorneys battle in court to protect the rights of the accused, while advocates for children battle to alter the judicial system to ease the pain of testifying for child witnesses and to protect children from sexual and other forms of abuse by adults and other children in a society in which violence is increasing.

The dangers to those accused of sexual abuse were illustrated by a landmark California case. In 1994 a jury awarded a father $500,000 against a psychotherapist whom he had accused of "conning his adult daughter into remembering childhood incidents of incest" that the father claimed never occurred. The trial took two months

and was the first in which a therapist who used the controversial technique of *recovered memory* was challenged by a nonpatient claiming to have been abused as the result of that procedure's use on a patient.[5]

SOURCE: Summarized by the author from media sources.
[1] "Frontline: Little Rascals: Was Justice Really Served?" *Washington Post* (18 July 1993), p. 7Y.
[2] "Day Care Owner Accepts Plea Bargain," *Atlanta Journal and Constitution* (22 January 1994), p. 4. All of the references to Elizabeth Kelly are from this source.
[3] "Fourth Person in Pre-School Case Is Sentenced for Sexual Abuse," *New York Times* (18 June 1994), p.6.
[4] "Suffer the Little Children: Lawsuits Target Churches for Sex Abuse by Clergy," *Trial* 29 (February 1993): 11–12.
[5] "Jury Awards Father Accused of Incest In Memory Therapy," *New York Times* (14 May 1994), p.1.

Mary Jo Buttafuoco, wife of Joseph Buttafuoco, with whom Fisher had sexual relations while she was a minor. Fisher, who has been dubbed the "Long Island Lolita," has been the subject of several books and movies and numerous tabloid headlines for her relationship with Buttafuoco. Fisher has indicated that she was sexually abused when she was a small child as well as later by a trusted family friend. She admits that she was sexually active at age fifteen and had an abortion at age sixteen. Some have argued that it is not reasonable to have criminal statutes to "protect" minors in such cases. Others insist that such minors are not mature enough to consent to sexual relations; thus, those who have sexual relations with them should be liable under the criminal law.

Buttafuoco was charged with statutory rape. Initially he denied the charges, but subsequently he entered a guilty plea. He was sentenced to six months in jail. Upon his release in March 1994, 300 people attended a party, complete with a five-foot-long, 400 pound cake. Buttafuoco's wife was wearing a one carat diamond and emerald ring given to her by her husband, who had the ring inscribed with these words: "I love you forever, Joey."

Incest

Incest refers to sexual intercourse between members of the immediate family who are prohibited by statute from marrying. Statutes may define the term in different ways. The Model Penal Code defines the crime as follows:

A person is guilty of incest, a felony of the third degree, if he knowingly marries or cohabits or has sexual intercourse with an ancestor or descendant, a brother or sister of the whole or half blood [or an uncle, aunt, nephew, or niece of the whole blood]. "Cohabit" means to live together under the representation or appearance of being married. The relationships referred to herein include blood relationships without regard to legitimacy, and relationship of parent and child by adoption.[58]

Incest may be prosecuted as other sexual crimes, too. For example, a father, who raped and sodomized his daughter and forced her to look at sexually explicit pictures in a magazine and then observe him and her mother engaging in sodomy and sexual intercourse, was prosecuted for *aggravated sexual abuse*, which may carry a more severe penalty.[59]

In many instances, utilizing other sexual abuse statutes permits criminal actions to be brought against male or female perpetrators whose victims are male. Male childhood sexual abuse victims have not received much attention, and there have been few prosecutions. But the problem was brought to national attention in 1990 when a prominent scholar and president of an eastern university resigned after being charged with making obscene phone calls. After pleading guilty, he received a suspended sentence on the condition that he continue with therapy and report to the court. Testifying that he was sexually abused as a child, he compared a child sexual abuse victim to a time bomb. "It might go off twenty-four hours later, twenty-four years later, but it will go off."[60]

Until recently, little was said publicly about incest, thought to be a crime committed infrequently and only by members of the lower class. Recent studies indicate, however, that the crime is not uncommon and is not limited to any particular socioeconomic class. Retrospective studies of adult women indicate that one out of ten were abused sexually by a member of her family.[61] Studies indicate also that cases of incest are highest among siblings.[62]

Continuous Child Sexual Abuse

California has a relatively new statute aimed at child sexual abusers. In part it provides as follows:

> (a) Any person who either resides in the same home with the minor child or has recurring access to the child, who over a period of time, not less than three months in duration, engages in three or more acts of substantial sexual conduct with a child under the age of 14 years at the time of the commission of the offense . . . or three or more acts of lewd or lascivious conduct under Section 288, with a child under the age of 14 years at the time of the commission of the offense is guilty of the offense of continuous sexual abuse of a child . . . .[63]

In March 1994 a California appellate court upheld an appellant's conviction and sixteen-year sentence under this statute.[64]

False Imprisonment and Kidnapping

False imprisonment and kidnapping are similar crimes in that both require restricting victims' freedom against their will. They differ in the elements required to establish the crimes, the seriousness of the offenses, and the punishments.

Under common law, **kidnapping** required the *asportation* (removal from one place to another) of victims from their own countries to another. **False imprisonment** did not require asportation. Sometimes called *false arrest*, false imprisonment referred to the unlawful confinement of another. Thus, kidnapping was the same as false imprisonment with the added element of asportation. Some jurisdictions do not define a separate crime of *false imprisonment*; likewise, some states do not define *kidnapping* as a separate crime if it is committed incidental to another crime.[65]

Asportation remains a required element of kidnapping in most jurisdictions, but statutes differ (as do court interpretations) concerning how much asportation is required. Consider the following case in which kidnapping was not the charge against the defendant but the issue of whether he had kidnapped his victim was introduced as an aggravating circumstance to enhance the penalty after his conviction for other crimes.[66]

People v. *Sheldon*

The evidence at issue indicated that defendant confronted Mrs. Mahan in her garage, forcibly pulled her into the house (adjoining the garage), and dragged her through the hall, kitchen, dining room and finally into the den. Although the record does not reveal the distances involved, it does appear that the asportation took place almost entirely within the Mahan home. Defendant contends that, for this reason, and regardless of the actual distance involved, the asportation did not amount to kidnapping. The people note that there is no "bright line" test for kidnapping, and that the offense may occur as long as the distance involved is not "slight," or "trivial." Moreover, as the People observe, even if the offense here may not have involved kidnapping, it certainly did involve some form of criminal activity (e.g., false imprisonment, assault) properly admissible as an aggravating circumstance . . . .

We agree with defendant that the asportation at issue was too minor to constitute kidnapping . . . .

Asportation might not be required if it can be shown that the offender had an intent to take the victim out of the state.[67] An appeals court in Maryland commented on the asportation issue:[68]

People v. *Adams*

The harm sought to be prevented is not movement of the victim, but his removal from one place to another and attendant increased risks to the victim. The actual distance the victim is transported does not necessarily correspond with the invasion of his physical interest. An asportation of 50 feet may in some cases expose the victim to precisely those abuses which kidnapping statutes are designed to prevent; in other cases, an asportation of 500 feet may alter the victim's situation not at all . . . .

[The court continued with its analysis by concluding that moving the victim does not constitute asportation unless] it has significance independent of the assault. And, unless the victim is removed from the environment where he is found, the consequences of the movement itself to the victim are not independently significant from the assault—the movement does not manifest the commission of a separate crime—and punishment for injury to the victim must be founded upon crimes other than kidnapping.

On appeal, that decision was affirmed in part and reversed in part, with the Michigan Supreme Court agreeing with the requirement of asportation but disagreeing that the victim had to be removed from the original environment. According to the court, "in one sense you can change the environment of the smallest room by intruding a criminal with a weapon, although in another sense it is still the same room."[69]

What is the purpose of this exercise in deciding when asportation has occurred? The courts are trying to avoid making a lesser crime (false imprisonment) into the more serious crime of kidnapping by finding the asportation element when it has nothing to do with the crime of kidnapping, or by creating two crimes (false imprisonment and kidnapping) when only one occurred.

Some kidnapping statutes require that the victim be isolated in a secret place; others may require only proof that there was an intent to isolate the victim. Some statutes define more than one degree of kidnapping, requiring aggravating circumstances for the more serious offense of first-degree kidnapping. Kidnapping a child for purposes of prostitution or pornography is an example of an aggravating circumstance; kidnapping for ransom is another. Frequently the classic kidnapping is accompanied by other crimes, such as extortion, ransom demands, terrorism and torture, and murder.[70]

Some jurisdictions define a separate crime of child stealing or parental kidnapping. Congress passed the Parental Kidnapping Prevention Act of 1980, which obligates states, under specified circumstances, to recognize child custody determinations of other states.[71] However, the Court has held that the statute does not give federal courts the power to resolve conflicting custody battle disputes between states. That problem, said the Court, is for Congress to decide through appropriate legislation if states refuse to cooperate with the provisions of the federal act. Thus, if two states disagree on custody in a given case, federal courts cannot solve that dispute in a civil action. Critics of the decision argue that this ruling makes U.S. courts powerless to deter parental kidnapping, for it will be easier for parents to kidnap the child and go to another jurisdiction to avoid the custody decision of the home state.[72]

Suppose a parent does just that—kidnaps the children and takes them to another state. Is that act kidnapping under the federal kidnapping law, also known as the Lindbergh Act (see Focus 6.6)? In 1993 a federal appellate court answered that question, holding that the federal statute does not permit kidnapping charges in the case of a mother accused of taking her children at gunpoint from their foster parents. In 1991 Grace Sheek and two friends traveled from Missouri to South Carolina to the foster home in which Sheek's two children were living. According to the foster mother, Mary Y. Floyd, Mrs. Sheek told the children she was taking them for ice cream. After she left, the friends bound the foster parents, threatened them with a pistol, and robbed them of $5,000. The friends were convicted of kidnapping, but the Fourth Circuit Court of Appeals ruled that the federal kidnapping law does not cover parents who abduct their own children. Mrs. Sheek is being detained in jail pending state charges, and the children have been returned to their foster home. The Floyds have adopted one of the children and are hoping to adopt the other. It has been argued that the federal statutes should be revised to include a crime of parental kidnapping, with lesser penalties than the current federal kidnapping statute, under which a conviction may result in life in prison.[73] Focus 6.6 discusses the background of this statute, along with recent cases of kidnapping.

Lower courts have disagreed concerning whether natural parents may be convicted for kidnapping a child under the various state statutes. In 1990, the Arizona Supreme Court upheld a father's convictions for sexual conduct with a minor, kidnapping, and child abuse. Under Arizona law, a conviction of kidnapping requires that the victim be restrained with the intent to commit a further act. The court held that the "further act" of child abuse was sufficient to sustain the kidnapping conviction.[74] Likewise, the Illinois aggravated kidnapping statute does not apply to a natural parent who takes a child as a victim.[75]

Terrorism and Related Crimes

In recent years an increasing number of acts that might be classified within the general term **terrorism** have occurred. These acts involve violence or the threat of violence aimed at arousing fear, alarm, dread, or coercion. Often terrorist acts are aimed at governments and the actual victims may be insignificant to the terrorists, but many recent acts of random violence against individuals may be considered a form of terrorism as well. A few are noted because of their prominence in recent years.[76]

Hate Crimes and Stalking

The 1990 Hate Crime Statistics Act defines *hate crime* as crimes "that manifest evidence of prejudice based on race, religion, sexual orientation, or

FOCUS 6.6   Kidnapping: An Overview

The 1932 kidnapping of the Lindbergh baby shocked the nation and the world, leading to the passage of a federal kidnapping statute (known as the *Lindbergh Act*) in the United States. In recent years kidnapping has become common enough that many wealthy people buy kidnapping insurance, described by one writer as "the most secretive insurance in the land."[1] Some of the nation's best-known kidnappings are as follows.

The Lindbergh Case

On 1 March 1932, twenty-month-old Charles A. Lindbergh, Jr. was kidnapped and killed. A ransom note demanding $50,000 was left on the windowsill of the nursery in the New Jersey home where the baby lived with his parents. Two years later police arrested Bruno Richard Hauptman after he purchased gas with a $10 bill from the ransom money. Hauptman was convicted, and in 1936 he was electrocuted in New Jersey's state prison. Hauptman's widow maintains her husband was innocent; she and her attorney are trying to clear his name. According to the attorney, "The trial of the century was probably the greatest fraud in the history of this country."[2] Mrs. Hauptman claims she was with her husband the night the baby was kidnapped and that they were not near the Lindbergh home. She has asked the New Jersey governor to declare that her late husband was convicted and executed unfairly.

The Mackle Kidnapping

In December 1968 Barbara Mackle, daughter of a wealthy South Florida developer, was kidnapped in Georgia and "buried" in a large coffinlike box with few amenities. She was alive eighty-three hours later when FBI agents freed her. The mastermind of the kidnapping was Steven Gary Krist, who was sentenced to life imprisonment for the crime. Krist, a brilliant man, took college courses during his prison term. After ten years in prison he was paroled, and in 1988 he was released from parole. Krist wants to become a doctor, but he has encountered rejection in his efforts to do so. A member of the Georgia Parole Board, who has become a fatherlike figure to Krist since his parole, insists that it is unfair to hold the kidnapping against Krist forever, that he has been an exemplary citizen since his release from prison, and that he should be permitted to pursue a profession. Mackle is married and lives in Florida with her husband and two children.[3]

The Weinstein Case

Reminiscent of the Mackle case, Harvey Weinstein, sixty-eight and chairman of the nation's largest manufacturer of tuxedos, was kidnapped and incarcerated in a pit six feet underground, with only a hose for air, water to drink, and fruit to eat. His kidnappers demanded and received $3 million. Weinstein was weak but alive and reasonably healthy when authorities freed him twelve days later. Police arrested a former employee of Weinstein, who allegedly masterminded the plan and executed it along with his brother, girlfriend, and brother-in-law. In May 1994 police arrested a fifth suspect, thought to be the one who forced Weinstein into the car and held a gun to his head. The case had not gone to trial when this section was completed..[4]

The Exxon Executive Case

In 1992 Sidney J. Reso, a top executive of Exxon Corporation, was kidnapped and murdered. In sentencing Arthur D. Seale to ninety-five years in prison and a five year term of supervised release, the judge said, "Your actions . . . were cold-blooded and calculated. To the extent you seek mercy you will be given the same you gave your innocent victim—none."[5] Seale's wife, Irene, was sentenced to twenty years in prison and a five-year term of supervised release for her role in the kidnapping and extortion. Arthur was fined $1.75 million, and Irene was fined $500,000, but those fines deviated from the federal sentencing guidelines and were thrown out by a federal appellate court in 1994.[6]

The Polly Klaas Case

Polly Klaas, a popular twelve year-old who was kidnapped from her home while she played a game with two school friends and her mother and half-sister slept down the hall, was buried in Petaluma, California, in December 1993. Polly's body was not found for two months after her kidnapping. It was discovered after officers arrested a career criminal, Richard Allen Davis, thirty-nine, who led them to the body. The Klaas case was publicized widely as law enforcement officers, family, friends, and volunteers searched for Polly. Her case represents one of the greatest fears of a parent: his or her child is not safe even at home. A nation mourned as Polly Klaas was buried. As one journalist noted,

Polly Klaas, kidnapped from her home, became a national symbol of random violence during the two months between the crime and the discovery of her body. Polly was twelve years old.

Even journalists, often callous in pursuit of grieving relatives, said they had been moved as never before by the Klaas family's plight, and many wept as they worked today. One television station withheld an exclusive report about Polly's death . . . until the police announced it, for fear that some family members did not yet know. And today, there were no satellite trucks lurking in wait outside the family's gray-and-white wood frame house, which was shuttered and silent but for a tinkling wind chime.[7]

In June 1994 eleven felony counts were filed against Davis, who faces the death penalty if convicted for the abduction and murder of Klaas.

[1.] "As Kidnappings Rise, Insurers Respond," *Miami Herald* (7 September 1993), p. 1.

2. "A Crime That Will not Die," *St. Petersburg Times* (2 February 1992), p. 2F.

3. "A Debt Paid in Full? Mackle Kidnapper Finds He Still Owes," *Miami Herald* (27 August 1991), p. 13; "Criminal Past Puts Career in Jeopardy," *Miami Herald* (2 July 1992), p. 1E.

4. "The Fifth Suspect: Man Charged in Weinstein Kidnapping," *Newsday* (23 May 1994), p. 21.

5. "Life Imposed in Exxon Official's Killing," *New York Times* (1 December 1992), p. 11.

6. United States v. Seale, 20 F. 3d 1279 (3d Cir. 1994).

7. "California Town Mourning After Girl's Body Is Found," *New York Times* (6 December 1993), p. 7.

ethnicity, including where appropriate the crimes of murder, non-negligent manslaughter; forcible rape; aggravated assault, simple assault; intimidation; arson; and destruction, damage or vandalism of property."[77]

Some states have enacted specific hate crime statutes, although some of those have been declared unconstitutional as a violation of the First Amendment right to Free Speech (see Appendix A). The Oregon Supreme Court upheld a state statute that makes it a crime for two or more people to injure another "because of their perception of that person's race, color, religion, national origin or sexual orientation." The court held that this statute is directed against conduct, not against speech.[78] In June 1993 the U.S. Supreme Court upheld a state statute that provides for enhanced sentences for persons convicted of crimes motivated by racial or other bias.[79]

An example of an ordinance that did not meet constitutional muster is seen in another case that illustrates the difference between *conduct* and *speech*. In *R.A.V. v. St. Paul*, the U.S. Supreme Court invalidated a St. Paul, Minnesota ordinance that prohibited displaying on public or private property a symbol that a person knows or should know will arouse alarm, anger, or resentment on the basis of race, color, creed, religion, or gender. In *R.A.V.*, a white teenager was accused of burning a cross in the yard of an African-American family. The Court found that the ordinance could have a chilling effect on the right to free speech because it permits only the expression of one side of an issue.[80]

The 1993 racial hate crime in Tampa, Florida, which resulted in the torching of an African-American tourist, focused attention once again on racial tensions in the United States. Two white drifters, Mark Kohut and Charles Rourk, were convicted of abducting Christopher Wilson, dousing him with gasoline and setting him on fire with his own lighter. They left a note at the scene, "one les nigger, more to do. KKK." Wilson was burned severely, and his injuries continue to require therapy and cause considerable pain. Despite the lack of physical evidence tied to the accused and a rocky trial in which the primary prosecutor resigned after a series of disagreements with the chief prosecutor, the defendants were convicted. Some jurors said they were convinced by the testimony of Wilson, who identified both defendants as his assailants.[81]

Some forms of behavior that do not rise to the level of physical injury nor fall within traditional criminal definitions but that may be frightening for the targeted person are covered now under *antistalking* statutes. Most states have enacted such statutes in recent years. The statutes vary consid-

Christopher Wilson suffered severe burns after he was doused with gasoline and set afire by two men who yelled racial epithets as they committed their crimes.

erably, but primarily they are designed to punish people who watch, follow, and harass others repeatedly over a period of time. Some of the statutes are too broad and will not pass constitutional tests. Others are narrowly drawn and probably will be upheld.[82]

Highway Violence

Because of the closeness of the elements of robbery to larceny-theft, robbery and carjacking are discussed in the next chapter, which focuses on property crimes. In many cases these crimes are violent crimes as well, resulting in serious bodily injury or death as well as creating fear for all who may become random victims.

In particular, violence on U.S. highways has captured headlines in the 1990s, especially in the heavily populated state of Florida, one of the top tourist destinations. The killing of foreign tourists in that state has led to international headlines proclaiming Florida as similar to a war zone. Particularly shocking was the killing of one English tourist and the injuring of another in September 1993 at a rest stop on Interstate 10 in North Florida. The other killings had occurred in heavily populated areas, generally Miami, with tourists targeted after they rented cars late at night at the airport. Investigation of the North Florida killing is focusing on African-

American teenagers who allegedly stole a car and attempted to rob the English couple. When the driver attempted to drive off, he was shot and killed, his passenger/companion injured.

SUMMARY

In one sense every crime is a crime against a person. This chapter continues the previous chapter's discussion of the *violent* crime of homicide by focusing on assault and battery and forcible rape and sodomy as well as crimes that may not be violent but that are considered very serious because they involve children (such as incest and statutory rape); or they seriously infringe on the freedom and, in many cases, raise the fear of others (such as kidnapping and false imprisonment). In this edition a new section on hate crimes and stalking as well as highway and other violence aimed at tourists highlights some of the most violent and recent crimes that have captured our attention and enhanced our fears. All of the crimes discussed in this chapter are either more prevalent today or just more obvious because of increased reporting by victims. Most of the crimes discussed in this chapter represent recent and significant changes in legislation and case law. These changes may contribute to increased reporting by victims.

Assault and battery and mayhem are violent crimes that involve inflicting bodily injury on others in an unlawful manner. These crimes may be minor or very serious, such as dismemberment, in the case of mayhem, or serious beatings, in the case of aggravated assault. A *simple assault and battery* may not involve any real physical injury but is a crime because it involves an unauthorized, offensive touching. Many cases of assault and battery are in the context of domestic violence, and only recently have we begun to recognize these acts as violent crimes rather than as domestic problems.

Forcible rape, which under the common law included only unlawful carnal knowledge of a female without her consent, has been changed by statute in some jurisdictions to include male victims and female offenders and to expand the definition of carnal knowledge beyond that of penile-vaginal intercourse. Some changes have been made in evidentiary requirements in the prosecution of rape cases. In many recent statutory changes, forcible rape and forcible sodomy are combined into crimes with such names as *aggravated sexual assault or abuse*.

Forcible rape and sodomy, as well as assault and battery, have been recognized recently in many jurisdictions as including acts that occur within the domestic setting. In the past most situations involving domestic violence were excluded from the criminal law and considered to be domestic problems, not crimes. Some states have repealed their marital rape and sodomy exemptions; others have interpreted their statutes to exclude the exemption in some cases, such as forced sexual relations with an estranged spouse.

Date rape is another violent crime that has received little attention until recently. Today it is recognized that the issue in a criminal case of alleged sexual assault and battery is not whether the victim knew the assailant but whether the victim agreed to the behavior at issue. This official recognition of date crime as a violent crime does not mean, however, that victims are necessarily more willing to report the crimes. Nor does it mean that police, prosecutors, judges, and jurors are more willing to believe that rape may occur within a marriage or other situation in which the complaining witness agreed to some social interaction with the alleged offender. Despite changes in evidence laws and attempts to sensitize court professionals as well as the general public, much remains to be accomplished in the reporting and prosecution of alleged rapes. On the other hand, we must not lose sight of defendants' rights, especially in an area in which corroborating evidence may not be available.

Another crime that has surfaced only recently as one that occurs with some regularity and contrary to prior beliefs is sexual abuse of children. This abuse occurs in all social classes. Today an alarming number of adults are reporting that they were abused as children, many by members of their own families. Such incidents were revealed in dramatic and tragic detail during the California trial of the Menendez brothers, who murdered their wealthy parents. Prosecutors argued the murders were for greed; defense attorneys argued that the brothers had been abused by their parents in many ways, including sexual, and that the brothers shot their parents because they feared their parents were going to kill them because of their threats to disclose this alleged abuse to other family members and the public.

Sexual abuse may and usually does cause serious psychological and even physical problems for children; some of those problems do not surface until later in life. Thus, it is important to prevent this crime as well as to detect it when it occurs and assist the victims in their difficult recovery. On the other hand, false allegations of sexual abuse, thought to be on the increase among children, particularly in child custody cases, may be devastating for the innocent parent or other person as well. Sorting out falsehoods from truth is extremely important but exceedingly difficult in many cases.

Kidnapping is a serious crime against the person. In one sense, it is identical to false imprisonment but with the added element of asportation. Modern kidnapping statutes do not require that the victim be taken to another country, as under the common law, but there is no general agreement on what is meant by the asportation element. There is no reason to think that this conflict will be settled soon. Some jurisdictions have abandoned the asportation element but do require that the victim be held secretly.

Neither kidnapping nor false imprisonment necessarily involves physical violence. However, both are serious crimes against the person because they may involve violence, usually create fear in their victims, and by definition involve restraint against the person's will. These crimes, like robbery, illustrate the problem of placing crimes in discrete categories. Robbery, which may but does not always involve violence, most frequently is viewed as a property crime instead of a violent crime against the person. It is discussed in the next chapter along with other property crimes.

The final section of this chapter covers several personal crimes that have become more visible in recent years and some of which have been defined only recently. Statutes designed to punish for stalking are designed to deter persons from harassing others by watching them continuously, creating fear that some violent acts may be taken. Statutes that punish hate crimes or that permit enhanced sentences when a crime is accompanied by hate that is aimed at racial, ethnic, or other suspect categories of persons are becoming the focus of attention as one side argues that such statutes are unconstitutional and the other side supports this increased effort to protect minorities from harassment. The terroristic activities of individuals and groups who prey upon the unsuspecting and innocent public in general (as in the case of the World Trade Center bombing) or upon groups, such as foreign tourists, are threats to all of society, and they appear to be increasing in frequency as well as in the total loss of life and property. More attention is given in the next chapter to these violent crimes that include property crimes as well.

STUDY QUESTIONS

1. Distinguish among *assault*, *battery*, and *mayhem*. Distinguish between *simple* and *aggravated battery*.
2. How does *domestic violence* compare to *assault and battery*?
3. What is meant by *reckless assault and battery*?
4. How do modern statutes differ from the common law definition of forcible rape? Of sodomy?
5. Discuss some of the problems involved in prosecuting cases of forcible rape and sodomy, paying particular attention to the basic elements of the crimes.
6. What is meant by *corroborating evidence*, and what is its role in sexual abuse prosecutions?
7. What are *rape shield statutes*? Evaluate the contributions or problems they bring to prosecutions for sexual abuse of adults and of children.
8. Should date rape be processed in the criminal justice system in a different way than rape by strangers? How about marital rape?
9. What is *statutory rape*, and what are its elements? Should any changes be made in the traditional statutory rape statutes? Why or why not?
10. What is *incest*?
11. Do you believe convictions for incest, statutory rape, date rape, and marital rape should carry the same penalties as those for sexual assault by strangers? Why or why not?
12. Should parental child kidnapping be a separate crime, or should it be prosecuted as kidnapping, requiring the same elements and carrying the same penalties as provided for any kidnapping?
13. Explain the importance of *asportation* in kidnapping cases.
14. Define *hate crime* and explain the concept, using a recent case. Contrast hate crime with *stalking*. What are the constitutional issues regarding statutes aimed at the behaviors included within hate crime activities and stalking?
15. If you were the Florida governor, what measures would you recommend to combat terrorism of tourists? How effective do you think those measures would be?

ENDNOTES

1. Model Penal Code, Section 211.1.
2. People v. Rocha, 479 P.2d 372 (Cal. 1971), n. 12.
3. Government of Virgin Islands v. Stull, 280 F.Supp. 460 (V.I. Dist. Ct. 1968), footnotes and citations omitted.
4. Model Penal Code, Section 211.2.
5. Federal Bureau of Investigation, *Crime in the United States, Uniform Crime Reports 1992* (Washington, D.C.: U.S. Department of Justice, 1993), pp. 31, 32.
6. See State v. Danforth, 385 N.W.2d 125 (Wis. 1986).
7. For an overview of domestic violence crimes, see Sue Titus Reid, *Crime and Criminology*, 7th ed. (New York: Holt, Rinehart and Winston, 1991), pp. 299–310. See also Richard J. Gelles and Claire Pedrick Cornell, *Intimate Violence in Families*, 2d ed. (Newbury Park, Calif.: Sage, 1990); and Lloyd Ohlin and Michael Tonry, ed. *Family Violence* (Chicago: University of Chicago Press, 1989). For a discussion of domestic violence in other countries, see David Levinson, *Family Violence in Cross Cultural Perspective* (Beverly Hills, Calif.: Sage, 1989).
8. Florida Statutes, Section 784.045 (1994).
9. Dixon v. State, 1992 Fla.App. LEXIS 2401; 17 Fla.L.W. D 700 (1992). That opinion of the three-judge panel was withdrawn by the full court, which substituted its opinion, excerpted in the text and recorded in 603 So.2d 570 (Fla.Ct.App.5th Dist. 1992), *review denied*, 613 So.2d 9 (Fla. 1992), footnotes and citations omitted.
10. Model Penal Code, Section 211.2.
11. Perkins v. United States, 446 A.2d 19 (D.C.App. 1982).
12. Model Penal Code, Section 211.1(2).
13. Idaho Criminal Code, Section 18-6605 (1994).
14. State v. Burnham, 769 P.2d 607 (Idaho App. 1989).
15. See, for example, State v. Tarrant, 80 N.E.2d 509 (Ohio App. 1948), excluding cunnilingus from the sodomy statute. Including the act was Locke v. State, 501 S.W.2d 826 (Tenn.Crim. 1973).
16. U.S. Code, Title 18, Chapter 109A, Section 2241 (1994).
17. U.S. Code, Title 18, Chapter 109A, Sections 2242, 2243, and 2244 (1994).
18. U.S. Code, Title 18, Chapter 109A, Section 2245 (1994).
19. State v. Gibson, 787 P.2d 1176 (Kan. 1990).
20. Kan. Stat. Ann., Article 35, Section 21-3518(1)(a) (1994).
21. Model Penal Code, Section 213.1(1).
22. Cal. Penal Code, Section 261 (1994).
23. Mich. Penal Code, Section 750.520b(1) (1994).
24. Mich. Penal Code, Section 750.520a(m) (1994).
25. U.S. Code, Title 18, Chapter 109A, Section 2241(a) (1994).
26. See, for example, People v. Karsai, 182 Cal.Rptr. 406 (Cal. 1982).
27. Mich. Penal Code, Section 750.520a(l) 1994.
28. State v. Moppin, 783 P.2d 878 (Kan. 1989), *superceded by statute as stated in* Norton v. State, 1991 Kansas App. (Kan.Ct.App. 1991). The statute is Kan. Stat. Ann., Article 35, Section 21-3501 (1992).
29. Chambers v. Lockhart, 872 F.2d 274, 276 (8th Cir. 1989), *cert. denied*, 493 U.S. 938 (1989).
30. See Schrum v. Commonwealth, 246 S.E.2d 893 (Va. 1978).
31. People v. Barnes, 721 P.2d 110 (Cal. 1986), *reh'g. denied*, 756 P.2d 795 (1986). See also State v. Willcoxson, 751 P.2d 1385 (Ariz.App. 1987), upholding the court's refusal to give a lengthy jury instruction indicating that rape victims must show resistance.

32. Commonwealth v. Berkowitz,—A.2d—(Pa. 1994). In general, see the discussion in "Focusing on the Offender's Forceful Conduct: A Proposal For the Redefinition of Rape Laws," *George Washington Law Review* 56 (January 1988): 403–404.

33. State v. Gibson, 787 P.2d 1176, 1180 (Kan. 1990). For a discussion of the lack of consent in rape cases, see Donald A. Dripps, "Beyond Rape: An Essay on the Difference Between the Presence of Force and the Absence of Consent," *Columbia Law Review* 92 (November 1992): 1780–1809.

34. People v. Gonzalez, 409 N.Y.S.2d 497 (N.Y.City Crim.Ct. 1978).

35. Vt. Stat. Ann., Title 13, Section 3255(a)(3)(B) (1994).

36. League v. Commonwealth, 385 S.E.2d 232 (Va.App. 1989), *adhered to on rehearing*, 392 S.E.2d 510 (Va.App. 1990).

37. State v. Barber, 766 P.2d 1288 (Kan. App. 1989).

38. Stephens v. Miller, 989 F.2d 264 (7th Cir. 1993), *reh'g. en banc, granted, vacated*, 1993 U.S.App. LEXIS 13463 (7th Cir. 1993).

39. State v. Saldana, 324 N.W.2d 227 (Minn. 1982).

40. State v. Myers, 359 N.W.2d 604 (Minn. 1984).

41. For recent information on rape victims, see Patricia A. Frazier, "A Comparative Study of Male and Female Rape Victims Seen at a Hospital-Based Rape Crisis Program," *Journal of Interpersonal Violence* 8 (March 1993): 74–76; and Grace Galliano et al., "Victim Reactions During Rape/Sexual Assault: A Preliminary Study of the Immobility Response and Its Correlates," in the same journal, pp. 109–114. See also the special section on rape in the June 1993 issue of that same journal and volume, especially the article by Patricia A. Resick, "The Psychological Impact of Rape," pp. 256–276.

42. See, for example, Lee Madigan and Nancy Gamble, *The Second Rape: Society's Continued Betrayal of the Victim* (New York: Lexington Books, 1991).

43. Violence Against Women Act of 1993. Final Status pending.

44. State v. Globe Communications Corporation, 622 So.2d 1066 (Fla.Dist. Ct.App.4th Dist. 1993). The statute is Florida Statutes, Section 794.03 (1994).

45. Susan Estrich, *A Woman's Place in the '80s, Real Rape* (Cambridge, Mass.: Harvard University Press, 1987).

46. People v. Evans, 379 N.Y.S.2d 912 (N.Y. 1975).

47. See Patricia Lopez, "He Said . . . She Said . . . An Overview of Date Rape from Commission through Verdict," *Criminal Justice Journal* 13 (Spring 1992): 275.

48. *The Chronicle of Higher Education* (16 October 1985), p. 35, quoted in Michael Clay Smith, *Coping with Crime on Campus* (New York: Macmillan, 1988), p. 121. See also Peggy Reeves Sanday, *Fraternity Gang rape: Sex, Brotherhood, and Privilege on Campus* (New York: New York University Press, 1990); and Mary P. Koss and John A. Gaines, "The Prediction of Sexual Aggression by Alcohol Use, Athletic Participation, and Fraternity Affiliation," *Journal of Interpersonal Violence* 8 (March 1993): 94–108.

49. See, for example, Marie B. Caulfield and David R. Riggs, "The Assessment of Dating Aggression: Empirical Evaluation of the Conflict Tactics Scale," *Journal of Interpersonal Violence* 7 (December 1992): 549–558; Riggs, "Relationship Problems and Dating Aggression: A Potential Treatment Target," *Journal of Interpersonal Violence* 8 (March 1993): 36–51; and Teresa M. Bethke and David M. DeJoy, "An Experimental Study of Factors Influencing the Acceptability of Dating Violence," *Journal of Interpersonal Violence* 8 (March 1993): 18–35.

50. Cal. Penal Code, Sections 262 and 264 (1994).

51. Warren v. State, 336 S.E.2d 221 (Ga. 1985), discussed in "Abrogation of A

Common Law Sanctuary for Husband Rapists: Warren v. State," *Detroit College of Law Review* 2 (Summer 1986): 599–612. See also David Finkelhor and Kersti Yllo, *License to Rape: Sexual Abuse of Wives* (New York: Free Press, 1987).

52. Liberta v. Kelly, 839 F.2d 77 (2d Cir. 1988), (citations omitted), *cert. denied*, 488 U.S. 832 (1988).

53. R. v. R., House of Lords (1991). 4 All ER 481; 3WLR 767; 94 CR App. Rep. 216 (1992) Crim.L.R.207.

54. "Marital-Rape Acquittal Upsets Activists," *Miami Herald* (19 April 1992), p. 11. See also Diana E. H. Russell, *Rape in Marriage*, Expanded edition (Bloomington, Indiana: Indiana University Press, 1990).

55. See People v. Hernandez, 393 P.2d 673 (Cal. 1964), and discussion in Chapter 3 of this text.

56. Michael M. v. Superior Court of Sonoma County, 450 U.S. 464, 471-2 (1981).

57. Jory v. State, 1994 Fla. App. LEXIS 5283 (Fla.Dist.Ct.App.5th Dist. 1994). The Florida statute is Fla. Stat., Section 794.011 (1994).

58. Model Penal Code, Section 230.2.

59. Donegan v. McWherter, 676 F.Supp. 154 (M.D.Tenn. 1987).

60. "Case Examines Length of Shadow Cast by Childhood Abuse," *Atlanta Constitution* (29 May 1990), p. 1B. See also Frank G. Bolton et al., *Males at Risk: The Other Side of Child Sexual Abuse* (Beverly Hills, Cal.: Sage, 1989). The former president has published an account of his experiences. See Richard Berendzen, *Come Here: A Man Copes with the Aftermath of Childhood Sex* (New York: Random House, 1993).

61. Laura Myers, "Incest: No One Wants to Know," *Student Lawyer* 9 (November 1980): 30. See also Anne L. Horton and Barry L. Johnson, eds., *The Incest Perpetrator: A Family Member No One Wants to Treat* (Beverly Hills, Cal.: Sage, 1989); and S. Giora Shoham, *Sex as Bait* (Albany, N.Y.: Harrow and Heston Publishers, 1989); Susan Roth and Elana Newman, "The Process of Coping With Incest for Adult Survivors: Measurement and Implications for Treatment and Research," *Journal of Interpersonal Violence* 8 (September 1993): 363–377.

62. See David Finkelhor, *Sexually Victimized Children*. See also Robert L. Geiser, *Hidden Victims: The Sexual Abuse of Children* (Boston: Beacon Press, 1979), and Joseph Shepher, *Incest: A Biosocial View* (New York: Academic Press, 1983).

63. Calif. Penal Code, Section 288.5 (1994).

64. People v. Maldonado, 23 Cal. App. 4th 46 (2d Dist. 1994), *review denied*, 1994 Cal. LEXIS 2978 (Cal. 1994).

65. See Apodaca v. People, 712 P.2d 467 (Colo. 1985).

66. People v. Sheldon, 771 P.2d 1330 (Cal. 1989), citations omitted, *rehearing denied* (Cal. 1989), *later proceeding* (Cal. 1989).

67. See Cal. Penal Code, Section 207 (1994).

68. People v. Adams, 192 N.W.2d 19 (Mich. App. 1971), *aff'd. in part, rev'd. in part*, 205 N.W.2d 415 (Mich. 1973), citations omitted.

69. People v. Adams, 205 N.W.2d 415, 421 (Mich. 1973).

70. For an analysis of kidnapping, see John L. Diamond, "Kidnapping: A Modern Definition," *American Journal of Criminal Law* 13 (Fall 1985): 1–36. For a brief but excellent discussion of the history and elements of the crime, see Stephen Kanter, "Kidnapping," in Sanford H. Kadish, ed., *Encyclopedia of Crime and Justice*, vol. 3 (New York: The Free Press, 1983), pp. 993–999. For a discussion of the kidnapping of Patty Hearst, see Shana Alexander, *Anyone's Daughter* (New York: Viking Press, 1979).

71. U.S. Code, Title 28, Section 1738A (1994).

72. Thompson v. Clay, 484 U.S. 174 (1988).

73. "Natural Mother Is Exempted From Federal Kidnap Statute," *New York Times* (2 April 1993), p. 11. The case is United States v. Sheek, 990 F.2d 150 (4th Cir. 1993).

74. State v. Viramontes, 788 P.2d 67 (Ariz. 1990).

75. See Ill. Crim. Stat., Chapter 38, Section 10-2(a) (1993). The case State v. Algarin, 558 N.E.2d 457 (Ill.App. 1990), *appeal denied*, 561 N.E.2d 695 (1990). For a discussion of parental kidnapping, see Michael V. Agopian, *Parental Child-Stealing* (Lexington, Mass.: D. C. Heath, 1981). See also Ruth Inglis, *Sins of the Fathers: A Study of the Physical and Emotional Abuse of Children* (New York: St. Martin's Press, 1978); and Geoffrey L. Greif and Rebecca L. Hegar, *When Parents Kidnap: The Families Behind the Headlines, Their Problems and Possible Solutions* (New York: Free Press, 1992).

76. For an overview of terrorism, see Sue Titus Reid, *Crime and Criminology*, 7th ed. (Ft. Worth, Tex.: Harcourt, Brace, 1994), pp. 432–442.

77. U.S. Code, Title 28, Section 534 (1994). For a discussion of this statute, see James B. Jacobs and Barry Eisler, "The Hate Crime Statistics Act of 1990," *Criminal Law Bulletin* 29 (March–April 1993): 99–123.

78. State v. Plowman, 838 P.2d 558 (Ore. 1992), *cert. denied*, 113 S.Ct. 2967 (1993).

79. State v. Mitchell, 113 S.Ct. 2194 (1993). For a recent discussion of enhanced sentencing for hate crimes, see "Hate Is Not Speech: A Constitutional Defense of Penalty Enhancement for Hate Crimes," *Harvard Law Review* 106 (April 1993): 1314–1331.

80. R.A.V. v. St. Paul, 112 S.Ct. 2538 (1992). For a discussion on the decision in a similar case in Georgia, see Note, "Antimask Laws: Exploring the Outer Bounds of Protected Speech Under the First Amendment—*State* v. *Miller*," *Washington Law Review* 66 (October 1991): 1139–1162, discussing State v. Miller, 398 S.E.2d 546 (Ga. 1990).

81. "Jury in Florida Convicts Two Whites of Burning Black Brooklyn Man," *New York Times* (8 September 1993), p. 1.

82. See, for example, the Florida statute, Fla. Stat., Section 784.048(3) (1994), providing that "any person who willfully, maliciously, and repeatedly follows or harasses another person" is guilty of stalking. Florida trial courts have split over the issue of whether this stalking law is constitutional, but in a recent decision the Third district Court of Appeals upheld the statute. See Pallas v. State, 636 So.2d 1358 (Fla.Dist.Ct.App.3d Dist. 1994). For a discussion of the deterrent effect of antistalking statutes, see Ellen F. Sohn, "Antistalking Statutes: Do They Actually Protect Victims?" *Criminal Law Bulletin* 30 (May-June 1994) : 203–241.

Chapter 7

Property Crimes

Outline

Key Terms

arson
asportation
bailee
blackmail
burglary
carjacking
confidence game

criminal trespass
embezzlement
extortion
false pretense
fence
forgery

fraud
home-invasion robbery
larceny by trick
larceny-theft
malicious mischief
robbery

Introduction

Modern property law cannot be understood fully without looking at its history, particularly through English common law. Life was much simpler when property laws first emerged. That simplicity is important in understanding how and why certain rules developed concerning property crimes and why some acts considered criminal today were considered acceptable business practices under the common law.

The English common law of property, like the common law of violent crimes, was influential in the development of property law in the United States. When U.S. common law was codified, many of the statutes were patterned after English common law. Despite changes that have resulted in criminalizing some acts that were not criminal under the common law, modern property laws retain many of the elements of the English common law. Thus, it is important to a discussion of property law to look briefly at English common law definitions and interpretations. It is important also to look at some generalities about each property crime and note specific definitions, such as those of the Model Penal Code, which have been influential in the evolution of modern property crimes.

Official FBI crime data indicate that among serious crimes, property crimes (burglary, larceny-theft, motor vehicle theft, and arson) are committed far more frequently than violent crimes (murder and nonnegligent manslaughter, forcible rape, robbery, and aggravated assault). Although the FBI and some states categorize *robbery* as a violent personal crime, some jurisdictions categorize it as a property crime. Because of its similarities to larceny-theft, robbery is discussed in this chapter along with another hybrid crime of property and violence, carjacking. This categorization is not meant to minimize the violation of the person that occurs when robbery and carjacking are committed, but rather to discuss them in the context of the elements they share with other property-related crimes. Less serious property crimes are discussed briefly in this chapter.

Serious Property Offenses

Larceny-Theft

Larceny-theft is the oldest common law theft crime, and it is the most frequently committed serious crime in the United States, with almost 8 million offenses known to police in 1992. Larceny-theft constituted 63 percent of all property crimes and 55 percent of all serious crimes, representing a 2.8 percent decrease from 1991 larceny-thefts. The estimated loss nationally from larceny-thefts in 1991 was $3.8 billion.[1]

Larceny means stealing. Under early common law, larceny was the only type of theft punishable as a crime, and its elements were construed carefully. Larceny was defined as the unlawful taking, carrying, leading, or riding away of property from the possession of another with the intent to steal. Many actions that we consider theft today were not included under early definitions of larceny. As one early case noted, it was not a crime to "make a fool of another" by deliberately delivering fewer goods than the purchaser had ordered.[2] Such deceptions were left to the civil, not the criminal law.

Under English common law, larceny was divided into *grand larceny* and *petit larceny*, with the difference being the value of the goods stolen. In a subsequent statute England abolished the distinction between grand and petit larceny. Until recently, most U.S. jurisdictions distinguished between grand and petit larceny, although the amounts involved varied considerably. But determining the value of property may be a problem, because the real value may exceed the actual cost. Usually market value is used as a measure of the property's value.[3]

Some jurisdictions differentiate grand and petit larceny by elements other than the monetary value of the stolen property. New York defines *petit larceny* quite simply: "A person is guilty of petit larceny when he steals property. Petit larceny is a class A misdemeanor." According to the commentary to that code, petit larceny is "in essence, simply the basic crime of larceny." The term therefore includes all thefts, including grand larceny, regardless of amounts or type of property stolen. In practice, the petit larceny statute is used to encompass thefts that do not amount to grand larceny.[4]

The New York Code previously designated three degrees of grand larceny and now delineates four degrees, all of which are felonies. *Grand larceny in the first degree*, the most serious larceny offense, requires obtaining property by extortion by placing the victim in fear of any one of several enumerated possibilities. In 1986 this section was amended to add a requirement that the property stolen must exceed $1 million. *Grand larceny in the second degree* requires that property valued in excess of $50,000 be stolen, while *grand larceny in the third degree* includes most thefts by extortion regardless of the amount of money involved as well as the theft of property valued in excess of $3000. *Grand larceny in the fourth degree* requires that one steal property that is valued in excess of $1000 or which includes one or more specified types of property. Examples are secret scientific materials, credit cards, or public records.[5]

Other jurisdictions have abandoned the grand versus petit larceny approach, abolished the use of the term *larceny*, and organized their codes around a consolidated theft statute. This approach follows that of the Model Penal Code.[6] But jurisdictions that take this approach, which is discussed in more detail later, may use the common law as a basis for defining theft. Thus, it is important to understand the common law of larceny.

Common Law Larceny

Under English common law, because of the seriousness of larceny-theft (which at times carried the death penalty), the elements of larceny were enumerated carefully. All elements had to be present to constitute the crime. Because of the seriousness of the offense of larceny-theft, however, many judges were reluctant to convict. Consequently, technicalities crept into the law, making some of the elements a disgrace and embarrassment. Attempts to erase these loopholes led one scholar to conclude that the "intricacies of this patchwork pattern are interesting as a matter of history but embarrassing as a matter of law-enforcement."[7] The elements of larceny are as follows:

1. a trespassory taking and
2. a carrying away (asportation)
3. of the personal property
4. of another
5. with the intent to steal.

Under the common law, technically no act can be larceny unless all of these elements are present. Modern statutes make some exceptions, at least in interpretations.

Trespassory Taking The critical element of larceny is the requirement of a *trespassory taking*, a term used in the common law to refer to the unlawful taking away of goods from the owner's possession. Apparently the common law crime of larceny was developed to deter people from committing thefts that might cause personal retaliation. It was assumed that if an owner saw someone taking away his property, he would take action that might become violent. If no trespassory taking occurred but someone outsmarted him and thereby misappropriated his personal property, he might be as angry as if there had been a trespassory taking; but it was not as likely that the offender would be available for immediate retaliatory action. Thus, the peace of society was less likely to be challenged, and consequently the common law provided civil but not criminal remedies.

As society became more complex, especially in business transactions, judges thought it necessary to expand larceny to cover thefts that did not involve trespassory takings. But instead of abolishing that element as a requirement for larceny, judges developed fictions in which a trespassory taking was assumed.The judicial fiction might operate like this. When a master delivered property to his servant to be used for the benefit of the master, it was argued that the servant had *custody* of the property but that the master retained *possession*, which in this situation was called *constructive possession*. Other forms of fiction developed, but the following example illustrates the problems created when judges began trying to expand the law of larceny without developing new offense categories.

In *Hufstetler* v. *State*, the defendant stopped at a service station and asked to have the gas tank of his car filled. The attendant pumped six and a half gallons of gas into the tank. At that time the total value of the gas was $1.94, which was below the requirement for grand larceny. The driver of the car drove off without paying for the gas. He was convicted of petit larceny and appealed, arguing that because the station attendant parted voluntarily with the possession and ownership of the gasoline, he was not guilty of petit larceny, one element of which is a trespass. In upholding the conviction, the court indicates that the owner retained constructive possession because actual possession was obtained by trick. "The obtaining of the property by the consent of the owner under such conditions will not necessarily prevent the taking from being larceny. . . . The trick or fraud vitiates the transaction, and it will be deemed that the owner still retained the constructive possession."[8] Larceny in this manner is called **larceny by trick**, meaning that because the actual possession was obtained by deception, the owner retained constructive possession. Thus, the trespassory taking from the possession of the owner was present.

Another exception to the requirement of actual possession crept into the law as judges attempted to deal with the problem that occurred when a **bailee**, a person to whom goods are entrusted, converted those goods to his own use. Technically the bailee was not taking the goods from the possession of the owner; thus, larceny had not occurred. The master-servant exception did not apply, because the bailee was an independent contractor.

New provisions were needed. The first solution was to rule that the bailee could be convicted of larceny if he broke the case of goods open and took some of the contents. Some judges reasoned that once the bailee broke the bulk, possession returned to the owner, whereas others argued that the bailee never had possession of the contents, only of the container. The practical result was that a bailee who misappropriated the entire package could not be charged with larceny because he had not taken the package unlawfully from the owner's possession. But if he broke open the package and took part of the contents, larceny was an appropriate charge, provided the other elements of larceny were present as well.[9]

These and other fictions led to later changes in the law of theft. Today, when a bailee misappropriates property, some states treat that act as larceny if the package is broken, but as embezzlement if it is not broken. Other states have a separate crime, *larceny by bailee*, to cover the misappropriation whether or not there was a breaking. Some have a general crime called *theft* that covers all these situations.

The element of taking is of significance in shoplifting. Suppose a student enters the university book store, picks up several pens, and puts them in his or her pocket before leaving. Has the element of *taking* occurred? May the student be charged with larceny-theft before leaving the premises? This issue arose in three New York cases. The facts differed in each case, but essentially they involved acts that might be considered shoplifting except that the accused had not left the stores when they were apprehended. In one of the cases the suspect took a book from the shelf of a bookstore, put it in his briefcase, and continued to browse. When confronted by an employee, he reacted by hitting that person with the case. It fell open, and the book fell out. In the excerpt below, the New York Court of Appeals explains its reasons for upholding each conviction. After citing the facts of each case, the court discussed the common law of property with its requirement of a taking, and then the modern evolution of the law away from actual taking to a requirement that the individual exercised control over the property "inconsistent with the continued rights of the owner," noting that it is expected that customers may examine or even try on articles.[10]

People v. *Olivo*

In many cases, it will be particularly relevant that defendant concealed the goods under clothing or in a container. Such conduct is not generally expected in a self-service store and may in a proper case be deemed an exercise of dominion and control inconsistent with the store's continued rights. Other furtive or unusual behavior on the part of the defendant should also be weighed. Thus, if the defendant surveys the area while secreting the merchandise or abandoned his or her own property in exchange for the concealed goods, this may evince larcenous rather than innocent behavior. Relevant too is the customer's proximity to or movement towards one of the store's exits. Certainly it is highly probative of guilt that the customer was in possession of secreted goods just a few short steps from the door or moving in that direction. Finally, possession of a known shoplifting device actually used to conceal merchandise, such as a specially designed outer garment or false-bottomed carrying case, would be all but decisive.

Of course, in a particular case, any one or any combination of these factors may take on special significance. And there may be other considerations, not now identified, which should be examined. So long as it bears upon the principal issue—whether the shopper exercised control wholly inconsistent with the owner's continued rights—any attending circumstance is relevant and may be taken into account . . . .

Quite simply, a customer who crosses the line between the limited right he or she has to deal with merchandise and the store owner's rights may be subject to prosecution for larceny.

Other circumstances are relevant to the required trespassory taking, and the law is very technical. But one other situation should be noted. What happens if you *find* property that belongs to another and decide to appropriate that property to your own use?

An early case considered the issue when property lost on the street was found and taken with the intent to keep. In 1878 an Ohio court said, "The title to the property, and its constructive possession, still remains in the owner; and the finder, if he takes possession of it for his own use, and not for the benefit of the owner, would be guilty of trespass."[11] If the finder intended to find the owner and return the property, there is no trespass, so that element of larceny is absent.

Most modern statutes have requirements for returning or at least making an effort to return known lost property. The Model Penal Code, which uses the term *theft* rather than *larceny*, provides:

> A person who comes into control of property of another that he knows to have been lost, mislaid, or delivered under a mistake as to the nature or amount of the property or the identity of the recipient is guilty of theft if, with purpose to deprive the owner thereof, he fails to take reasonable measures to restore the property to a person entitled to have it.[12]

A Carrying Away (Asportation) The second element of larceny is that the goods must be taken away, called **asportation**, which means moving things from one place to another. This element may be satisfied by the slightest movement. If the defendant attempts to take the article away and does not succeed, the element is not complete and larceny has not occurred. Thus, a defendant who removed a coat from a store dummy and tried to take it away but could not do so because it was attached by a chain was not guilty of larceny.[13]

The asportation requirement of common law larceny is not very important today because most modern codes follow the Model Penal Code provision that a person is guilty of theft "if he unlawfully takes, or exercises unlawful control over, movable property of another with purpose to deprive him thereof."[14] Some jurisdictions provide greater penalties when the article is taken from the person; some call this act a separate crime, such as *larceny from the person* or *pickpocketing*.

Personal Property of Another The third and fourth elements of common law larceny are that the article must be the personal property of another person. The phrase *of another* means that abandoned property and wild animals are not included. Under the common law, personal property referred only to *tangible personal property*. Trees, minerals, crops, and other items of real property could not be the subject matter of larceny. If those items were severed, larceny could occur, but the severance and the larceny had to be two separate acts.

Today, some jurisdictions do not require the separate actions to constitute larceny; some statutes include trees and other items of *real property* within the definition of theft. In most cases, electricity and gas are considered property subject to larceny, but labor and services are not covered unless specified by statute.[15]

Some statutes cover services. The Model Penal Code covers theft of services, defined to include "labor, professional service, transportation, telephone or other public service, accommodation in hotels, restaurants or elsewhere, admission to exhibitions, use of vehicles or other movable property."[16]

The evolution of statutes to include theft of services is an interesting indicator of how our society is changing. In 1986, New York expanded its statute covering theft of services to include the "intent to avoid payment of the lawful charge for admission to any theatre or concert hall, or with intent to avoid payment of the lawful charge for admission to or use of a chair lift, gondola, rope-tow or similar mechanical device utilized in assisting skiers in transportation to a point of ski arrival or departure."[17]

Some modern cases have considered the issue of what constitutes property for purposes of theft. For example, consider the defendant who was employed as a computer operator who had access to the city's leased computer terminal and computer storage. During the course of his employment, he began a private business but used the computer at work to store his business files. Subsequently he was fired and charged with nine counts of theft for his use of the city computer for his private business. He was convicted and appealed.

The appellate court reversed his conviction on the grounds that he had not taken any property of value from the city; that is, he had not stolen property. The computer was leased at a fixed charge; thus, his use of the computer for his private business did not cost his employer additional costs, and the disks and storage space were erasable and reusable. He benefitted in his private business from the use of the city computer, but he did not take any property from the city.[18] Some jurisdictions have enacted statutes aimed specifically at computer crimes, which are discussed in Chapter 11.

With the Intent to Steal The final element of common law larceny is that the defendant must have had an intent to deprive the owner of the property.

In a very early case involving a seventeen-year-old who took a bicycle, as he said, "to get even with the boy, and of course, I didn't intend to keep it," the California Supreme Court reversed the conviction and emphasized the common law position that the intent must be an intent to deprive the owner of the property permanently, as indicated in the brief excerpt from *People v. Brown*.[19]

People v. *Brown*

The [trial] court told the jury that larceny may be committed, even though it was only the intent of the party taking the property to deprive the owner of it temporarily....But the test of law to be applied to these circumstances for the purpose of determining the ultimate fact as to the man's guilt or innocence is, did he intend to permanently deprive the owner of his property? If he did not intend to do so, there is no felonious intent, and his acts constitute but a trespass. While the felonious intent of the party taking need not necessarily be an intention to convert the property to his own use, still it must in all cases be an intent to wholly and permanently deprive the owner thereof.

If larceny requires an intent to deprive an owner of property permanently, what would you do with the typical joyride, in which the defendants testified that they took the car only for the purpose of driving it for a short period and then intended to return it to its owner? Most states have handled this problem by enacting special statutes to cover joyriding and similar offenses. The Model Penal Code provides, "A person commits a misdemeanor if he operates another's automobile, airplane, motorcycle, motorboat, or other motor-propelled vehicle without consent of the owner." It is an affirmative defense if the actor had a reasonable belief that the owner would have consented to the operation had he or she known of it.[20]

The intent to deprive permanently is retained as an element of theft in many jurisdictions that now refer to *theft* rather than *larceny-theft*. The Model Penal Code defines *deprive* as any of the following:

(a) to withhold property of another permanently or for so extended a period as to appropriate a major portion of its economic value, or with intent to restore only upon payment of reward or other compensation; or

(b) to dispose of the property so as to make it unlikely that the owner will recover it.[21]

MODERN THEFT CODES

We have analyzed the common law elements of larceny because most of those elements are retained in modern theft statutes, and frequently common law is used to interpret statutes. In recent years many jurisdictions have enacted legislation more specific than common law larceny-theft. These specific statutes reflect the problems that arose when attempts were made to apply the common law definition of larceny-theft to modern theft crimes.

Some of the problems have been noted already. For example, services were excluded from the personal property requirement of larceny-theft. Some jurisdictions have included theft of services under a special statute, while others, such as New York, have expanded their current statutes to include theft of services. In addition, the theft section of New York's Penal Code includes a statute prohibiting fortune-telling, a misdemeanor. The statute excludes people who engage in fortune-telling "as part of a show or exhibition solely for the purpose of entertainment or amusement." The statute, formerly included under "disorderly conduct," is aimed at preventing those who mislead and "annually bilk a gullible public of many millions of dollars."[22]

Today a common approach is to combine all theft-related crimes into one crime of *theft*, as in the Model Penal Code. The MPC specifies types of theft: theft by unlawful taking or disposition; theft by deception; theft by extortion; theft of property lost, mislaid, or delivered by mistake; the receiving of stolen property; theft of services; theft by failure to make required disposition of funds received; and unauthorized use of automobiles and other vehicles.[23]

The Model Penal Code approach permits combining many kinds of theft into a few categories. A contrasting approach is to have numerous larceny statutes covering the various types of larceny. Jurisdictions differ also in whether they include theft-type crimes, such as embezzlement, fraud, false pretense, forgery, counterfeiting, and those involving stolen property, within the general theft statute or whether they have separate statutes. The crimes included by the FBI in its collection of official data on larceny-theft are enumerated in Figure 7.1, which contains a graph indicating the percentage distribution of each type.

Burglary

Another major property crime is **burglary**. Official data on burglary indicated a decrease in 1992 as compared to 1991, with the number of offenses down 5.6 percent. Burglary accounted for 21 percent of the total Index Crimes and 24 percent of property crimes. Most of the burglaries, two out

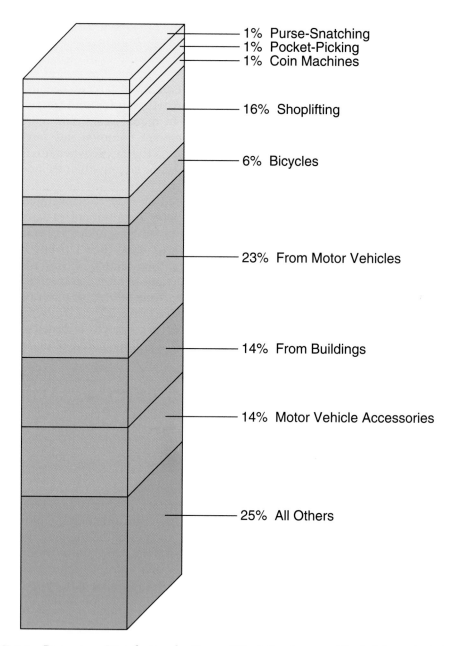

1% Purse-Snatching
1% Pocket-Picking
1% Coin Machines

16% Shoplifting

6% Bicycles

23% From Motor Vehicles

14% From Buildings

14% Motor Vehicle Accessories

25% All Others

FIGURE 7.1   Percentage Distribution by Type of Theft For Larceny-Theft Crimes in 1992
SOURCE: Federal Bureau of Investigation, *Crime in the United States, Uniform Crime Reports 1992*
(Washington, D.C.: U.S. Department of Justice, 1993), p. 47.

of every three, occurred in residential dwellings. The average loss per burglary was $1,278.00, and the total loss in the country was estimated at about $3.8 billion.[24]

Along with arson, common law burglary was classified as an offense *against the habitation and occupancy*. Today both arson and burglary are statutory crimes. The statutory definitions of burglary and arson go far beyond the common law definitions and elements, but the common law is important to an understanding of modern statutes.

Before examining the elements of common law burglary, it is necessary to distinguish residential burglary from robbery, discussed later. It is common for a victim of household burglary to say, "I was robbed." This statement is incorrect; each of the crimes has some distinct elements. For example, robbery, discussed later in the chapter, requires taking property *from the person or presence of the victim*. Burglary does not require this element. Robbery requires the use of *force or threat of force*, which is not required for burglary.

Burglary of a home may and often does occur when no one is home. But a burglary may lead to a robbery. Household burglary is one of the most serious of crimes, not only because of the illegal entry into the home, but also because a substantial proportion of violent crimes that occur in the home occur during burglaries. Burglary is important also because offenders who commit this crime may be involved in crime for years. Focus 7.1 contains information on the extent to which some criminals engage in burglary as a "career."[25]

COMMON LAW BURGLARY

Common law burglary referred to breaking and entering the dwelling of another in the nighttime with the intent to commit a felony. Under the common law, a *breaking* did not require destruction of any part of the property in order to enter, but it did require a "breaking, removing, or putting aside of something material, which constitutes a part of the dwelling house, and is relied on as a security against intrusion."[26] The emphasis on security is important. If the door were already open, entering by that means did not constitute a breaking. If the door were closed but unlatched, opening the door constituted a breaking. In some jurisdictions, if the door were partially open and if it were necessary to open it further to enter, breaking was deemed to have occurred.[27]

Under some circumstances, such as obtaining entry by fraud, by threatening the use of force, by going through a chimney, or by having a servant or some other person within the structure open the door, it was argued that *constructive force* sufficient to constitute a breaking had occurred. The breaking had to involve a *trespass*. That is, the person who entered did not have permission to enter, and therefore entry was unlawful. Furthermore, the entry must have been accomplished by means of the breaking. Therefore, it would not be sufficient if the offender broke the window to enter but actually entered the dwelling through a door that had been left open by the owner.

FOCUS 7.1   Burglary as a Career

In 1987 several news accounts focused on burglary as a career. Based on interviews with burglars, the articles supported conclusions by social scientists: a few burglars commit a large proportion of the burglaries. But these news accounts go further than data and tell us something about the "profession" of burglary as viewed by those who have chosen this line of work.

Three inmates in the Texas Department of Corrections claimed that they were responsible for more than 5,000 burglaries in Dallas. Although these claims are impossible to substantiate, authorities tend to believe them. The inmates considered burglary to be their profession. One burglar kept regular hours, working in the morning from 9 until 11:45 and then taking afternoons off to work on his golf game. The burglars utilized methodical and purposeful procedures. They would drive through neighborhoods checking to see who was home and then double-check by using a crisscross directory to get the phone number and call. Once a target home was selected, the burglars would kick open the door and work rapidly, usually securing what they wanted (jewelry, silver, cash, or videocassette recorders) and be gone within five minutes.[1]

In Chicago, a twenty-three-year-old man claimed to have committed 1,500 burglaries within two years. He began his burglary workdays at dusk and worked most of the day, staying out of the wealthiest neighborhoods because his car would be too obvious there. Michael Sherrill claims that he was deterred by burglar alarms, a large dog, or the sound of a stereo. In such cases, he would move to another, easier target. Sherrill worked until 9 or 10 at night "or until his car trunk was full." Sherrill took as much as $1,000 worth of drugs per day, and his burglary career enabled him to support this habit.[2]

In July 1987, police in Tulsa, Oklahoma, found evidence of a burglary operation in which suspects, with elaborate computer technology, compiled information on targeted homes of doctors and lawyers. They had data on the activity patterns of these targeted victims as well as their neighbors and already had burglarized numerous dwellings when the police discovered the ring.[3]

[1] Steve Blow, "Stealing for a Living," *Dallas Morning News* (15 February 1987), p. 22.
[2] "Man's Confession Gives Insight into How Burglars Work," *Dallas Morning News* (10 December 1986), p. 41.
[3] Landon Jones and Amber Merchant, "Arrests Yield Evidence of Computerized Burglaries," *Tulsa Tribune* (10 July 1987), p. 1. For a classic study of the professional thief, see Edwin H. Sutherland, *The Professional Thief* (Chicago: University of Chicago Press, 1937). For more recent studies, see Joan Petersilia et al., *The Prison Experience of Career Criminals* (Santa Monica, Cal.: Rand Corporation, 1980).

The second element of common law burglary was an *entering*. The requirement of an entry could be satisfied if any part of the person of the intruder entered; it was not necessary that the person go into the dwelling. The entry requirement could be accomplished by the use of a tool, provided that the tool was for the purpose of committing the intended felony. Using an auger to drill a hole through a floor to steal grain by letting the grain fall into a sack constituted an entry. It would not be an entry if the offender inserted a tool into the dwelling to effect his or her own entry but did not actually enter.[28] Entry could be accomplished constructively by sending in someone who was not legally capable of committing a crime, such as a child, a trained monkey or other animal, or an insane person, to commit the felony.

The third element of common law burglary required that the *dwelling of another* be entered. Under the common law, burglary was limited to acts that occurred within the home, referred to as the *dwelling* or the *dwelling place*. There was some precedent that a church could be the subject of burglary, because it was the home of the Almighty, and this common law position was accepted in a 1964 Maryland case.[29] Usually a dwelling was a place where someone slept regularly; occasional sleeping was not sufficient. If the building were used regularly during one season (for example, a summer home), that would suffice, provided the possessor intended to return another summer. The dwelling requirement was met if someone slept regularly in an office or other structure; it was the regular sleeping that was critical to this element of the offense.

Included within the definition of *dwelling* were pertinent buildings that were "within the curtilage," such as a garage, barn, stable, or cellar, or those buildings generally included within the fence of the property. If there were no fence, the buildings would have to be reasonably close enough to the dwelling to be fenced. One final requirement was that the dwelling place had to be that of another. Burglary did not encompass breaking and entering your own property with the intent to commit a felony.

Common law burglary required that the crime occur during the nighttime, usually defined as from sunset until sunrise or when the countenance of a person could not be discerned. Both the breaking and the entering had to occur at night, although they did not have to occur on the same night; one might break on one night and enter on a subsequent night.

The final element of common law burglary was that of the intent to commit a felony, usually larceny. Any felony would suffice. It was sufficient if one entered the building to commit the felony but did not actually do so. It was the unlawful breaking and entering *with the intent of* committing the felony that constituted burglary. If the felony (for example, larceny) were completed, the offender could be charged with and convicted of both larceny and burglary.

If the individual entered the dwelling without an intent to commit a felony and once inside decided to commit a felony, he or she might be convicted of that felony but not of burglary. The intent to commit the felony must have been present at the time of the unlawful breaking and entering. The intent to commit a misdemeanor would not be sufficient; there must have been an intent to commit a felony.

STATUTORY BURGLARY

Most jurisdictions have enacted burglary statutes. Some of the common law requirements are retained in burglary statutes; others are modified. Most no longer require a breaking, although they may require *unlawfully remaining*. Any illegal entrance may be sufficient. Most include any structure and do not retain the common law requirement of a dwelling, although they may provide greater penalties for those who burglarize a dwelling. The distinction between night and day is retained in some statutes; in others it is eliminated or made relevant only to punishment.

Some jurisdictions define grades of burglary, such as aggravated burglary or burglary of the first and second degree; or they classify certain types of burglary as a felony of the first, second, or third degree and provide differential sentences depending on the perceived seriousness of the type of burglary.

The Model Penal Code is an example of a modern burglary statute that differs from the common law in several respects. It provides as follows:

> (1) *Burglary Defined*. A person is guilty of burglary if he enters a building or occupied structure, or separately secured or occupied portion thereof, with purpose to commit a crime therein, unless the premises are at the time open to the public or the actor is licensed or privileged to enter. It is an affirmative defense to prosecution for burglary that the building or structure was abandoned.
>
> (2) *Grading*. Burglary is a felony of the second degree if it is perpetrated in the dwelling of another at night, or if, in the course of committing the offense, the actor:
>> (a) purposely, knowingly or recklessly inflicts or attempts to inflict bodily injury on anyone; or
>> (b) is armed with explosives or a deadly weapon.
>
> Otherwise, burglary is a felony of the third degree. An act shall be deemed "in the course of committing" an offense if it occurs in an attempt to commit the offense or in flight after the attempt or commission.[30]

The M.P.C. definition does require an *entering*. New York includes *unlawfully remaining* as an alternative to entering, permitting a charge of burglary when a person "knowingly enters or remains unlawfully in a building with intent to commit a crime therein." In New York, there are three degrees of burglary, with the above phrase defining all degrees. It is the sole definition of third-degree burglary. To constitute first- or second-degree burglary, other elements must be met. Those elements range from being "armed with explosives or a deadly weapon" to displaying "what appears to be a pistol, revolver, rifle, shotgun, machine gun or other firearm," with some exceptions following that phrase. In essence, the New York statute is grading burglary in terms of the total circumstances in which it occurs, with special reference to the potential for danger. All three degrees of burglary are felonies in New York.[31]

Both the M.P.C. and the New York statutes deviate from the common law requirement of *intent to commit a felony* in that both refer only to the *intent to commit a crime*. Thus, a burglary conviction could be based on an intent to commit a misdemeanor. Others, such as Montana, use the terminology *with the purpose to commit an offense therein*. Montana's statute requires knowingly remaining unlawfully as well as knowingly entering unlawfully.[32]

In *State* v. *Christofferson*, the defendant gained entry to the house by deceit; he told a student who lived there that the mother, whom he knew, told him to check on the student and one child, who had remained in the home with the student when the mother left town. Apparently the mother did not tell the defendant to go into the house, but he was admitted to the house by the student. Later the defendant twice told the student he was leaving, but he did not do so. Instead, he went to the daughter's bedroom and engaged in what Montana calls *felony sexual intercourse without consent*. The court upheld the defendant's convictions for that crime and for burglary, the latter based on the fact that he remained in the home unlawfully and with the purpose of committing an offense.[33]

In 1990, the U.S. Supreme Court considered the meaning of the word *burglary* in the context of the Career Criminals Amendment Act of 1986 of the Anti-Drug Abuse Act of 1986. The amendment provides for an enhanced penalty for persons convicted under the Anti-Drug Abuse Act if they have three prior convictions for specified types of offenses, including burglary. But the act did not define *burglary*.[34] The Court disagreed with the argument that the word *burglary* should be defined as it is defined in the state in which the former act took place. Acknowledging that state statutes differ, the Court noted that there are common elements of burglary and adopted the following definition: "We conclude that a person has been convicted of burglary...if he is convicted of any crime, regardless of its exact definition or label, having the basic elements of unlawful or unprivileged entry into, or remaining in, a building or structure, with intent to commit a crime."[35]

Modern statutes may differ from the common law regarding whether they permit a conviction on the burglary charge *and* on the crime for which the illegal entry was made. Some jurisdictions retain the common law provision but limit it to situations in which the burglary was committed with the intent to commit a *serious* (usually defined as a felony) crime.[36]

In recent years some jurisdictions have enacted new statutes to cover the entry of a dwelling with the purpose of committing a robbery. This new approach to crimes against the person and the habitation is discussed later in this chapter.

Motor Vehicle Theft

In the official crime data of the FBI, thefts *from* vehicles are included under *larceny-theft*, but theft *of* motor vehicles is a separate category of serious property crime, defined as "the theft or attempted theft of a motor vehicle." This definition includes

> the stealing of automobiles, trucks, buses, motorcycles, motorscooters, snowmobiles, etc. The definition excludes the taking of a motor vehicle for temporary use by those persons having lawful access.

The number of offenses falling within this category in the 1992 *Uniform Crime Reports (UCR)* data was 1,610,834, a 3.1 percent decrease from 1992. Despite this decrease, the 1992 rate of motor vehicle thefts represents a 47 percent increase over the 1983 rate and an 8 percent increase over the 1988 rate.[37]

For obvious reasons, the common law of motor vehicle theft is not a subject of discussion in this or other sources. The importance of vehicles in modern society, leading to the frequent theft of these important possessions, necessitated redefining criminal statutes to include this crime. Despite the inconvenience that results from being victimized by a motor vehicle thief and the probability that the property will not be returned undamaged, little is known about those who commit this crime. Nor is much attention paid to the law of motor vehicle theft.

In 1988 the Bureau of Justice Statistics published a report of its analysis of motor vehicle thefts between 1973 and 1985. Some of the results of that study are reprinted in Focus 7.2.

In 1992 New Jersey officials faced the growing number of motor vehicle thefts with a range of proposals. The state's attorney general blamed the increase in car thefts and subsequent violence by juveniles confronted by police (some juvenile car thieves pull weapons or ram the stolen cars into police cars) on a "wayward group of youths" for whom "the ramming of police cruisers...has become a perverse form of recreation." The attorney general indicated that the state would target specifically the less than 100 juveniles who had committed more than 1,000 car thefts. "These offenders must know that there will be sure and certain punishment for their anti-social acts."[38]

In 1993 New Jersey officials and legislators continued their efforts to combat motor vehicle thefts, of which 60 percent are committed by juveniles (under eighteen), with the typical thief a person aged sixteen. In June of that year the legislature enacted a package of bills providing for stiffer penalties for car theft. Among other provisions, the statutes require extended prison terms for persons who use stolen cars to commit certain crimes.

An increase in auto thefts by juveniles, some of whom commit violent acts in the course of these crimes, has led some states to target such acts with curfews and other provisions.

FOCUS 7.2 Motor Vehicle Theft

In a special report on motor vehicle theft prepared by the Bureau of Justice Statistics, the BJS director said, "Motor vehicle theft is of great concern to most Americans. The cost of this crime to victims and to society as a whole is considerable." Some of the findings of that study are as follows:

• The number of motor vehicles stolen declined 33% during the 1973–85 period, from 9 to 6 per 1,000 registered vehicles.

• Motor vehicle thefts, whether completed or attempted, most often took place at night; vehicles were most often parked near the victim's home, in noncommercial parking lots, or on the street.

• A household member was present in about 9% of all motor vehicle theft incidents, and in 3% the offender either threatened or physically attacked the victim.

• Attempted thefts were more likely than completed thefts to occur at night, have a household member present, result in property damage, and be reported to police by someone outside the household.

• Stolen motor vehicles were recovered in 62% of the incidents.

• Almost 9 in 10 completed motor vehicle thefts were reported to police. The percentage of thefts reported increased as the value of the stolen property increased.

• In half of all completed motor vehicle thefts, property worth $2,455 or more was stolen; in more than 1 in 4 thefts, property worth at least $5,000 was stolen; and in 1 in 10 the loss was $10,000 or more.

• Losses from completed motor vehicle thefts after recoveries and reimbursements by insurance companies amounted to $16.1 billion, or $1.2 billion annually.

• Blacks, Hispanics, households headed by persons under age 25, people living in multiple-dwelling units, residents of central cities, and low-income households were among those most likely to be victimized by motor vehicle theft.

• Those least likely to experience a motor vehicle theft included those 55 and older, people who owned their own homes, and those living in rural areas.

SOURCE: Bureau of Justice Statistics, *Motor Vehicle Theft* (Washington, D.C.: U.S. Department of Justice, May 1988), p. 1.

Jail terms are to be imposed on repeat offenders. Mandatory penalties are provided for juveniles who are involved in motor-vehicle-related crimes. For example, a juvenile convicted of aggravated assault as a result of joy riding, or of eluding police, must serve a minimum of sixty days. Repeat joy riders must serve at least thirty days. The first offense of stealing a motor vehicle, joy riding, or eluding police calls for a sixty-day mandatory community service sentence. Persons who use stolen cars to commit the crimes of robbery, burglary, escape, drug distribution, aggravated or sexual assault, eluding police, kidnapping, or manslaughter face longer prison terms than those specified for any of those crimes committed without the use of a stolen car.[39]

Arson

Arson is classified as a serious property crime in the official crime data collected by the FBI, but it did not attain that status until 1978. Arson is a serious crime, causing significant property damage and, in some cases, injury and death. But it is difficult to acquire sufficient evidence for arson convictions, as much, if not all, of the evidence of a crime may be destroyed by the fire.[40]

Officials warn that arson data may reflect better reporting and investigating procedures rather than actual changes in occurrence. Despite these difficulties, we do have official data on arson in recent years, with 102,009 arsons reported to police in 1992, representing virtually no change over the number reported in 1991. Arson is defined by the *UCR* as "any willful or malicious burning or attempt to burn, with or without intent to defraud, a dwelling house, public building, motor vehicle or aircraft, personal property of another, etc."[41]

In recent years more attention has been given to arson since the occurrence of several cases involving large numbers of deaths have occurred. Some of those crimes are summarized in Focus 7.3.

In the fall of 1993 fires swept through Laguna Beach, Malibu, and other California neighborhoods, forcing evacuation of many and causing the deaths of three Malibu residents, destroying over 1,000 structures (including many expensive homes) and over 200,000 acres. Arson is suspected in at least nineteen of the twenty-six fires. Forty-four-year-old Thomas Lee Larsen, also known as *Fedbuster*, was arrested for threatening to set fires "in revenge for the Government seizure of his property." Larsen entered a plea of not guilty, but he was refused bail. Subsequently he entered a guilty plea to six counts of sending threatening letters to commit arson. Larsen, a convicted child molester, was sentenced to forty months in prison.[42]

Increasing attention is being given to the crime of *arson for hire*, believed by some to become more prevalent in difficult economic times. The sociological and psychological causes of arson are of concern, too. For example, in 1992 a Florida drifter indicted and tried for multiple counts of arson of Florida churches and linked with church arsons in Tennessee, was found not guilty by reason of insanity. Patrick Lee Frank claimed that he committed arson of churches because he thought church computers were trying to control him and that as a child in Tennessee he was sexually abused by a church member. Frank was committed indefinitely to a federal psychiatric hospital.[43]

Another feature of arson that police are contending with in some areas, such as Miami, Florida, is the practice of juveniles who steal cars, set them on fire, and jump out just in time to avoid injury or death. It is claimed that to increase their thrills, some juveniles will drive the

FOCUS 7.3   The Tragedy of Fire

In 1903 the deadliest fire in U.S. history claimed the lives of 575 people in the Iroquois Theater fire in Chicago. In 1992 survivors of the second-largest fire in U.S. history gathered in Boston to mark the fiftieth anniversary of the Cocoanut Grove nightclub fire which they escaped on 28 November 1942. That fire claimed the lives of 491 people.[1] Recognition of the lack of adequate safety precautions, which increased the death toll in these fires, led to improved fire codes and enforcement of those codes. Improved fire codes are important, but they cannot always eliminate human tragedies, especially when fires are set deliberately. A few recent examples are noted.

San Juan Hotel Fire, December 1986

When three members of Local 901 of the International Brotherhood of Teamsters set fire to Puerto Rico's Dupont Plaza Hotel, all they wanted was a small fire that would put pressure on the hotel's management to come to terms with the union. What they got was a runaway blaze that started in the hotel's ballroom and raced up the elevator shafts, killing ninety-seven people as it roared through the hotel.

The fire moved through the ground level of the hotel so fast that many occupants were not able to reach emergency exits. Rescuers found corpses propped up at the bar. Some of the hotel's guests on higher floors made it to the roof where they were rescued by helicopter. Others scaled walls or jumped out of windows only to find themselves in the pool area with a locked gate. Some scaled the fence and barbed wire to reach safety.[2]

Three Teamsters were arrested and admitted their involvement in setting the fire. Hector Escudero Aponte confessed that he set fire to a can of Sterno fuel under a pile of furniture in the hotel's ballroom. Jose Francisco Lopez was found to have incited the others to start the fire. Armando Jimenez Rivera admitted that he obtained the fuel to start the blaze.

In a rare move, federal district Judge Jose A. Fuste gave the defendants harsher sentences than the prosecutors requested. For their involvement in the deadliest fire in North America in forty years, Aponte was sentenced to two concurrent ninety-nine-year terms; Lopez to ninety-seven years; and Rivera to seventy-five years. The U.S. Supreme Court upheld these sentences, but subsequently Judge Fuste reduced the sentences. An appeal to vacate the sentences was denied in 1993.[3]

Bronx Social Club Fire, March 1990

Eighty-seven people were asphyxiated or burned to death as fire raged quickly through the Happy Land Social Club, an illegal Bronx, New York social club that had been ordered closed due to fire code violations. This was the worst fire since the Puerto Rico fire discussed above. Police arrested a suspect who had been ejected from the club and reportedly was there arguing with his former girlfriend.

Julio Gonzalez, thirty-six, a Cuban immigrant, was charged with 178 counts of murder, arson, and related crimes. He was convicted and sentenced to twenty-five years to life in prison on each of eighty-seven counts of felony murder and murder, the sentences to be served concurrently. Gonzalez is eligible for parole after he serves twenty-five years. The owner entered a guilty plea to two misdemeanor counts of building code violations and was sentenced to fifty hours of community service and a $150,000 fine.[4]

Rescuers retrieve the bodies of those who died in the toy factory fire in 1993 in Thailand.

Nakhon Pathom, Thailand, May 1993

At least 240 people were killed in a doll factory fire that may have been the result of arson. This fire is thought to be the most destructive factory fire since 1911 when 146 people lost their lives in the Triangle Shirtwaist Company in New York City. The factory did not have a fire alarm system or proper fire escapes, and no fire drill had ever been held. Most of the victims were young women, who constitute approximately 80 percent of the workers in Thailand's low-wage factories.[5]

1. "Cocoanut Survivors Mark Anniversary," *Tampa Tribune* (29 November 1992), p. 9.
2. "Anatomy of a Disaster: The Dupont Plaza Hotel Fire," *American Bar Association Journal* 73 (1 August 1987): 100.
3. United States v. Jimenez-Rivera, 842 F.2d 545 (1st Cir. 1988), *cert. denied*, 487 U.S. 1223 (1988), *post-conviction proceeding*, 1993 U.S. App. LEXIS 23567 (1st Cir. 1993).
4. "Happy Land Arsonist Sentenced to 25 Years to Life for 87 Deaths," *New York Times* (20 October 1991), p. 8.
5. "Arson is Suspected in Factory Inferno," *Tallahassee Democrat* (13 May 1993), p. 6; *Chicago Tribune* (25 March 1993), p. 10.

burning car into a canal. In only a two-month period in 1993, Miami-area fire departments reported that 108 stolen cars were burned by arsonists.[44]

COMMON LAW ARSON

Common law arson referred to the malicious burning of the dwelling of another. The definition of dwelling for purposes of this crime was identical to that applicable to common law burglary. The requirement *of another* referred to possession, not ownership. If a landlord burned a dwelling rented to a tenant, the element would be satisfied because the tenant had a legal right to possession of that dwelling.

The common law required that the dwelling be burned, but it did not have to be burned completely. Earlier cases established the requirement that there must be a burning, not just a smoking or a maliciously set fire that was put out before any of the dwelling was burned. In 1885 a North

Carolina court held that the following testimony did not support burning sufficient to establish common law arson (although it might be sufficient to establish attempted arson). "A part of the boards of the kitchen floor was scorched black, but not burnt. The faggot [a badge that had been placed on the floor of the kitchen] was nearly consumed, but no part of the wood of the floor was consumed."[45]

A final requirement of common law arson was a criminal intent. Negligence was not sufficient to establish arson; nor was there a felony arson crime analogous to felony murder. A fire that resulted from the commission of another crime was not arson. Nor did one commit arson by burning his own dwelling. However, if in the process of burning his own dwelling the owner created an unreasonable fire hazard for other dwellings—one or more of which burned—the property owner could be charged with arson for the burning of the other's dwelling.

The criminal intent element did not require malice toward the property owner or the property in question. It required either the intent to burn the dwelling, the knowledge that a fire would burn the dwelling, or setting a fire without excuse or justification that created an obvious hazard to the dwelling of another.

STATUTORY ARSON

Although some jurisdictions retain the common law definition of arson, others have expanded the crime to include the burning of many structures other than dwellings and burning one's own structures. Some statutes eliminate the requirement of actual burning and permit an arson charge when damage is caused by an explosion that does not result in a fire or when a fire that is started purposely does not burn the structure in question. However, it must be shown that the actor had the intent to damage or destroy that structure.

The Model Penal Code has some of these changes. The Code explains that common law arson was a felony that at times carried the death penalty because it created a risk for human life. Consequently, the M.P.C. retains the more severe penalties for acts that are likely to injure human health or life and relegates acts such as the destruction of personal property not likely to endanger humans, to the lesser crime of *criminal mischief*.

The Model Penal Code classifies arson as a felony of the second or third degree or a misdemeanor, depending on the risk involved. The less serious offense involves the act of failing to control or report a dangerous fire. Arson that is a second-degree felony consists of reckless burning or exploding, whereas the most serious arson offense is starting a fire or causing an explosion with the purpose of

> (a) destroying a building or occupied structure of another; or
>
> (b) destroying or damaging any property, whether his own or another's, to collect insurance for such loss. It shall be an affirmative defense to prosecution under this paragraph that the actor's conduct did not recklessly endanger any building or occupied structure of another or place any other person in danger of death or bodily injury.[46]

New York has four degrees of arson. The first degree includes arson of a building occupied by another not involved in the crime when the offender knows that the circumstances are such that someone is likely to be in that building. The fourth degree involves reckless arson.[47]

In addition to arson statutes, most jurisdictions have statutes providing criminal penalties for those who destroy real or personal property maliciously. Attempts to commit arson are criminal, too.

Less Serious Property Crimes

In addition to the FBI Index property crimes of larceny-theft, burglary, motor vehicle theft, and arson, the FBI collects data on less serious personal and property crimes. In addition, states have various statutes covering less serious property crimes. Some of those categories of crime are discussed here. It is important to understand that the term *less serious* does not mean that the crime has a lesser economic impact on society. For example, the first crimes discussed, embezzlement and fraud, result in greater economic losses than larceny-theft and burglary. But embezzlement and fraud do not arouse the fear and anger for the general public that occurs with burglary and larceny-theft.

Embezzlement and Fraud

Acts that today are defined as embezzlement and fraud were not included in common law larceny, because a person already in lawful possession of property could not be charged with larceny. Statutory requirements were necessary to bring under the criminal law the acquisition of another's property by misappropriation or misapplication when the actor already had legal control of the property.

Embezzlement refers to misappropriating or misapplying property or money that was already entrusted to the individual, whereas **fraud** includes obtaining and converting money by false pretense. Because these crimes are general theft crimes that can be committed by many people, they are discussed here briefly. Various types of fraud and embezzlement are more characteristic of business crimes and organized crime, however, and are discussed in Chapter 11.

Embezzlement requires *conversion*, which is a serious interference with the owner's property, not merely a movement of that property. Although some statutes define the property that may be subject to embezzlement in the same way as property subject to larceny, other jurisdictions define the crime more broadly, some even including real property.[48] Some jurisdictions have a separate statute to cover embezzlement by public officials, making the penalty more severe for these people than for nonpublic officials.

Today some jurisdictions do not distinguish between larceny and embezzlement. The Virginia Criminal Code provides that:

> If any person wrongfully and fraudulently use, dispose of, conceal or embezzle any money, bill, note, check, order, draft, bond, receipt, bill of lading or

any other personal property, tangible or intangible, which he shall have received for another or for his employer, principal or bailor, or by virtue of his office, trust, or employment, or which shall have been entrusted or delivered to him by another or by any court, corporation or company, he shall be deemed guilty of larceny thereof,...and proof of embezzlement under this section shall be sufficient to sustain the charge.[49]

Although embezzlement is considered larceny (or part of a general theft statute) in some jurisdictions, others define it as a separate crime.

The elements that must be proved in a fraud case were enumerated by one court as follows:

1. a representation;
2. its falsity;
3. its materiality;
4. the speaker's knowledge of its falsity or ignorance of its truth;
5. the speaker's intent that it should be acted upon by the person and in the manner reasonably contemplated;
6. the hearer's ignorance of its falsity;
7. the hearer's reliance upon its truth;
8. the right of the hearer to rely upon it;
9. the hearer's consequent and proximate injury or damage.[50]

There are many kinds of fraud, such as securities fraud, mail fraud, consumer fraud, and fraud by government officials, which are discussed in Chapter 11. Mention should be made, too, of an increasingly noticed type of fraud today—**confidence games**. There is a difference of opinion on the distinction between confidence games and false pretense, discussed below. Today the trend is to abolish the separate crime of confidence games. There is debate over the meaning of the crime, too. One court has defined *confidence game* as follows:

> Obtaining of money or property by means of some trick, device, or swindling operation in which advantage is taken of the confidence which the victim reposes in the swindler. The elements of the crime are: (1) an intentional false representation to the victim as to some present fact, (2) knowing it to be false, (3) with intent that the victim rely on the representation, (4) the representation being made to obtain the victim's confidence and thereafter his money and property, (5) which confidence is then abused by defendant.[51]

False Pretense

Similar to fraud is the crime of **false pretense**. *False pretense* is a statutory crime; thus, the definition can vary from jurisdiction to jurisdiction. Generally, the crime refers to obtaining title to property by falsely representing facts to the owner with the intent to defraud that person.

The crime of false pretense was necessary to cover a loophole in the common law of larceny; for if by false pretense a person obtained title to property but did not get possession of that property, a larceny had not been committed. Parliament created the crime of *false pretense* to cover this act. Most U.S. jurisdictions followed the English precedent. The Model Penal

Code calls it *theft by deception* and enumerates the actions considered to be deception. There are five elements:

1. a false representation of a past or present fact
2. that causes the victim
3. to pass the title of the property
4. to the wrongdoer
5. who
   a. knows the representation to be false and
   b. thereby intends to defraud the victim.[52]

Some of these elements need further explanation. With regard to the first, the requirement that the statement be false means that even if the representation is false when made but later becomes true, it does not meet the requirement. The representation must be false at the same time as the property is obtained. The false representation must be made about a material fact (one that is essential to the case); it may be communicated orally or in writing.

Traditionally the false representation had to relate to a past or a present but not a future fact; thus, promises did not count. So, for example, if you walk into my office and tell my secretary that you are the president's son and that you are there to pick up a book for him, which he will pay for the next day, the former but not the latter statement will qualify for this first element. If you are not the president's son, you have misrepresented a present fact; but even if your statement that the president will pay for the book in the future is false, it does not establish this first element of false pretense.

The reason for not including false promises was the concern that the crime would be used against someone who did not make a false promise but, due to changes in circumstances, could not live up to the bargain. For example, a person could not pay a bill and thus became a debtor; but at the time the financial transaction was made, the individual had the intent to pay that bill in the future. Today's trend is to consider false promises or other false statements of future intentions to meet the requirement for false representations of a fact. This point is stated in the Model Penal Code's formulation of the crime of false representation, which it calls *theft by deception*, which states in part:

> A person is guilty of theft if he purposely obtains property of another by deception. A person deceives if he purposely:
> (1) creates or reinforces a false impression, including false impressions as to law, value, intention or other state of mind; but deception as to a person's intention to perform a promise shall not be inferred from the fact alone that he did not subsequently perform the promise;...[53]

Thus, the M.P.C. requires more than lack of performance of a promise to prove false pretense or theft by deception.

The second and third elements of false pretense are that the false representation must be the reason the victim passes the title to the property; that is, the victim's act is done in reliance on the actor's misrepresentation. Title must be passed to the wrongdoer; simple possession is not sufficient, although that would be sufficient for the crime of larceny by trick. Under the common law *property* included tangible personal property and money; the modern trend is to include all items that may be the subject of larceny. The Model Penal Code defines *property* in its theft statutes as "anything of value, including real estate, tangible and intangible personal property, contract rights, choses-in-action and other interests in or claims to wealth, admission or transportation tickets, captured or domestic animals, food and drink, electric or other power."[54]

The final element of false pretense is the mental element of the actor. Generally statutes require that the misrepresentation must be made *knowingly* or *with the intent to defraud* and that mental element must occur at the same time as the transfer of title, even if it did not occur at the time the misrepresentation was made.[55]

Forgery and Counterfeiting

Forgery has been explained as follows.

> The law against forgery is designed to protect society from the deceitful creation or alteration of writings on whose authenticity people depend in their important affairs. A person who, with the purpose of deceiving or injuring, makes or alters a writing in such a way as to convey a false impression concerning its authenticity is guilty of forgery in its contemporary sense.[56]

Forgery and false pretense are similar because both require an intent to defraud. They are dissimilar because forgery is complete even though the potential victim is not defrauded of money or property. Thus, one may forge a document but not have the opportunity to pass it on to another.

Under the Model Penal Code, one is guilty of forgery if, "with purpose to defraud or injure anyone, or with knowledge that he is facilitating a fraud or injury to be perpetrated by anyone, the actor: (a) alters any writing of another without his authority." The word *writing* includes "printing or any other method of recording information, money, coins, tokens, stamps, seals, credit cards, badges, trade-marks, and other symbols of value, right, privilege, or identification."[57]

In most cases forgery is associated with money or securities. There are other crimes relating to forgery, such as counterfeiting, but the trend today is to follow the Model Penal Code recommendation of combining counterfeiting and uttering into one forgery statute. *Uttering* refers to publishing or passing on a forged or otherwise bad document. The crime of *uttering a forged instrument* is common. Generally the crime of uttering or passing bad checks is a separate crime, for a person may commit this crime without forging the document. That is, the signature may be genuine, but there are insufficient funds in the account for the check to be good. The Model Penal Code has a separate provision for the crime of issuing or passing a bad check, which is a misdemeanor.[58]

Some statutes provide that writing a false or bogus check is a felony. Some require that the check must be more than a specified amount, whereas others require that more than one check is involved.

Stolen Property: Buying, Receiving, Possessing

Many thieves, particularly professional thieves, do not steal property they intend to use. They depend on the **fence** to be the instrument for disposing of the stolen property in a profitable manner. In early common law, the person who received stolen property from the thief could not be convicted of a crime, but the importance of controlling the fence led to statutes making the receipt of stolen property a crime. Generally these statutes are interpreted to mean that, in addition to knowing the property is stolen, receipt of the property must be with the intent to deprive the owner of that property.[59]

The crime of receiving stolen property has four elements:

1. receiving
2. stolen property
3. knowing it to be stolen and
4. with the intent to deprive the owner of the property.

To sustain a conviction for this crime, the prosecution must prove each of these elements and prove that the knowledge, conduct, and criminal intent concurred in time. The element of *receiving* may be broadly interpreted. The Model Penal Code refers to "receives, retains, or disposes of" and states that *"receiving* means acquiring possession, control or title, or lending on the security of the property." The element of *knowing it to be stolen* also includes *or believing that it probably has been stolen,* and that knowledge may be inferred from situations.[60] The knowledge that the received property is stolen and the intent to deprive may be inferred from circumstances.

Some jurisdictions specify types of receivers, such as junk dealers, and provide greater penalties for them than for people who are not usually in the business of receiving stolen property. Some provide greater penalties for larger amounts (grand receiving) as compared to smaller amounts (petit receiving), analogous to penalties for grand and petit larceny.

Some states divide criminal possession of stolen property into degrees. Until recently New York had three degrees of stolen property; that has been changed to five degrees. Criminal possession of stolen property in the first and second degrees are felonies; in the third, fourth, and fifth degrees, they are misdemeanors. The value of the property is a critical element. To constitute a first-degree violation, the property value must exceed $1 million, compared to $1,000 for a fourth-degree violation. No value amount is specified for the fifth degree.[61]

Malicious Mischief

The malicious destruction or infliction of damage to the property of another constitutes **malicious mischief**. It is similar to larceny in that it involves a crime against the property of another person but dissimilar in that it does not require taking the property away or intending to deprive the owner of possession.

Unlike larceny, malicious mischief may target real property. Another difference is that, in some jurisdictions, malicious mischief requires destruction of the property. Malicious mischief is similar to arson, too. Both involve damage to property, but malicious mischief does not require burning, a requirement of arson.

In modern codes, malicious mischief may be defined broadly. In addition to malicious damage to real or personal property, the California Penal Code includes such acts as cruelty to animals, unauthorized entry of property, obstruction of university teachers, and abandonment of a dog or cat.[62]

The Model Penal Code consolidates the common law crime of criminal mischief and other statutes that relate to destruction of property into a statute entitled *criminal mischief*, which includes purposeful as well as negligent damage to property by use of fire, explosives, flood, avalanche, collapse of building, release of poison gas, radioactive material, or other harmful or destructive force or substance.[63]

Criminal Trespass

Some jurisdictions provide for punishment of people who criminally trespass on land but whose actions are not sufficient to sustain convictions for malicious mischief or burglary. **Criminal trespass** involves the entering or remaining unlawfully in or on the premises of another (this could include land, boats, or other vehicles) under certain circumstances (specified by statute). It does not require the destruction of property involved in malicious mischief or the intent to commit a crime required by burglary.[64]

One recent example of an arrest for criminal trespass illustrates the way in which this crime might be enforced. A high school senior was charged with criminal trespass when he arrived at the prom dressed as a woman. Brett Martin, eighteen, wore a "red, sequined, spaghetti-strapped dress" that his sister had worn to the prom the previous year. Martin wore make-up and a wig as well. The prosecutor who dropped the charges said, "We looked around at the cost of time and money to prosecute and decided it was out of proportion to the charge."[65]

Copyright Infringement

Common law copyright refers to an individual's rights to protection of his or her intellectual or artistic property to give that individual first right of publication or to prevent publication of those works. Intellectual property is protected through formal statutory provisions, resulting in the issuance of a formal copyright. Violation of that copyright subjects the offender to civil and criminal penalties. There are some exceptions; some copying is permitted, but in general formal permission is required to reproduce works that are protected by a copyright.

The federal copyright statute provides in part:

Subject matter of copyright: In general

(a) copyright protection subsists, in accordance with this title, in original works of authorship fixed in any tangible medium of expression, now known or later developed, from which they can be perceived, reproduced, or otherwise communicated, either directly or with the aid of a machine or device. Works of authorship include the following categories:

(1) literary works;

(2) musical works, including any accompanying words;

(3) dramatic works, including any accompanying music;

(4) pantomimes and choreographic works;

(5) pictorial, graphic, and sculptural works;

(6) motion pictures and other audiovisual works;

(7) sound recordings; and

(8) architectural works.[66]

Copyright violations occur frequently, but they are difficult to detect unless committed on a large scale. The previous edition of this text was the object of a copyright violation when a midwestern police department made over 300 unauthorized copies, added a page indicating that the book was a training manual (to be used for a promotional test), and distributed the copies to law enforcement officers who wanted to qualify for promotion to sergeant. The publisher, which owns the copyright on the text, settled without filing suit. The author, who is a beneficial owner under the U.S. copyright statute, sued for additional damages. That case was settled shortly before it was scheduled for trial.[67]

Hybrid Crimes against the Person and Property

The previous two chapters discuss crimes against the person; this chapter focuses on property crimes. It is obvious, however, that not all crimes fit neatly into one or the other of these categories. This section covers several crimes that overlap both categories; they may involve property, but also they involve violence against the person at least to the extent that they arouse fear in their potential victims.

Robbery

Robbery, the felonious taking of property from the person or in the immediate presence of a person by means of force or threat, is a common law property crime older than larceny. Today the trend is to consider robbery as a violent crime against the person. The FBI categorizes robbery as one of the four violent crimes, but the FBI indicates the property as well as violent aspect of robbery in this statement: "While the object of a robbery is to obtain money or property, the crime always involves force or threat of force, and many victims suffer serious personal injury."[68]

In a report on robbery, the director of the Bureau of Justice Statistics said,

Robbery ranks among the most serious and feared criminal offenses because it involves both threatened or actual violence and loss of property to the victim. It also occurs much more frequently than either rape or homicide. Although many robberies do not result in physical harm to the victim or extensive loss, fully one in three involves actual injury, ranging from bruises and black eyes to life-threatening gunshot or knife wounds, and one in eight involves thefts of $250 or more.[69]

But robbery involves theft, too, and larceny is a lesser included offense within robbery. For that reason, historically many legal scholars and legislative codes have classified robbery as a property crime. In this text it is considered a hybrid crime against the person and his or her property.

As Figure 7.2 indicates, robbery rates and offenses have fluctuated over the years, with a decrease occurring in the latest official data, representing a 3 percent decline in the robbery rate and a 2 percent decline in robbery offenses in 1992 as compared to 1991. The decline is welcome but should not be considered a trend. Furthermore, the number of robberies in 1992 was 33 percent above the 1983 total and 24 percent higher than the 1988 total.[70]

Robbery is categorized as a *violent crime* in the FBI's Index offenses. In 1992 it accounted for 5 percent of all Index crimes and 35 percent of all violent crimes. It is estimated that the loss attributed to robberies in 1992 was $565 million, with an average of $840 per robbery. An average of $3,325 was taken in each bank robbery. Most of the robberies (56 percent) occurred on

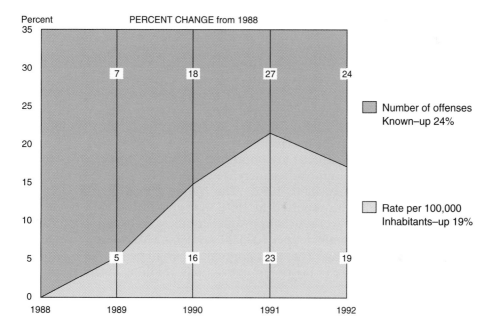

FIGURE 7.2   Robbery: Offenses and Trends
SOURCE: Federal Bureau of Investigation, *Crime in the United States, Uniform Crime Reports 1992* (Washington, D.C.: U.S. Department of Justice, 1993), p. 28.

streets and highways, with an additional 21 percent occurring in commercial and financial establishments and 10 percent in residences. Firearms were used in 40 percent of 1992 robberies, and strong-arm tactics were used in 40 percent. Knives or other cutting instruments were used in 11 percent, with other dangerous weapons used in the remainder of robberies.

Persons under twenty-five were involved in 62 percent of the 1992 robberies cleared by arrest. Ninety-one percent of the arrestees were men; 61 percent were African American, and 38 percent were white.

Despite the overall decrease in robberies in 1992, there was a slight increase (1 percent) in bank robberies and miscellaneous robberies, and between 1988 and 1992 bank robberies increased by 44 percent, by far the largest increase in any robbery category. An Associated Press report referred to the increase in bank robberies between 1990 and 1991 as "epidemic." The report cited various authorities who suggest that the increasing drug problem explains some of the rise in bank robberies. Others suggest that an increase in robbery is to be expected when unemployment increases. The growth of branch banking is another factor, a factor that makes bank robberies easier and more convenient. Branch banks are located closer to highways, making escape easier. The report indicated that bank robberies "skyrocketed" in Illinois after the state approved branch banking.[71]

Commenting on the ease of escaping a bank robbery, a California official said, "You rob a bank, take a right turn and in 32 seconds you're on the freeway."[72] Yet, bank robberies can be dangerous even for offenders. In January 1993 a gunman and a hostage were killed in a shootout after a bank robbery in New York City.[73] Furthermore, banks have surveillance cameras; so the risk of conviction may be greater for those tried for bank robbery than for other crimes. So why rob banks? As the veteran bank robber of earlier days, Willie Sutton, said, "Because that is where the money is." He was partially correct.

Large sums may be robbed from armored cars as well. In late 1993 robbers got $8 million from an armored car company in Brooklyn. One week later three armed men wearing ski masks took an estimated $10 million from a Brink's company armored car in Rochester, New York. Two years previously armed robbers had taken approximately $10.8 million from a Rochester armored car driver.[74]

Convenience stores are another frequent target for robberies. Convenience store robberies increased steadily between 1988 and 1991 but declined by 2 percent in 1992. The National Institute for Occupational Safety and Health reported in 1991 that jobs in the food retail business (which includes working at convenience stores) ranked second in the jobs with the most homicides per 100,000 workers. This category was surpassed only by taxi driving. That year approximately 10 percent of Florida's death row inmates were in prison for convictions of killing during a convenience store robbery.[75]

Robbery of tourists in Florida has become a problem of international as well as state concern. In 1991 two armed robbers on a motorcycle pulled up beside a rented convertible and stole $100,000 in Rolex watches from a German tourist. While one robber held a gun to the head of the driver, another grabbed a purse, which contained the watches. This incident occurred less than two weeks after a smash-and-grab robbery and shooting of a British couple, an act that drew international attention to the problems tourists faced in South Florida, especially when they were driving rental cars. The problems escalated during the following two years, with several deaths of tourists occurring during the robberies. In the fall of 1993 the problems moved north, with an English tourist losing his life at a rest stop about thirty-five miles from the state's capital in North Florida. The tourist and his companion had stopped for a brief nap at approximately 2:30 a.m. when they were approached by armed men demanding their money. The driver attempted to drive off and was shot in the neck and killed. His companion was wounded. Teenagers have been charged in these crimes.

Florida officials reacted to these crimes against foreign tourists by changing regulations concerning rental cars (no longer are they identified by a "Z" on the license tag), placing armed guards in all rest areas, issuing warnings, and making other efforts to preserve its multibillion dollar tourist industry.

ELEMENTS OF ROBBERY

Robbery has all of the elements of larceny, plus the requirement that the property must be taken from the person or presence of the victim. Force or intimidation must occur. The requirement of *from the person or presence of the victim* means that the possessor of the property must be close enough that the victim could exercise control over the property and prevent the robbery except for the presence of force or intimidation.

The Model Penal Code defines robbery as follows:

(1) *Robbery Defined.* A person is guilty of robbery if, in the course of committing a theft, he:
   (a) inflicts serious bodily injury upon another; or
   (b) threatens another with or purposely puts him in fear of immediate serious bodily injury; or
   (c) commits or threatens immediately to commit any felony of the first or second degree.
   An act shall be deemed "in the course of committing a theft" if it occurs in an attempt to commit theft or in flight after the attempt or commission.
(2) *Grading.* Robbery is a felony of the second degree, except that it is a felony of the first degree if in the course of committing the theft the actor attempts to kill anyone, or purposely inflicts or attempts to inflict serious bodily injury.[76]

The requirement of force or intimidation causes difficulty in distinguishing robbery from larceny-theft. Is a quick purse snatching robbery or larceny? Cases differ, but generally it depends on how quickly the snatching occurs. If the purse is grabbed so quickly that the victim does not even miss it, the act may be interpreted as larceny, not robbery.[77] But if the victim is aware of the act and struggles to retain the purse, the act may be classified as a robbery.[78]

Pickpocketing was included in the category of larceny-theft, although if the victim realizes what is happening and struggles to prevent the crime but is overcome by the actor, the crime may be robbery, not larceny-theft.[79] If the offender uses force to render the victim helpless and then commits larceny, even if the force used is drugs, the act may be robbery.[80]

The use of intimidation to commit a theft may constitute robbery. Actual violence is not required; threats will suffice. The threat need not be directed at the victim. It could be directed at the victim's family, but the threat must be of an immediate injury. It is not sufficient to issue a general threat to harm their families at some point in the future.[81]

Unlike larceny-theft statutes, most robbery statutes do not distinguish acts by the value of what is taken. In robbery it is the threat or actual use of violence that is crucial. Robbery statutes, however, may grade the crime in terms of aggravating factors, such as the use of an accomplice, actual injury, or the use of a dangerous weapon. *Simple robbery* may be distinguished from *aggravated robbery*, which requires an aggravating circumstance. Robbery statutes may be classified by degrees, as they are in New York, which has robbery in the first, second, and third degrees.[82]

Some interesting litigation occurs over the elements of robbery. If aggravated robbery requires the use of a dangerous weapon, without a definition of "dangerous weapon," what would you include in that category? Would you include a stapler? One court held that, because it was used to inflict serious bodily harm on the robbery victim, a stapler qualified as a dangerous weapon.[83] Another held that a toy gun would suffice.[84] In fact, the Police Executive Research Forum (PERF) estimates that approximately 15 percent of all "armed" robberies are committed with the use of toy guns.[85]

Is an unloaded gun a dangerous weapon? The U.S. Supreme Court has held that it is, giving three reasons, "each independently sufficient," for its decision. In the first place, a gun is "typically and characteristically dangerous," and it is manufactured and sold for purposes that are dangerous. Thus, it is reasonable to assume that the gun is to be used for dangerous purposes "even though it may not be armed at a particular time or place." In the second place, "the display of a gun instills fear in the average citizen." Thus, it creates in a reasonable person an immediate fear that danger will occur. Third, "a gun can cause harm when used as a bludgeon."[86]

Some of the elements of robbery, along with a comparison of robbery and theft, are illustrated in the following excerpt from an earlier California case.[87]

People v. *Butler*

Defendant was charged by information with the murder of Joseph H. Anderson and with assault with intent to murder William Russell Locklear. A jury convicted defendant of first-degree felony murder and of assault with a deadly weapon; it fixed the penalty for the murder at death. This appeal is automatic.

We have determined that error in the guilt phase of the trial deprived defendant of his primary defense to the charge of first-degree felony murder. The judgment of conviction of murder must therefore be reversed.

Joseph H. Anderson operated a catering service in Los Angeles at the time of his death, and William Locklear assisted him. On the evening of May 18, 1965, Locklear was at Anderson's home where he planned to remain for the night. He testified that the doorbell rang shortly after midnight while he was in the bedroom. He heard little for 20 to 30 minutes after that because he was in the shower. When he returned to the bedroom he heard Anderson call, "Bill, he's got a gun." Anderson then entered the bedroom followed by defendant, whose hand was in his coat pocket. Locklear did not see a gun until two or three minutes later when defendant produced one from "someplace." Anderson attempted to seize the gun, it fired and Anderson fell. Locklear tried to apprehend defendant but was himself shot and lost consciousness. Defendant was gone when Locklear regained consciousness.

Defendant testified that he met Anderson several weeks before the killing and that Anderson employed him on one occasion to do catering work. Anderson did not pay him for the work, and when he requested payment Anderson asked him to wait a few days. On the evening of May 18th, defendant went to Anderson's home to obtain payment. While the two were sitting in the living room discussing the debt, Anderson made an incedent proposal and, when defendant rejected it, offered to double the money he owed defendant. Defendant also refused this offer telling Anderson he needed his money and wished only to be paid.

Defendant also testified that at this point Anderson agreed to pay him, but they had two or three drinks together before Anderson started toward the bedroom to get the money. Anderson apparently changed his mind and returned to discuss his earlier proposition. Defendant persisted in his refusal, and Anderson again went to the bedroom. Defendant testified that when he entered the bedroom a few seconds later, Anderson approached him with a pistol. He had not previously been aware of Locklear's presence, but he then saw Locklear lying on the bed. Defendant stated that he had armed himself before going to Anderson's home because he had heard stories about Anderson's brutality, and that when he saw a gun in Anderson's hand, he brought out his own to defend himself. Anderson called to Locklear that defendant had a gun and threw a towel or bathrobe at defendant. Defendant testified that he did not intend to shoot, but as the towel was thrown at him, Anderson grabbed his arm and the gun fired. After Anderson was shot, Locklear jumped up and as he came forward defendant shot him too. Defendant then ran to the living room and back to the bedroom where he looked for money. Finding none, he took a wallet and ran from the house.

No evidence of premeditation or deliberation was adduced by the prosecution. The court instructed the jury that since these elements were not present, it could find first-degree murder only if defendant committed the killing in the perpetration of a robbery.

Defendant testified that he did not intend to rob Anderson when he went to the house, but intended only to recover money owed to him. Over his objection, the prosecutor argued to the jury, "If you think a man owes you a hundred dollars, or fifty dollars, or five dollars, or a dollar, and you go over with a gun to try to get his money, it's robbery." And, "If you go into a man's home and merely because he's supposed to owe you some money, you take money from him at gunpoint, you have robbed him." Again objecting to further argument by the prosecutor that a robbery was committed even if defendant believed Anderson owed him money, defendant suggested that a necessary element of theft, the intent to steal, was requisite to robbery, but was overruled by the court.

Defendant's objection was well taken. "Robbery is the felonious taking of personal property in the possession of another, from his person or immediate presence, and against his will, accomplished by means of force or fear." An essential element of robbery is the felonious intent or *animus furandi* that accompanies the taking. Since robbery is but larceny aggravated by the use of force or fear to accomplish the taking of property from the person or presence of the possessor the felonious intent requisite to robbery is the same intent common to those offenses that, like larceny, are grouped in the Penal Code designation of "theft." The taking of property is not theft in the absence of an intent to steal, and a specific intent to steal, i.e., an intent to deprive an owner permanently of his property, is an essential element of robbery.

Although an intent to steal may ordinarily be inferred when one person takes the property of another, particularly if he takes it by force, proof of the existence of a state of mind incompatible with an intent to steal precludes a finding of either theft or robbery. It has long been the rule in this state and generally throughout the country that a bona fide belief, even though mistakenly held, that one has a right or claim to the property negates felonious intent.

A belief that the property taken belongs to the taker or that he had a right to retake goods sold is sufficient to preclude felonious intent. Felonious intent exists only if the actor intends to take the property of another without believing in good faith that he has a right or claim to it. Defendant testified that in going to Anderson's home "my sole intention was to try to get my money, and that was all." The jury was properly instructed that if the intent to take the money from Anderson did not arise until after Anderson had been fatally wounded, the killing could not be murder in the perpetration of robbery.

Since the jury returned a verdict of first-degree murder it believed defendant intended to take money from Anderson by force before the shooting occurred. Accordingly, defendant's only defense to robbery-murder was the existence of an honest belief that he was entitled to the money. The trial court's approval of the prosecutor's argument that no such defense exists removed completely from the consideration of the jury a material issue raised by credible, substantial evidence. It precluded any finding that an intent to steal was absent. Defendant had a constitutional right to have every significant issue determined by a jury. The denial of that right was a miscarriage of justice within the meaning of the California Consitution and requires reversal.

Mosk, Justice (Dissenting)

I dissent.

Penal Code section 211 defines robbery as "the felonious taking of personal property in the possession of another, from his person or immediate presence, and against his will, accomplished by means of force or fear." This code section was enacted in 1872 and has remained unchanged since that date.

It is significant that the section requires the taking be from the *possession* of another, and makes no reference whatever to *ownership* of the property.

The question here, then, is whether the defendant may assert *ipse dixit* [assertion made by the individual without any other authority] his belief that he was entitled to an unpaid debt taken from another by force or fear as a defense to a charge of robbery, and by extrapolation as a defense to a charge of murder committed in the course of a robbery. While there is some authority suggesting this query be answered in the affirmative, there has been no explicit holding of this court on the issue.

Thus, the question is ultimately one of basic public policy, which unequivocally dictates that the proper forum for resolving debt disputes is a court of law, pursuant to legal process—not the street, at the business end of a lethal weapon. Had this defendant been entrusted with the contents of the deceased's wallet, and had he appropriated them to his own use, believing he was entitled to keep the funds in payment of wages or a debt, that belief would have furnished him no defense to a charge of embezzlement. By parity of rationale, the claim of offset denied to the trusted employee who dips into the company cashbox should be denied to one who, like this defendant, enforces his demands at gunpoint. To hold otherwise would be to constitute him judge and jury in his own cause....

In a bucolic western sense or in the wooly atmosphere of the frontier in the nineteenth century, the six-shooter may have been an acceptable device for do-it-yourself debt collection. If the law permitted a might-makes-right doctrine in that milieu, it is of dubious adaptability to urban society in this final third of the twentieth century.

HOME-INVASION ROBBERY

In July 1993 three men arrested in three states became the first to be charged with violating Florida's recently enacted statute prohibiting **home-invasion robbery**. The three were alleged to have attacked a couple shortly after they returned to their home from a class reunion. The three were captured after the bank for which the male victim was a branch manager offered a $50,000 reward for information that would lead to an arrest in the case.[88]

Florida statutes define *home-invasion robbery* as "any robbery that occurs when the offender enters a dwelling with the intent to commit a robbery and does commit a robbery of the occupant therein." This act is a first-degree felony. In enacting this statute (along with one on carjacking, discussed below), the legislature amended several Florida statutes to include these crimes. For example, the murder statute was amended to provide that both carjacking and home-invasion robbery are murder when death results.[89]

Carjacking

The crime is an old one, but it has a new name. Today we speak of **carjacking** when we refer to the theft of an auto by use of force, especially deadly weapons. In previous days we called the crime *robbery*. The escalation of such crimes, along with the brutality of many, as discussed in Focus 7.4, has led many states and the federal government to enact statutes to cover carjacking.

Florida's carjacking statute provides for two degrees of carjacking, depending on whether a firearm or other deadly weapon is used. The statute defines *carjacking* as:

> the taking of a motor vehicle which may be the subject of larceny from the person or custody of another, with intent to either permanently or temporarily deprive the person or the owner of the motor vehicle, when in the course of the taking there is the use of force, violence, assault, or putting in fear.[90]

In September 1993 the director of the FBI announced that his agency would be viewing violent automobile theft as a new priority in the "Operation Safe Streets" anticrime program. The Operation Safe Streets program was begun in early 1992 when 300 FBI agents were reassigned from foreign counterintelligence to work on domestic violence and gang-related violence.[91]

As Focus 7.4 indicates, Congress has enacted a federal carjacking statute. That statute applies only to the theft of a motor vehicle "that has been transported, shipped or received in interstate or foreign commerce." Federal courts have not agreed on whether the interstate commerce aspect of the statute is constitutional. A Pennsylvania court has held that it is; a Tennessee court has held that it is not constitutional.[92]

The federal statute provides for a penalty of not more than fifteen years in prison unless serious bodily injury is caused, in which case the penalty is not more than twenty-five years. If death results, the penalty is "any

FOCUS 7.4   Carjacking: A New Crime?

Pam Basu of Maryland was driving her twenty-two-month-old daughter to her first day of preschool on 8 September 1992 when Bernard Miller, age seventeen, and Rodney Solomon, his twenty-seven-year-old accomplice, beat her and forced her from her car at a stop sign. In her effort to grab her baby, Basu's arm was caught in her seat belt. She was dragged over a mile before her assailants dislodged her from the car. Later the baby was found by the side of a road, in her car seat, and unharmed.

In April 1993 the jury deliberated over eleven hours over two days before finding Miller guilty of murder and other charges stemming from the incident in which Basu was killed. In August 1993 Solomon was convicted of murder and six other charges stemming from the incident. Miller was sentenced to life in prison. He could be paroled in seventeen and one-half years. Had he not been only sixteen at the time of the crime, he could have been sentenced to death. Solomon was sentenced to life in prison for the murder and eighty years in prison for robbery, kidnapping, and assault. He could have received the death penalty.[1]

The increasing number of carjackings in New Jersey led officials to form an anticarjacking police squad, Tactical Auto Recovery Group and Enforcement Team (TARGET), a squad of twenty-five officers with special training in terrorism, defensive driving, use of special weapons and equipment, and cultural sensitivity. These officers are assigned to special areas during special times when most carjackings are likely to occur. They have access to a helicopter to spot stolen cars more quickly. To avoid high-speed chases, these officers target stolen cars with paint guns, which spray blue or yellow flourescent paint. These cars may be identified quickly by other citizens, whose cooperation in notifying authorities of the location of the cars is expected.[2]

In April 1993 the first suspects charged under the new federal carjacking statute (see text for discussion) were convicted in Florida. Jermaine Foster, nineteen, Gerard Booker, twenty-two, and Alf Catholic, twenty-one, were sentenced to life without parole for their respective roles in the abduction of three men and the execution of two of them.[3]

Florida's "carjacking capital," Jacksonville, had eight reported carjackings in a three-day period in August 1993, for a total of 127 carjackings through 17 August 1993.[4]

[1.] "Youth is Convicted of Murder in Maryland Carjacking Case," *New York Times* (25 April 1993), p. 16; "Man Guilty in Fatal Carjacking," *New York Times* (15 August 1993), p. 16; "Man Sentenced to Life for Carjacking Death," *New York Times* (20 August 1993), p. 7.
[2.] "Twenty-Five Newark Police Officers to Work in Anti-Carjacking Squad," *Criminal Justice Newsletter* 22 (16 November 1992), p. 5.
[3.] The federal carjacking statute is part of the Anti Car Theft Act of 1992, U.S.Code, Title 18, Section 2119 (1994).
[4.] "Jacksonville Has Eight Carjackings in Three Days," *Orlando Sentinel* (17 August 1993), p. 5B.

number of years up to life." In addition, the statute increased existing penalties for importation and exportation of stolen vehicles as well as trafficking in stolen vehicles. Penalties for up to fifteen years in prison are pro-

Memorial for two Japanese students killed during a carjacking in Los Angeles.

vided for knowingly owning, operating, maintaining, or controlling a "chop shop." The first trial under this federal statute was begun in Orlando, Florida in February 1993. As Focus 7.4 indicates, the defendants were convicted.

Extortion or Blackmail

A final hybrid crime that is related to property is **extortion** or **blackmail**. Common law robbery, which carried the death penalty, was restricted to threats of *immediate* harm. This left threats of future actions uncovered. Under the common law and in most of the early statutes, *extortion* was limited to the unlawful taking of money by public officials who did so "by colour of their offices." Congress extended this definition of extortion "to include acts by private individuals pursuant to which property is obtained by means of force, fear, or threats."[93] The federal statute defines *extortion* as "the obtaining of property from another, with his consent, induced by wrongful use or threatened force, violence, or fear, or under color of official right."[94]

Some extortion statutes are part of a general theft statute. The Model Penal Code is an example of this approach. The M.P.C. illustrates also the expanded definition of extortion. Under the M.P.C. a person is guilty of theft by extortion if he obtains the property of another by threatening to

1. inflict bodily injury on anyone or commit any other criminal offense; or
2. accuse anyone of a criminal offense; or

3. expose any secret tending to subject any person to hatred, contempt or ridicule, or to impair his credit or business repute; or

4. take or withhold action as an official, or cause an official to take or withhold action; or

5. bring about or continue a strike, boycott or other collective unofficial action, if the property is not demanded or received for the benefit of the group in whose interest the actor purports to act; or

6. testify or provide information or withhold testimony or information with respect to another's legal claim or defense; or

7. inflict any other harm which would not benefit the actor.[95]

Extortion is similar to the crime of *bribery*, which is discussed in a subsequent chapter.[96]

SUMMARY

Although the fear of being victimized by violent crimes is greater than the fear associated with property crimes, property crimes claim the largest number of victims in the country. It is not easy to separate the two kinds of crimes, for many property crimes, such as robbery, extortion, burglary, and arson may involve personal violence, even death. Nevertheless, for purposes of analysis, crimes are divided into categories. This chapter discusses those crimes generally considered to be crimes against property.

Property rights were extremely important in the common law. The emergence and development of crimes to protect property has been closely related to those rights. Some of the restrictions on the elements or requirements for the crimes do not make much sense in modern times. Some of those have changed; others remain. Thus, it is important to understand the common law of property crimes.

One of the most complicated and fascinating of the common law crimes, larceny-theft, illustrates the importance of the common law. Although all the common law elements of this crime are no longer required, some remain. Others are important in interpreting modern statutes. Likewise, the common law division of larceny-theft into grand and petit larceny is retained in some jurisdictions.

Common law larceny-theft required a trespassory taking and a carrying away of the personal property of another with the intent to steal. The requirement of trespassory taking prevented the inclusion of some crimes that evolved over the years. To cover these "new" crimes, judges began to invent fictions such as *constructive possession* to refer to the property a master had delivered to his servant to be used for the benefit of the master. If that servant misappropriated the property, his act could be included within common law larceny-theft.

The common law requirement of asportation, or taking away, generally has been replaced today with a requirement that the offender exercise unlawful control over property even if it is not carried away, provided he or she does so with the intent and purpose of depriving the owner of that property. Under the common law, the property stolen had to be the personal property of another, meaning tangible personal property. Modern statutes have extended larceny-theft to some real property, services, admission to exhibitions, and many other areas.

The common law interpretation of *intent to steal* as requiring an intent to deprive the owner of his property permanently has been retained in some and abolished in other jurisdictions to permit inclusion of crimes such as joyriding. Another way of handling this element, however, has been to create separate offenses for acts such as joyriding.

Burglary is another property offense in which the common law definition and interpretations are important to an understanding of modern statutes. Today, the common law requirement of breaking and entering may be met in some statutes by the act of remaining on the property illegally. The breaking requirement may be met by entering illegally. The requirement that the structure be the dwelling of another has been extended to include other buildings.

The common law required nighttime for burglary; most modern statutes omit that requirement. Today the common law requirement of an intent to commit a felony may include an intent to commit a misdemeanor. Even when modern statutes have abandoned or changed some of the common law elements of burglary, the influence of these older crimes is seen in the differentiation of the crime by degrees. Although it may not be required that the burglar enter a home for the crime to be complete, entering a home may result in a higher degree of burglary and a harsher sentence.

Although larceny-theft includes the theft of parts from motor vehicles, the theft of motor vehicles constitutes a separate category of serious property crimes in the FBI's *Uniform Crime Reports*. The chapter includes a brief discussion of this crime. The final serious property crime, arson, is discussed in terms of its common law background as well as modern statutory approaches. Some of the most deadly fires caused by arson are discussed.

The second major section of the chapter covers less serious property offenses. These crimes are labeled *less serious* by the FBI, but they may create a significant problem for their immediate victims as well as for society in general. For example, embezzlement and fraud (both discussed in more detail in a subsequent chapter along with other business crimes) may involve millions of dollars, compared to far smaller losses from larceny-theft. A number of lesser property crimes are discussed individually. Although the modern trend is toward consolidating theft-type offenses into fewer categories, some jurisdictions retain the common law larceny-theft category, which excluded such offenses as larceny by trick, fraud, false pretense, forgery, and embezzlement. These jurisdictions have separate statutes for these offenses. Other jurisdictions have abandoned the use of the term *larceny-theft* and refer only to *theft* crimes, which may be subdivided into many categories.

The last major section of the chapter includes what we call *hybrid crimes against the person and property*. Scholars differ in their treatment of the major crime in this category, robbery. In this text robbery is discussed as a property crime because larceny-theft may be a lesser included offense of robbery; thus, it is necessary to understand the elements of larceny-theft in order to understand the elements of robbery. But often robbery involves violence as well as larceny-theft. Robbery may occur during the commission of larceny-theft if the additional element of putting the victim in fear of imminent harm is present. If the threat is to future harm, the crime of *extortion* may have been committed. Robberies within homes are particularly frightening, and recently *home-invasion robbery* statutes have been enacted to cover this crime. In recent years the use of force or the threat of force for theft of motor vehicles has become such a problem that some jurisdictions have enacted special legislation to cover *carjacking*.

This chapter contains an overview of property crimes. All of these crimes could be discussed at much greater length. All involve intricate and complicated legal issues. Some of the crimes are committed by businesses or government. They may involve accomplices or in some other way be associated with major topics of discussion that provide the focus of subsequent chapters. More attention is given to some of these property crimes in Chapter 11.

STUDY QUESTIONS

1. Generally, what is meant by the common law term *larceny-theft?*
2. Distinguish *petit* and *grand larceny* under the common law and under the New York statute.
3. Should the amount paid or the market value of a stolen item have any effect on the sentence of a convicted offender? Why or why not?
4. What did the common law mean by (a) a *trespassory taking*, (b) *asportation*, and (c) *with the intent to steal?*
5. What is the difference between *actual* and *constructive possession?*
6. How does *burglary* differ from *larceny-theft?* What are some of the ways in which modern burglary statutes differ from the common law approach?
7. What are the elements of arson? Why is the crime considered a serious one?
8. What is meant by *larceny by trick?*
9. How does the larceny element of *taking* apply to shoplifting?
10. How have modern statutes changed the common law definition of larceny-theft?
11. Why would embezzlement and fraud not fit in the common law category of larceny-theft?
12. What is meant by the following element of false pretense—*a false representation of a past or present fact?* How do the common law and modern law differ regarding this element?
13. How does *forgery* differ from *false pretense?*
14. What is *malicious mischief?*
15. Should *robbery* be classified as a violent or a property crime? Explain your answer.

16. How does *robbery* differ from *extortion*?
17. What is meant by *home-invasion robbery* and *carjacking*, and why do we need separate statutes for these crimes?

ENDNOTES

1. Federal Bureau of Investigation, *Crime in the United States, Uniform Crime Reports 1992* (Washington, D.C.: U.S. Government Printing Office, 1993), pp. 43, 44.
2. Rex v. Wheatly, 97 E.R. 746 (1761).
3. Wayne R. LaFave and Austin W. Scott, Jr., *Criminal Law*, 2d ed. (St. Paul, Minn.: West, 1986), pp. 718-720.
4. New York Penal Code, Title J, Section 155.25 (1994).
5. New York Penal Code, Title J, Section 155.30 *et. seq.* (1994).
6. Model Penal Code, Section 223.0.
7. Rollin M. Perkins, *Criminal Law*, 3d ed. (Mineola, N.Y.: Foundation Press, 1982), p. 291. For a history of the development of the law of theft, see Jerome Hall, *Theft, Law and Society*, rev. ed. (Indianapolis: Bobbs-Merrill, 1952), Chapters 1–4; LaFave and Scott, *Criminal Law*, pp. 700–801.
8. Hufstetler v. State, 63 So.2d 730 (Ala.App. 1953).
9. The Carrier's Case, Y.B. 13 Edw. IV, f.9, pl.5 (Star Chamber 1473).
10. People v. Olivo, 420 N.E.2d 40 (N.Y.App. 1981), footnotes, cases and citations omitted.
11. Brooks v. State, 35 Ohio St. 46 (1878).
12. Model Penal Code, Section 223.5.
13. People v. Meyer, 17 P. 431 (Cal. 1888).
14. Model Penal Code, Section 223.2(1).
15. See People v. Menagas, 11 N.E.2d 403 (Ill. 1937) (electricity); and State v. Gisclair, 382 So.2d 914 (La. 1980) (services are not covered).
16. Model Penal Code, Section 223.7(1).
17. New York Penal Code, Title J, Section 165.15(8) (1994).
18. State v. McGraw, 480 N.E.2d 552 (Ind. 1985).
19. People v. Brown, 38 P. 518 (Cal. 1894).
20. Model Penal Code, Section 223.9.
21. Model Penal Code, Section 223.0(1).
22. Arnold D. Hechtman, commentary following the statute, New York Penal Code Ann., Section 165.35 (1993).
23. Model Penal Code, Section 223.
24. *Uniform Crime Reports 1992*, pp. 38, 39.
25. For recent studies on burglary, see the following: Richard Wright et al., "A Snowball's Chance in Hell: Doing Fieldwork With Active Residential Burglars," *Journal of Research in Crime and Delinquency* 29 (May 1992): 148–161; James Garofalo and David Clark, "Guardianship and Residential Burglary," *Justice Quarterly* 9 (September 1992): 443–463; Scott Decker et al., "Perceptual Deterrence Among Active Residential Burglars: A Research Note," *Criminology* 31 (February 1993): 135–147; and Paul F. Cromwell et al., *Breaking and Entering: An Ethnographic Analysis of Burglary* (Beverly Hills, Calif.: Sage, 1991).
26. State v. Boon, 35 N.C. 244, 246 (1852).
27. See Jones v. State, 537 P.2d 431 (Okla.Crim.App. 1975).
28. See Walker v. State, 63 Ala. 49 (1879).

29. McGraw v. Maryland, 199 A.2d 229 (Md. 1964), *cert. denied*, 379 U.S. 862 (1964).

30. Model Penal Code, Section 221.1.

31. New York Penal Code, Sections 140.20-140.30 (1993).

32. Montana Code Ann., Section 45-6-204 (1994).

33. State v. Christofferson, 775 P.2d 690 (Mont. 1989).

34. Section 1402 of Subtitle I (the Career Criminals Amendment Act of 1986) of the Anti-Drug Abuse Act of 1986, U.S. Code, Title 18, Section 924(e) (1994).

35. Taylor v. United States, 495 U.S. 575 (1990).

36. See Model Penal Code, Section 221.1(3).

37. *Uniform Crime Reports 1992*, pp. 49, 50. For a recent analysis of auto thefts, see Erkki Koskela and Matti Virén, "An Economic Model of Auto Thefts in Finland," *International Review of Law and Economics* 13 (1993): 179–191.

38. "New Jersey Announces Plans to Stop New Wave of Car Thefts," *Criminal Justice Newsletter* 23 (17 August 1992): 4.

39. "New Jersey Plans Auto-Crime Laws," *New York Times* (19 February 1993), p. 12; "Tougher Car-Theft Laws Signed Including Penalties for Juveniles," *New York Times* (4 June 1993), p. 5B.

40. For a discussion of evidence in arson investigations, see Edward J. Imwinkelried, "Forensic Science: Forensic Evidence in Arson Cases: Part I," *Criminal Law Bulletin* 28 (November–December 1992): 554–561; and "Part II," *Criminal Law Bulletin* 29 (January–February 1993): 70–75.

41. *Uniform Crime Reports* 1992, pp. 53, 54.

42. "U.S. Holds Los Angeles Man In Threats of Revenge Fires," *New York Times* (9 November 1993), p. 9; "Metropolitan Digest:...Suspect in 'Fedbuster' Letter Threats Pleads Not Guilty," *Los Angeles Times* (30 November 1993), p. 2B; "Metropolitan Digest:...Los Suspect in Arson Threats Denied Release on Bail," *Los Angeles Times* (2 December 1993), p. 2B; "Guilty Plea Entered in 'Fedbuster' Letters Case," *Los Angeles Times* (11 January 1994), p. 6B.

43. See, for example, Anthony Olen Rider, *The Firesetter: A Psychological Profile* (Washington, D.C.: U.S. Department of Justice, 1984). For a discussion of the Florida case, see "Church Arsonist Insane, Sent to Mental Hospital," *Miami Herald* (5 January 1993), p. 5B.

44. "Teen Trend: Arson," *Miami Herald* (17 June 1993), p. 1B.

45. State v. Hall, 93 N.C. 571, 573 (1885).

46. Model Penal Code, Section 220.1.

47. New York Penal Code, Title J, Section 150.05 *et seq* (1994).

48. See People v. Roland, 26 P.2d 517 (Cal.App. 1933).

49. Va. Code Ann., Section 18.2-111 (1994).

50. Avco Financial Services v. Foreman-Donovan, 772 P.2d 862 (Mont. 1989).

51. United States v. Brown, 309 A.2d 256, 257 (D.C.App. 1973). For an analysis of fraud, see the following: Paul E. Tracy and James Alan Fox, "A Field Experiment on Insurance Fraud in Auto Body Repair," *Criminology* 27 (August 1989): 589–603; and Kitty Calavita and Henry N. Pontell, "'Heads I Win, Tails You Lose': Deregulation, Crime, and Crisis in the Savings and Loan Industry," *Crime and Delinquency* 36 (July 1990): 309–341.

52. Model Penal Code, Section 223.3.

53. Model Penal Code, Section 223.3(1). The term *deceive*, however, does not include falsity as to matters having no pecuniary significance or puffing by statements unlikely to deceive ordinary persons in the group addressed.

54. Model Penal Code, Section 223.0 (6).

55. See Clarke v. People, 171 P. 69 (Colo. 1918).

56. Peter Goldberger, "Forgery," in *Encyclopedia of Crime and Justice*, vol. 2, ed. Sanford H. Kadish (New York: Free Press, 1983), p. 795.
57. Model Penal Code, Section 224.1(1)(a),(c).
58. Model Penal Code, Section 224.5.
59. For a discussion of the history of this crime, see Hall, *Theft, Law and Society*, pp. 52–60, LaFave and Scott, *Criminal Law*, pp. 765–766, and Peter A. Bell, "Fencing and Receiving Stolen Goods: Legal Aspects," in *Encyclopedia and Crime and Justice*, vol. 2, ed. Kadish, pp. 789–790.
60. Model Penal Code, Section 223.6.
61. New York Penal Code, Title J, Sections 165.40-165.54 (1994).
62. Cal. Pen. Code, Section 594-625(b) (1994).
63. Model Penal Code, Section 220.3.
64. See Model Penal Code, Section 221.2.
65. "Charge Dropped for Boy Who Wore Dress to Prom," *Orlando Sentinel* (8 May 1993), p. 11.
66. U.S. Code, Chapter 17, Section 102 (1994).
67. For a discussion of the legal aspects of copyright violations, see June C. Ginsburg, "No 'Sweat'? Copyright and Other Protections of Works of Information after *Feist* v. *Rural Telephone*," *Columbia Law Review* 92 (March 1992): 338–388; and "Creations and Commercial Value: Copyright Protection of Works of Information," *Columbia Law Review* 90 (November 1990): 1865–1938. For a discussion of a state copyright statute, see Barbara A. Petersen, "Copyright and State Government: an Analysis of Section 119.083, Florida's Software Copyright Provision," *Florida State Law Review* 20 (1992): 441–485.
68. *Uniform Crime Reports 1992*, p. 27.
69. Steven R. Schlesinger, quoted in Bureau of Justice Statistics, *Robbery Victims* (Washington, D.C.: U.S. Department of Justice, April 1987), p. 1.
70. The data from this and the following paragraphs come from *Uniform Crime Reports 1992*, pp. 26, 27, 29.
71. "Bank Heists Soar as Times Get Tough," *Tampa Tribune* (17 February 1992), p. 3.
72. Quoted in "The Bank Robbery Boom: The S&L Theives Didn't Get all the Money: Now Stickup Men Want the Rest," *Newsweek* (9 December 1991), p. 63.
73. "Gunman and Hostage Killed in Shootout After Bank Robbery," *New York Times* (30 January 1993), p. 32Y.
74. "Three Gunmen Rob Brink's Car, Get $10 Million," *Miami Herald* (6 January 1993), p. 6; "Brooklyn Robbers Get $8 Million in Armored-Car Company Holdup," *New York Times* (29 December 1992), p. 1.
75. "Convenience Store Jobs: At Night and at Risk," *New York Times* (7 April 1991), p. 1. For an analysis of Florida convenience store robberies, see Stewart D'Alessio and Lisa Stolzenberg, "A Crime of Convenience: The Environment and Convenience Store Robbery," *Environment and Behavior* 22 (March 1990): 255–271.
76. See Model Penal Code, Section 222.1.
77. See People v. Patton, 389 N.E.2d 1174 (Ill. 1979).
78. See Lear v. State, 6 P.2d 426 (Ariz. 1931).
79. See Bauer v. State, 43 P.2d 203 (Ariz. 1935).
80. People v. Dreas, 153 Cal.App. 3d 623 (1st App.Dist.Div.4, 1984).
81. People v. Rudelt, 179 N.Y.S.2d 916 (N.Y.App. 1958).
82. New York Penal Code, Title J., Sections 160.00-160.15 (1994).
83. Cummings v. State, 384 N.E.2d 605 (Ind. 1979), *aff'd. without opinion*, Cummings v. Duckworth, 843 F.2d 500 (7th Cir. 1988).

84. United States v. Martinez-Jimenez, 864 F.2d 664 (9th Cir. 1989), *cert. denied*, 489 U.S. 1099 (1989). For a discussion, see "Use a Toy Gun, Go to Prison," *Golden Gate University Law Review* 20 (1990): 167–173. See also United States v. Cannon, 903 F.2d 849 (1st Cir. 1990), *cert. denied*, 498 U.S. 1014 584 (1990); and United States v. Garrett, 3 F.3d 390 (11th Cir. 1993), *cert. denied*, 114 S.Ct. 1100 (1994).

85. "Toys, Imitation Guns Often Used in Robberies, PERF Study Shows," *Criminal Justice Newsletter* 21 (16 July 1990): 4.

86. McLaughlin v. United States, 476 U.S. 16 (1986). For a discussion of armed robbery, see Thomas Gabor and Andre Normandeau, *Armed Robbery: Cops, Robbers, and Victims* (Springfield, Ill.: Charles C. Thomas, 1987).

87. People v. Butler, 421 P.2d 703 (Cal. 1967), footnotes and citations omitted.

88. "Trio Are First to be Charged Under 'Home Invasion' Law," *Tallahassee Democrat* (21 July 1993), p. 8.

89. The home-invasion robbery statute is codified in Florida Stat., Section 812.135 (1993). The murder statute is Section 782.04 (1994).

90. Florida Stat., Section 812.133 (1)(A)(1) (1994).

91. "FBI Announces Plans for Anti-Carjacking Task Forces," *Criminal Justice Newsletter* 23 (1 September 1992): 5.

92. See United States v. Watson, 815 F.Supp. 827 (E.D.Pa. 1993), upholding the statute; and United States v. Cortner, 834 F.Supp. 242 (M.D.Tenn. 1993), holding that the statute violates the U.S. Constitution. The statute is codified at U.S. Code, Title 18, Section 2119 (1993).

93. Evans v. United States, 112 S.Ct. 1881 (1992).

94. U.S. Code, Title 18, Section 1951(b)(2) (1994).

95. Model Penal Code, Section 223.4.

96. For recent analyses of extortion, see the Symposium on blackmail and extortion in the *University of Pennsylvania Law Review* 141 (May 1993).

Chapter 8

Crimes against Public Order and Morality

Outline

Key Terms

adultery
bigamy
breach of the peace
disorderly conduct
fighting words
forcible entry and
    detainer

fornication
libel
obscenity
prostitution
riot
rout

seduction
slander
sodomy
unlawful
    assembly
vagrancy

Introduction

Most criminal law casebooks written for law schools, as well as most criminal law texts written for the college and university audience, do not discuss misdemeanors. This text is an exception. Even though by definition misdemeanors are less serious offenses than felonies, some are extremely important in terms of the frequency with which they occur or the important constitutional rights they may involve. In its introduction to a chapter that includes most of the crimes included in this chapter, the Model Penal Code makes this declaration: "Offenses in this category affect a large number of defendants, involve a great proportion of public activity, and powerfully influence the view of public justice held by millions of people."[1]

Likewise, although there are few prosecutions for adultery, bigamy, seduction, consensual sodomy, and fornication, statutes regulating these offenses may infringe on fundamental constitutional rights. Enforcement of the statutes may violate individual rights. These offenses, along with prostitution, represent areas in which there is no agreement concerning whether the criminal law should be used to regulate the activity. Violation of any of these laws may lead to more serious problems, such as extortion and blackmail.

Although space does not permit an extensive discussion of constitutional law, it is important to keep the subject in mind while reading this chapter. Chapter 1 discusses briefly the relationship of the U.S. Constitution to criminal law. It examines the *void for vagueness* doctrine, which is illustrated with a recent case involving loitering, one of the crimes discussed in this chapter. It looks at the *overbreadth doctrine*. These doctrines require that statutes must be written so that reasonable people know what they mean, and they must be specific regarding the conduct prohibited. The statute may not reach beyond conduct that may be prohibited constitutionally and include conduct that is protected by the Constitution. Frequently these issues arise in cases involving *free speech*. Although the First Amendment (see Appendix A) states that Congress shall pass "no law" inhibiting free speech, the interpretation has been that some speech and some actions that convey speech are not covered by that amendment and may be regulated.

Another constitutional doctrine important to this chapter is the right of privacy. Unlike free speech and assembly, this right is not articulated clearly in a particular amendment. Rather, it emanates from several amendments, including the First, Third, Fourth, Fifth, and Ninth (see Appendix A), as discussed by the Supreme Court in *Griswold* v. *Connecticut*, which invalidated criminal statutes concerning the prescribing and use of birth control devices by married persons.[2]

This chapter is important in that it discusses offenses that go to the heart of a free society, offenses that force us to consider under what circumstances the rights of individuals should prevail over the alleged need to protect society. Thus, some argue that consensual sexual relations between any two adults, regardless of their gender or the type of acts in which they engage, is their own business provided their acts are conducted in private. Others argue that the criminal law should be used to deter some of these acts even when they occur within marriage.

The chapter is divided into two major sections: crimes against public order and crimes against public morality.

Crimes against Public Order

Early common law was concerned with preserving peace and order to the extent that in England most statutes concluded with the phrase "to preserve the peace of the King" or "against the peace of the King." In the United States many early statutes contained the phrase "against the peace and dignity of the state." These phrases emphasized the need to preserve the peace and tranquility of society. To do that it was thought necessary to criminalize behaviors that might incite people to fight or retaliate in other ways.

All crimes might be considered offenses against the peace of the king or of the state, but common law and modern statutes use "offenses against the public peace and order" to refer to those offenses that are punishable criminally primarily because they invade society's peace and tranquility.[3]

Breach of the Peace

Breach of the peace results from an act that disturbs the public tranquility or order. In common law the category covered numerous actions, but the main thrust of the crime was to include acts that otherwise were not defined as criminal but that tended to disturb peace and tranquility. If otherwise the acts were defined as crimes, generally most were prosecuted as those crimes.

A breach of the peace statute that was held to be constitutional was the subject of litigation in a 1967 Georgia case in which the defendant said, "You son of a bitch, I'll choke you to death." He was prosecuted under a statute that prohibited "opprobrious words or abusive language, tending to cause a breach of the peace." The court held that the words of that phrase "have a definite meaning as to the conduct forbidden, measured by common understanding and practice, and are not unconstitutionally vague, indefinite or uncertain."[4]

In contrast, a 1985 decision held as unconstitutionally vague a Kentucky statute aimed at breach of the peace behavior: "No person shall upbraid, insult or abuse any teacher of the public schools in the presence of the school or in the presence of a pupil of the school."[5] In *Commonwealth* v. *Ashcraft* an obviously upset father stormed into the classroom late one afternoon after most students had gone. In the presence of the remaining children, including his daughter, he yelled criticisms at the teacher.

In *Ashcraft* the Kentucky Court of Appeals held that the statute was vague and that it infringed on the First Amendment right of communication (see Appendix A). Parents have a right to criticize teachers. The court noted that the statute as worded made it a crime for parents to criticize teachers or coaches at home or at school or elsewhere in the presence of children. "A parent could be prosecuted for insulting a teacher at a dinner table in the presence of his child/student.... Likewise, one can be penalized for insulting or abusing a teacher at the school when no students are present."[6]

Peaceful demonstrations are protected by the first Amendment. The woman in the first picture has been involved in demonstrations in front of the White House for eight years.

In *Ashcraft* there was no evidence that the father was violent or was becoming violent. The statute, designed to prevent breaching the peace, was so vague that it was used to go beyond the state's legitimate right to keep peace. It infringed on the father's First Amendment right to criticize his daughter's teacher.

Some statutes covering disturbance of the peace are aimed at controlling noise. The California statute is an example. It provides as follows:

> Any of the following persons shall be punished by imprisonment in the county jail for a period of not more than 90 days, a fine of not more than four hundred dollars ($400), or both such imprisonment and fine:
> (1) Any person who unlawfully fights in a public place or challenges another person in a public place to fight.
> (2) Any person who maliciously and willfully disturbs another person by loud and unreasonable noise.
> (3) Any person who uses offensive words in a public place which are inherently likely to provoke an immediate violent reaction.[7]

Most modern codes contain statutes aimed at preventing people from disturbing the public peace and order. California's code covers most of the offenses discussed in this chapter (in addition to others), and is used as an example.[8]

Fighting

Attempts to avoid fighting, which creates a disturbance of peace and order, are illustrated by the California Penal Code above. This statute prohibits unlawful fighting or challenging to fight in a public place, maliciously disturbing others by unreasonably loud noises, and the use of fighting words. The last prohibition is an important and frequently litigated area of law and requires more attention.

By **fighting words** the U.S. Supreme Court means words that have a tendency to incite violence by the person to whom they are directed. Fighting words do not constitute speech that is protected by the First Amendment; rather, they are viewed as words designed to inflict harm rather than to communicate ideas. As such, fighting words are more analogous to a punch in the mouth than to the communication of ideas. They are designed to elicit immediate violent reaction, not to arouse people to thought and debate. In 1942, in *Chaplinsky* v. *New Hampshire*, the U.S. Supreme Court considered the subject of fighting words and enunciated its position in this excerpt from the case.[9]

Chaplinsky v. *New Hampshire*

Appellant, a member of the sect known as Jehovah's Witnesses, was convicted in the municipal court of Rochester, New Hampshire, for [these fighting words spoken to the complainant]. "You are a God damned racketeer" and "a damned Fascist and the whole government of Rochester are Fascists or agents of Fascists." . . .

There is no substantial dispute over the facts. Chaplinsky was distributing the literature of his sect on the streets of Rochester on a busy Saturday afternoon. Members of the local citizenry complained to the City Marshall, Bowering, that Chaplinsky was denouncing all religion as a "racket." Bowering told them that Chaplinsky was lawfully engaged, and then warned Chaplinsky that the crowd was getting restless. Some time later, a disturbance occurred. The traffic officer on duty at the busy intersection started with Chaplinsky for the police station, but did not inform him that he was under arrest or that he was going to be arrested. On the way they encountered Marshall Bowering, who had been advised that a riot was under way and was therefore hurrying to the scene. Bowering repeated his earlier warning to Chaplinsky, who then addressed to Bowering the words set forth in the complaint.

Chaplinsky's version of the affair was slightly different. He testified that, when he met Bowering, he asked him to arrest the ones responsible for the disturbance. In reply, Bowering cursed him and told him to come along. Appellant admitted that he said the words charged in the complaint, with the exception of the name of the Deity. . . .

[I]t is well understood that the right of free speech is not absolute at all times and under all circumstances. There are certain well-defined and narrowly limited classes of speech, the prevention and punishment of which have never been thought to raise any Constitutional problem. These include the lewd and obscene, the profane, the libelous, and the insulting or "fighting" words—those which by their very utterance inflict injury or tend to incite an immediate breach of the peace. It has been well observed that such utterances are no essential part of any exposition of ideas, and are of such slight social value as a step to truth that any benefit that may be derived from them is clearly outweighed by the social interest in order and morality. "Resort to epithets or personal abuse is not in any proper sense communication of information or opinion safeguarded by the Constitution, and its punishment as a criminal act would raise no question under that instrument."

> We are unable to say that the limited scope of the statute as thus construed contravenes the Constitutional right of free expression. It is a statute narrowly drawn and limited to define and punish specific conduct lying within the domain of state power, the use in a public place of words likely to cause a breach of the peace. . . .
>
> Argument is unnecessary to demonstrate that the appellations "damned racketeer" and "damned Fascist" are epithets likely to provoke the average person to retaliation, and thereby cause a breach of the peace.

In later cases the Court has retreated somewhat from the presumption in *Chaplinsky* that fighting words incite people to violence. In *Terminiello* v. *Chicago*, decided in 1949, the Court upheld the trial court's jury instruction that the statute in question "stirs the public to anger, invites dispute, brings about a condition of unrest or creates a disturbance." The Court indicated that part of the purpose of speech is to arouse debate and invite dispute. Although in *Terminiello* the statute was held unconstitutional because it was vague and too broad, thereby enabling the Court to avoid deciding whether the speech in question was protected by the First Amendment, the case represents a reluctance to broaden the fighting words doctrine.[10]

In *Feiner* v. *New York*, decided in 1951, the Court upheld the conviction of Feiner, who was convicted of disorderly conduct when he described President Truman as a "bum," called the Syracuse mayor a "champagne sipping bum," and referred to the American Legion as a "Nazi Gestapo." Feiner urged black people to "rise up in arms and fight for equal rights." According to the Supreme Court, "these racial statements stirred up a little excitement. Some of the onlookers made remarks to the police about their inability to handle the crowd and at least one threatened violence if the police did not act. There were others who appeared to be favoring petitioner's arguments."

The Court said Feiner's arrest was not effected as a censor to his speech but rather as an effort to maintain the peace. "It is one thing to say that the police cannot be used as an instrument for the suppression of unpopular views, and another to say that, when as here the speaker passes the bounds of argument or persuasion and undertakes incitement to riot, they are powerless to prevent a breach of the peace."[11]

The line between permissible and impermissible speech in such situations is difficult to draw, however, as illustrated by the U.S. Supreme Court's 1963 decision in *Edwards* v. *South Carolina*. In *Edwards* the Court refused to hold as fighting words the religious and patriotic songs of demonstrators who were urging the audience to go to segregated lunch counters in protest. The Court acknowledged that an expansion of the *Feiner* holding could permit authorities to suppress unreasonably the civil rights demonstrations by contending that the audience was becoming restive and potentially dangerous.[12]

In analyzing these earlier cases, we must look carefully at the facts and what might be expected to occur as a result of the alleged fighting words.

Police may not suppress words because they (or others) do not agree with those words; something more must be present.

Some insight comes from a later case, *Cohen* v. *California*, decided in 1971. The Court reversed the conviction of Cohen, who, in protest of the draft, walked into a Los Angeles courthouse wearing a jacket on which were imprinted the words "Fuck the Draft." The Court concluded that in the context in which this occurred, there was not a substantial invasion of privacy (people in public must expect to see and hear some words and signs of which they may not approve) "in an intolerable manner." Nor were the words a "direct personal insult" directed specifically at the hearer. Nor were the police, in arresting Cohen, as in the case of *Feiner*, attempting "to prevent a speaker from intentionally provoking a given group to a hostile reaction."[13]

In terms of the future status of the fighting words doctrine, it appears that in reviewing allegations of fighting words, the Court will look carefully at the makeup of the audience to whom the words are directed, the results that occur, and the wording of the statute that serves as the basis for the criminal charge. The Court has not overruled *Chaplinsky*, but it has proceeded with caution in recent cases, holding similar statutes unconstitutional for overbreadth or vagueness rather than reaching the First Amendment free speech issue. In *Lewis* v. *City of New Orleans*, the Court refused to sustain the conviction of a defendant who referred to a police officer as a "goddamn motherfucking police." According to the Court, words that convey or are intended to convey disgrace are not, for that reason alone, fighting words.[14]

These and other cases appear to indicate that although the Court still recognizes the fighting words doctrine, a conviction under this doctrine will be examined closely.

Disorderly Conduct

There is no common law crime of disorderly conduct, although many acts that were included in the common law breach of peace crime are typical of acts covered by modern disorderly conduct statutes. Today most jurisdictions have a statute providing for criminal punishment of certain minor offenses, sometimes enumerated, and in many jurisdictions these are called *disorderly conduct statutes*. These statutes vary considerably from one jurisdiction to another. They may include offenses, such as drunkenness or fighting, that are defined as specific crimes or included within breach of the peace statutes in other jurisdictions.

Sometimes disorderly conduct statutes are confused with or considered synonymous with *vagrancy*, discussed later. A disorderly conduct statute may specify that being vagrant is an example of the proscribed conduct. On the other hand, vagrancy statutes may refer to people behaving in a disorderly manner. In any particular jurisdiction, it is important to check the wording and interpretation of the statute. It is important also to determine whether disorderly conduct statutes are vague or overbroad. The general constitutional issues applicable to both disorderly conduct and vagrancy statutes are discussed after each crime is analyzed.

One court has defined **disorderly conduct** as:

> A term of loose and indefinite meaning (except when defined by statutes), but signifying generally any behavior that is contrary to law, and more particularly such as tends to disturb the public peace or decorum, scandalize the community, or shock the public sense of morality. An offense against public morals, peace or safety.[15]

In an attempt to avoid the vagueness characteristic of many disorderly conduct and vagrancy statutes, the Model Penal Code specifies conduct that may be considered disorderly. The relevant section is as follows:

> (1) *Offense Defined*. A person is guilty of disorderly conduct if, with purpose to cause public inconvenience, annoyance or alarm, or recklessly creating a risk thereof, he:
>> (a) engages in fighting or threatening, or in violent or tumultuous behavior, or
>> (b) makes unreasonable noise or offensively coarse utterance, gesture or display, or addresses abusive language to any person present; or
>> (c) creates a hazardous or physically offensive condition by any act which serves no legitimate purpose of the actor.
>
> "Public" means affecting or likely to affect persons in a place to which the public of a substantial group has access; among the places included are highways, transport facilities, schools, prisons, apartment houses, places of business or amusement, or any neighborhood.[16]

The M.P.C. narrows the coverage as compared to the traditional statutes, but the language is broad enough to encompass a wide variety of behavior. The commentary to that section indicates that it was intended to cover such conduct as "setting off 'stink bombs,' strewing garbage, nails, or noxious substances in public passages, turning off lights in an occupied theatre, and an endless variety of public annoyances that mischief can conceive."[17]

Under the M.P.C. how would you react to an arrest under the following facts? Laurie Palmer, a forty-year-old mother, grandmother, and intensive-care nurse was arrested for disorderly conduct and impeding traffic. Her offense of was that she refused to skate (rollerblade) on the sidewalk rather than on a four-lane road. Ms. Palmer took the position that she was protecting the rights of pedestrians by staying off the sidewalk, where she did not belong, as she was not a pedestrian. She argued that in addition sidewalks are too narrow for rollerblading, and that they are unsafe as many are not maintained properly. The governmental relations chair of the International In-Line Skating Association assisted Ms. Palmer in preparing her case (she could not afford an attorney), arguing that an in-line skater is more like a bicyclist than a pedestrian in terms of speed, maneuverability, and stopping ability. Palmer skates up to fifteen miles-per hour.[18] In October 1992 Palmer was struck by a car while she rollerbladed on a public street. She received minor injuries to her arm when she left a parking lot and entered the street. She was struck by the car's passenger-side mirror. Palmer was given a written warning for improper use of a highway by a pedestrian.[19]

Vagrancy and Loitering

The common law crime of **vagrancy** referred to people who wandered about from place to place without any visible means of support, refusing to work even though able to do so, and living off the charity of others. Vagrancy as a crime dates back for centuries, focusing on the idle. Early English statutes required able-bodied people to work and made it a crime for them to wander about the country looking for higher wages or avoiding work. But idleness continued to be a major problem, particularly in England.[20]

Most vagrancy laws are broader than disorderly conduct laws, and many vagrancy laws have been declared unconstitutional. Vagrancy statutes have been attacked as permitting police to exercise too much discretion, which has led to discrimination against racial and ethnic minorities and the homeless, who may have characteristics and behavior of which the majority and the affluent and powerful may disapprove. Today there is some support for institutional efforts to assist homeless people, but as Focus 8.1 indicates, problems remain.

Vagrancy and disorderly conduct statutes may be unconstitutional because they are vague or overbroad, an issue discussed in Chapter 1, in which the U.S. Supreme Court case from California, *Kolender* v. *Lawson*, was analyzed. That case involved a black jogger arrested frequently for disorderly conduct under a statute that prohibited loitering or wandering about without apparent reason or business and refusing to identify oneself when asked to do so by peace officers.

Although the California statute in *Kolender* specified "if the surrounding circumstances are such as to indicate to a reasonable man that the public

In some cities there is social pressure to remove the homeless from public places, but some legislative attempts to do so have been declared unconstitutional.

FOCUS 8.1   The Homeless: How Should Society React?

Anger and shock were the reactions of many when in May 1990 the New York Transit Authority announced its new policy of ejecting all panhandlers and homeless people from the subways, Grand Central Terminal, and Pennsylvania Station, the only "home" many of these people had. Basing its policy on a federal court decision that begging is not a constitutionally protected type of free speech, the Authority began enforcing its policy in early June 1990. In November 1990, the Supreme Court refused to hear this case, thus leaving intact the decision of the federal appeals court that upheld the ban on subway begging.[1] As the accompanying text indicates, attorneys for the homeless have taken other approaches to challenging treatment of the homeless.

Who are the "street people?" A Bureau of Justice Statistics report indicates that despite the stereotype that they are alcoholics, drug addicts, criminals, and mentally ill persons, many are individuals who experienced economic problems recently and do not have jobs or other means of economic support. Some remain on the streets even when shelters are provided because shelters may have high crime rates or close during the day, therefore giving the individuals shelter only part of the time and forcing them to return to the streets during the day.[2]

There is social and political pressure to assist the homeless and to remove beggars from public places. Police are limited in their power to remove these individuals, as many of the statutes traditionally used for this purpose have been declared unconstitutional.

Therefore, police may look for drug or alcohol abuse, for example, in jurisdictions that have ordinances against public intoxication or other related offenses. For example, between August and December of 1993, law enforcement officers in San Francisco wrote 3,400 citations for "such long-ignored violations as 'intent to camp' and public intoxication." If the street people ignore the citations, they are arrested.[3]

In 1993, Seattle, Washington residents enacted an ordinance making it a civil offense to sit on the sidewalk during the day in front of a business. Other city ordinances have been drafted, covering such acts as urinating in public, loitering, and aggressive panhandling, all designed to make it easier for police to arrest street people. Advocates for street people argue that such ordinances make it a crime to be poor, and many of these ordinances are being challenged in the courts.[4]

Street people will continue to present problems for a society torn between the belief that they are people who will not work, who are dangerous to the rest of society, and who should be removed from the streets and the realization that many of these people have no other alternatives and therefore are social problems, not criminals.

[1] Young v. New York City Transit Authority, 903 F.2d 146 (2d Cir. 1990), *cert. denied*, 498 U.S. 984 (1990).
[2] Peter Finn, "Street People," Bureau of Justice Statistics (Washington, D.C.: National Institute of Justice, 1988), p. 1.
[3] "In Three Progressive Cities, It's Law vs. Street People," *New York Times* (12 December 1993), p. 16.
[4] Ibid.

safety demands such identification," the Court held that the statute was unconstitutional because it vested too much discretionary power in the police. The statute "encourages arbitrary enforcement by failing to describe with sufficient particularity what a suspect must do in order to satisfy the statute."[21] In an earlier case, *Papachristou* v. *City of Jacksonville*, the Court invalidated a vagrancy ordinance, holding that the ordinance was vague and that one result of that vagueness was to give police too much discretion.[22]

Papachristou v. *City of Jacksonville*

This case involves eight defendants who were convicted in a Florida municipal court of violating a Jacksonville, Florida vagrancy ordinance. . . . For reasons which will appear, we reverse. . . .

Those generally implicated by the imprecise terms of the ordinance—poor people, nonconformists, dissenters, idlers—may be required to comport themselves according to the life-style deemed appropriate by the Jacksonville police and the courts. Where, as here, there are no standards governing the exercise of the discretion granted by the ordinance, the scheme permits and encourages an arbitrary and discriminatory enforcement of the law. It furnishes a convenient tool for "harsh and discriminatory enforcement by prosecuting officials, against particular groups deemed to merit their displeasure." It results in a regime in which the poor and the unpopular are permitted to "stand on a public sidewalk . . . only at the whim of any police officer."

A presumption that people who might walk or loaf or loiter or stroll or frequent houses where liquor is sold, or who are supported by their wives or who look suspicious to the police are to become future criminals is too precarious for a rule of law. . . .

Of course, vagrancy statutes are useful to the police. Of course they are nets making easy the round-up of so-called undesirables. But the rule of law implies equality and justice in its application. Vagrancy laws of the Jacksonville type teach that the scales of justice are so tipped that even-handed administration of the law is not possible. The rule of law, evenly applied to minorities as well as to majorities, to the poor as well as to the rich, is the great mucilage that holds society together.

Some modern statutes use the term *loitering* rather than vagrancy. They may be found unconstitutional if they are vague or overbroad; they may be upheld if they are clear. For example, a municipal loitering ordinance modeled after that of the Model Penal Code was upheld against charges of vagueness and overbreadth. In *Milwaukee* v. *Nelson*, the Wisconsin Supreme Court upheld an ordinance that makes it an offense to loiter "in a place, at a time, or in a manner not usual for law-abiding individuals under circumstances that warrant alarm for the safety of persons or property in the vicinity."[23] Likewise, the California statute that prohibits loitering "in or about any toilet open to the public for the purpose of engaging in or soliciting any lewd or lascivious or any unlawful act" has been upheld against charges of vagueness.[24]

In contrast, a Tampa, Florida ordinance that prohibited loitering "in a manner and under circumstances manifesting the purpose" to solicit prostitution, was declared unconstitutional by the Florida Supreme Court in 1993. The decision was 4-3, with the majority writing three opinions, with little agreement on why the ordinance was unconstitutional. Some of the reasons given were that the ordinance was too broad, too vague, too harsh compared to similar Florida statutes, and violative of due substantive process. The ordinance could be interpreted to prohibit "known prostitutes" from hailing a cab, waving to a friend, or engaging in other protected behavior without incurring the possibility of an arrest.[25]

Focus 8.1 discusses a New York Transit Authority ban on begging that was upheld against a constitutional challenge. The attorney for those challenging the regulation questioned the state's loitering statute and got a more favorable result. In 1992 the same court ruled that the portion of the New York statute that defines as loitering a person who "loiters, remains or wanders about in a public place for the purpose of begging" violates the free speech guarantee of the First Amendment (see Appendix A). The state statute was distinguished from the Transit Authority regulation, with the court noting that in the latter case the prohibition was narrow. It applied only to subways, leaving persons other avenues for communicating to the public about the problems of the homeless (or about any other issue). In contrast, the state statute prohibits begging throughout the state, thus inhibiting the free speech rights of those who might want to communicate to the public the problems of homeless people.[26]

Public Intoxication and Drug Incapacitation

Chapter 4 examines substance abuse and the issue of whether it is a disease or an act of free will. That discussion focuses on the use of intoxication (both alcohol and other drugs) as a defense to criminal acts. In this chapter the focus is on the practice of *criminalizing* substance abuse in public. The emphasis is on the aspect of disturbing public order or morality not only by the appearance of these people in public but in the concern that they may hurt others or try to entice others to engage in substance abuse. Further, statutes regulating public drunkenness and drug incapacitation may be used to remove people from the streets. Whether designated as a separate crime or one falling under the general categories of disorderly conduct, vagrancy, or disturbing the peace, the public abuse of alcohol and drugs is another category of criminal activity that raises serious debate as well as constitutional issues.

In *Powell* v. *Texas*, the Supreme Court upheld Powell's conviction based on its conclusion that his being drunk in public was an act, not a condition.[27] As long as the Court holds that position, in all probability public drunkenness statutes will be upheld. Presumably they are enacted to preserve public peace, order, and morals, but the reasonableness of having these statutes is questioned.

Many of those arrested for public drunkenness are "homeless, penniless, and beset with acute personal problems."[28] Most are arrested more than once. Many spend so much time in jail that they have been described as "serving a life sentence on the installment plan." They are not aided by being placed in jail. As a result of enforcing criminal laws in this area, police are diverted from other more important functions.

Some jurisdictions have enacted statutes that emphasize treatment and rehabilitation instead of prosecution of public drunkenness. The Georgia statute, enacted in 1974, illustrates this trend, although Georgia, like many other states, has not provided sufficient treatment facilities for these cases: "It is the policy of this State that alcoholics may not be subjected to criminal prosecution because of their consumption of alcoholic beverages but rather should be afforded a continuum of treatment in order that they may lead normal lives as productive members of society."[29]

Despite the fact that most states have enacted legislation to decriminalize public drunkenness, many people are held in jail for this offense, mainly because so many jurisdictions have no other facilities for detaining and treating people who are apprehended for public drunkenness and related offenses.

Some state courts have held that jailing public drunks violates their state constitutional rights. Excerpts from the 1982 West Virginia case of *State* v. *Zegeer* illustrate this position.[30]

State v. Zegeer

Relying on the protections mandated by the West Virginia Constitution, we hold that no chronic alcoholic can be criminally prosecuted for public drunkenness.

Most states have adopted the Uniform Alcoholism and Intoxication Treatment Act that deals with alcoholism as a disease. Others stopped short of decriminalization, and instead developed diversionary systems for both alcoholics and public drunks. In each of these states, when the courts failed to act, the uniform act, or a variant thereof, was soon adopted. We urge our Legislature to enact a comprehensive plan for dealing with alcoholics in a humane and beneficial manner....[The court discusses the conditions under which the defendant was confined in this case.]

No one expects jails to be luxury hotels, or as editorialists delight in claiming, country clubs. But we cannot permit human beings to be penned en masse with dangerous, oftentimes murderous, companions in filthy cages without flushing commodes, with no place to sleep but concrete floors spewn with human excrement, vomit and rodents or insects. Jail conditions are often evaluated by the cumulative effect of intolerable conditions, and using a "totality of the circumstances" test, we notice that many jails in this State are unfit for humans....

We ... conclude that jailing of alcoholics for public intoxication is unconstitutional. The State is obliged to develop alternative methods for dealing with public drunkenness and alcoholics.

In its discussion of the history of criminalizing public intoxication and drug incapacitation, the Model Penal Code notes that the former has long been a crime, the latter only recently. Some public drunkenness prohibitions are contained in state statutes; others are in city or county ordinances. Historically these prohibitions have differed considerably. Some cover non-public drunkenness; others exclude private intoxication, the approach the M.P.C. takes. The M.P.C. notes also the concern discussed earlier in conjunction with defenses to criminal acts. In the words of the M.P.C.,

> The underlying concern in this area is the proper role of the penal law in dealing with persons suffering from chronic alcoholism, narcotics addiction, or other drug dependency. These conditions create a kind of pharmacological compulsion that, to some extent at least, may overpower the will of the individual so affected. There are obvious problems in assigning punishment for behavior that is in some meaningful sense not voluntary, just as there are obvious difficulties in attempting to differentiate the person who could not restrain himself from the person who merely did not do so.[31]

The M.P.C. incorporates the following model statute defining the crime. The crime is a misdemeanor only if the defendant has two previous convictions under this section; otherwise it is a violation, a lesser offense. "A person is guilty of an offense if he appears in any public place manifestly under the influence of alcohol, narcotics or other drug, not therapeutically administered, to the degree that he may endanger himself or other persons or property, or annoy persons in his vicinity."[32]

Unlawful Assembly, Rout, and Riot

Under the common law, unlawful assembly, rout, and riot were misdemeanors. **Unlawful assembly** referred to the meeting of three or more persons to disturb the public peace, with the intention of participating in a forcible and violent execution of an unlawful enterprise or of a lawful enterprise in an unauthorized manner. To constitute unlawful assembly, the group did not have to carry out its purpose; but if it took steps to carry out the plan, those involved committed a **rout**. If it carried out the plan, they committed a **riot**.

The word *rout* and the word *route* come from the same word, and *rout* is used to indicate that those who have unlawfully assembled are "on their way."[33] The word *riot* may be defined as "a tumultuous disturbance of the peace by three or more persons assembled and acting with a common intent; either in executing a lawful private enterprise in a violent and turbulent manner, to the terror of the people, or as executing an unlawful enterprise in a violent and turbulent manner."[34]

The English Riot Act of 1714 made it a capital felony for twelve or more persons to continue together for an hour after an official proclamation that people should disperse because of an existing riot. The official command to disperse was known as *reading the riot act* and involved this statement:

> Our sovereign Lady the Queen chargeth and commandeth all persons being assembled immediately to disperse themselves and peaceably to depart to their habitations or to their lawful business, upon the pains contained in the

Act made in the first year of King George for preventing tumults and riotous assemblies. God save the Queen.[35]

Some modern statutes retain the crimes of unlawful assembly and riot; fewer retain rout. California retains all three, although the definitions differ somewhat from the common law crimes. As indicated in Focus 8.2, California defines unlawful assembly as requiring two or more persons, whereas the common law required three or more. The statutes vary from jurisdiction to jurisdiction.

Statutes regulating unlawful assemblies, routs, and riots are justified as necessary to preserve peace and order, but they may be used also to harass and suppress political protestors. Unlawful assemblies and riots range from deadly scenes to relatively peaceful demonstrations. In recent years, abortion clinics and college campuses have been frequent targets of protests, some of which have been lawful but others of which have resulted in arrests for unlawful activities.

The federal riot statute focuses on people who cross state lines to create disorder and disturb the peace. It is based on the presumption that outside agitators play a major role in creating urban disturbances.[36]

Riots are usually classified as misdemeanors, although some jurisdictions provide that aggravated riots are felonies. Some provide for additional penalties if defendants commit other crimes, such as carrying weapons, during the riots. Some statutes contain related crimes, such as *inciting to riot*. For example, New York's penal code includes a section entitled "Inciting to Riot," which criminalizes the urging of ten or more people to "engage in tumultuous and violent conduct of a kind likely to create public alarm." This offense is a misdemeanor.[37]

Some statutes divide riots into categories according to seriousness, such as first-degree riot, second-degree riot, and so on. For example, New York has two degrees of riots. Riot in the second degree is a misdemeanor, but first-degree riot is a felony. The major difference between the two is that first-degree riot requires that ten or more other people be involved (compared to four or more in second-degree riot) and that someone other than those involved in the riot be injured or that property damage occur as a result of the riot.[38]

Carrying Weapons

Violence discussed in earlier chapters has led to vigorous debates over gun control in the United States, one of the most violent countries in the Western world. Over two decades ago two scholars claimed,

> Americans own a greater number and variety of firearms than the citizens of any other Western democracy, and they also use their guns to assault, maim, and kill one another much more often. Thus violence in the United States is more serious, and a possible means of reducing that violence—gun control—is more difficult to achieve than in other industrialized countries. It is this special significance of firearms in American life that has led to the great gun control debate.[39]

FOCUS 8.2   Unlawful Assembly, Rout, and Riot: The California Statutes

Section 404. "Riot"

(a) Any use of force or violence, disturbing the public peace, or any threat to use such force or violence, if accompanied by immediate power of execution, by two or more persons acting together, and without authority of law, is a riot.

(b) As used in this section, disturbing the public peace may occur in any place of confinement. Place of confinement means any state prison, county jail, industrial farm, or road camp, or any city jail, industrial farm, or road camp.

Section 404.6. Urging Riot

Every person who with the intent to cause a riot does an act or engages in conduct which urges a riot, or urges others to commit acts of force or violence, or the burning or destroying of property, and at a time and place and under circumstances which produce a clear and present and immediate danger of acts of force or violence or the burning or destroying of property, is guilty of a misdemeanor. ...

Section 405a.

The taking by means of a riot of any person from the lawful custody of any peace officer is a lynching.

Section 406. "Rout" Defined

Whenever two or more persons, assembled and acting together, make any attempt or advance toward the commission of an act which would be a riot if actually committed, such assembly is a rout.

Section 407. "Unlawful Assembly" Defined

Whenever two or more persons assemble together to do an unlawful act, or do a lawful act in a violent, boisterous, or tumultuous manner, such assembly is an unlawful assembly.

Section 409. Remaining Present at Place of Riot, etc., after Warning to Disperse

Every person remaining present at the place of any riot, rout, or unlawful assembly, after the same has been lawfully warned to disperse, except public officers and persons assisting them in attempting to disperse the same, is guilty of a misdemeanor.

SOURCE: Cal. Penal Code, Title 11, Section 404, *et. seq.* (1994).

Under the common law, because of the danger of breaching the peace if weapons were carried, it was a misdemeanor to "terrify the good people of the land by riding or going armed with dangerous or unusual weapons." The emphasis was on terrifying the king's citizens.[40]

Today most U.S. jurisdictions have statutes regulating carrying weapons, but they differ so much that it is not possible to generalize. Most include carrying concealed weapons, and many do not go beyond that offense. Two commentators have recounted the example of a law student who, after carefully studying the state statutes prohibiting carrying *concealed* weapons, strapped a weapon on his belt in full view and walked about town. He was arrested quickly. Upon reciting his recently acquired knowledge of the law, he was shocked to discover that he was violating a city ordinance that prohibited the carrying of weapons, concealed or unconcealed.[41]

Modern statutes regulate the sale, possession, and carrying of weapons. The most restrictive at that time, the Morton Grove (Illinois) ordinance, which bans both the sale and ownership of handguns, was upheld by a lower federal court. The U.S. Supreme Court refused to review the case, thus leaving the lower court decision that the ordinance does not violate the federal constitution.[42] The following year, the Illinois Supreme Court held that the Morton Grove ordinance did not violate the Illinois state constitution.[43]

The increased violence with guns, especially among juveniles, has led to renewed arguments for gun control. In September 1993, after a five-day special session on juvenile violence, Colorado enacted a statute that bans teenagers (persons under the age of eighteen) from possessing handguns except when the guns are used for hunting, firearms instruction, and target practice. The first offense is a misdemeanor, and a juvenile who is found in illegal possession of a handgun may be detained in jail for a minimum of ten days.[44]

Earlier discussions mentioned the recently enacted Brady Handgun Violence Prevention Act, named for James Brady, who was wounded seriously when John Hinckley attempted to assassinate President Ronald Reagan. The statute requires a five-day waiting period for the purchase of handguns. Shortly after the passage of that bill (which incurred many hurdles in Congress), President Clinton's administration suggested requiring licensing of all gun owners. Attorney General Janet Reno was instructed to study the idea. Said Reno, "It should be at least as hard to get a license to possess a gun as it is to drive an automobile."[45]

Enacting gun control laws, however, may not achieve the desired results. Lack of funds for enforcement may render the Brady Bill ineffective. Experts estimate that adequate enforcement of the statute would cost hundreds of billions of dollars along with additional billions "to pay for prenatal care, primary education, domestic violence prevention and other programs aimed at preventing another generation of children from turning to a life of crime."[46]

Even if sufficient funds are appropriated, there is no guarantee that gun control measures will have a significant impact on crime prevention. Two years after a ban on military-style assault weapons, a measure sold to the public as a crime-fighting weapon, New Jersey officials admitted that the ban had not had any measurable effect. Only approximately 2,000 of the tens or even hundreds of thousands of assault weapons thought to be in the state were accounted for during those two years.[47]

Obstructing a Highway or Public Passage

Public authorities have the right to regulate the flow of traffic and people on public streets, highways, and sidewalks; but this right to keep peace and order may not infringe upon the right to free speech and expression.

Statutes designed to regulate obstructing highways or public passages may not be so broad or vague that they grant excessive discretion to those charged with enforcing the statutes.

Most problems arise when authorities attempt to suppress demonstrations they consider unpopular. An example illustrating this problem is provided by a brief excerpt from *Cox* v. *Louisiana*. Cox was arrested and charged with four offenses: criminal conspiracy, disturbing the peace, obstructing public passages, and picketing before a courthouse. He was convicted of the latter three. Cox was the leader of a group of demonstrators who marched to the courthouse to protest the jailing of their friends for picketing. They were peaceful in their demonstration, did not block the street, and moved to the west side of the street when told to do so by police. But at noon Cox told the crowd to go to the lunch counters to protest racial discrimination.

The sheriff told Cox that although his protest to that point had been more or less peaceful, "what you are doing now is a direct violation of the law, a disturbance of the peace, and it has to be broken up immediately." Cox and the demonstrators did not break up the demonstration; police exploded a tear gas bomb, at which point the demonstrators dispersed quickly. The next day Cox was arrested. In this excerpt, the Court addresses its comments to Cox's conviction for obstructing public passages.[48]

Cox v. Louisiana

The rights of free speech and assembly, while fundamental in our democratic society, still do not mean that everyone with opinions or beliefs to express may address a group at any public place and at any time. The constitutional guarantee of liberty implies the existence of an organized society maintaining public order, without which liberty itself would be lost in the excesses of anarchy. The control of travel on the streets is a clear example of governmental responsibility to insure this necessary order. A restriction in that relation, designed to promote the public convenience in the interest of all, and not susceptible to abuses of discriminatory application, cannot be disregarded by the attempted exercise of some civil right which, in other circumstances, would be entitled to protection. One would not be justified in ignoring the familiar red light because this was thought to be a means of social protest .... A group of demonstrators could not insist upon the right to cordon off a street, or entrance to a public or private building, and allow no one to pass who did not agree to listen to their exhortations....

[The Court noted that authorities have the right to limit demonstrations by time, place, duration, or manner provided those limitations do not involve unfair discrimination and are uniformly and consistently based on the facts of each case.]

But here it is clear that the practice in Baton Rouge allowing unfettered discretion in local officials in the regulation of the use of the streets for peaceful parades and meetings is an unwarranted abridgment of appellant's freedom of speech and assembly secured to him by the First Amendment, as applied to the States by the Fourteenth Amendment. It follows, therefore, that appellant's conviction for violating the statute as so applied and enforced must be reversed.

The Model Penal Code requires that for a violation to occur, the person must have refused a "reasonable official request or order to move."[49]

Other Offenses against Public Order

Under the common law or under modern statutes or both there are a variety of other offenses against public order. For example, *disturbance of public assembly* is a criminal offense in some jurisdictions. Because the societal order might be disturbed if people attempt to disrupt public meetings, there are some statutes prohibiting these activities. The Model Penal Code section, "Disrupting Meetings and Processions," is an example. "A person commits a misdemeanor if, with purpose to prevent or disrupt a lawful meeting, procession or gathering, he does any act tending to obstruct or interfere with it physically, or makes any utterance, gesture or display designed to outrage the sensibilities of the group."[50]

The Model Penal Code prohibits the desecration of venerated objects, another act that might disturb societal order. This offense is described as follows:

> A person commits a misdemeanor if he purposely desecrates any public monument or structure, or place of worship or burial, or if he purposely desecrates the national flag or any other object of veneration by the public or a substantial segment thereof in any public place. "Desecrate" means defacing, damaging, polluting or otherwise physically mistreating in a way that the actor knows will outrage the sensibilities of persons likely to observe or discover his action.[51]

Recently, however, state and federal statutes prohibiting flag burning per se have been declared unconstitutional in the context of cases in which the flag was burned as a political protest.[52]

Abuse of corpse is another crime thought to be disruptive of public order, and the occurrence of this crime is not as uncommon as might be expected. Under the common law and under modern statutes, individuals who abuse a corpse may be prosecuted criminally as well as subjected to civil suits. The Model Penal Code has a criminal provision providing that "except as authorized by law, a person who treats a corpse in a way that he knows would outrage ordinary family sensibilities commits a misdemeanor."[53] In 1992 a funeral home returned a body to a relative when the bill for cremation was not paid. In Richmond, Texas, when Larry Bojarski paid Evans Mortuary $299 of the $683 for his father's cremation, he was told that if he did not pay the balance the body would be returned. When Bojarski had not paid three days later, his father's body was left at the front door of his apartment, covered with a sheet. Newell Evans, owner of Evans Mortuary, was charged with abuse of corpse.[54] In 1991 two leaders of a gang of grave robbers were sentenced to death in the People's Republic of China after they stole gold, silver, and jade.[55]

Abuse of animals is another public order crime that has been in the news recently. The Model Penal Code provides that with the exception of veterinary practices and activities carried on for scientific research, it is a misdemeanor if purposely or recklessly a person: "(1) subjects any animal to cruel mistreatment; or (2) subjects any animal in his custody to cruel neglect; or (3) kills or injures any animal belonging to another without legal privilege or consent of the owner."[56]

The issue of animal abuse has arisen in the context of what constitutes acceptable research in contrast to animal cruelty, but there have been recent cases of alleged animal abuse outside of the research arena. In August 1993, animal cruelty charges were filed in Pensacola, Florida against three men accused of ritualistic mutilations and killings of cats by a satanic cult. Subsequently the charges were dropped after one witness recanted his testimony and two others refused to testify.[57]

The U.S. Humane Society reports that cat torture is on the rise. Cats have surpassed dogs as the preferred pet in the United States.[58] In California the maximum three-year penalty for animal abuse was given to a man who killed, grilled, and ate his neighbor's dog. The defendant testified that he committed these acts because he did not have any money and had not eaten in two days.[59] In Florida, however, a defendant was placed on probation, fined $500, and ordered to pay $398.25 in restitution and to serve one hundred hours of community service for cutting off the penis of a dog while the dog was mating. The defendant was ordered to read the numerous letters the judge received about the case prior to its resolution.[60] Finally, a Pennsylvania man was arrested for allegedly plucking a peacock. Some say this is dangerous to the animal, which has blood vessels at the end of its tail. Others say it is like plucking your own hair. The accused in this case was jailed for the night and faced felony charges of cruelty to zoo animals, theft, and receiving stolen property. The male peacock "uses its colorful feathers to attract the female" and was near a group of females when he was plucked.[61]

Forcible entry and detainer is another crime against public order. A person who enters land forcibly or being there peacefully, uses force to remain, may be a threat to public peace and security. Forcible entry and detainer was a common law offense and is a statutory offense in many jurisdictions today. Although there are two separate offenses (because a forcible detainer can exist without a forcible entry), usually the offense is referred to as one.

The Model Penal Code contains a *criminal trespass* provision that is similar to forcible entry and detainer statutes. Under this provision, it is a misdemeanor (if committed in a dwelling at night; otherwise it is a petty misdemeanor) to enter or remain surreptitiously in any building or occupied structure knowing that you do not have a privilege or license to do so. It is an offense also to enter and remain in any place to which notice against trespass has been given (under certain circumstances) when the actor knows that he or she is not licensed or privileged to do so.[62] As a result of campus disruptions and demonstrations, some states enacted legislation making it a crime to enter forcibly and to remain in campus buildings and structures.

One final example of a crime against the public order that has received considerable attention in recent years is *harassment*. Some jurisdictions criminalize various harassment techniques, such as insults, challenges, phone calls, or other means of inciting an individual to violence, subjecting another to offensive touching, engaging in alarming conduct, or making repeated communications anonymously or at times or in places that are inconvenient to the recipient.

An example of a statute that prohibits harassment is that of New York, reprinted in Focus 8.3. New York has a statute prohibiting *aggravated harassment*, which applies to harassment conducted by mechanical or electronic means. Aggravated harassment in the second degree includes making a telephone call, "whether or not a conversation ensues, with no purpose of legitimate communication." The call, along with other acts that constitute second-degree harassment, must be done "with intent to harass, annoy, threaten or alarm another person." Second-degree harassment includes also the acts of one who "strikes, shoves, kicks, or otherwise subjects another person to physical contact, or attempts or threatens to do the same because of the race, color, religion, or national origin of such person.[63] In 1992 the New York legislature added the grades of harassment to the statute and changed the language from "he" to "he or she," thus making it clear that women may be charged with harassment.

With the recent awareness of the extent and seriousness of sexual and racial harassment, many college and university faculties and administrators have instituted harassment policies that define unacceptable behavior on campus or in other settings in which university employees or students may be interacting in an official capacity. These policies have been accompanied by administrative procedures that make it easier to enforce the regulations, while encouraging alleged racial and sexual harassment victims to file complaints. Penalties for those who are found to be in violation of the policies may be severe, such as dismissal for faculty or students who initiate the forbidden behavior. Some of these policies state that dating between a subordinate and a superordinate constitutes a presumption that the superordinate in the relationship pressured the alleged victim to engage in sexual behavior.

Generally these campus regulations fall under administrative, not criminal law, but in some settings sexual harassment is a crime as well as a violation of administrative or civil law. For example, a Florida statute criminalizes a sexual relationship by a psychotherapist (and certain other specified health-care personnel) with a patient. Consent is not a defense. The act is a felony of the third degree, and conviction may result in a five-year prison term for a first offense and a fifteen-year term for a second offense.[64]

This brief discussion of harassment illustrates the fact that offenses against public order may and often are sex-related. The next section focuses on acts that are not considered serious enough to be major crimes but offensive enough at least to some to be included within the criminal law.

FOCUS 8.3 The Crime of Harassment: The New York Statutes

Section 240.25. Harassment in the First Degree

A person is guilty of harassment in the first degree when he or she intentionally and repeatedly harasses another person by following such person in or about a public place or places or by engaging in a course of conduct or by repeatedly committing acts which places [sic] such person in reasonable fear of physical injury.

Harassment in the first degree is a class B misdemeanor.

Section 240.26. Harassment in the Second Degree

A person is guilty of harassment in the second degree when, with intent to harass, annoy or alarm another person:

1. He or she strikes, shoves, kicks or otherwise subjects such other person to physical contact, or attempts or threatens to do the same; or
2. He or she follows a person in or about a public place or places; or
3. He or she engages in a course of conduct or repeatedly commits acts which alarm or seriously annoy such other person and which serve no legitimate purpose.

Harassment in the second degree is a violation.

SOURCE: New York Penal Code, Title J, Section 240.25 *et seq.* (1994).

Offenses against Public Morality

The discussion of the purposes of criminal law in Chapter 1 looks briefly at the arguments for and against including morality within the criminal law. Certainly criminal law should encompass forced sexual behavior, but should it include sexual behavior in which consenting adults engage? If so, to what extent should the law cover these behaviors? Should it prohibit all sexual behavior between unmarried persons? Or should it extend only to acts that involve a person under the age of legal consent? If so, what should be the age of consent?

The problem of what to include and what to exclude from the criminal law probably engenders more debate in the area of moral behavior than in any other area. Historically, many of the behaviors discussed in this chapter were considered within the area of morality to be governed by the church and not by the state. In Roman law, the word *crime* comes from a word meaning fault, sinning, an act against morality.

The early criminal statutes of the American colonies and subsequently the United States were strict and patterned after Biblical laws. In the Massachusetts Code of 1648, the death penalty was used for rape and adultery as well as for many other acts. The Puritans equated sin and crime, and frequently they prosecuted offenders for sexual crimes. Of the 370 prosecutions in one Massachusetts county between 1760 and 1774, 210 were for fornication. After the American revolution, prosecutions focused on property crimes rather than sex crimes.[65]

Despite the declining number of prosecutions for sexual offenses, these offenses remained in the criminal law. Within the past two decades some jurisdictions have decriminalized some of the behaviors, such as private consensual sexual behavior between unmarried adults. But the debate remains over who should control morality—the church, the state, or neither. The recent AIDS (acquired immune deficiency syndrome) epidemic has refocused attention on sexual behavior and the law.

Prostitution

Prostitution, illegal in this country in all but some rural counties in Nevada, historically has been accepted—in some societies, even esteemed. It has been essential in societies that permit premarital and postmarital sexual behavior by men with women who are not their marital partners, while insisting that women should not engage in such behavior. It has been argued that the prostitute serves the role in society of preserving families and the chastity of other women.[66]

In 1993 a San Francisco committee was appointed to study the feasibility of establishing city-run brothels. City officials appointed the committee in response to complaints from merchants and residents complaining about those who sell sex on the streets. Three prostitutes serve on the committee, which is to file a report in 1994. At issue is whether it would be preferable to have the city license brothels and check the health of prostitutes as well as tax their earnings as a way to remove streetwalkers. For the most part law enforcement officers have ignored those streetwalkers, who violate the law by selling sex. Those who have been arrested are released in a very short time because the jails are crowded. But residents and business owners complain that the presence of streetwalkers endangers their safety

Heidi Fleiss, called the "Hollywood Madame," entered a not-guilty plea after her arrest on prostitution-related charges.

and welfare, especially when violence and drugs accompany prostitutes into the area.[67]

In addition to the argument that prostitution may contribute to family welfare is, of course, the contrary argument that prostitution endangers the well-being of the family. Another view of prostitution is to consider it solely in economic terms: prostitutes are responding to the demand for their services. A Tallahassee, Florida public school substitute teacher, charged in 1992 with twenty-two counts of prostitution-related charges, was featured on talk shows nationally as she talked about her "business." Coral Velisek entered a no-contest plea to the charges and was placed on probation after serving thirty days in jail and paying a fine. Velisek explained her involvement, along with that of the women who worked for her, in terms of economic necessity. "I need the money to buy groceries...pay the light bill...fix the car...take my kid to the doctor." Velisek argued that police should be fighting violent crime, not trying to arrest women who are "just trying to make ends meet."[68] The 1993 arrest of Heidi Fleiss, discussed in Focus 8.4 refers also to the economic aspect of prostitution.

Prostitution is viewed by others as a way of exploiting women and children. A *Time* magazine feature story in June 1993 had a cover picture of a customer and a bar girl in Bangkok, and carried this headline, "Sex For Sale: An Alarming Boom in Prostitution Debases the Women and Children of the World." According to this article, prostitution is a multibillion-dollar business throughout the world. "Souls do not count, only bodies, debased over and over, unmindful of social cost or disease."[69]

Statutes regulating prostitution vary. So do definitions of the term, although basically it refers to indiscriminate sexual intercourse for hire.

FOCUS 8.4 Heidi Fleiss: The Hollywood Madam?

She has been called the most powerful woman in Hollywood since her arrest on prostitution-related charges. Heidi Fleiss, twenty-seven-year-old daughter of a pediatrician, mixed with some of Hollywood's most powerful and influential people. She was arrested at her $1.6 million mansion and charged with operating a high-class call girl ring in the Los Angeles area. She entered a plea of not guilty to five counts of pandering and one count of possessing cocaine for sale. She was released on $100,000 bond.

A few weeks after her arrest Fleiss began to talk about her business, noting the economic issue with the statement that perhaps "I put a lot of people through college, maybe. A lot of people got to go on with their careers. A lot of girls got to be who they really wanted to be."[1] Thus far Fleiss has not named any of her clients, but it is reasonable to believe that many people in Hollywood are nervous that at some point she may do so. Fleiss was scheduled to go on trial in September 1994.

[1.] "Heidi Talks About Heidi, and Hollywood Listens," *New York Times* (20 August 1993), p.7; CNN News (16 March 1994).

Prostitution was not a common law crime in some countries, and it remains legal in many countries, although some acts associated with prostitution, such as *pandering* (procuring a female for a house of prostitution) or soliciting may be criminal.

By definition some statutes limit prostitution to women; others include men or use a neutral term, such as gender, the position of the Model Penal Code. The M.P.C. includes patronizing a prostitute and living off a prostitute under specified circumstances as criminal offenses. The Model Penal Code includes a lengthy list of situations that fall under the prohibition of *promoting prostitution*.[70]

Statutory prohibitions of prostitution may be extensive. In New York, for example, where prostitution is defined as engaging or agreeing or offering "to engage in sexual conduct with another person in return for a fee," prostitution is a misdemeanor. Despite an extensive list of acts included under the title of *prostitution offenses* in the New York Penal Code, authorities report that most of the prostitution-related arrests in New York City are for violation of *loitering for the purpose of engaging in a prostitution offense*. This section of the New York Penal Code criminalizes the act of remaining in or wandering about public places while repeatedly beckoning to, or repeatedly stopping, people on the sidewalk or in passing vehicles "for the purpose of prostitution, or of patronizing a prostitute." The provision has been upheld.[71] Likewise, the New York statute that prohibits *engaging in or soliciting another person to engage in deviate sexual intercourse* has been upheld when applied to male homosexuals.[72]

Problems of interpreting statutes aimed at controlling the sale of sex are demostrated by a 1986 Pennsylvania case. Following the excerpt we will see how the case was used by analogy in a 1991 case.[73]

Commonwealth v. *Robbins*

This is an appeal from judgment of sentence entered after a jury convicted appellant of prostitution. A sentence of one year probation and a $750 fine was imposed. Appellant was charged [with the statute that makes it an offense to] "knowingly promote prostitution of another by owning, controlling, managing, supervising or otherwise keeping, alone or in association with another, a house of prostitution or a prostitution business."

The jury found appellant in violation of this section for her co-owner status of the Body Clinic, an establishment where semi-nude female employees perform massages on nude male customers for a fee. The "massage" included masturbation of the genitalia. . . .

[Appellant contended that the term *sexual activity* was not defined adequately in the statute and thus did not include the behavior in question. The court noted the definition of prostitution, a third-degree misdemeanor, which includes being an inmate of a house of prostitution or otherwise engaging in sexual activity as a business.] Sexual activity is defined as "includ[ing] homosexual and other deviate sexual relations."

In essence, appellant asserts she had no notice and fair warning as required by due process that she was violating the law by allowing manual genital stimulation for the payment of money. . . .

[The court discusses the meaning of reasonable notice and the prohibition against vague statutes.] However, the constitutional prohibition against vagueness does not invalidate every statute which could have been drafted with greater precision. Due process requires only that the law give sufficient warning so that individuals may conform their conduct so as to avoid that which the law forbids.

[The court discusses constitutional issues, notes that statutes enjoy a presumption of constitutionality, and discusses two prior cases, quoting one as follows:]

> In the mind of a man of 'common intelligence' the term sexual activity clearly encompasses masturbation as a business. Indeed...it is difficult to believe that any man of common intelligence would consider the massaging of the genitals of an unclothed man by a nude or partially nude female to be anything other than sexual activity. . . .

We believe there is no question that appellant had notice and fair warning, as required by due process, that she was violating the law by allowing manual sexual stimulation for the payment of money. This is clearly not a situation where the conduct prohibited is so intangible or vague as to require men of common intelligence to guess at its meaning and differ as to its application.

The statute in question was enacted to provide an ascertainable standard of conduct directed at a defined evil; such evil being the commercial exploitation of sexual gratification. Furthermore, since the term "sexual activity" is undefined by the statute, we are obliged to construe that term according to its common and approved usage. When the term "sexual activity" is examined in light of the statute's underlying purpose of prohibiting commercial exploitation of sexual gratification and also in light of its common and approved usage, there is no doubt that masturbation for hire falls within the statute's proscription. Therefore we find section 5902(a) is not unconstitutionally vague so as to cause appellant to seriously believe that she was not providing some form of sexual gratification for the payment of money.

If masturbation as described in the above case constitutes "sexual activity," how would you categorize self-masturbation as described in a subsequent case that came before the same court? *Commonwealth* v. *Bleigh* and other cases decided at the same time involved convictions made on the basis of evidence secured by detectives who visited an adult bookstore. The bookstore had booths from which patrons could view sexually explicit movies or see a live female dancer. "The booths contained a telephone, a waste can, and a roll of toilet paper. The patrons and the dancers were separated by a pane of glass. As such, they communicated by phone."[74]

Two detectives visited the bookstore on separate occasions and entered the booths, paying money to view a live female dancer, who removed her clothes and masturbated. Among the many issues on appeal, the significant one for this discussion was whether self-masturbation constitutes *sexual activity* under the Pennsylvania statute. Since the term *sexual activity* is not defined, the court looked at the history of prostitution and the history of the legislative revision of the prostitution statute to include the phrase *homosexual and other deviate sexual relations*. The court concluded that the purpose of adding that phrase was to clarify the common law approach by adding homosexual and other deviate acts. The legislature did not intend to eradicate the common meaning of *prostitution*. After reviewing the cases interpreting the prostitution statute, the court concluded that self-masturbation is not included. The addition of the phrase *homosexual and other deviate sexual relations* implies that the term *sexual activity* "requires the physical interaction of two or more people." This case did not involve such interaction. "As such, the conduct is more akin to commercial voyeurism; it is not, however, prostitution." The court reversed the convictions.

The fact that the behavior in question does not constitute prostitution does not mean it is not criminal. It might fall under another statute aimed at protecting public morality, such as statutes that regulate lewdness and indecency.

Lewdness and Indecency

Several words, such as *lewd*, *obscene*, *lascivious*, *lecherous*, and *indecent* have been used to describe a variety of behaviors that some people find offensive to the extent that the criminal law is invoked to try to curb them. These words may be used to describe such acts as appearing nude in public or living openly and notoriously with a member of the opposite gender without being married (also called *illicit* or *lewd cohabitation*). Although some may consider these behaviors serious violations of law, generally they are defined as misdemeanors and carry only slight penalties.

Lewdness may refer to certain sexual behaviors. *Lewd and lascivious behavior* might be used to describe sexual acts between members of the same gender even when those acts occur in private. *Lewd and lascivious* may be used to refer to heterosexual or homosexual acts that are considered serious offenses. In many jurisdictions this approach is used to criminalize sexual behavior with children. For example, the Idaho Criminal Code prohibits "lewd conduct with minor child under sixteen." This conduct is described as "manual-anal contact, or manual-genital contact, whether between persons of the same or opposite sex, or who shall involve such minor child in any act of bestiality or sado-masochism as defined" [in a previous section of the statute.][75]

Some lewdness statutes are difficult to interpret, particularly when the statute requires *intent* as an element of the crime. The intent issue is illustrated by *State* v. *Rocker*, a case based on allegedly lewd behavior and brought under a statute prohibiting a common nuisance. In *Rocker*, the male defendants were arrested for indecent exposure after police observed them sunbathing nude on an Hawaiian beach. They were not engaging in any sexual behavior. Their convictions for creating a common nuisance were upheld on appeal.

The appellate court emphasized that to sustain a conviction "there must be an indecent exposure of the person in a public place where it may be seen by others if they pass by. . . . Sunbathing in the nude is not per se illegal. It must be coupled with the intent to indecently expose oneself." The intent is a general, not a specific, one. Thus, if the evidence indicates that the exposure was made under circumstances in which the actor was likely to be seen by others, the intent to engage in a common nuisance may be inferred. In this case, there was sufficient evidence that the beach was used by the public to support a conviction.[76]

The California Supreme Court has held that nude sunbathing on an isolated beach by people who were not engaging in sexual acts was not sufficient to support a conviction for willful or lewd exposure of the body's private parts.[77] In 1993 a federal court dismissed charges of lewdness against eight defendants who were arrested for being nude in a park at Canaveral National Seashore in Florida. According to the court, basing its ruling on a Florida Supreme Court case, the Florida statute that prohibits public nudity does not prohibit all public nudity. Rather, a charge under the statute requires that the public exposure of sexual organs must relate to "a lascivious exhibition of those private parts."[78]

An earlier federal decision, however, upheld the convictions of young people who, after skinny dipping in a national forest, were arrested while eating watermelons and sunbathing nude. The court said it was not "persuaded by such nostalgic authorities as James Whitcomb Riley's 'The Old Swimming Hole' or Mark Twain's *Adventures of Huckleberry Finn*."[79]

In 1992 twenty-two Princeton students were sentenced for running nude through the small town of Princeton, New Jersey. For years it has been the custom on that campus that when the first snow falls the sophomores run nude through campus at midnight. Some run through the town, too, but when the police were told that the 1991 run would be a large one, they warned the students to stay on campus. Some ventured out into the town, running through restaurants and other establishments to the shock of local residents. The judge who sentenced the students was enraged at their behavior, the investigation of which required one-fourth of the thirty-two member local police force. The students were charged with lewdness and faced a six-month jail sentence if convicted. They were permitted to plead to a municipal ordinance, fined $100, and ordered to perform community service. The students will not have a criminal record. They promised that more would run the next year but wear ski masks.[80] The first snow came earlier during the 1992-93 academic year at Princeton, and in December 200 students participated in the "Nude Olympics," but only two were arrested. They were charged with lewdness, disorderly conduct, and theft of a gallon of ice-cream. University officials indicated they would like to see the tradition end but that although they cannot condone the behavior, "It's not behaviour we feel we can prevent.'" According to a Princeton freshman, during the 1993-94 academic year's first snow, "It happened, but no arrests were made."[81]

Sodomy

The debate over the use of the criminal law to attempt to regulate private, consensual sexual behavior between adults has escalated as the result of the Supreme Court decision in *Bowers* v. *Hardwick*. In that case the Court upheld the Georgia statute prohibiting **sodomy**, defined by that statute as "any sexual act involving the sex organs of one person and the mouth or anus of another" and providing for a penalty of imprisonment for not less than one nor more than twenty years upon conviction.[82]

Bowers v. *Hardwick* involved these facts. Hardwick was engaged in sexual activity with another man in his own bedroom when a police officer arrived to serve a warrant for arrest on another charge, saw the two men, and arrested them. After a preliminary hearing, the district attorney decided not to prosecute, but Hardwick brought suit in the federal district court, challenging the constitutionality of the statute insofar as it criminalized consensual sodomy. He asserted that he was a practicing homosexual, "that the Georgia sodomy statute . . . placed him in imminent danger of arrest, and that the statute for several reasons violates the Federal Constitution." The U.S. Supreme Court disagreed and held that the statute did not violate the fundamental rights of homosexuals.

Bowers v. *Hardwick* has led to protests by homosexuals, but it is important to understand that the case is not just about the rights of homosexuals. It is about the rights of all adults to engage in consensual sexual behavior in private.

RATIONALE FOR SODOMY STATUTES

The historical background for regulating sodomy, along with the modern reasons for it, is discussed in this excerpt from *Commonwealth* v. *Bonadio*.[83]

Commonwealth v. *Bonadio*

[The defendants were arrested while performing oral and anal sex on the stage at an "adult" pornographic theater. They were charged with voluntary deviate sexual intercourse and/or conspiracy to perform the same. Deviate sexual intercourse was defined by statute as "sexual intercourse per os or per anus between human beings who are not husband and wife, and any form of sexual intercourse with an animal."]

The threshold question in determining whether the statute in question is a valid exercise of the police power is to decide whether it benefits the public generally. The state clearly has a proper role to perform in protecting the public from inadvertent offensive displays of sexual behavior, in preventing people from being forced against their will to submit to sexual contact, in protecting minors from being sexually used by adults, and in eliminating cruelty to animals. To assure these protections, a broad range of criminal statutes constitute valid police exercises, including proscriptions of indecent exposure, open lewdness, rape, *involuntary* deviate sexual intercourse, indecent assault, statutory rape, corruption of minors, and cruelty to animals. The statute in question serves none of the foregoing purposes and it is nugatory to suggest that it promotes a state interest in the institution of marriage. The Voluntary Deviate Sexual Intercourse Statute has only one possible purpose: to regulate the private conduct of consenting adults. Such a purpose, we believe, exceeds the valid bounds of the police power while infringing the right to equal protection of the laws guaranteed by the Constitution of the United States and of this Commonwealth.

With respect to regulation of morals, the police power should properly be exercised to protect each individual's right to be free from interference in defining and pursuing his own morality but not to enforce a majority morality on persons whose conduct *does not harm others*. Many issues that are considered to be matters of morals are subject to debate, and no sufficient state interest justifies legislation of norms simply because a particular belief is followed by a number of people, or even a majority. Indeed, what is considered to be "moral" changes with the times and is dependent upon societal background. Spiritual leadership, not the government, has the responsibility for striving to improve the morality of individuals. Enactment of the Voluntary Deviate Sexual Intercourse Statute, despite the fact that it provides punishment for what many believe to be abhorrent crimes against nature and perceived sins against God, is not properly in the realm of the temporal police power. . . .

[The court ruled also that the statute was defective in that it established a separate category of consensual sexual acts that were criminal only when the parties were unmarried, without establishing a proper justification for that differentiation.]

MODERN SODOMY STATUTES

To avoid the problem of vagueness that was typical of earlier sodomy statutes, some jurisdictions have revised their statutes to include specifics. For example, California changed its sodomy statute from one referring to "the infamous crime against nature, committed with mankind or with any animal" (for which one could be punished in the state prison for not less than one year) to "sexual conduct consisting of contact between the penis of one person and the anus of another person." California does not define sodomy as a punishable offense unless it is committed under any one of numerous specified circumstances, such as those involving force, violence, or duress; or acts committed with an underage person, a mentally incompetent person, or a person known by the actor to be unconscious.[84]

Until recently all states had laws prohibiting sodomy, but over one-half of the states have revised these statutes. Sodomy statutes are being challenged in many states, and with some success. Texas is one of the latest battlegrounds. The Texas statute was upheld by a federal court in 1986, following the *Bowers* v. *Hardwick* decision by the U.S. Supreme Court.[85]

In 1993 a Texas trial court held that Texas's sodomy statute is unconstitutional and cannot be used as grounds to deny employment to lesbians and homosexuals in the police department. The Third Court of Appeals affirmed that decision, holding that the sodomy statute violate the individual's right of privacy under the Texas constitution. On appeal of that decision, the State argued that the issue was hypothetical as no prosecutor had charged anyone with a criminal offense under the sodomy statute.[86]

The Texas Supreme Court reversed and remanded the case with instructions to the lower court to dismiss the case. The Supreme Court ruled that neither it nor the lower courts had jurisdiction to invalidate the statute under the facts presented in the case of *State* v. *Morales*. "A naked declaration as to the constitutionality of a criminal statute alone, without a valid request for injunctive relief, is clearly not within the jurisdiction of a Texas court sitting in equity." Thus, the Texas sodomy statute remains in effect, with the state's supreme court refusing to invalidate that statute for technical reasons. The issue of whether a sodomy statute violates the right of privacy guaranteed by that state's constitution was not decided.[87] In Texas sodomy is a misdemeanor, punishable by a maximun fine of $200.[88]

Kentucky's sodomy statute, which prohibits "deviate sexual intercourse with another person of the same sex," has been declared unconstitutional. The Kentucky Supreme Court held that the statute violates privacy rights secured by the state's constitution. "We may not sympathize, agree with, or even understand the sexual preference of homosexuals in order to recognize their right to equal treatment before the bar of justice."[89]

Seduction, Fornication, and Adultery

Seduction, fornication, and adultery are acts that at one time have been criminalized in the United States. All refer to consensual sexual behavior that society has thought to be dangerous to its general welfare.

Although under common law **seduction** was not an offense, many jurisdictions established the offense by statute. Technically, *seduction* refers to the act of seducing, a word familiar to most people. In earlier days seduction was a felony; where the laws remain today, generally seduction is a misdemeanor. Some statutes provide that a subsequent marriage between the two parties negates the crime.

The Model Penal Code retains a seduction provision, which requires breach of a promise to marry, permits no defense for subsequent marriage, and does not require that the victim be chaste. There are age restrictions for the unlawful act to qualify as seduction.[90] The modern trend is to repeal seduction statutes.[91]

Fornication is another sex act that is considered a crime against public morals in some jurisdictions. The word *fornication* comes from *fornix*, a Latin word for brothel. It means unlawful sexual intercourse between two unmarried persons. In some states, the term applies also to a single person involved in unlawful sexual intercourse with a person who is married to someone else. Other states define the acts of both in that situation as *adultery*. Fornication statutes are enforced infrequently.

Adultery is another sexual act believed to be immoral by many and included in the criminal codes of many jurisdictions. Like most other sex crimes, *adultery* has various definitions. Some jurisdictions define adultery as sexual intercourse between two people if one is married to someone else. Some jurisdictions hold that only the married party in that relationship is committing adultery. In earlier laws, only the married woman was committing adultery; the behavior was not criminal for a married man.

Today, some jurisdictions distinguish between *single adultery*, in which only one party is married, and *double adultery*, in which both parties are married to other persons. Like fornication, adultery was not a common law crime, although it was an ecclesiastical offense. The trend today is toward decriminalizing adultery. Some jurisdictions criminalize adultery only when the acts are "open and notorious."[92] Others have abolished adultery statutes,[93] and the statutes that remain are enforced infrequently.

One notable exception occurred in 1990 in Wisconsin. Donna Carroll, who was going through a divorce and custody battle, allegedly stated in court that she had had a sexual encounter with a man other than her husband. Through her attorneys, she denied making that statement, but the prosecutor claimed that sufficient evidence of adultery existed and in the face of that evidence, "for me to decide not to prosecute would be, in effect, to declare the statute null and void. And that is not my role as district attorney."[94]

Carroll's attorney argued that the adultery statute violated his client's rights to privacy, due process, and freedom from cruel and unusual punishment (the statute provided for a penalty of up to two years in the state penitentiary and a $10,000 fine). In addition, he claimed a violation of equal protection because Carroll's ex-husband, who admitted that he had an affair while he was married to her, was not prosecuted for adultery. The prosecutor decided not to file charges against the ex-husband after a special prosecutor investigating his situation decided that the acts probably took place outside Wisconsin. Carroll's partner was not charged with adultery either.[95] Carroll accepted a plea bargain requiring her to perform forty hours of community service and attend parental counseling sessions in exchange for dismissal of the adultery charge.[96]

Bigamy

Like adultery, **bigamy** is considered a crime against the family. Like adultery and fornication, bigamy was not a common law crime, although it was an ecclesiastical offense. In 1603 the British Parliament criminalized bigamy, making it a felony punishable by death. *Bigamy* may be defined as knowingly and willingly contracting a second marriage when the individual is aware that another marriage is undissolved. Historically bigamy has been criminalized in the United States, although few prosecutions have occurred. Under the Model Penal Code, bigamy is a misdemeanor, but *polygamy*, defined as marrying or cohabiting with more than one spouse at a time in purported exercise of the right of plural marriage, is a third-degree felony. Polygamy involves several marriages, whereas bigamy involves only two.[97]

The New York statute is typical of bigamy statutes that consider the offense to be a serious crime, a felony. "A person is guilty of bigamy when he contracts or purports to contract a marriage with another person at a time when he has a living spouse or the other person has a living spouse. Bigamy is a class E felony." Adultery is a misdemeanor.[98]

Pornography and Obscenity

It is appropriate to end this chapter with a discussion of criminal statutes that are enacted to preserve the morality of society, which are very difficult to enforce, and which may violate basic constitutional rights such as the First Amendment right to free speech and the right to privacy (see Appendix A). In *Stanley* v. *Georgia*, the Supreme Court held that "mere private possession of obscene matter" in one's own home is not a crime, but the Court emphasized the right of states to regulate obscenity in other contexts.[99] Although the Supreme Court has spent considerable time over the years defining what is *speech* for purposes of the First Amendment, for this discussion, it is sufficient to understand that words, pictures, films, and other depictions may or may not be protected by the First Amendment.

Material that is obscene does not have First Amendment protection; thus, it is important to know the definition of *obscene*. The Supreme Court has established tests to determine what is and what is not obscene, but those tests have generated considerable controversy and are subject to interpretation.[100]

The Court defined **obscenity** in a 1973 case, *Miller* v. *California*, which requires that all three of the following conditions be met:

1. The average person, applying contemporary community standards, would find that the work, taken as a whole, appeals to the prurient interest [in sex]; and
2. the work depicts or describes, in a patently offensive way, sexual conduct specifically defined by the applicable state [or federal] law; and
3. the work, taken as a whole, lacks serious literary, artistic, political, or scientific value.[101]

The Court rejected a national standard; thus the preceding are to be interpreted according to local standards. In establishing this obscenity test, the Court rejected a requirement of its earlier test—that to be obscene the material in question must be "utterly without redeeming social value."[102]

Obscenity Statutes

The most frequent method of prosecution in alleged obscenity cases is through obscenity statutes, with the general test of obscenity as just stated. Some cases are prosecuted under public nuisance statutes, zoning ordinances, and civil rights statutes, all of which have problems. Prosecutors have brought actions under prostitution statutes, arguing that the materials (or acts, as in the case of live sex shows) promote prostitution.[103] In October, 1990, the Supreme Court let stand the use of a federal antiracketeering law to force the closing of three adult bookstores and nine video rental shops in Virginia, thus expanding the government's ability to prosecute for obscenity.[104]

The Attorney General's Commission on Pornography (also called the Meese commission, named after its chairperson, then-Attorney General Edwin Meese) issued its two-volume final report in 1986. The commission pointed out that the United States and most states have laws that prohibit the sale, distribution, or exhibition of obscene materials as defined in *Miller*. The statutes are similar; the differences occur in "how, how vigorously, and how often these laws are enforced." The commission noted that evidence indicates unquestionably that "with few exceptions the obscenity laws on the books go unenforced."[105] .

Pornography and the Sexual Exploitation of Children

The Meese commission stated that "what is commonly referred to as 'child pornography' is not so much a form of pornography as it is a form of sexual exploitation of children. The distinguishing characteristic of child pornography . . . is that actual children are photographed while engaged in some form of sexual activity, either with adults or with other children."[106]

To combat such sexual exploitation, many jurisdictions have enacted statutes aimed solely at child pornography. The federal statute is used as an example of legislation in this area. Referred to as the Child Protection Act of 1984, the statute was enacted in 1978 and amended by Congress in 1984 (as well as subsequently), relying upon the following findings:

1. Child pornography has developed into a highly organized, multi-million-dollar industry which operates on a nationwide scale;
2. Thousands of children including large numbers of runaway and homeless youth are exploited in the production and distribution of pornographic materials; and
3. The use of children as subjects of pornographic materials is harmful to the physiological, emotional, and mental health of the individual child and to society.[107]

The federal statute is a lengthy one. The statute imposes liability upon parents and guardians as well as on coercers, producers, and distributors of child pornography. Focus 8.5 reproduces the provisions concerning sexual exploitation of children, including the penalties, a fine of not more than $100,000 for an individual's first offense (not more than $250,000 for an organization) and/or imprisonment for not more than ten years. The statute provides also for forfeiture of any property or proceeds obtained, used, or produced. It defines numerous terms of the statute and specifies the types of sexual behavior that are covered, which includes conduct that is genital-genital, oral-genital, anal-genital, or oral-anal, whether between persons of the same or opposite sex; bestiality; masturbation; sadistic or masochistic; abuse; or lascivious exhibition of the genitals or pubic area of any person.[108]

The constitutionality of this federal statute has been upheld against allegations that the statute is vague and too broad.[109] But in 1993 a federal circuit court held that the statute is unconstitutional because it does not require that defendants *know* that at least one of the performers is under

FOCUS 8.5 Sexual Exploitation of Children: The Federal Statute

Section 2251. Sexual Exploitation of Children

(a) Any person who employs, uses, persuades, induces, entices, or coerces any minor to engage in, or who has a minor assist any other person to engage in, or who transports any minor in interstate or foreign commerce, or in any Territory or Possession of the United States, with the intent that such minor engage in any sexually explicit conduct for the purpose of producing any visual depiction of such conduct, shall be punished as provided under subsection (d), if such person knows or has reason to know that such visual depiction will be transported in interstate or foreign commerce or mailed, or if such visual depiction has actually been transported in interstate or foreign commerce or mailed.

(b) Any parent, legal guardian, or person having custody or control of a minor who knowingly permits such minor to engage in, or to assist any other person to engage in, sexually explicit conduct for the purpose of producing any visual depiction of such conduct shall be punished as provided under subsection (d) of this section, if such parent, legal guardian, or person knows or has reason to know that such visual depiction will be transported in interstate or foreign commerce or mailed or if such visual depiction has actually been transported in interstate or foreign commerce or mailed.

(c)(1) Any person who, in a circumstance described in paragraph (2), knowingly makes, prints, or publishes, or causes to be made, printed, or published, any notice or advertisement seeking or offering —

(A) to receive, exchange, buy, produce, display, distribute, or reproduce, any visual depiction, if the production of such visual depiction involves the use of a minor engaging in sexually explicit conduct and such visual depiction is of such conduct; or

(B) participation in any act of sexually explicit conduct by or with any minor for the purpose of producing a visual depiction of such conduct; shall be punished as provided under subsection (d).

(2) The circumstance referred to in paragraph (1) is that —

(A) such person knows or has reason to know that such notice or advertisement will be transported in interstate or foreign commerce or mailed; or

(B) such notice or advertisement is transported in interstate or foreign commerce or mailed.

(d) Any individual who violates this section shall be fined not more than $100,000, or imprisoned not more than 10 years, or both, but, if such individual has a prior conviction under this section, such individual shall be fined not more than $200,000, or imprisoned not less than five years nor more than 15 years, or both. Any organization which violates this section shall be fined not more than $250,000.

SOURCE: U.S. Code, Title 18, Section 2251 (1994).

the age of eighteen and thus a minor.[110] And, in 1993 the U.S. Supreme Court vacated the judgment in the case of *Knox* v. *United States*, in which Stephen A. Knox had been convicted of violating the federal statute. Knox, a Pennsylvania State University graduate student, was convicted under the child pornography statute because he was in possession of three videos depicting young girls in gym clothes and bathing suits. The Supreme Court had agreed to hear the case but reversed itself in an unexpected decision that sent the case back to the lower court to reconsider in light of the recent statement by the Clinton administration. That statement enunciates the view that if children are wearing clothing, photographs of them cannot be considered pornographic under the federal statute unless the child's genitals are revealed through sheer or very tight clothing. According to the administration, Congress intended that the word *lascivious* in the federal statute require that a child be portrayed "lasciviously engaging in sexual conduct as distinguished from lasciviousness on the part of the photographer or consumer."[111]

The Child Protection Act, along with many others that attempt to regulate sexual behavior, has been the focus of overzealous conduct by law enforcement authorities attempting to enforce the statute. Focus 3.6 in Chapter 3 discusses the recent U.S. Supreme Court case of *Jacobson* v. *United States* in the context of the entrapment defense. That focus should be reviewed for its information on child pornography.

In January 1993, Larry Lane Bateman, a former teacher at Phillips Exeter Academy in Concord, New Hampshire, was sentenced to five years in prison without possibility of parole. After he serves his prison sentence Bateman will be on probation for three years. Bateman was convicted of two counts of possession and two counts of shipment of child pornography in interstate commerce. A fine of up to $250,000 on each count was waived because Bateman has no assets, but he was assessed a payment of $150 to a federal fund for crime victims. Bateman admitted that he possessed videos of child pornography but denied that he shipped them in interstate commerce. Although he apologized to his students, family, and friends for any pain he might have caused, he questioned who were the victims of his acts.

> If I had strangled a child, if somebody had been hurt; if somebody's property had been destroyed, then there certainly would be a victim. . . . Where are the victims?[112]

Recent Developments Regarding Obscenity Laws

In 1990, the Miami-based musicians group known as 2 Live Crew were arrested and charged with violating Florida's obscenity laws. A federal court judge ruled that their album, *As Nasty as They Wanna Be*, was obscene. This was the first musical album banned by a U.S. court, but an appellate court reversed the decision. The U.S. Supreme Court refused to hear the case, thus leaving the appellate decision that the material is not obscene.[113] In another Florida case, after two months of investigation during which prosecutors analyzed over 600 obscenity cases, prosecutors decided not to charge Suzy Smith, a twenty-three-year-old public access producer, with a crime. Smith had outraged numerous people when she aired a video of a punk rock musician defecating onstage. Smith was suspended from the station for one year for violating a policy against showing "turgid genitalia" on public access programs.[114]

In the fall of 1990, the director of a Cincinnati art gallery was charged and tried on obscenity charges stemming from the exhibition of the works of Robert Mapplethorpe. Apparently this was the first charge of this type. After a trial that gained widespread national publicity, the jury returned a verdict of acquittal. There have been some successes in obscenity prosecutions, especially since the federal government established a spectial section in the Criminal Division of the Justice Department to fight pornography. Since its inception in 1987, the government "has obtained 135 convictions, 50 involving mail-order companies." Despite these successes, pornography remains a lucrative business.[115]

In recent years the U.S. Supreme Court has decided some significant cases on obscenity. In 1989, a unanimous Court held that a statute that banned telephone messages that are *indecent* but not *obscene* is a violation of the First Amendment right to free speech, but the Court held also that a total ban on *obscene* phone calls is constitutional. In *Sable Communications of Cal., Inc.* v. *FCC*, the Court did not distinguish between *indecent* and *obscene*; the definition of *obscene*, therefore, remains as articulated in *Miller*, discussed earlier.[116]

In 1990, the Court carved out an exception to the rule announced in *Stanley*, discussed earlier, by holding that states may criminalize possessing pornographic photographs of children. In *Osborne* v. *Ohio*, the Court reversed Osborne's conviction on the basis of inadequate jury instructions but upheld the constitutionality of Ohio's statute that forbids owning or viewing pornography of children. The Court said that the statute seeks to protect innocent victims of child pornography, and the state "hopes to destroy a market for the exploitative use of children." The Court noted that the Ohio statute, unlike some others, was narrowly drawn and includes only minors "who are not the person's child or ward" and who are "in a state of nudity."[117]

The government has used another prosecutor's tool in obscenity cases, and that is the federal RICO statute, discussed in a subsequent chapter. Among other provisions, that statute permits forfeiture of the profits from the illegal activity. In *Alexander* v. *United States*, Ferris Alexander, who owned a chain of adult-oriented bookstores, was ordered to forfeit the entire chain, including fixtures and inventory, along with $9 million "acquired through racketeering activities." Alexander was convicted of selling seven obscene magazines and tapes. He was fined over $100,000 and costs and was sentenced to six years in prison. He appealed on the issue of forfeiture. The Supreme Court held that the forfeiture was a legitimate punishment, not a violation of the defendant's First Amendment right (see Appendix A). The Court stated that Alexander's "assets were forfeited because they were directly related to racketeering, and thus they differ from material seized or restrained on suspicion of being obscene without a prior judicial obscenity determination." The case was remanded to determine whether the forfeiture was excessive under the Eighth Amendment (see Appendix A).[118]

SUMMARY

This chapter includes a wide range of offenses, many of which are misdemeanors. But some of those offenses, such as public intoxication, may consume enormous amounts of law enforcement time and facilities. For example, jailing public drunks contributes significantly to jail overcrowding. Many of the offenses included in this chapter are important in that they may and often do infringe on basic constitutional rights, such as free speech and privacy. On the other hand, it is argued that these offenses threaten public order, the sanctity of the family, and general morality. Therefore, they must be preserved. But enforcement is lax in many areas, and discretionary enforcement is extensive, leaving room for illegal discrimination. This chapter raises the critical issue of how we draw the line between individual rights and society's needs (or desires) as well as how we control actions that may be very private in nature.

The first substantive crime discussed, breach of the peace, illustrates the philosophy behind the common law crimes included in this chapter. The crime was designed to cover acts not otherwise criminalized that might disrupt society's peace and tranquility. Breach of the peace has been retained as a crime by most states, although the definitions vary. Like many of the other crimes included in this chapter, breach of the peace statutes may be written too broadly or vaguely, in which case they will be declared unconstitutional.

The preservation of peace and order may be threatened by language as well as by actions. The criminal law attempts to avoid these problems by criminalizing *fighting words*, a crime that comes dangerously close to violating the First Amendment right to free speech. Consequently, considerable litigation has occurred as courts interpret the variously worded statutes, paying particular attention to whether they violate constitutional rights.

Historically it has not been uncommon for society to attempt to suppress unpopular views and keep certain types of people out of sight. Statutes covering disorderly conduct, vagrancy, and public abuse of alcohol and drugs are used for this purpose. Many of these statutes are vague, leaving police with wide discretion in deciding whether or not to arrest. In recent years some of these statutes have been declared unconstitutional. Either they criminalize *status* (or condition) in contrast to *willful acts* because they are vague, or they are so broad that individuals cannot know in advance whether their behavior is covered by the statutes. Many disorderly conduct and vagrancy statutes are declared unconstitutional, but these statutes may be used effectively to control order and will stand if worded properly. Such statutes may be utilized to harass, too, and the same is true of laws regulating public intoxication.

Some jurisdictions have decriminalized some of these acts; for example, public drunkenness. In other jurisdictions courts have held the statutes unconstitutional. The discussion of substance abuse should be reviewed in the context of earlier discussions of the intoxication defense and of deterrence. Deterrence is one of the prime philosophies used today to justify including the behaviors discussed in this chapter within the scope of criminal law. Yet some research indicates a lack of deterrent effect in these areas.

The desire to protect society from physical dangers to people and property that may result from some gatherings has led to statutes encompassing unlawful assemblies, routs, and riots. Once again, however, these statutes must be examined carefully to be sure that they do not conflict with the constitutional rights to assemble and to communicate ideas.

Criminal laws that cover carrying weapons are a real topic of controversy today. Against the beliefs of many that they have a "right" to carry weapons to protect themselves is the argument that society has an interest in protecting the health and welfare of its citizens and should be able to penalize those who carry weapons without authorization.

A wide variety of other offenses are thought to threaten the public, including obstructing public highways, disturbing public assemblies, desecrating venerated objects, abusing corpses, cruelty to animals, and forcibly entering the property of another or remaining on the property without proper authorization.

Another major category of offenses covered in this chapter includes acts that some people think should be criminalized to protect public morality. Despite one's beliefs about whether consensual sexual activities between adults should be covered by the criminal law, it is important to understand the full implications of criminalizing these offenses. Many of these offenses are important far beyond their effects on their immediate victims or society; some or all of them may be the source of other crimes such as extortion, blackmail, and organized crime. This is particularly the case with prostitution and consensual homosexual sodomy. Both involve human sexual behavior that may be engaged in by consenting adults in private with no financial arrangements, but both may involve commercialized sex as well. Because most people who are involved in prostitution or homosexual relations fear public disclosure of their activities, they are particularly vulnerable to extortion and blackmail.

The offenses are controversial, however. In the case of commercialized sex, there is strong argument that society has an interest in protecting the social welfare by preventing the spread of disease, preserving the family structure, and upholding its moral structure. Yet, there is strong argument that criminalizing sexual activity does not achieve these goals and infringes on individual personal rights. The U.S. Supreme Court, in the controversial case of *Bowers* v. *Hardwick*, which involved private, consensual sodomy by two male adults, indicates that it is constitutionally permissible for the state to criminalize the behavior in question.

It is difficult to draft and interpret indecency and lewdness statutes to achieve the desired goal of protecting people from being forced to view sexual behavior that they choose to avoid. These statutes risk becoming so broad as to prohibit behavior, such as cohabitation, of which many approve today.

Some of the crimes discussed in this chapter are aimed primarily at preserving the family structure. Seduction (now abolished in most states), fornication, adultery, and bigamy are examples. Although some states have abolished statutes criminalizing fornication and some have abolished adultery statutes, many have retained statutes prohibiting these acts. But the statutes are seldom enforced.

In addition, pornography and obscenity statutes pose the question of what should be private behavior and what should be regulated by the criminal law. Over the years courts have disagreed in their interpretation of what is and is not permissible in this area. This chapter emphasizes the Meese commission's conclusions about the use of pornography and obscenity to exploit children sexually. Those conclusions led to the passage of federal statutes aimed at the protection of children. A brief discussion of recent court interpretations of obscenity statutes concludes this discussion.

This chapter focuses on some of the most controversial areas of criminal law. By their nature, some of the offenses are delicate and sensitive. But they are extremely important, for they touch on some of our most valued rights—the right to privacy and the right to procreation, which involves the right to sexual expression. Others involve the right to free speech and all the ramifications that right involves. It is important to remember that these and other rights may be regulated by the state or federal government under some circumstances. The critical issue is whether the statutes are aimed at protecting the welfare of society and whether they violate basic constitutional rights. Finally, it is important to assure that statutes such as those discussed in this chapter, most of which are not enforced rigorously, are not used for the purpose of harassing the homeless or racial, ethnic, or other minorities.

STUDY QUESTIONS

1. Discuss the origin of *breach of the peace* statutes and the circumstances under which these and related statutes may be unconstitutional.
2. What is meant by the *fighting words* doctrine?
3. What are the potential constitutional hazards of disorderly conduct and vagrancy statutes? Do we need these statutes? Why or why not? Could they be reworded to avoid constitutional problems?
4. To what extent should public intoxication and drug incapacitation be regulated by the criminal law? What has the Supreme Court said about this issue? What are the recent developments in these areas?
5. Distinguish between *rout* and *riot*. Should both be criminal?
6. How would you distinguish *rioting* from *inciting to riot* in terms of seriousness? What is *unlawful assembly*?
7. Should citizens be allowed to carry guns to protect themselves? If your answer is yes, what, if any restrictions would you advocate?
8. How is the right to free speech affected by statutes prohibiting obstructing a highway or other public passage?

9. Although it may be offensive to some people if others abuse a corpse, are cruel to animals, or desecrate venerated objects, would the law's deterrent effect be greater if these behaviors were part of the civil law only, giving victims a right to compensation from those who victimize them? What does the criminal law add?

10. List all behaviors that you think should be covered by *criminal*, as opposed to *civil*, harassment statutes.

11. Discuss some of the problems of enforcing statutes that prohibit prostitution. Should prostitution be decriminalized? Why or why not?

12. What are the reasons for including *cohabitation* within the criminal law? Should this be changed? Should *lewdness* and *indecency* statutes be abolished?

13. Discuss the Supreme Court's holding and rationale in *Bowers* v. *Hardwick*. What are the implications of this decision?

14. Which, if any, of the following behaviors—seduction, fornication, adultery, and bigamy—should remain within the criminal law? Which should be removed? Which should be defined more clearly?

15. What is *obscenity*? What is the Meese Commission on Pornography? What has been its impact on statutory changes?

16. Should we distinguish between pornography involving adults and that involving children? Discuss the Supreme Court's position on this subject.

ENDNOTES

1. American Law Institute, *Model Penal Code and Commentaries*, Part II, vol. 3 (Philadelphia: American Law Institute, 1980), Article 250, "Riot, Disorderly Conduct, and Related Offenses," p. 309.
2. Griswold v. Connecticut, 381 U.S. 479 (1965).
3. For a discussion see Rollin M. Perkins and Ronald N. Boyce, *Criminal Law*, 3d ed. (Mineola, N.Y.: The Foundation Press, 1982), pp. 477-497. This source is the basis of this discussion.
4. Wilson v. State, 156 S.E.2d 446 (Ga. 1967), *cert. denied*, 390 U.S. 911 (1968), *and later proceeding*, Gooding v. Wilson, 405 U.S. 518 (1972).
5. Ky. Rev. Stat., Section 161.190 (1994).
6. Commonwealth v. Ashcraft, 691 S.W.2d 229, 232 (Ky.App. 1985).
7. Cal. Penal Code, Title 11, Section 415 (1994).
8. Cal. Penal Code, Title 11, Sections 403-420 (1994).
9. Chaplinksy v. New Hampshire, 315 U.S. 568 (1942), footnotes and citations omitted.
10. Terminiello v. Chicago, 337 U.S. 1 (1949), *reh'g. denied*, 337 U.S. 934 (1949).
11. Feiner v. New York, 340 U.S. 315, 317, 321 (1951).
12. Edwards v. South Carolina, 372 U.S. 229 (1963).
13. Cohen v. California, 403 U.S. 15, 20 (1971), *reh'g. denied*, 404 U.S. 876 (1971).
14. Lewis v. City of New Orleans, 415 U.S. 130, 133 (1974).
15. State v. Cherry, 173 N.W.2d 887, 888 (Neb. 1970).
16. Model Penal Code, Section 250.2.
17. Model Penal Code, Section 250.2, Commentary.
18. "Rollerblading Leads Woman to Court," *New York Times* (23 September 1992), p. 13.
19. "Rollerblader Hit by Car Is Still Facing Traffic Charges," *Hartford Courant* (27 October 1992), p. 6B.

20. For a history of vagrancy laws, see Jeffrey S. Adler, "A Historical Analysis of the Law of Vagrancy," *Criminology* 27 (May 1989): 209-230.

21. Kolender v. Lawson, 461 U.S. 352 (1983). The statute was Cal. Penal Code, Title 11, Section 647(e) (1994).

22. Papachristou v. City of Jacksonville, 405 U.S. 156 (1972).

23. Milwaukee v. Nelson, 439 N.W.2d 562 (Wis. 1989), *cert. denied*, 495 U.S. 858 (1989).

24. People v. Superior Court (Oswell), 758 P.2d 1046 (Cal. 1988), *reh'g. denied*, 1988 Cal. LEXIS 1484 (Cal. 1988).

25. Wyche v. State, 619 So.2d 231 (Fla. 1993); and Holliday v. City of Tampa, Florida, 619 So.2d 244 (Fla. 1993). The Tampa ordinance is Section 24-61 (1987). Florida's loitering statute is Fla. Stat., Section 856.021 (1994). Florida's prostitution and solicitation statute is Fla. Stat., Section 796.07(3)(b) (1994).

26. Loper v. New York City Police Department, 999 F.2d 699 (2d Cir. 1993), *affirming* 802 F.Supp. 1029 (S.D.N.Y. 1992). For a discussion of loitering laws that prohibit begging, see Helen Hershkoff, "Aggressive Panhandling Laws," *American Bar Association Journal* 79 (June 1993): 40-41. With regard to the right of homeless people to sleep in public places, see "A Right to Sleep Outside? Laws Designed to Keep Homeless Out of Public Areas Spur Lawsuits," *American Bar Association Journal* 79 (August 1993): 38. See also William Trosch, "The Third Generation of Loitering Laws Goes to Court: Do Laws That Criminalize 'Loitering With the Intent to Sell Drugs,' Pass Constitutional Muster?" *North Carolina Law Review* 71 (January 1993): 513–578.

27. Powell v. Texas, 392 U.S. 514 (1968).

28. President's Commission on Law Enforcement and Administration of Justice, *Challenge of Crime in a Free Society* (Washington, D.C.: U.S. Government Printing Office, 1967), p. 233.

29. Ga. Code Ann., Title 37, Section 37-8-1 (1994).

30. State v. Zegeer, 296 S.E.2d 873, 878-881 (W.Va. 1982).

31. American Law Institute, *Model Penal Code and Commentaries*, Part II, vol. 3, pp. 378–379.

32. Model Penal Code, Section 250.5.

33. People v. Judson, 11 Daly 1, 83 (N.Y.C.P. 1849).

34. State v. Abbadini, 192 A. 550, 551-552 (Del. 1937).

35. Judge Stephen, *A History of the Criminal Law of England*, p. 203, n. 1 (1883), quoted in Perkins and Boyce, *Criminal Law*, p. 486.

36. U.S. Code, Title 18, Section 2101 (1994). For a case upholding the constitutionality of the act on the grounds that rioting or incitement to riot is not protected by the First Amendment, see National Mobilization Committee to End War in Vietnam v. Foran, 411 F.2d 934 (7th Cir. 1969), and United States v. Dellinger, 472 F.2d 340 (7th Cir. 1972), *cert. denied*, 410 U.S. 970 (1973).

37. New York Penal Code, Section 240.06 (1994).

38. New York Penal Code, Sections 240.05 and 240.06 (1994).

39. James Lindgren and Franklin E. Zimring, "Guns, Regulation of," in Sanford H. Kadish, ed., *Encyclopedia of Crime and Justice*, vol. 2 (New York: Free Press, 1983), p. 836.

40. Perkins and Boyce, *Criminal Law*, p. 492.

41. Ibid.

42. Quilici v. Village of Morton Grove, 695 F.2d 261 (7th Cir. 1982), *cert. denied*, 464 U.S. 863 (1983).

43. Kalodimos v. Village of Morton Grove, 470 N.E.2d 266 (Ill. 1984).

44. "Colorado Bans Juveniles From Possessing Handguns," *Miami Herald* (13 September 1993), p. 3. The statute is C.R.S. 18-12-108.5 (1994).

45. "Administration Floats Proposal For Licensing All Gun Owners," *New York Times* (10 December 1993), p. 1; "Guns R Us; Gun Violence and Gun Control," *Scholastic Update* 126 (11 February 1994): 18. The statute is codified in U.S. Code, Title 18, Section 922 *et.seq.* (1994).

46. "Brady Bill May Be Ineffective Without Funds," *St. Petersburg Times* (29 November 1993), p. 1.

47. "New Jersey's Ban on Assault Guns Has Little Effect on Violence," *New York Times* (20 June 1993), p. 14.

48. Cox v. Louisiana, 379 U.S. 536 (1965).

49. Model Penal Code, Section 250.7(2).

50. Model Penal Code, Section 250.8.

51. Model Penal Code, Section 250.9.

52. See, for example, Texas v. Johnson, 491 U.S. 397 (1989) and United States v. Eichman, 496 U.S 310 (1990). See also "Waiving Rights and Burning Flags: The Search for a Valid State Interest in Flag Protection," *Harvard Civil Rights-Civil Liberties Law Review* 25 (1990): 591-624.

53. Model Penal Code, Section 250.10.

54. The case was on hold pending a court review of the issue of whether three television reporters should be ordered to testify at the trial. See "Body-dumping Trial on Hold," *Houston Chronicle* (17 August 1993), p. 14.

55. "Grave Robbing Brings Death Sentence for Two," *Miami Herald* (27 May 1991), p. 8.

56. Model Penal Code, Section 250.11.

57. "Police Arrest Three in Ritual Cat Killings," *Tallahassee Democrat* (8 August 1993), p. 2D; *St. Petersburg Times* (2 February 1994), p. 4B.

58. "Cat Torture on the Rise, Reports Say," *Orlando Sentinel* (18 August 1992), p. 5B.

59. "Man Who Ate Neighbor's Dog Sentenced," *Tampa Tribune* (25 January 1992), p. 3.

60. "Man Gets Probation in Dog Multilation," *Tampa Tribune, Marion/Alachua* (9 October 1992), p. 1.

61. "Man Arrested for Plucking Peacock," *Tallahassee Democrat* (27 May 1992), p. 3; "Man Jailed for Plucking Peacock," UPI Press Release (26 May 1992).

62. Model Penal Code, Section 221.2.

63. New York Penal Code, Title J, Section 240.30 (1994).

64. Fla. Stat., Section 491.0112 (1994).

65. William E. Nelson, "Emerging Notions of Modern Criminal Law in the Revolutionary Era," in *Crime, Law, and Society*, ed. Abraham S. Goldstein and Joseph Goldstein (New York: Free Press, 1971), p. 73.

66. See Freda Adler, "The Oldest and Newest Profession," in *Sisters in Crime: The Rise of the New Female Criminal*, by Freda Adler (New York: McGraw-Hill Book Co., 1975), pp. 55-83.

67. "Are City-Run Brothels the Answer?" *Miami Herald* (28 November 1993), p. 7. For a negative response to this question, see "Will San Francisco Become a Municipal Pimp?" *San Francisco Examiner* (18 February 1994), p. 23; "Get Prostitutes Off the Streets, Into Brothels Where They Belong," *Arizona Republic* (2 June 1994), p.2.

68. Coral Velisek, "Should We Allow Sex for Money? The Tallahassee Madam Says Yes," *Tallahassee Democrat* (13 September 1993), p. 12.

69. "The Skin Trade," *Time* (21 June 1993), p. 45. For a feminist analysis of prostitution, see Annette Jolin, "On the Backs of Working Prostitutes: Feminist Theory and Prostitution Policy," *Crime & Delinquency* 40 (January 1994): 69-83.

70. Model Penal Code, Section 251.2(2).

71. People v. Smith, 378 N.E.2d 1032 (N.Y.App. 1978), upholding New York Penal Code, Section 240.37 (1994).

72. See, for example, People v. Uplinger, 444 N.Y.S.2d 373 (City Court of N.Y. 1981), upholding New York Penal Code, Section 240.35(3) (1994).

73. Commonwealth v. Robbins, 516 A.2d 1266 (Pa. 1986), *appeal denied*, 527 A.2d 538 (Pa. 1987).

74. Commonwealth v. Bleigh, 586 A.2d 450 (Pa. 1991), *appeal denied*, 596 A.2d 154 (Pa. 1991).

75. Idaho Crim. Code, Title 18, Section 18-1508 (1992).

76. State v. Rocker, 475 P.2d 684 (Hawaii 1970).

77. *In re* Smith, 497 P.2d 807 (Cal. 1972).

78. United States of America v. A Naked Person, discussed in "Just Being Nude Isn't Lewd, Judge Rules," *Miami Herald* (20 November 1993), p. 9B.

79. United States v. Hymans, 463 F.2d 615 (10th Cir. 1972).

80. "Twenty-Two Naked 'Olympians' Sentenced," *Miami Herald* (14 June 1992), p. 11. For a discussion of public nudity, see Craig J. Forsyth, "Parade Strippers: A Note on being Naked in Public," *Deviant Behavior* 13, no. 4 (1992): 391-404. For a general discussion of nudity, see Herald Price Fahringer, "Equal in All Things: Drawing the Line on Nudity," *Criminal Law Bulletin* 29 (March-April 1993): 137-146.

81. "Naked Affront," *The Times* (21 December 1992), no page given. Final quotation is from a private conversation with Clint Pickett.

82. The statute is codified at Ga. Code Ann., Section 26-2002 (1994). See also Bowers v. Hardwick, 478 U.S. 186 (1986), *reh'g. denied*, 478 U.S. 1039 (1986).

83. Commonwealth v. Bonadio, 415 A.2d 47 (Pa. 1980).

84. Cal. Penal Code, Section 286 (1993).

85. Baker v. Wade et al., 769 F.2d 289 (5th Cir. 1986).

86. Dallas v. England, 846 S.W.2d 957 (Tex.App.3d Dist. 1993), *writ dismissed without prejudice* (May 5, 1994), *and reh'g. of writ of error overruled* (June 9, 1993).

87. State v. Morales, 826 S.W.2d 201 (Tex.App. 1992), *rev'd. and remanded*, 869 S.W.2d 941 (Tex. 1994).

88. Tex. Penal Code, Section 21.06 (1993). A bill introduced into the Texas legislature in early 1992 would have repealed this statute, effective 1 September 1993, but that bill did not pass. House Bill 652, No. TX73RHB 652, Filed 2/2/93. For a discussion see "Sodomy Laws Challenged," *American Bar Association Journal* 79 (July 1993): 38.

89. Watson v. State, 842 S.W.2d 487 (Ky. 1992).

90. See Model Penal Code, Section 213.3.

91. See for example, Cal. Penal Code, Section 268, repealed 1984.

92. See Ariz. Crim. Code, Section 13-1409 (1994). This statute applies also to cohabitation.

93. See, for example, Cal. Penal Code, Section 268, repealed 1984.

94. William E. Schmidt, "Treating Adultery as a Crime: Wisconsin Dusts Off Old Law," *New York Times* (30 April 1990), p. 1.

95. Ibid. See also Wis. Stat., Section 944.16 (1994).

96. "Adulterer Accepts Penance to Avoid Trial," *Daily Telegraph* (9 May 1990), p. 1.

97. For an analysis of a state's right to prohibit polygamy versus the individual's right to practice religious beliefs that permit polygamy, see Barlow v. Blackburn, 798 P.2d 1360 (Ariz.App. 1990), *review denied*, 1990 Ariz. LEXIS 248 (Ariz. Oct. 31, 1990).

98. New York Penal Code, Section 255.15 (1993). The adultery statute is New York Penal Code, Section 255.17 (1994).

99. Stanley v. Georgia, 394 U.S. 557 (1969), *on remand*, 167 S.E.2d 756 (1969).

100. See, for example, Roth v. United States, 354 U.S. 476 (1957), *reh'g. denied*, 355 U.S. 852 (1956), *overruled*, Miller v. California, 413 U.S. 15 (1973), and Paris Adult Theatre I v. Slaton, 413 U.S. 49 (1973), *reh'g. denied*, 414 U.S. 881 (1973), *remanded*, 201 S.E.2d 456 (1973), *cert. denied*, 418 U.S. 939 (1974).

101. Miller v. California, 413 U.S. 15 (1973), *reh'g. denied*, 414 U.S. 881 (1973).

102. Memoirs v. Massachusetts, 383 U.S. 413 (1966).

103. For a discussion of these methods, see Lori Douglass Hutchins, "Pornography: The Prosecution of Pornographers Under Prostitution Statutes—A New Approach," *Syracuse Law Review* 37 (1986): 977-1002.

104. United States v. Pryba, 900 F.2d 748 (4th Cir. 1990), *cert. denied*, 498 U.S. 924 (1990).

105. Attorney General's Commission on Pornography, *Final Report*, (Washington, D.C.: U.S. Department of Justice, July 1986), pp. 364, 366, 367. For discussions of the effects of pornography, see Richard Delgado and Jean Stefancic, "Pornography and Harm to Women," *Ohio State Law Journal* 53 (1992): 1037-1055; and Justine Juson and Brenda Lillington, "Recognizing the Expressive Value and the Harm in Pornography," *Golden Gate University Law Review* 23 (1993): 651-678. For a discussion of pornography in the workplace, see Morrison Torrey, "We Get the Message—Pornography in the Workplace," *Southwest University Law Review* 22 (1992): 53-103.

106. *Final Report*, Ibid., p. 405.

107. S.R.Rep.No. 438, 95th Cong., 2nd Sess. (1978), *reprinted* in *1978 U.S. Code Cong. & Ad. News* 40, 41-54, and in United States v. Reedy, 632 F.Supp. 1415, 1417 (W.D. Okla. 1986), *aff'd.*, 845 F.2d 239 (10th Cir. 1988), *cert. denied*, 489 U.S. 1055 (1989). The federal statute is codified in U.S. Code, Title 18, Sections 2251, *et. seq*. (1993).

108. U.S. Code, Title 18, Section 2251, *et. seq*. (1994).

109. See United States v. Reedy, 632 F.Supp. 1415 (W.D.Okla. 1986), *aff'd.*, 845 F.2d 239 (10th Cir. 1988), *cert. denied*, 489 U.S. 1055 (1989).

110. United States v. X-Citement Video Inc., 982 F.2d 1285 (9th Cir. 1992), *cert. granted*, 114 S.Ct. 1186 (1994). For an analysis, see Robert F. Schwartz, "Federal Child Pornography Law's Scienter Requirement," *Harvard Civ. Rts.- Civ. Lib. Review* 28 (1993): 585-600.

111. "Child Smut Conviction Is Thrown Out," *New York Times* (2 November 1993), p. 11. The case is United States v. Knox, 977 F.2d 815 (3d Cir. 1992), *cert. granted*, Knox v. United States, 113 S.Ct. 2926 (1993), *vacated, dismissed, vacated, remanded*, 114 S.Ct. 375 (1993) *and reaff'd.*, 1994 U.S. App. LEXIS 13919 (3d Cir. June 9, 1994). See also "Clinton Seeks Wider Pornography Laws," *New York Times* (12 November 1993), p. 8.

112. "Teacher Gets Five Years in Child-Pornography Case," *New York Times* (14 January 1993), p. 12.

113. Skywalker Records, Inc., v. Navarro, 739 F.Supp. 578 (S.D.Fla. 1990), *reversed sub. nom.*, 960 F.2d 134 (11th Cir. 1992), *cert. denied*, 113 S.Ct. 659 (1992).

114. "Cable TV Producer Off Hook," *St. Petersburg Times* (7 May 1993), p. 1B.

115. "Despite Six-Year U.S. Campaign, Pornography Industry Thrives," *New York Times* (4 July 1993), p. 10.

116. Sable Communications of California, Inc. v. FCC, 492 U.S. 115 (1989). For a discussion, see "First Amendment—Disconnecting Dial-A-Porn: Section 223(b)'s Two Pronged Challenge to First Amendment Rights," *The Journal of Criminal Law and Criminology* 80 (Winter 1990): 968-995.

117. Osborne v. Ohio, 495 U.S. 103 (1990), *reh'g. denied*, 496 U.S. 913 (1990), *on remand*, 557 N.E.2d 1210 (Ohio 1990). See also Commonwealth v. Oakes, 518 N.E.2d 836 (Mass. 1988), *cert. granted*, 486 U.S. 1022 (1988), *vacated*, 491 U.S. 576 (1989), *on remand*, 551 N.E.2d 910 (Mass. 1990).

118. Alexander v. Thornburgh, 943 F.2d 825 (8th Cir. 1991), *vacated, remanded*, 113 S.Ct. 2766 (1993), *reh'g. denied*, 113 S.Ct. 295 (1993).

Chapter 9

Crimes against the Administration of Government

Outline

Key Terms

bribery
compounding a crime
contempt
counterfeiting
embracery
escape

false swearing
misprision of felony
misprision of treason
obstruction of justice
official misconduct in
    office

perjury
sedition
subornation of perjury
treason
under color of law

Introduction

In primitive societies, the offenses discussed in this chapter did not exist. Simple societies needed protection from outsiders, but most problems within societies were handled informally. As societies became more complex and developed formal laws and governments, they faced the necessity of dealing with those people who tried to disrupt the legal and governmental structures. Additionally, there was the possibility that government and government officials might mistreat citizens. This chapter discusses crimes against the administration of government and crimes committed by government officials in connection with their official duties.

Some introductory criminal law texts do not cover the crimes discussed in this chapter. To omit these crimes is to leave the reader with an inaccurate perception of crime in the United States. It is tempting to emphasize only those serious crimes that threaten us as individuals—crimes of violence and crimes against property. But an increasing number of government officials are being indicted and prosecuted for crimes associated with their offices.

Crimes committed against the administration of justice may be serious. These crimes, such as treason and sedition, may affect the security of all citizens. Some of the crimes may involve violence, even death. All of the crimes make the administration of government more difficult.

Treason

The most serious crimes against the administration of government are those that attempt to overthrow the government. These consist of treason and related offenses. **Treason**, attempting to overthrow the government of which one is a member or betraying that government to a foreign power, was thought to be such a serious offense that it was included in the U.S. Constitution, the only crime defined in that document. Article III, Section 3 provides: "Treason against the United States, shall consist only in levying War against them, or in adhering to their Enemies, giving them Aid and Comfort. No Person shall be convicted of Treason unless on the Testimony of two Witnesses to the same overt Act, or on Confession in open Court."

The Constitution provides that Congress has the power to legislate punishment for treason. The U.S. Criminal Code's chapter entitled "Treason, Sedition, and Subversive Activities" contains numerous sections defining the relevant crimes and their punishments. The punishment for treason against the United States is death or imprisonment for not less than five years and a fine of not less than $10,000. A person convicted of treason under the federal code may not hold any office in the U.S. government. The constitutionality of the death penalty for treason has been questioned by scholars.[1]

In his commentary on the laws of England William Blackstone noted that implicit in the word *treason* is "betraying, treachery, or breach of faith." It refers not only to an act against the king and government but also to situations in which an inferior betrays a superior. Thus, under the English common law, for a wife to kill her lord or husband, a servant his master or mis-

Aldrich H. Ames, C.I.A. officer accused (along with his wife) of spying for Moscow, entered a guilty plea and was sentenced to life in prison.

tress, or a clergyman his prelate was treason, although these offenses were called *petit treason*.[2] For that offense the penalty was drawing and hanging for a male offender, drawing and burning for a female. *Drawing* referred to dragging the offender by horse to the place of execution. Because of the brutality of this punishment, petit treason did not become part of U.S. legal tradition.

Killing the king constituted an act of *high treason* and was punishable by death. But because the crime was considered so serious, Blackstone argued that it should be "most precisely defined. For if the crime of high treason be indeterminate, this alone...is sufficient to make any government degenerate into arbitrary power."[3]

Fewer than fifty cases of treason have been prosecuted in the United States, although some cases have been brought under other statutes. Julius and Ethel Rosenberg, accused of providing protected information to the Soviet Union, were convicted of conspiracy to violate the federal Espionage Act. *Espionage*, or spying, is defined by the federal code as "gathering, transmitting or losing" national defense information with the intent or reasonable belief that the information will be used against the United States. The Rosenbergs were executed in 1953.[4]

In 1993 the American Bar Association observed the fortieth anniversary of the Rosenbergs' executions with a mock trial. In the "retrial" of the "trial of the century," the Rosenbergs were acquitted, with the jury ruling that the prosecution's case was "shabby."[5]

Elements of Treason

Treason has been labeled the worst of all crimes.[6] Because of its seriousness, it is defined carefully and consists of three elements:

1. an allegiance owed to the government (which may be state or federal);
2. an act that violates the offender's allegiance; and
3. a criminal intent.

A person who is not a U.S. citizen cannot commit treason against the United States as by definition treason requires an allegiance to the government. This requirement applies even if the person has had U.S. citizenship and either lost or renounced it.[7] The owed allegiance must be breached by an overt act; treasonous thoughts are not sufficient. As the Constitution specifies, the allegiance may be breached by levying war against the country or by aiding and comforting the enemy. Aiding and comforting the enemy may consist of acts such as providing arms and other supplies for the enemy to use against the United States or delivering deserters and prisoners to the enemy.

The criminal intent for treason may be shown by proving an awareness that the actions in question would assist the enemy in its efforts against the United States.[8] One final constitutional requirement for conviction of treason is a confession in open court or the testimony of two witnesses.

Most states have treason statutes that apply to offenses against the state government. These statutes may not violate the U.S. Constitution's provisions; otherwise, states have discretion in framing their statutes or constitutional provisions regarding treason. The California statute illustrates one state's reaction to treason:

> Treason against this state consists only in levying war against it, adhering to its enemies, or giving them aid and comfort, and can be committed only by persons owing allegiance to the state. The punishment of treason shall be death or life imprisonment without possibility of parole....[9]

Treason-Related Crimes

The concealment of the known treason of another, called **misprision of treason**, is punishable under federal and most state statutes. The California Penal Code provides, "Misprision of treason is the knowledge and concealment of treason, without otherwise assenting to or participating in the crime. It is punishable by imprisonment in the state prison."[10]

Several other offenses are related to treason. The federal code includes inciting a rebellion against the United States, seditious conspiracy, advocating the overthrow of the government, willfully interfering with the armed forces, recruiting for service against the United States, and enlistment to serve against the United States.[11]

State statutes include related offenses as well; some have been held unconstitutionally broad or vague. California's prohibition against displaying a red flag "in any public place...as a sign, symbol or emblem of opposition to organized government" was held to be unconstitutional because this prohibition might include "peaceful and orderly opposition to government by legal means and within constitutional limitations."[12]

Another crime related to treason is **sedition**, defined by the federal criminal code as knowingly or willfully advocating, abetting, advising, or teaching the duty, necessity, desirability, or propriety of overthrowing, putting down, or destroying the government by force or violence or by assassinating any officer of the government or with that criminal intent to print, publish, edit, issue, circulate, sell, distribute, or publicly display written or printed matter designed to overthrow the government.[13] Thus, sedition is a communication or agreement aimed at stirring up treason or defaming the government.

Generally sedition takes the form of written expression and as such is called *seditious libel*, but the federal criminal code prohibits *seditious conspiracy* as well. Although there have been few prosecutions for these offenses in recent years, the prosecutions that do occur are publicized nationally. In 1987 and 1988 national attention was focused on a federal trial for seditious conspiracy and other crimes that involved several members of a white supremacist movement who were charged, among other crimes, with conspiring to overthrow the U.S. government, replace it with a white supremacist state, and kill a federal judge and a federal agent. The trial in Fort Smith, Arkansas, was only the fourth time in forty years that the federal government had prosecuted a case involving sedition. An all-white jury acquitted the defendants on all charges, although six of the defendants are serving prison time for other crimes. Focus 9.1 contains the details of other trials that involved sedition, treason, or espionage.

Perjury

Under the common law, **perjury** referred only to false statements willfully made under oath in a judicial proceeding. According to Blackstone, perjury was limited to situations in which "a *lawful* oath is administered, in some *judicial* proceeding, to a person who swears *willfully, absolutely* and *falsely*, in a matter *material* to the issue or point in question." The law considered all other perjuries "unnecessary at least, and therefore will not punish the breach of them."[14]

In early common law the punishment for perjury was death; later the penalty was banishment or cutting out the offender's tongue; still later forfeiture of goods, and finally, at the time Blackstone was writing, the punishment was fine and imprisonment. Additionally, the convicted perjurer was not permitted to give sworn testimony in court again.

Subornation of perjury, also a common law crime, involved procuring someone to commit perjury. It carried the same penalties as perjury. Although the original common law crimes of perjury and subornation of perjury were limited to statements made under official oath in judicial proceedings, as other kinds of sworn statements gained recognition the English courts developed additional crimes to cover the offenses, but they did not carry the term *perjury*. Many of these false statements were included in the offense of **false swearing**, which included false statements that would have been perjury but for the fact that they were not made in a judicial proceeding.

Both perjury and subornation of perjury are crimes under the federal code,[15] along with the crime of *false declarations before grand jury or court*.[16] This statute was the basis of a 1987 appeal in which the conviction of a fed-

FOCUS 9.1 Sedition, Treason, Espionage: Recent Cases

Sedition, treason, and espionage are viewed as the most serious crimes a citizen can commit against the government. The reaction of governments to convictions for these crimes indicates the seriousness with which they are viewed. A few recent examples illustrate.

In April 1993 thirty-two disciples of a blind Muslim cleric were convicted by a military court in Haekstap, Egypt. The defendants were convicted of attempting to topple the government by attacking tourism and thus destroying the financial mainstay of that government. Seven of the defendants were sentenced to hang; the rest received twenty-five-year prison sentences. Seventeen were acquitted.[1]

The cleric, Sheik Omar Abdel-Rahman, has been linked by U.S. officials with the bombing of the World Trade Center in New York City in 1993, killing six people and injuring more than 1,000. In March 1994 four Islamic fundamentalists were found guilty of causing the explosion. Fifteen other Islamic extremists, including the Sheik, will be tried for conspiracy in that bombing. They will be tried also for a plot to bomb the United Nations building as well as a bridge and tunnels that connect New York and New Jersey. That trial was scheduled to begin in September 1994.[2]

Earlier in 1993 two KGB turncoats were executed for treason after they assisted the U.S. government while they were employed at the Soviet Embassy in Washington. One claimed he cooperated with the FBI "for ideological reasons." The other claimed to be a victim of a "classic FBI entrap-ment scheme designed to take advantage of the insatiable appetite of low-paid Soviet agents and diplomats for Western consumer goods."[3]

Clayton J. Lonetree, a Marine sergeant, was convicted of espionage for his role in disclosing secrets about the U.S. Embassy in Moscow while having an affair with a Soviet woman. Lonetree, who was sentenced to twenty-five years in prison and demoted to the rank of private, appealed his conviction to the highest court of appeals in the military justice system, the U.S. Court of Military Appeals in Washington, on the grounds that his attorney, William J. Kunstler, misled him about the possibility of a plea agreement. Lonetree was fined $5,000 and received a dishonorable discharge along with the loss of all military pay and allowance. In October 1993 a military judge reduced Lonetree's sentence, an act that made him eligible for parole. Lonetree is the first marine convicted of spying against the United States.[4]

Although he was charged with defrauding the government, the defendant indicated that had he engaged in the acts alleged, it would have been *treason*. Retired Army General Wallace Nutting, the only four-star general to be indicted for a federal crime, was charged with defrauding the Defense Department out of $40 million by producing shoddy ammunition, faking test results, and billing the department for work that was not done. Nutting was acquitted of the charges but stated, "As far as I am concerned, a government official stole two and one-half years of my life." He quoted a former official during the Nixon administration who was acquitted of criminal charges, "So where do I go to get my reputation back?"[5]

In October 1993 Catholic bishops rejected the charges brought by Cuba's official press, which had alleged that the bishops' criticisms constituted treason. "We categorically reject the serious accusations of treason because they are slanderous," said the bishops. Some members of the Cuban Catholic clergy had called on Cuba to eliminate the "exclusive and omnipresent character of the official ideology," as well as to lift the restrictions on civil rights "and halt excessive controls by the state security forces."[6]

In April 1994 Aldrich H. Ames admitted that he gave intelligence information to Soviet officials. He was given the most severe penalty the law allows: life in prison with no possibility of parole. Rosario Ames, arrested along with her husband on charges of espionage conspiracy, denied that she knew anything about her husband's activities. Sentencing in her case was pending at the time this text went to press.[7]

[1.] "Court Convicts Thirty-Two Disciples of Cleric," *Tampa Tribune*, (23 April 1993), Nation World, p. 6.
[2.] "Now the Hard Part of the Crime Fight: Money; New York's Verdict Against Terrorism," *U.S. News & World Report* 116 (14 March 1994): 14.
[3.] "KGB Turncoats Were Executed," *Tampa Tribune* (23 February 1993), p. 3.
[4.] "Military Court Hears Appeal of Marine in Spy Case," *New York Times* (13 May 1991), p. 7; "Marine in Espionage Case Now Eligible for Parole," *New York Times* (31 October 1993), p. 21.
[5.] "A Four-Star Acquittal for This General," *St. Petersburg Times* (4 August 1993), p. 1.
[6.] "Catholic Bishops Dismiss Charges in Official Press," *Agence France Presse* (7 October 1993), p. 1.
[7.] "Guilty, but Unremorseful," *Miami Herald* (29 April 1994), p. 1. "Angry Rosario Ames Denies Role as a Spy," *St. Petersburg Times* (20 April 1994), p. 3.

eral judge in Mississippi was upheld. In *United States* v. *Nixon*, the Fifth Circuit Court of Appeals upheld the conviction of Judge Walter H. Nixon, who, according to the appellate court, "had for some years prior to the incidents at issue herein been dissatisfied with his modest judicial salary, and had looked for means of augmenting it." The judge found a source in a successful investor in oil and gas properties. At a modest price, the judge purchased an interest in three oil wells. By the time he was convicted, his investment had increased sixfold. The investor's son was involved in drug sales. It was with regard to that case that the judge perjured himself before a federal grand jury. In *Nixon*, the court stated the elements of perjury: "The Government must prove that the defendant's statements were material, that they were false, and that, at the time they were made, the defendant did not believe them to be true."[17] In 1993 Nixon, age sixty-four, was permitted to return to the practice of law in Mississippi after he passed the state bar exam. He had been disbarred in 1990 after his perjury conviction.[18]

If the government does not prove that the allegedly false statements are *material*—that is, related to the issue under consideration—the defendant may not be convicted. The judge decides whether the evidence is material. If the judge is overturned on this issue on appeal after a conviction, that conviction must be reversed.[19]

It is important to understand that an element of perjury is that the allegedly false information is made under an oath or affirmation during official proceedings. According to the Model Penal Code commentary, it is "these ingredients that make the conduct involved in perjury especially serious." The commentary classifies perjury as "the most serious of several offenses designed to protect the integrity of information on which the government will rely." It notes, however, that many penalties are disproportionate to the offense. In most jurisdictions perjury is classified as a felony. The M.P.C. classifies perjury as a felony in the third degree.[20]

Several cases of alleged perjury among government officials have come to light in recent years. A widely publicized perjury trial was that of Michael Deaver, former President Reagan's chief of staff and longtime confidant. Deaver was charged with five counts of perjury and convicted of three. Focus 9.2 contains information on the Deaver trial and other recent perjury cases of national and international significance.

In addition to statutes on perjury, subornation of perjury, and false swearing, many state codes and the Model Penal Code include statutes prohibiting such offenses as unsworn falsification to authorities, false alarms to agencies of public safety, false reports to law enforcement authorities, tampering with witnesses and informants or retaliation against them, tampering with or fabricating physical evidence, tampering with public records or information, and impersonating a public servant.[21]

Bribery

Beginning in antiquity and continuing through early English and American literature are the prohibitions against the offense that today is called **bribery**, defined as the offering, giving, receiving, or soliciting anything of value for the purpose of influencing action by public officials. As a common law misdemeanor, bribery was limited to actions concerning judicial officials (a judge or another person performing judicial functions). It applied only to the judge who took the bribe.

By legislation bribery was extended to the *briber*, or bribe giver, as well as the *bribee*, or bribe taker. In addition, the offense was extended beyond bribing a judicial official to include other public officials, and attempted bribery became an offense as well. "Whatever it is a crime to take, it is a crime to give; they are reciprocal. And...the attempt is a crime; it is complete on the side who offers it."[22]

Early U.S. common law extended bribery to include the giver as well as the taker. It included public officers and those who were not public officers but who were performing public functions or duties when the gift involved a corrupt intention to influence the discharging of that public duty. By statute in many jurisdictions, bribery has been broadened so that today the offense includes three types: official, quasi-official, and occupational bribery.

Types of Bribery

Official bribery laws in the United States have gone beyond the English limitation of judicial officers to include other public officials or those performing official duties, including servants or employees and deputies of

FOCUS 9.2 Perjury by Government Officials: Some Recent Cases

Several cases of alleged perjury involving government officials have come to the nation's attention in recent years. Arizona governor Evan Mecham was indicted on six felony counts, including perjury before a grand jury. Mecham was impeached by the Arizona House and convicted by the Arizona Senate, making him the first U.S. governor in fifty-nine years to be impeached and removed from office. In his criminal trial, the jury found him not guilty.

Unnamed associates of Judge Douglas H. Ginsburg, who withdrew his nomination for appointment to the U.S. Supreme Court after he admitted to having used marihuana on several occasions, were accused of lying to government officials when asked whether Judge Ginsburg had used marihuana. No criminal prosecutions followed, but the FBI indicated that it would revamp its procedures for investigating candidates for public office.

Anthony R. Ameruso, transportation commissioner of New York City, was convicted of perjury when testifying under oath before a panel investigating government corruption. Ameruso was ordered to perform 1,000 hours of community service.

Former Illinois governor Daniel Walker pleaded guilty to fraud, perjury, and misapplication of funds charges stemming from his false statements to a bank board investigative committee. Walker was freed after serving almost eighteen months of a seven-year prison term.

Former White House aide and close friend of former President and Mrs.

Reagan Michael Deaver was convicted of perjury based on false testimony made to a congressional subcommittee and a federal grand jury that were investigating his lobbying activities. Deaver's trial, which lasted seven weeks, resulted in three convictions and two acquittals on five perjury charges. Deaver was fined $100,000 and placed on three years' probation.

In 1989, former Georgia congressman Patrick L. Swindall was convicted of nine counts of perjury before a grand jury and sentenced to a year in prison.

Elizabeth Irene Richardson, convicted of perjury in February 1990, was ordered to apologize in public ads to Gary Nitsch, against whom she testified for raping her. She later admitted to friends that the alleged rape was a hoax to get the attention of her husband who traveled frequently and, she claimed, neglected her. Prior to her admission, the case was dropped for lack of sufficient evidence.

Richardson was ordered to purchase a one-half page advertisement in every newspaper and purchase an ad on every radio station in the county. She elicited the assistance of the Nebraska Civil Liberties Union lawyers on the issue of whether this "scarlet letter" approach to sentencing is constitutional. She was sentenced to 180 days in jail to be followed by two years' probation.

In September 1993 the Fourth Circuit Court of Appeals upheld the perjury and fraud convictions of Dr. Cecil B. Jacobson, who was convicted of using his own sperm to inseminate women who came to his fertility clinic.

He tricked other women into thinking they were pregnant. Jacobson was convicted of fifty-two counts of fraud and perjury. Jacobson, who told his patients that he was using donor sperm, may have fathered as many as seventy-five children.[1] In May 1994 the U.S. Supreme Court refused to hear Jacobson's appeal.

And, in September 1993 a former U.S. government informant was indicted for eight counts of perjury for allegedly lying about the responsibility of the U.S. government in the 1988 fatal bombing of Pan Am Flight 103, which crashed over Lockerbie, Scotland on 21 December 1988, killing all 259 persons on board and another eleven persons on the ground. Arrest warrants have been issued by the United States and Great Britain for two Libyans allegedly involved in the bombing. As of press time, both men had been indicted but were in Libya, whose ruler, Moammar Gadhafi, had refused to grant extradiction to enable the United States and Britain to prosecute the men.[2]

SOURCE: Summarized by the author from media sources.
[1] "Conviction Upheld in Fertility Case," *New York Times* (8 September 1993), p. 11B. The case is United States v. Jacobson, 785 F.Supp. 563 (E.D.Va. 1992), *related proceeding*, 826 F.Supp. 155(E.D.Va. 1992), and *later proceeding*, 1993 U.S.App. LEXIS 22534 (4th Cir. 1993), *and subsequent civil proceeding*, James v. Jacobson, 6 F.3d 233 (4th Cir. 1993).
[2] "Tipster Indicted in Pan Am 103 Case," *Washington Times* (22 September 1993), p. 13; "Clinton to Honor Pan Am Victims: Memorial to Flight 103 Reflects Commitment Against Terrorism," *Washington Post* (20 December 1993), p. 6.

public officials. The trend is toward expanding the category of official bribery to include people who serve as jurors, witnesses, and electors.

Bribery is considered a serious crime. It constitutes one of two offenses (the other being treason) designated by the Constitution as grounds for impeaching a president, vice president, and all civil officers of the United States.[23]

Certain functions, although not official, are considered so important that some jurisdictions have extended criminal statutes to include *quasi-bribery*, or bribery of people such as

1. officers or employees of public institutions;
2. officers or members of any legislative caucus, political convention, committee, or political gathering having for its purpose the nomination of candidates for public office; or
3. representatives of a labor organization.

An example of a statute aimed at representatives of a labor organization is New York's statute, which provides that a "person is guilty of bribing a labor official when, with intent to influence a labor official in respect to any of his acts, decisions or duties as such labor official, he confers, or offers or agrees to confer, any benefit upon him." Bribing a labor official in New York is a felony.[24]

A final category of bribery is *occupational bribery*. Many duties that are neither official nor quasi-official are important enough to society that we wish to protect the integrity of decision making in areas such as commercial accounts, other business or professional areas, and sports. The importance of preventing bribery because of its impact on the moral fiber of society is perhaps surpassed only by its involvement in organized crime, discussed in Chapter 11. But in this brief excerpt from *United States* v. *Perrin*, the court reminds us of the connection.[25]

United States v. *Perrin*

[C]ommon experience has taught us that organized crime does not limit bribery to bribery of public officials. Few will ever forget the most notorious commercial bribe in American history—the bribing of the 1919 Chicago White Sox baseball team. In that sad episode, Abe Attell, supposedly an employee of the New York gambler Arnold Rothstein, bribed eight players of the Chicago White Sox to throw the first and second games of the 1919 World Series to the Cincinnati Reds. Attell paid Eddie Cicotte, Oscar "Happy" Felsch, Chick Gandil, "Shoeless" Joe Jackson, Freddy McMullin, Charles "Swede" Risberg, George "Buck" Weaver, and Claude Williams about $70,000 for their participation in the scheme.[26]

In its 1986 final reports, the President's Commission on Organized Crime emphasized the role of organized crime in sports bribery. These cases are prosecuted under the following federal statute:

> (a) Whoever carries into effect, attempts to carry into effect, or conspires with any other person to carry into effect any scheme in commerce to influence, in any way, by bribery any sporting contest, with knowledge that the purpose of such scheme is to influence by bribery that contest, shall be fined not more than $10,000, or imprisoned not more than five years, or both.[27]

Elements of Bribery

In addition to defining who may be bribed, statutes require as an element of bribery that there be a criminal intent. This is the most important element of the crime, for if it cannot be shown that the giver gave to the official for the purpose of influencing a decision, there is no bribery. If the recipient is the defendant, it must be shown that he or she received the gift with the intent of being influenced in making a decision affecting the one who offered the gift. It is possible, of course, that one party has the requisite criminal intent and the other does not. In that case, only the party with the *mens rea* may be convicted of bribery. The evil motive or intent may be proved by circumstantial evidence.

A bribery conviction requires also that the money be given to the official to influence action over which that person has some *official* control. For example, the federal statute defines *official act* as "any decision or action on any question, matter, cause, suit, proceeding or controversy, which may at any time be pending, or which may by law be brought before any public official, in such official's official capacity, or in such official's place of trust or profit."[28] Thus, in a case in which defendant was convicted of bribery after he became involved in a private scheme to sell group automobile insurance to labor unions as part of a negotiated benefit in union contracts, the appellate court reversed the conviction. The court noted that although the conduct of the defendant, who was the Assistant to the Secretary for Labor Relations at the Department of Housing and Urban Development (HUD), was reprehensible, it did not constitute bribery. Although the defendant served as a liason between his office in HUD and organized labor, group automobile insurance was not a subject that had or would come before him for decision. This action was not a part of his *official acts* at HUD.[29]

Bribery Laws and Political Influence

In 1962, during the administration of President John F. Kennedy, Congress revised the federal bribery statute, with one purpose being to exact greater control on political influence resulting from campaign contributions. A critique of the statute notes that the "seemingly expansive reach of the bribery statute has effectively discouraged the explicit, quid pro quo arrangements involving the exchange of campaign contributions for political favors," but that extensive influence resulting from campaign contributions still leads to political corruption. "Reform of the federal bribery statute is essential to end the invidious form of corruption that now permeates Capitol Hill."[30]

Controlling undue influence on political officials is difficult. According to the Supreme Court, bribery laws "deal with only the most blatant and specific attempts of those with money to influence governmental action."[31] Furthermore, it is important for citizens to communicate their ideas and have some influence over their public officials. Thus, a statute aimed at controlling undue influence must not be so broad as to have a chilling effect on this important communication. On the other hand, federal and state statutes should be sufficiently specific to cover excessive influence over public officials through, for example, campaign contributions. One critic believes that significant change is unlikely.

> Although campaign finance reform proposals circulate through the halls of Capitol Hill, any drastic change in the system, with or without reform, probably will not occur. Media costs, political consulting fees, and the overall increase in the sophistication of political campaigns will require the continued consumption of large amounts of campaign dollars. Unfortunately, however, the change in the nature of campaign financing has institutionalized not only the role and leverage of PACs, [political action committees] but also the opportunities for corruption in the system.[32]

Related Offenses

Bribery may merge with other crimes analyzed previously or discussed subsequently. Examples are *misconduct in office, accepting unlawful gratuities, compounding a crime, conspiracy, obstruction of justice,* and *extortion.* In some cases the offense in question may be prosecuted as one of these crimes or as bribery or both. Focus 9.3 summarizes several recent cases that involve charges of bribery, and in some cases other crimes as well.

Mario Biaggi, a congressman from New York City, was found guilty of federal charges involving unlawful gratuities but was acquitted of the more serious charges of bribery and conspiracy to commit bribery in a case involving his acceptance of two vacations paid for by a New York political boss. Biaggi, who was convicted also of obstructing justice in the government's efforts to investigate the case, referred to his conviction as follows: "The jury convicted me of 'tipping.'. . . I'm not a waiter. I'm a congressman. I will continue to be a congressman."[33]

In Biaggi's case, the jury was instructed that *bribery* is payment to an official to influence an official act, whereas a gratuity is a reward for an act. Biaggi was sentenced to two and one-half years in prison and was ordered to pay a $500,000 fine.

Another common law crime related to bribery was **embracery**, a misdemeanor referring to a corrupt attempt to influence a juror by means of promises, money, persuasions, or similar techniques. Today many jurisdictions include this offense under a separate title such as *corrupt influencing of jurors* or include it within the crime of *obstructing justice*, discussed below.

Official Misconduct in Office

Official misconduct in office refers to any willful, unlawful behavior by public officials in the course of their official duties. This may involve failure to act, or *nonfeasance;* engaging in a wrongful act that the official has no right to do, or *malfeasance;* or improperly performing an act that the official has a right to do, *misfeasance.*

Official misconduct in office is a common law crime punishable by imprisonment, fine, or, in some circumstances, removal from office. Some offenses, such as bribery, are designated as separate crimes. They are not covered by the crime of official misconduct, although an official may be convicted for both if, after accepting a bribe (the crime of bribery, assuming all the elements are met), the official carries out the bribe, at which point misconduct in office has been committed.[34]

Elements of Official Misconduct

The first element of official misconduct is that the actor must be a public official or one acting in that capacity. The misconduct must occur during the course of that officer's official duties or **under color of law**. This important concept means that even if the official is acting beyond the scope of the office, the action is taken under the guise of the office; that is, as if permissible by virtue of that office. This element was tested in an earlier federal case and was brought under the previous criminal civil rights statute.

Crews v. *United States* involved a defendant described by the appellate court that upheld his conviction as the "Town Marshall...and also the Constable of the District that embraced the Town. He was 'the law,' twice

FOCUS 9.3 Bribery and Related Offenses: A Recent View

B.C.C.I. Investigation

In July 1992 indictments were filed against Clark M. Clifford and Robert A. Altman, both charged with bribery and related charges in connection with the corrupt Bank of Credit and Commercial International (B.C.C.I). Clifford served as Secretary of Defense under President Lyndon Johnson and as a campaign adviser to Harry S. Truman. Altman, also a banker and a lawyer, was a younger protege of Clifford. He is married to actress Lynda Carter.

Circumstances involving the now-defunct B.C.C.I. resulted in the largest bank scandal in history, in which an estimated $20 billion was stolen, lost, or misappropriated. The case against Altman was tried in 1993, resulting in acquittals on all counts. The case was extremely complicated, with 15,000 pages of transcript and over forty witnesses. Clifford was too ill to stand trial in 1993, and in November of that year the prosecutor recommended dropping all criminal charges against him because of his bad health. Both Clifford and Altman face civil charges in the case. In June 1994 twelve former top executives of the B.C.C.I. were convicted of fraud and mismanagement, sentenced to up to fourteen years in prison, and ordered to pay $9.13 billion in restitution to the bank's major shareholder. It is unlikely that any of that money will be collected, however, as the defendants say they are broke.[1]

Judge Collins Guilty of Bribery

In 1993 the U.S. Supreme Court refused to hear the appeal of U.S. District Judge Robert F. Collins, civil rights leader and one of the few African-American judges in the South. The decision meant that Collins, who began serving his six-year, ten-month prison term in December 1991, would remain in prison.[2] Judge Collins and his co-conspirator were convicted of accepting a bribe of $100,000 in exchange for reducing the sentence of a drug dealer. Collins was convicted of bribery, obstructing justice, and conspiracy. He refused to resign his position on the federal bench, and in June 1993 the federal judiciary asked the House of Representatives to consider impeachment proceedings, the only method for removing federal judges from office, since they are appointed for life. That proceeding was begun in July 1993, but Collins had not been impeached when this text went to press.

Italian Bribery Scandal

State and private businesses and approximately 1,500 individuals from those organizations were investigated in one of the worst bribery scandals alleged in Italian history. Some officials implicated in the scandal resigned from public office, and several persons scheduled to testify regarding the alleged bribery committed suicide. The Justice Ministry was expected to offer amnesty to those public officials who confessed, resigned, and paid back any bribes in which they were involved. In December 1993 Italian law enforcement officials arrested a leading industrialist, Mario Schimberni, seventy, who was placed under house arrest because of his age. Schimberni is accused of corruption by diverting $300 million from one account to another.

It has been estimated that the alleged scandal could have cost Italians over $20 billion and that bribes ranged from "everything from a contract to renovate a cemetery, to supplying a school's heating oil, to ordering pencils for the clerks." [3]

Bribery in Miami, Florida

In the fall of 1993 the former mayor of Miami Beach, Florida, Alex Daoud, began serving a five-year sentence for bribery, obstruction of justice, and evading taxes. The bribery charge was based on the acceptance of a $10,000 payment from a former boxing promoter and drug trafficker, a charge for which Daoud was found guilty in 1992 at which time he was acquitted of nine other charges. In 1993 Daoud entered a guilty plea to obstruction of justice, another count of bribery, money laundering, and tax evasion (failing to report $160,000 of income in 1988).[4]

The bribery count to which Daoud entered a guilty plea involved accepting a $5,000 payment from a bank in exchange for his vote on a zoning variance for the bank's president, David Paul. Paul was convicted on sixty-eight out of sixty-nine counts of banking fraud, dealing primarily with spending $3.2 million of CenTrust money on the remodeling of his personal residence. Three months later he entered guilty pleas to twenty-nine counts of financial fraud concerning primarily securities fraud. An additional trial to determine forfeiture was set for the Spring of 1994. It was delayed when lawyers argued over the facts.[5]

The U.S. Probation Office recommended that Paul be sentenced to twenty-two years in federal prison, but Paul received a light sentence. For ten months he must spend weekends and holidays in a federal prison. In June 1994 William Christopher Berry, who was indicted along with Paul, was acquitted of any wrongdoing in the CenTrust scandal. This acquittal could affect Paul's sentencing.[6]

[1.] "Innocent As Charged," Time (30 August 1993), p. 34; "Request: Drop Clifford Case," St. Petersburg Times (3 November 1993), p. 7.
[2.] Collins v. United States, 972 F.2d 1385 (5th Cir. 1992), cert. denied, 113 S.Ct. 1812 (1993).
[3.] "Broad Bribery Investigation Is Ensnaring the Elite of Italy," New York Times (3 March 1993), p. 1; "An Italian Defense Official Arrested in Bribery Scandal," New York Times (11 April 1993), p. 4.
[4.] "Daoud Pleads Guilty to Four Charges," Miami Herald (1 July 1993), p. 1B; "Daoud Gets Five Years for 'Big Mistake,'" Miami Herald (9 September 1993), p. 1B.
[5.] "David Paul: Horatio Alger or Thief?" Miami Herald (13 October 1993), p. 1C; "David Paul Convicted of Fraud," Miami Herald (25 November 1993), p. 1; "Paul Pleads Guilty to Securities Charges," Miami Herald (11 February 1994), p. 1C; "Bickering Among Lawyers Stalls Paul's Forfeiture Trial," Miami Herald (16 June 1994), p. 1C. .
[6.] "Stiff Term Urged for David Paul," Miami Herald (18 March 1994), p. 1C; "Jury Acquits Ex-CenTrust Official," St. Petersburg Times (8 June 1994), p. 1E.

fortified." The defendant, who was not wearing his cap denoting his position (which he argued he always wore when on duty), was not driving a patrol car, was not wearing a uniform, and was not wearing a badge, argued that he was not acting under color of law when he interacted with the victim.

The defendant administered a bullwhip to the victim and then drove him to a highway bridge, where he forced the victim to jump off into the water, telling him he had a 50–50 chance of surviving. It was high odds for a man who protested that he could not swim. The victim drowned. It was argued that the homicide was "solely one of personal vengeance and entirely devoid of official character or authority and, therefore, not within the purview of the statute." The appellate court disagreed. After analyzing all of the facts of the case carefully, the court reached the conclusion stated in this excerpt.[35]

Crews v. *United States*

An officer of the law should not be permitted to divest himself of his official authority in actions taken by him wherein he acts, or purports, or pretends, to act pursuant to his authority, and where one, known by another to be an officer, takes the other into custody in a manner which appears on its face to be in the exercise of authority of law, without making to the other any disclosure to the contrary, such officer thereby justifies the conclusion that he was acting under color of law in making an arrest.

To sustain a conviction for official misconduct, it must be shown that the officer's act was accompanied by *mens rea*, an evil intent; an act performed because of ignorance and in good faith will not qualify. The act itself must be unlawful, an act of corruption, or one of depravity, perversion, or taint—an act requiring an evil intent or motive.[36]

Criminal Punishment for Violating Civil Rights

The U.S. Code's criminal provision for the punishment of those who violate civil rights is as follows:

> Whoever, under color of any law, statute, ordinance, regulation, or custom, willfully subjects any inhabitant of any State, Territory, or District to the deprivation of any rights, privileges, or immunities secured or protected by the constitution or laws of the United States, or to different punishments, pains, or penalties, on account of such inhabitant being an alien, or by reason of his color, or race, than are prescribed for the punishment of citizens, shall be fined not more than $1,000 or imprisoned not more than one year, or both; and if death results shall be subject to imprisonment for any term of years or for life.[37]

This statute was violated in the 1968 case of *Miller* v. *United States*.[38]

Miller v. *United States*

This is a police brutality case. The appellants William Miller and Paul Vallee were deputy sheriffs of Jefferson Parish, Louisiana. They were charged with the infliction of summary punishment upon two men in their custody and convicted by a jury of violating 18 U.S.C.A. Section 242.

The evidence at trial showed that on the night of October 24, 1966, Miller and Vallee participated in the arrest of James Dyle and Lee Gauthe on suspicion of burglary. Although the two deputies were instructed by a superior officer to take Dyle and Gauthe to the police station lockup, they drove instead to a secluded alley and attempted to extract confessions from the suspects. Their methods of interrogation were somewhat bizarre. According to one deputy who testified for the government, Miller opened the rear door of the police patrol car and Vallee activated his "K-9" police dog causing it to bite Dyle. The dog had been trained to strike at whatever part of a man's body was indicated by its handler. Vallee utilized this training by slapping Dyle in various places and then standing aside while the dog attacked him. Dyle was tormented in this manner for about seven or eight minutes until the arrival of Vallee's superior. The suspects were then taken to the West Bank Lockup in Gretna, Louisiana, and there Vallee again turned his dog on Dyle. Miller, for his part, lifted Gauthe by his feet, and holding him upside down, pounded his head against the lockup floor.

Miller and Vallee both appeal their convictions and their two year suspended sentences. Only two of their contentions seem to us to merit discussion.

First, appellants contend that 18 U.S.C.A. Section 242 is inapplicable to their subhuman and vicarious animalism. They argue that the visitation of the statute arises only when race, color or alienage is involved. Our reply is that appellants misread the statute....So long as the deputies deprived Dyle and Gauthe under color of law of the constitutional right not to be summarily punished without due process of law, 18 U.S.C.A. Section 242 was violated. All people regardless of taint or degradation so long as they are inhabitants of a state, territory or district are within the statute's protective embrace. Even suspected criminality or accomplished incarceration furnish no license for the destruction of guaranteed constitutional rights.

Many acts fall within official misconduct by public officials; but violation of civil rights actions have captured considerable attention in recent years, although many of the cases are civil actions filed under the federal Civil Rights Acts, known as Section 1983 actions, named after the applicable section of the civil code.[39] Criminal prosecutions have become more prominent, too, as illustrated by the discussion of policing in Focus 9.4.

Obstruction of Justice

In early common law, interference with the orderly processes of the civil and criminal courts was a misdemeanor known as **obstruction of justice**. The crime could take many forms, including tampering with the jury, interfering with an officer who is attempting to perform official duties, suppressing or refusing to produce evidence, intimidating witnesses, and bribing judges, witnesses, and jurors.

FOCUS 9.4   Police Brutality and the Case of Rodney King

The 1991 beating of Rodney King, an African-American suspect, by Los Angeles police officers was captured on video by an amateur photographer. A state trial in nearby Simi Valley resulting in the acquittal of the officers was followed by three days of intense rioting in Los Angeles, resulting in the deaths of over fifty persons and property damage in excess of $1 billion.[1]

Subsequently the officers were tried in federal court, accused of violating King's civil rights under federal statutes. Some attorneys and legal scholars questioned the appropriateness of this trial, arguing that it violated the federal constitutional prohibition against double jeopardy. Other scholars do not believe that the U.S. Supreme Court will agree with this position.[2]

A different result was reached after Miami police officer William Lozano was acquitted of manslaughter charges in the deaths of two African Americans in Miami, an incident that led to rioting in Miami immediately after the shooting in 1989. Lozano was convicted in his first trial (in Miami), but that conviction was reversed on appeal. After several changes of venue, the second trial was held in Orlando, Florida, in 1993, and Lozano was acquitted. Despite pressure from some to do so, prosecutors declined to file federal civil rights charges against Lozano. Prior to the announcement of that decision, Roy Black, Lozano's attorney, spoke about the issue of double jeopardy with these words:

The men who founded this country put the double jeopardy clause in the Constitution to protect citizens from unwarranted persecution by the government. The founders knew that if you put someone through multiple prosecutions, eventually you can break him.[3]

In the federal case in Los Angeles, two officers, Timothy Wind and Officer Theodore Brisno, were acquitted. Sergeant Stacey Koon and Officer Laurence Powell were convicted. Koon and Powell began serving their two and one-half year prison terms at a minimun security institution in October 1993, but in August 1994 a federal appeals court ordered resentencing because the trial judge failed to follow the sentencing guidelines.[4]

In April 1994 a Los Angeles jury awarded King $3.8 million in damages for the beating, but in August 1994 a judge ruled that King owes $237,958 in legal fees to the Los Angeles School District because his naming of them in a lawsuit was a frivolous act.[5]

1. "Rioting in Los Angeles Is Relived As Jury Views Videos on Beatings," *New York Times* (29 August 1993), p. 14.
2. For a discussion of the pros and cons of this issue, see Darlene Ricker, "Double Exposure: Did The Second Rodney King Trial Violate Double Jeopardy?" *American Bar Association* 79 (August 1993): 66–69.
3. Ibid., p. 69.
4. United States v. Koon, 1994 U.S.App. LEXIS 22588 (9th Cir. 1994).
5. "Rodney King Hit with $237,958 Bill for School District," *Rocky Mountain News* (13 August 1994), p. 34.

These acts and others are recognized today by criminal statutes in most jurisdictions. They may be prosecuted as obstruction of justice crimes or as related crimes such as contempt, conspiracy, perjury, embracery, bribery, or extortion. The crime may be committed by judicial and other officials and might constitute official misconduct in office.

In some jurisdictions, the crime of obstruction of justice may extend to legislative and administrative agencies, although a federal court has held this is not the case with the federal statute.[40] The Model Penal Code includes obstructing, impairing or perverting "the administration of law or other governmental function."[41]

Former Arizona governor Evan Mecham was convicted of obstruction of justice based on his attempt to thwart a death-threat investigation. He became the first U.S. governor to be impeached and removed from office in fifty-nine years. In 1993 a Tennessee judge free on $20,000 bond while awaiting sentencing for convictions in connection with his sexual assaults of several women in his courthouse was ordered to jail after it was alleged that he was trying to obstruct justice by asking his attorneys to contact witnesses to change their testimonies. The judge was convicted and sentenced to twelve to twenty-five years in prison, fined $25,000, and ordered to pay the government $1,500 a month from his state pension during his imprisonment.[42]

In 1991 Senator Edward Kennedy and several of his friends, including William Barry, were investigated for obstruction of justice in allegedly misleading police who were investigating allegations of rape against Kennedy's nephew, Dr. William Kennedy Smith. Smith was acquitted; no one was indicted for obstruction of justice.[43]

The Federal Statute

Under the federal statute, obstruction of justice contains six sections, entitled as follows:

> *Section 1503.* Influencing or Injuring Officer or Juror generally.
> *Section 1511.* Obstruction of State or Local Law Enforcement.
> *Section 1512.* Tampering with a Witness, Victim, or an Informant.
> *Section 1513.* Retaliating Against a Witness, Victim, or an Informant.
> *Section 1514.* Civil Action to Restrain Harassment of a Victim or Witness.
> *Section 1515.* Definitions for Certain Provisions.[44]

These statutes have been litigated frequently. In a 1987 case, a federal appellate court upheld the convictions of two attorneys charged with violating Section 1503 as well as the federal conspiracy statute. The evidence indicated that both attorneys tried to convince a convicted drug dealer that on payment of $50,000 they would have his four-year prison sentence reduced to fifteen months. The defendants were sentenced to five years for each conviction, with the sentences to be served concurrently.[45]

In a 1990 case, a federal court upheld a conviction for obstruction of justice under the federal code, Section 1503 just cited, as well as a conviction for conspiracy to obstruct justice (but sent the case back for resentencing), as described in this excerpt from *United States* v. *Moree*.[46]

United States v. Moree

In 1987 Robert Joiner, then Highway Commissioner for the Southern District of Mississippi, was indicted on eleven counts of extortion, bribery, and tax evasion. Earlier that year a federal grand jury had indicted Sim Ed Moree, a supervisor in Marion County, Mississippi, on charges of malfeasance while in public office. The indictments of both men occurred as part of "Operation Pretense," an investigation into corruption among Mississippi's public officials by the Federal Bureau of Investigation ("FBI").

In December 1987, Moree's original indictment was dismissed without prejudice to allow the government to list additional charges. After the dismissal and before he was reindicted, Moree approached Joiner with the story that the dismissal of his indictment had been secured by certain persons for a fee of $25,000. For $160,000, Moree claimed, these same persons would receive a maximum three-year sentence with two years suspended and a $25,000 fine. Moree told Joiner that he could not name these individuals and that they would work only through Moree. Joiner reported the offer to his attorney, who contacted the FBI.

With Joiner's cooperation, Agent King of the FBI conducted surveillance of conversations and meetings between Joiner and Moree which produced six audio tapes of Moree discussing the same offer with Joiner. Moree never divulged the identity of any coconspirator. The FBI did learn that Moree's brother, Ben Moree, watched Joiner's car during two of the meetings and followed Joiner after one of the meetings. During their third meeting, Moree accepted from Joiner $50,000 in cash which had been provided by the government. When Moree left the motel room, King arrested him. King then walked across the road to Ben Moree, who had been watching Joiner's car from his parked truck. Ben told King that he did not know the purpose of the meetings between his brother and Joiner, but that Sim Ed had told him to watch Joiner's car.

Sim Ed Moree was convicted of conspiring to obstruct justice and endeavoring to obstruct justice. . . . Moree appeals both his conviction and sentence. . . .

Moree contends that the government produced insufficient evidence to convict him of endeavoring to obstruct justice under 18 U.S.C., Section 1503. He states that no proof was offered of his ability or intention to fix Joiner's trial or of his ability to foresee the danger to the public's right to try Joiner which the success of his scam would cause. Moree's contention is frivolous. It is hard to imagine a more invidious obstruction of justice than an offer to bribe officials in control of the judicial system to fix the result of a trial. Had Moree's scam succeeded in deceiving Joiner, it cannot be seriously doubted that Joiner would have taken a different approach to his trial, including the entry of a falsely-induced guilty plea. Nor can it be doubted that Moree could foresee these unprofitable consequences for Joiner. The jury was presented with sufficient evidence to find Moree guilty of endeavoring to obstruct justice.

State Prosecutions

Defendants may be prosecuted for obstructing justice in state courts as well. A 1982 South Dakota case indicates that obstruction of justice by interfering with a police officer (a rather common type of charge under these statutes) may be accomplished without actual force. When police were trying to subdue several people who were disturbing the peace, one officer told the defendant to move out of the way. The defendant replied that he had "a right as a citizen to be there." The officer repeated his order twice; the defendant remained. He was arrested and subsequently convicted of obstructing justice.

In upholding the defendant's conviction, the South Dakota Supreme Court ruled that a threat to use "violence, force, physical interference, or obstacle would be sufficient to establish a violation of the statute." The court found that the defendant's refusal to move from the officer's path amounted to a physical interference with the officer's carrying out his duties to disperse the unruly crowd and therefore was an obstruction of justice.[47]

Counterfeiting

Counterfeiting means to forge, copy, or imitate coins, paper money, or anything else of value (such as stamps) without authority and with the intent to defraud. The crime involves an offense against property as well as an obstruction of justice. The federal code has a one-page listing of statutes under *Counterfeiting* and *Forgery*.

The crime of counterfeiting is the making of false money (or other value); a special intent to defraud is not required (although if shown it could constitute a separate offense). Being in possession of counterfeit materials also is a crime, though a lesser one, and often will require knowledge of the counterfeit nature of the materials. The federal statute regulating *uttering counterfeit foreign obligations or securities* requires the element of "knowingly and with intent to defraud" to constitute the crime of uttering, passing, or putting off "in payment or negotiation, any false, forged, or counterfeited bond, certificate, obligation, security, treasury note, bill, or promise to pay. . . ."[48]

Recent incidents of counterfeiting on a large scale in The People's Republic of China have been reported. In October 1993 half of twenty-one suspects in an alleged counterfeiting ring were arrested and $400,000 in fake cash was confiscated. The suspected leader of the troup, Meng Qingyu, was arrested in August. He boasted that "every time we printed, our forgeries got better." A Beijing newspaper indicated that the police crackdowns on counterfeiting were not sufficient.[49] Another news source claimed that the recording industry could be destroyed by the extensive counterfeiting of compact discs (CDs) in China. "These factories have the capacity to produce fifty-four million pirated compact discs a year and they are doing so."[50]

Resisting Arrest

According to the Model Penal Code, resisting arrest is "perhaps the most common form of obstruction of justice." At the time the American Law

Institute formulated its model code on this crime, state statutes varied greatly, some stated as broadly as covering any act of a public official or law enforcement officer in the discharge of official duty. Thus, one court upheld the conviction of a defendant who refused to "move along" when so ordered by the police, stating that any act "calculated in any appreciable degree to hamper or impede the police in the performance of their duties as they saw them" constituted a criminal offense.[51] Other statutes focused only on resisting arrest by a law enforcement officer.

It can be argued that individuals should be allowed to use peaceful means to resist an unlawful arrest because any unlawful restraint of liberty is unacceptable. On the other hand, it has been argued that the judicial process is sufficient for those who are arrested unlawfully and therefore they should not be able to take action to resist the arrest. The Model Penal Code does not permit resisting arrest by a *known* police officer even if that arrest is illegal. It provides for a criminal penalty only if the resistance creates a "substantial risk of bodily injury to the public servant or anyone else, or employs means justifying or requiring substantial force to overcome the resistance." The statute applies to an act committed "for the purpose of preventing a public servant from effecting a lawful arrest or discharging any other duty."[52]

The framers of the M.P.C. were attempting to avoid criminalizing any attempt to resist a lawful arrest. "This language exempts from liability nonviolent refusal to submit to arrest and such minor acts of resistance as running from a policeman or trying to shake free of his grasp. The policy judgment underlying this curtailment of coverage is that authorizing criminal punishment for every trivial act of resistance would invite abusive prosecution."[53]

The defined seriousness of resisting arrest, like the definition of the crime, varies. In New York, resisting arrest is a misdemeanor, although assaulting an officer with resulting injury is a felony.[54] Under the federal criminal code, the penalty for resisting arrest is increased if a deadly or dangerous weapon is used during the commission of the crime.[55]

Some states have passed "no-sock" rules; in those jurisdictions you may not resist even an unlawful arrest. Others permit resistance, but that resistance must be reasonable under the circumstances.[56] In jurisdictions that do not permit reasonable resistance to unlawful arrest, if a person who resists with force is charged with assault and battery, that person may invoke the defenses of resisting arrest or self-defense.

Escape and Related Offenses

Technically **escape** means to flee from, to avoid, to get away, but in some jurisdictions the crime is limited to getting away from police or prison authorities. That is, escape refers only to a person already in custody who leaves. Used in that sense, a person who is not yet arrested because he or she flees when a police officer approaches technically has not committed the crime of escape. In reality, however, escape is used more broadly. According to an earlier case, "The term 'escape' is not to be taken in its technical sense, which would imply, as is argued, that previously the person was in the officer's custody and had eluded his vigilance. It must be understood in its popular sense, which is, 'to flee from, to avoid, to get out of the way, etc.' "[57]

Even if one considers the word *escape* to apply only if the person is in custody or at least has been arrested, it is important to understand that *arrest* may occur when the officer has only touched the suspect. Thus, if "A, holding a warrant for the arrest of B, comes up behind B, taps B on the shoulder, and says 'I arrest you' [and B starts running and escapes], B is arrested." B's running constitutes an escape.[58]

The common law offense of escape is accomplished without force; the use of force converts the act to *breach of prison*, a more serious offense than the misdemeanor of escape. Modern statutes vary in their definitions; some include only fleeing from prisons or jails, whereas others include fleeing from arrest. The Model Penal Code uses the language "unlawfully removes himself from official detention or fails to return to official detention following temporary leave granted for a specific purpose or limited period." *Official detention* in the code includes detention for law enforcement purposes, including those found to be delinquent, and detention for extradition or deportation. It does not include probation or parole or "constraint incidental to release on bail." In the M.P.C., knowingly permitting or facilitating an escape is a crime, too. The M.P.C. provides penalties for providing inmates with escape implements and a penalty for inmates who are in possession of such implements.[59]

The New York statute illustrates a state code. This statute has three degrees of escape. Escape in the first degree (a felony) requires escape from a detention facility and that the accused be charged with or convicted of a felony. Second-degree escape is a felony but carries a lower maximum penalty. Third-degree escape is a misdemeanor.[60]

New York's penal code contains two degrees of *absconding from temporary release*, two degrees of *promoting prison contraband*, and separate statutes for *absconding from a furlough program* and *absconding from a community treatment facility*.[61]

Elements of Escape

In general, escape may be committed only if the actor is in *lawful* custody. Escape may occur also when a prisoner takes an unauthorized leave from an honor farm or fails to return from an authorized community visit or furlough, as indicated by the New York statutes. Because escape is a continuing offense, escapees may be charged with offenses if they fail to return to custody even though the original escapes are justified; that is, if prison conditions are such that inmates are in danger of serious bodily injury or death and if they have reported this to authorities who have not taken action. In these narrowly drawn circumstances in which escape may be justified, escapees must turn themselves in to authorities within a reasonable period after the escape.[62]

Escape requires a *physical act* of departing; therefore, refusal to work is a punishable offense within a prison but generally does not constitute escape. The *intent* requirement is met if it can be shown that the person went beyond the legal physical limits of confinement. "Accordingly, we hold that the prosecution fulfills its burden...if it demonstrates that an escapee knew his actions would result in his leaving physical confinement without permission."[63]

What, then, constitutes a lawful escape? In *People* v. *Trujillo*, the defendant claimed that he escaped from prison when he was threatened by inmates who demanded sexual favors after he had been gang-raped by six inmates. He said he reported the attacks to prison officials but that nothing was done. At his trial, the judge excluded all evidence that defendant wished to offer about the previous gang rape. On appeal, the conviction was reversed on the grounds that the defendant should have been allowed to introduce that evidence in support of his duress defense claim.[64]

In contrast, in an Iowa case the inmate's escape conviction was upheld even though he claimed he was attacked homosexually and that his life was threatened. The court adopted the rationale of a California case that established these rules for establishing a limited necessity-defense for escaping from prison:

1. Specific threats of death, bodily injury or sexual assault have been made;
2. The inmate did not have time to complain to authorities or had done so with no response;
3. There was insufficient time to resort to the courts for resolution of the issue;
4. The inmate did not use force or violence on innocent personnel or on prison personnel; and
5. Immediately after escaping, the inmate surrendered to law enforcement authorities.

In the Iowa case, the inmate was caught in hiding twenty-four hours after the escape and thus did not meet the fifth requirement.[65]

Related Crimes

The U.S. Fugitive Felon Act "makes it a federal crime to flee a state to avoid prosecution for a state felony and provides that violations...may be prosecuted only in the federal district in which the original state crime was allegedly committed." In addition, the act provides punishment for aiding and abetting the crime.[66] Focus 9.5 relates the facts of two well-known fugitives who eluded arrest, one for a long time and the other only briefly.

A related statute is the Parental Kidnapping Prevention Act of 1980, which permits federal authorities to issue warrants for parents who flee a state's jurisdiction to avoid prosecution for parental kidnapping, an increasingly common problem whose solution has eluded state authorities.[67]

Some offenses related to escape, such as aiding an escape or permitting an escape (for example, through negligence) have been mentioned already. Other related offenses are refusing to aid an officer, violating probation or parole, and jumping bail. Some jurisdictions provide separate penalties for these offenses. The Model Penal Code contains an offense that includes bail jumping and defaulting in required appearance, providing that a person

FOCUS 9.5   *Fugitives from Justice*

Two recent cases illustrate the success and perhaps the failure of becoming a fugitive from justice. The first involves Katherine Ann Power. For twenty-three years she fled law enforcement officials, becoming the subject of the longest womanhunt in U.S. history. She made the "Ten Most Wanted" list for fourteen years after she eluded arrest for her part in a bank robbery and the murder of a police officer who was the father of nine young children. In 1993 the woman known to her husband and

The longest womanhunt in history ended after twenty-three years when Katherine Ann Power surrendered to authorities in 1993. Power was accused of murder but was allowed to plead to manslaughter in the death of a police officer, along with charges of robbery.

teenage son as Alice Metzinger turned herself in to authorities who knew her as Katherine Ann Power.

During the years prior to her surrender Power turned to therapy in an effort to cope with her depression, a depression so deep that her therapist called her suicidal and described her as "the most clinically depressed person I've ever seen." Her participation in the robbery and murder haunted her to the point that eventually she surrendered. Her lawyer negotiated her surrender, which included a plea bargain under which Power entered a guilty plea to the lesser charge of manslaughter and to bank robbery. She is expected to spend less than five years in prison on her eight-to-twelve-year prison term.[1]

At the time of this writing, some argue that the second case is not a fugitive from justice; law officials disagree.

On Friday, 17 June 1994, police planned to arrest former football great O. J. Simpson for the brutal slayings of his ex-wife and one of her friends. Simpson's attorney had agreed that Simpson would surrender as soon as he was examined by his physicians. But Simpson and his long-time friend Al Cowlings slipped out of the house in which attorney Robert Shapiro and others were discussing the case. With Cowlings at the wheel of Simpson's Ford Bronco, the two began a drive that led police on a slow and orderly "chase" on Los Angeles freeways while millions watched in awe as news media reported that Simpson was in the back seat, holding a gun to his head.

As word of the pursuit spread, many went to the freeways to cheer O. J. and Al on their journey, apparently headed for Simpson's mother's home. Others went to Simpson's home to show their support for a hero they did not believe capable of killing. The saga ended when Cowlings drove back to Simpson's home, where both surrendered to police after negotiations with officers. The following Monday Simpson entered a not guilty plea to the murder charges. Simpson was denied bail and jailed. Cowlings was released after posting bail. Simpson could face the death penalty but, although prosecutors say they have a strong case for murder with special circumstances, it is question-able whether a defendant so popular as Simpson would ever face that punishment.[2]

[1] Summarized from media sources. For more information, see "The Return of the Fugitive," *Time* (27 September 1993), p. 60; and "Woman's Surrender in '70 Killing Ended After Year of Negotiations," *New York Times* (19 September 1993), p. 17.

[2] Summarized from media sources. For more information, see "Charged in 2 Murders, O. J. Simpson Vanishes," *New York Times* (18 June 1994), p. 1; "Prosecutor Sees Simpson Case As 'Solid' One," *New York Times* (20 June 1994), p. 1; "A Grim O. J. Simpson pleads 'Not Guilty' in Two Murders," *New York Times* (21 June 1994), p.1.

who is at liberty, either on bail or without bail, "upon condition that he will subsequently appear at a specified time and place, commits a misdemeanor if, without lawful excuse, he fails to appear at that time and place." The seriousness of the offense increases if the failure to appear involves a required appearance on a felony charge or for a disposition on a felony charge and if the individual failed to appear for the purpose of avoiding apprehension, trial, or punishment.[68]

Contempt

Contempt refers to willfully disobeying or disregarding a public official or engaging in behavior that disrupts, embarrasses, or humiliates the court or obstructs the judicial or other process. Contempt citations may be issued by the judicial or legislative branches of government. Contempt may be committed by any person; it is not limited to public officials. A variety of behaviors may constitute contempt. Focus 9.6 relates the facts of one contempt case.

The federal code defines *contempt* as follows:

1. misbehavior of any person in its presence or so near thereto as to obstruct the administration of justice;
2. misbehavior of any of its officers in their official transactions;
3. disobedience or resistance to its lawful writ, process, order, rule, decree, or command.

Conviction is punishable by fine or imprisonment.[69]

Other statutes refer to acts that embarrass, hinder, show disrespect, or obstruct the court (in contempt of court) or legislative process (contempt

FOCUS 9.6   Attorney Held in Contempt for Courtroom Language

An attorney admonished not to use any of a list of specific words during his defense of defendants charged with criminal trespass at an abortion clinic was held in contempt of court twenty times for his use of those words. The questions in which he utilized some of the forbidden words are as follows:

Is that the place where they empty the contents of a woman's uterus?

Are you familiar with those facilities where two persons go in and only one person comes out alive?

Can't we ask anything about the baby-killing, Your Honor?

What time do the first victims arrive?

How do you feel about making a living off the blood of babies?

Are your paychecks bloodstained?

Is the unborn baby a life you have sworn to protect?

Did you feel any obligation to protect the children who would be killed that day?

Officer, were you an unborn baby at some time in your life?

Wasn't the safety corridor the place where babies were taken to be killed?

Isn't that a poster of the unborn child sucking its thumb?

Zal [the attorney] occasionally was given one contempt citation for several questions. In sum, Zal was held in contempt twenty times.

It is not disputed that Zal knowingly and intentionally flouted the trial court's orders excluding certain defenses. At oral argument, Zal candidly admitted that he violated the orders in service of a "higher law." Zal's intent was to reach the jury on the precluded defense and prompt it to use its powers of nullification. The prohibited words were taken from Zal's attempts to accomplish the same mischief in previous cases.

[The case was on appeal on several issues, and the appellate court affirmed the lower court].

SOURCE: Zal v. Steppe, 968 F.2d 924 (9th Cir. 1992), *amended*, 1992 U.S. App. LEXIS, 17413 (9th Cir. 1992), *cert. denied*, 113 S.Ct. 656 (1992).

of Congress or other legislative bodies). It has been held that courts have inherent power to "enforce compliance with their lawful orders through civil contempt."[70]

Contempt may be classified as *direct* or *constructive, civil* or *criminal. Direct contempts* are those committed directly in the presence of the court (or legislative body), such as the use of foul language toward the judge. *Constructive or indirect contempts* are acts committed outside the court but that still degrade the proceedings. For example, when jurors violate the judge's order not to communicate with anyone other than other jurors or the bailiff while they are out of the courtroom, they may be cited for constructive contempt.

Much of the law of contempt applies to *civil* contempt and is not germane to this text, although it is significant to note that a person cited for civil contempt of court may be incarcerated, as illustrated by the Morgan-Foretich custody battle over their daughter, Hilary. Dr. Elizabeth Morgan spent two years in jail for civil contempt imposed by the judge when she refused to disclose the location of Hilary. Dr. Morgan claimed that the child's father, Dr. Eric Foretich, sexually abused the child during unsupervised visitation; she refused to let him see the child. She was released from jail only after Congress enacted a statute limiting jail terms to one year in civil contempt cases. The child was located later with her grandparents in New Zealand, where a court ordered that she must remain. Dr. Morgan moved to New Zealand to be with her child, and subsequently the father announced that in view of the New Zealand court ruling, he was abandoning his custody fight.

Dr. Morgan's father, psychiatrist William J. Morgan, has accused the police of taking bribes from Foretich and blames them for not arresting him. In August 1993, after someone broke into Morgan's office and stole files concerning the bitter custody battle, he renewed his claims of a conspiracy between the police and Foretich. In October 1993 Hilary's other grandparents, the Foretiches, "filed a libel and defamation suit against Capital Cities /ABC Inc. and the Landsburg Co., a Los Angeles–based production company, for their roles in creating and broadcasting a television docudrama about" the custody case between Hilary's parents. The suit alleges that the movie makes false accusations that the grandparents abused Hilary. The defendants deny the claim.[71]

Civil contempt refers to willful disobedience of a court order that was made for the benefit of the other party before the court (or legislative body). Civil contempt citations are in response to offenses that harm another party, not the court itself. *Criminal contempt* is imposed for acts that are viewed as offenses against the court (or legislative body), such as disruptive behavior during a trial or other proceeding. Some acts may constitute both civil and criminal contempt. In some cases, it is difficult to determine which is most appplicable.

This problem was illustrated in a case involving a university professor who served on a faculty evaluation committee. In that capacity he was ordered to answer questions in a deposition in the course of a sex-discrimination suit against the Board of Regents. When he refused to answer the questions, he was cited for criminal contempt, sentenced to ninety days in prison, and fined $100 per day for thirty days.

Originally a contempt citation was considered criminal, but later contempt was changed to civil because the purpose of the citation was not to punish or vindicate but to coerce the professor to testify. It was held that a coercive, nonpunitive fine is appropriate in civil contempt cases and that a jail or prison term is appropriate, too, as long as relief is permitted if the person decides to comply with the order for which the citation was granted. Finally, a person may not be jailed for contempt beyond the period of usefulness of the ordered testimony.[72]

Although some courts have held that criminal contempt is something "in the nature of, but not, a crime,"[73] the U.S. Supreme Court has indicated that contempt is a crime. In facing the issue of whether a defendant who requested one was entitled to a trial by jury when charged with criminal contempt, the Court made this comment in *Bloom* v. *Illinois*.[74]

Bloom v. *Illinois*

Until *United States* v. *Barnett*, the Court consistently upheld the constitutional power of the state and federal courts to punish any criminal contempt without a jury trial. These cases construed the Due Process Clause and the otherwise inclusive language of Article III and the Sixth Amendment as permitting summary trials in contempt cases because at common law contempt was tried without a jury and because the power of courts to punish for contempt without the intervention of any other agency was considered essential to the proper and effective functioning of the courts and to the administration of justice. . . .

[W]e must once again confront the broad rule that all criminal contempts can be constitutionally tried without a jury. Our deliberations have convinced us...that serious contempts are so nearly like other serious crimes that they are subject to the jury trial provisions of the Constitution, now binding on the States, and that the traditional rule is constitutionally infirm insofar as it permits other than petty contempts to be tried without honoring a demand for a jury trial. We accept the judgment of [our earlier cases] that criminal contempt is a petty offense unless the punishment makes it a serious one; but, in our view, dispensing with the jury in the trial of contempts subjected to severe punishments represents an unacceptable construction of the Constitution.

[The Court held that, because the defendant was sentenced to two years in prison, a severe sentence, he was entitled to his requested trial by jury.]

In a more recent case, the Supreme Court dealt with the issue of punishment in comparing civil and criminal contempt. In *Hicks* v. *Feiock*, the Court said:[75]

Hicks v. *Feiock*

[T]he critical features are the substance of the proceeding and the character of the relief that the proceeding will afford. "If it is for civil contempt the punishment is remedial, and for the benefit of the complainant. But if it is for criminal contempt the sentence is punitive, to vindicate the authority of the court." The character of the relief imposed is thus ascertainable by applying a few straightforward rules. If the relief provided is a sentence of imprisonment, it is remedial if 'the defendant stands committed unless and until he performs the affirmative act required by the court's order,' and is punitive if 'the sentence is limited to imprisonment for a definite period.' If the relief provided is a fine, it is remedial when it is paid to the complainant, and punitive when it is paid to the court, though a fine that would be payable to the court is also remedial when the defendant can avoid paying the fine simply by performing the affirmative act required by the court's order. These distinctions lead us to the fundamental proposition that criminal penalties may not be imposed on someone who has not been afforded the protections that the Constitution requires of such criminal proceedings, including the requirement that the offense be proved beyond a reasonable doubt.

Like many crimes, contempt may be only one offense for which a defendant may be charged or only one method of handling a particular situation. The frequently cited case of *Illinois* v. *Allen* illustrates this point. In this case, the defendant, charged with armed robbery, insisted on handling his own defense. But as the excerpt below indicates, he threatened the judge while showing disrespect. He was ordered removed from the courtroom and the trial continued in his absence, with appointed counsel handling the defense. Although the case is concerned primarily with the right to counsel and whether that right precludes the trial judge's order in this case, it illustrates a pattern of facts in which a criminal contempt citation may be issued or be considered inadequate to solve the problem.[76]

Illinois v. *Allen*

Before trial, the judge acceded to Allen's wish to conduct his own defense, although court-appointed counsel would "sit in and protect the record." During the [questioning of potential jurors] Allen "started to argue with the judge in a most abusive and disrespectful manner" when the judge directed him to confine his questioning to matters relating to the prospective juror's qualifications. The judge then asked appointed counsel to proceed with the examination, upon which Allen continued to talk and concluded his remarks by saying to the judge, "When I go out for lunchtime, you're going to be a corpse here." The judge then warned Allen that he would be removed from the courtroom if there was another outbreak of that sort. Allen continued to talk back, saying, "There's not going to be no trial, either. I'm going to sit here and you're going to talk and you can bring your shackles out and straight jacket and put them on me and tape my mouth, but it will do no good because there's not going to be no trial." After more abusive remarks, the judge ordered the trial to proceed in Allen's absence.

[Allen was permitted to return the next day; another outburst led to his removal and he was brought in only for identification purposes;

later he was permitted to return and stay provided he behaved. The Supreme Court continued.]

The Court of Appeals felt that the defendant's Sixth Amendment right to be present at his own trial was so "absolute" that, no matter how unruly or disruptive the defendant's conduct might be, he could never be held to have lost that right so long as he continued to insist upon it. . . We cannot agree. . . .

It is essential to the proper administration of criminal justice that dignity, order, and decorum be the hallmarks of all court proceedings in our country. The flagrant disregard in the courtroom of elementary standards of proper conduct should not and cannot be tolerated. We believe trial judges confronted with disruptive, contumacious, stubbornly defiant defendants must be given sufficient discretion to meet the circumstances of each case. No one formula for maintaining the appropriate courtroom atmosphere will be best in all situations. We think there are at least three constitutionally permissible ways for a trial judge to handle an obstreperous defendant like Allen: (1) bind and gag him, thereby keeping him present; (2) cite him for contempt; (3) take him out of the courtroom until he promises to conduct himself properly. [The Court said the evidence indicated that a criminal court citation would not have been sufficient in this case; therefore, removing him from the court was acceptable.]

Other Offenses against the Administration of Government

Several other offenses against the administration of government are included in various statutes. **Misprision of felony** refers to the act of failing to report or prosecute a known felony and taking positive steps to conceal that crime. According to the federal code, "Whoever, having knowledge of the actual commission of a felony cognizable by a court of the United States, conceals and does not as soon as possible make known the same to some judge or other person in civil or military authority under the United States, shall be fined not more than $500 or imprisoned not more than three years, or both."[77] This statute was interpreted by one federal court as follows:

> In order to sustain a conviction for misprision of a felony, the government must prove that a felony was committed, that [the defendant] had knowledge of the felony, that he failed to notify authorities, and that he took an affirmative step to conceal the crime. . . . [M]ere failure to report a felony is not sufficient. Violation of the misprision statute additionally requires some positive act designed to conceal from authorities the fact that a felony has been committed.[78]

Compounding a crime refers to an agreement for consideration not to prosecute or inform on another who has committed a felony. The Model Penal Code presents an example.

A person commits a misdemeanor if he accepts or agrees to accept any pecuniary benefit in consideration of refraining from reporting to law enforcement authorities the commission or suspected commission of any offense or information relating to an offense. It is an affirmative defense to prosecution under this Section that the pecuniary benefit did not exceed an amount which the actor believed to be due as restitution or indemnification for harm caused by the offense.[79]

SUMMARY

This chapter explores a variety of offenses against the orderly administration of government, including legislative as well as judicial processes. It begins with treason, the highest crime against the government. To be convicted of treason against the U.S. government, a defendant must owe an allegiance to the federal government. An act must be committed that violates that allegiance, and there must be a criminal intent. Two witnesses must testify to the crime unless the defendant confesses.

Treason may be committed against a state as well. States are free to define this crime within their own statutes as long as those statutes do not violate the U.S. Constitution. Like the federal government, some state constitutions include treason, thereby indicating the seriousness of the offense.

Several crimes related to treason are discussed. *Misprision of treason* refers to concealing a known treasoner. *Sedition*, a crime that was prosecuted more frequently in the early years of the United States, has been limited by court interpretations of the First Amendment right to free speech. But that right does not include the right to communications aimed at stirring up treason or defaming the government.

The common law crimes of *perjury* and *subornation of perjury*, limited to false statements under oath in a judicial proceeding, have been expanded by statutes to cover other proceedings, such as grand jury and congressional hearings. Some jurisdictions accomplish the same purpose by enacting separate statutes, such as *false swearing* or *false declarations before a grand jury*, rather than expanding the common law crime of perjury.

In the English common law, *bribery* was more limited in scope that it is today. Common law bribery referred to offering, receiving, giving, or soliciting anything of value for the purpose of influencing action by *public officials*. It referred only to the judge who took the bribe. Modern statutes have extended bribery to include the one who makes as well as the one who receives the bribe. Some statutes have extended the crime to include people other than public officials.

In many cases bribery is combined with other crimes, such as *official misconduct in office*, which refers to any willful, unlawful behavior by public officials in the course of their official duties. To be convicted of official misconduct in office, however, an official must have been acting *under color of law;* that is, during the course of official duties. Another crime that makes administration of justice more difficult is *obstructing justice*. This crime takes many forms. Some of the more common forms are tampering with a jury to try to influence jurors' votes; suppressing or refusing to produce evidence relevant to a trial; and interfering with an officer while he or she is attempting to perform official duties. It may include bribery, the attempt to bribe, or the conspiracy to bribe a public official.

Counterfeiting and *being in possession of counterfeit goods* constitute federal and state crimes. Resisting arrest or other law enforcement orders, like other crimes discussed in this chapter, may differ in degree of seriousness and penalties from state to state. These crimes, along with *escape*, may be interpreted differently. Escape statutes have been interpreted by some recent decisions to exclude escapes by prisoners made as the result of reasonable fears for their safety while incarcerated. But where courts have precluded conviction for escape in these cases, they have detailed the circumstances to which the statutes do not apply. Generally, this means that the inmates must turn themselves in to authorities within a reasonable period after the escape.

Criminal contempt, the willful disobeying or disregarding of the orders of a judicial or legislative official, provides a powerful weapon for public officials (for example, judges) in controlling what happens in court or in legislative session. Witnesses, defendants, even attorneys who refuse to obey the orders of the court may be cited for criminal or civil contempt and punished accordingly.

Other crimes, such as misprision of felony and compounding a crime are included within the broad category of crimes referring to the administration of government.

The crimes discussed in this chapter, like those of some of the other chapters, may overlap other offenses. In particular, this is true of the relationship between offenses against the administration of government and the crimes discussed in Chapter 10. A defendant may be charged with aiding and abetting, soliciting, or conspiring to commit offenses against the administration of government as well as other crimes. It is important, therefore, to devote a chapter to anticipatory offenses.

STUDY QUESTIONS

1. Explain the elements of *treason,* and contrast that crime with *misprision of treason*.
2. What is *sedition*? What are the First Amendment problems with prosecuting defendants for this crime? Define *espionage*.
3. Distinguish *perjury, subornation of perjury*, and *false swearing*.
4. Explain the different types of bribery and how modern bribery statutes differ from the English common law offense.
5. Discuss the impact of bribery statutes on politics.
6. What is meant by *official misconduct in office*? How does the phrase *under color of law* affect the crime? Discuss one example.
7. Explain what is meant by the crime *obstruction of justice*.
8. What is meant by *counterfeiting*?
9. Why do we criminalize *resisting arrest*? When, if ever, is it lawful to resist arrest?
10. What are the elements of *escape*?
11. What is the purpose of the federal Fugitive Felon Act and the Parental

Kidnapping Prevention Act of 1980?

12. Distinguish between *civil* and *criminal contempt* and *direct* and *constructive contempt*. Is a prison sentence appropriate for civil contempt? For criminal attempt? Are there any procedural differences in imposing a prison sentence for each?

13. Explain what is meant by *misprision of felony* and *compounding a crime*.

14. Some of the crimes discussed in this chapter (or at least some of the degrees of those crimes) are misdemeanors, not felonies. Do you think this is a proper categorization of the seriousness of these offenses? Explain.

ENDNOTES

1. See James G. Wilson, "Chaining the Leviathan: The Unconstitutionality of Executing Those Convicted of Treason," *University of Pittsburgh Law Review* 45 (1983): 99–179. This article includes a summary of the evolution of the treason statute. The federal treason statute is contained in the U.S. Code, Title 18, Section 2381 (1994).

2. William Blackstone, *Commentary on the Laws of England*, vol. 4 (Special Edition, Birmingham, Ala.: Legal Classics Library, 1983), p. 75.

3. Ibid.

4. Rosenberg v. United States, 346 U.S. 273 (1952). The federal Espionage Act is found in U.S. Code, Title 18, Section 793 *et seq.* (1994). For a discussion of treason, see James Willard Hurst, *The Law of Treason in the United States* (Westport, Conn.: Greenwood Press, 1971). For a brief discussion of this crime, see James Willard Hurst, "Treason," in *Encyclopedia of Crime and Justice*, vol. 4, ed. Sanford H. Kadish (New York: Free Press, 1983), pp. 1559–1562. For information on espionage, see H. H. A. Cooper and Lawrence J. Redlinger, *Catching Spies: Principles and Practices of Counterespionage* (Boulder, Colo.: Paladin Press, 1988).

5. "A Different Verdict," *Houston Chronicle* (11 August 1993), p. 2.

6. Hanauer v. Doane, 79 U.S. 342, 347 (1870).

7. Kawakita v. United States, 343 U.S. 717 (1952), *reh'g. denied*, 344 U.S. 850 (1952).

8. D'Aquino v. United States, 192 F.2d 338 (9th Cir. 1951), *cert. denied*, 343 U.S. 935 (1952).

9. Cal. Penal Code, Section 37 (1994).

10. Cal. Penal Code, Title 3, Section 38 (1994).

11. U.S. Code, Title 18, Sections 2383, *et seq.* (1994).

12. Stromberg v. California, 283 U.S. 359 (1931).

13. U.S. Code, Title 18, Section 2385 (1994).

14. Blackstone, *Commentaries on the Laws of England*, Vol. 4, p. 137.

15. See U.S. Code, Title 18, Sections 1621 and 1622 (1994).

16. U.S. Code, Title 18, Section 1623 (1994).

17. United States v. Nixon, 816 F.2d 1022 (5th Cir. 1987), *cert. denied*, 484 U.S. 1026 (1988).

18. "Disbarred Judge Returns to Law," *Tallahassee Democrat* (26 September 1993), p. 3.

19. See United States v. Adams, 870 F.2d 1140 (6th Cir. 1989), *reh'g. denied*, 1989 U.S. App. LEXIS 4271, and *on remand*, 722 F.Supp. 408 (W.D. Tenn. 1989), reversing a conviction on this issue, and State v. Paxson, 861 F.2d 730 (D.C. App. 1988), affirming the conviction.

20. Model Penal Code, Section 241.1 and Commentary.

21. See Model Penal Code, Sections 241.3–241.9.

22. Lord Mansfield, quoted in Rollin M. Perkins and Ronald N. Boyce, *Criminal Law*, 3d ed. (Mineola, N.Y.: Foundation Press, 1982), p. 527. See this source for more background information on bribery. See also John T. Noonan, Jr., *Bribes* (New York: Macmillan, 1984).

23. U.S. Constitution, Article II, Section 4.

24. New York Penal Code, Section 180.15 (1994).

25. United States v. Perrin, 580 F.2d 730, 733 (5th Cir. 1978), *aff'd.*, 444 U.S. 37 (1979).

26. After the bribe was discovered, a small boy is said to have approached "Shoeless" Joe Jackson and exclaimed, "Say it ain't so, Joe." *Chicago Herald and Examiner* (30 September 1920), cited in United States v. Perrin, 580 F.2d 730, 734 (5th Cir. 1978), note 6, *aff'd.*, 444 U.S. 37 (1979).

27. U.S. Code, Title 18, Section 224 (1993). See also President's Commission on Organized Crime, *Organized Crime and Gambling* (Washington, D.C.: U.S. Government Printing Office, June 1985), pp. 847–849.

28. U.S. Code, Title 18, Section 201(a)(3) (1994).

29. United States v. Muntain, 610 F.2d 964 (D.C.App. 1979).

30. Comment, "The Federal Bribery Statute and Special Interest Campaign Contributions," *Journal of Criminal Law and Criminology* 79 (Winter 1989): 1347, 1348.

31. Buckley v. Valeo, 424 U.S. 1, 28 (1976). The federal bribery statute is codified in U.S. Code, Title 18, Section 201 (1994).

32. Comment, "The Federal Bribery Statute and Special Interest Campaign Contributions," p. 1373.

33. Quoted in the *Tulsa Tribune* (23 September 1987), p. 2. See also "Charges of Favoritism, Tests of Credibility at House Ethics Panel," *Washington Post* (15 December 1987), p. 21.

34. See Wells v. State, 129 S.W.2d 203 (Tenn. 1939).

35. Crews v. United States, 160 F.2d 746, 750 (5th Cir. 1947).

36. State v. Seitz, 14 A.2d 710, 711 (Del. 1940).

37. U.S. Code, Title 18, Section 242 (1994).

38. Miller v. United States, 404 F.2d 611 (5th Cir. 1968), *cert. denied*, 394 U.S. 963 (1969), footnotes and citations omitted.

39. Civil actions are brought under U.S. Code, Title 42, Sections 1983 and 1985 (1993). For a discussion of civil liability regarding civil rights issues as related specifically to police, see Victor E. Kappler, *Critical Issues in Police Civil Liability* (Prospect Heights, Illinois: Waveland, 1993).

40. See United States v. Brown, 688 F.2d 596 (9th Cir. 1982).

41. Model Penal Code, Section 242.1.

42. "Convicted Judge Returned to Jail," *New York Times* (20 February 1993), p. 19; *New York Times* (13 April 1993), p. 15.

43. "Spotlight on the Senator: What Did Teddy Know?" *Newsweek* (27 May 1991), p. 21; "Jury Clears Friend of Kennedy Family," *New York Times* (20 December 1991), p. 10.

44. U.S. Code Ann., Title 18, Section 1503 *et seq.* (1994).

45. United States v. Machi, 811 F.2d 991 (7th Cir. 1987).

46. United States v. Moree, 897 F.2d 1329 (5th Cir. 1990), *appeal after remand*, 928 F.2d 654 (5th Cir. 1991).

47. State v. Wiedeman, 321 N.W.2d 539 (S.D. 1982).

48. U.S. Code, Title 18, Section 479 (1994).

49. "Largest Ever Counterfeiting Ring Rounded up in China," United Press International news release (4 October 1993), BC cycle.

50. "Chinese Factories Turn out Counterfeit CDs by the Million," *The Gazette* (Montreal) (7 October 1993), p. 9D.

51. State v. Taylor, 118 A.2d 36, 48 (N.J. 1955), quoted in the Model Penal Code Commentary, p. 212.

52. Model Penal Code, Section 242.2.

53. Model Penal Code and Commentaries, Part 2, vol. 3, p. 214.

54. New York Penal Code, Sections 205.30 and 120.05 (1994).

55. U.S. Code, Title 18, Section 111 (1994).

56. See, for example, State v. Mulvihill, 270 A.2d 277 (N.J. 1970).

57. Lewis v. State, 40 Tenn. 127, 147 (1859).

58. American Law Institute, *Restatement of the Law, Torts 2d*, vol. 1, Section 112, Comment (St. Paul, Minn.: American Law Institute Publishers, 1965), pp. 112–113.

59. Model Penal Code, Sections 242.6 and 242.7.

60. New York Penal Code, Sections 205.05, 205.10, and 205.15 (1994).

61. New York Penal Code, Section 205.16, *et. seq.* (1994).

62. See United States v. Bailey, 444 U.S. 394 (1980), *cert. denied sub. nom.*, 459 U.S. 853 (1982). With regard to prison escapes, see Herbert Fingarette, "Victimization: A Legalist Analysis of Coercion, Deception, Undue Influence, and Excusable Prison Escape," *Washington and Lee Law Review* 42 (Winter 1985): 65–118.

63. United States v. Bailey, 444 U.S. 394 (1980), *cert. denied sub. nom.*, 459 U.S. 853 (1982).

64. People v. Trujillo, 586 P.2d 235 (Colo.App. 1978).

65. State v. Reese, 272 N.W.2d 863 (Iowa 1978), following People v. Lovercamp, 118 Cal.Rptr. 110 (Cal.4th Dist. 1974).

66. United States v. Thurman, 687 F.2d 11 (3d Cir. 1982). The statute is codified in U.S. Code, Title 18, Section 1073 (1993).

67. See Beach v. Smith, 535 F.Supp. 560 (S.D.Cal. 1982), *later proceeding*, 743 F.2d 1303 (9th Cir. 1984). The statute is codified in U.S. Code, Title 28, Section 1738A.

68. Model Penal Code, Section 242.8.

69. U.S. Code, Title 18, Section 401 (1994).

70. Shillitani v. United States, 384 U.S. 364 (1966).

71. "Metropolitan: That's Politics," *Washington Times* (18 August 1993), p. 3B; "Foretich, et al., v. Capital Cities/ABC Inc., et al.," *Legal Times* (11 October 1993), p. 13.

72. *In re* Dinnan, 625 F.2d 1146 (5th Cir. 1980).

73. Flannagan v. Jepson, 158 N.W. 641, 642 (Iowa 1916).

74. Bloom v. Illinois, 391 U.S. 194, 195 (1968), citations omitted.

75. Hicks v. Feiock, 485 U.S. 624 (1988), *remanded*, 215 Cal.App.3d 141 (4th Dist. 1989), *rev. denied*, 1990 LEXIS 112 (Cal. 1990).

76. Illinois v. Allen, 397 U.S. 337 (1970), *reh'g. denied*, 398 U.S. 915 (1970).

77. U.S. Code, Title 18, Section 4 (1994).

78. United States v. Davila, 698 F.2d 715 (5th Cir. 1983), *reh'g. denied*, 703 F.2d 557 (5th Cir. 1983).

79. Model Penal Code, Section 242.5.

Chapter 10

Anticipatory Offenses and Parties to Crime

Outline

Key Terms

abettor
accessory after the fact
accessory before the
    fact
accomplice
aid and abet
attempt
complicity

conspiracy
criminal facilitation
criminal protector
criminal solicitation
inchoate crimes
inciter
perpetrator

Pinkerton rule
principal
principal in the
    first degree
principal in the
    second degree
Wharton rule

Introduction

The first four chapters of this text introduce criminal law—its elements and its defenses. Chapters 5-9 focus on specific crimes, many of which were common law crimes carried over into statutory crimes. These crimes of violence and of property—constituting felonies, misdemeanors, or even less serious offenses—exist only when the criminal *act* and the criminal *state of mind* concur to produce a *result*.

It is possible, however, that individuals may engage in acts that are dangerous to society because they indicate an inclination to commit a crime even though the target crime is never accomplished. For example, an attempt to commit rape is a serious threat to the potential victim and society even if rape is not committed. Such anticipatory, uncompleted acts, or incipient crimes, which frequently lead to other crimes, are called **inchoate crimes** and consist of criminal *solicitation*, criminal *attempts*, and criminal *conspiracy*. Because all are considered a threat to society, it is important to consider each in light of the purposes of criminal law discussed previously.

If deterrence is a goal, will deterrence be accomplished by criminalizing inchoate crimes? Is deterrence more likely if the criminal code permits a defense of abandonment or renunciation to any or all of the inchoate crimes? Is it reasonable for society to demand retribution from those who *plan* to commit a crime or who *conspire* with another to commit that crime but who never go any further? What about attempts? Should a lack of success in attempted murder enable the actor to be free of criminal liability?

In reviewing the purposes of criminal law, it is important to consider whether all who are involved in a crime should have the same criminal liability. Should punishment be more severe for the individual who instigates, plans, leads, and makes arrangements to commit a crime than it is for a person who only assists during the latter stages of the criminal act? The role of various parties to crimes is another focus of this chapter. It is clear that many statutes impose criminal liability for inchoate crimes. It is clear also that in many cases the law distinguishes among parties to a crime in terms of the role each played in the commission of that crime.

Criminal Solicitation

Criminal solicitation is the asking, inciting, ordering, urgently requesting, or enticing of another person to commit a crime. The solicited crime does not have to be committed for the crime of solicitation to occur. Perhaps most familiar among such crimes are soliciting a bribe or soliciting for prostitution, but the act may involve soliciting for murder or other serious crimes. Solicitation was a misdemeanor in the English common law.

The need for the crime of solicitation, apart from the crime for which the solicitation is made, is explained in the New York State Criminal Code's commentary to its criminal solicitation statute. If A entices B to kill X, and B does kill X, both A and B may be charged with *murder*. If A entices B to kill X and B attempts to do so but fails, both A and B may be charged with *attempted murder*. If B succumbs to the enticement and agrees to murder X and if A and B discuss how the murder should be committed, but B does not even attempt to murder X, both A and B may be charged with *conspiracy to commit murder*. But if A urges, entices, encourages, demands, or uses other methods of persuading B to kill X, but B does not succumb, B has not committed a crime. Unless there is a solicitation statute, A has not committed a crime either.

To deal with this last example, some jurisdictions sought to punish A under attempt statutes. If A wanted X's barn burned and asked B to do that and gave him a match, A was charged with attempted arson, although he had not attempted to commit the crime. Clearly another provision was needed. New York solved the problem by passing a criminal solicitation statute: "A person is guilty of criminal solicitation. . . when, with intent that another person engage in conduct constituting a crime, he solicits, requests, commands, importunes or otherwise attempts to cause such other person to engage in such conduct."[1]

When the statute was passed, New York had three degrees of criminal solicitation, with the crime considered more serious as the crime solicited became more serious. Later, criminal solicitation was divided into five degrees, with the relative ages of the solicitor and the solicitee taken into consideration.[2] The degrees of solicitation and penalties for the crime were increased in 1978 "because of the growing number of cases in which adults utilized juveniles in criminal activities to limit their own exposure to prosecution."[3]

The framers of the Model Penal Code articulated this reason for including criminal solicitation. "Purposeful solicitation presents dangers calling for preventive intervention and is sufficiently indicative of a disposition towards criminal activity to call for liability."[4]

Elements and Defenses

Criminal solicitation requires a purpose to promote or facilitate the commission of a crime as well as a command, encouragement, demand, request, or other means of enticing another to commit the crime. That incitement may be directed at a crowd, not just a particular individual.

In some jurisdictions the communication of criminal solicitation may qualify even if it is not accomplished. According to the Model Penal Code, "It is immaterial. . . that the actor fails to communicate with the person he solicits to commit a crime if his conduct was designed to effect such communication."[5] The rationale is that the harm to society occurs when a person attempts to communicate criminal solicitation but is not very successful in doing so. The M.P.C. includes uncommunicated solicitation as criminal solicitation; other statutes classify this as *attempted criminal solicitation*. The following case illustrates.[6]

State v. *Lee*

Defendant appeals his conviction for solicitation to commit robbery in the first degree. He argues that a letter that was not delivered can support, at most, a conviction for attempted solicitation. We agree.

In July, 1989, defendant, while in jail, wrote letters to an acquaintance who was in the Hillcrest Juvenile Center, outlining plans to rob a store and a residence. The letters were intercepted by Hillcrest personnel and never reached their intended recipient. The first intercepted letter stated:

> I wrote about two weeks ago. I guess you didn't get it. So, I'll tell you again. The job I got set up will get us some guns. On the other page is a picture of the place. And then I want to go to Washington. Okay.

The letter also described plans for robbing a store and burglarizing a residence. The other letter intercepted at Hillcrest also discussed plans for a "job." Defendant admitted that he wrote the letters.

Defendant first argues that there was insufficient evidence to convict him of solicitation. He contends that the evidence was insufficient for the court to find that he had the requisite "intent of causing another to engage in specific conduct constituting a crime" [as required by statute]. Defendant failed to move for a judgment of acquittal, and we decline to address the issue.

Defendant next contends that, because the letters were never received by the addressee, he did not commit the crime of solicitation, but only attempted solicitation. Solicitation is defined in [the state statute]:

> A person commits the crime of solicitation if with the intent of causing another to engage in specific conduct constituting a crime punishable as a felony or as a Class A misdemeanor or an attempt to commit such felony or Class A misdemeanor the person commands or solicits such other person to engage in that conduct.

The statute contains two elements: *mens rea* and *actus reus*. Defendant was found by the trial court to have the specified state of mind. He argues, however, that the *actus reus* proved by the state was insufficient to support a conviction, because the intercepted letters do not constitute a completed solicitation.

The statute provides that a person is guilty of solicitation if that person "commands or solicits" another to engage in criminal conduct constituting a felony or a Class A misdemeanor. However, the terms "command" or "solicit" are not defined in the statute, and it is unclear whether they include circumstances where a communication is not received. Our function is to construe the statute to carry out the legislature's intent. The issue of an unreceived solicitation is not specifically discussed in the commentary to the statute. It is noted in the commentary, however, that the terms 'request' and 'encourage' were not included in the statute, because the drafters were concerned that such language might be "too open-ended."

It is also noted in the commentary that the word "solicits" was used "because it is an historic legal term that would carry with it the traditional limitations that are intended." At common law, solicitation probably required that the communication be completed:

> What if the solicitor's message never reaches the person intended to be solicited, as where an intermediary fails to pass on the communication or the solicitor's letter is intercepted before it reaches the addressee? The act is nonetheless criminal, although it may be that the solicitor must be prosecuted for an attempt to solicit on such facts.

Solicitation in the Oregon Penal Code was based in part on the Model Penal Code. Significantly, the legislature did not adopt the provision of the Model Penal Code that specifically provides that solicitation may be based on an incomplete communication.

We conclude that a completed communication is required to prove the crime of solicitation. Accordingly, defendant's conviction for solicitation was error. An attempt to solicit is necessarily included in the completed crime. Because the trial court found defendant guilty of acts constituting attempted solititation, no new trial is required.

Conviction for solicitation vacated; remanded with instructions to enter a judgment of conviction for attempted solicitation and for resentencing.

Some jurisdictions require that the crime solicited must be a serious one—for example, a felony—whereas others, such as the Model Penal Code, follow the common law and include any crime. Penalties vary, with some statutes providing a lesser penalty for solicitation than for the solicited crime. Others, such as the Model Penal Code, provide the same penalty as that for the most serious crime solicited, with the exception of capital crimes and first-degree felonies. In those cases, the attempt may be punished as a second-degree felony. This provision applies also to criminal attempt and criminal conspiracy.[7] Some jurisdictions require corroboration of witnesses or circumstances to substantiate the *mens rea* for criminal solicitation.

The *mens reas* for criminal solicitation is one of specific intent. Thus, it is not sufficient to joke to another about committing a crime, even if that person commits the crime suggested. To constitute the crime of solicitation, the communication must be made with the intent to entice the target party to commit the crime. According to the Model Penal Code, "It is not enough for a person to be aware that his words may lead to a criminal act or even to be quite sure they will do so; it must be the actor's purpose that the crime be committed."[8]

Some states permit the defense of renouncing criminal solicitation. For example, Arizona permits the defense but requires that there must be a voluntary *and* complete renunciation of the criminal intent, which may be shown by meeting *both* of these requirements:

1. Notification of the person solicited.
2. Giving a timely warning to law enforcement authorities or otherwise making a reasonable effort to prevent the conduct or result solicited.[9]

The Model Penal Code, which also permits the defense of renunciation to criminal solicitation, requires that the solicitor persuade the solicitee not to commit the crime or in some other way prevent "the commission of the crime, under circumstances manifesting a complete and voluntary renunciation of his criminal purpose."[10] Presumably this action means that the person no longer is dangerous to society, and therefore punishment is not necessary.

Criminal Attempt

In some states that do not have criminal solicitation statutes, earlier courts held that criminal soliciting could be penalized under criminal **attempt** statutes. But criminal attempt requires that the actor go beyond mere preparation to commit a crime, and this is not true of solicitation. "To constitute an attempt there must. . . be an act of perpetration. . . . However, solicitation is preparation rather than perpetration."[11] Because criminal attempt requires going beyond "mere preparation," it may be viewed as a serious act for which criminal punishment should be provided. Criminal attempt involves a step toward the commission of a crime *and* a specific intent to commit that crime.

Although in early English common law attempt was not a crime, it was recognized as a common law crime in a 1784 decision that involved a defendant renter who set a lighted candle and combustible materials inside the rental house with the intent to burn it. The prosecution did not allege that the house burned; so, the crime of arson was not complete. Against the defense that there was no crime of attempting to commit a crime, the court held, "The intent may make an act, innocent in itself, criminal; nor is the completion of an act, criminal in itself, necessary to constitute criminality."[12]

In a later case, the English court recognized the crime of attempt by stating that "All offenses of a public nature, that is, all such acts or attempts as tend to the prejudice of the community, are indictable."[13] Attempt was recognized as a misdemeanor whether the attempt was to commit a misdemeanor or a felony.

Today most states have statutes criminalizing attempts to commit crimes. The nature of the statutes varies. Some follow the Model Penal Code's definition (see Focus 10.1), referring to any crime. Some require that the attempt must have been to commit a *serious* crime, a felony, or any of an enumerated list of serious crimes.

In previous codes, a separate offense would be listed, for example, attempted rape or attempted murder. Today the trend is toward one general attempt statute.[14] The penalties for attempts vary. In New York the penalty for attempt varies according to the crime attempted. Some jurisdictions use a formula such as a penalty consisting of one-half the penalty of the attempted crime. The Model Penal Code provides the same penalty as the attempted crime with the exception that an attempt to commit a capital

FOCUS 10.1   Criminal Attempt: The Model Penal Code

Section 5.01. Criminal Attempt

(1) **Definition of Attempt**. A person is guilty of an attempt to commit a crime if, acting with the kind of culpability otherwise required for commission of the crime, he:

    (a) purposely engages in conduct which would constitute the crime if the attendant circumstances were as he believes them to be; or

    (b) when causing a particular result is an element of the crime, does or omits to do anything with the purpose of causing or with the belief that it will cause such result without further conduct on his part; or

    (c) purposely does or omits to do anything which, under the circumstances as he believes them to be, is an act or omission constituting a substantial step in a course of conduct planned to culminate in his commission of the crime.

(2) **Conduct Which May Be Held Substantial Step Under Subsection (1)(c)**. Conduct shall not be held to constitute a substantial step under Subsection (1)(c) of this Section unless it is strongly corroborative of the actor's criminal purpose. Without negating the sufficiency of other conduct, the following, if strongly corroborative of the actor's criminal purpose, shall not be held insufficient as a matter of law:

    (a) lying in wait, searching for or following the contemplated victim of the crime;

    (b) enticing or seeking to entice the contemplated victim of the crime to go to the place contemplated for its commission;

    (c) reconnoitering the place contemplated for the commission of the crime;

    (d) unlawful entry of a structure, vehicle enclosure in which it is contemplated that the crime will be committed;

    (e) possession of materials to be employed in the commission of the crime, which are specially designed for such unlawful use or which can serve no lawful purpose of the actor under the circumstances;

    (f) possession, collection or fabrication of materials to be employed in the commission of the crime, at or near the place contemplated for its commission, where such possession, collection or fabrication serves no lawful purpose of the actor under the circumstances;

    (g) soliciting an innocent agent to engage in conduct constituting an element of the crime.

(3) **Conduct Designed to Aid Another in Commission of a Crime**. A person who engages in conduct designed to aid another to commit a crime which would establish his complicity under Section 2.06 if the crime were committed by such other person, is guilty of an attempt to commit the crime, although the crime is not committed or attempted by such other person. . . .

crime or a felony of the first degree is a felony of the second degree and punished accordingly.[15]

Elements of Attempt

The first element of attempt is that the defendant must have had the requisite *mens rea* or criminal intent. Focus 10.2 contains the facts of a case that raises the issue of the intent requirement for attempt.

The intent required for attempt is a specific intent.[16] It is not sufficient that the defendant had a general criminal intent. "One cannot attempt to commit an act which one does not intend to commit."[17] Legally one cannot attempt to commit a crime that does not require a specific intent. Thus, criminal attempt excludes crimes that are the result of recklessness. The "crime of attempted reckless endangerment is nonexistent as it is a nonintent offense."[18]

The problem with the intent requirement occurs when the defendant has been charged with attempted murder but the victim of the crime has not died. One may be convicted of murder without proof of a specific intent to kill that particular victim. As stated previously, a conviction is appropriate in some cases in which the defendant has not exhibited an intent to kill but has engaged in reckless behavior indicating indifference to human life or has manifested an intent only to inflict great bodily harm although death occurred. However, with these same facts and a victim who does not die, a charge of attempted murder is inappropriate. "[W]hile a person may be guilty of murder though there was no actual intent to kill, he cannot be guilty of an attempt to commit murder unless he has a specific intent to kill."[19]

Charges of attempting to commit a crime, such as attempted murder, may be appropriate in some cases.

FOCUS 10.2   May an Involuntary Act Be Intended?

One of the elements of the crime of attempt is that the act requires a criminal intent. The intent issue arose in a case involving a defendant who went to the home of a person he had met previously, robbed the victim at gunpoint, and then fired several shots, wounding but not killing the victim. The defendant was charged with robbery and attempted murder; he was convicted of robbery and attempted involuntary manslaughter (as a lesser included charge in attempted murder). The defendant claimed on appeal that he shot out of fear for his own life and that, further-

more, there is no such crime as attempted involuntary manslaughter.

The appellate court agreed with the defense, indicating that it is impossible legally to commit attempted involuntary manslaughter, because attempt requires an intent and involuntary manslaughter by definition is an unintentional killing. It is logically impossible to attempt to commit an involuntary act.[1]

[1.] See Bailey v. State, 688 P.2d 320 (Nev. 1984). See also Curry v. State, 792 P.2d 396 (Nev. 1990).

Under these facts, attempt to commit the crime (murder) requires a higher intent than is required for conviction of the target crime. This position has been questioned, with leading authorities in the field of criminal law pointing out the harm to society caused when people who are grossly negligent in their conduct escape criminal liability because the attempt statutes do not cover their acts. Other scholars note that even if the criminal law is used in such cases, perhaps it should be done in ways other than by redefining the crime of attempt.[20]

A similar problem may occur even if the victim does not die. The intent requirement for murder may be found in felony murder, a death that occurs when one is committing another felony (sometimes a serious felony is required), but some courts have held that the intent requirement for attempted murder is not met by implied malice or felony murder.[21]

The second element of attempt is that there must be a criminal act. U.S. criminal law does not permit criminal punishment for thoughts. Some act (or failure to act where there is a legal duty to act) must be taken. Usually courts require that the defendant went beyond *preparation* and moved toward *perpetration* of the crime, distinguished by an earlier court as follows: "The preparation consists in devising or arranging the means or measures necessary for the commission of the offense; the attempt is the direct movement toward the commission after the preparations are made."[22]

The difference between preparation and perpetration is of critical legal significance in that unless perpetration has occurred, there is no criminal attempt. In the following excerpt from *United States* v. *Cartlidge*, the federal court discusses various tests for making this determination. The defendant in *Cartlidge* was a former law enforcement officer who argued that the evidence used to convict him of taking a bribe to provide protection for a purported marijuana smuggling operation was not sufficient to support his conviction for attempting to aid and abet (discussed later in this chapter) in the possession and distribution of marijuana. The court disagreed.

The appellate court held that the defendant's acts of "silence and providing warnings when needed, promising assistance, assurances of ability to provide protection against law enforcement interference, and supplying information about a convenient time for the operation, coupled with the acceptance of payment for these services" went beyond preparation and supported an attempt to aid and abet a federal crime. The court's discussion of the issue is enlightening.[23]

United States v. *Cartlidge*

A recurrent problem in determining whether a defendant has committed an attempt is "pinpointing the time in the unfolding of a criminal plan at which the actor becomes liable for an attempt." The execution of a crime, other than one committed impetuously, involves planning and preparation. Like the jurisprudence of most states, federal law defines the threshold of criminality as the time when the defendant has gone beyond those preliminary activities and committed the additional act that constitutes the proscribed attempt even though he has not yet committed the contemplated crime. . . .

Most states have adopted the subjective [in contrast to the objective-criminality approach. Thus the Model Penal Code defines an attempt as "an act or omission constituting a substantial step in a course of conduct planned to culminate in . . . commission of [a] crime." The drafters of the Model Penal Code note that this approach emphasizes what the defendant has already done rather than what remains to be done, imposes liability only if some firmness of criminal purpose is shown, and permits the defendant's conduct to be assessed in the light of the statements. It also recognizes that an attempt to aid in the commission of a crime is sufficient for criminal sanction, and several statutes explicitly condemn such conduct....

Cartlidge contends that the evidence against him, even if wholly believed, was sufficient only to prove that he took a bribe, not that he attempted to aid and abet in the distribution of marijuana. Cartlidge's acceptance of three payments was evidence of receipt of a bribe, but it was also a step in a plan to aid in the distribution of a controlled substance. Cartlidge also gave information about the propitiousness of the planned date, furnished information, albeit erroneous, that federal agents could not conduct an investigation without his knowledge, and promised to shield those whom he thought to be drug dealers. These activities are sufficient to show that he had moved beyond preparation. They were substantial steps strongly corroborative of criminal intent.

The Model Penal Code requires that a *substantial step* be made to constitute criminal attempt. As Focus 10.1 indicates, that substantial step must be "strongly corroborative of the actor's criminal purpose." The M.P.C. lists activities, such as lying in wait, or possession of materials that might be used to commit the crime, that might show a criminal purpose.

Focus 10.3 contains quotations from several courts that have drawn the line between preparation and perpetration. A close reading of those statements indicates the difficulty one might have in making a decision, for the guidelines are not very clear and may afford no greater insight than the Model Penal Code's approach of a substantial step.

The substantial step requirement is particularly difficult in attempt cases involving sex crimes. Compare these cases. In the first, defendant offered a woman $100 to find a young girl with whom he could have sexual intercourse. Subsequently he negotiated with an undercover officer for the purchase of a young girl; offered the agent $150 to furnish the girl; chose a young girl from photos supplied by the agent, rented a room and purchased vaseline to use as a lubricant, and drove toward the apartment where the girl was allegedly waiting. He was arrested and charged with attempted sexual assault, for which he was convicted. Do you agree with that decision? Had he taken a substantial step toward perpetration, not just preparation?

The appellate court upheld the conviction. Emphasizing that in its previous decisions the court had held that "mere indecent advances, solicitations, or importunities do not amount to an attempt [to rape]," and that "mere preparation to commit a crime is insufficient to constitute an attempt," the court upheld the conviction with this statement: "[W]hen the design of a person to commit a crime is clearly shown, slight acts done in furtherance of that crime will constitute an attempt. . . . In the present case, we have the clearest evidence of appellant's intent to commit sexual assault on the young girl. He stipulated that this was his intent."[24]

In the second case, the defendant was convicted of attempted rape after he ordered a woman to take off her clothes. She was wearing jeans and could not get them off over her boots; so he ordered her to perform oral sex on him. He then put her in the trunk of his car, drove around for several hours, and let her out. He was convicted of assault and battery with intent to kill, attempted rape, forcible sodomy, robbery with a firearm, and kidnapping. The appellate court upheld all but the conviction for attempted rape, which it reversed on the grounds that defendant did not take a substantial step towards committing rape. "It must be such act or acts as will apparently result, in the usual and natural course of events, if not hindered by extraneous causes, in the commission of the crime itself."[25]

The final example illustrates a decision upholding one but not another attempt conviction. The defendant stopped a thirteen-year-old girl who was riding her bike from her parents' home, where she had been helping her mother with a garage sale, to another garage sale down the street. The defendant asked her to help him find his dog; she refused. He offered her money to do so; she refused. He offered more money; she refused. He said

---

FOCUS 10.3 Preparation or Attempt? Courts Seek a Definition

When faced with the issue of whether a defendant has gone beyond preparation and committed an act sufficient to constitute the crime of attempt, courts must devise tests. Here are a few of the guidelines articulated by various courts over the years.

1. "The act must reach far enough towards the accomplishment of the desired result to amount to the commencement of the consummation."[1]

2. "[W]here the intent to commit the substantive offense is. . . clearly established ..., acts done toward the commission of the crime may constitute an attempt, where the same acts would be held insufficient to constitute an attempt if the intent with which they were done is equivocal and not clearly proved."[2]

3. "Acts in furtherance of a criminal project do not reach the stage of an 'attempt' unless they carry the project forward within dangerous proximity to the criminal end to be attained."[3]

4. "The question whether an accused is guilty of an attempt to commit a crime is determined by his intentions and actions, and is unaffected by the circumstance that by reason of some unforeseen obstacle he was prevented from achieving his purpose. He is guilty if he has with criminal intent made some positive steps, beyond mere preparation, looking to the performance of an act which, if perpetrated, would be a crime."[4]

[1.] People v. Miller, 42 P.2d 308, 309 (Cal. 1935).
[2.] People v. Berger, 280 P.2d 136, 138 (Cal.1st Dist. 1955).
[3.] People v. Ditchik, 41 N.E.2d 905 (N.Y. 1942).
[4.] People v. Sullivan, 173 N.Y. 122 (N.Y.App. 1903).

---

he would go to her home and ask her parents if she could help him and asked her to get into his truck so he could drive her home. She refused.

The defendant followed the victim to her home. She told her mother what had happened, and the police were called. The defendant denied that he had any improper intentions, but the evidence showed that he did not have a dog and that previously he had been convicted of rape of a thirteen-year-old girl. Do you believe the facts constitute sufficient evidence to convict him of attempted kidnapping and attempted rape, as the circuit court decided? The Oregon appellate court upheld the conviction for attempted kidnapping in the second-degree but reversed the conviction for attempted rape. The Oregon Supreme Court reversed and affirmed the circuit court, meaning that both convictions stand.[26]

It was decided quite early that the defendant's act does not have to be the *last* act in the chain of causation to constitute an attempt. "[I]t is not necessary to constitute an attempt that the act done should be the last proximate one for the commission of the offence attempted."[27] Modern courts have upheld this view.[28] Courts have articulated several tests or measures that may be used to determine how close the act must be to the attempted crime to constitute an attempt.[29]

Defenses

Two defenses available in attempt cases are *abandonment* and *impossibility*. If two of the purposes of criminal law are to deter people from committing criminal acts and to punish those who commit crimes, what position should the law take when people abandon their plans to commit a crime? Should it make a difference whether the abandonment is voluntary or involuntary? Do you agree that "anywhere between the conception of the intent and the overt act toward its commission, there is room for repentance; and the law in its beneficence extends the hand of forgiveness."[30]

Read the facts of *People* v. *Staples*, reprinted in Focus 10.4, before proceeding with this discussion. That frequently cited case presents some of the basic issues in deciding whether an attempt has been committed or whether there has been sufficient abandonment that the crime was not committed.

If on his own the defendant in *Staples* abandoned the intent to commit burglary, why should he be punished? On the other hand, if his statements about abandonment were merely self-serving, why not punish him? Does his abandonment create in your mind a *reasonable doubt* whether he intended to commit burglary? Was he fantasizing about committing the perfect crime but never really intended to carry it out? Recall that a criminal intent is a necessary element of attempt. Would you argue that this defendant never went beyond mere preparation and therefore the second element of attempt, an act in furtherance of that intent, did not occur?

The appellate court in *Staples* took the position that when the defendant started drilling, he began the "breaking" element of burglary and thus had committed an act in preparation for that crime. The attempt conviction was upheld. Some courts do recognize abandonment as a defense if there is evidence that abandonment is voluntary and complete. Most courts do not recognize this defense when abandonment is the result of getting caught or of someone finding out about the act.

The Model Penal Code provides for the abandonment defense.[31] Where the defense is allowed, it is construed strictly, and most defendants do not succeed with this defense. In its discussion of this defense, the M.P.C. indicates that it was not clear at the time this section was formulated whether most jurisdictions recognized renunciation or abandonment as a defense to attempt. Where it was recognized, courts appeared to distinguish between *voluntary* and *involuntary* abandonment, with the former referring to a real change of heart or purpose and the latter referring to a case of fear of getting caught. "There has been no doubt that such an abandonment [involuntary] does not exculpate the actor from attempt liability otherwise incurred."[32]

A more plausible defense to attempt is *factual* or *legal impossibility*. In 1864 an English decision held that a man could not be convicted of attempted larceny simply by proof that he inserted his hand into the victim's pocket with intent to steal. According to the court, "[A]n attempt to

FOCUS 10.4 People v. Staples

The facts of this case are as follows. Staples, under an assumed name and while his wife was out of town, rented an office located over the mezzanine of a bank from 23 October 1967 to 23 November 1967. The defendant knew that the bank's vault was below the mezzanine.

The landlord had ten days before commencement of the rental to complete repairs and painting, but during that period, defendant Staples took some items into the office, including drilling tools, two acetylene gas tanks, a blow torch, a blanket, and a linoleum rug. The landlord saw these items from time to time when he checked on repairs.

The defendant found out that no one was in the building on Saturdays. On Saturday, 14 October 1967, he drilled two groups of holes into the floor of the office above the mezzanine room. He stopped drilling before the holes went through the floor. He came back to the office several times, thinking he would slowly drill down farther. Each time he left he covered the holes with the linoleum rug.

The defendant installed a lock on the closet and intended to, and perhaps did, place his tools in that closet. But he left the keys to the lock on the premises. Around the end of November and apparently after November 23, the landlord notified the police of the tools and turned the office over to them. The defendant was arrested on 22 February 1968. After he was told his rights, he gave a statement that included the following.

Saturday, the 14th. . . I drilled some small holes in the floor of the room. Because of tiredness, fear, and the implications of what I was doing, I stopped and went to sleep.

At this point I think my motives began to change. The actual [*sic*] commencement of my plan made me begin to realize that even if I were to succeed a fugitive life of living off of stolen money would not give the enjoyment of the life of a mathematician however humble a job I might have.

I still had not given up my plan however. I felt I had made a certain investment of time, money, effort and a certain psychological [*sic*] commitment to the concept.

I came back several times thinking I might store the tools in the closet and slowly drill down (covering the hole with a rug of linoleum square). As time went on (after two weeks or so), my wife came back and my life as bank robber seemed more and more absurd.

Do you think the defendant had abandoned his attempt to commit burglary, for which he was convicted? The appellate court noted that the case was unusual in that in the typical attempt case the defendant is intercepted or caught in the act. "Here, there was no direct proof of any actual interception."

SOURCE: People v. Staples, 85 Cal. Rptr. 589 (Cal.2d Dist. 1970).

commit a felony can only be made out when, if no interruption had taken place, the attempt could have been carried out successfully."[33] Such broad language was rejected in 1892, when it was held that the inability of the pickpocket to steal from an empty pocket did not preclude his conviction of attempted larceny.[34]

Most U.S. courts hold that a defendant may be charged with an attempted crime when *physical or factual impossibility* exists, but not when *legal impossibility* exists. Although it may be difficult to determine the difference in any particular case, the following excerpt from *Booth* v. *State* refers to some examples.[35]

Booth v. *State*

What is a "legal impossibility" as distinguished from a "physical or factual impossibility" has over a long period of time perplexed our courts and has resulted in many irreconcilable decisions and much philosophical discussion by legal scholars.

The reason for the "impossibility" of completing the substantive crime ordinarily falls into one of two categories: (1) Where the act if completed would not be criminal, a situation which is usually described as a "legal impossibility," and (2) where the basic or substantive crime is impossible of completion, simply because of some physical or factual condition unknown to the defendant, a situation which is usually described as a "factual impossibility.". . .

Examples of the so-called "legal impossibility" situations are:

(a) A person accepting goods which he believes to have been stolen, but which were not in fact stolen goods, is not guilty of an attempt to receive stolen goods.

(b) It is not an attempt to commit subornation of perjury where the false testimony solicited, if given, would have been immaterial to the case at hand and hence not perjurious.

(c) An accused who offers a bribe to a person believed to be, but who is not, a juror is not guilty of an attempt to bribe a juror.

(d) A hunter who shoots a stuffed deer believing it to be alive is not guilty of an attempt to shoot a deer out of season.

Examples of cases in which attempt convictions have been sustained on the theory that all that prevented the consummation of the completed crime was a "factual impossibility" are:

(a) The picking of an empty pocket.

(b) An attempt to steal from an empty receptacle or an empty house.

(c) Where defendant shoots into the intended victim's bed, believing he is there, when in fact he is elsewhere.

(d) Where the defendant erroneously believing that the gun is loaded points it at his wife's head and pulls the trigger.

(e) Where the woman upon whom the abortion operation is performed is not in fact pregnant.

The defense of impossibility might arise also in relationship to the actor's state of mind; that is, whether the actor had the required *mens rea* to commit the attempt. Thus, in most cases impotency is considered a factual impossibility and therefore not a defense to attempted rape. It might be a defense, however, if the would-be rapist had known for some time that he was impotent and not capable of having sexual intercourse. In jurisdictions in which the traditional definition of rape is still in effect, he might not have the requisite *mens rea* for attempted rape.[36]

One final type of impossibility is *inherent impossibility*, usually illustrated by the hypothetical case of the doctor who comes to the United States from another country and attempts to use voodoo to kill a person. Because *murder* by voodoo is impossible, the doctor should not be charged with attempted murder. As one court noted:

> If a statute simply made it a felony to attempt to kill any human being, or to conspire to do so, an attempt by means of witchcraft, or a conspiracy to kill by means of charms and incantations, would not be an offense within such a statute. The poverty of language compels one to say "an attempt to kill by means of witchcraft," but such an attempt is really no attempt at all to kill. It is true the sin or wickedness may be as great as an attempt or conspiracy by competent means; but human laws are made, not to punish sin, but to prevent crime and mischief.[37]

The Spread of AIDS: Attempted Murder?

The rapid spread of the deadly HIV virus that causes AIDS (acquired immune deficiency syndrome) has affected all of our social institutions, including our legal system. In August 1993 a Fort Lauderdale, Florida man won a civil judgment of $18 million from his wife, an exotic dancer who knew she was HIV-positive but did not tell her husband. The large award is rare, and the case is thought to be the first in which a woman has been found liable for knowingly infecting her husband. Collecting that amount of money is unlikely, but one target was her $300,000 homeowner's insurance policy.[38]

Civil liability for the spread of AIDS is one issue. Another is criminal liability. Should a person who knows he or she is HIV-positive, or has AIDS, be charged with a crime for engaging in activities that might lead to the infection of others? Numerous state legislatures have answered this question in the affirmative by enacting statutes criminalizing such actions. But there are problems with such special statutes, and in 1993 the Texas legislature repealed that state's statute enacted in 1989, which prohibited an act called *exposing to AIDS/HIV*, which is a third-degree felony. The statute had been used infrequently, and legislators thought it would be more appropriate to prosecute such actions under attempted murder or assault statutes.[39]

Under a statute similar to that of Texas, Salvadore Gamberella, an unemployed shipyard welder in Louisiana, was convicted and sentenced to ten years in prison. Salvadore testified that he told his girlfriend that he had AIDS; she said he did not tell her. The jury took only twelve minutes to find the defendant guilty. Both Salvadore and his girlfriend are dying of AIDS.[40]

These statutes and convictions may not be surprising in light of the seriousness of the disease and the fact that the statutes are designed to deter people from having sexual relations without notifying their partners of known exposure to the HIV virus. Some authorities argue that it is quite a different matter to prosecute for attempted murder in these cases, but this is being done, and convictions are being upheld.

In Texas a drifter with AIDS was convicted of attempted murder when he spat on a correctional officer twice and hit the officer in the lips, nostrils, eyes, and cheeks. In a case the American Civil Liberties Union calls the "most outrageous AIDS-related case ever," Curtis Weeks was accused of looking directly at the officer and telling him that he, Weeks, was "HIV-4." "The complainant believed that appellant intended to kill him." This excerpt from the opinion of the appellate court that upheld the conviction of attempted murder and the life sentence imposed for that crime indicates why the court found the elements of attempted murder had been proved.[41]

Weeks v. *State*

Under [Texas statutes] the essential elements of an attempt offense are that: a person, with specific intent to commit an offense, does an act amounting to more than mere preparation that tends, but fails, to effect the commission of the offenses intended. To prove attempted murder, it is sufficient to show that the accused had the intent to cause the death of the complainant and that he commited an act, which amounted to more than mere preparation, that could have caused the death of the complainant but failed to do so. The State was required to prove that appellant's intent, when he spit on the officer, was to cause the officer's death; that appellant was infected with HIV at the time he spit on the officer; and that this act was more than mere preparation which tended, but failed to effect the commission of the offenses intended, which was the officer's death.

It is undisputed that appellant spit twice on the officer and that appellant was infected with HIV at the time. The record reflects that appellant believed he could kill the complainant by spitting his HIV infected saliva on him. The issue, then, before this court is whether sufficient evidence, when viewed in the light more favorable to the verdict, was presented to the jury showing that appellant could have transmitted HIV by spitting on the officer.

[The court discussed the testimony of the expert witnesses and noted that it was in the province of the jury to believe those who testified that the HIV virus may be spread through saliva.]

In March 1993 a New Jersey court upheld the conviction and twenty-five year sentence (without eligibility for parole for over twelve years) of Gregory Dean Smith, convicted of attempted murder, aggravated assault, and terroristic threats. Smith bit a corrections officer. In this case, as in the *Weeks* case, there was conflicting expert testimony regarding the spread of the HIV virus though saliva.[42] Likewise, in *Scroggins* v. *State*, a Georgia court upheld the conviction of an appellant who was HIV-positive when he bit and spat at a police officer. Scroggins was convicted of aggravated assault with intent to murder and sentenced to ten years in prison. Scroggins, who was only 5 feet 3 inches and weighed 113 pounds, testified

Ignacio A. Perea, Jr., was convicted of attempted murder by a Florida jury based on charges that he knew he had AIDS when he committed the crime of rape.

that he bit the officer because he was being choked and the officer was cutting off his air supply.[43]

Two Florida cases are relevant to this discussion, too. A mother who has AIDS and repeatedly bit her daughter was charged with attempted murder but permitted to plead no contest to aggravated child abuse. Pamela Super, twenty-one, was sentenced to fifty-one weeks in jail, followed by a year of house arrest and two years of probation. The attempted murder charge was dropped after doctors indicated that the chances of transmitting the HIV virus through saliva were minimal.[44]

Finally, the case of Ignacio Perea Jr. received national media attention in 1993-1994. Perea, who has AIDS, was accused of raping three young boys. He was charged with rape, kidnapping, and attempted first-degree murder. The more serious charge of attempted *first-degree* murder was possible because the alleged crime of attempted murder occurred during the commission of another felony. It was alleged also that because anal intercourse was involved there was a greater chance of transmission of the deadly virus than through other means. Perea's attorney raised the critical question, "How can you attempt or try to do something you never intended to do?" Gay rights and other advocates argue that charging attempted murder in such cases involves misapplying attempt statutes and arouses public hysteria concerning the deadly virus. In 1994 Perea was sentenced to five life terms for attempted murder, rape, and kidnapping.[45]

Criminal Conspiracy

Conspiracy is a crime in almost all U.S. jurisdictions, but the statutes vary significantly. Like criminal solicitation and criminal attempt, criminal conspiracy is an inchoate crime; but unlike these other crimes, conspiracy permits criminal prosecution for the behavior of others as well as for one's own acts. A further distinction between criminal attempt and conspiracy is that, unlike attempt, which merges into the crime (thus, a defendant cannot be convicted of both attempt to commit robbery and robbery of the same person), in conspiracy in most jurisdictions a defendant could be convicted of conspiracy *and* of the crime that was the object of the conspiracy.

Following the Model Penal Code approach, some statutes do not permit two convictions. The Model Penal Code provides that when the conspiracy has only one motive (A and B conspire to murder X), the conspirators may be punished for one but not both crimes. But if A and B conspire to murder X, Y, and Z on separate occasions, A and B may be convicted of those murders *and* of conspiracy to commit murder.[46]

Conspiracy may be distinguished from attempt also in that attempt requires some preparation, whereas in some jurisdictions the *act* required for conspiracy is the *agreement*. Therefore, it is possible that a defendant could be convicted of conspiracy to commit robbery under circumstances that would not justify conviction of attempted robbery.

Criminal conspiracy is a favorite crime of many prosecutors, and as far back as 1925 was called "the darling of the prosecutor's nursery."[47] Conspiracy received this label because of procedural reasons that are beyond the scope of this text, but also because the definition of the crime permits prosecutions in cases in which it would be impossible to prove the elements of criminal attempt. Because it is defined broadly, conspiracy is a useful tool for prosecutors.

The Problem of Definition

Many students become frustrated by the lack of agreement in law. The study of law would be so much easier if there were fewer ambiguities. As many commentators have noted, the law of conspiracy is no exception to this problem. It would be a misrepresentation of the facts to suggest a simple and definite statement defining the crime of conspiracy. "The definition of a crime does not represent the end of the search but is merely a convenient starting point for the consideration of the problems involved."[48] This is true particularly with conspiracy.

A good starting point is a brief look at common law conspiracy. Conspiracy was not a recognized crime in *early* common law. When it emerged, it was defined narrowly, but over the years the definition was expanded. For purposes of this discussion, an 1832 definition is significant. In that year, an English lord stated that an indictment for conspiracy required that a defendant must be charged either with conspiracy "to do an unlawful act or a lawful act by unlawful means."[49] Although the word *unlawful* could have been understood as meaning *criminal*, the English and American courts interpreted it more broadly, to include acts that are "corrupt, dishonest, fraudulent, immoral, and in that sense illegal, and it is in the combination to make use of such practices that the dangers of this offense consist."[50]

Some jurisdictions retain the common law definition even though they have codified the law; where that occurs, conspiracy is defined broadly as an agreement (or combination or confederation) to engage in an unlawful act or to engage in a lawful act by unlawful means. Some jurisdictions specify that the conspiracy must be to commit a *crime*, as required by the Model Penal Code,[51] whereas others specify the type of crime.

The New York Penal Code serves as an example of a modern conspiracy statute. New York specifies six degrees of conspiracy, with the definition of each degree specifying the type of crime that must be the subject of the conspiracy and indicating the type of felony that this conspiracy would be. *Conspiracy in the first degree* is defined as follows:

> A person is guilty of conspiracy in the first degree when, with intent that conduct constituting a class A felony [the most serious felonies] be performed, he, being over 18 years of age, agrees with one or more persons under 16 years of age to engage in or cause the performance of such conduct.
>
> Conspiracy in the first degree is a class A-1 felony.[52]

The purpose of adding this degree of conspiracy was to decrease the number of adults who use juveniles in criminal activities to limit their exposure to prosecution.

Not all jurisdictions separate conspiracy into degrees, but most consider conspiracy to be a serious crime. The group involvement makes the crime more serious than other inchoate crimes. The abandonment of one individual's interest in pursuing criminal activity may not in any way deter the activity from taking place by the others; furthermore, it is reasonable to assume that in many cases co-conspirators encourage each other in other criminal activities.

Elements of Conspiracy

ACTUS REUS

The first element of conspiracy is that there must be an act. The act may be the *agreement*, which is the essence of conspiracy. Close analysis of the alleged agreement is important to determine (1) whether more than one party was involved, (2) whether the requisite criminal intent was present, and (3) whether there were one or more conspiracies. The agreement does not have to be a written one; usually it is not. It may be inferred from the facts and circumstances of the case.

Depending on the jurisdiction's definition of conspiracy, the nature of the agreement may have to be criminal or unlawful, covering acts that are not defined as crimes. Despite the broad language of some conspiracy statutes, many courts have upheld such language. This broad language gives prosecutors greater latitude to prosecute in this area, but the U.S. Supreme Court has held that a statute prohibiting conspiracies "to commit any act injurious to the public health, to public morals, or to trade, commerce or for the perversion or obstruction of justice or the due administration of the law" is vague unless narrowed by the state court.[53]

Proving the existence of an agreement in a criminal conspiracy trial may be difficult. After the prosecution presents all its evidence on the issue, the judge tells the jury which test is to be used to determine whether an agreement existed. In a 1985 federal case, the court stated the *objective standard* used in that jurisdiction to determine the existence of an agreement. That test is whether *any* rational trier of fact (for example, a judge or juror) could conclude beyond a reasonable doubt that an agreement existed. This is to be distinguished from the *subjective test*, which asks in effect whether *you*, the trier of fact, could have found the agreement.[54]

An issue that may be even more complicated than whether any agreement existed is the issue of whether more than one agreement was in effect. This may be very important for procedural reasons beyond the scope of this text. Of importance here is the fact that if the prosecutor charges the defendants with more than one conspiracy but can prove only one or charges only one and the evidence indicates more than one agreement, the defendants may be entitled to an acquittal. In addition, the number of agreements may be important in the imposition of punishment.

It is not always easy to determine whether one or more conspiracies existed. Consider, for example, a complex series of transactions, such as occurred in *United States* v. *Bruno*, a frequently cited case despite the fact that it was decided in 1939 and reversed on other grounds. *Bruno* can be analyzed by both methods of determining the nature and scope of a conspiracy and whether one or more conspiracies existed: the *chain* and the *wheel or circle*.[55]

In *Bruno*, eighty-eight defendants were indicted for conspiracy to import, possess, and sell narcotics over a long period. The evidence indicated that smugglers in New York City imported the drugs and sold them to middlemen who distributed the drugs to two groups of retailers, one group in Texas and Louisiana and the other in New York. These transactions are diagrammed in Figure 10.1.

The smugglers in *Bruno* committed the crime of importing; the middlemen committed the crime of illegal distribution, and the two groups of retailers committed the crime of selling drugs illegally. The retailers argued that because there was no evidence that they had any contact with each other or with the smugglers, they were not involved in a conspiracy with the smugglers.

The court in *Bruno* held that only one conspiracy existed and that despite the lack of contact between the retailers and the smugglers, they each knew the other had to exist in order to complete the crime of smuggling, possessing, and distributing drugs. This *chain* of activities indicated the existence of only one large conspiracy. Each retailer could be held criminally liable for every sale of narcotics made by other retailers as well as for the crime of smuggling.

Bruno may be analyzed also by the second method of determining the extent of a conspiracy or the number of conspiracies—the *wheel or circle*, diagrammed in Figure 10.1. The middlemen, or distributors, in *Bruno* may be viewed as the central hub of the wheel, with the smugglers and each

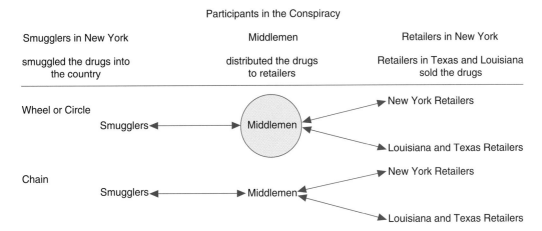

Participants in the Conspiracy

Smugglers in New York	Middlemen	Retailers in New York
smuggled the drugs into the country	distributed the drugs to retailers	Retailers in Texas and Louisiana sold the drugs

FIGURE 10.1   The Wheel-and-Chain Approach to the Agreement Requirement of a Criminal Conspiracy

SOURCE: Diagrammed by the author from the facts of United States v. Bruno, 105 F.2d 921 (2d Cir. 1939), *rev'd. on other grounds*, 308 U.S. 287 (1939).

group of retailers constituting spokes on the wheel. Although there was no communication between the New York retailers and the Texas and Louisiana retailers or between either of those groups of retailers and the smugglers, all communicated with the distributors. The court said that communication would be sufficient to establish an agreement to violate drug laws.

The retailers in *Bruno* argued unsuccessfully that there could not be only one conspiracy, as the government had charged, because neither group of retailers knew of the existence of the other and neither had communicated with the smugglers. The court held that only one conspiracy existed. According to the court, it was of no concern to the smugglers who or how many retailers were involved. They knew there had to be retailers for the drugs to be sold.

The court held also that the retailers knew they were a necessary part of "a scheme of distribution, and the others, [retailers] whom he knew to be convenient to its execution, were as much parts of a single undertaking or enterprise as two salesmen in the same shop."[56]

Under the common law and under some state statutes the *agreement* is sufficient; no further act is required. Some statutes require that in addition to the agreement there must be an *overt act*. For example, the federal code requires that of those involved in the agreement, "one or more. . . [must] do any act to effect the object of the conspiracy."[57] In upholding a conviction under this section, a federal court stated what the federal code requires for a criminal conspiracy conviction under this section.

> The essence of a conspiracy is an agreement by two or more persons to commit a substantive offense coupled with an overt act in furtherance of the

offense. The intent required to be proved is the intent necessary to the substantive offense. In this case, [the defendant] was charged. . . with conspiracy to defraud the United States. Thus, the intent required was that necessary to defraud the United States.[58]

The federal code does not require an overt act for criminal conspiracy under the Comprehensive Drug Abuse Prevention and Control Act,[59] but it does require an overt act for conspiracy to murder.[60]

When a conspiracy statute requires an overt act, normally the requirement is not as stringent as that required for an attempt. Often it is intended to permit any of the actors a chance to abandon their participation and avoid prosecution.[61] An example of a sufficient overt act is the purchase of stamps needed to carry out a conspiracy to commit murder by poison sent through the mail.[62]

Some states specify that an act in addition to an agreement is required only for some conspiracy crimes. Consider the Arizona statute:

> A person commits conspiracy if, with the intent to promote or aid the commission of an offense, such person agrees with one or more persons that at least one of them or another person will engage in conduct constituting the offense and one of the parties commits an overt act in furtherance of the offense, except that an overt act shall not be required if the object of the conspiracy was to commit any felony upon the person of another, or to commit an offense under [two other sections.][63]

When an overt act is required it is not always necessary that all co-conspirators engage in the overt act; an act on the part of one may be sufficient to establish this element of the crime.[64]

LIMITATIONS ON PARTIES TO CONSPIRACY

Four important limitations to parties to conspiracy exist: the Wharton rule, husband-and-wife rule, the two-or-more rule, and the corporation rule. The **Wharton rule**, named after its author, Francis Wharton,[65] specifies that when individuals engage in crimes that by definition require more than one person, they may not be prosecuted for conspiracy to commit those crimes. A third party must be involved for a conspiracy to exist. Crimes that qualify under this rule are acts such as adultery, bigamy, and incest. The Wharton rule has been rejected by the Model Penal Code, which takes the position that any inchoate agreement to commit a crime should be punished as a conspiracy.[66]

A second limitation is the *husband-and-wife rule*. In common law, husband and wife were considered one, not two, persons, and because conspiracy requires two or more persons, a husband and his wife could not conspire to commit a crime. This position was accepted in the United States in earlier days, based primarily on the assumption that the husband "owned" his wife, who was under his control. As other laws relating to the relationship between husband and wife have changed, so has the law of conspiracy. Today a wife may act independently of her husband, so the two of them may commit conspiracy.[67]

A third limitation on parties to conspiracy is the *two-or-more rule*, requiring that for a conspiracy to exist two or more persons must be involved. Although it is obvious that the definition of conspiracy precludes one person from conspiring alone, courts have taken different positions on what happens if, for example, one of two alleged conspirators is acquitted. Technically, if there are only two alleged conspirators and one is acquitted, the other may not be convicted, as there would be only one party to the conspiracy. Some courts have taken this position.[68]

Other courts look to the *reason* why a second alleged co-conspirator was not convicted. If one defendant were granted immunity in exchange for testifying against the second co-conspirator, a conspiracy conviction may be upheld on the defendant without immunity.[69]

Although it might seem unfair to uphold the conspiracy convictions of a defendant whose alleged co-conspirators were acquitted in separate trials but not uphold those convictions if those acquittals occur in the same trials, the argument for taking this position is that it is necessary to maintain internal consistency. Logically, the same jury could not acquit one of two alleged conspirators and convict the other, for the second one would not have had anyone with whom to conspire. But if two juries reach different conclusions, internal consistency is not compromised.

This traditional unilateral rule has been criticized. The Model Penal Code, which requires agreement *by* the defendant but not agreement *between* two or more persons, does not follow the rule.[70] The case of *United States* v. *Thomas* is in agreement.[71]

United States v. *Thomas*

[Thomas was convicted of possession of cocaine with intent to distribute; conspiracy to distribute cocaine; and possession with intent to distribute. He appealed the conspiracy conviction and his sentences. This excerpt speaks only to the conspiracy conviction.]

Thomas argues that his conspiracy conviction must be reversed because his co-defendant and alleged co-conspirator, Battle, was acquitted. Thomas claims that under the common law "rule of consistency," he cannot be convicted of conspiracy where his co-conspirator is found innocent in the same trial.

Thomas' argument fails because the Supreme Court has made it clear that a defendant cannot challenge his conviction merely because it is inconsistent with a jury's verdict of acquittal on another count....[The defendant then argued that the cited and quoted Supreme Court cases do not apply to his case, and the court responded:]

We disagree. Because of the reasoning provided by the Supreme Court we are forced to find otherwise. According to the Supreme Court, [in its most recent statement, in *United States* v. *Powell*] inconsistent verdicts

> should not necessarily be interpreted as a windfall to the Government at the defendant's expense. It is equally possible that the jury, convinced of

> guilt, properly reached its conclusion on the compound offense, and then through mistake, compromise, or lenity, arrived at an inconsistent conclusion on the lesser offense.
>
> This explanation applies equally as much to this case as to *Powell*. . . . Enough evidence exists of a conspiracy between Battle and Thomas to uphold the jury's verdict against Thomas. We thus reject Thomas' argument that his conviction should be overturned because Battle was acquitted.

Whether the unilateral or plurality approaches are used determines whether a conspiracy charge may be brought when the defendant has conspired with a person who has no intention of carrying out the conspiracy; for example, a police officer. Modern cases have held that this situation does not preclude a conspiracy conviction against the party with the criminal intent.[72]

A final limitation on parties to conspiracy is the *corporation rule*. Corporations may commit conspiracy with other corporations or with a natural person, although there are problems with the two-or-more rule. When two corporations and an officer of each are charged, there is no problem, for there are two or more *separate persons* involved in the conspiracy. Likewise, when a corporation is indicted for conspiracy, along with one of its officers and an officer from another corporation, the two-or-more requirement is met.

The problem arises when a corporation and one of its officers is charged with conspiracy. Very early cases established that this does not constitute a conspiracy.[73] Nor is there conspiracy in a case involving two corporations and one agent acting for both corporations. In both of these cases, only *one human actor* is involved, so there can be no agreement between two or more persons.

The two-or-more requirement arises also when two or more agents of the *same corporation* are involved. A 1952 civil case held that this does not meet the two-or-more requirement for civil conspiracy; that holding might be applied as well to criminal conspiracy.[74] More recently, however, some courts have held that this would meet the two-or-more requirement for a conspiracy.[75]

MENS REA

The criminal intent element required for conspiracy is a source of controversy. The Model Penal Code notes that the traditional definition of this inchoate crime "said nothing about the actor's state of mind except insofar as the concept of agreement itself carries certain implications about his attitude toward the crime."[76] Perhaps this is because the intent to agree is difficult to distinguish from the agreement itself.

It is not sufficient to show that the conspirators intended to agree. It must be proved that the conspirators intended to accomplish an unlawful objective, which is the object of the conspiracy. The elements of the unlawful objective must be met. The Model Penal Code drafters use this example. Suppose A and B plan to bomb a building to destroy that structure. They know there are people inside and that in all probability those people will be killed by their actions. They do not intend to kill those people, so they do not have the intent to kill required for most murder convictions. If they bomb the building and people die as a result, under many state statutes they may be convicted of murder. But they may not be convicted of conspiracy to commit murder, only of conspiracy to bomb the building. In responding to this illustration, one commentator has said that clearly a "conspiracy to commit a particular substantive offense cannot exist without *at least* the degree of criminal intent necessary for the substantive offense itself."[77]

Another problem that exists with regard to the *mens rea* requirement of conspiracy is what to do with alleged conspirators who merely provided goods or services to others who used them for unlawful purposes. Conspiracy requires *intent*, not just *knowledge*; so it would seem that knowledge that the goods and services would be used for unlawful purposes would not be sufficient.

Supreme Court cases on this point may seem inconsistent. In 1940 in *United States* v. *Falcone*, the Court held that selling sugar and yeast to buyers known to be engaging in a conspiracy to make illegal liquor was not sufficient to make the sellers part of the conspiracy.[78] But in 1943 in *Direct Sales Co.* v. *United States*, the Court upheld the conspiracy conviction of a drug manufacturer and wholesaler who sold large quantities of morphine to a specific doctor over a long period of time and must have known that the doctor could not have needed that much for legal distribution.[79]

In later cases other courts have found the intent required for conspiracy by emphasizing the facts of *Direct Sales*, along with additional facts such as inflated prices, failure to keep required records of sales of restricted products (such as drugs), and the percentage of a seller's business accounted for by the illegal sales.[80]

One final *mens rea* requirement in conspiracy cases in some jurisdictions is that the parties must have had a *corrupt motive*. Thus, if the parties did not know they were violating a statute, they might argue successfully that they were not guilty of a conspiracy, which, by definition, implies that the agreement "must have been entered into with an evil purpose, as distinguished from a purpose to do the act prohibited, in ignorance of the prohibition."[81]

Not all courts agree, however, noting that normally ignorance of the law is not an excuse. Others take the position that if the conspiracy is to commit a *malum prohibitum* rather than a *mala in se* act, the corrupt motive doctrine applies. This is based on the assumption that a person should be aware that there are laws against the latter type of crimes.[82]

Defenses to Conspiracy

Most courts hold that impossibility is not a defense to conspiracy.[83] Some, using the analogy of attempt, hold that legal—but not factual—impossibility is a defense.[84] In many jurisdictions withdrawal is permitted as a defense to conspiracy, although in any particular situation withdrawal may be difficult to prove. Jurisdictions vary on their statutory requirements to prove the defense, and courts vary on their interpretations of these statutes.

The Model Penal Code permits a conspirator to abandon the agreement "if and only when he advises those with whom he conspired of his abandonment or he informs the law enforcement authorities of the existence of the conspiracy and of his participation therein."[85] The U.S. Supreme Court disapproved of that rule, saying that "Affirmative acts inconsistent with the object of the conspiracy and communicated in a manner reasonably calculated to reach co-conspirators have generally been regarded as sufficient to establish withdrawal or abandonment."[86]

Other Issues in Conspiracy

An important issue that arises in conspiracy cases is the extent to which one is liable for the crimes of co-conspirators. In the leading case of *Pinkerton* v. *United States*, the Supreme Court established that a co-conspirator may be held accountable for the acts of fellow conspirators even though the requirements of liability for the acts of accomplices (discussed later) are not met. Some of the offenses for which Pinkerton was convicted were committed without his knowledge and while he was in prison.[87]

The **Pinkerton rule** has been criticized. The drafters of the Model Penal Code argued that it could result in gross distortion. If anyone who gets involved in a conspiracy is responsible for *all* criminal acts of co-conspirators, a relatively uninvolved person could become criminally liable for many crimes.[88] Some courts dodge this problem by limiting liability for crimes of co-conspirators to reasonably foreseeable acts.

Another issue concerns the duration of the conspiracy. Liability for the crimes of co-conspirators lasts only as long as the conspiracy. The conspiracy is considered to continue "up to the abandonment or success."[89] In a particular case, that point might be hard to determine, but it is very important, for a number of procedural issues are affected by the time at which the conspiracy ended. Both the duration of the conspiracy and the extent of liability for the crimes of co-conspirators, in the case of a particular defendant, are affected by whether that defendant withdraws successfully or abandons the conspiracy.

One final point of importance in conspiracy cases is that conspiracy cases may be (and usually are) extremely complicated. Frequently conspiracy charges are combined with charges for substantive crimes; the cases are numerous; many involve illegal drug sales. It is beyond the scope of this text to examine all of the complications of a conspiracy trial, but a brief statement of the facts and issues of a 1990 case illustrates the issue.

United States v. *Torres* involved twelve defendants charged with a total of thirty-two counts, including the following crimes: conspiring to distribute and to possess with intent to distribute more than a kilogram of heroin; operating a continuing criminal enterprise (discussed in Chapter 11); distributing heroin, or possessing heroin with the intent to distribute it; possession of cocaine with intent to distribute it; using and carrying a firearm in connection with drug trafficking; making apartments controlled by them available for the unlawful manufacture, distribution and storage of heroin; tax evasion; and obtaining specified property constituting and derived from proceeds of drug trafficking. The case involved legal procedural issues such as electronic wiretapping, jury instructions, sufficiency of the evidence, and others. Defendants challenged their sentences as well. The appellate opinion in the case is forty-seven published pages. The listing of defendants, the counts for which each was charged, and their sentences constitute three and one-half printed pages.[90]

Parties to Crime

The law has long recognized criminal liability for people other than those who commit criminal acts. Individuals may assist, aid and abet, incite, or encourage others to commit criminal acts. The word ***complicity*** is used to describe people who share in the guilt even though they do not engage in the criminal act. They are **accomplices** to the crime, meaning that they aid or assist in some way.

Accomplices assume criminal liability in terms of their degree of participation in the criminal activity. They may receive a lesser punishment than the principal. The common law had definite categories for participants or parties to crimes. Statutory law differs to some degree; both are examined.

Common Law Classifications

The common law classified parties to crimes. These categories were important for procedural reasons, and they are retained in some statutes today. The categories are *principal in the first degree*, *principal in the second degree*, *accessory before the fact*, and *accessory after the fact*.

Principals are those persons involved in the commission of a crime. **Principals in the first degree** are those who perpetrate crimes either through their own acts or by use of inanimate objects or innocent people. **Principals in the second degree** incite or abet the commission of crimes and are present actually or constructively. Persons are present constructively when, without being present, they assist the principals of the first degree at the moment the crimes are being committed. In many crimes, it is common for the principal in the second degree of a bank robbery to be posted away from the bank, ready to signal when the coast is clear.

An **accessory before the fact** incites or abets but is not present actually or constructively when the crime is committed. An example is someone who provides counsel or tools for the commission of a crime. An **accessory after the fact** is one who, knowing that a felony has been committed, receives, relieves, comforts, or assists the felon for the purpose of hindering apprehension and conviction. In addition to these categories, the common law had a category of *accessory at the fact*; but that category was merged later with principal in the second degree, because the English courts recognized that all who were present and aiding and abetting at the crime were second-degree principals.

A few further distinctions need to be made about the common law categories. The terms *perpetrator*, *abettor*, *inciter*, and *criminal protector* must be defined and compared to the common law categories. This is done in Focus 10.5, which indicates also that the categories differ in terms of whether the crime was a misdemeanor or a felony. Treason was a special case, with all participants considered principals.

Modern Statutory Treatment

Generally, modern statutes do not distinguish between principals (either degree) and accessories before the fact. All three are treated as principals. Accessories may be convicted even if the principal has not been convicted, although there are some exceptions.[91] Many of the statutes have abandoned the common law terminology and specify that an accomplice is accountable legally for the conduct of another. The federal code defines principals as follows:

> (a) Whoever commits an offense against the United States or aids, abets, counsels, commands, induces or procures its commission is punishable as a principal.
> (b) Whoever willfully causes an act to be done which ifdirectly performed by him or another would be an offense against the United States is punishable as a principal.[92]

The purpose of this statute is explained in this brief excerpt from *United States* v. *Mann*.[93]

United States v. Mann

The aiding and abetting statute ... does not establish a separate crime, but rather is an alternative charge that permits one to be found guilty as a principal for aiding or procuring someone else to commit the offense. A jury may find a person guilty of aiding and abetting even though he or she did not commit all the acts constituting the elements of the substantive crime charged. Nonetheless, as an element of the offense of aiding and abetting, the government must prove that someone committed the underlying crime. It is not a prerequisite to a conviction for aiding and abetting, however, that the principal be tried and convicted, or even that the principal be identified. In fact, an aider and abettor's conviction may be upheld even though the principal is acquitted of the underlying offense. In such cases, however, it is clear that although the principal was not convicted, the underlying offense was committed.

[The conviction for aiding and abetting another to knowingly, with intent to defraud, have possession of "device-making equipment in manner affecting interstate commerce" was reversed because the jury was not instructed and therefore not given the opportunity to decide whether the underlying offense was committed.]

FOCUS 10.5 Parties to Crimes: Common Law Categories

Using the terms "perpetrator," "abettor," "inciter" and "criminal protector" with the meanings thus arbitrarily assigned [as follows], the common law classification of principals and accessories may be expressed in this form:

1. In treason, perpetrators, abettors, inciters and criminal protectors are all principals "because of the heinousness of the crime," and different degrees of principals are seldom even mentioned.
2. In felony:
   a. Perpetrators are principals in the first degree.
   b. Abettors are principals in the second degree.
   c. Inciters are accessories before the fact; and
   d. Criminal protectors are accessories after the fact.
3. In misdemeanors:
   a. Perpetrators, abettors and inciters are all principals, because the law "does not descend to distinguish the different shades of guilt in petty misdemeanors."
   b. Criminal protectors are not punishable as such.

[The authors define perpetrator, abettor, inciter, and criminal protector as follows:]

Perpetrators are those who, with the requisite *mens rea*, actually commit the criminal acts or who are directly responsible for those acts. **Abettors** are persons who, with the requisite *mens rea* and being actually or constructively present (although a few courts have not required this element), encourage, promote, instigate, or stand ready to assist the perpetrator. Abettors are sometimes called aiders and abettors, but some commentators suggest that that is verbose; the term *abettor* is sufficient.

An **inciter** refers to one who, "with *mens rea*, aids, counsels, commands, procures or encourages another to commit a crime, or with *mens rea*, supplies him with the weapons, tools or information needed for his criminal purpose, the one not being present either actually or constructively at the moment of perpetration."

Criminal protectors are those who are in no way "tainted with guilt of a crime when perpetrated but who, with full knowledge of the facts," after the crime has been committed, either conceal the offenders or give them assistance in avoiding detection and prosecution.

SOURCE: Rollin M. Perkins and Ronald N. Boyce, *Criminal Law*, 3d ed. (Mineola, N.Y.: The Foundation Press, 1982), p. 726, citations and bold print omitted. Reprinted with permission.

The federal code has a separate provision for accessory after the fact.[94] The Model Penal Code provides that an actor is guilty of an offense if committed by that person or another for whom he or she is legally accountable, or both.[95]

Accomplice Liability

Because most jurisdictions have merged first- and second-degree principals and accessory before the fact, all to be treated as principals to the offense, it is possible to look at the elements of accomplice liability. Accessories after the fact include such crimes as compounding a felony and misprision of felony, which are discussed in an earlier chapter.

There are three basic elements to accomplice liability. One is mentioned earlier—whether it is necessary to find the principal guilty before convicting the accomplice. The other two elements are those of other crimes, the act and the mental state.

ACTUS REUS

Often a fine line is drawn between doing enough and not doing enough to constitute the act required for complicity. The easier cases are those in which the alleged accomplice provides a hotel room for a prostitute, provides a gun for a murderer, drives the getaway car for the robber, or supplies the necessary technological information for the computer thief. More difficult is the person who is present and appears to approve and who has some legal duty to act but does not do so. A West Virginia case held that a passenger in an automobile committed the *tort* of aiding and abetting by providing alcohol and drugs for the driver whose negligent driving resulted in a fatal head-on collision.[96] Although this was a civil, not a criminal, case, criminal liability could result if the prosecutor chose to file charges. More recently, the Supreme Judicial Court of Maine upheld the conviction of a defendant as an accomplice to operating under the influence of intoxicating liquor when the defendant, who had been drinking heavily, asked another person who was under the influence to drive his truck. The court noted that the state's definition of accomplice does not limit the crimes to which it applies.[97]

Each case must be decided on its facts. The case of *Pace v. State* illustrates the problem, while giving some general statements about guidelines for determining whether the alleged accomplice has committed the requisite act.[98]

Pace v. *State*

[The defendant was convicted of aiding and abetting a robbery.]

[T]he record shows the following: appellant, his wife and two infant children were in a car driving from South Bend to LaPorte. Eugene Rootes was riding with them. The appellant was driving with his wife and one child in the front seat. Rootes and appellant's other child were in the back seat. While in South Bend, appellant after asking his wife for permission stopped to pick up a hitchhiker, Mr. Reppert, who sat next to Rootes in the back seat with one of appellant's infant children. Later Rootes pulled a knife and took Reppert's wallet. After driving further, Reppert got out of the car. Rootes then took his watch. The appellant said nothing during the entire period and they continued driving. . . .

The main question ... is what evidence beyond the mere presence of person at the scene of a crime is sufficient to sustain a conviction as an accessory before the fact? This court has previously stated that negative acquiescence is not enough to constitute a person guilty of aiding and abetting the commission of a crime. Consequently, this court has always looked for affirmative conduct either in the form of acts or words from which reasonable inferences of a common design or purpose to effect the commission of a crime might be drawn....

In the facts at bar we have found no evidence or reasonable inferences therefrom which might demonstrate that the appellant aided and abetted in the alleged crime. While he was driving the car, nothing was said, nor did he act in any manner to indicate his approval or countenance of the robbery. While there is evidence from which a jury might reasonably infer that he knew the crime was being committed, his situation was not one which would demonstrate a duty to oppose it. We do not intend to draw any hard and fast rules in this area of the law. Each case must be reviewed on its own facts; in so doing we hold that the verdict is not sustained by substantial evidence of probative value and is therefore contrary to law.

Judgment reversed.

MENS REA

Jurisdictions differ also regarding the *mens rea* requirement of complicity. Generally alleged accomplices are required at a minimum to have the *mens rea* required for the offenses for which they are alleged to be accomplices. In addition, most jurisdictions require an *intent to aid* in the commission of the crime.[99] This intent requirement becomes difficult in reality, for frequently it is difficult to distinguish between one who intends only to sell a product or a service and one who intends to do that to facilitate a crime. If a motel owner rents rooms to individuals, knowing that they intend to use those rooms for illegal purposes, has the owner *intended* only a financial transaction or intended to facilitate a crime?

Few cases have been decided on this issue, and the two leading ones disagree. *Backun* v. *United States*, decided in 1940, provides that "The seller may not ignore the purpose for which the purchase is made if he is advised of that purpose, or wash his hands of the aid that he has given the perpetrator of a felony by the plea that he has merely made a sale of merchandise."[100]

An earlier case, *United States* v. *Peoni*, decided by the Second Circuit in 1938, indicated, "All the words used—even the most colorless, 'abet'— carry an implication of purposive attitude towards "the crime."[101] That case is cited with approval in a 1990 case, stating that aiding and abetting "requires some proof that the accused either participated in or assisted, encouraged, solicited, or counseled the crime." The court in *State* v. *Randles* went on to state:

> Mere knowledge of a crime and assent to or acquiscence in its commission does not give rise to accomplice liability. Failure to disclose the occurrence of a crime to authorities is not sufficient to constitute aiding and abetting. Rather, under the Idaho Criminal Code, failure to report a felony makes a person guilty only as an accessory, not as an accomplice.[102]

Several ways to solve the conflict between *Peoni* and *Backun* have been suggested. The Model Penal Code limits accomplice liability to instances in which there exists "the purpose of promoting or facilitating the commission of an offense." Thus, it must be shown that the accomplice affirmatively desired to encourage or assist the principal.[103]

Other courts have held that it is sufficient that accomplices know their acts will assist in the commission of crimes, although they do not necessarily desire that result. Still others permit finding that accomplices have the requisite criminal intent if they act recklessly knowing that the reckless behavior will facilitate the commission of a crime. These people may be just as dangerous to society as those who *intend* the dangerous result. Some permit this result only in the case of *serious* crimes. Some courts have specified other conditions that must be considered, such as what stake the accomplice has in the outcome of the venture. A defendant who will share in the financial proceeds of the venture presumably would have the intent to aid.[104]

One other approach to the intent issue in accomplice liability is to enact a statute for **criminal facilitation**, which means to make it easier for another person to engage in a criminal act. New York has four degrees of criminal facilitation, with *criminal facilitation in the first degree* defined as follows:

> A person is guilty of criminal facilitation in the first degree when, believing it probable that he is rendering aid to a person under 16 years of age who intends to engage in conduct that would constitute a class A felony, he, being over 18 years of age, engages in conduct which provides such person with means or opportunity for the commission thereof and which in fact aids such person to commit such a class A felony.[105]

New York enacted this statute in an attempt to curb the increasing number of adults who were using young people in criminal activities to minimize or limit their own exposure to prosecution.

Other Issues of Accomplice Liability

As in the Wharton rule in conspiracy, in most cases of accomplice liability individuals are not held criminally liable as an accomplice when they assist principals to commit crimes that by definition require two people, such as prostitution, which requires a prostitute and a customer. In the Model Penal Code provision, a person is not an accomplice to an offense when "the offense is so defined that his conduct is inevitably incident to its commission."[106]

Generally the defense of abandonment is recognized in accomplice liability. To sustain this defense, the defendant must show that the complicity was abandoned in a timely manner. The Model Penal Code's provision for abandonment states that the actor must terminate the complicity before the commission of the offense and that such termination either wholly deprives the accomplice's act of any effectiveness in the commission of the offense or the actor gives timely warning to law enforcement officials or makes other reasonable efforts to prevent the commission of the offense.[107]

One final issue is the scope of accomplice liability. Traditionally an accomplice has been held criminally liable for all crimes that might reasonably result in complicity, even though the principal's crimes go beyond those crimes contemplated by the accomplice. It may be argued, however, that this position extends criminal liability beyond the requirement of a criminal state of mind. The traditional rule is rejected by the Model Penal Code. That position is followed by a minority of the states.[108]

SUMMARY

After nine chapters that discuss the meaning and purpose of the criminal law and the liability of principals for a wide variety of criminal offenses, this chapter focuses on anticipatory crimes and the criminal liability of people who are connected to crimes but who are not principals in the traditional sense. An understanding of the crimes discussed in this chapter provides additional reasons for thinking about the meaning and purpose of the criminal law and for reexamining how far that law should go to deter, to promote justice, to punish, or to accomplish any other purpose deemed relevant to criminal law.

Some of the crimes discussed in this chapter may be categorized as *inchoate* or *anticipatory* in that the actual crime is never committed. Inchoate crimes are important, however, for in many cases they lead to the commission of other crimes. An individual who is thwarted in an attempted robbery may try again—and succeed. But even the failures are threats to society, as well as to potential victims.

Criminal solicitation permits punishing people who are the instigators of crimes but who do not commit those crimes. The solicitor may be the prime reason the crime is committed. Because of the potential seriousness of solicitation, some states have very strict requirements for a successful abandonment or renunciation defense.

It is not always easy to distinguish *solicitation*, which involves preparation, and *attempt*, which involves perpetration along with the required criminal state of mind. The facts of each case must be analyzed carefully to determine whether there is any direct movement toward committing a crime—in other words, whether there is an attempt. The Model Penal Code requires that a *substantial step* be made toward the commission of a crime in order for it to be classified as an attempt.

Abandonment and legal impossibility are two defenses that may be permitted in criminal attempt cases. Both require careful consideration of the facts. Frequently it is difficult to determine whether the alleged criminal abandoned the attempt or just failed to achieve the goal of committing a crime successfully. Likewise, it may be difficult to determine the difference between *factual impossibility*, which usually is not a defense, and *legal impossibility*, which may be a valid defense.

A new feature of this chapter is the discussion of criminalizing the knowing transmission of the HIV virus that causes the deadly disease, AIDS. The chapter discusses several cases in which attempted murder has been charged, a conviction obtained, and an appellate court has upheld the conviction. The use of attempt crimes in such cases is questionable, although there appears to be general agreement that other crimes, such as aggravated assault, are appropriate.

Criminal conspiracy occupies a significant portion of this chapter, for it is a crime that is utilized frequently by prosecutors today. Because some jurisdictions permit prosecution and conviction for a substantive crime (such as murder) *and* conspiracy (such as conspiracy to commit murder), conspiracy is a very important tool for prosecutors. Conspiracy is important, too, because this crime may be prosecuted successfully even when the predicate crime did not occur. A person may be found guilty of conspiracy to commit burglary even though the burglary was not committed. Conspiracy is a favorite charge of prosecutors also because it is defined broadly. Most conspiracy statutes are sufficiently precise to pass constitutional scrutiny but sufficiently broad to encompass a wide range of acts.

Conspiracy requires an *agreement* between two or more parties. In most jurisdictions the agreement is sufficient to constitute the *act* required for a crime, but some jurisdictions require an overt act in addition to the agreement. The agreement required for conspiracy is not an easy element to prove. It does not have to be a written agreement; in fact, conspiracy agreements are seldom written. Nor does the agreement have to be communicated to each person in the alleged conspiracy.

The *wheel* and the *chain* methods may be used to decide whether an agreement existed between parties that may not have had any contact with each other at all. But if they all had contact with a central hub (the wheel approach), in some cases it can be inferred that a reasonable person in that situation would know there were others involved.

Conspiracies may be limited by the Wharton rule, referring to crimes that require a specific number of people. Adultery requires two people; therefore, if only two people are involved, under the Wharton rule there cannot be a conspiracy to commit adultery. Although in the past husbands and wives could not conspire because legally they were one person, that rule has been changed.

Corporations may be charged with conspiracy provided the "two-or-more rule" is not violated. The key is to determine whether one or two human actors is involved in the alleged criminal agreements. Although any alleged conspiracy may have begun with more than one party to the agreement, that may change when one party is acquitted. If only one party is left without an acquittal, that individual may not be tried for conspiracy in many jurisdictions. Exceptions may be made, depending on the nature of the acquittal.

The *mens rea* requirement for conspiracy presents problems. The conspirators not only have to have an intent to agree but also an intent to accomplish the criminal purpose. Usually the degree of intent required is that required for the substantive crime. Intent may be inferred, however, from the alleged conspirator's *knowledge* of the situation. In addition, some jurisdictions require an *evil purpose* or motive.

Another reason that conspiracy is a popular crime with prosecutors is that it permits punishment of individuals for crimes committed by others. Some of these crimes may go beyond the original agreement. This rule, called the *Pinkerton rule*, has been criticized severely. Some jurisdictions handle the Pinkerton rule problem by limiting criminal liability of an individual for the criminal acts of a co-conspirator only if those acts are reasonably foreseeable.

The final section of this chapter focuses on parties to crimes. Jurisdictions differ in how they categorize such crimes, but generally these categories exist: principal in the first degree, principal in the second degree, accessory before the fact, and accessory after the fact. Today most jurisdictions do not distinguish either degree of principals and accessories before the fact; all are treated as principals.

Like other crimes included in this chapter, defining the elements of a *principal* may be difficult. An act is required. Usually courts look for *affirmative acts* in contrast to mere acquiescence to an act. The *mens rea* required for a principal may be hard to determine, but usually it will require at least the level of *mens rea* required for the offense to which the actor is an alleged accomplice. Some jurisdictions require proof of an *intent to aid*. Some look to see what stake the accomplice has in the outcome of the illegal venture. Others try to avoid these problems by drafting a separate statute to cover *criminal facilitation*.

All of the crimes discussed in this chapter may be related to the rest of a jurisdiction's criminal code. It is important to check that code carefully before deciding how anticipatory crimes and parties to crimes are applied in that jurisdiction. The crimes discussed in this chapter may be related to the crimes discussed in subsequent chapters, including the broad categories of business or corporate crimes, organized crime, and illegal drug trafficking.

STUDY QUESTIONS

1. Why does a criminal code need to include *criminal solicitation*?
2. Comment in detail on this statement: one charged with solicitation to burn a house may not be convicted of that crime if the house does not burn.
3. Discuss the elements and the defense for criminal solicitation.
4. Distinguish between *criminal solicitation* and *criminal attempt*.
5. Explain how the act and intent elements of a crime relate to the crime of criminal attempt. Explain what is meant by the *substantial step* requirement imposed by some criminal attempt statutes or judicial interpretations of those statutes.
6. What must occur for a defendant to establish abandoning a criminal attempt? What is the difference between *voluntary* and *involuntary abandonment*?
7. What is meant by *impossibility* in criminal law? Distinguish between *factual impossibility* and *legal impossibility*.

8. What do you think is the most appropriate charge to bring against persons who know they are HIV-positive or already have AIDS and who engage in activities, such as sexual behavior or biting, that may spread the virus to others?
9. Why are prosecutors so fond of conspiracy statutes?
10. Discuss the *actus reus* required for conspiracy.
11. What is the difference between the *wheel* and the *chain* analogies? How do they relate to conspiracy?
12. What is meant by the *Wharton rule*? Should it be abolished?
13. Under what circumstances may corporations be prosecuted for conspiracy?
14. Briefly discuss the problems with requiring a criminal intent or *mens rea* for conspiracy.
15. To what extent may conspirators be held criminally responsible for the crimes of their co-conspirators? How does the *Pinkerton rule* apply to this question? Do you think this rule should be followed? Why or why not?
16. How long does a conspiracy last? How do you know when it ended? Why are conspiracy cases so complicated?
17. Distinguish among these terms: *principals in the first degree, principals in the second degree, accessory before the fact* and *accessory after the fact, perpetrator, abettor, inciter,* and *criminal protector*.
18. Explain the *actus reus* and the *mens rea* in accomplice liability crimes.

ENDNOTES

1. New York Penal Code, Section 100.00, *et seq*. (1994).
2. New York Penal Code, Section 100.13 (1994).
3. Arnold D. Hechtman, Practices Commentaries, New York Penal Code, Section 100.13 (1993).
4. Model Penal Code, Comment to Section 5.02.
5. Model Penal Code, Section 5.02(2).
6. State v. Lee, 804 P.2d 1208 (Or.App. 1991), *review denied*, 812 P.2d 827 (1991), citations and footnotes omitted.
7. Model Penal Code, Section 5.05(1).
8. Commentary to Model Penal Code, Section 5.02, p. 371.
9. Ariz. Rev. Stat., Section 13-1005(B) (1994).
10. Model Penal Code, Section 5.02(3).
11. Gervin v. State, 371 S.W.2d 449 (Tenn. 1963).
12. Rex v. Scofield, Cald. 397 (1784).
13. Rex v. Higgins, 2 East 5 (1801).
14. See, for example, New York Penal Code, Section 110.00 (1994).
15. Model Penal Code, Section 5.05(1).
16. See Keys v. State, 766 P.2d 270 (Nev. 1988).
17. People v. Terry, 479 N.Y.S.2d 278 (2d Dept. 1984).
18. People v. Trepanier, 446 N.Y.S.2d 829 (4th Dept. 1982).
19. Merritt v. Commonwealth, 180 S.E. 395 (Va. 1935).
20. Wayne R. LaFave and Austin W. Scott, Jr., *Criminal Law*, 2d ed (St. Paul, Minn.: West Publishing Co., 1986), p. 502.
21. See, for example, People v. Guerra, 708 P.2d 1252 (Cal. 1985).

22. People v. Murray, 14 Cal. 159 (Cal.Ct.Sess. 1859).

23. United States v. Cartlidge, 808 F.2d 1064, 1066–7, 1068–9 (5th Cir. 1987), footnotes and citations omitted.

24. Van Bell v. State, 775 P.2d 1273 (Nev. 1989), *reh'g. denied* (21 August 1990).

25. Schultz v. State, 749 P.2d 559 (Okla.Crim. 1988), citations omitted.

26. State v. Walters, 783 P.2d 531 (Or.App. 1989), *reversed*, 804 P.2d 1164 (Ore. 1991), *cert. denied*, 501 U.S. 1209 (1991).

27. People v. Sullivan, 65 N.E. 989 (N.Y.App. 1903).

28. See People v. Bracey, 360 N.E.2d 1094 (N.Y. 1977), *remanded*, 396 N.Y.S.2d 329 (2d Dept. 1977).

29. For a discussion, see LaFave and Scott, *Criminal Law*, pp. 504–509.

30. State v. Hayes, 78 Mo. 307 (1883).

31. Model Penal Code, Section 5.01(4).

32. Model Penal Code, Commentary to Section 5.01, Part I, Vol. 2, p. 356.

33. Regina v. Collins, 9 Cox C.C. 497 (1864).

34. Regina v. Ring, 17 Cox C.C. 491 (1892).

35. Booth v. State, 398 P.2d 863 (Okla.Crim. 1984), case names and citations omitted.

36. See Waters v. State, 234 A.2d 147 (Md.App. 1967), and State v. Ballamah, 210 P. 391 (N.M. 1922).

37. Attorney General v. Sillem, 159 Eng. Rep. 178 (1863).

38. "Man with HIV Wins $18 Million—from Ex-Wife," *Miami Herald* (26 August 1993), p. 11. See also "Tide of Lawsuits Portrays Society Ravaged by AIDS," *New York Times* (23 August 1992), p. 1.

39. "Texas AIDS Law Off Books in '94: No Convictions Obtained in Statute's Brief History," *Houston Chronicle* (5 September 1993), p. 1C.

40. "Man Who Exposed a Woman to H.I.V. Gets 10-Year Term," *New York Times* (16 December 1992), p. 24. See also "Man Is First Convicted in Louisiana for Putting Partner at Risk of H.I.V.," *New York Times* (28 November 1992), p. 6.

41. Weeks v. State, 834 S.W.2d 559 (Tex.App.Eastland 1992), cases, citations, and notes omitted; *petition for discretionary review ref'd.*, (14 October 1992).

42. Smith v. New Jersey, 621 A.2d 493 (N.J.Super. 1993), *certification denied sub. nom.*, 634 A.2d 523 (N.J. 1993). See also "HIV Exceptionalism, Or, Making Plague Pay," *New Jersey Law Journal* (29 March 1993), p. 20.

43. "Man Bites Cop," *American Bar Association Journal* 76 (March 1990): 32; Scroggins v State, 401 S.E.2d 13 (Ga.App. 1990).

44. "Mom with AIDS Sentenced for Biting Her Child," *Orlando Sentinel* (23 April 1993), p. 1B.

45. "HIV–Positive Status Brings Attempted Murder Charges in More Sex Cases," *Los Angeles Times* (29 August 1993), p. 27. See also "Rape Trial Considers Lethal Use of AIDS," *Miami Herald* (6 July 1993), p. 1B; "AIDS Trial Delayed to Give Defense Time," *Miami Herald* (7 July 1993), p. 3B.

46. Model Penal Code, Section 1.07(1)(b).

47. Harrison v. U.S., 7 F.2d 259 (2d Cir. 1925).

48. Rollin M. Perkins and Ronald N. Boyce, *Criminal Law*, 3d ed. (Mineola, N.Y.: Foundation Press, Inc., 1982), p. 681.

49. Rex v. Jones, 110 Eng. Rep. 485 (1832).

50. State v. Burnham, 15 N.H. 396 (1844).

51. See Model Penal Code, Section 5.03(1).

52. New York Penal Code, Section 105.17 (1994).

53. Musser v. Utah, 333 U.S. 95 (1948).

54. United States v. Brown, 776 F.2d 397 (2d Cir. 1985), *cert. denied*, 475 U.S. 1141 (1986).

55. United States v. Bruno, 105 F.2d 921 (2d Cir. 1939), *rev'd. on other grounds*, 308 U.S. 287 (1939).

56. United States v. Bruno, 105 F.2d 921 (2d Cir. 1939), *rev'd. on other grounds*, 308 U. S. 287 (1939). See also United States v. Townsend, 924 F.2d 1385 (7th Cir. 1991), *post-conviction proceeding sub. nom.*, 769 F.Supp. 1482 (N.D. Ill. 1991).

57. U.S. Code, Title 18, Section 371 (1994).

58. United States v. Zimmerman, 832 F.2d 454, 457 (8th Cir. 1987).

59. U.S. Code, Title 21, Section 963 (1994).

60. U.S. Code, Title 18, Section 1117 (1994).

61. See People v. Zamora, 557 P.2d 75 (Cal. 1976).

62. See People v. Corica, 130 P.2d 164 (Cal.App. 1942).

63. Ariz. Rev. Stat., Section 13-1003A (1994).

64. United States v. Robinson, 503 F.2d 208 (7th Cir. 1974), *cert. denied*, 420 U.S. 949 (1975), *later proceeding*, Beard v. Mitchell, 604 F.2d 485 (75h Cir. 1979), *cert. denied*, Beard v. O'Neal, 469 U.S. 825 (1984).

65. Francis Wharton, *Wharton's Criminal Law*, 14th ed., vol. 2, ed., Charles E. Torcia (New York: Lawyers Cooperative, 1978).

66. Model Penal Code, Comment to Section 5.04, pp. 482–483.

67. See, for example, United States v. Dege, 364 U.S. 51 (1960), *reh'g. denied*, 364 U.S. 854 (1960).

68. See State v. Valladares, 664 P.2d 508 (Wash. 1983).

69. Hurwitz v. State, 92 A.2d 575 (Md. 1952).

70. Model Penal Code, Section 5.03(1).

71. United States v. Thomas, 900 F.2d 37 (4th Cir. 1990), most citations omitted. The citation for United States v. Powell is 469 U.S. 57 (1984). See also United States v. Andrews, 850 F.2d 1557 (11th Cir. 1988) (*en banc*), *cert. denied*, 488 U.S. 1032 (1989); and United States v. Byerley, 999 F.2d 231 (7th Cir. 1993).

72. State v. St. Christopher, 232 N.W.2d 798 (Minn. 1975).

73. Union Pacific Coal Co. v. United States, 173 F. 737 (8th Cir. 1909).

74. Nelson Radio & Supply Co. v. Motorola, 200 F.2d 911 (5th Cir. 1952), *cert. denied*, 345 U.S. 925 (1953).

75. See, for example, United States v. Hartley, 678 F.2d 961 (11th Cir. 1982), *cert. denied*, 459 U.S. 1170 (1983).

76. Model Penal Code Comment to Section 5.03, p. 403.

77. "Developments in the Law—Criminal Conspiracy," *Harvard Law Review* 72 (1959): 939.

78. United States v. Falcone, 311 U.S. 205 (1940).

79. Direct Sales Co. v. United States, 319 U.S. 703 (1943).

80. See, for example, People v. Lauria, 59 Cal.Rptr. 628 (2d Dist.Cal. 1967).

81. People v. Powell, 63 N.Y. 88 (1875).

82. For a discussion, see LaFave and Scott, *Criminal Law*, pp. 540–541.

83. See United States v. Giordano, 693 F.2d 245 (2d Cir. 1982).

84. Ventimiglia v. United States, 242 F.2d 620 (4th Cir. 1957).

85. Model Penal Code, Section 5.03(7)(c).

86. United States v. United States Gypsum Co., 438 U.S. 422 (1978).

87. Pinkerton v. United States, 328 U.S. 640 (1946), *reh'g. denied*, 328 U.S. 818 (1946).

88. Model Penal Code, Tent. Draft 1, p. 21.

89. United States v. Kissel, 218 U.S. 601 (1910).

90. United States v. Torres, 901 F.2d 205 (2d Cir. 1990), *cert. denied sub. nom.*, 498 U.S. 906 (1990).

91. See People v. Taylor, 527 P.2d 622 (Cal. 1974).

92. U.S. Code, Title 18, Section 2 (1994).
93. United States v. Mann, 811 F.2d 495 (9th Cir. 1987), citations omitted.
94. U.S. Code, Title 18, Section 3 (1994).
95. Model Penal Code, Section 2.06.
96. Price v. Halstead, 355 S.E.2d 380 (W.Va. 1987).
97. State v. Stratton, 591 A.2d 246 (Me. 1991).
98. Pace v. State, 224 N.E.2d 312 (Ind. 1967).
99. People v. Beeman, 674 P.2d 1318 (Cal. 1984).
100. Backun v. United States, 112 F.2d 635, 637 (4th Cir. 1940).
101. United States v. Peoni, 100 F.2d 401, 402 (2d Cir. 1938).
102. State v. Randles, 787 P.2d 1152, 1155 (Idaho 1990).
103. Model Penal Code, Section 2.06(3)(a).
104. See State v. Gladstone, 474 P.2d 274 (Wash. 1970).
105. New York Penal Code, Section 115.08 (1994).
106. Model Penal Code, Section 2.06(6)(b).
107. Model Penal Code, Section 2.06(6)(c).
108. See Model Penal Code, Section 2.06(4).

Chapter 11

Focal Areas of Crime Control through Criminal Law

Outline

Key Terms

antitrust violations
buffer
computer crime
corporate crime
criminal group
false pretense
fraud

infiltrated
insider information
insider trading
La Cosa Nostra
Mafia
money laundering

organized crime
racketeering
RICO
securities
syndicate
white-collar crime

Introduction

Crime is recognized widely as a serious problem in the United States, but there is little agreement over how to cope with the problem. From time to time the federal government, state governments, and law enforcement agencies focus on one or more target areas of criminality. Legislatures and Congress enact tougher legislation. Law enforcement agencies crack down on law breakers in an effort to gain greater control over those crimes. This chapter looks at three major areas that are focal points of crime control at federal and state levels: business or white-collar crime, organized crime, and drug trafficking.

It is important to understand that most of the specific crimes discussed in this chapter are not new or unique; any or all of them could be discussed under other headings. For example, computer crime is a theft or property crime; it can be and is committed by individuals not associated with businesses. It is discussed in this chapter because of its frequent association with business crimes.

The uniqueness of this chapter, then, is not in the specific crimes per se but in the relationship those crimes have toward areas of criminality that, due to their perceived seriousness and difficulty to control, are targeted as requiring special attention. The commission of these crimes may not be so obvious to us, but the impact on society as a whole in terms of cost, human injury and life, and corruption of the general ethical and moral fiber of society, is enormous.

Crimes of the Business World

The earlier discussion of property crimes noted that historically, under a laissez-faire attitude of "let the buyer beware," individuals were expected to examine carefully every business deal. If they were outsmarted, they were not crime victims. Today, with a much more complicated social and business system, criminal law has become more realistic and more protective of business people and other consumers. Some acts considered smart business deals and thus not illegal in previous times are covered by the criminal law today. Changing technology has altered the nature of criminality, too, bringing new possibilities for committing crimes, creating the need for new criminal statutes. Theft by computer is a good example of an area of criminality in which traditional statutes are not sufficient.

Various terms have been used to describe the crimes discussed in this section. The term **white-collar crime** is used frequently to refer to business crimes. Sociologist Edwin H. Sutherland coined the term in his 1939 presidential address before the American Sociological Association. Sutherland defined *white-collar crime* as "a crime committed by a person of respectability and high social status in the course of his occupation." This definition involves two essential elements: the status of the actor, which is acquired by or at least related to a profession with a high social status, and the commission of the act within the scope of that business. Excluded would be acts such as murder, manslaughter, or robbery, "since these are not customarily a part of occupational procedures." Sutherland excluded acts such as confidence games committed by wealthy people who are members of the underworld, "since they are not persons of respectability and high social status."[1]

Under federal law, *white-collar crime* is defined as "an illegal act or series of illegal acts committed by nonphysical means and by concealment or guile, to obtain money or property, to avoid the payment or loss of money or property, or to obtain business or personal advantage."[2] In its 1983 annual report, the U.S. Attorney General's Office defined *white-collar crime* as follows:

> White-collar crimes are illegal acts that use deceit and concealment—rather than the application or threat of physical force or violence—to obtain money, property, or service; to avoid the payment or loss of money; or to secure a business or personal advantage. White-collar criminals occupy positions of responsibility and trust in government, industry, the professions, and civil organizations.[3]

The term **corporate crime** is another term used in reference to business crimes.[4] It is a narrower term than *white-collar crime*, focusing on *organizational crime*. The terms have been distinguished as follows:

> If a policymaking corporate executive is acting in the name of the corporation and the individual's decision to violate the law is for the benefit of the corporation, as in price-fixing violations, the violation would constitute corporate crime.
> If on the other hand, the corporate official acts against the corporation, as in the case of embezzlement, and benefits in a personal way from his official connections with the corporation, his acts would constitute white-collar or occupational crime.[5]

This chapter uses the term *business crimes* to cover both corporate and white-collar crimes. The variety of business crimes is immense. Only a few are explored here.

Basis of Liability for Business Crimes

Individual liability for any of the crimes committed by people in the course of business may be determined by the same principles discussed earlier regarding criminal liability. Some crimes have special elements that must be proved in each case. When individuals are charged with bribery, extortion, employee theft, fraud, false pretense, tax evasion, or any other business crime, any elements peculiar to that crime must be proved along with the required act, mental element, and causation. The same is true when several people are charged, as in conspiracy.

The rules change when a corporation is charged with a crime or when a corporate executive is charged with a crime committed by an employee. In addition, a distinction must be made between allegations of criminal and tort liability. At this point it is necessary to recall Chapter 1's discussion of the similarities between torts and crimes.

A brief review of Chapter 2's discussion of criminal liability without fault is crucial to this chapter as well. That discussion noted that there are three types of liability without fault or areas in which an individual may be held liable for a crime without a criminal intent or without even having knowledge that a crime is being committed.

Under a *strict liability* theory, a person may be held criminally liable for such acts as statutory rape without knowing the victim is under the legal age or for selling liquor to a minor without knowing the buyer is a minor. Under *vicarious liability* theory, individuals may be held criminally liable for the crimes of those who work for them, such as employers' liability for employees who sell food or drugs that are in violation of pure food and drug laws and that result in the injury or death of consumers.

Enterprise liability theory, also called *corporate liability*, provides that under some circumstances corporate officers and officials may be held criminally liable for the acts of their employees. Although historically corporations have been held liable for negligence and other torts, many legal issues are involved in holding them liable for criminal acts. Historically, corporations were not held liable for homicide, although as far back as 1909 the Supreme Court upheld the constitutionality of holding a corporation criminally liable for the acts and omissions of its agents. In *New York Central and Hudson River Railroad Co. v. United States*, the Court permitted imputing the criminal intent of a corporate agent to the corporation.[6] This case was a break with the traditional common law approach that corporations could not be held criminally liable, although their agents could. As corporations became more powerful and more dangerous, legislatures and courts began to recognize corporate criminal liability.

In recent years there has been an increasing number of indictments and prosecutions against corporations for violent crimes such as homicide. Focus 11.1 contains one of the indictments in the case against Ford Motor Company for reckless homicide in deaths stemming from an accident involving a 1973 Ford Pinto. Although Ford was acquitted of all criminal charges, the case gained widespread attention and put corporate America on notice that reckless acts causing deaths may lead to the prosecution of the corporation for criminal homicide.[7]

Corporate agents may be held criminally liable for the acts of other employees within the corporation,[8] but the corporate agent may not be convicted if he or she can prove a lack of power to control the situation. When criminal liability is imposed on corporate agents for the acts of their employees, most courts limit punishment to penalties such as a fine. The classic case of *Commonwealth v. Koczwara* held that although a tavern owner could be fined for his bartender's violation of liquor laws, he could not be imprisoned.[9]

The Model Penal Code provides for corporate liability in three areas, with the broadest base of liability "incurred as a consequence of conduct by an agent of the corporation acting on behalf of the corporation and within the scope of his employment." That liability is "limited to violations and to offenses defined by statutes outside the criminal code that plainly evidence a legislative purpose to impose liability on a corporation."[10]

Because many business crimes are prosecuted under federal law, federal statutes are used to illustrate most of the crimes discussed here. States prosecute these crimes, too, but their statutes vary. Furthermore, there is

FOCUS 11.1 Ford Motor Company Indicted for Reckless Homicide

On 14 March 1980, a jury found Ford Motor Company not guilty on all three charges of reckless homicide in connection with the deaths of three teenagers who died in a Ford Pinto when it burned after being hit by another car. This was the first time a corporation was prosecuted for homicide stemming from a products liability case. The indictment that follows indicates the state's charges regarding the dangerous design of the Pinto. Although Ford was exonerated of criminal charges, the company has paid millions of dollars in torts cases resulting from injuries and deaths sustained by drivers and passengers in Ford Pintos.

Here is the indictment, or true bill, the official document that begins a criminal case for which a grand jury must act.

State v. Ford Motor Co.

Indictment in Four Counts Charging Three Counts of Reckless Homicide, a Class D Felony and One Count of Criminal Recklessness, a Class A Misdemeanor

The Grand Jurors of Elkhart County, State of Indiana, being first duly sworn upon their oaths do present and say:

Count 1

That Ford Motor Company, a corporation, on or about the 10th day of August, 1978, in the County of Elkhart, State of Indiana, did then and there through the acts and omissions of its agents and employees acting within the scope of their authority with said corporation recklessly cause the death of Judy Ann Ulrich, a human being, to-wit: that the Ford Motor Company, a corporation, did recklessly authorize and approve the design, and did recklessly design and manufacture a certain 1973 Pinto automobile, Serial Number F3T10X298722F, in such a manner as would likely cause said automobile to flame and burn upon rear-end impact; and the said Ford Motor Company permitted said Pinto automobile to remain upon the highways and roadways of Elkhart County, State of Indiana, to-wit: U.S. Highway Number 33, in said County and State; and the said Ford Motor Company did fail to repair and modify said Pinto automobile; and thereafter on said date as a proximate contributing cause of said reckless disregard for the safety of other persons within said automobile, including, the said Judy Ann Ulrich, a rear-end impact involving said Pinto automobile did occur creating fire and flame which did then and there and thereby inflict mortal injuries upon the said Judy Ann Ulrich, and the said Judy Ann Ulrich did then and there languish and die by incineration in Allen County, State of Indiana, on or about the 11th day of August, 1978.

And so the Grand Jurors aforesaid, upon their oaths aforesaid, do say and charge that the said Ford Motor Company, a corporation, did recklessly cause the death of the said Judy Ann Ulrich, a human being, in the manner and form aforesaid, and contrary to the form of the statutes in such cases made and provided, to-wit: Burns Indiana Statutes, Indiana Code Section 35-42-1-5; and against the peace and dignity of the State of Indiana.

considerable overlap among criminal, civil, and administrative laws covering business crimes.

Mail and Wire Fraud

Numerous acts are included within the crime of **fraud.** Some of these are discussed in Chapter 7, for they overlap with *theft.* But fraud may be defined specifically as well. Focus 11.2 contains the Model Penal Code definition of fraudulent acts pertaining to business practices.

Normally fraud is prosecuted in state courts by state prosecutors. But the use of modern technological devices that transport across state lines has created the need for federal law to standardize law and prosecutions in this area. The mail fraud statute, originally passed in 1872, is the oldest of the federal statutes that cover crimes traditionally considered to be state problems. The wire fraud statute was enacted in 1952. Both are reprinted in Focus 11.3. These statutes criminalize using the mails or wires to carry out a scheme to defraud victims of money or other property rights.

Federal mail and wire fraud statutes differ from **false pretense** in that one element of the latter is the success of the effort. To constitute mail or wire fraud, the actor does not have to succeed. Mail and wire fraud statutes constitute a very important tool in the government's efforts to combat white-collar crime, for the statutes are broad and flexible. In 1984, Congress added a section on bank fraud to the federal statute.[11]

Many fraud and related types of crimes are prosecuted today under state statutes or under other federal statutes, but the case load under the mail-fraud statute is high, covering traditional frauds in addition to more recent prosecutions for use of the mails to commit bribery and extortion. The statute has been used also to prosecute commercial and political corruption as well as frauds committed within corporate, governmental, or non-business settings.

In 1987 the Supreme Court narrowed the scope of the 115-year-old federal mail fraud statute, thus limiting prosecutorial powers that lead to uncertainty regarding the status of political corruption cases prosecuted or pending under this statute. In *McNally* v. *United States*, the Court reversed the convictions and ten-year prison sentences of a former Kentucky state official and a businessman who were charged with mail fraud in an insurance contract kickback scheme. The jury was instructed that they could convict the defendants of mail fraud if they found evidence that the defendants had defrauded the people and the government of Kentucky of their right "to have the Commonwealth's affairs conducted honestly." The Court said that the purpose of the statute is to protect money and property, not intangibles. But *McNally* was overruled by legislation in 1988 when Congress amended the wire fraud statute to include "a scheme or artifice to deprive another of the intangible right of honest services."[12]

After the Supreme Court's decision in *McNally*, numerous politicians convicted under the mail or wire fraud statutes petitioned courts to have those convictions reversed. Some were successful. In *United States* v. *Italiano*, the defendant's conviction was reversed and vacated on the basis of *McNally's* substantial limitation of the mail fraud statute to schemes to

FOCUS 11.2 Fraud in Business Practices: The Model Penal Code Provision

Section 224.7. Deceptive Business Practices

A person commits a misdemeanor if in the course of business he:

1. uses or possesses for use a false weight or measure, or any other device for falsely determining or recording any quality or quantity; or
2. sells, offers or exposes for sale, or delivers less than the represented quantity of any commodity or service; or
3. takes or attempts to take more than the represented quantity of any commodity or service when as buyer he furnishes the weight or measure, or
4. sells, offers or exposes for sale adulterated or mislabeled commodities. "Adulterated" means varying from the standard of composition or quality prescribed by or pursuant to any statute providing criminal penalties for such variance, or set by established commercial usage. "Mislabeled" means varying from the standard of truth or disclosure in labeling prescribed by or pursuant to any statute providing criminal penalties for such variance, or set by established commercial usage; or
5. makes a false or misleading statement in any advertisement addressed to the public or to a substantial segment thereof for the purpose of promoting the purchase or sale of property or services; or
6. makes a false or misleading written statement for the purpose of obtaining property or credit; or
7. makes a false or misleading written statement for the purpose of promoting the sale of securities, or omits information required by law to be disclosed in written documents relating to securities.

It is an affirmative defense to prosecution under this Section if the defendant proves by a preponderance of the evidence that his conduct was not knowingly or recklessly deceptive.

SOURCE: Copyright 1992 by The American Law Institute. Reprinted with the permission of the American Law Institute.

deprive individuals of their money and property. In *Italiano* the jury instruction had a heavy emphasis on the intangible right of citizens to fair and honest government.[13]

In 1989, in *Schmuck* v. *United States*, the Supreme Court upheld the conviction of a defendant who was convicted of mail fraud after rolling back odometers. The Court indicated that for a conviction under this statute, the mails do not have to be an essential element of the crime as long as the mails are incident to an essential part of the scheme.[14]

A successful mail- and wire-fraud case requires that the government prove three elements: (1) a scheme or artifice formed with the intent to defraud; (2) using or causing the mails or wire to be used (3) in furtherance

FOCUS 11.3 Federal Mail and Wire Fraud Statutes

Frauds and Swindles[1]

Whoever, having devised or intending to devise any scheme . . . to defraud . . . for the purpose of executing such schemes . . . places in any post office or authorized depository for mail matter, any matter or thing whatever to be sent or delivered by the Postal Service, or takes or receives therefrom, any such matter or thing, or knowingly causes to be delivered by mail . . . any such matter or thing, shall be fined not more than $1,000 or imprisoned not more than five years, or both.

Fraud by Wire, Radio, or Television[2]

Whoever, having devised or intending to devise any scheme . . . transmits or causes to be transmitted by means of wire, radio, or television communications in interstate or foreign commerce, any . . . signals . . . for the purpose of executing such scheme . . . shall be fined not more than $1,000 or imprisoned not more than five years, or both.

[1] U.S. Code, Title 18, Section 1341 (1994).
[2] U.S. Code, Title 18, Section 1343 (1994).

of the scheme. The first element no longer may be satisfied by intangibles; the scheme must involve money or property. The government does not have to show that the scheme was successful or even that victims suffered losses, but only that the defendant had the *specific* intent to defraud.[15]

To satisfy the use requirement, the second element, the defendant does not have to be *directly* involved in using the mail or wire; nor does the victim have to receive the information through either. But there must be evidence that either the mail or wire actually was used and that its use was a reasonably foreseeable result of the defendant's actions. The final element does not require that the mails or wire be essential to the scheme but only that one be useful to the defendant or closely related to the scheme.

Because mail and wire fraud require a specific intent, a defense is a showing of a good-faith effort to obey the law. It is a defense as well to show that the mailing or use of wire was not in furtherance of a scheme to defraud.[16]

The Travel Act

Another statute that may be used widely and involves extensive prosecutorial discretion is the Travel Act. The Travel Act prohibits traveling in foreign or interstate commerce or using any facility in interstate commerce, including the mail, with the intent to do any of the following:

(1) distribute the proceeds of any unlawful activity; or
(2) commit any crime of violence to further any unlawful activity; or
(3) otherwise promote, manage, establish, carry on, or facilitate the promo-

tion, management, establishment, or carrying on, of any unlawful activity, and thereafter performs or attempts to perform any of the acts specified in subparagraphs (1), (2), and (3).[17]

This statute would be considerably broader if not for the fact that the statute defines the word *unlawful* to include unlawful gambling, liquor, narcotics, prostitution, extortion, bribery, or arson. The primary purpose of the Travel Act is to control the activities of people who live in one state and conduct illegal activities in another. It is aimed primarily at organized crime but is used also in prosecuting corporate crimes not associated with organized crime, along with attempts to bribe public officials.

The Travel Act requires that the government prove three elements. First, the defendant traveled in or used interstate or foreign commerce. Second, the defendant had the intent to commit the acts included, and third, the defendant did commit the illegal acts defined by the statute.

There has been considerable litigation and disagreement among the courts on the meaning of these elements. Violation requires a specific intent; thus a good-faith belief that the underlying act was not criminal is a defense. Another defense is to show that the activity was not part of a business enterprise, which is a requirement of the statute.

Environmental Crimes

Protection of the environment for future generations as well as for those of us enjoying life today has become a matter of extensive local, state, and national concern. Although civil actions are available, the criminal law is being utilized in an effort to prevent environmental pollution. (See Focus 11.4). Civil penalties may not carry stigma; civil cases may last for years; and businesses may consider the resulting fines just another cost of doing business. Thus, the deterrent effect of civil penalties may be limited. Further, the effect of prosecution may not be significant. For example, in the Exxon case, discussed in Focus 11.4, a government study reports that much of the over $1 billion fine assessed Exxon had been squandered. According to the General Accounting Office, almost 15 percent of the money paid by Exxon thus far "has been spent to reimburse government agencies and Exxon itself for expenses." Recently some steps were taken to ensure that the future money paid by Exxon is used for the primary purpose of the fine: to restore the coastal waters of the area.[18]

The federal government and many state governments have passed hundreds of criminal laws aimed at preventing environmental pollution, and within the past decade, enforcement has been stricter. The U.S. Justice Department established an Environmental Crimes Section in an effort to enforce the Resource Conservation and Recovery Act (RCRA), which authorizes felony sanctions for illegal dumping of toxic waste.[19] States, too, have enacted legislation in this area, but it varies widely.[20] Perhaps the most familiar of the federal statutes that provide penalties for environmental pollution is the Clean Air Act (CAA), which delegates power to the Environmental Protection Agency (EPA) to establish air quality control standards.

FOCUS 11.4 Crackdown on Environmental Pollution: The Use of Criminal Statutes—Recent Cases

It was the worst oil spill in U.S. history, and the nation reacted with shock and dismay when the Valdez, an Exxon tanker, ran aground in Alaska and dumped nearly 11 million gallons of crude oil into Prince William Sound. The captain, Joseph J. Hazelwood, was acquitted of the most serious charges against him, which included reckless endangerment, criminal mischief, and operating a vessel while intoxicated. Hazelwood, who had gone below to his cabin and left a third mate in charge of the tanker's voyage through the sound, was thought to have been drinking; but the jury did not believe the state proved that he was drunk.

Hazelwood was convicted of a single charge of misdemeanor negligence (for negligent discharge of oil) for which he was sentenced to spend 1,000 hours in the oil spill cleanup and pay the state of Alaska $50,000 in restitution. In 1992 the conviction was reversed on the grounds that the federal law that required Hazelwood to report the oil spill granted him immunity from prosecution. Hazelwood's attorney, claiming that his client was vindicated, referred to the oil spill as a maritime accident and the prosecution as a politically motivated one. In 1993 the Alaska Supreme Court upheld the lower court's decision on immunity but held

A worker hired by Exxon tests a heated water spray hose to clean oil-covered rocks on Smith Island in Prince William Sound. The largest oil spill in U.S. history occurred when Exxon's tanker, the Valdez, went aground.

that the immunity is limited by a procedural rule (the "inevitable discovery rule"). The case was sent back to the court of appeals for reconsideration of the conviction for negligent discharge of oil in light of this ruling.[1]

Exxon Corporation was indicted for two felonies involving violation of the Ports and Waterways Safety Act and the Dangerous Cargo Act for allegedly allowing incompetent crew members to operate the Valdez and employing physically and mentally incompetent personnel. The corporation faced misdemeanor charges for violation of the Clean Water Act, the Refuse Act, and the Migratory Bird Treaty Act. The indictment alleged that over 700 miles of water and shoreline were polluted and that over 36,000 migratory birds, including 100 bald eagles, were killed as a direct result of the oil spill. After a series of negotiations and plea bargains, all claims were settled when Exxon agreed to pay large fines and restitution over a ten-year period. In December 1993, however, an independent geochemist reported that not all of the damage to Prince William Sound was caused by oil from the Exxon tanker. At that point Exxon had already paid about $3 billion in fines, with another $3.5 billion remaining to be paid for over 5,000 claims. If the geochemist is correct, the penalties against Exxon will have to be altered. The geochemist claims that some of the damage may have been caused by a 1964 oil spill that received little attention at the time.[2]

After a month-long civil trial, in June 1994 a jury found that Exxon acted recklessly in permitting Hazelwood, who had a history of alcoholism, to command the Valdez. The jury found also that Hazelwood was reckless and negligent on the afternoon of the oil spill. The next phase of the civil trial is to determine the amount of damages that must be paid to plaintiffs in the lawsuit.[3]

These criminal indictments represent a trend in the efforts of federal as well as state law enforcement agencies to get tough on polluters. Among other cases, Ashland Oil was fined $2.25 million for violating the Rivers and Harbors Act; Texaco was fined $750,000 for violations under the Outer Continental Shelf Lands Act; Ocean Spray Cranberries was fined $400,000 for twenty-one violations of the Clean Water Act.[4]

In 1990 Eastman Kodak was fined $2.15 million in criminal and civil penalties for violating New York's environmental laws. The company pleaded guilty to two misdemeanor violations for illegally disposing of hazardous waste and failing to report the toxic spill until five days after the spill was discovered. Additionally, Kodak had to pay $150,000 to local emergency planning committees.

In November 1990, Evelyn Berman Frank, head of a New York company charged with illegal sewage-sludge dumping, was sentenced to five years' probation and 500 hours of community service for her role in the offense.[5]

[1.] "Hazelwood's Conviction Overturned," *American Bar Association Journal* 78 (October 1992): 25; "A New Slant on Exxon Valdez Spill," *New York Times* (1 December 1992), p. 1C. The case is Hazelwood v. State, 836 P.2d 943 (Alas.App. 1992), *aff'd. in part, rev'd. in part, and remanded for further proceedings*, 866 P.2d 827 (Alas. 1993).
[2.] "Hazelwood's Conviction Overturned," ibid. See also Daniel A. Farber, "The Global Environment and the Rehnquist Court," *Trial* 28 (August 1992): 73–77.
[3.] "Jury Finds Exxon Acted Recklessly in Valdez Oil Spill," *New York Times* (14 June 1994), p. 1.
[4.] "Battling Crimes Against Nature," *Time* (12 March 1990), p. 54.
[5.] "Barge Owner Gets Probation for Harbor Dumping," *New York Times* (7 November 1990), p. 1.

Environmental pollution may include pollution of the inside working environment or other safety problems in various industries. As far back as 1911, businesses were put on notice that they might be prosecuted for crimes when they provided dangerous work environments. Factory owners were charged with manslaughter after over 140 women died in the Triangle Shirt Waist fire in New York.[21]

In 1970 Congress passed OSHA (Occupational Safety and Health Act); but in contrast to the significant resources provided for the enforcement of federal environmental control, little has been done by the federal government to provide for enforcement of OSHA. Consequently, prosecutions at the state level have been significant. In 1980, New York–based Warner-Lambert, a chewing gum manufacturing plant, and its manager were charged with manslaughter for the deaths of six employees. The deaths resulted from an explosion and fire, possible dangers of which the company had been prewarned. For technical reasons regarding the evidence, they were not held criminally liable.[22]

After a discussion of prosecutions under California's OSHA statute, two scholars concluded that although the "number of prosecutions may be small, . . . like a barking dog, their very presence may deter thousands of violations." In distinguishing the *criminal* from the *civil* (which may exist also) nature of these violations, the authors stated:

> None of these cases . . . involved intentional deaths. They were all the result of either a reckless or negligent act, or a failure to act. Nonetheless, in each case the defendant violated his duty of care to another human being. Under California law, the acts or omissions were criminal. The deaths or injuries were not accidents.[23]

Whether to bring charges under criminal or civil statutes (or both) is debatable. Theoretically civil cases are easier to win, but even they are expensive and difficult. Many lawyers were shocked in late 1993 as they sat in a Columbus, Georgia courtroom where plaintiffs in a case against DuPont Company settled their cases for $4.25 million (one hundred times less than the damages sought) just prior to the return of a jury verdict. These lawyer-observers represent farmers in over 400 other lawsuits against DuPont and realized that this settlement could weaken their respective cases. One month later an Arkansas jury returned a verdict of $10.65 million in damages against DuPont and in favor of thirty-one tomato farmers. These cases involve a DuPont-manufactured fungicide, Benlate DF, which is alleged to be the cause of plant damage. Earlier Dupont had settled over $500 million in claims against the company for crop damages allegedly caused by Benlate, but in 1992 the company stopped settling the claims, arguing that new tests indicated the fungicide was not the cause of crop damage.[24]

Environmental pollution and, to a lesser extent, safety in the work place are growing concerns. The laws that govern them are complicated. Violations invoke widespread public debate and concern because of the resulting injuries and deaths as well as environmental pollution. Whether to pursue environmental pollution under the civil or criminal law (or both) is a debatable issue.[25]

Antitrust Violations

Most states and the federal government have statutes protecting trade and commerce from unlawful restraints, monopolies, price fixing, and price discriminations. These acts are referred to as ***antitrust violations***. Although there are several federal statutes, most federal antitrust violations are prosecuted under the Sherman Antitrust Act, passed by Congress in 1890.[26]

The primary purpose of Section 1 of the Sherman Antitrust Act is to prevent companies from joining together to fix prices. Litigation arises, however, over the meaning of *price fixing* and how to distinguish between the legal exchange of information between legitimate businesses, such as trade associations that disseminate trade news and data, and illegal exchanges of information that lead to unreasonable restraint of trade.[27] Section 2 of the Act is aimed at controlling monopolies. Litigation here has focused on defining the product market, the geographic market, and the market share.

The Sherman Act contains provisions for criminal prosecutions (brought by the Justice Department) and civil proceedings (brought by the Federal Trade Commission). Also, there are provisions for privately injured parties to sue for damages; if successful, they may recover attorney fees *and* treble damages. If their actual damages are high, paying three times those damages is a stiff penalty. It may be argued that this penalty is a greater deterrent than criminal prosecutions in some cases.[28]

Securities Fraud

The exchange of securities is a highly regulated business in the United States. **Securities** include stocks, bonds, notes, and other documents that are representative of a share in a company or a debt of the company. Although there are several federal statutes covering the exchange of securities, two are used most frequently for prosecution of securities violations.

The Securities Act of 1933 requires that securities to be sold to the public must be registered. Complete information must be given concerning the stock offering and the issuer.[29] The Securities Exchange Act of 1934 regulates the operation of over-the-counter trading and the buying and selling of stock. It specifies the information that must be published concerning stocks listed on the national securities exchange.[30] These statutes and others are administered by the Securities and Exchange Commission (SEC).

Also prosecuted under these acts are closely related crimes such as mail and wire fraud, conspiracy, aiding and abetting, and the making of false statements. These two federal security statutes prohibit the use of any device, scheme, or artifice to defraud; the making of an untrue statement of facts material to the buying and selling of the securities; the omission of information that would result in a misleading statement; and acts that operate to defraud or deceive the stock purchaser. Intent is a material element of the crimes under these securities statutes. To constitute a violation, the defendant must use interstate commerce through the mails or other methods. The object of the transaction in question must be a security as defined by the acts.

Administrative, civil, and criminal remedies are provided by the securities acts. Initial investigations into possible violations of the statutes (or the rules promulgated by the SEC in accordance with the administrative powers delegated to that agency by Congress) are conducted by the SEC. The Justice Department has sole jurisdiction to prosecute criminal violations under these statutes.

INSIDER TRADING

Because of the attention given nationally to **insider trading** prosecutions in recent years, this particular securities violation deserves special attention. Insider trading is the most frequent type of violation, although there is no way of knowing the extent of these violations.

Prosecutions for insider trading began increasing with the appointment of John Shad as SEC chairman in 1981. The SEC began a highly publicized campaign to inform everyone about insider trading and prosecutions for the offense. Congress enacted the Insider Trading Sanctions Act of 1984, which increased the penalties for this crime. Among other sanctions, the insider faces civil fines of up to four times the amount of the money earned from insider trading. The maximum criminal fine has been increased from $10,000 to $100,000.[31] In 1988 Congress enacted another statute aimed specifically at insider trading; that statute increased penalties for insider trading.[32]

Insider trading is the act of trading in the securities market when the trader has information that has not yet been made available to the investing public. **Insider information** is information known to securities officers before it is available to the public. If in accordance with SEC regulations the insiders do not publicize the information available to them and then trade on the basis of that information, they may be prosecuted criminally as well as face civil fines and other penalties. The *disclose or abstain* rule exists presumably to make trading more equitable; it is unfair for insiders to make profits based on information not available to the public. Such trading violates a *fiduciary* (one who manages money for another and has special responsibilities as a result) *duty.*

Many Americans were stunned in the 1980s by insider trading cases in which some of the most powerful traders in the stock market were charged. The Wall Street scandal broke in May 1986 when mergers-and-acquisitions specialist Dennis B. Levine was charged with having used his advance knowledge of fifty-four impending mergers to make millions of dollars off the trading of stocks. Levine was sentenced to two years in federal prison, a lenient sentence because he cooperated with the government.[33]

Levine gave the government evidence of the illegal insider trading of Ivan F. Boesky, a leading Wall Street stock market speculator, who in turn cooperated in leading the federal prosecutors to other violators. In exchange for an agreement that other charges against him would be dropped, Boesky pleaded guilty to one charge of conspiracy to "make false, fictitious and fraudulent statements" to the government.

Ivan Boesky, convicted for his role in insider trading, served his prison term and has been cooperating with the government on other cases since his release.

In 1987, Boesky was sentenced by Judge Morris F. Lasker, considered by many to be the most lenient judge in New York. Boesky, who could have been sentenced to a five-year prison term and been fined, received a three-year prison term. Boesky was not fined by Judge Lasker, but he had agreed previously to pay $100 million as a civil penalty, one-half to go to the U.S. Treasury and one-half to be placed in escrow to handle the investors' claims. Released from prison in the spring of 1990, Boesky has become a key government witness in other cases of insider trading.

In 1993 Boesky was back in court, this time attempting to get money from his ex-wife. The one-time wealthy financier said he was penniless and asked the court for $20,000 per week in "interim financial support" in May 1993, when the judge granted his wife a divorce on the grounds of cruel and inhumane treatment. At stake were the assets of Seema Boesky, reported to equal $100 million. The case was settled out of court in June, when Seema agreed to pay Ivan $20 million (he had asked for $50 million), a $2.5 million home in California, and yearly payments of $180,000 for the remainder of his life.[34]

On 13 February 1987, Martin A. Siegel, a thirty-eight-year-old investment banker with an outstanding career and an even more promising future, pleaded guilty in Manhattan to two felony charges: conspiracy and tax evasion in connection with his part in an insider trading scheme. Siegel agreed to give up $9 million in cash and stock as part of his plea bargain with federal prosecutors, who dropped other charges against him because of his cooperation with authorities in securing evidence on other violators. Because of his cooperation with the prosecution and his contrition for his crimes, Siegel was sentenced to two months in prison, one of the shortest sentences in the Wall Street insider trading cases.

Ira B. Sokolow, a thirty-two-year-old investment banker, was convicted and sentenced to one year and a day in prison and three years' probation after he admitted that he sold information about pending takeovers to Levine. In April 1990 the "junk bond" king, billionaire Michael R. Milken, entered guilty pleas to six felony charges of insider trading and conspiracy. Milken, former head of the junk bond division of now-defunct Drexel Burnham, proclaimed his innocence until he entered his plea. At that time he apologized for his crimes but not for the junk bond market he had created and that had financed many of the corporate takeovers of the 1980s. Earlier Drexel had reached a settlement with federal prosecutors to end the largest probe in history of a securities firm. Drexel agreed to pay $650 million in fines and to plead guilty to six felony counts of mail, wire, and securities fraud. Part of that fine ($300 million) goes to the government, which spent $10 million prosecuting the case up to that point, and $350 million was to be set aside for victims of Drexel's crimes.[35]

In November 1990, Milken was sentenced to a ten-year prison term, the longest prison sentence imposed in the Wall Street scandal. In addition, Milken was ordered to serve 1,800 hours of community service after his prison term.[36] In 1991 the judge who sentenced Milken to ten years in prison recommended that he be eligible for parole after serving three years. In 1993 Milken was released from prison after serving only twenty-two months. He is working in a DARE (Drug Abuse Resistance Education) program in Los Angeles and teaching a class in management finance. During his first class, the still-wealthy and highly charismatic Milken proclaimed, "If there's no risk, there's no future."[37]

The insider cases continue in both civil and criminal courts. In 1993 both Milken and Boesky testified in a civil case involving Miami, Florida financier Victor Posner and his son, Steven, in which the SEC alleged that the Posners conspired with Milken and Boesky to make an illegal purchase of the Fischbach Corporation. In testifying at this trial, Milken denied that he had any illegal dealings with the Posners. The SEC sought to bar the Posners from serving as directors or corporate officers and sought the Posners' forfeiture of the $4 million they earned in salaries while at Fischbach.[38]

In December 1993 a federal judge ruled in favor of the SEC and barred both Posner and his son from ever serving as officers or directors of any public companies. The Posners were ordered to repay the nearly $4 million they had received from the Fischbach Corporation. The judge was not impressed with Milken's testimony, concluding that he was evasive and that he gave the appearance of "someone who cannot, and therefore will not, accept the fact that he has done wrong." Milken insisted that he had told the truth during his testimony.[39] In late December 1993 Posner settled an income-tax evasion conviction by donating $2.1 million to several charities in South Florida.[40]

Computer Crimes

During the past two decades computers have played an increasingly important role in everyday life. In many ways they have made business easier; in some cases, when the computer is not functioning properly, transactions stop, creating frustrating waiting periods.

Computers have made life more convenient, too; money may be obtained from machines as well as from banks. But with these and other conveniences have come problems. Privacy is more likely to be invaded now that extensive personal data are kept in various computer files. Although computers have been used to process valuable data leading to the apprehension of criminals, they have created serious problems and a new field of crime for individuals and for businesses to combat.

The conviction of college student, Robert Morris, Jr., for his role in disrupting computers, emphasized the extensive damage that can be done by one computer hacker. Morris, a graduate student at Cornell University, wanted to demonstrate the weaknesses of computer security. He unleashed a computer "worm" program into a group of computer networks that connect universities and other institutions, including military and government computers. It was not intended that the worm would interfere with daily computer operations, but the result was that the affected computers ceased functioning, causing an estimated $200 to $53,000 dollars in damage at each location. Morris faced up to five years in prison and a $250,000 fine, but he was placed on three years' probation, fined $10,000, and ordered to perform 400 hours of community service. Included in the latter was an assignment to answer the phone for a bar association. Morris appealed his conviction but lost, with the appellate court rejecting his argument, among others, that he did not intend to cause harm. The court indicated that the statute requires only the intent to use the computer in an unauthorized manner. An intent to cause harm is not required.[41]

Unlike Morris, who acted alone and apparently had no intent to harm, apparently some of the more recent computer hackers engaged in their crimes for purposes of intimidation and harassment. Several nationwide computer hacker groups exist, and the members appear to enjoy the company of other hackers, although some like to annoy those hackers. In 1992 five members of the M.O.D. (Masters of Deception), a group of New York–based computer hackers, entered guilty pleas to numerous federal computer crimes. These hackers were charged with stealing information from some of the most sophisticated computer systems in the country and selling that information to private investigators. Prosecutors argued successfully that these hackers engaged in computer crimes for the purpose of harassing and intimidating their victims.[42]

In late 1993 two men were sentenced to two and one-half years in federal prison as a result of their guilty pleas in rigging a fake automated teller machine, which they used to make over $100,000 in illegal withdrawals. The fake machine was used to copy personal identification numbers, which were used to make counterfeit identification cards. Those cards were used for illegal withdrawals. In addition to the prison terms, which resulted from negotiated pleas, the defendants were ordered to pay $464,000 in restitution to their victims.[43]

Computer crime refers to crimes committed by the use of a computer. Computers are used to commit theft and embezzlement. "In all parts of the country, computers have been tools in crimes of unprecedented economic cost, from electronic funds transfer fraud to inventory loss." Estimates of the annual societal loss from computer crimes vary, but one estimate is between $3 and $5 billion annually. Computers are being used not only as tools for traditional theft crimes; they are becoming increasingly important in "the illegal activities of drug networks. Drug traffickers use them to communicate with each other, record their transactions, and transfer and launder money."[44] Computers are being used also for counterfeiting documents such as checks and securities.[45]

STATUTES REGULATING COMPUTER CRIMES

In 1978 Florida and Arizona became the first states to enact computer crime statutes. Today most states have enacted similar statutes, as indicated in Focus 11.5. Despite several attempts, Congress did not pass a computer crime statute until 1984. Prior to that time, computer crimes were prosecuted under about forty federal statutes. Because these statutes were written for other purposes, many problems arose when they were applied to computer crimes. Examples of statutes were those covering wire and mail fraud, theft and embezzlement, and the transportation of stolen property. The Federal Computer Crime Control Act is part of the general revision of the federal criminal code, known as the Comprehensive Crime Control Act of 1984. It contains three general categories of forbidden acts. The code prohibits knowingly accessing a computer without authorization or, after having authorization, accessing a computer and using it to obtain information beyond the scope of that authorization for the purpose of:

1. gaining information declared essential for national defense or foreign relations or certain types of specified restricted data for the purpose of injuring the United States or benefitting a foreign country;
2. obtaining "information contained in a financial record of a financial institution . . . or . . . a file of a consumer reporting agency on a consumer," or
3. using, modifying, destroying, or disclosing information in, or presenting the authorized use of the computer "if such computer is operated for or on behalf of the Government of the United States and such conduct affects such operation."[46]

There are some specified limitations on the extent to which these last two provisions apply.

The statute includes attempts and conspiracies to commit the enumerated crimes. Penalties, including fines and prison terms, are based on the type of computer offense and whether it is a first or subsequent offense. The maximum prison term is twenty years.[47]

It is possible that this statute, along with state statutes, does not deter people from committing computer crimes. The crimes are difficult to

FOCUS 11.5   State Computer Crime Statutes

In late 1988, Robert T. Morris, a Cornell University graduate student, shut down a nationwide computer network with what rapidly became the best-known computer worm in history. Prosecuted in federal court for violation of the federal computer crime statute, Morris eventually received a fine and probation. But his actions cut loose a torrent of public discussion on the adequacy of the criminal justice system to deal with predators as skillful as but more malicious than Morris.

Computer technology is omnipresent in contemporary American life. We pump gas from computerized pumps; receive computerized bills from public utilities for service that is largely computerized; receive computerized grocery checkout lists, which are part of computerized inventory control systems; take off, fly, and land in planes guided by computers; telephone friends on the other side of the country on computerized telecommunications systems; get telephone calls from computers; read articles, including this one, written on computers.

State and federal legislators are fully aware that we have entered the computer age. In the ten years before the Morris worm, forty-eight of the fifty state legislatures and the U.S. Congress had passed some form of computer crime statute. Morris probably could have been prosecuted in every state in which his worm entered a computer, for either unauthorized access or computer damage.

The article discusses the evolution of state computer crime statutes, including definitions of terms, offenses, elements of computer crimes, penalties, venue, civil remedies, and other miscellaneous features, before discussing computer worms and viruses, as indicated here.

Computer Worms and Viruses

The beginning of this article referred to the computer worm used by Robert Morris to penetrate a national network. Even though most states already had computer crime statutes, several state legislatures amended their statutes to include detailed descriptions of Morris' techniques.

The Morris worm was an independent program that penetrated computers on the network and replicated itself, rapidly overloading the individual computers, first making them sluggish and then causing them to crash. The worm created temporary files that disappeared when the affected computers were shut down, and it did not steal information or destroy files. In the jargon of the industry, because Morris' program was an independent program, it was a "worm." A computer "virus" is a piece of computer code attached to another program.

California's amendment, which refers to both worms and viruses under the rubric "computer contaminant," is illustrative of the new provisions adopted after the Morris incident:

(10) "Computer contaminant" means any set of computer instructions that are designed to modify, damage, destroy, record, or transmit information within a computer, computer system, or computer network without the intent or permission of the owner of the information.

They include, but are not limited to, a group of computer instructions commonly called viruses or worms, which are self-replicating or self-propagating and are designed to contaminate other computer programs or computer data, consume computer resources, modify, destroy, record, or transmit data, or in some other fashion usurp the normal operation of the computer, computer system, or computer network.

Maine and Texas both added "computer virus" to their definitions, and Minnesota added "destructive computer program" to its definitions. Illinois put its new prohibition under "computer tampering."

Conclusion

Justice Holmes considered the States laboratories for working out a variety of approaches to problems confronting our society. The computer crime statutes just discussed are an excellent example of what he was talking about. In a very short period of time—short, that is, as far

as lawmaking goes—almost all States have adopted legislation dealing directly and explicitly with computer crime. They have chosen to add these statutes to existing law, rather than to substitute them for prior criminal prohibitions and civil remedies, broadening the options available to prosecutors and civil litigants.

These laws are detailed in definition and comprehensive in scope. But if anything characterizes the criminals at whom these laws are aimed, it is their own ingenuity in finding cracks and loopholes in computer systems and networks. The next decade will provide a test of the strength and precision of these computer laws.

SOURCE: Hugh Nugent, *State Computer Crime Statutes*, National Institute of Justice (Washington, D.C.: U.S. Department of Justice, November 1991), pp. 1, 10, footnotes omitted.

detect. Prosecution requires highly technical information, and most apprehended offenders are middle- or upper-class people, the types not often prosecuted in criminal justice systems despite the recent emphasis on prosecuting white-collar criminals. Some companies do not want the publicity of prosecuting their employees for crimes that, it might be argued, they could have avoided with more extensive checking of references.

The use of computers to commit crimes ties together this discussion of business crimes with the next two focuses of the chapter—organized crime and drugs. As already noted, computers are used extensively in drug trafficking, which is connected with organized crime in many instances. Likewise, many of the other crimes discussed here are part of organized crime. It is not possible to separate these areas entirely, as the first paragraph of this next section indicates.

Organized Crime

In 1983 the late Donald R. Cressey, a noted criminologist, answered his own question about what the Presidential Crime Commission of the year 2113 would say about organized crime by stating, "My hunch is this commission will not even have a task force on organized crime. By that time, what we call organized crime will be considered what we call white-collar crime."[48]

Gilbert Geis, a sociologist who has written extensively about white-collar crime, emphasized the closeness between organized crime and some corporate crime in his recent analysis of Sutherland's concept of white-collar crime, noted in the beginning of this chapter. According to Geis, Sutherland's concept was vague, but Sutherland was "most concerned with the illegal abuse of power by upper-echelon businessmen in the service of their corporations."[49]

Other scholars, in recent writings, insist that if white-collar crime and organized crime are defined in terms of the "motives and methods of the offense" rather than in terms of "the status of the offenders," the similarities will be obvious. This approach is applied to an analysis of savings and loan fraud, "arguably the largest set of white-collar heists in history," resulting in the demonstration that the "*modus operandi* of much executive misconduct approximates the organized crime model."[50]

In many cases it is difficult to draw the line between organized crime and white-collar crime, for as noted by the most recent President's Commission on Organized Crime, organized crime has **infiltrated** many legitimate businesses.[51] Consequently, organized crime is another national and state legislative and law enforcement target, with the Federal Bureau of Investigation (FBI) and the Department of Justice having designated organized crime as one of its main target areas, along with white-collar crime and drug trafficking.[52] The history of the government's attempts to combat organized crime may be seen with a brief glance at the commissions appointed to study the problem.

Commission Reports

Several government commissions have investigated organized crime. Brief excerpts from their conclusions are found in Focus 11.6. The Committee to Investigate Crime in Interstate Commerce, popularly known as the Kefauver Committee, found widespread involvement of organized crime in illegal businesses. Stating that a nationwide **syndicate** existed, the committee reported that this syndicate, called the **Mafia,** claimed power in many large U.S. cities. Its leadership, depending on muscle and murder, controlled lucrative rackets. The vast sums of money available from the rackets allowed the leadership group family members to influence, bribe, intimidate, or murder its opposition.[53]

The McClellan Committee (the Select Committee on Improper Activities in the Labor or Management Field) reported widespread involvement of organized crime in labor unions.[54] The 1967 reports of the President's Committee on Law Enforcement and Administration of Justice claimed that organized crime not only had gained extensive influence in illegitimate businesses but had infiltrated many legitimate businesses.[55] In its 1973 report, the National Advisory Committee on Criminal Justice Standards and Goals emphasized the infiltration of organized crime into many areas of American life.[56]

In July 1983, President Reagan expressed his concern by appointing a nineteen-member commission to study organized crime. Headed by Judge Irving R. Kaufman of the U.S. Court of Appeals for the Second Circuit, the

FOCUS 11.6   The Impact of Organized Crime

The Kefauver Committee, 1953

"Organized crime affects the lives of millions of Americans, but because it desperately preserves its invisibility many, perhaps most, Americans are not aware how they are affected, or even that they are affected at all. The price of a loaf of bread may go up one cent as the result of an organized crime conspiracy, but a housewife has no way of knowing why she is paying more."[1]

The President's Commission on Law Enforcement and Administration of Justice, Task Force on Organized Crime, 1967

"The core of organized crime activity is the supplying of illegal goods and services—gambling, loan sharking, narcotics, and other forms of vice—to countless numbers of citizen customers. But organized crime is also extensively and deeply involved in legitimate business and in labor unions. Here it employs illegitimate methods—monopolization, terrorism, extortion, tax evasion—to drive out or control lawful ownership and leadership and to exact illegal profits from the public. And to carry on its many activities secure from governmental interference, organized crime corrupts public officials."[2]

The National Advisory Committee on Criminal Justice Standards and Goals, 1973

"No one is beyond the reach of the illegal efforts of organized crime. The picture of organized crime in America that emerges . . . is one of an elusive, changing, nationwide activity involving crim-inal, quasi-criminal, and deceptively legitimate individuals. . . . Organized crime appears to be a conspiratorial effort to profit from the operations of American commerce without abiding by laws or paying taxes."[3]

Irving R. Kaufman, Chairman, the President's Commission on Organized Crime, 1983

"Organized crime has become a scourge of modern society with direct responsibility for a host of social ills. . . . Organized crime victimizes tens of thousands of working people each year. . . .

Organized crime in its traditional form poses a sufficient danger to justify an in-depth investigation and analysis. Today, however, we are also confronted with new forms of illegal activity. . . .

The threat of organized crime today also differs from the past by reason of its sheer size. The menace is larger and still growing."[4]

[1.] *Senate Special Committee to Investigate Organized Crime in Interstate Commerce*, 3d Interim Rep., H. Rep. No. 307, 82d Cong., 1st Sess. 150 (1951), pp. 170–171.
[2.] The President's Commission on Law Enforcement and Administration of Justice, Task Force Report, *Organized Crime* (Washington, D.C.: U.S. Government Printing Office, 1967), p. 1.
[3.] National Advisory Committee on Criminal Justice Standards and Goals, *Organized Crime* (Washington, D.C.: Government Printing Office, 1973), Foreword, p. 21.
[4.] Irving R. Kaufman, chairman, the President's Commission on Organized Crime, Public Hearing, 29 November 1983, published in President's Commission on Organized Crime, *Organized Crime: Federal Law Enforcement Perspective* (Washington, D.C.: U.S. Government Printing Office, 1983), pp. 4–5.

commission's mandate was a broad one, as indicated in Focus 11.7. The commission's interim and final reports provide the basis for many of the discussions in this chapter. The commission spent nearly $5 million in its two and one-half years of existence, which were characterized by significant internal disagreements, with nine members accusing the committee of mismanaging time, staff, and money.[57]

Defining Organized Crime

Like most concepts in criminal law, **organized crime** is no exception to the problem of a lack of definitional consensus. In the past the term has been used almost synonymously with *professional crime*. It distinguished amateur from professional criminals. More recently, organized crime has been used to refer to highly structured, disciplined, and self-perpetuating associations of people who bind together for the purpose of making huge profits through illegal and legal means while utilizing graft and corruption in the criminal justice arena to protect their activities from criminal prosecution.

The 1967 President's Commission on Law Enforcement and Administration of Justice defined organized crime as "a society that seeks to operate outside the control of the American people and their working government." It is an organization of thousands of criminals who operate in a very complex organizational structure. They have rules that are even more rigid and more strictly enforced than the rules of legitimate government. The main goals are money and power, and organized crime infiltrates legitimate as well as illegitimate businesses.[58]

A few years after the 1967 commission report, the Task Force on Organized Crime of the National Advisory Committee on Criminal Justice Standards and Goals considered the definition of organized crime and refused to define the concept to include all of the criminal activities covered by state and federal statutes. Instead, that task force enumerated characteristics of organized crime.[59]

The 1983 presidential commission delineated two crucial components of organized crime: the criminal group and the buffer. The **criminal group** (also called the *cartel, corporation, family, gang, gumi, and triad*) "is a continuing, structured collectivity of defined members utilizing criminality, including violence, to gain and maintain profit and power." The criminal group has six characteristics: continuity, structure, defined membership, criminality, violence, and power as its goal.

The second component of organized crime, the **buffer,** protects the criminal group from effective prosecution by corrupting judges, lawyers, politicians, law enforcement officials, financial advisors, financial institutions, gaming establishments, and other national and international businesses. Additionally, people serve in support groups, working for a particular criminal group and sometimes waiting to become members of the criminal group. There are four categories of support groups:

1. *Specialist support* includes individuals and groups who perform specific tasks to facilitate organized crime activities, including pilots, chemists, arsonists, and saboteurs.

FOCUS 11.7 The President's Commission on Organized Crime

The President's Commission on Organized Crime was established by Executive Order on 28 July 1983. The Executive Order directed the commission to

1. make a full and complete national and region-by-region analysis of organized crime;
2. define the nature of traditional organized crime as well as emerging organized crime groups, the sources and amounts of organized crime's income, and the uses to which organized crime puts its income;
3. develop in-depth information on the participants in organized crime networks;

4. evaluate federal laws pertinent to the effort to combat organized crime;
5. advise the president and the attorney general with respect to its findings and actions that can be undertaken to improve law enforcement efforts directed against organized crime;
6. make recommendations concerning appropriate administrative and legislative improvements and improvements in the administration of justice; and
7. report to the president from time to time as requested and to submit its final report by 1 March 1986.

SOURCE: Public Law 98-368.

---

2. *Supply support* includes the providers of organized crime's illicit goods and services.

3. *User support* includes the users of organized crime's illicit goods and services, including drug users and patrons of the local bookie.

4. *Social support* includes individuals and organizations that grant power and an air of legitimacy to organized crime generally and to certain criminal groups and their members specifically; for example, public officials who solicit the support of organized crime figures; business leaders who do business with organized crime; social and community leaders who invite organized crime figures to social gatherings; and members of the media and entertainment industries who portray the criminal group or organized crime in a favorable or glamorous light.[60]

Finally, as the discussion below indicates, organized crime has been defined historically in terms of the ethnicity and background of its participants, primarily Italians. Sociologists have criticized this approach.[61]

Structure of Organized Crime

The history and structure of organized crime have been hotly debated, with some arguing that it is controlled by one syndicate, the Mafia. The earlier Kefauver commission took that position.[62] Others deny that the Mafia exists.[63] The 1967 president's commission concluded that there are twenty-four groups, known as families, with the membership of each ranging from twenty to 700. That commission presented a detailed diagram and explanation of the hierarchical structure of the organized crime family, ranging from the lower-level *lieutenants*, who "operate the illegal enterprises on a commission basis or own illicit or licit businesses under the protection of the family," to the head of the family, the *boss*.[64]

The 1967 presidential commission reported that the name of the organization had been changed from Mafia to **La Cosa Nostra** (LCN), meaning "our thing." The 1986 report of the latest presidential commission did not define precisely either Mafia or La Cosa Nostra. Although it centered its investigation on LCN, that commission concluded that organized crime is much broader than LCN. But the commission stated that LCN infiltrates legitimate business more frequently than other organized crime groups.[65]

The 1986 trial and conviction of eight men who were top leaders in the *commission* (which serves primarily as a judicial body) and is the top ruling body, shed more light on the structure of organized crime. During opening statements in September 1986, the defense conceded that the Mafia does exist and that there is a commission, but argued that these facts did not mean the defendants were guilty of the crimes charged — **racketeering** patterns that included murders, loan sharking, labor payoffs, and extortion in the concrete industry. All eight were convicted and given long prison terms.[66]

In 1988 Anthony (Fat Tony) Salerno, boss of the Genovese crime family, was acquitted of some charges but convicted of racketeering (along with eight other defendants). Salerno died in prison in 1992 of complications from a stroke. He was serving terms of seventy and 100 years for separate convictions. It is believed that during the 1980s Salerno ran the largest numbers racket in Harlem and that those businesses made about $50 million a year. It is said also that during the 1964 riots in Harlem, in one area in which Salerno owned a shop, all store windows were smashed except those belonging to Salerno. According to criminologist Howard Abadinsky, "Even in the middle of a riot, people knew better."[67]

The government has been successful in other prosecutions of high-level organized crime members. In 1988 the reputed crime boss of Philadelphia and Atlantic City, Nicodemo Scarfo, Jr., and sixteen of his associates were convicted, leading to the claim that prosecutors had won the "most sweeping mob conviction ever." The defendants were charged with "committing or participating in nine murders and four attempted murders as well as conspiracy to commit racketeering, extortion, illegal gambling, loansharking and drug trafficking."[68]

The 1987 acquittal of John Gotti, claimed by the government to be the leader of the most powerful of the organized crime families and charged with federal racketeering and conspiracy, was called the "first major setback in [the government's] recent assault on organized crime."[69] On 9 February 1990 Gotti was acquitted of assault and conspiracy charges, his third acquittal in four years. In December 1990, Gotti was indicted for racketeering, gambling, loansharking, bribery, and four murders. He was accused of plotting the 1985 murder of Paul Castellano so that Gotti could become the head of the most powerful Mafia family.[70] Gotti's 1992 trial drew widespread media attention, with noted persons holding vigil outside the courthouse in which Gotti and his codefendant were tried and convicted of thirteen counts. Even after his conviction, some stated that Gotti was a very nice man; his codefendant stated at Gotti's sentencing that "if there were more men like John Gotti on this earth, we would have a better country."[71]

In October 1993 the convictions were upheld on appeal, with the judge accusing one of Gotti's attorneys of being a potential witness and perhaps an accomplice to some of Gotti's crimes. The attorney denied any wrong-doing and indicated his belief that he could get the conviction overturned. In 1994 the U.S. Supreme Court refused to hear the appeal. Gotti's attorney, Bruce Cutler, was sentenced to ninety days of house arrest, fined $5,000, suspended from legal practice for 180 days in the Eastern judicial district of New York, and ordered to perform 200 hours of community service for each of three years' probation. Cutler received these penalties for speaking to reporters against the judge's orders in one of Gotti's trials.[72]

Gotti is incarcerated in Marion, Illinois in one of the most secure of all federal prisons, but he is reported to be running the Gambino family from that prison.[73] His associates have carried on the work of the Gambino family, too, but in March 1993, despite numerous allegations of jury tampering, Robert Bisaccia was convicted of charges stemming from his position as a Gambino family captain. One juror was offered $500 to vote for acquittal; the car of another was riddled with bullets, but the jury convicted Bisaccia and six other members of the Gambino family of racketeering charges. Three jurors, who were intimidated by the events, were dismissed before the case went to the jury.[74]

In May 1993 Thomas Gambino, for whose father the Gambino organized crime family is named, was convicted of racketeering and racketeering conspiracy. In June two of his distant cousins, brothers John and Joseph Gambino, were convicted of bail jumping (they forfeited $5 million in bail in 1992 but were caught later), but the jury could not reach a verdict on the more serious charges of racketeering, murder, loan sharking, gambling, and conspiracy. The judge declared a mistrial. In January 1994 the Gambino brothers pleaded guilty to various crimes committed between 1975 and 1992. In June of that year they were sentenced to fifteen years in prison on racketeering charges, including murder and drug trafficking. They are not eligible for parole during that period.[75]

Anthony Salvatore Casso, thought to be one of the most dangerous organized crime leaders in the United States today, was captured in January 1993. Casso had disappeared shortly before his scheduled trial in 1990. He was apprehended as he stepped out of the shower and taken into custody wearing a towel. He and Salvatore Avellino, Jr. were charged "in the 1989 killings of two men who had fought the mob cartel that authorities say dominates the private trash-collection industry on Long Island."[76]

Organized Crime and Money Laundering

Special attention is given here to one area of organized crime involvement: **money laundering.** Frequently huge profits made through the sale and distribution of illicit drugs and other illegal ventures are laundered to make them appear legitimate. The process includes disguising the illegal source and illegal application of income as well as concealing the existence of illegal income. The term *money laundering* comes from references criminals make to the process of laundering "dirty" money so that it looks "clean."

In the past, not all money laundering was illegal. The illegal acts were prosecuted under the Bank Secrecy Act, which required banks to report any domestic transaction of more than $10,000. The organized crime commission concluded that the act was not sufficient. The penalties were too light, and the act did not permit needed government surveillance to detect money-laundering schemes.[77]

In 1986, Congress enacted legislation making money laundering a crime. The Money Laundering Control Act of 1986 imposes criminal penalties for anyone who knowingly uses proceeds from unlawful activity to conduct a financial transaction (1) to conceal the nature or ownership of the proceeds or (2) to avoid transaction reporting requirements. Both criminal and civil penalties are provided. The statute was amended in 1988.[78]

The money-laundering statute is complicated and has been criticized severely. In 1994 the U.S. Supreme Court held that the willfulness requirement of the statute requires the government to prove that the defendant "acted with the knowledge that the structuring he or she undertook was unlawful, not simply that the defendant's purpose was to circumvent a bank's reporting obligation."[79]

The Group of Seven, a group concerned with money laundering and representing several industrial countries, has proposed "a broad set of regulatory and banking reforms . . . to combat the growing problem of concealing illegal narcotics profits in banks and other financial institutions." A report based on an investigation of money laundering estimates that $85 billion per year may be laundered from illegal drugs and quickly reinvested.[80] The American Bankers Association has reported that U.S. bankers spend more than $129 million a year in an effort to prevent money laundering.[81]

Money laundering is a problem in white-collar crime as well as in organized crime. Those who attended the meeting of the National Institute on White-Collar Crime in 1990 were told that money laundering is the crime of the decade. Most of those in attendance were the white-collar defense bar. They were told, "You will all prosper beyond your wildest dreams."[82]

Focus 11.8 gives a brief description of the extent of money laundering in the world, along with information about the role of the BCCI (Bank of Commerce and Credit International) in money laundering.[83]

Controlling Organized Crime through RICO

Prior to the passage of **RICO**, discussed later, federal and state prosecutors could and did prosecute alleged organized criminals for individual crimes, such as extortion, gambling, production and sale of drugs, and murder. But Congress felt it necessary to provide another tool against organized crime.

After two decades of attempts, Congress passed its massive effort to combat organized crime, the Racketeer Influenced Corrupt Organization Act

FOCUS 11.8   International Money Laundering

The Money-Laundering Industry

In the summer of 1991, perhaps only the dismantling of the Soviet Union received greater national media attention than the shutdown of the Bank of Commerce and Credit International (BCCI) by regulators in several countries. BCCI was convicted of money laundering in Tampa, Florida. In addition, BCCI has, as part of a global plea agreement, pled guilty in the District of Columbia to conspiracy to commit racketeering acts involving money laundering, fraud, and tax evasion, and in New York to charges of money laundering, fraud, bribery, and theft.

The bank has been called "the most pervasive money-laundering operation and financial supermarket ever created," a "marathon swindle," and a "steering service for [Colombian] drug traffickers to deposit hundreds of millions of contraband dollars outside the country." Currently the target of investigations in several countries, BCCI will surely rank as one of the most complex schemes of its kind. Even so, BCCI is only one example of the pervasive, worldwide money laundering industry that exists today.

It is probably impossible to determine how much money is laundered either domestically or internationally each year. One way to gain some perspective on the problem is to consider estimates of drug trafficking revenues. Worldwide, people spend as much as $500 billion annually on illegal drugs, with up to $200 billion spent in the United States.

According to the U.S. Department of the Treasury, drug traffickers launder an estimated $100 billion each year in this country alone, with much of the activity channeled through financial institutions. Although drug trafficking fuels the money-laundering industry, any assessment of the problem must also consider the funds laundered from other crimes, including fraud offenses, securities manipulation, illegal gambling, bribery, extortion, tax evasion, illegal arms sales, political pay-offs, and terrorism. When these crimes are also considered, estimates of the amount of money laundered annually run as high as $300 billion.

SOURCE: Barbara Webster and Michael S. McCampbell, *International Money Laundering: Research and Investigation Join Forces*, National Institute of Justice (Washington, D.C.: U.S. Department of Justice, September 1992), p. 1, footnotes omitted.

(RICO), which was part of the Organized Crime Control Act of 1970. This statute has been called the *new darling* of the prosecutor's nursery, replacing conspiracy in that position. RICO got this title because it is written broadly and therefore constitutes a potentially powerful prosecutorial tool.[84] In enacting RICO, Congress stated: "It is the purpose of this Act to seek the eradication of organized crime in the United States . . . by providing enhanced sanctions and new remedies to deal with the unlawful activities of those engaged in organized crime."[85]

RICO may be distinguished from other statutes that are used to prosecute organized crime in that RICO is broader. Unlike other statutes, RICO does not create specific *individual* offenses but operates on a *pattern* of offenses, which is discussed later. In addition, RICO allows enhanced penalties, such as the forfeiture provision, which provides that when a person is convicted under RICO, "any interest he has acquired or maintained in violation of" the RICO statute may be subjected to forfeiture. This means the government may order that the personal or real property acquired from money derived through criminal racketeering be forfeited to the government.[86] RICO differs also in that penalties may be cumulative. Defendants may receive penalties for the underlying crime (such as extortion) as well as for the RICO violation.[87]

One final distinction is that RICO provides different civil penalties, such as permitting some plaintiffs to recover treble damages. This means that instead of the usual procedure of permitting successful plaintiffs to recover the extent of their business and property losses from defendants who violated RICO, they may recover three times those damages. Successful plaintiffs may recover court costs and reasonable attorney fees from the defendants.[88] This section has been interpreted broadly and used widely in civil litigation.[89]

RICO prohibits

1. the use of income derived from a *pattern of racketeering* to acquire an interest in an *enterprise;*
2. acquiring or maintaining an interest in an enterprise through a pattern of racketeering activity;
3. conducting or participating in an enterprise's affairs through a pattern of racketeering activity; and
4. conspiring to commit any of these offenses.[90]

As noted, in many cases it is impossible to separate business crimes from organized crime. RICO has been used to prosecute doctors, labor union leaders, government officials, and many other professionals, as well as business people charged with civil and criminal acts covered by the statute. "The wider use of the law is part of a move by Federal prosecutors away from the traditional, narrow definition of 'organized crime' toward a broader grouping that takes account as well of crooked business executives and other white-collar offenders."[91]

ELEMENTS OF RICO

The RICO statute begins by listing the crimes that may form the basis of a RICO offense. Twenty-four federal and eight state crimes are included. These crimes are referred to as *predicate crimes*, because they constitute a predicate, or basis, for a RICO violation.[92]

In 1984 Congress added *dealing in obscene material* as a predicate crime because of the significant increase in the sale and production of hard-core pornography. This section was challenged and upheld in *United States* v. *Pryba*, decided in 1990.[93] Also added were currency violations and three automobile-theft offenses. Each predicate crime may constitute a *racketeering activity*. But the RICO statute requires a *pattern* of racketeering activity. It is not aimed at individual violators but rather at those who have committed at least *two predicate offenses* within a ten-year period, one of which occurred after RICO became effective.[94] The statute does not specify what is necessary to make two or more federal crimes a pattern. In *H. J. Inc.* v. *Northwestern Bell Telephone Company*, the Court faced that issue in a civil RICO action. RICO is used frequently as a basis for a civil case because of the high penalties—treble damages plus court costs and attorney fees. Although trial procedures and proof distinguish civil and criminal RICO actions, the Court's interpretation of the meaning of the *pattern* requirement in a civil case has applicability to a criminal RICO case.[95]

The Court noted that Congress had not specified what it meant by *pattern*, looked at the legislative history of the statute, and concluded that Congress intended that statute to cover *continuing* racketeering activity. The key phrase in the Court's analysis is *continuity plus relationship*. The Court held that

> In order to prove a pattern of racketeering activity, a plaintiff or prosecutor must show at least two racketeering predicates that are related *and* that amount to, or threaten the likelihood of, continued criminal activity. Proof of neither relationship nor continuity requires a showing that the racketeering predicates were committed in furtherance of multiple criminal schemes.[96]

According to the statute, an *enterprise* includes "any individual, partnership, corporation, association or other legal entity, and any union or group of individuals associated in fact although not a legal entity." According to the Supreme Court in *United States* v. *Turkette*, the enterprise must have an ongoing formal or informal organization whose associates function as a continuing unit. Legal enterprises are included.[97]

Litigation under RICO may be complex, but this excerpt from *United States* v. *Weinberg* gives a picture of the extent of the offenses, some of the issues that may be raised, and one of the types of offenses that any of us might experience. The case illustrates the use of RICO to prosecute white-collar or business crimes that constitute patterns of racketeering but that are not necessarily associated with organized crime.[98]

United States v. Weinberg

Defendant is named in a sixteen-count superseding indictment. Count One charges that defendant violated the Racketeer Influenced and Corrupt Organizations Act ("RICO"), by conducting the affairs of an enterprise — his real estate business—through a pattern of racketeering. Seven predicate acts of racketeering are alleged.

The first four predicate acts arise from defendant's ownership of a building . . . . The First Act of Racketeering charges defendant with employing various forms of harassment and deception in a scheme to force and fraudulently induce elderly and low-rent tenants to vacate their apartments. The Second Act of Racketeering charges a fraudulent scheme to overcharge tenants by violating New York's rent control and stabilization laws and misrepresenting to tenants the requirements of those regulations. The Third Act of Racketeering charges defendant with defrauding the purchaser of the building by falsely stating that the rents had been legally set and by misrepresenting the condition of the building. As part of this scheme, defendant allegedly paid $10,000 to the building superintendent in exchange for the latter's providing misleading information to agents of the purchaser. . . .

The next two predicate acts involve a building. . . . It is alleged that defendant fraudulently received money from insurance companies by hiring an individual to commit arson at the building. . . .

The Seventh Act of Racketeering involves a two-family home. . . . It is alleged that defendant arranged to have the house vandalized and then filed a fraudulent insurance claim for the damage. . . .

[There were numerous mail fraud charges as well. Among other findings, the appellate court held that the allegations of the complaint alleged sufficiently the existence of a criminal enterprise and a pattern of racketeering; thus, the charges under RICO were appropriate.]

It is important to understand that RICO was intended by Congress to reach serious violators—major violators who engage in a pattern of racketeering activity. As noted, however, the statute is worded broadly, and the Court has found it necessary to place some limits on the interpretation of some of the broad language. In 1993 the Court held that generally professional advisors to businesses, such as accountants, do not participate in those businesses to the extent that they should be included within the reach of RICO.[99]

FORFEITURES

In the discussion above it is mentioned that the government may require forfeitures of personal and real property acquired or maintained by money acquired through illegal patterns of racketeering. RICO is not the only federal statute that permits forfeitures; about one hundred statutes contain a forfeiture provision. It is estimated that 80 percent of individuals who lose property through forfeiture laws are never charged with crimes and that the value of the seized property in 1992 was $531 million. Many innocent persons lose property through RICO and other forfeiture statutes. The government seizes not only the means of illegal production of goods and the illegal goods (such as drugs) but the homes in which the material is found and the vehicles used to transport the illegal materials. These forfeitures may occur without prior notice, and the individual who wants the property back has the burden of proving that it should not have been confiscated. Before a hearing will be held on that issue, the owner of the forfeited property must post a bond of 10 percent of the value of the property. Some conservative lawmakers are proposing legislation to curtail such forfeitures so that innocent people do not suffer.[100]

The Supreme Court has shown concern recently with the potential unfairness of forfeitures, as illustrated by two decisions during the 1992–93 term. Looking at RICO and another forfeiture law, the Court ruled that seized property must not be excessive when compared to the seriousness of the crimes in question. The Court views forfeiture of property as punishment and applies the cruel and unusual clause of the Eighth Amendment (see Appendix A) to the analysis of those forfeitures.[101] Earlier in its 1992–93 term the Court had ruled in a Florida case involving civil forfeiture proceedings in which the government had taken a house alleging that it was purchased with money from illegal drug trafficking. The case involved jurisdictional questions beyond the scope of this text, but the result was to bolster the right of persons to appeal when the government seizes their property.[102] In its 1993–94 term, the Court decided another forfeiture case, holding that unless there are exigent circumstances, the government must give notice and permit one the opportunity for a hearing before real property subject to civil forfeiture is seized.[103]

Asset forfeitures occur frequently in cases involving illegal drug trafficking. "In particular, civil forfeiture schemes have been increasingly employed in the 'war on drugs.'"[104] Traffic in illegal drugs constitutes one of the most serious social problems in the world today, and the last part of this chapter focuses on substance abuse and drug trafficking.

Substance Abuse and Drug Trafficking

It has been estimated that substance abuse (including cigarettes, alcohol, and other drugs) is responsible for 500,000 deaths in the United States each year. Substance abuse destroys families, increases health care costs, contributes to violence—especially gang violence—and overwhelms the social institutions of this country, especially the educational and criminal justice systems.[105] The number of drug-related cases in state and federal courts has increased significantly in the past decade. This increase, combined with longer sentences, has been the primary factor contributing to prison and jail overcrowding. The proportion of prison populations incarcerated for drug offenses has increased (from 9 percent to 22 percent between 1986 and 1991) while the proportion for violent offenses has decreased (from 55 percent to 45 percent); yet, violent crimes have been increasing. A report of the American Bar Association reviews these facts and concludes that "The criminal justice system in this country is on the fast track to collapse." These changes have affected minorities more negatively than others, shown by the 23 percent increase in arrests compared to a 10 percent increase for nonminorities.[106] Some have argued that these problems are a result of the government's war on drugs.

The U.S. War on Drugs

In a 1992 publication the *New York Times* reviewed the twenty years of the U.S. "war on drugs." The article concluded that despite the estimated $70 billion cost of the war in its first twenty years, drug-related crime is "far worse than it was twenty years ago. . . . It may be too harsh to say the war has been lost. But on many fronts there seems to have been little progress."[107]

Former President Reagan and his administration continued the war on drugs. In June 1982 the president appointed a nineteen-member special group of government agency heads and instructed them to report back to him with suggestions on how to fight drug abuse.[108] In 1986 President Reagan signed into law the Anti-Drug Abuse Act of 1986 (see Focus 11.9), which increased penalties for federal drug-related offenses and provided funding for drug prevention, education, and treatment. The statute provides also for drug education programs and alcohol and drug abuse treatment, prevention, and rehabilitation programs. This legislation has been held constitutional.[109]

As part of the war on drugs, Congress passed the Anti-Drug Abuse Act of 1988, which directed the president to examine the extent and nature of the drug problem and to propose policies for dealing with the problem. An Office of National Drug Control Policy (ONDCP) was established in the Executive Office of the President, with the director appointed by the president and confirmed by the Senate. In September 1989 President Bush issued his President's National Drug Control Strategy, in which he called for a "larger and more flexible information base in order to help us refine and target our counterdrug efforts." In January 1990 ONDCP Director William J. Bennett, also known as the *Drug Czar*, released an updated version of the president's drug-control strategy, with this comment: "Prevention and treatment, however successful, require the support of drug enforcement activities that lead to the arrest of drug traffickers, that stop drugs from being smuggled into the country, and that keep dealers off the streets."[110]

President Bush's drug-control strategy contained provisions for federal grants to state and local agencies for law enforcement purposes, along with numerous provisions for attempts at drug enforcement. It was praised strongly by some and criticized bitterly by others, but no significant effects were seen in the fight against drugs, leading some to argue for legalization of drugs.[111] The Drug Czar responded that legalization is an idea "seductively simple," and an argument "so dumb only intellectuals would believe" it.[112]

Focus 11.10 tracks government activities regarding drugs between 1965 and 1990. Since 1990 some changes have occurred. In that year Bennett resigned his position. He was succeeded by Robert Martinez, former Florida governor, who was succeeded by President Clinton's appointment, Lee P. Brown, former New York City police commissioner, who has toned down the war-approach language to illegal drugs. Attorney general Janet Reno has indicated that she favors a reversal of long mandatory minimums for minor drug crimes and an emphasis on treatment rather than punishment, a position she took and implemented when she was federal prosecutor in Dade County, Florida, which includes Miami.[113]

President Clinton has kept a relatively low profile about drugs despite his frequent references to being tough on crime. When U.S. Surgeon General Joycelyn Elders suggested that we study legalizing drugs, a move that might reduce crime, her comments were not embraced by the White House. In 1994, Elders' son, Kevin M. Elders, was convicted of drug violations.[114]

FOCUS 11.9 Major Federal Antidrug Bills Enacted in the Past Decade

The 1984 Crime Control Act—

- expanded criminal and civil asset forfeiture laws;
- amended the Bail Reform Act to target pretrial detention of defendants accused of serious drug offenses;
- established a determinate sentencing system; and
- increased federal criminal penalties for drug offenses.

The 1986 Anti-Drug Abuse Act—

- budgeted money for prevention and treatment programs, giving the programs a larger share of federal drug-control funds than previous laws;
- restored mandatory prison sentences for large-scale distribution of marihuana;
- imposed new sanctions on money laundering;
- added controlled substances' analogs (designer drugs) to the drug schedule;
- created a drug law enforcement grant program to assist state and local efforts; and
- contained various provisions designed to strengthen international drug-control efforts.

The 1988 Anti-Drug Abuse Act—

- increased penalties for offenses related to drug trafficking, created new federal offenses and regulatory requirements, and changed criminal procedures;
- altered the organization and coordination of federal antidrug efforts;
- increased treatment and prevention efforts aimed at reduction of drug demand;
- endorsed the use of sanctions aimed at drug users to reduce the demand for drugs; and
- targeted for reduction drug production abroad and international trafficking in drugs.

The Crime Control Act of 1990—

- doubled the appropriations authorized for drug law enforcement grants to states and localities;
- expanded drug control and education programs aimed at the nation's schools;
- expanded specific drug enforcement assistance to rural states;
- expanded regulation of precursor chemicals used in the manufacture of illegal drugs;
- provided additional measures aimed at seizure and forfeiture of drug trafficker assets;
- sanctioned anabolic steriods under the Controlled Substances Act; and
- included provisions on international money laundering, rural drug enforcement, drug-free school zones, drug paraphernalia, and drug enforcement grants.

SOURCE: Bureau of Justice Statistics, *Drugs, Crime, and the Justice System: A National Report* (Washington, D.C.: U.S. Department of Justice, December 1992), p. 86.

Illegal Drug Trafficking

Earlier discussions of drugs in this text focus on substance abuse as a *defense* to criminal liability. The focus here is on criminal law violations. These are concerned mainly with *drug trafficking*, although it is important

FOCUS 11.10   Major Federal Legislation and International Conventions Aimed at Drug Control, 1965–1990

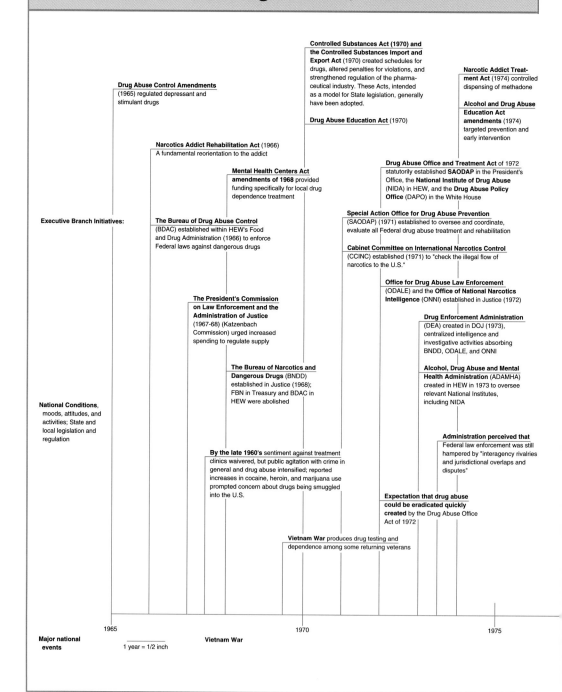

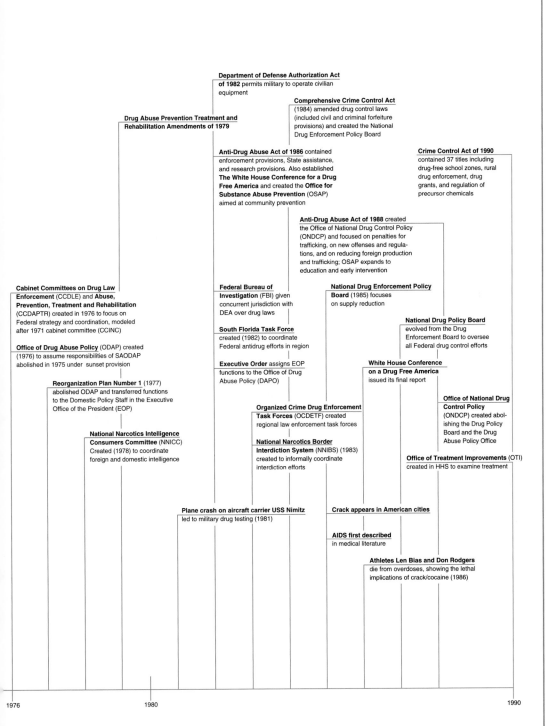

Department of Defense Authorization Act of 1982 permits military to operate civilian equipment

Comprehensive Crime Control Act (1984) amended drug control laws (included civil and criminal forfeiture provisions) and created the National Drug Enforcement Policy Board

Drug Abuse Prevention Treatment and Rehabilitation Amendments of 1979

Anti-Drug Abuse Act of 1986 contained enforcement provisions, State assistance, and research provisions. Also established **The White House Conference for a Drug Free America** and created the **Office for Substance Abuse Prevention** (OSAP) aimed at community prevention

Crime Control Act of 1990 contained 37 titles including drug-free school zones, rural drug enforcement, drug grants, and regulation of precursor chemicals

Anti-Drug Abuse Act of 1988 created the Office of National Drug Control Policy (ONDCP) and focused on penalties for trafficking, on new offenses and regulations, and on reducing foreign production and trafficking; OSAP expands to education and early intervention

Cabinet Committees on Drug Law Enforcement (CCDLE) and **Abuse, Prevention, Treatment and Rehabilitation** (CCDAPTR) created in 1976 to focus on Federal strategy and coordination, modeled after 1971 cabinet committee (CCINC)

Office of Drug Abuse Policy (ODAP) created (1976) to assume responsibilities of SAODAP abolished in 1975 under sunset provision

Reorganization Plan Number 1 (1977) abolished ODAP and transferred functions to the Domestic Policy Staff in the Executive Office of the President (EOP)

National Narcotics Intelligence Consumers Committee (NNICC) Created (1978) to coordinate foreign and domestic intelligence

Federal Bureau of Investigation (FBI) given concurrent jurisdiction with DEA over drug laws

South Florida Task Force created (1982) to coordinate Federal antidrug efforts in region

Executive Order assigns EOP functions to the Office of Drug Abuse Policy (DAPO)

Organized Crime Drug Enforcement Task Forces (OCDETF) created regional law enforcement task forces

National Narcotics Border Interdiction System (NNIBS) (1983) created to informally coordinate interdiction efforts

National Drug Enforcement Policy Board (1985) focuses on supply reduction

National Drug Policy Board evolved from the Drug Enforcement Board to oversee all Federal drug control efforts

White House Conference on a Drug Free America issued its final report

Office of National Drug Control Policy (ONDCP) created abolishing the Drug Policy Board and the Drug Abuse Policy Office

Office of Treatment Improvements (OTI) created in HHS to examine treatment

Plane crash on aircraft carrier USS Nimitz led to military drug testing (1981)

Crack appears in American cities

AIDS first described in medical literature

Athletes Len Bias and Don Rodgers die from overdoses, showing the lethal implications of crack/cocaine (1986)

1976   1980   1990

SOURCE: Bureau of Justice Statistics, *Drugs, Crime, and the Justice System: A National Report* (Washington, D.C.: U.S. Department of Justice, December 1992), pp. 82–83.

to note that both drug possession and drug trafficking offenses are extensive and that attempts to enforce laws regulating the use and sale of controlled substances constitute a large percentage of appeals in both the federal and state systems. Some of these appeals are based on controversies over the *substantive* criminal law; but most of them involve *procedural* issues, which are beyond the scope of this text.

Drug cases, especially those that involve drug trafficking, are complicated. It is not unusual for other crimes, such as conspiracy, to be involved. Furthermore, many of the charges involve attempt crimes, such as *attempt to distribute a controlled substance*. Drug trafficking involves billions of dollars as well.[115]

Drugs and Organized Crime

The production and distribution of illegal drugs is by no means limited to organized crime. A successful effort to curb the problem must have a broader focus than organized crime. However, drugs constitute one area in which organized crime is involved extensively. Therefore it is important to look at the connection.

The 1983 commission concluded that illicit traffic in drugs is the most serious organized crime problem in the world, that it generates billions of dollars in business each year, and that it is supported by an increasing demand for illicit drugs. The commission emphasized the need for cooperation from the public.

> Ultimately, the curse of drug abuse will be broken but only by a nationwide dedication to persistent and unyielding assaults on both supply and demand. The supply is already under siege by our enforcement, diplomatic, and intelligence communities. Because an end to consumption is our ultimate goal, it is a concerted and direct attack on demand that must be mounted.[116]

Attacking organized crime is one way to attack the drug problem, but the latest president's commission indicated that this approach alone will not be sufficient. The commission made numerous recommendations for action that should be taken by governments, media and entertainment industries, health professionals, law enforcement officials, schools, churches, parents, civic organizations, and businesses.[117] Many of these recommendations are already in place, perhaps with drug testing being the most controversial.[118]

SUMMARY

This chapter, which ends the discussion of specific crimes covered by federal and state substantive criminal laws, focuses on three areas in which special legislative and administrative efforts have been made to cope with crime: business crimes, organized crime, and substance abuse and drug trafficking. Discussion of these areas indicates the overlap between federal and state concerns as well as the magnitude of the crime problem.

Ironically, although efforts to reform criminal laws and enforce those laws for the crimes discussed in this chapter far exceed the efforts in all other areas, these concerns rarely are discussed in criminal law texts either at the law school or undergraduate level. Yet, a substantial portion of the time of any local, state, or federal law enforcement officer may be spent in one or more of these areas, and courts are clogged mainly because of the litigation in the latter area, substance abuse and drug trafficking. Finally, prisons are overcrowded mainly because of drug offenders. This is not to suggest that we should ease our efforts to fight the war on drugs or the other areas discussed in this chapter, but rather to emphasize the importance of including these areas in our study of criminal law.

This chapter begins with a focus on crimes that may be committed by individuals within businesses or by the corporate organization. Such crimes are referred to as *white-collar crimes, corporate crimes*, or *business crimes*. Some of the crimes included in that section are discussed also in the chapter on property crimes. Here the focus is on committing those crimes in the course of business.

Corporate criminal liability raises the critical issue of holding a corporation responsible for the criminal acts of its employees and the even more critical issue of how far the system can go in the actual punishment of a corporation or its executives when employees engage in criminal acts in conjunction with their jobs. Here again deterrence is important, with the underlying assumption of corporate criminal liability being that this is at least one way to deter criminal acts.

Many of the crimes discussed in this chapter, such as mail and wire fraud, antitrust violations, and securities fraud, by definition are federal crimes, or at least thought to be best solved at the federal level. They are crimes that cross state boundaries and not only involve crime beyond the reach of a particular state's control but that are also far-reaching in their impact on society. Federal legislation has been required to prosecute in many of these areas.

Some of the crimes discussed in this chapter, such as those in securities fraud (particularly insider trading), have captured national attention because of the high social status of the people prosecuted. The huge sums of money and the vast networks involved in insider trading indicate that these crimes may have a serious impact on society as well as on individual investors who may have lost money as a result.

As technology changes, making our lives easier to some extent, crime changes as well. The extensive use of computers has decreased our privacy and made it possible for individuals to embezzle large sums of money as well as to engage in counterfeiting documents more easily than in the past. Statutory efforts to combat computer crimes are discussed.

The extensiveness of business-related crimes and the potential dangers these crimes have on society suggest that more attention be given to the study of business crimes. Their interrelationship with organized crime led to the second major focus of the chapter.

Organized crime has been studied for years, and concern with the topic has led to the creation of several presidential commissions. A brief look at the commission reports began our study of organized crime. The studies emphasized the involvement of organized crime in illegitimate businesses such as prostitution, gambling, and drugs. But the most recent commissions have emphasized that organized crime has infiltrated legitimate businesses and that its impact in these ventures is growing.

Defining organized crime is not easy. In some ways organized crime is similar to business crimes. Some definitions emphasize the characteristic of operating outside the government; others define organized crime in terms of characteristics but make no attempt to enumerate the crimes that might be included.

The most recent commission report views organized crime in terms of two characteristics that distinguish it from other crimes: the *criminal group*, which utilizes crimes of violence and of property to gain and maintain profits and power, and the *buffer*, which utilizes corruption of public officials and business people to protect the criminal group from effective prosecution. Four categories of support groups assist in the success of organized crime.

Scholars disagree on the internal structure of organized crime. But there is agreement that the groups or families are highly structured into power positions and that, whether or not the Mafia, the La Cosa Nostra, or another family is in control, organized crime has infiltrated legitimate as well as illegitimate businesses in the United States and has had a significant effect on the structure of U.S. businesses.

The influence of organized crime may be seen in such activities as drugs, money laundering, pornography, prostitution, gambling, and labor racketeering, as well as legitimate activities ranging from construction to sports. This chapter focuses on organized crime and money laundering, the "crime of the 1990s," and one that is characteristic of business crimes and drug trafficking that are not always associated with organized crime.

Attempts to control organized crime involve prosecution for specific crimes such as murder, extortion, fraud, drug trafficking, prostitution, and many others. More recently, the government has sought prosecution in the Racketeering Influenced and Corrupt Organizations Act (RICO) because of its wider scope and enhanced penalties. RICO permits prosecution for both the individual predicate crimes as well as the *enterprise* activities if a sufficient pattern of activities can be established.

Substance abuse and drug trafficking, the third and final focus of crime control discussed in this chapter, are examined primarily in the context of recent administrative drug-control strategies. These strategies have not been effective in curbing drug-related crimes, however, and the punitive aspect of the policies has resulted in clogging criminal justice systems. We await President Clinton's proposed solutions to the problem, but we have been told that it will be a treatment, not punishment approach, at least with regard to offenses involving possession of small amounts of illegal drugs.

This chapter completes the text's analysis of specific crimes and combinations of crimes, but one of the major problems in criminal law is what to do once the offender is convicted. The next chapter analyzes the various sentencing options available in U.S. systems of criminal law. It is a fitting subject to follow the discussions in this chapter, for the changes in sentencing, especially of drug offenders, have created serious problems. For example, some federal judges are refusing to handle drug cases because they require judges to impose long mandatory minimum sentences upon conviction. Senior Judge Jack Weinstein of the Eastern District of New York, explains. "I simply cannot sentence another impoverished person whose destruction has no discernible effect on the drug trade."[119]

Weinstein's sentiments were echoed by U.S. Supreme Court Justice Anthony M. Kennedy, who is not known to be a liberal, when he said, "I am in agreement with most judges in the federal system that mandatory minimums are an imprudent, unwise and often unjust mechanism for sentencing."[120]

The attempt to win the war on drugs has led to severe sentencing policies; the next chapter provides a basis for discussing whether that is a wise approach.

STUDY QUESTIONS

1. Distinguish among the terms *white-collar crime*, *corporate crime*, and *business crime*. Would you suggest another term, or would you use one of these terms as the best to cover the crimes discussed in this chapter?
2. What did Edwin Sutherland mean by *white-collar crime?* Analyze his position in light of modern developments in this area.
3. Why is it important to study business-related crimes?
4. Distinguish among *strict liability*, *vicarious liability*, and *enterprise liability*.
5. What is the Travel Act?
6. What is OSHA, and why is it important? Do you think prosecutions under OSHA should be increased? If so, under what circumstances? If not, why not?
7. What is the purpose of the Clean Air Act? Which government agency is responsible for its enforcement?
8. Discuss the relationship of the Sherman Antitrust Act to current antitrust violations.
9. What is *insider trading?* Discuss recent developments in federal prosecutions in this area.
10. How severe should criminal punishments be for wealthy people who are convicted of insider trading? How do you react to Ivan Boesky's sentence? Michael Milken's sentence?
11. What is *computer crime?* Discuss the legislative efforts to combat this new type of crime.
12. Explain briefly the findings of the presidential commissions on organized crime prior to the 1980s.
13. Why did President Reagan appoint another commission? What did it accomplish?
14. Explain the recent commission's analysis of organized crime in terms of the *criminal group*, the *buffer*, and *support groups*. Discuss the relationship of these terms to the Mafia and La Cosa Nostra.
15. What is *money laundering?* How is it related to organized crime?

16. When prosecutors bring charges against people allegedly involved in organized crime, why might they prefer RICO to statutes defining specific crimes, such as extortion?
17. Explain what is meant by *predicate crimes* and *criminal enterprise* under RICO. What is a *pattern* of activity?
18. What is the relationship between drugs and organized crimes?
19. Summarize the drug-control efforts of Congress and the executive branch within the past decade.

ENDNOTES

1. Edwin H. Sutherland, *White-Collar Crime* (New York: Holt, Rinehart and Winston, 1959, 1961, paperback ed.; originally published in 1949 by the Dryden Press), p. 9.
2. U.S. Code, Title 42, Section 3791 (1994).
3. Attorney General of the United States, *Annual Report* (1983), p. 39.
4. See Marshall B. Clinard and Peter C. Yeager, *Corporate Crime* (New York: Free Press, 1980), p. 17.
5. Marshall B. Clinard, *Illegal Corporate Behavior* (Washington, D.C.: Government Printing Office, October 1979), p. 18.
6. New York Central and Hudson River Railroad v. United States, 212 U.S. 481 (1909).
7. For a discussion of this case, see Francis Cullen et al., *Corporate Crime Under Attack: The Ford Pinto Case and Beyond* (Cincinnati: Anderson Publishing Co., 1987). For information on one of the civil cases filed against Ford, see Grimshaw v. Ford Motor Company, 174 Cal.Rptr. 348 (4th Dist. 1981).
8. See, for example, United States v. Park, 421 U.S. 658 (1975).
9. Commonwealth v. Koczwara, 155 A.2d 825 (Pa. 1959), *cert. denied,* 363 U.S. 848 (1960).
10. Model Penal Code, Section 2.07, Explanatory Note.
11. U.S. Code, Title 18, Section 1344 (1994).
12. McNally v. United States, 483 U.S. 350 (1987), *on remand,* United States v. Gray, 705 F.Supp. 1224 (E.D.Ky. 1988), *overturned by statute,* Anti Drug Abuse Act of 1988, U.S. Code, Title 18, Section 1346 (1988).
13. United States v. Italiano, 837 F.2d 1480 (11th Cir. 1988), *later proceeding,* 701 F.Supp. 205 (M.D.Fla. 1988), *aff'd.,* 894 F.2d 1280 (11th Cir. 1990), *cert denied,* 498 U.S. 896 (1990).
14. Schmuck v. United States, 489 U.S. 705 (1989), *reh'g. denied,* 490 U.S. 1076 (1989).
15. See Pritchard v. United States, 386 F.2d 760 (8th Cir. 1967), *cert. denied.,* 390 U.S. 1004 (1968), and United States v. Reid, 533 F.2d 1255 (D.C.Cir. 1976).
16. See U.S. Code, Title 18, Section 1341 *et seq.* (1994).
17. U.S. Code, Title 18, Section 1952 (1994).
18. "Report: Exxon Penalty From Oil Spill Wasted," *Miami Herald* (23 August 1994), p. 3.
19. For a discussion, see Christopher Harris et al., "Criminal Liability for Violations of Federal Hazardous Waste Law: The 'Knowledge' of Corporations and Their Executives," *Wake Forest Law Review* 23 (1988): 203–236.
20. For a discussion of the need for uniformity in state laws, see John DeCicco and Edward Bonanno, "A Comparative Analysis of the Criminal Environmental Laws of the Fifty States: The Need for Statutory Uniformity as a Catalyst for Effective Enforcement of Existing and Proposed Laws," *Criminal Justice Quarterly* 9 (Summer 1988): 216–220.

21. Ira Reiner and Jan Chatten-Brown, "When It Is Not an Accident, but a Crime: Prosecutors Get Tough with OSHA Violations," *Northern Kentucky Law Review* 17, no. 1 (1989): 85–103. For additional information, see this entire journal, which contains a symposium on Workplace Safety for the 1990s. See also *Chicago Tribune* (25 March 1993), p. 10.

22. People v. Warner-Lambert Co., 434 N.Y.S.2d 159 (1980), *cert. denied*, 450 U.S. 1031 (1981).

23. Reiner and Chatten-Brown, "When It Is Not an Accident, but a Crime," p. 103.

24. "Low Settlement Seen as DuPont Win," *American Bar Association Journal* 79 (November 1993): 34.

25. See G. Nelson Smith, III, "Waking the Sleeping Giant: The Use of the Felony Sanctions Under CERCLA to Ensure Compliance with Environmental Laws," *Creighton Law Review* 26 (1993): 449–477.

26. U.S. Code, Title 15, Sections 1–7 (1994).

27. See Symposium, "Trade Associations and the Antitrust Law," *Brooklyn Law Review* 46 (Winter 1980): 181–247; and Edward B. Rock, "Corporate Law Through an Antitrust Lens," *Columbia Law Review* 92 (April 1992): 497–570.

28. For a discussion of deterrence of antitrust actions, see Herbert Hovenkamp, "Antitrust's Protected Classes," *Michigan Law Review* 88 (October 1989): 1–48. See also Steven A. Saltzburg, "The Control of Criminal Conduct in Organizations," *Boston University Law Review* 71 (March 1991): 71.

29. U.S. Code, Title 15, Section 77a *et seq.* (1994). For an analysis of several issues relating to the SEC, see the symposium published in *Washington and Lee Law Review* 4 (1990); and the series of articles published in *Fordham Law Review* 61 (May 1994).

30. U.S. Code, Title 15, Section 78a *et seq.* (1994).

31. U.S. Code, Title 15, Section 78c (1994).

32. For discussions of legal problems with insider trading, see the symposium on insider trading in the *American Criminal Law Review* 26 (1988). The statute is codified in U.S. Code, Title 15, Section 780 (1994).

33. For more information on insider trading, see Elyse Diamond, "Outside Investors: A New Breed of Insider Traders?" *Fordham Law Review* 60 (May 1992): 319–357; and Steven R. Salbu, "Regulation of Insider Trading in a Global Marketplace: A Uniform Statutory Approach," *Tulane Law Review* 66 (March 1992): 837–872.

34. "Boesky Gets $20 Million from His Former Wife," *Miami Herald* (10 June 1993), p. 3C.

35. For more information on junk bonds, see "Insider Trading in Junk Bonds," *Harvard Law Review* 105 (May 1992): 1720–1744.

36. "Milken Gets 10 Years for Wall St. Crimes," *New York Times* (22 November 1990), p. 1.

37. "Judge Who Gave Milken Ten Years Backs a Parole After He Serves Three," *New York Times* (20 February 1991), p. 1C; "An Unfettered Milken Has Lessons to Teach," *New York Times* (16 October 1993), p. 1.

38. "Milken Testifies on Posners' Behalf," *Los Angeles Times* (29 June 1993), p. 2D.

39. "Posner, Son Barred from Running Firms," *Washington Post* (2 December 1993), p. 11B.

40. "Tax Evader Pays Final Dues: $2.1 Million," *Tallahassee Democrat* (22 December 1993), p. 1C.

41. United States v. Morris 928 F.2d 504 (2d Cir. 1991), *cert. denied*, 112 S.Ct. 72 (1991).

42. "Urban Hackers Charged in High-Tech Crime," *New York Times* (23 July 1992), p. 1.

43. "Two Sentenced in $100,000 Automatic Teller Machine Fraud," *New York Times* (21 December 1993), p. 12.

44. Catherine H. Conly and J. Thomas McEwen, "Computer Crime," *NIJ Reports* (January/February 1990): 2. For a more extensive analysis of computer crime, see August Bequai, *Computer Crime* (Lexington, Mass.: D. C. Heath, 1978). For a discussion of computer security, see John M. Carroll, *Computer Security*, 2d ed. (Stoneham, Mass.: Butterworth, 1987); and Dorothy B. Francis, *Computer Crime* (Bergenfield, N.J.: E. P. Dutton, 1987).

45. "Computers Used in a New Crime: Desktop Forgery," *New York Times* (8 October 1990), p. 1.

46. Federal Computer Crime Control Act, U.S. Code, Title 18, Section 1030 (1994).

47. U.S. Code, Title 18, Section 1030(c) (1994).

48. Donald R. Cressey, quoted in James W. Meeker et al., "White-Collar and Organized Crimes: Questions of Seriousness and Policy," *Justice Quarterly* 4 (March 1987): 73.

49. Gilbert Geis, "White-Collar Crime: What Is It?" in *White-Collar Crime Reconsidered*, ed. Kip Schlegel and David Weisburd (Boston: Northeastern University, 1992), p. 35.

50. Kitty Calavita and Henry N. Pontell, "Savings and Loan Fraud As Organized Crime: Toward a Conceptual Typology of Corporate Illegality," *Criminology* 31 (November 1993): 519–548; quotations are on pp. 520 and 529.

51. President's Commission on Organized Crime, Report to the President and Attorney General, *The Edge: Organized Crime, Business, and Labor Unions* (Washington, D.C.: U.S. Government Printing Office, 1986). For an overview of the infiltration of organized crime into legitimate business, see Howard Abadinsky, *Organized Crime*, 3d ed. (Chicago: Nelson-Hall, 1990), pp. 349–395.

52. For a general discussion of the FBI historically as well as an analysis of its recent emphasis on white-collar crime and organized crime, see Tony Poveda, *Lawless and Reform: The FBI in Transition* (Pacific Grove, Cal.: Brooks/Cole Publishing Company, 1990).

53. Estes Kefauver, *Crime in America* (Garden City, N.Y.: Doubleday, 1951); see also Morris Ploscowe, ed., *Organized Crime and Law Enforcement* (New York: Grosby Press, 1952).

54. Robert F. Kennedy, *The Enemy Within* (New York: Harper & Row, 1960).

55. The President's Commission on Law Enforcement and Administration of Justice, *The Challenge of Crime in a Free Society* (Washington, D.C.: U.S. Government Printing Office, 1967). See also that commission's Task Force Report, *Organized Crime*.

56. National Advisory Committee on Criminal Justice Standards and Goals, *Organized Crime* (Washington, D.C.: U.S. Government Printing Office, 1973).

57. "Crime Panel Issues Its Final Report," *New York Times* (2 April 1986), p. 1.

58. President's Commission on Law Enforcement and Administration of Justice, *The Challenge of Crime in a Free Society* (Washington, D.C.: U.S. Government Printing Office, 1967).

59. See National Advisory Commission on Criminal Justice Standards and Goals, *Organized Crime: Report of the Task Force on Organized Crime* (Washington, D.C.: U.S. Government Printing Office, 1976), pp. 7–8.

60. President's Commission on Organized Crime, *America's Habit* (Washington, D.C.: U.S. Government Printing Office, 1983), Appendix A, no page numbers.

61. See, for example, Calavita and Pontell, "Savings and Loan Fraud."

62. See U.S. Senate Special Committee to Investigate Organized Crime in Interstate Commerce, *Third Interim Report,* Senate Report No. 307, 83d Cong.,

1st Sess. (Washington, D.C.: U.S. Government Printing Office). The report is abridged in Kefauver, *Crime in America*.

63. Giovanni Schiavo, *The Truth About the Mafia* (New York: Vigo Press, 1962). For other accounts of the Mafia, see Francis A. J. Ianni and Elizabeth Reuss-Ianni, eds., *A Family Business: Kinship and Social Control in Organized Crime* (New York: Russell Sage, 1972); Howard Abadinsky, *The Mafia in America: An Oral History* (New York: Praeger, 1981); and Dwight C. Smith, Jr., *The Mafia Mystique* (Lanham, Md.: University of America Press, 1990). For more recent accounts of organized crime in general, see Abadinsky, *Organized Crime*, 3d ed.

64. Francis A. J. Ianni and Elizabeth Reuss-Ianni, "Organized Crime," in *Encyclopedia of Crime and Justice*, vol. 3, ed. Sanford H. Kadish (New York: Free Press, 1983), p. 1101. The commission's discussion of the organized crime family structure is contained in *The Challenge of Crime in a Free Society*, pp. 193–196.

65. President's Commission on Organized Crime, *The Edge: Organized Crime, Business, and Labor Unions*, p. xviii.

66. "The Mafia of the 1980s: Divided and Under Seige," *New York Times* (11 March 1987), p. 1.

67. "Anthony (Fat Tony) Salerno, 80, A Top Crime Boss, Dies in Prison," *New York Times* (29 July 1992), p. 12.

68. "Reputed Mob Leader and Sixteen Others are Convicted," *New York Times* (21 November 1988), p. 11.

69. "Gotti Is Acquitted by a Federal Jury in Conspiracy Case," *New York Times* (14 March 1987), p. 1.

70. "Gotti Accused of Role in Mafia Slaying," *New York Times* (13 December 1990), p. 16.

71. "Gotti Sentenced to Life in Prison Without the Possibility of Parole," *New York Times* (24 June 1992), p. 1.

72. "Gotti, Aide, Convictions are Upheld," *Orlando Sentinel* (11 October 1993), p. 9. See also United States v. Frank Locascio and John Gotti, 6 F.3d 924 (2d Cir. 1993), *cert. denied*, 114 S.Ct. 1645 (1994).

73. "Court Is Asked to Name Trustees to Run Union Local Tied to Gotti," *New York Times* (22 June 1994), p. 5B.

74. "Despite Fears of Jury Tampering, Six Convicted in Mob Trial," *New York Times* (7 March 1993), p. 8.

75. "Federal Jury in Gambino Case Deadlocks on Major Charges," *New York Times* (5 June 1993), p. 16. For more information on the Gambino organized crime family, see John H. David, *Mafia Dynasty: the Rise and Fall of the Gambino Crime Family* (New York: Harper Collins, 1993).

76. "FBI Arrests Mafia Chieftain In a Hideaway in New Jersey," *New York Times* (20 January 1993), p. 16; "Reputed Mafia Leaders Charged in Killings," *New York Times* (13 April 1993), p. 5B.

77. See *The Cash Connection: Organized Crime, Financial Institutions, and Money Laundering* (Washington, D. C.: U.S. Government Printing Office, 1984), pp. 7–27. The Final report is *The Edge*. See also Clifford L. Karchmer, "Money Laundering and the Organized Underworld," in Herbert E. Alexander and Gerald E. Caiden, *The Politics and Economics of Organized Crime*, (Lexington, Mass.: Lexington Books, 1985), pp. 37–48.

78. U.S. Code, Title 18, Sections 1956–1957 (1994).

79. Ratzlaf v. United States, 114 S.Ct. 655 (1994), *remanded*, 16 F.3d 1078 (9thCir. 1994). See also G. Richard Strafer, "Money Laundering: The Crime of the '90s," *American Criminal Law Review* 27 (Summer 1989): 149–207.

80. "Group of Seven Asks Money-Laundering Curbs," *New York Times* (20 April 1990), p. 1C.

81. "Banks spent $129 Million to Fight Money Laundering, Trade Group Says," *Miami Herald* (25 May 1990), p. 1C.

82. "Money Laundering Looms Large in White-Collar Prosecutions," *Criminal Law Reporter* 46 (21 March 1990): 1525.

83. See also Clifford Karchmer and Douglas Ruch, *State and Local Money Laundering Control Strategies,* National Institute of Justice (Washington, D.C.: U.S. Department of Justice, October 1992). For a series of articles on money laundering, see the Symposium, "The Anti-Money Laundering Statutes: Where from Here?" in *Alabama Law Review* 44 (1993): 657–861.

84. U.S. Code, Title 18, Sections 1961–1968 (1994).

85. Section 1 of Public Law 91-452, 84 Stat. 922 (1994).

86. U.S. Code, Title 18, Section 1963(a)(b) (1994).

87. See United States v. Hampton, 786 F.2d 977, 980 (10th Cir. 1986).

88. U.S. Code, Title 18, Section 1964(c) (1994).

89. See, for example, Sedima, S.P.R.L. v. Imrex Company, Inc., 473 U.S. 479 (1985). See also G. Richard Strafer et al., "Civil RICO in the Public Interest: 'Everybody's Darling,'" *American Criminal Law Review* 19 (1981–1982): 655–718.

90. U.S. Code, Title 18, Section 1962 (1994).

91. Jeff Gerth, "U.S. Expanding Use of '70 Crime Statute," *New York Times* (8 December 1978), p. 1D.

92. See United States v. Licavoli 725 F.2d 1040 (6th Cir. 1984), *cert. denied sub. nom.,* 467 U.S. 1252 (1984).

93. United States v. Pryba, 900 F.2d 748 (4th Cir. 1990), *cert. denied,* 498 U.S. 924 (1990).

94. U.S. Code, Title 18, Section 1961(5) (1994).

95. H. J. Inc. v. Northwestern Bell Telephone Company, 492 U.S. 229 (1989).

96. H. J. Inc. v. Northwestern Bell Telephone Company, 492 U.S. 229 (1989).

97. United States v. Turkette, 452 U.S. 576 (1981), *remanded,* 656 F.1d 5 (1st Cir. 1981), *and later proceeding,* 604 F.Supp. 667 (D.Mass. 1985).

98. United States v. Weinberg, 656 F.Supp. 1020, 1023, (E.D.N.Y. 1987), citations and footnotes omitted.

99. See Reves v. Ernst & Young, 113 S.Ct. 1163 (1993).

100. "A Law Run Wild: Conservative Lawmaker Seeks Asset Forfeiture Limits," *American Bar Association Journal* 79 (October 1993): 24. See also "Congress Weighs Due Process in Asset Forfeiture Actions," *Criminal Justice Newsletter* 24 (15 June 1993): 3.

101. See Austin v. United States, 113 S.Ct. 2801 (1993) and Alexander v. United States, 113 S. Ct. 2755 (1993), *reh'g. denied,* 114 S.Ct. 295 (1993).

102. Republic National Bank v. United States, 113 S.Ct. 554 (1992).

103. See United States v. James Daniel Good Real Property, 114 S.Ct. 492 (1993).

104. Marc B. Stahl, "Asset Forfeiture, Burdens of Proof and the War on Drugs," *Journal of Criminal Law and Criminology* 83 (Summer 1992): 274–337; quotation is on p. 274.

105. "Substance Abuse Is Blamed for 500,000 Deaths," *New York Times* (24 October 1993), p. 20.

106. Henry J. Reske, "Priorities Wrong? Report: Drug War Filling Prisons," *American Bar Association Journal* 79 (April 1993): 33. For a discussion of the lesser impact drug laws have had on smaller jurisdictions, see John M. Klofas, "Drugs and Justice: The Impact of Drugs on Criminal Justice in a Metropolitan Community," *Crime & Delinquency* 39 (April 1993): 204–224.

107. "Twenty Years of War on Drugs, and No Victory Yet," *New York Times* (14 June 1992), p. 7.

108. "Drive on Drug Abuse Opens," *New York Times* (23 June 1982), p. 9.

109. Anti-Drug Abuse Act of 1986, Section 1 *et seq*, 100 Stat. 3207; U.S. Code, Title 21, Section 801 (1993). See United States v. Jackson, 863 F.2d 1168 (4th Cir. 1989).

110. Quoted in "New Drug Strategy Continues Expansion of Justice System," *Criminal Justice Newsletter* 21 (1 February 1990): 5.

111. For a discussion of legalizing drugs, see Kathryn Ann Farr, "Revitalizing the Drug Decriminalization Debate," *Crime and Delinquency* 36 (April 1990): 223–237; James A. Inciardi, ed., *The Drug Legalization Debate* (Newbury Park, Calif.: Sage, 1991); Rod L. Evans and Irwin M. Berent, eds., *Drug Legalization: For and Against* (Lasalle, IL.: Open Court Publishing Company, 1992); and Richard Lawrence Miller, *The Case for Legalizing Drugs* (New York: Praeger, 1991).

112. Quoted in "Drug Czar Criticizes Legalization," *Tallahassee Democrat* (14 December 1989), p. 1.

113. "Reno Moving to Reverse Stiff Sentencing Rule for Minor Drug Crimes," *New York Times* (5 May 1993), p. 12; "Nation's Drug War Dwindles To A Skirmish," *The Times-Picayune* (6 March 1994), p. 4; "Drug Users: Jail Them or Treat Them?/ The Drug Fix," *USA Weekend* (10 April 1994), p. 4.

114. For a discussion of drug policy, see Ronald L. Akers, "What Do We Do About Drugs?" *Criminal Justice Review* 17 (Autumn 1992): 280–290.

115. Bureau of Justice Statistics, *Drugs, Crime, and the Justice System: A National Report* (Washington, D.C.: U.S. Department of Justice, December 1992), p. 36.

116. President's Commission on Organized Crime, *America's Habit,* p. 12.

117. President's Commission on Organized Crime, Report to the President and the Attorney General, *America's Habit: Drug Abuse, Drug Trafficking, and Organized Crime* (Washington, D.C.: U.S. Government Printing Office, March 1986), pp. 482–486.

118. In general, see Eric D. Wish and Bernard A. Gropper, "Drug Testing by the Criminal Justice System: Methods, Research, and Applications," in *Drugs and Crime,* ed. Michael Tonry and James Q. Wilson (Chicago: University of Chicago Press, 1990), pp. 321–392. It appears that the U.S. Supreme Court will not find drug testing unconstitutional for applicants for public jobs. The Court refused to review a case involving applications for the position of attorney with the U.S. Department of Justice. See Willner v. Thornburgh, 738 F.Supp. 1 (D.D.C. 1990), *vacated,* 928 F.2d 1185 (1991), *cert. denied,* 112 S.Ct. 669 (1991). See also David S. Weinberg, "Another Random Drug Test or the Latest Infringement on the Fourth Amendment Rights of American Workers?" *Northwestern University Law Review* 87 (1993): 1087–1119.

119. "Senior Judge Declines Drug Cases," *American Bar Association Journal* 79 (July 1993): 22.

120. "Will the Real Janet Reno Please Stand Up?" Let's Straighten Out Federal Sentencing Laws," *Los Angeles Times* (21 March 1994), p. 6B.

Chapter 12

Sentencing and the Criminal Law

Outline

Key Terms

aggravating circumstances	indeterminate sentence	presumptive sentencing
cruel and unusual punishment	intensive probation supervision (IPS)	probation recidivism
determinate sentence	mitigating circumstances	restitution
felony murder	pardon	revenge
fine	parole	sentence
good-time credits	plea bargaining	sentence disparity
habeas corpus		sentencing guidelines
house arrest		

Introduction

The first chapter of this text begins with a brief discussion of the historical reasons for punishment: revenge, retribution, deterrence, incapacitation, and rehabilitation, noting that rehabilitation has been losing its position of prominence in the past two decades. In its place are retribution, to which some refer as just deserts, and deterrence. These are *philosophies* of sentencing or punishment, and all have had a place of importance at some period in history. That place of prominence changes as other social, economic, and political conditions change. The philosophy in vogue at the time is reflected in the nature and types of sentences that society utilizes for convicted offenders.

In the past two decades, considerable attention has been given to sentencing. The emphasis in many jurisdictions on *punishment* rather than rehabilitation, along with the concern that sentencing should be more uniform, has led to significant changes in criminal codes. Some states have revised their entire codes, even to the extent of deleting many crimes, adding others, and consolidating still others (see Focus 12.1).

Some jurisdictions, including the federal, have established sentencing guidelines. Some of these guidelines recommend harsher penalties. Some are a reflection of previous sentence practices; others are statements of what sentence practices should be.

Mandatory sentences are more prevalent today, with some jurisdictions replacing previous indeterminate sentences with mandatory minimum or maximum sentences. These sentencing limits have been decided legislatively to remove much of the discretion that previously was delegated to judges at the sentencing hearing. But in recent years many have begun questioning mandatory sentences, especially mandatory minimums, which have contributed to one of the highest incarceration rates in the world, resulting in serious prison overcrowding. In Florida, for example, one study has described the result of mandatory sentences as creating a "very chaotic and ineffective prison system where very little treatment, supervision or punishment is being administered." Florida's system has been described as the "worst of both worlds when nonviolent, petty property and drug offenders

FOCUS 12.1 Legislative Statements of the Purpose of Sentencing

Until recent legislation, many state statutes did not state the purpose of sentencing. The movement away from the rehabilitative ideal and the indeterminate sentence toward a sentencing philosophy based on just deserts and deterrence, however, has been reflected in some of the revised codes. California and Washington are examples.

In California, the first state to adopt the indeterminate sentence and the one in which it was used most extensively, the legislature revised the criminal code in 1976, with punishment as its goal.[1]

The legislature finds and declares that the purpose of imprisonment for crime is punishment. This purpose is best served by terms proportionate to the seriousness of the offense with provision for uniformity in the sentences of offenders committing the same offense under similar circumstances. The Legislature further finds and declares that the elimination of disparity and the provision of uniformity of sentences can best be achieved by determinate sentences fixed by statute in proportion to the seriousness of the offense as determined by the Legislature to be imposed by the court with specified discretion.

In 1981 Washington enacted a comprehensive revision of its criminal code, the Sentencing Reform Act of 1981, in which the legislature for the first time stated the purpose of sentencing. The emphasis is on retribution, or just deserts. Specifically, the legislature made this declaration in the first section of the sentencing act.[2]

The purpose of this chapter is to make the criminal justice system accountable to the public by developing a system for the sentencing of felony offenders which structures, but does not eliminate, discretionary decisions affecting sentences, and to add a new chapter to Title 9 RCW designed to:

1. Ensure that the punishment for a criminal offense is proportionate to the seriousness of the offense and the offender's criminal history;
2. Promote respect for the law by providing punishment which is just;
3. Be commensurate with the punishment imposed on others committing similar offenses;
4. Protect the public;
5. Offer the offender an opportunity to improve him or herself; and
6. Make frugal use of the state's resources.

[1] California Penal Code, Section 1170(a)(1) (1994).
[2] Revised Code of Washington, Section 9.94A.010 (1994).

---

are sentenced inappropriately to prison while dangerous criminals are released early" [to make room for more inmates].[1]

Attorney General Janet Reno promised to examine mandatory minimums early in her tenure, but that recommendation did not appear in President's Clinton's anticrime bill presented to Congress in late 1993. One legal scholar commented on that issue.

> This seems odd, since our streets and cities are becoming less safe. As in years past, a steady drumbeat of statistics shows that violent crime continues to increase. Since Americans clearly have more crime to worry about than ever, why is nothing being tried?
>
> The answer is that the political debate about crime always has been about fear. It never has been about real solutions.[2]

Despite this conclusion, various approaches to sentencing have been tried and continue to dominate criminal justice systems. In addition to changes in sentence lengths, alternatives to incarceration, such as fines, restitution, probation, and community work service, are featured in some of the new sentencing structures. But what is most obvious is that the extensive controversies over sentencing have led to extremely divergent approaches to sentence reform. Therefore, it is impossible to indicate in this chapter what all jurisdictions are doing. A few state systems are discussed, along with the federal system, in which major sentencing changes have been made and questioned extensively. Earlier changes in the federal system were described as follows (see Appendix D for the later changes):

> Congress is of two minds on sentencing reform. One mind is dispassionate and learned, deliberating for decades in search of a rational, comprehensive solution. The other is impulsive, reckless, driven by unquenchable political passions, and impatient with its plodding alter-ego.[3]

Despite the emphasis in this chapter on criminal law rather than criminal procedure, some attention is given to constitutional issues of sentencing. The recent reforms have raised numerous questions about sentencing, and the substantive criminal law must be understood in the context of what is and is not permissible according to interpretations of the federal and state constitutions.

Determining Sentences

A **sentence** is the judgment pronounced formally by the court and imposed upon a defendant who pleads guilty or who is found guilty after a trial. The type and length of the sentence may be determined in one of several ways: legislatively, judicially, or administratively.

Sentence Models

Most sentencing involves a combination of these three models, but for analytical purposes, each is defined. In the *legislative model*, the type and length of sentence for each crime is determined by the legislature and codified into the criminal law. In the purest form of this model, no discretion is permitted in sentencing. For example, upon conviction of first-degree burglary, a defendant must be sentenced to ten years in the state prison. That term cannot be reduced administratively by prison officials or by **parole** boards, which generally have the power to release prisoners before the end of their sentences.

Sentences established by the legislature are called **determinate sentences**, in contrast to **indeterminate sentences**, in which the legislature either does not set a term and leaves the decision entirely up to judges, or sets minimum and maximum terms and leaves the decision to judges to set the actual sentence in each case. In the purest form of this model, referred to as the *judicial model*, judges are the final determiners of sentences; that is, no administrative releases are permitted.

In reality the pure forms of legislative and judicial sentencing occur only rarely. Even with the push for determinate sentencing, most states left some discretionary sentence power with judges. Some have retained at least part of the *administrative model*, in which parole boards may grant early releases or prison administrators may reduce time served by granting **good-time credits** to inmates who do not violate prison rules.

The administrative model was prominent during the period when the philosophy of rehabilitation was popular. Rehabilitation is based on the philosophy that offenders should be sent to prison for an indeterminate period, during which they should receive treatment. When they are rehabilitated, they should be released. Allegations of abuse of the rehabilitation approach, along with a belief that the philosophy could not work anyway, led to a deemphasis on rehabilitation.

In any of these sentencing models, the power to determine the length of sentences served may be altered by other factors. Power may be given to the governor (or the president, in the case of federal crimes) to commute a life sentence to a term of years or to commute a death sentence to life. The governor (or president) may have the power to grant a **pardon**, an act of grace that exempts the offender from punishment (or further punishment if some time has already been served). Focus 12.2 features some of these procedures. Some legislatures have given governors authority to order the release of inmates when prisons reach their court-imposed maximum populations. This permits the system to incarcerate new (and presumably more dangerous) inmates.

Presumptive Sentencing

In **presumptive sentencing** the legislature specifies the normal sentence for each crime, and judges are permitted to deviate only under specified types of circumstances or by giving written reasons or both.

In its 1976 report, the Twentieth Century Task Force on Criminal Sentencing recommended presumptive sentencing based on a detailed study of sentencing. Presumptive sentencing is based on the assumption that "a finding of guilty of committing a crime would predictably incur a particular sentence unless specific mitigating or aggravating factors are established." Presumptive sentencing enables the legislature to "retain the power to make those broad policy decisions that can be wisely and justly made about crime and do not involve the particulars of specific crimes and criminals." At the same time, it allows the sentencing judge "some degree of guided discretion

FOCUS 12.2 Executive Clemency: Some Recent Cases

It was predicted by some scholars that the move toward determinate sentencing, especially mandatory minimum sentences, would necessitate the expansion of executive clemency by governors or the U.S. president, but this has not been the case in all jurisdictions.[1] Many of the acts of executive clemency are not controversial; some go unnoticed. For example, shortly before the end of his term, President Reagan issued seventeen pardons, bringing his total of pardons issued to 380. Of the seventeen, only one, George M. Steinbrenner 3d, was well known. Steinbrenner, owner of the New York Yankees, was pardoned for his convictions for illegal contributions to Richard M. Nixon's 1972 campaign. Other pardons at that time were given to persons convicted of intent to distribute cocaine, possessing and concealing whiskey, receiving stolen property, copyright infringements, falsifying tax returns and aiding in preparation of falsified tax returns, and other offenses.[2]

Much more controversial were the pardons issued by President George Bush shortly before he left office in 1993. On Christmas Eve, 1992, Bush issued pardons to Caspar Weinberger, former defense secretary, and others charged with crimes in the Iran-Contra scandal. An earlier presidential pardon drew fire, too. President Gerald Ford pardoned Richard Nixon for his role in the Watergate scandal.

Normally executive clemency is not reviewable, meaning that the president or governor has unlimited power to grant pardons or commute sentences.

An exception may be made if the law requires conditions that are ignored by the pardoning agent. In 1992 a judge overturned eleven of the nearly one hundred clemency decisions made by Ohio's governor, Richard F. Celeste, before he left office. According to the attorney general who reviewed the cases, in the eleven cases that were reversed the former governor had not followed legal requirements concerning recommendations from the Ohio Adult Parole Authority. Attorneys for the inmates argued that the power to grant clemency was unrestricted.

Governor Celeste gained national media attention when he granted clemency to twenty-five women who had killed or assaulted their spouses or companions after years of physical abuse. Those decisions were not challenged.[3] Chapter 3 of this text discusses subsequent Ohio legislative changes concerning the battered woman syndrome. Women who were convicted under similar circumstances have been granted clemency in other states, including eight in Maryland. Similar efforts have been made in at least twenty states, although some of these efforts have not been successful.[4]

[1] See Kathleen Dean Moore, *Pardons: Justice, Mercy, and the Public Interest* (New York: Oxford University Press, 1989).
[2] "Steinbrenner Pardoned by Reagan For '72 Election Law Violations," *New York Times* (20 January 1989), p. 7.
[3] "Ohio Judge Overturns Clemency Granted to Death-Row Prisoners," *New York Times* (16 Feb. 1992), p. 17l.
[4] "The Whole Truth?: Was She a Battered Wife Who Killed in Self-Defense? The Case Rests," *Chicago Tribune* (3 October 1993), p. 5.

to consider and weigh those pertinent factors that cannot be wisely evaluated in the absence of the particular crime and criminal."[4]

In presumptive sentencing, according to attorney Richard Singer, the "burden on appeal would be *against* the deviate sentence, which would be upheld only if the appellate tribunal were substantially convinced that the abnormal sentence was justified." Singer concludes, "In considering presumptive sentencing, two points are especially important: First, presumptive sentencing does not abolish judicial discretion, and second, the proper mechanism for establishing the presumptive sentence guidelines, after full public hearing and careful consideration of what *might* be done in sentencing, is a sentencing commission."[5]

Voluntary Sentencing Guidelines

Presumptive sentencing may be accomplished through the use of a sentencing commission, which establishes *sentencing guidelines*. These guidelines may be viewed as a way to control judicial discretion without abolishing it and as a means of correcting the disparity that can result from individualized sentencing. Basically, this is what happens. A judge has an offender to sentence. The judge may consider the offender's background, the nature of the offense, or other variables without any guidelines. When sentencing guidelines are used, the difference is that the relevance of the variables considered may have been researched and quantified. In addition, the judge has a benchmark of a reasonable penalty in each case. The judge may decide it is reasonable to deviate from the guidelines; in that situation, reasons should be given.

Leslie T. Wilkins has defined *sentencing guidelines* as follows: "Guidelines are summaries of the experience of all members of the bench to the particular court system and provide for a basic minimum of information necessary to indicate the usual penalty which was awarded in similar cases."[6]

From such data, a table may be constructed, indicating the recommended sentence or range of sentences for a particular offense in that jurisdiction. This approach is based upon an empirical analysis of what *has been done* in the jurisdiction, not a philosophy of what *ought to be done*.

Guidelines need not be based on previous sentences. They may be developed on the basis of any reasons deemed appropriate. For example, some states have experimented with appointing advisory committees, usually consisting of judges, to develop guidelines to serve as *voluntary* sentencing guidelines for judges. "Some judges favor voluntary guidelines, even though they believe judges should retain full discretion over each individual sentence."[7]

Legislative Guidelines

One of the solutions to the problem of developing guidelines on the basis of past sentencing decisions is to establish guidelines under strong legislative directions and to provide for appellate judicial review of the application of guidelines. Judicial review would be available to the prosecution as well as to the defense. It is argued that such reviews "will go far towards eliminating disparities and introducing rationality in sentencing."[8] This approach is illustrated by recent reforms, both at the state and federal levels. State reforms differ from state to state, and any attempt to summarize them might be confusing to the beginning student. Therefore, two states, Washington and Pennsylvania, are used as examples of state sentencing guidelines. That discussion is followed by an analysis of the federal sentencing guidelines and reactions to them.

State Sentencing Guidelines

Washington State's Sentencing Reform Act

After much controversy and a five-year study, the Washington legislature enacted its Sentencing Reform Act of 1981, described by one scholar as "the most comprehensive—and in many respects the most thoughtful—sentencing reform measure enacted in the United States in the last half-century."[9]

The Washington legislature rejected the underlying assumptions of the indeterminate sentencing approach, which permitted tailoring of sentences to the individual needs of a particular defendant. But the legislature recognized that it is impossible (and undesirable) to attempt to eliminate all judicial discretion. The purpose of the 1981 sentencing reform, as indicated in the Washington statute, is reprinted in Focus 12.1.

The result in Washington was legislative formulation of presumptive sentences that retain considerable judicial discretion but within the framework of legislative standards. The judge's sentencing decision is final (and in that sense, the sentence is a determinate, not an indeterminate, one), but if it deviates from the legislative standards, reasons must be given for the deviation, and the decision is subject to judicial review.

In Washington the permissible range within which a judge may impose a sentence is based on the seriousness of the crime for which the defendant is being sentenced and the length and seriousness of that defendant's criminal history. Once that range is determined, the statute permits a judge "to impose any sentence within the range that [he or she] deems appropriate." The judge does not have to state reasons for this decision and may use any information that is not constitutionally impermissible.[10]

A judge may sentence *outside* the range appropriate for a particular defendant, thereby departing from the sentencing guidelines, if **mitigating** or **aggravating circumstances** exist. Under specified conditions, this "exceptional sentence" would be subject to judicial review. The Washington statute indicates some circumstances that may be considered by judges imposing an exceptional sentence, although the list, reproduced in part in Focus 12.3, is not meant to be exhaustive.[11]

Pennsylvania's Sentencing Guidelines

Several states are considering proposals for changing sentencing guidelines and procedures. Pennsylvania, which followed the first state (Minnesota) to adopt sentencing guidelines, is an example.[12] In the fall of 1993 the

FOCUS 12.3 Aggravating and Mitigating Circumstances in Sentencing

The Washington Sentencing Reform Act of 1981 provides that judges may impose sentences outside the sentencing guidelines after considering aggravating or mitigating circumstances such as provided by statute.[1]

Some of the illustrations are as follows:

(1) Mitigating Circumstances

(a) To a significant degree, the victim was an initiator, willing participant, aggressor, or provoker of the incident.

(b) Before detection, the defendant compensated, or made a good faith effort to compensate, the victim of the criminal conduct for any damage or injury sustained.

(c) The defendant committed the crime under duress, coercion, threat, or compulsion insufficient to constitute a complete defense but which significantly affected his or her conduct.

(d) The defendant, with no apparent predisposition to do so, was induced by others to participate in the crime.

(e) The defendant's capacity to appreciate the wrongfulness of his conduct or to conform his conduct to the requirements of the law was significantly impaired (voluntary use of drugs or alcohol is excluded).

(f) The offense was principally accomplished by another person and the defendant manifested extreme caution or sincere concern for the safety or well-being of the victim.

(g) The operation of the multiple offense policy of RCW 9.94A.400 results in a presumptive sentence that is clearly excessive in light of the purpose of this chapter. . . .

(2) Aggravating Circumstances

(a) The defendant's conduct during the commission of the current offense manifested deliberate cruelty to the victim.

(b) The defendant knew or should have known that the victim of the current offense was particularly vulnerable or incapable of resistance due to extreme youth, advanced age, disability, or ill health.

(c) The current offense was a major economic offense or series of offenses, so identified by a consideration of any of the following factors:

(i) The current offense involved multiple victims or multiple incidents per victim;

(ii) The current offense involved attempted or actual monetary loss substantially greater than typical for the offense;

(iii) The current offense involved a high degree of sophistication or planning or occurred over a lengthy period of time;

(iv) The defendant used his or her position of trust, confidence, or fiduciary responsibility to facilitate the commission of the current offense.

(d) The current offense was a major violation of the Uniform

Controlled Substances Act . . . (VUCSA), related to trafficking in controlled substances, which was more onerous than the typical offense of its statutory definition. The presence of ANY of the fol-

lowing may identify an offense as a major [violation of the VUCSA]: [the statute lists eight factors relating to drugs].

1. Revised Code of Washington, Section 9.94A.390 (1994).

Pennsylvania Commission on Sentencing recommended to that state's legislature that provisions be made for alternative punishments for nonviolent offenders (such as drug offenders, who may profit more from treatment than incarceration) in order to leave crowded prison space for violent offenders. According to the commission, Pennsylvania faces a prison overcrowding problem of epidemic proportion. The plan was endorsed by the state's corrections commissioner, who stated that "Our sentencing policies need to recognize that prisons have as much potential to do harm as they do to do good."[13]

In 1994 Pennsylvania adopted new sentencing guidelines. Unlike prior guidelines, the new ones place a greater emphasis on alternative sentences such as community service, house arrest, and treatment for substance abuse.[14]

The Federal Approach

Sentencing guidelines do not have to be based on past judicial experiences; nor must compliance be voluntary rather than mandatory. They may be based on the appointment of a sentencing commission and a thorough study of sentencing problems, recommendations, and legislative action on the guidelines. This is the approach taken in the federal system as the result of the Sentencing Reform Act of 1984, a part of the federal criminal code revision that was passed after years of discussion and multiple drafts.[15]

The new federal sentencing act amends the sentencing provisions of Title 18 of the United States Code. One of the most important provisions is the establishment of a commission to develop sentencing guidelines. That commission issued a preliminary report in 1986 and a final report in April 1987.

The U.S. Sentencing Commission

The U.S. Sentencing Commission consists of seven voting and two nonvoting, ex officio members. The commission was required by law to submit its initial guidelines by 13 April 1987, which it did. Those guidelines were to become law unless Congress enacted another law prior to 1 November 1987. Congress did not enact another law. The commission is a permanent agency. It may submit amendments to the sentencing guidelines each year between the beginning of a regular congressional session and May 1. Those amendments become effective within 180 days unless Congress passes a law to the contrary. The Statutory Mission of the commission is reprinted in part in Focus 12.4.

FOCUS 12.4 Statutory Mission of the U.S. Sentencing Commission

[In 1987 the mission of the U.S. Sentencing Commission was stated in part as follows:]

The Comprehensive Crime Control Act of 1984 foresees guidelines that will further the basic purposes of criminal punishment by deterring crime, incapacitating the offender, providing just punishment, and rehabilitating the offender. It delegates to the commission broad authority to review and rationalize the federal sentencing process.

The statute contains many detailed instructions as to how this determination should be made, but the most important of them instructs the commission to create categories of offense behavior and offender characteristics. An offense behavior category might consist, for example, of "bank robbery/committed with a gun/$2,500 taken." An offender characteristic category might be "offender with one prior conviction who was not sentenced to imprisonment."

The commission is required to prescribe guideline ranges that specify an appropriate sentence for each class of convicted people to be determined by coordinating the offense behavior categories with the offender characteristic categories. The statute contemplates the guidelines will establish a range of sentences for every combination of categories. Where the guidelines call for imprisonment, the range must be narrow. The maximum imprisonment cannot exceed the minimum by more than the greater of 25 percent or six months.

The sentencing judge must select a sentence from within the guideline range. If, however, a particular case presents atypical features, the Act allows the judge to depart from the guidelines and sentence outside the range. In that case, the judge must specify reasons for departure.

If the judge sentences within the guideline range, an appellate court may review the sentence to see if the guideline was correctly applied. If the judge departs from the guideline range, an appellate court may review the reasonableness of the departure. The Act requires the offender to serve virtually all of any prison sentence imposed, for it abolishes parole and substantially restructures good behavior adjustments.

SOURCE: U.S. Sentencing Commission, "Sentencing Guidelines for United States Courts," *Federal Register* 52, no. 92 (Wednesday, 13 May 1987), p. 18047.

According to the commission's statement, it was working within the basic framework of the statute's mandate. Of primary importance was the establishment of a sentencing structure that would "enhance the ability of the criminal justice system to reduce crime through an effective, fair sentencing system." The first problem was to devise a system that would ensure honesty in sentencing and, as the commission noted, remove the "confusion and implicit deception" that results from an indeterminate sentencing system combined with good-time credits. The combination of these two features results in much shorter sentences being served than the commission thought reasonable.[16] Theoretically the federal sentencing guidelines eliminate the unfairness and uncertainty of the indeterminate sentence by abolishing parole and limiting early release by reducing the effect of good-time credits. Allegedly fairness is achieved by numbers, with offenses grouped by categories (for example, offenses involving persons and offenses involving property). A basic-offense point value is assigned, and, in making that assignment, the sentencing judge is to look at the total circumstances involved when the offense was committed.

Although the use of numbers may give the appearance of science, not art, the system can get very complicated and subjective in the actual assessment of those numbers. For "all other things being equal" is rarely, if ever, the case. The commission noted that the more categories and factors involved, the more unworkable the system becomes. But a system tailored to meet every conceivable factor is unworkable, too.

The commission recognized that it may be impossible to achieve two of the goals established by Congress: uniformity and proportionality. To achieve *uniformity*, Congress intended for the sentencing structure to result in a narrowing of the wide disparity in sentences received by defendants committing the same offenses in different federal jurisdictions. *Proportionality* means that the sentence imposed should be commensurate with the severity of the offense; an armed robbery might not be like an unarmed robbery because of the differences in circumstances.

The preliminary guidelines presented to Congress in late 1986 were criticized as being too complicated. The final version simplified the guidelines somewhat and gave judges more discretion in departing from the guidelines. However, one commissioner criticized the guidelines (from which he dissented) as resulting in "equal sentences for unequal crimes." The commissioner argued that some important factors are ignored in the guidelines.

> For example, an offender who slips something into his girlfriend's drink and attempts to have sexual intercourse with her, but is stopped, is treated the same as an offender who stalks his intended rape victim for two weeks, rapes her at knife point, knocks her unconscious, and sets fire to her apartment before leaving, but she is rescued unharmed.[17]

The Sentencing Commission continues its research and recommendations. There is every expectation that its guidelines will remain controversial. This experience, by far the most extensive of all legislative attempts at revamping sentencing structures, indicates the difficulties of trying to combine goals of proportionality, uniformity, and fairness. To mandate that, in addition to the above goals, the guidelines be designed to achieve the goals of incapacitation, retribution, deterrence, and rehabilitation may be more than any system can be expected to deliver.

Litigation of the Federal Guidelines

Despite the fact that most federal judges and some members of the Sentencing Commission proposed a nine-month delay in implementing the commission's guidelines, Congress did not delay, and the guidelines became law on 1 November 1987. Defense attorneys began challenging the constitutionality of the guidelines as soon as possible. Many of the initial suits were in San Diego, where federal public defenders attacked the guidelines vigorously. But lawsuits were filed throughout the country, and federal courts disagreed on the constitutionality of the guidelines. While the federal courts were deciding cases on the guidelines, federal judges, prosecutors, and defense attorneys faced the issue of what to do with a complicated system that many had not had time to digest. Nor did they know what to expect, as lower federal courts were not uniform in their decisions when the guidelines were challenged.

The U.S. Supreme Court upheld the constitutionality of the federal sentencing guidelines in its 1989 decision in *Mistretta* v. *United States*. Justice Blackmun's opinion for the Court included an informative but lengthy discussion of the history of federal sentencing, after which he stated the following:[18]

Mistretta v. *United States*

Before settling on a mandatory-guideline system, Congress considered other competing proposals for sentencing reform. It rejected strict determinate sentencing because it concluded that a guideline system would be successful in reducing sentence disparities while retaining the flexibility needed to adjust for unanticipated factors arising in a particular case. The Judiciary Committee rejected a proposal that would have made the sentencing guidelines only advisory.

The Act, as adopted, revises the old sentencing process in several ways:

1. It rejects imprisonment as a means of promoting rehabilitation, and it states that punishment should serve retributive, educational, deterrent, and incapacitative goals.
2. It consolidates the power that had been exercised by the sentencing judge and the Parole Commission to decide what punishment an offender should suffer. This is done by creating the United States Sentencing Commission, directing that Commission to devise guidelines to be used for sentencing, and prospectively abolishing the Parole Commission.
3. It makes all sentences basically determinate. A prisoner is to be released at the completion of his sentence reduced only by any credit earned by good behavior while in custody.
4. It makes the Sentencing Commission's guidelines binding on the courts, although it preserves for the judge the discretion to depart from the guideline applicable to a particular case if the judge finds an aggravating or mitigating factor present that the Commission did not adequately consider when formulating guidelines. The Act also requires the court to state its reasons for the sentence imposed and to give "the specific reason" for imposing a sentence different from that described in the guideline.

5. It authorizes limited appellate review of the sentence. It permits a
   defendant to appeal a sentence that is above the defined range,
   and it permits the Government to appeal a sentence that is below
   that range. It also permits either side to appeal an incorrect application of the guideline.

Thus, guidelines were meant to establish a range of determinate sentences for categories of offenses and defendants according to various
specified factors, "among others." The maximum of the range ordinarily may not exceed the minimum by more than the greater of 25
percent or six months, and each sentence is to be within the limit provided by existing law.

[The opinion explained the Sentencing Commission and its authority and proceeded to discuss the facts of this case.]. . .

Petitioner [John M. Mistretta] argues that in delegating the power to
promulgate sentencing guidelines for every federal criminal offense to
an independent Sentencing Commission, Congress has granted the
Commission excessive legislative discretion in violation of the constitutionally based nondelegation doctrine. We do not agree. . . .

[The Court went into a lengthy discussion of the separation-of-pow-
ers and other issues raised by petitioner Mistretta.]. . .

We conclude that in creating the Sentencing Commission—an
unusual hybrid in structure and authority—Congress neither delegated excessive legislative power nor upset the constitutionally mandated
balance of powers among the coordinate Branches. The Constitution's
structural protections do not prohibit Congress from delegating to an
expert body located within the Judicial Branch the intricate task of
formulating sentencing guidelines consistent with such significant
statutory direction as is present here. Nor does our system of checked
and balanced authority prohibit Congress from calling upon the accu-
mulated wisdom and experience of the Judicial Branch in creating
policy on a matter uniquely within the ken of judges. Accordingly, we
hold that the Act is constitutional.

Mistretta held that the establishment of a sentencing commission that
promulgated guidelines that Congress accepted as law did not violate the
constitutional separation of powers, did not compromise the independence
of the federal judiciary, and did not constitute an unconstitutional delega-
tion of congressional powers. Many other issues remained undecided, however, and the litigation continues, with some defense attorneys saying that
the litigation had just begun, suggesting that it will take years for these
issues to be resolved.[19] Their predictions are accurate; issues continue to be
litigated; federal courts continue to differ in their decisions, creating the
need for the U.S. Supreme Court to hear more sentencing cases arising
under the reform act. The Court has decided some cases; some are too technical for discussion in an introductory text, but the Court has upheld various aspects of the guidelines, such as the Commission's Policy Statements[20]

and the Commission's Guidelines. The 1993 decision on Guidelines commentary is excerpted here to explain the Court's position.[21]

Stinson v. United States

The Sentencing Reform Act of 1984, as amended, created the Sentencing Commission, and charged it with the task of "establish[ing] sentencing policies and practices for the Federal criminal justice system. The Commission executed this function by promulgating the Guidelines Manual. The Manual contains text of three varieties. First is a guideline provision itself. The Sentencing Reform Act establishes that guildelines are "for use of a sentencing court in determining the sentence to be imposed in a criminal case." The guidelines provide direction as to the appropriate type of punishment—probation, fine, or terms of imprisonment—and the extent of the punishment imposed. Amendments to guidelines must be submitted to Congress for a 6-month period of review, during which Congress can modify or disapprove them. The second variety of text in the Manual is a policy statement. The Sentencing Reform Act authorizes the promulgation of "general policy statements regarding application of the guidelines" or other aspects of sentencing that would further the purposes of the Act. The third variant of text is commentary, at issue in this case. In the Guidelines Manual, both guidelines and policy statements are accompanied by extensive commentary. Although the Sentencing Reform Act does not in express terms authorize the issuance of commentary, the Act does refer to it. . . . The Sentencing Commission has provided in a guideline that commentary may serve these functions: commentary may "interpret [a] guidelines or explain how it is to be applied," "suggest circumstances which. . . may warrant departure from the guidelines," or "provide background information, including factors considered in promulgating the guideline or reasons underlying promulgation of the guideline."

As we have observed, "the Guidelines bind judges and courts in the exercise of their uncontested responsibility to pass sentence in criminal cases." The most obvious operation of this principle is with respect to guidelines themselves. The Sentencing Reform Act provides that, unless the sentencing court finds an aggravating or mitigating factor of a kind, or to a degree, not given adequate consideration by the Commission, a circumstance not applicable in this case, "[t]he court shall impose a sentence of the kind, and within the range," established by the applicable guidelines. [The Court referred to *Williams* v. *United States*, in which it had held that policy statements were binding]. . . .

In the case before us, the Court of Appeals determined that these principles do not apply to commentary. The conclusion that the commentary now being considered is not binding on the courts was error. . . .

It does not follow that commentary is binding in all instances. If, for example, commentary and the guideline it interprets are inconsistent in that following one will result in violating the dictates of the other, the Sentencing Reform Act itself commands compliance with the guideline. [The Court discussed some of the suggestions various courts have made for determining when commentary must be followed. The Court applied that discussion to the facts of this case, which involved the issue of whether a defendant who pled guilty to a five-count indictment of bank robbery was sentenced properly as a career offender under United States Sentencing Commission Guidelines Manual, which requires, among other things, that "the instant offense of conviction [be] a crime of violence." While the case was on appeal the Sentencing Commission added a sentence to the commentary, excluding the felon-in-possession offense from the "crime of violence" definition. The Court of Appeals affirmed the sentence, holding that the Commission's commentary was not binding on federal courts. The U.S. Supreme Court vacated that decision and remanded the case for consideration in light of its holding that the Commission's commentary to the Sentencing Guidelines is binding on federal courts.]

APPLICATION TO JUVENILES

In its 1991-1992 term the Supreme Court resolved a split among the federal circuits and held that the Federal Sentencing Guidelines apply to juveniles in that juveniles may not be sentenced to longer terms under the Federal Juvenile Delinquency Act than they would receive if they were tried as adults under the federal sentencing guidelines.

United States v. *R.L.C.* involved a sixteen-year-old who was charged with involuntary manslaughter. He was found to be a juvenile delinquent under the Federal Juvenile Delinquency Act and was sentenced to three years. He appealed, arguing that if he had been tried as an adult, under the federal sentencing guidelines he would have received a maximum sentence of eighteen months. The Eighth Circuit agreed, as did the U.S. Supreme Court.[22]

When Congress enacted the Federal Juvenile Delinquency Act in 1938, the purpose was to establish a separate system for juveniles, based primarily on the belief that young offenders can be rehabilitated. "Many of them can be reclaimed and made useful citizens if they are properly treated and cared for, and not permitted to mingle with mature and perhaps hardened criminals."[23] This position supported the original reason for establishing a separate court system for juveniles, but earlier Supreme Court decisions had eroded this position in general with reference to state decisions in juvenile cases.[24] In *United States* v. *R.L.C.*, the Supreme Court made other inroads into the traditional approach of treating juveniles differentially but in a way that increases the impact of the criminal justice system upon them. To the contrary, two noted criminologists, Travis Hirschi and Michael Gottfredson, take the position that we do not need two criminal justice systems, one for adults and one for juveniles, but that it is the latter that should prevail for all. Basing their conclusion on their social control theory approach to explaining behavior, these social scientists argue that for most cases, we should assume "that the function of the criminal justice system is to manage offenders, not to build a case against them that can be used only after they have passed beyond the age of maximal criminality." Hirschi and Gottfredson conclude:

> Although our theory suggests to many that we have a profoundly pessimistic view of human nature and a profoundly cynical view of the ability of the state to change the behavior of its citizens for the better, the fact is that we see no evidence of darkly sinister motives operating behind most criminal acts, and we are actually impressed by the relatively fleeting nature of the years of high criminal activity. Given that the cause of crime is low self-control, all that is required to reduce the crime problem to manageable proportions is to teach people early in life that they will be better off in the long run if they pay attention to the eventual consequences of their current behavior.[25]

Results of Federal Sentencing Guidelines

A noted authority on sentencing, Michael Tonry, states his analysis of federal sentencing guidelines bluntly, arguing that they "have failed." They have not met the stated goals of eliminating unwarranted sentence disparity and achieving sentence uniformity, and they have not gained the support of those who implement them: federal judges. The guidelines "are the most controversial and disliked sentencing reform initiative in United States history."[26] These criticisms deserve further analysis.

In 1992 the U.S. Sentencing Commission published the results of its self-evaluation of the results of the federal sentencing guidelines, an evaluation mandated by Congress. The Commission concluded that sentence disparity had been reduced. According to the commission's chair, "This, in itself, is a significant achievement and an important step toward a fairer and more effective criminal justice system." Nearly two-thirds of federal judges surveyed found the guidelines "mostly appropriate" as did 83 percent of the assistant U.S. attorneys. However, "90 percent of the federal defenders and 60 percent of the private defense attorneys surveyed said the guideline sentences are "mostly inappropriate."[27]

In another congressionally mandated study, the GAO (General Accounting Office) reported that the guidelines have reduced but not eliminated **sentence disparity**. Unwarranted factors such as gender, race, marital status, employment status, and age have continued to play a role in sentencing. "Our analyses. . . suggest that under the guidelines, not all unwarranted disparity in sentencing has been eliminated." Further, the guidelines remain highly controversial among those who must implement them.[28]

Tonry maintains that the Sentencing Commission study is "so beset by methodological and conceptual problems that little can be learned from its quantitative analyses" and that "on methodological grounds, GAO asserts that it is impossible to reach many general conclusions about disparities."[29] One conclusion is clear to all, however, and that is that the guidelines have resulted in longer sentences being served. The major findings of the first in-depth analysis of federal sentencing since the implementation of the guidelines in 1987 are reprinted in Focus 12.5.

FOCUS 12.5 Federal Sentencing in Transition, 1986-90

Federal sentencing practices changed substantially during the last half of the 1980s. Before the 1986 and 1988 anti-drug abuse laws that stiffened sanctions, the Sentencing Reform Act of 1984 (Public Law 98-473, 98 Stat. 1837 [1984], called "the Act" in this report) had already set in motion alterations of federal practices. Among other reforms, the Act established the U.S. Sentencing Commission to develop guidelines, which scale punishments to the gravity of the offense and the offender's criminal record. The guidelines apply to federal prisoners who committed their crimes on or after November 1, 1987.

Under the guidelines federal prisoners are no longer released from prison to parole by the U.S. Parole Commission. Instead, judges impose prison sentences that are served in full, except for time off that prisoners earn for good behavior. Offenders are supervised following their release from prison only if a judge requires it as a part of the sentence.

Cases subject to the Act ("guideline cases") began to appear in appreciable numbers in 1988, the year after the guidelines went into effect. During 1988, 17 percent of the offenders convicted in federal district courts were guideline cases.[1] In 1989 the proportion increased to 51 percent, and in 1990, to 65 percent. This report summarizes the main trends in federal sentencing. It compares sentences imposed before the Act in 1986–87 with those imposed between January 1988 and June 1990, when an increasing percentage of defendants were subject to the guidelines and faced stiffer mandatory sentences. The report also examines time actually served by offenders released from Federal prison between 1986 and 1990.

The main findings include:
• The percentage of convicted federal offenders receiving a prison sentence, which may have included a period of probation, rose from 52 percent during 1986 to 60 percent in the first half of 1990.
• Offenders sentenced under the sentencing guidelines were more likely to go to prison than those sentenced before the guidelines went into effect: 74 percent of the guideline cases in 1990, compared to 52 percent of the preguideline cases in 1986.
• The number and percentage of federal offenders sentenced to prison increased primarily after 1988. Among those sentenced in federal district courts, the increased number of drug offenders accounted for most of the increase in sentences to prison.
• The average length of federal sentences to incarceration decreased between 1986 and 1990 for crimes other than drug offenses. However, because offenders sentenced under the provisions of the Act are not eligible for release on parole, the more recently committed offenders were likely to be incarcerated longer than their predecessors.
• The use of probation sentences decreased from 63 percent in 1986 to 44 percent in the first half of 1990.
• Federal prisoners first released in 1990 served an average of 19 months

(75 percent of their court-imposed sentences). This was 29 percent longer than the average term served by prisoners first released in 1986.

SOURCE: Douglas C. McDonald and Kenneth E. Carlson, *Federal Sentencing in Transition, 1986-90*, Bureau of Justice Statistics (Washington, D.C.: U.S. Department of Justice, June 1992), p. 1, footnote omitted.

A second criticism of the federal guidelines is that many persons who must implement them view them with disfavor. This disfavor has been expressed most strongly by federal judges who have resigned their positions due to frustrations with the guidelines. For example, in 1992 U.S. District Judge Louis Oberdorfer, age seventy-three, announced his retirement with a written statement to his colleagues, which stated in part that he was "influenced by the diminution of our role as federal judges as a result of the endless street crime, drug trials, mandatory sentencing laws and guidelines, and the Court of Appeals' tendency not to respect our findings and our judgement." The latter reference was to a case in which Judge Oberdorfer thought the defendant might be rehabilitated and had assessed a penalty of sixty months rather than the ninety-seven to 121 months specified by the federal guidelines. Judge Oberdorfer's resignation was preceded by the 1990 resignations of two other judges, Thomas Scott of Miami and J. Lawrence Irving of San Diego, both of whom indicated that they resigned because of the limitations placed by federal guidelines on their sentencing decisions in individual cases.[30]

Other judges have taken a different approach. Two senior federal judges in New York City have refused to hear drug cases. Unlike other judges, these semiretired judges have the power to decide which cases they will hear. Judge Whitman Knapp and Judge Jack B. Weinstein indicated in 1993 that they would refuse to hear drug cases because of their frustration over the mandatory minimum sentences, which they do not think are effective in combatting drug offenses. They agreed to hear drug cases referred to them by other judges, but they indicated they would refer the cases back to those judges for sentencing. Both used the word "futility" to describe federal sentencing guidelines for drug cases. In the fall of 1993 Judge Weinstein was named Lawyer of the Year by the *National Law Journal*, despite the fact that after his refusal to hear drug cases, several members of Congress called for his resignation.[31]

In 1993 a federal judge ruled that a thirty-year sentence required by the federal guidelines for a career criminal convicted of a new drug charge was unconstitutional, constituting cruel and unusual punishment (discussed later in this chapter). U.S. District Judge Harold H. Greene gave the defendant a ten-year sentence instead, indicating that was an appropriate length for the relatively small amount of drugs for which the defendant was convicted in the instant case (and presumably in his former convictions, given the short sentences he had received). Judge Greene wrote a twenty-one-page opinion in which he stated that he and other judges were not upset over the federal sentencing guidelines because they remove judicial discretion per se but because they result in the "loss of the ability to do justice." Greene continued:

> Most judges feel a profound and severe sense of wrong when they have to sit by, powerless, while sentences are imposed in their names and by their voices which are entirely at odds with what justice and basic concepts of morality and equity require.[32]

A few days after Judge Greene's decision, the Supreme Court decided *Stinson* v. *United States*, excerpted and discussed earlier in this chapter. Judge Greene's decision was upheld on appeal.[33]

These and other actions demonstrate the controversy surrounding mandatory sentences, especially mandatory minimum sentences. Attorney General Janet Reno has indicated that she will analyze the situation. A coalition of thirty national organizations has called for numerous changes in criminal justice systems, including "halting the trend toward mandatory minimum sentencing in the federal system."[34] (See Appendix D for Congressional sentencing changes.)

Tonry concludes that any reasonable person analyzing the federal system will realize that the sentencing guidelines have failed. "I express no view on why. . . [they] failed. Finger-pointing can serve no purpose. What is important now is to admit the failure and begin the effort to recreate a federal sentencing system that is efficient and fair, evenhanded and discriminating."[35]

Sentencing Reform: An Analysis

In addition to sentencing reform in the federal system, major sentencing reforms have occurred in most states in recent years. Some are so recent that it is too early to analyze their impact. Others have been studied extensively by social scientists, although lower courts have shown little consensus in some of the constitutional challenges to sentencing reform. However, it is possible to suggest some overall results of sentencing reform.

The first result is that recent sentencing reform has deemphasized rehabilitation as a proper goal for sentencing and reinstituted retribution as a proper objective. As noted earlier, some jurisdictions state this change in their reform statutes. On the other hand, in 1992 and 1993 we saw some scholars, administrators, and politicians return to a rehabilitation emphasis. For example, Attorney General Reno, Lee P. Brown, senior drug policy aide to the president, and President Clinton talked about treatment rather than long sentences for some drug offenders, indicating that rehabilitation is a reasonable goal in some cases.[36]

There is some evidence that although the public remains punitive toward crime, there is some concern for rehabilitation, especially with young, poor, and minority defendants, according to one study that questioned about attitudes toward six crimes: robbery, rape, molestation, burglary, drug sale, and drug possession.[37] There is evidence, too, that prison administrators and other correctional personnel remain somewhat supportive of rehabilitative efforts.[38]

The second result is that sentencing reform does not always achieve one of its explicit or implicit goals: eliminating arbitrariness, discrimination, and disparity from the system. This result has been discussed with regard to the federal system but applies to state sentencing as well.[39] Discretion is not eliminated even when judicial discretion is curbed. There are multiple areas of discretion within criminal justice systems, and sentencing guidelines do not reach those areas.

Attempts to eliminate or reduce judicial sentencing discretion, such as the Washington Sentencing Reform Act, highlight some discretionary issues involved in structured sentencing. Although the Washington statute is more structured than its predecessor, take a look at Focus 12.3 and consider carefully some of the words and phrases used in describing mitigating and aggravating circumstances. How are they to be interpreted? The answer is by the discretion of the sentencing judge. In addition, judges have great discretion when sentencing *within* the ranges of the legislative guidelines. Despite the provision for judicial review in the Washington code, wide discretion is left to judges. Whether they exercise that discretion is another matter.

Discretion goes beyond the judge, however. Many of the sentencing reforms will have little or no effect on prosecutorial discretion. Prosecutors may refuse to prosecute a particular case or control the nature and number of charges that will be filed. Prosecutors have wide discretion in **plea bargaining** with defendants. Juries have considerable discretion. If they think a determinate sentence that would be imposed after a guilty verdict is unreasonable, they may refuse to convict.

Another problem is that most sentencing reforms utilizing sentencing guidelines provide that the guidelines apply only to prison or jail sentences, with wide discretion permitted in the imposition of alternative sentences, discussed later. According to Norval Morris, "The criticisms that the sentencing commission gives of its own work include their recognition that the cases riding the line between imprisonment and nonincarcerative punishments are still handled in the same unstructured, ill-informed manner."[40]

Other results may occur. When sentencing reform results in longer sentences, it intensifies the already overcrowded conditions of most prisons. Furthermore, mathematical approaches to sentencing give the appearance of being precise and more scientific than previous methods, but arbitrariness and discrimination may creep into the system when guidelines contain ambiguous words that must be interpreted in the context of a specific case.

Sentencing may be so complicated that judges, prosecutors, and defense attorneys do not understand the system or must spend considerable time learning the system. Although sentencing reform in some manner has occurred in most jurisdictions and in the federal system, the systems vary, which means that *sentence disparity* may continue when the various jurisdictions are compared. Finally, as long as the time served by an inmate may be reduced by *good-time credits* or by a parole board acting on those or other factors, disparity may exist.

The solution to this problem in some jurisdictions has been to abolish parole as a form of early release. This is the approach taken by the federal system and several states, although some states, such as Florida, which had abolished parole in 1983, reinstated it because of severe prison overcrowding.[41] The solution of abolishing parole, however, removes one method that has been used to alleviate prison overcrowding or to reduce the harshness of sentences in particular cases.

Although recent sentencing reforms have focused on jail and prison terms, there has been an accompanying concern with sentencing alternatives as well.

Intermediate Sanctions

In recent years the pressures of prison populations have led some scholars to an emphasis on intermediate sanctions, such as day fines, intensive probation supervision, boot camps, electronic monitoring, and house arrest.[42] These sanctions may be used instead of traditional sentences such as incarceration, capital punishment, and probation. Intermediate sanctions may be used in conjunction with probation. In addition to the scholarly emphasis on intermediate sanctions, governments have focused on this trend, too. Emphasis on intermediate sanctions is a new funding priority for the State Justice Institute (SJI) for its 1994 fiscal year. "The goal is to help states analyze their current sentencing practices and show judges how to take an active role in development of a wider array of sentencing options, if needed."[43] Legislatures have emphasized intermediate sanctions, too. For example, in 1993 Rhode Island's legislature approved legislation for intermediate sanctions, including intermediate probation supervision, community service, and reintegration centers for offenders.[44] Focus 12.6 gives an overview of the movement toward intermediate sanctions.

Fines

The imposition of a *fine*, sentencing the defendant to pay a financial penalty to the state (or federal government), is provided in many criminal statutes. Fines may be assessed to pay the state for prosecution costs. In recent years the *day fine* has gained prominence. The term describes a fine based on the individual's daily earnings. Day fines are common in some European and South American countries. They are considered more equitable because the fines are based on the ability to pay rather than the traditional approach in the United States, which based fines on the crime committed.

The day-fine programs in Staten Island (New York) and Milwaukee (Wisconsin) have been analyzed.[45] Some of the conclusions of the Staten Island study are as follows:

> Day fines were successfully introduced into routine sentencing. . . .
> The introduction of day fines did not appreciably affect judges' sentencing decisions during the pilot year. . . .
> After introduction of the day fine, average fines imposed for penal law offenses rose 25 percent. . . .

FOCUS 12.6 Intermediate Sanctions

Intermediate sanctions, ranging in severity from day fines to "boot camps," are interventions that are beginning to fill the sentencing gap between prison at one extreme and probation at the other. Lengthy prison terms may be inappropriate for some offenders; for others probation may be too inconsequential and may not provide the degree of supervision necessary to ensure public safety.

By expanding sentencing options, intermediate sanctions enable the criminal justice system to tailor punishment more closely to the nature of the crime and the criminal. An appropriate range of punishments can make it possible for the system to hold offenders strictly accountable for their actions.

These are important goals when one also considers the strains being placed every day on a criminal justice system that currently incarcerates more than 1.2 million adults and releases three times that number to some form of community supervision, primarily probation. Demands on traditional probation in major cities are probably increasing more dramatically than on jails and prisons; caseloads of up to 200 offenders per probation officer are not uncommon.

Criminal justice officials in many parts of the country are looking to intermediate sanctions as a means of meeting these challenges without threatening public safety. Through drug testing, electronic monitoring, and heightened supervision, intermediate sanctions increase control of certain offenders supervised in the com-

munity. And by offering other options for punishing low-risk offenders, they ensure that prisons will continue to incarcerate those offenders who pose an unacceptable risk to the public.

Intermediate sanctions also expand the opportunities to affect offenders' present and future behavior, by offering drug treatment and educational and vocational training, as well as opportunities for offenders to make restitution, perform community service, and maintain employment while serving their sentences.

Given the potential benefits of intermediate sanctions, in 1986 the National Institute of Justice (NIJ) launched a major and ongoing initiative to explore the types of offenders and supervision conditions most appropriate for such sanctions and to examine the sanctions' impact on deterring criminal behavior. As part of this initiative, the Institute has awarded grants to study and evaluate a variety of programs across the country that make use of intermediate sanctions. In 1990, NIJ sponsored an Intermediate Punishments Conference in conjunction with the State Justice Institute and National Institute of Corrections. The conference brought together criminal justice experts, governmental officials, and researchers from across the country to explore the spectrum of intermediate sanctions and their potential for improving justice and public safety.

SOURCE: Voncile B. Gowdy, *Intermediate Sanctions,* National Institute of Justice (Washington, D.C.: U.S. Department of Justice, 1992), pp.1-2, footnotes omitted.

> The total amount of the fines imposed by the court in penal law cases increased by 14 percent during the pilot year (from $82,060 to $93,856). . . . As expected, there was more variation among individual fine amounts when they were calculated using the day-fine system.[46]

One legal issue regarding fines has been resolved by the Supreme Court. In colonial America, imprisoning a debtor for inability to pay a debt was a common practice, so it is not unusual that incarcerating defendants who do not pay their fines became common once again. In 1983 the Supreme Court addressed this issue in *Bearden* v. *Georgia*. In the excerpt that follows, Justice Sandra Day O'Connor, writing for the Court, discusses the legal issues in this case along with the established precedent cases.

The defendant in *Bearden* was ordered by the trial court to pay a $500 fine and $235 in restitution while serving a probationary term after he pleaded guilty to the felonies of burglary and theft by receiving stolen property. The money was to be paid on a schedule. When the defendant failed to meet one of the deadlines, his probation was revoked. He was sent to prison for failure to make the monetary payment.[47]

Bearden v. *Georgia*

Since other courts have held that revoking the probation of indigents for failure to pay fines does violate the Equal Protection Clause, we granted certiorari to resolve this important issue in the administration of criminal justice. . . .

The rule . . . [established by prior cases] is that the State cannot "impos[e] a fine as a sentence and then automatically conver[t] it into a jail term solely because the defendant is indigent and cannot forthwith pay the fine in full." In other words, if the State determines a fine or restitution to be the appropriate and adequate penalty for the crime, it may not thereafter imprison a person solely because he lacked the resources to pay it. [Prior cases have] carefully distinguished this substantive limitation on the imprisonment of indigents from the situation where a defendant was at fault in failing to pay the fine. . . .

This distinction, based on the reasons for non-payment, is of critical importance here. If the probationer has willfully refused to pay the fine or restitution when he has the means to pay, the State is perfectly justified in using imprisonment as a sanction to enforce collection. Similarly, a probationer's failure to make sufficient bona fide efforts to seek employment or borrow money in order to pay the fine or restitution may reflect an insufficient concern for his crime. In such a situation, the state is likewise justified in revoking probation and using imprisonment as an appropriate penalty for the offense. But if the probationer has made all reasonable efforts to pay the fine or restitution, and yet cannot do so through no fault of his own, it is fundamentally unfair to revoke probation automatically without considering whether adequate alternative methods of punishing the defendant are available.

Recent studies indicate that fines are permitted in almost all U.S. jurisdictions and that this punishment is "less drastic, far less costly to the public, and perhaps more effective than imprisonment or community service." Until recently, fines were not utilized widely because of a lack of understanding of how to administer them properly. Problems of jail and prison overcrowding, along with increased knowledge of the effectiveness and widespread use of fines in Western European countries, have led to increased use of this sentencing alternative.[48]

Restitution and Community Service

Restitution and community service are used increasingly for sentencing alternatives. The use of restitution, requiring the offender to reimburse the victim financially or with services, has had a long history. In many instances restitution is combined with community service. In recent years, with the increasing development of victim compensation programs, victims in some jurisdictions have been permitted to participate in restitution decision making.

Restitution may be implemented in a variety of ways. The provisions among the states vary. In some, restitution may be imposed in addition to a fine; in others, it may be a condition of probation or conditional discharge. Some limit restitution to less serious offenses; others confine it to property losses. Some combine financial restitution with work service. The federal Victim and Witness Protection Act of 1982 (VWPA), as amended in subsequent years, includes a restitution provision for federal cases. That provision has been the subject of considerable litigation.[49]

Community work service statutes and practices vary widely, too. Some provide that work may be assigned while a person is on probation. Some permit work service in lieu of a fine or in addition to a fine. The statutes may be quite general in defining what constitutes community service. For example, according to Washington's Sentencing Reform Act of 1981, "'Community service' means compulsory service, without compensation, performed for the benefit of the community by the offender."[50] That definition leaves considerable discretion to judges to define what is and is not community service and what is beneficial. In most cases, as long as the orders do not violate constitutional provisions regarding sentences, the sentencing orders are upheld.

In most jurisdictions defendants convicted of certain crimes, such as violent personal crimes, are not eligible for community service as an alternative to incarceration. Similar exclusions may apply to probation as well.

Shock Incarceration or Boot Camps

The concept of *shock incarceration* has existed for years although called by other terms. In 1965, Ohio became the first state to adopt *shock probation*, which involved a judge-imposed sentence of a brief period of incarceration followed by probation.[51] Technically the term *shock probation* is incorrect, as probation is a sentence that does not involve incarceration. Thus, today we speak of *shock incarceration*. Shock incarceration is implemented primarily in boot camps, which are military-style places of incarceration. Boot camp inmates must follow strict codes of discipline, which resemble military training. Generally they participate in the incarceration program for 120 days (some programs are longer), followed by supervision in the community. In addition to strict physical discipline and exercise programs, offenders participate in academic programs, drug and alcohol treatment programs, and counseling.

Boot camps are used primarily for young, nonviolent first offenders who have not committed major felonies, although the programs differ widely. Boot camps are based on the assumption that strict, brief introductions to prison serve a deterrent purpose as well as save money for the state (or federal government). It is assumed that participants will learn skills and adopt attitudes that will enable them to lead law-abiding lives.

Boot camps have gained favor in recent years. In the 1989 New York City mayoral race, boot camps were a major focus, with all candidates favoring them.[52] In the 1990s numerous jurisdictions instituted or planned to institute boot camp programs. In 1991 a New York correctional group praised that state's boot camp program and urged its expansion. The Correctional Association of New York, a nonprofit group that has the power to visit correctional facilities and report their findings to the legislature and which has been very critical of New York correctional facilities, reported on visits to boot camps. The group concluded that the staff in those facilities is "energetic, able, intelligent, and most important, dedicated to a rehabilitative goal." Further, boot camps save money because participants are there for only six months. The association recommended that the programs be expanded to include offenders over thirty. "Older prisoners, for example, including repeat offenders, are often ready, even eager for rehabilitation."[53]

A correctional officer lines up inmates for inspection in New York's boot camp prison for low-level drug offenders.

In the 1993-94 Congressional efforts to enact new crime legislation, the boot camp concept was a prime focus. By the end of 1993 the Senate and the House had passed bills, but the two had yet to settle their differences. The Senate bill provided $3 billion to assist states in developing their own boot camp systems. This compared to a $600 million allocation in the House version. In April 1994 House members voted on a bill that increased allocations for boot camps to $3.6 billion, along with other changes, but Congress had not enacted a final crime statute by the time of this writing. Furthermore, skeptics were beginning to question whether boot camps could accomplish the goals for which they are designed. The evidence is mixed.[54] (See Appendix D for an update.)

There is evidence that offenders who complete shock incarceration programs have improved social attitudes compared to those who drop out of the programs or those who are incarcerated in regular programs, but it is not clear that these changes are sufficient to effect marked changes once they return to society unsupervised.[55]

Preliminary data from a recent analysis of three federally funded boot camp programs indicate a high rate of attrition, but researchers insist that boot camps have not had sufficient time to prove their worth. The American Correctional Association is surveying all boot camp programs in the United States and developing standards for these programs. Those standards should be available in 1994, but the ACA has reported an initial finding that boot camp programs do not reduce costs despite the shorter time served by offenders in these programs compared to those who are incarcerated in prisons and jails. The boot camp programs are "more program- and staff-intensive," and that raises costs.[56]

A contrary conclusion has been drawn by the GAO (U.S. General Accounting Office), which indicates that boot camps are less expensive than regular incarceration, although it is too early to tell whether they result in lower **recidivism** rates. The GAO cites these figures, among others, to support its conclusion. In New York the average daily cost for an inmate in a medium-security institution is $60; for a minimum-security prison, $51; and for a boot camp, $69. But overall, the boot camp inmate costs the state $19,000 less than an offender placed in a traditional prison. "New York estimated that its boot camps have saved the state $83 million in operating costs as of September 1991, plus another $93 million in prison construction costs." The GAO acknowledged that whether boot camps result in an overall reduction in correctional costs depends on whether they are used as a *replacement* for traditional incarceration.[57]

A 1993 publication by Doris Layton MacKenzie and her colleagues, who have conducted extensive research on boot camps, noted that since 1983, twenty-six states had opened forty-one boot camp programs. These researchers evaluated the Louisiana boot camp programs. They found positive changes in inmates' attitudes but noted that more time is needed for accurate analyses of recidivism rates. The boot camp programs cost more per day than traditional imprisonment, but the total length of time for shock incarceration is less, resulting in a cost of $13,784 less for the in-prison phase of boot camp as compared to the regular incarceration. The parole phase costs $5,956 more for the shock incarceration/boot camp program, resulting in a total savings of $7,828 for each offender who participates in this program as compared to traditional incarceration. The researchers warn, however, that there are other costs to consider, such as staff selection and training, demands on staff time, prison construction, and so on that must be considered in comparing the costs of the two approaches.[58]

The concept of boot camps is spreading rapidly, with programs in operation in thirty states, ten local jurisdictions, and the federal government by the end of 1993.[59] Until recently, most of the programs were in state prisons (with one conducted by the Federal Bureau of Prisons), but in recent months the boot camp concept has been expanded to local and regional jails as well. These programs have as their primary goals relieving overcrowding, rehabilitation, and improving community relations as well as jail operations. It is too early to determine whether these goals are being met, but there is some criticism of boot camps, and in June 1994 it was announced that one was closing. The first National Guard boot camp for problem teenagers was closed in Connecticut after an investigation disclosed that the camp was characterized by inadequate staffing as well as reports of drug use, violence, and gang activity among the teenagers. Officials emphasized that the camp's closing was not an indictment of its educational program and expressed hope that the camp might be reopened. The problems were attributed to inadequate selection procedures and supervision.[60]

House Arrest and Electronic Monitoring

In a 1985 case a federal judge wrote an excellent opinion in which he considered the purposes of punishment and concluded that in the case before him for sentencing, the imposition of a prison sentence and a large fine were not necessary to accomplish those purposes. Indeed, imprisonment might exacerbate the situation. Note his remarks in this excerpt from the case. The judge's action was unusual in 1985; today **house arrest**, in which offenders are permitted to remain in the community but only if they observe restrictions that limit leaving their residences, is more common. Before reading this excerpt it might be helpful to review the discussion of the purposes of punishment in Chapter 1.[61]

United States v. *Murphy*

The sentencing of Maureen Murphy requires, in the court's opinion, a sentence not heretofore used in this District and almost never used in the country in the federal court. . . .

The penalty is home detention. Respect for public opinion, the need to explain the reasons for the sentence to the defendant and others and the desirability of providing data for the Federal Sentencing Commission just appointed by the President require a more extensive statement than usual.

After a full trial Ms. Murphy was found guilty of a violation of the Racketeer Influenced and Corrupt Organizations Act (RICO), mail fraud and obstruction of justice charges. For many years as confidential secretary to Norman Teitler, a lawyer, she assisted in committing frauds against insurance companies and helped obtain inflated medical and other expenses following auto accidents. When the Grand Jury began its investigation she attempted to induce key witnesses to change their testimony.

Obviously these crimes are serious. They threaten the very foundation of the effective administration of justice in polluting the sources of information available to the Grand Jury. In addition, the corruption of the civil litigation process by lawyers, doctors and others cannot, and will not, be condoned or tolerated.

A sentence such as this must be approached with some general philosophical background. [The judge discussed prison overcrowding and the cost of incarceration and the realization that we cannot continue imposing long prison terms indefinitely]. . . .

The goals of punishment are incapacitation, rehabilitation, specific deterrence of the individual defendant, general deterrence of those who might commit crimes without the threat of punishment and, finally, the related goals of providing an outlet for the expression of strong disapproval or unacceptable conduct together with the catharsis of a specific statement of public condemnation together with punishment.

Incapacitation of those who are dangerous must, of course, continue to be our policy.

Rehabilitation in general takes place more effectively outside prison walls. Federal probation officers in this District have the resources and skill to exercise strict control, supply training and help with jobs. Cutting the person off from family, friends and jobs during this process is counterproductive.

Specific deterrence is important, but where it does not require incapacitation, particularly among non-professional criminals, it can be accomplished without long incarceration. A taste of jail may be enough under such circumstances.

General deterrence is a factor we know little about. For most crimes of white collar corruption it may not be necessary to provide substantial prison terms. Heavy fines, disgrace, and loss of licenses to practice professionally will help deter. More important is vigilance of those who should be apprehending and prosecuting the white collar criminals. Putting our money in swift and sure prosecution rather than in prison terms appears to be cost effective.

With these principles in mind, we turn to the defendant's background. Already related are the nature of her crimes. In total, she is subject to $56,000 in fines and 50 years in prison. She is now 35 years old, a high-school graduate. She attended local parochial school. She was raised in a close-knit, harmonious and religious family setting by hard-working parents. Her father was a New York City Sanitation

Department Engineer. She studied at secretarial schools and is, by all accounts, an excellent and bright worker who has always been steadily employed. Her assets are $150.00 in a savings account and a 1976 Pontiac. She has never been married and lives alone. . . .

Obviously the maximum fine could never be paid and would accomplish nothing except to make it impossible for the defendant to live and rehabilitate herself. The maximum terms of imprisonment provided by the statutes are much too long to even be considered seriously for this relatively young person who has never, so far as we know, committed another crime.

Putting her in prison for any substantial length of time will undoubtedly help to destroy her. The conditions of imprisonment, even in the best prisons for women, are reprehensible.

Accordingly, the court assesses a fine of $5,000 payable as Probation directs over the next five years. It sentences the defendant on Counts 2, 10, and 27 to 5 years on each count, concurrent, suspending execution of sentence and placing her on probation. Home detention is a condition of the probation on Counts 2, 10 and 27.

She is sentenced to 2 years of home detention on Count One in place of imprisonment. . . .

The defendant will be required to remain in her apartment, or other place of abode. She may not change her residence without the consent of Probation. She may leave only as permitted by Probation for medical reasons, employment and religious services and essential shopping for food and the like. She may go directly to and from her job and seek a new job only as permitted by Probation. She is at all times subject to strict supervision, to surprise visits by Probation and strict control. . . .

Should the defendant not comply strictly with Probation's orders, she will be ordered to serve out her prison term. She is reminded that the prison term is now suspended, not cancelled.

There will be some who will believe that this sentence is much too lenient. Others will believe it too humiliating. Public humiliation is a part of the punishment. Obviously there is serious danger of depression and worse in the case of home detention. Probation will arrange for suitable psychiatric and other appropriate services for defendant to forestall such problems.

In many respects the colonial use of stocks and equivalent punishment in other societies served a useful goal in providing swift disapproval as a deterrent. It is obvious that some form of this disapproval is required under modern conditions. How it can be accomplished is not clear. Obviously we will not tolerate branding and the carrying of signs. The matter is a difficult one and will require experimentation and modification of procedures in the light of experience.

The nation's largest community control program involving house arrest is in Florida, where a 1993 evaluation report indicated that in the past decade more than 40,000 offenders were placed on community control, many in

This electronic monitoring device is worn by offenders who are permitted to live outside prison provided they meet specified conditions, such as house arrest, which can be monitored by this device.

house arrest programs. The degree of control/supervision is high, with a minimum of twenty-eight contacts monthly and case loads ranging from twenty to twenty-five. The report recognizes the occurrence of some net widening (including in community control programs some offenders who otherwise would not have been incarcerated, some recidivism, including technical violations of probation conditions, and the high cost of intensive supervision and small case loads. Yet, the investigators conclude that the overall effect in the Florida Community Control Program (FCCP) has been positive. "With an estimated prison diversion rate of 54 percent, community control is cost effective despite the combined effect of net widening and the punishments imposed on almost 10 percent of FCCP participants for technical violations."[62]

Some house arrestees are monitored electronically.[63] In 1990 it was estimated that electronic monitoring devices were being used in forty states and that approximately 10,000 offenders were involved. These devices are much less expensive than incarceration and involve greater control than ordinary probation. Electronic monitoring has been implemented to some degree in all states, but the types of programs differ significantly, as do their success rates.[64] There is evidence that electronic monitoring has some success with drug offenders, and that for offenders convicted of driving under the influence, electronic monitoring is more cost-effective and more reasonable than jail sentences. Electronic monitoring "offers all the advantages of a community-based sanction while providing even greater incapacitation benefits than does jailing."[65]

In 1993 New York City officials announced their plans to reorganize the manner of handling the city's 60,000 probationers. Electronic monitoring is being used more extensively for the minor offenders, while the city is making significant expansions in its use of intensive probation supervision (discussed below) of more serious offenders. "The change in New York City, which has one of the largest probation departments in the nation, will amount to a working laboratory in the search for less costly alternatives to prison."[66]

Probation

The intermediate sanctions just discussed have been developed to provide sentencing options between the extremes of incarceration (or capital punishment) and the more lenient approach of probation, the most frequently imposed sanction. Although some argue that probation is a condition, not a sentence, courts disagree. Probation is a sentence imposed by a judge after adjudication of guilt.[67]

Probation involves permitting the offender to remain in the community, usually under minimum supervision, for a specified period of time under specified circumstances. In some cases probation is combined with electronic monitoring; in others, intensive personal supervision is utilized.

Data and Examples

According to the Bureau of Justice Statistics, during 1990, 2,670,234 U.S. adults were on probation, representing a 5.9 percent increase over the previous year. In that same year one in every forty-three U.S. adults was under some form of correctional supervision, with approximately two-thirds of those on probation. The BJS is preparing a report of later data, but that report is not yet available.[68]

Despite the increase in the use of probation in recent years, probation is not popular with the general public, many of whom want offenders incarcerated although they are ambivalent about spending tax dollars to make that possible.[69] Media reports of shocking cases arouse public passion on the issue. Of particular note recently was the probation sentence of a nineteen-year-old white supremacist in Texas. Christopher William Brosky was sentenced to probation after his conviction for murdering an African-American male. An outcry of public outrage and protest followed the decision, which was the result of technical error. The all-white jury had recommended five years in prison followed by ten years on probation. But Texas law does not permit a jury to recommend probation if it recommends a prison sentence of less than ten years. Thus, in this case, by law the judge had to impose only the probation sentence.[70] Subsequently, Brosky was tried on a related charge (federal conspiracy), convicted by a racially mixed jury, and sentenced to forty years in prison and a $5,000 fine.

FELONY PROBATION AND INTENSIVE PROBATION SUPERVISION

In recent years, primarily because of prison overcrowding, some jurisdictions have begun a policy of *felony probation*, in which some serious offenders are placed on probation rather than sentenced to prison.[71] Felony probation may be combined with another recent innovation in probation, **intensive probation supervision (IPS)**. IPS is aimed primarily at diverting convicted persons from overcrowded jails and prisons, but it has other objectives as well. With smaller case loads and more supervision given to each probationer, greater success may be expected. There is some evidence that this is a correct assumption. It is thought, too, that IPS improves the public image of probation because additional supervision is emphasized.[72]

IPS programs differ, but most have at least the following requirements:

- some combination of multiple weekly contacts with a supervising officer;
- random and unannounced drug testing;
- stringent enforcement of probation/parole conditions; and

- a requirement to participate in relevant treatment, hold a job, and perhaps perform community service.[73]

Whether IPS programs are effective depends on how they are implemented and how the goals are defined and measured. There is evidence that some programs are effective as surveillance and as intermediate sanctions, providing greater supervision and offering alternative sanctions between the extremes of incarceration and traditional probation (or parole). They may not be as effective if goals are to reduce prison populations and overall costs.[74] The same is true of recidivism. Increased monitoring may result in increased observation of technical violations.[75] A study conducted by the General Accounting Office (GAO) concluded that IPS programs have "some merit" despite the fact that the programs have been oversold in terms of what they might accomplish overall.[76]

As noted earlier, New York City is expanding the use of IPS as well as of electronic monitoring, with officials counting on a savings from the latter approach to provide more funds for IPS. The most serious offenders who are on probation are required to report twice weekly for "at least two hours of peer-group counseling shepherded by teams of probation workers, far greater attention than the few minutes a month currently afforded to them." It is argued that this new focus "on violence-prone criminals, before they do something worse on the streets, is the best investment of scarce resources."[77]

Capital Punishment

Obviously the most severe sentence is capital punishment. The U.S. Supreme Court has interpreted the Constitution as placing some restrictions on capital punishment, but in 1972, in *Furman* v. *Georgia*, the Court held that capital punishment is not per se unconstitutional. When the sentence is imposed in an arbitrary and discriminatory manner, however, it is unconstitutional. In *Furman*, the Court left open the possibility that other statutes could be drafted and could survive constitutional scrutiny.[78]

By 1976 many states had enacted new capital punishment statutes. In that year, in *Gregg* v. *Georgia*, the Court upheld the constitutionality of death penalty statutes that require a consideration of aggravating and mitigating circumstances before imposition of the penalty. That same year the Court had invalidated a statute that provided for *mandatory* imposition of capital punishment.[79]

Figure 12.1 graphs the increase in the number of persons on death row between 1953 and 1992, showing the sharp increase since the 1976 decision. Executions have increased also, with over 200 conducted between 1976 and 1994. Between January 1 and 16 September 1993, thirty-two inmates were executed in the United States, more than in any year since forty-seven were executed in 1962. Fourteen of those 1993 executions were in Texas, four in Virginia, and three in Florida.[80] The fifteenth Texas execution occurred in September, followed by another in November 1993.

Various studies indicate that the American public favors capital punishment, although there is some evidence that when given an alternative of life

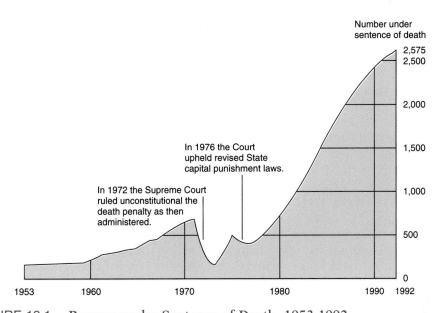

Number under
sentence of death

In 1976 the Court
upheld revised State
capital punishment laws.

In 1972 the Supreme Court
ruled unconstitutional the
death penalty as then
administered.

FIGURE 12.1   Persons under Sentence of Death, 1953-1992

SOURCE: Lawrence A. Greenfeld and James J. Stephan, *Capital Punishment 1992*, Bureau of Justice Statistics (Washington, D.C.: U.S. Department of Justice, December 1993), p. 2.

without possibility of parole, the percentage of those favoring capital punishment decreases significantly.[81] It is not uncommon to see spectators holding vigil, singing and dancing, while others cry and pray at execution sites. Some have proposed television of executions; an attempt was made to do so in California, but a court refused.[82]

The 1994 crime statute increases the number of crimes calling for the death penalty, while scholars and others debate the morality of capital punishment[83] and conduct research on the effects of capital punishment.[84]

Politicians have gotten involved in the death penalty debate, too. As Focus 4.4 in Chapter 4 notes, the Florida governor's office was involved in a highly political death penalty case. In 1992 Pope John Paul II sent a letter to Texas Governor Ann Richards, protesting the scheduled execution of Johnny Frank Garrett. Garrett, who was convicted of raping and murdering a seventy-six-year-old nun, was given a reprieve from his scheduled January execution, but one month later he was executed after the governor was overruled by the Texas Board of Pardons and Paroles, which voted unanimously against commuting the sentence.

In 1993 two state governors argued over who should have custody of Thomas Grasso, who was sent to Oklahoma after he was convicted of murder in New York. Grasso had been convicted previously of murder in Oklahoma, where he was sentenced to die. New York wanted him back to serve his twenty years-to-life sentence. Grasso wanted to remain in Oklahoma and be executed. "I did it. The state says I deserve it. Why prolong it?"[85] New York won at least temporarily. Oklahoma sent Grasso back to New York to serve his term while the state decided whether to appeal the decision that blocked his Oklahoma execution. Twelve hours before Grasso was scheduled to die in October 1993, a federal court ruled that he be sent back to New York to serve his sentence there prior to execution.[86]

In December 1993 the U.S. Supreme Court agreed to decide two capital punishment cases from California. Both involve the imposition of the death penalty by juries. The defense in the cases argued that the California statute is vague with regard to instruction to juries concerning mitigating and aggravating factors to be considered in deciding whether to impose the death penalty. The 1978 statute indicates that jurors are to consider a variety of factors if they are relevant but does not specify whether those factors are mitigating or aggravating factors. Thus, for example, the factor of *age* might work for or against the defense. Another issue is the provision that juries are to consider "the circumstances of the crime" without any specification regarding the meaning of that phrase. In addition, the defense argued that telling the jury to consider "the presence or absence of criminal activity by the defendant which involved the use or attempt use of force or violence" does not constitute sufficient instruction to the jury on how to evaluate the prior criminal record of the defendant. On the last day of the 1993–94 term the Court upheld the California death penalty statute against charges that it is unconstitutionally vague. Had the Court not done so, all 383 California death row inmates would have had to be resentenced.[87]

Constitutional Issues of Sentencing

Appellate courts are hesitant to interfere with legislative or judicial sentencing powers, but they do hear and decide sentences on appeal if it appears that those sentences violate defendants' *constitutional* rights.

The Eighth Amendment's ban on cruel and unusual punishment and the Fourteenth Amendment's prohibition against violating equal protection and due process (see Appendix A) provide the basis for the constitutional rights discussed in this section. Most due process issues are procedural and are not discussed here.

Equal Protection Issues

Sentences may not violate defendants' rights to equal protection under the law. The issue arises in many cases, particularly with regard to race and gender, both of which are examined. First, it is necessary to understand that by requiring equal protection in sentencing, the Constitution does not require that all defendants be treated *identically*. "The belief no longer prevails that every offense in a like legal category calls for an identical punishment without regard to the past life and habits of a particular offender."[88] Equal protection in sentencing means that, when there are differences, the bases for sentencing must be factors other than, for example, race or gender.

In the U.S. Supreme Court building in Washington, D.C., the justices hear and decide numerous cases on the issue of whether certain punishments are constitutional.

RACE AND SENTENCING

Allegations of violating equal protection in sentencing minorities, particularly when capital punishment is involved and the defendant is African American, have been made frequently over the years. The issue was faced by the Supreme Court in 1987 in *McCleskey* v. *Kemp*, which involved an African-American defendant sentenced to death in Georgia for murdering a white police officer. McCleskey argued unsuccessfully that a statistical study by University of Iowa law professor David C. Baldus supported his argument that he had been discriminated against because of his race *and* the race of his victim. In this excerpt, the Court gives its reaction to the argument.[89]

McCleskey v. *Kemp*

This case presents the question whether a complex statistical study that indicates a risk that racial considerations enter into capital sentencing determinations proves that petitioner McCleskey's capital sentence is unconstitutional under the Eighth or Fourteenth Amendment. . . .

McCleskey's first claim is that the Georgia capital punishment statute violates the Equal Protection Clause of the Fourteenth Amendment. He argues that race has infected the administration of Georgia's statute in two ways: persons who murder whites are more likely to be sentenced to death than persons who murder blacks, and that black murderers are more likely to be sentenced to death than white murderers. As a black defendant who killed a white victim, McCleskey claims that the Baldus study demonstrates that he was discriminated against because of his race and because of the race of his victim . . . this claim must fail. . . .

McCleskey also argues that the Baldus study demonstrates that the Georgia capital sentencing system violates the Eighth Amendment. . . . [The Court reviewed its previous decisions on cruel and unusual punishment, particularly with respect to the death penalty.]

In sum, our decisions . . . identified a constitutionally permissible range of discretion in imposing the death penalty. First, there is a required threshold below which the death penalty cannot be imposed. In this context, the State must establish rational criteria that narrow the decision maker's judgment as to whether the circumstances of a particular defendant's case meets the threshold. Moreover, a societal consensus that the death penalty is disproportionate to a particular offense prevents a State from imposing the death penalty for that offense. Second, States cannot limit the sentencer's consideration of any relevant circumstance that could cause it to decline to impose the penalty. In this respect, the State cannot channel the sentencer's discretion, but must allow it to consider any relevant information offered by the defendant. . . .

At most, the Baldus study indicates a discrepancy that appears to correlate with race. Apparent disparities in sentencing are an inevitable part of our criminal justice system. The discrepancy indicated by the Baldus study is a "far cry from the major systemic defects identified in *Furman.*" . . . Where the discretion that is fundamental to our criminal process is involved, we decline to assume that what is unexplained is invidious. In light of the safeguards designed to minimize racial bias in the process, the fundamental value of jury trial in our criminal justice system, and the benefits that discretion provides to criminal defendants, we hold that the Baldus study does not demonstrate a constitutionally significant risk of racial bias affecting the Georgia capital-sentencing process. [In addition, the Court rejected the Eighth Amendment claims against cruel and unusual punishment].

Four justices dissented in *McCleskey*. Among others, Justice Brennan wrote that he believed McCleskey had conclusively "demonstrated precisely the type of risk of irrationality in sentencing that we have consistently condemned in our Eighth Amendment jurisprudence." [90]

McCleskey was executed in 1991 after thirteen years on death row. He continued his appeals beyond that of the above case, but in *McCleskey* v. *Zant*, the U.S. Supreme Court declared that the abuse of *habeas corpus*, which McClesley employed, promotes "disrespect for the finality of convictions" and thus "disparages the entire criminal justice system."[91] The writ of *habeas corpus*, which means "you have the body," is a procedure used frequently by inmates to question the legality of their confinement. By filing the writ, inmates are arguing that they are being incarcerated illegally and thus should be released. In recent years the Court has been restraining the use of the writ, especially in capital cases, which tend to go on for years before final resolution of all legal issues. The Supreme Court's position on *habeas corpus* has been criticized by many, including federal judges,[92] but a committee appointed in 1988 by Chief Justice Rehnquist concluded that:

> Capital cases should be subject to one complete and fair course of collateral review in the state and federal system, free from the time pressure of impending execution, and with the assistance of competent counsel for the defendant. When this review has concluded, litigation should end.[93]

In 1992 the Supreme Court indicated further its growing impatience with numerous appeals in individual capital punishment cases. On 22 April 1992 the Court issued an unprecedented order, which paved the way for the first California execution in twenty-five years. The Court ordered that "No further stays of Robert Alton Harris's execution shall be entered by the Federal courts except upon order of this Court." The *New York Times* referred to the Court's order as its "rush to kill," and suggested that "If executions deter murders, the Harris execution. . . should usher in a wave of civil peace. And if the state can really get serious about executing the 330 men and women on its death row, there'll be perfect tranquility in time for the Millennium."[94] Harris was executed subsequently.

In a further move in January 1993, the Court ruled that death-row inmates making late claims should be heard by courts only in "truly persuasive" cases. In his dissent, Justice Harry Blackmun, who read his dissenting opinion from the bench, interpreted the majority's actions as sanctioning the execution of innocent people, a move "periously close to simple murder." However, at the end of its 1993–94 term the Court held that federal district judges may postpone executions of convicts who have exhausted their state remedies in order to give those individuals an opportunity to secure an attorney to represent them on a federal appeal. Justice Blackmun, who retired from the Court that day, wrote the opinion for the majority.[95]

The issues surrounding the writ of *habeas corpus* arise primarily in capital punishment cases, as does the issue of race discrimination, but race discrimination has been alleged in other areas of sentencing as well. Earlier we discussed problems with mandatory minimum sentences. There is evidence that these sentences have a greater impact on minorities than on whites, with African Americans impacted even more than Hispanics. "The difference found across race appears to have increased since 1984."[96]

In 1993 the U.S. Justice Department appealed the decision of a federal district judge who ruled that the federal mandatory minimum-sentence guidelines negatively impact African Americans sentenced in crack-and-powder-cocaine cases. Judge Lyle E. Strom of Omaha, Nebraska, "is the first Federal judge to cite racial disparity in departing from the guidelines" although there has been at least one similar ruling by a state judge interpreting state sentencing guidelines. The appeal will not be heard until 1994.[97] There is evidence also that among juveniles, African Americans are more negatively impacted by sentencing.[98]

Evidence of racism in sentencing is recognized by some courts. In December 1989 the Texas Court of Criminal Appeals set aside the conviction of Clarence Lee Brandley, who was on death row in Texas and who twice came within hours of execution. According to the judge who wrote the opinion, Brandley's trial was sloppy, potentially racist, and a "subversion of justice." In 1989 Brandley was released.[99]

Scholars have alleged racial discrimination in sentencing as well as in other phases of the criminal justice system. In a 1993 publication, Coramae Richey Mann reviews and analyzes former and current literature on race and sentencing and concludes that

> racial minority suspects disproportionately become defendants and as defendants are disproportionately sent to prison or disproportionately executed. . . . How many studies will it take to achieve the necessary and appropriate policies to alleviate the disparate treatment of U.S. racial minorities? If only one Native, Hispanic, Asian, or African American is imprisoned, shot, gassed, electrocuted, hanged, or lethally injected because of a racist system, of what use are studies after the fact? To paraphrase Pepinsky, the humanness of the issue has been empirically sucked dry; it is time to restore it through ameliorative action.[100]

GENDER AND SENTENCING

It is improper to discriminate against defendants because of their gender. If men and women commit similar offenses under similar circumstances, they should receive the same sentences unless there is a rational reason why they should be treated differently because of gender.

In *State v. Chambers* the New Jersey Supreme Court considered a statute that provided for differential sentencing of men and women; female offenders were to be sentenced for an indeterminate term in a situation in which male offenders would be given a minimum-maximum term for the same offense. A woman who pled guilty to a bookmaking charge and who received the mandatory indeterminate sentence could be imprisoned for as long as five years under the statute, whereas a man would receive a sentence of not less than one nor more than two years. The excerpt gives the state's rationale for this differential in sentencing and the response of the court.[101]

State v. Chambers

At the post-conviction hearing . . . the State attempted to satisfy the burden of showing a substantial empirically grounded justification for the disparate statutory sentencing schemes. However, almost all of the witnesses agreed that there was no sound penological basis justifying indeterminate sentences for women and minimum-maximum sentences for males for the same offense.

Most of the witnesses affirmatively stated that they could find no basis for concluding that it takes longer to rehabilitate females than to rehabilitate males, or that females were better subjects for rehabilitation than males. . . .

> Analyzing the proofs, the most that has been shown is that there are differences in the emotional behavior of men and women. However, basically, there are no innate differences in capacity for intellectual achievement, self-perception or self-control, or the ability to change attitude and behavior, adjust to social norms and accept responsibility.

Some distinctions are permissible when sentencing men or women. The point is that the state must show a rational reason for making such distinctions. Consider this example. A man in Illinois claimed that the state violated the Equal Protection Clause of the Constitution in providing for a greater penalty for a man convicted of incest with his stepdaughter than for a woman convicted of incest with her stepson. The conviction was confirmed on appeal, with the appellate court indicating that the state had a rational reason for the distinction — the prevention of pregnancy in the case of a female victim. The U.S. Supreme Court refused to hear the case, thus allowing the ruling to stand.[102]

There is extensive literature on the issue of whether race or gender discrimination exists in the criminal justice system, and there is widespread disagreement over the conclusions. The key is not whether *differences* exist, but *why* they exist. For example, recent research has indicated that although gender differences exist in sanctioning of female and male children and teens in the home and in the school, the evidence does not support that finding in the justice system.[103] On the other hand, studies in Florida, Massachusetts, and other states report bias against women in most areas of the criminal justice system.[104] Still others argue that what appears to be differential treatment by gender may reflect differences in appropriate variables, such as the nature and type of offense or background of offenses as well as changes in the methodology of the research.[105] As one scholar notes:

> Only small differences in sentence length by sex were observed; for the most part these are explained by the different criminal behaviors of men and of women. For both men and women, the most important determinant of sentence length is the type and seriousness of the offense.[106]

In studying possible discrimination in the justice system, research must be analyzed in terms of all relevant variables—such as seriousness of the crime and prior convictions—that are permissible for distinctions. It cannot be assumed that differences equal discrimination.

Proportionality

The Eighth Amendment prohibition against cruel and unusual punishment (see Appendix A) has been interpreted to mean that a sentence must be proportionate to the offense. Proportionality may involve *type* or *length* of offense. This issue arises most often with respect to the death penalty. The major case is *Coker* v. *Georgia*. In this excerpt, the Supreme Court explains why the death penalty is disproportionate for the crime of raping an adult female.[107]

Coker v. Georgia

Georgia is the sole jurisdiction in the United States at the present time that authorizes a sentence of death when the rape victim is an adult woman, and only two other jurisdictions provide capital punishment when the victim is a child.

We do not discount the seriousness of rape as a crime. It is highly reprehensible, both in a moral sense and in its almost total contempt for the personal integrity and autonomy of the female victim and for the latter's privilege of choosing those with whom intimate relationships are to be established. Short of homicide, it is the "ultimate violation of self." . . . Rape is without doubt deserving of serious punishment; but in terms of moral depravity and of the injury to the person and to the public, it does not compare with murder, which does involve the unjustified taking of human life. The murderer kills; the rapist, if no more than that does not. Life is over for the victim of the murderers; for the rape victim life may not be nearly so happy as it was, but it is not over and normally is not beyond repair. We have the abiding conviction that the death penalty, which "is unique in its severity and revocability" is an excessive penalty for the rapist who, as such, does not take human life.

The proportionality issue arises also with respect to sentence length. Although most appellate courts defer to trial judges on this issue, some sentencing decisions are reversed on appeal. For example, a lower federal court reversed the sentence of a defendant who received a ten-year sentence (the maximum allowed by law) for conviction of illegal drug possession. When arrested, the defendant possessed only half of his daily dosage of drugs, a clear indication, said the court, that he was not intending to sell the drugs. Although possession was illegal, the court said the sentence was disproportionate in that it was

> at least twice as long as the *maximum* federal sentence for such major felonies as extortion, blackmail, perjury, assault with a dangerous weapon or by beating, arson (not endangering a human life), threatening the life of the President, and selling a man into slavery. It is severe both in its length and in its callous disregard for appellant's obvious need for treatment.[108]

A contrary conclusion was reached on appeal in a New York case, which indicates the reluctance of courts to interfere with legislatively established minimum and maximum sentences. The court had struck down sentences on the proportionality issue involving sentencing under the 1973 drug law, which provided a mandatory indeterminate sentence of a number of years to life in the case of drug offenders. The court held that a maximum sentence of life in such cases violated the Eighth Amendment ban against cruel and unusual punishment (see Appendix A).

On appeal, the Second Circuit reversed the lower court in a long opinion in which the court discusses the respective roles of the legislature and the judiciary in determining sentence length. The court concluded:

> No decision of the Supreme Court, this court or the highest court of the State of New York has found a sentence of imprisonment to transgress the Eighth Amendment merely because of its length. There may well be such a case but this is surely not it. In view of the extraordinary crisis faced by the State of New York, caused by the crime of drug trafficking, we cannot agree with the district court that the punishments meted out to the appellees here are constitutionally defective.[109]

The proportionality issue arises also in habitual offender or recidivism statutes, which provide for an increased penalty once a defendant has been convicted of multiple offenses. The U.S. Supreme Court faced the issue in 1980, when the justices looked at the Texas statute permitting a life sentence to be imposed under the recidivist statute.

Rummel v. *Estelle* involved a defendant who had been convicted in the state courts and sentenced to prison on two previous occasions for two separate felonies. William James Rummel had been convicted of fraudulent use of a credit card to obtain $80 worth of goods or services and on another occasion of passing a forged check in the amount of $28.36. Upon conviction of his third felony, obtaining $120.75 by false pretense, he received a mandatory life sentence. The Supreme Court held that the life sentence was not disproportionate to the offense when prior convictions were considered.[110]

In *Solem* v. *Helm*, the Supreme Court held that a life sentence was disproportionate to the crime for which it was imposed. The Court said it was not permissible to impose a life sentence on a defendant who was convicted of a seventh nonviolent felony, passing a $100 bad check. The Court distinguished the facts of *Helm* from those of *Rummel*. In *Rummel*, the defendant had a chance for parole, but in *Helm*, the defendant was sentenced to life in prison with no possibility of parole.

In *Helm* the Supreme Court stated objective criteria on which such decisions are to be based.

> In sum, a court's proportionality analysis under the Eighth Amendment should be guided by objective criteria, including (i) the gravity of the offense and the harshness of the penalty; (ii) the sentences imposed on other criminals in the same jurisdiction; and (iii) the sentences imposed for commission of the same crime in other jurisdictions.[111]

In 1991, the Supreme Court decided a Michigan case in which Ronald Allen Harmelin argued that the state's mandatory sentence of life imprisonment without possibility of parole for possession of more than 650 grams of cocaine is unconstitutional. Harmelin, a forty-five-year-old first offender, who faced the rest of his life in prison, argued that his conviction for possession of approximately one and one-half pounds of cocaine was not as serious as other crimes for which the mandatory penalty was not so stiff. Harmelin argued that under *Solem* v. *Helm*, his sentence was unconstitutional. The state argued that *Solem* v. *Helm* should be overruled because the proportionality test stated in that case is too subjective and therefore permits judicial arbitrariness. The Supreme Court upheld the Michigan statute.[112]

The Supreme Court has held that in the sentencing process in death penalty cases, a proportionality review is not required. The issue arose in 1984 when the Court heard a California case in which the federal court had reversed the conviction of a defendant sentenced to death. The lower court said the sentence was invalid because the state had not conducted a proportionality review, meaning the state had not attempted to find out whether other similarly situated defendants received the death penalty. Emphasizing that the California statute required that, before the death penalty can be imposed on a defendant the jury must find at least one special circumstance pointing to the need for that penalty, the U.S. Supreme Court concluded that a proportionality review was not required.[113]

In May 1993 the District of Columbia Court of Appeals held that the Sentencing Commission had overstepped its authority when it required automatic imposition of a sentence three times as long as the congressional ten-year mandatory minimum sentence for repeat drug offenders.[114] In October 1993 the U.S. Supreme Court agreed to hear a case involving the issue of whether defendants facing sentencing under the Armed Career Criminal Act may challenge the validity of the three (or more) earlier state convictions for violent felonies or serious drug offenses that subject them to the mandatory fifteen-year-sentence (with a maximum of life in prison) when convicted of owning or transporting a gun. Lower federal courts disagreed on the issue, and in the case of Darren J. Custis, the Court agreed to hear arguments concerning whether Custis could challenge his previous robbery and burglary convictions. Custis contended that the earlier convictions could not be the basis for an enhanced penalty because he did not have adequate legal representation when he entered guilty pleas to those earlier offenses. He maintained that he was not informed fully of the consequences of his pleas. Custis faced only three years in prison for the current offense, but if sentenced under the habitual criminal provision of the Armed Career Criminal Act, he faced a twenty-year sentence. The U.S. Supreme Court held that in enacting the Armed Career Criminal Act Congress did not intend to permit defendants to challenge their earlier state convictions except under limited circumstances (convictions obtained in violation of the right to counsel). In addition to considering the intent of Congress in enacting the statute, the majority opinion (written by Chief Justice Rehnquist for six members of the Court) indicated concern with the finality of judgments and the adminstrative overhead that would be involved in permitting the type of collateral attacks of former convictions requested by the defendant.[115]

Cruel and Unusual Punishment

The basis for reversing most sentences is the Eighth Amendment's prohibition against the infliction of **cruel and unusual punishment** (see Appendix A), but the definition of that concept is not clear. We have seen that sentences may be unconstitutional because they are too long in proportion to the offense, because the type of sentence is excessive when compared to the nature of the offense, or because defendants are discriminated against because of their race or gender. Some types of sentences or probation conditions may be considered cruel and unusual as well. For example, California courts have refused to uphold an order of contraception in some probation cases.[116] In a widely discussed recent case, Darlene Johnson was sentenced to three years' probation. Among other conditions, she was to be implanted with Norplant, a birth control implant only recently approved by the FDA at the time of Johnson's sentencing. Her case was featured on "60 Minutes," in many national magazines and journals, and on "L.A. Law." The case became moot in March 1992, when Ms. Johnson was sentenced to prison for violation of one of the other terms of her probation.[117]

In other cases judges have ordered tubal ligations of women; several are reported each year. Most are withdrawn after they are protested by many; some are declared unconstitutional by courts, some of which refer back to the landmark decision in 1942 when the U.S. Supreme Court invalidated an Oklahoma statute that provided for mandatory sterilization of offenders convicted of a third crime of moral turpitude. In *Skinner* v. *Oklahoma*, the Court proclaimed procreation as "one of the basic civil rights of man."[118]

Some courts cite their state's constitutional provisions in invalidating mandatory sterilization as a sentence. The high court in South Carolina has held that sterilization violates the state's prohibition against cruel and unusual punishment.[119] Surgical or chemical castration of male sex offenders has been imposed, too, but in a recent case the judge withdrew this probation condition when he could not find a doctor who would perform the surgery. Texas judge Michael T. McSpadden ordered surgical castration on a defendant who volunteered to undergo the surgery if the judge would not impose incarceration. Judge McSpadden advocates castration as a deterrent to sex crimes, but his position has been described by the director of the Texas Civil Rights Project as "bestowing his judicial blessing upon a practice as barbaric as it is misguided." A bill was introduced into the Texas legislature to provide for castration of sex offenders, but it failed.[120]

In 1993 Barbara Gross agreed to a tubal ligation as a condition of probation after she and her husband pleaded guilty to sexual abuse of their four children. Judge Lynn Brown of the criminal court of Washington County, Tennessee, said that the fact that the defendant volunteered to be sterilized made the probation condition legal. Others disagree, arguing that a pick-pocket cannot agree to have his hands cut off as an alternative to incarceration; likewise, a woman cannot agree to sterilization as a condition of probation. Gross had her baby; it was not known whether she had a tubal ligation, but Judge Brown said that until the defendant or her lawyer come to court and make a motion to modify the probation condition, it must stand.[121]

Sentences may be considered cruel and unusual if they are imposed without considering characteristics of the offender, the offense, and mitigating factors. This issue arises most often in capital punishment cases. In *Sumner* v. *Shuman*, Justice Harry A. Blackmun, writing for the majority, said that the Eighth Amendment's prohibition against cruel and unusual punishment guarantees to all defendants facing capital punishment the right "to present any relevant mitigating evidence that could justify a lesser sentence." The case involves an inmate serving a life sentence who was convicted under a statute providing a mandatory death sentence for an inmate convicted of murder while serving a life sentence without parole. According to Blackmun, even under these facts, the sentencing court must consider the record, character, age, the influence of drugs, alcohol, or extreme emotional disturbance, and any other relevant mitigating factors before imposing the death penalty. Blackmun concluded:

> Just as the level of an offender's involvement in a routine crime varies, so too can the level of involvement in a violent prison incident. . . . An inmate's participation may be sufficient to support a murder conviction, but in some cases it may not be sufficient to render death an appropriate sentence, even though it is a life-term inmate.[122]

The Supreme Court has held that it is permissible to impose capital punishment on a person who was involved in a felony murder but who did not commit the murder or intend for the murder to be committed, provided that person was a *major participant* in the felony and acted with reckless indifference to human life. **Felony murder** refers to an unlawful killing that occurs during the commission of a felony. The concept permits murder convictions of all those participating in the felony even though they were not involved in the actual killings but raises the issue of whether capital punishment for all participants would be cruel and unusual punishment.

Tison v. *Arizona* involved two defendants, brothers, who, along with another brother, took weapons to their father and another inmate in the Arizona State Prison and assisted in the escape of the two inmates, knowing that those inmates had killed in an earlier escape attempt. The defendants participated with the escapees in kidnapping and robbing a family, and although they did not participate in the murder of that family, they stood by and did nothing to prevent the murders.[123]

In *Tison*, the Court distinguished its earlier case, *Enmund* v. *Florida*, in which the Court held that capital punishment was not permissible in the case of a felon who did not participate in or intend the resulting murder.[124] The Court reasoned that the defendant in *Enmund* was a *minor participant* in the armed robbery; he was not on the scene of the murder; he did not attempt to kill; and he did not have the required mental state for murder, compared to the defendant in *Tison*, who may be found to have exhibited reckless disregard for human life. *Tison* was sent back for more findings on that issue.

The Supreme Court has held that imposing capital punishment on a person who was fifteen at the time the murder was committed constitutes cruel and unusual punishment, thus overturning the sentence of William Wayne Thompson of Oklahoma. Thompson was convicted of killing his brother-in-law in a brutal murder. The victim was shot twice; his throat, chest, and abdomen were slashed, and he had multiple bruises and a broken leg. The body was chained to a concrete block and thrown in the river.[125]

The electric chair is one method of capital punishment still in use in the United States. The Supreme Court has recognized this method as appropriate.

Three other men over the age of eighteen were convicted and sentenced to death in this murder. The Court's opinion in the *Thompson* case does not answer the question of where the line is to be drawn in deciding whether capital punishment is cruel and unusual in light of a defendant's age.

The Supreme Court has held that a mildly retarded person may be executed, thus refusing to reverse the conviction in *Penry* v. *Lynaugh*. Penry had an IQ of a seven-year-old. He was found competent to stand trial. In *Ford* v. *Wainwright*, the Court had held that it is cruel and unusual punishment to execute the insane or "someone who is unaware of the punishment they are about to suffer and why they are to suffer it."[126] But in comparing the cases, the Court said the following:[127]

Penry v. *Lynaugh*

Such a case is not before us today. Penry was found competent to stand trial. In other words, he was found to have the ability to consult with his lawyer with a reasonable degree of rational understanding, and was found to have a rational as well as factual understanding of the proceedings against him. In addition, the jury rejected his insanity defense, which reflected their conclusion that Penry knew that his conduct was wrong and was capable of conforming his conduct to the requirements of the law. . . .

On the record before the Court today, however, I cannot conclude that all mentally retarded people of Penry's ability—by virtue of their mental retardation alone, and apart from any individualized consideration of their personal responsibility—inevitably lack the cognitive, volitional, and moral capacity to act with the degree of culpability associated with the death penalty. Mentally retarded persons are individuals whose abilities and experiences can vary greatly. . . .

In light of the diverse capacities and life experiences of mentally retarded persons, it cannot be said on the record before us today that all mentally retarded people, by definition, can never act with the level of culpability associated with the death penalty.

Penry remains on Texas' death row.[128]

In May 1990, Dalton Prejean, a retarded convict who killed a police officer, was executed in Louisiana. Prejean was seventeen when he committed the crime; he had the IQ of a thirteen-year-old.[129] In 1993 Robert Sawyer, a Louisiana offender who had an IQ of 68, became the first person to be executed by lethal injection in Louisiana, which previously had used the electric chair for capital punishment cases.[130]

The Court has held, however, that an insane offender may not be executed.[131] In 1993 the Louisiana Supreme Court held that an inmate who is insane may not be medicated forcibly for the purpose of becoming sane enough to be executed. The case of Michael Owen Perry had been to the U.S. Supreme Court, which sent it back to the Louisiana trial court for reconsideration in light of the high Court's decision in *Washington* v. *Harper*, which held that an inmate can be medicated by force only if that is in the inmate's best medical interest. For example, if forced medication is necessary to prevent the inmate from committing suicide, it is permissible.[132] In *Washington* v. *Harper*, the Louisiana court said that forced medication for the purpose of execution would violate the cruel and unusual punishment clause as well as violate the offender's right to privacy.

Another issue on cruel and unusual punishment concerns the method of execution. Westley Allan Dodd, an admitted child molester, was executed by hanging in Washington in 1993. Dodd admitted that he molested children, an act he enjoyed and engaged in frequently. "I liked molesting children and did what I had to do to avoid jail so I could continue molesting." After hearing some of the details in court, "hardened reporters who covered the case sought counseling to help them handle what they had heard." A therapist who treated the offender said that he "ought to fry." The Washington constitution prohibits "cruel" punishment (in contrast to the U.S. Constitution, which prohibits "cruel and unusual" punishment), and the American Civil Liberties Union argued in the Dodd case that hanging is a cruel punishment.[133]

A new twist in public opinion about the death penalty arose during the final stages of this text's production. As mentioned earlier in the text, O. J. Simpson, famed football player, was arrested for the brutal murders of his ex-wife Nicole Brown Simpson and her friend Ronald Goldman. After a preliminary hearing, the judge ruled that the prosecution had enough evidence to charge Simpson with those murders. Public opinion concerning whether they thought Simpson committed the murders varied as the evidence unfolded in the media and in court. It was not uncommon, however, to hear public comments that the death penalty would be inappropriate in the case of O. J. Simpson if he were tried for these murders and convicted. As noted defense attorney Roy Black stated, "We save the death penalty for people we hate."[134]

While the debate on the guilt or innocence of O. J. Simpson continued before the watchful eyes of millions throughout the world, the U.S. Congress struggled with a 1,463 page anticrime bill that was stalled because of a five-page provision concerning the death penalty. This provision, called the *racial justice act*, would permit death row inmates challenging their sentences to cite statistical trends as well as the facts of their individual cases. The controversial bill provides for additional prison construction as well as for 100,000 additional police officers, along with other provisions. Another controversial provision is the "three strikes and you are out" approach to sentencing, which provides for a mandatory life sentence upon conviction of a third felony.[135] A compromise bill was passed after this book went to press (see Appendix D).

A final issue regarding cruel and unusual punishment should be noted, and that is the issue of corporal punishment. Corporal punishment is not a legally recognized punishment in U.S. criminal justice systems today. The last corporal punishment statute to be repealed was that of Delaware, which permitted whippings until 1973. Some scholars have recommended a return to corporal punishment, arguing that it would be fair and just.[136]

Corporal punishment is a common punishment in some countries, however, as illustrated by Singapore's policy of caning. In 1994, after New Jersey teen Michael Fay, eighteen, confessed to acts of vandalism and related crimes in Singapore, he was sentenced to be caned six times, spend four months in prison, and pay a $2,220 fine. Fay was living with his mother in Singapore when the alleged acts occurred. Fay's parents are divorced, and

Michael Fay, American teenager, arrives at a Singapore court where his sentencing appeal was heard. Among other punishments, Fay was sentenced to be caned.

his father, who lives in the United States, says he urged his son to plead guilty, pay the fine, and leave. George Fay said he was led to believe that caning would not be part of the sentence.

Caning was part of the sentence, and Americans were not as outraged as Michael's father thought they would be. In fact, many indicated that the punishment was appropriate, arguing that crime in the United States might decrease if corporal punishment were reinstituted. Michael and his parents argued that the confession was coerced and that Michael was innocent. There is some independent evidence to support their appeal, but Singapore officials denied that any coercion occurred. The sentence—reduced to four strokes—was carried out. Singapore government officials disagree that caning is cruel and tortuous punishment, and they emphasized that a doctor is present during the punishment and that if at any time the subject appears to be having physical difficulty, the caning is stopped until he (women are not sentenced to caning in Singapore) recovers.[137]

In June 1994 Fay was released from prison and returned to the United States to live with his father.

SUMMARY

This text begins with an examination of the purpose of criminal law, a discussion that includes an overview of revenge, incapacitation, retribution, and its modern counterparts, just desserts, rehabilitation, and deterrence. The punishment philosophy that dominates at any given time is reflected in sentencing philosophies. Thus, with the recent trend toward retribution and deterrence has come a movement away from the indeterminate sentencing structure. The purpose of this chapter is to discuss that change of events.

Allegations of legislative and judicial sentence disparity and judicial leniency resulted in public pressure to exert controls over sentencing judges and to influence legislative changes in sentence lengths. The chapter examines sentence types and sentencing guidelines. The essence of the federal mandate and subsequent proposed guidelines is to decrease sentencing discretion and to abolish parole release over a period of time. Although mitigating and aggravating circumstances of a crime and characteristics of an offender may be considered in sentencing, the U.S. Sentencing Commission developed statistical data and tables designed to minimize the disparity that results when any or several individualized factors are considered. It is an attempt to avoid the harshness of a system that sentences every offender of a particular crime, for example, robbery, to the same sentence. But it is an attempt also to eliminate extreme disparity that may result in a less structured system. The guidelines and the Sentencing Commission remain controversial. The Supreme Court has upheld the constitutionality of the commission's mandate, but many legal issues about the guidelines remain unresolved.

In addition to revising sentencing structures relating to incarceration, some modern sentencing reforms have included an emphasis on alternative sentencing. The provision of fines, restitution, community work service, probation (especially with intensive supervision), and house arrest (with or without electronic monitoring) as alternatives to incarceration may decrease prison and jail overcrowding and have the additional benefits of reducing costs. But any of these alternatives may be perceived as too lenient and too dangerous; thus, in many jurisdictions they are limited to nonviolent offenders. Most recently, many jurisdictions have been placing an emphasis on boot camp programs for young offenders, hoping that shock incarceration for a relatively brief period under strict supervision will deter those young people from criminal activity upon release. Some believe the programs are working; others are not so sure. Probably the answer is unavailable; it is too early to assess the long-term results of modern-day boot camps.

Capital punishment has reemerged as an alternative to long-term incarceration, although the appeal process in capital cases may result in a long sentence being served before the capital sentence is carried out. Capital punishment raises many constitutional issues, and frequently the Supreme Court is asked to resolve those issues. One current emphasis of the Court is to reduce the appeals process by restricting the use of *habeas corpus* writs among capital offenders.

The U.S. Supreme Court has held capital punishment unconstitutional under some circumstances. Capital punishment may not be permitted in situations that result in cruel and unusual punishment, such as for the rape of an adult that does not lead to murder. Aggravating and mitigating circumstances must be considered; a felony murder conviction alone may not be sufficient for imposing capital punishment on all involved in the crime, and the sentence may not be imposed arbitrarily or in a discriminatory manner. It is permissible to execute a mildly retarded person, but it is unconstitutional to execute an insane person. The difficulty, of course, is deciding when these impermissible criteria exist.

This completes our analysis of criminal law, a subject of great complexity and extreme importance. This discussion provides only an overview of the subject; criminal law varies among jurisdictions, and in some cases that variance is significant. It is possible to gain only an overview of the general issues, problems, and trends in such a vast field that changes rapidly. Many issues related to these discussions are left to a text in criminal procedure; some are primarily criminological in nature, whereas others relate primarily to the correctional system. All are interrelated and important to a comprehensive understanding of U.S. criminal justice systems.

STUDY QUESTIONS

1. Explain how *punishment philosophy* relates to sentencing.
2. Explain the differences in these sentencing models: legislative, judicial, and administrative. Relate your answer to *specific* sentencing reforms discussed in this chapter.
3. What is *presumptive sentencing*? Give examples.
4. If sentencing guidelines are used, should they be based on a jurisdiction's previous sentencing practices or on ideal sentencing practices? If the latter, how would you propose to draft the guidelines? How much discretion would you allow? Discuss in relationship to the federal system.

5. Washington state legislators claim that their 1981 sentencing code revision represents a move from indeterminate to determinate sentencing. Analyze that statement.

6. Describe the U.S. Sentencing Commission, its purpose, and its problems. What is the constitutional status of the sentencing guidelines the commission proposed?

7. Of the sentencing alternatives discussed in this chapter, which do you think are most appropriate for violent crimes and which for nonviolent crimes? Explain your answer.

8. What are some of the results of sentencing reform?

9. What are some of the *equal protection* issues in sentencing?

10. What is meant by *proportionality* in sentencing? What has the Supreme Court held on this concept?

11. What is meant by *aggravating and mitigating circumstances*? What is the Supreme Court's position on this issue?

12. List what you think would be aggravating and mitigating circumstances that you think should be considered in imposing capital punishment. Should aggravating and mitigating circumstances be considered in determining other sentences?

13. What is your reaction to the execution of juveniles? Of mentally retarded persons?

14. Do you think corporal punishment, such as caning, is cruel and unusual punishment?

ENDNOTES

1. "NCCD Says Mandatory Sentencing Made Florida Prisons 'Chaotic,'" *Criminal Justice Newsletter* 22 (15 August 1991): 1, 2.

2. David A. Harris, "What Happened to Crime? Why Politicians Don't Want To Talk About It Anymore," *American Bar Association Journal* 79 (October 1993): 138.

3. Henry Scott Wallace, "Mandatory Minimums and the Betrayal of Sentencing Reform: A Legislative Dr. Jekyll and Mr. Hyde," *Federal Probation* 57 (September 1993): 9.

4. Twentieth Century Fund Task Force on Criminal Sentencing, *Fair and Certain Punishment*, with a background paper by Alan M. Dershowitz (New York: McGraw-Hill, 1976), pp. 19–20.

5. Richard Singer, "In Favor of 'Presumptive Sentences' Set by a Sentencing Commission," *Crime and Delinquency* 24 (October 1978): 402, 421.

6. Leslie T. Wilkins, "Sentencing Guidelines to Reduce Disparity?" *The Criminal Law Review* (April 1980): 202. See also Leslie T. Wilkins et al., *Sentencing Guidelines Structuring Judicial Discretion: Report on the Feasibility Study* (Washington, D.C.: National Institute of Law Enforcement and Criminal Justice, LEAA, 1978).

7. Richard Singer, *Sentencing*, National Institute of Justice (Washington, D.C.: U.S. Department of Justice, 1988), p. 3.

8. Louis B. Schwartz, "Options in Constructing a Sentencing System: Sentencing Guidelines Under Legislative or Judicial Hegemony," *Virginia Law Review* 67 (May 1981): 640.

9. David Boerner, *Sentencing in Washington: A Legal Analysis of the Sentencing Reform Act of 1981* (Seattle: Butterworth Legal Publishers, 1985), p. 1–1.

10. Rev. Code Wash., Section 9.94A.370 (1994).

11. For a recent analysis of the Washington Sentencing Reform Act and its results, see Glenn Olson, "Forecasting the Long-Term Impact of Washington's Sentencing Guidelines: A Roller Coaster Ride," *Crime & Delinquency* 38 (July 1992): 330–356.

12. For a recent discussion of Minnesota's guidelines, see Nelson Black, "The Minnesota Sentencing Guidelines: the Effect of Determinate Sentencing on Disparities in Sentencing Decisions," *Law & Inequality* 10 (1992): 217–251.

13. "Pennsylvania Begins Overhaul of Sentencing Guidelines," *Criminal Justice Newsletter* 19 (1 October 1993): 1–2.

14. "Sentencing Guidelines Renew Debate," *Legal Intelligencer* (26 July 1994), p. 6.

15. The Sentencing Reform Act was passed as part of the Comprehensive Crime Control Act of 1984, Pub.L.No. 98–473, 98 Stat. 1837, 1976 (1984), and is codified with its subsequent amendments in U.S. Code, Title 18, Sections 3551 *et. seq* (1994), and U.S. Code, Title 28, Sections 991–998 (1994).

16. The discussion here and later of the major issues and how the commission proposes to resolve them comes from the opening statements of the proposed guidelines, is published in the *Federal Register*, vol. 52 (13 May 1987): 18048-18053. A more recent account is found in Ilene H. Nagel, "Structuring Sentencing Discretion: The New Federal Sentencing Guidelines," *Journal of Criminal Law and Criminology* 80 (Winter 1990): 883–899.

17. "Sentencing Plan Under Fire: Redrafted Guidelines Again Criticized as Too Harsh," *American Bar Association Journal* (1 July 1987): 21.

18. Mistretta v. United States, 488 U.S. 361 (1989), cases, citations, and footnotes omitted.

19. See "Defense Lawyers Will Continue to Fight Sentencing Guidelines," *Criminal Justice Newsletter* 10 (15 February 1989): 1.

20. See Williams v. United States, 112 S.Ct. 1112 (1992), *remanded*, 966 F.2d 208 (7th Cir. 1992).

21. Stinson v. United States, 113 S.Ct. 1913 (1993), citations and footnotes omitted.

22. See United States v. R.L.C., 112 S.Ct. 1329 (1992). For a discussion see Tiffany M. Erwin, "United States v. R.L.C.: the Supreme Court Applies a Band-Aid Where Major Surgery Is Needed," *Criminal Law Bulletin* 29 (July–August 1993): 317–355. The Eighth Circuit opinion is United States v. R.L.C., 915 F.2d 320 (8th Cir. 1990). For a contrary result in the Ninth Circuit, see United States v. Marco L., 868 F.2d 1121 (9th Cir. 1988).

23. S.Rep. No. 1989, 75th Congress., 3d Sess. 1 (letter appended), as cited in Erwin, ibid., p. 320. The statute is the Federal Juvenile Delinquency Act, U.S. Code, Title 18, Section 5031–5042 (1994).

24. For a brief overview of the criminal justice status of juveniles, see Sue Titus Reid, *Criminal Justice*, 3d ed. (New York: Macmillan, 1993), pp. 708–751. See also *In re* Gault, 387 U.S. 1 (1967): *In re* Winship, 397 U.S. 358 (1970); McKeiver v. Pennsylvania, 403 U.S. 528 (1971); Breed v. Jones, 421 U.S. 519 (1975); and Schall v. Martin, 467 U.S. 253 (1984).

25. Travis Hirschi and Michael Gottfredson, "Rethinking the Juvenile Justice System," *Crime & Delinquency* 39 (April 1993): 262–271; quotations are on pp. 270 and 271.

26. Michael Tonry, "The Failure of the U.S. Sentencing Commission's Guidelines," *Crime & Delinquency* 39 (April 1993): 131–149; quotation is on p. 131.

27. "Sentencing Guidelines Reduce Disparities, Commission Says," *Criminal Justice Newsletter* 23 (3 February 1992): 3–4.

28. *Sentencing Guidelines: Central Questions Remain Unanswered*, (GAO/GGD-92-93), available from the U.S. General Accounting Office, Box 6015, Gaithersburg, MD, 20877, discussed in "Sentencing Guidelines Said to

Reduce, Not Eliminate, Disparity," *Criminal Justice Newsletter* 23 (3 August 1992): 6, 7.

29. Tonry, "The Failure of the U.S. Sentencing Commission's Guidelines," pp. 132–133.

30. "Federal Judge Quits Over Law on Sentencing," *Miami Herald* (4 July 1992), p. 7, referring to United States v. Harrington, 947 F.2d 956 (D.D.C. 1991), *remanded*, 808 F.Supp. 883 (D.D.C. 1992).

31. "Two Judges Decline Drug Cases, Spark Mandatory Minimum Debate," *Criminal Justice Newsletter* 24 (3 May 1993): 4; "Controversial Judge Gets Lawyer of the Year Honor," *Orlando Sentinel* (21 December 1993), p. 16.

32. "U.S. District Judge Rejects Sentencing Guideline Minimum," *Criminal Justice Newsletter* 24 (3 May 1993): 5, 6.

33. United States v. Spencer, 817 F.Supp. 176 (D.D.C. 1993), *aff'd., remanded*, 25 F. 3d 1105 (D.C.Cir. 1994).

34. "Thirty Organizations Call for Shift in Criminal Justice Policy," *Criminal Justice Newsletter* 24 (15 July 1993), p. 3. For more information, see the following sources: "Janet Reno at Bar Convention: A Conquering Hero," *New York Times* (9 August 1993), p. 9; "Chorus of Judicial Critics Assail Sentencing Guides," *New York Times* (17 April 1992), p. 1; "Federal Judges Denounce Mandatory Drug Sentences," *Miami Herald* (9 June 1992), p. 12.

35. Tonry, "The Failure of the U.S. Sentencing Commission's Guidelines," p. 148.

36. See "Reno: Offer Drug Users Treatment, not Prison," *Miami Herald* (8 May 1993), p. 10; "Clinton Sets Out to Combat Drugs by Rehabilitation," *New York Times* (21 October 1993), p. 1; and "Dealing with Dealers: Rehabilitation, Not Jail," *New York Times* (20 January 1993), p. 12B.

37. See Richard C. McCorkle, "Research Note: Punish and Rehabilitate? Public Attitudes Toward Six Common Crimes," *Crime & Delinquency* 39 (April 1993): 240–252.

38. See Francis T. Cullen et al., "The Correctional Orientation of Prison Wardens: Is the Rehabilitative Ideal Supported?" *Criminology* 31 (February 1993): 69–92; and David Lester, Michael Braswell, and Patricia Van Voorhis, *Correctional Counseling*, 2d ed. (Cincinnati, OH: Anderson, 1992).

39. For a series of articles on sentencing reform in the states, see *University of Colorado Law Review* 64 (1993): 645–847.

40. Norval Morris, "Alternatives to Imprisonment: Failures and Prospects," *Criminal Justice Research Bulletin*, Vol. 3, no. 7 (Huntsville, Texas: Sam Houston State University Criminal Justice Center, 1987).

41. See "Florida Plan: More Prisons and Restoration of Parole," *Criminal Justice Newsletter* 21 (16 January 1990): 2. Florida reinstated a Parole Commission in 1990, Fla. Stat., Section 947.01 (1994).

42. See the following sources: Belinda R. McCarthy, ed., *Intermediate Punishments: Intensive Supervision, Home Confinement, and Electronic Surveillance* (Monsey, N.Y.: Criminal Justice Press, 1987); Norval Morris and Michael Tonry, *Between Prison and Probation: Intermediate Punishments in a Rational Sentencing System* (New York: Oxford, 1990); and James M. Bryne et al., eds., *Smart Sentencing: The Emergence of Intermediate Sanctions* (Newbury Park, Calif.: Sage, 1994).

43. "Intermediate Sanctions A New Priority for Justice Institute," *Criminal Justice Newsletter* 24 (1 October 1993): 4. The statute is R.I. Pub. Laws 205 (1994).

44. "Rhode Island Legislature Approves Intermediate Sanctions," *Criminal Justice Newsletter* 24 (2 August 1993), p. 4. The statute is R. I. Gen. Laws 12-19-23.2 (1994).

45. See Douglas C. McDonald et al., eds. *Day Fines in American Courts: The Staten Island and Milwaukee Experiments*, National Institute of Justice (Washington, D.C.: U.S. Department of Justice, 1992).

46. Laura A. Winterfield and Sally T. Hillsman, *The Staten Island Day-Fine Project*, National Institute of Justice (Washington, D.C.: U.S. Department of Justice, January 1993), p. 3, emphasis deleted.

47. Bearden v. Georgia, 461 U.S. 660 (1983), footnotes and citations omitted.

48. Sally T. Hillsman et al., *Fines as Criminal Sanctions*, National Institute of Justice (Washington, D.C.: U.S. Department of Justice, September 1987), p. 1.

49. The act is codified in U.S. Code, Title 18, Sections 3663 and 3664 (1994). For recent decisions concerning the restitution provision, see Hughey v. United States, 495 U.S. 411 (1990), *remanded*, 907 F.2d 39 (1990), *superceded by statute* as stated in United States v. Arnold, 947 F.2d 1236 (5th Cir. 1991); and United States v. Munoz-Flores, 495 U.S. 385 (1990).

50. Rev. Code Wash., Section 9.94A.030(7) (1994).

51. Ohio Rev. Code, Section 2947.061 (1994).

52. "Candidates in Accord: Boot Camp for Criminals," *New York Times* (19 July 1989), p. 12.

53. "Observations and Proposals Regarding New York State's Shock Incarceration Program," available from the Correctional Association of New York, 135 East 15th Street, New York, NY, 10003, quoted in "New York Correctional Group Praises Boot Camp Programs," in *Criminal Justice Newsletter* 27 (1 April 1991): 4.

54. "As Boot Camps for Criminals Multiply, Skepticism, Grows," *New York Times* (18 December 1993), p. 1; "House Endorses Tougher Measures on Crime," *New York Times* (20 April 1994), p. 9. See Appendix D for an update.

55. See the study of Doris Layton MacKenzie et al., "Characteristics Associated with Successful Adjustment to Supervision: A Comparison of Parolees, Probationers, Shock Participants, and Shock Dropouts," *Criminal Justice and Behavior* 19 (December 1992): 437–454. For an analysis of attitude changes, see Velmer S. Burton et al., "A Study of Attitudinal Change Among Boot Camp Participants," *Federal Probation* 57 (September 1993): 46-52. For a critique of boot camps, see Merry Morash and Lila Rucker, "A Critical Look at the Idea of Boot Camp as a Correctional Reform," *Crime & Delinquency* 36 (April 1990): 204–222.

56. "High Attrition Rates Found at OJJPD-Funded Model Boot Camps," *Criminal Justice Newsletter* 24 (1 July 1993): 5, 6.

57. "GAO Says Boot Camps Cut Costs, But Recidivism Not Yet Clear," *Criminal Justice Newsletter* 24 (17 May 1993): 4.

58. Doris Layton MacKenzie et al., *An Evaluation of Shock Incarceration in Louisiana*, National Institute of Justice (Washington, D.C.: U.S. Department of Justice, June 1993): 6.

59. "As Boot Camps for Criminals Multiply, Skepticism Grows."

60. James Austin et al., *The Growing Use of Jail Boot Camps: The Current State of the Art*, National Institute of Justice (Washington, D.C.: U.S. Department of Justice, October 1993), p. 5. For a discussion of the Connecticut boot camp closing, see "Connecticut Closes Boot Camp Built to Assist Troubled Youths," *New York Times* (11 June 1994), p. 8.

61. See Richard A. Ball, C. Ronald Huff, and J. Robert Lilly, *House Arrest and Correctional Policy* (Beverly Hills, Calif.: Sage, 1988); United States v. Murphy, 108 F.R.D. 437 (E.D.N.Y. 1985). For a recent analysis of the effects of home confinement, see Stephen J. Rackmill, "An Analysis of Home Confinement as a Sanction," *Federal Probation* LVIII (March 1994): 45–52.

62. Dennis Wagner and Christopher Baird, *Evaluation of the Florida Community Control Program*, National Institute of Justice (Washington, D.C.: U.S. Department of Justice, January 1993): 1, 5. For a discussion of the psychological and legal problems of home confinement, see Dorothy K. Kagehiro, "Psycholegal Issues of Home Confinement," *St. Louis University Law Journal* 37 (1993): 647–674.

63. For a discussion of the issues surrounding house arrest and electronic surveillance, see Joseph B. Vaughn, "Planning for Change: The Use of Electronic Monitoring as a Correctional Alternative," in *Intermediate Punishments: Intensive Supervision, Home Confinement, and Electronic Surveillance*, ed. Belinda R. McCarthy (Monsey, N.Y.: Criminal Justice Press, 1987), pp. 153–168; and Rolando V. del Carmen and Joseph B. Vaughn, "Legal Issues in the Use of Electronic Surveillance in Probation," *Federal Probation* 50 (1986): 60–69.

64. See, for example, Terry L. Baumer et al., "A Comparative Analysis of Three Electronically Monitored Home Detention Programs," *Justice Quarterly* 10 (March 1993): 121–142.

65. J. Robert Lilly et al., "Electronic Monitoring of the Drunk Driver: A Seven-Year Study of the Home Confinement Alternative," *Crime & Delinquency* 39 (October 1993): 462–484; quotation is on p. 478. For an analysis of EM with drug offenders, see Annette Jolin and Brian Stipak, "Drug Treatment and Electronically Monitored Home Confinement: An Evaluation of a Community-Based Sentencing Option," *Crime & Delinquency* 38 (April 1992): 158–170.

66. "Some New Yorkers on Probation Will Begin Reporting to Machines," *New York Times* (24 May 1993), p. 1.

67. See United States v. Corpuz, 953 F.2d 526 (9th Cir. 1992).

68. Louis Jankowski, *Probation and Parole 1990*, Bureau of Justice Statistics (Washington, D.C.: U.S. Department of Justice, November 1991), p. 1.

69. For a discussion, see Edwin M. Lemert, "Visions of Social Control: Probation Considered," *Crime & Delinquency* 39 (October 1993): 447–461.

70. "Second Trial Allowed in Skinhead Case," *New York Times* (19 May 1993), p. 9.

71. See Joan Petersilia et al., *Granting Felons Probation: Public Risks and Alternatives* (Santa Monica, Calif.: Rand, 1985), p. v.

72. For a discussion of IPS, see the following: Frank S. Pearson and Alice Glasel Harper, "Contingent Intermediate Sentences: New Jersey's Intensive Supervision Program," *Crime and Delinquency* 36 (January 1990): 75–86; Joan Petersilia, "Conditions that Permit Intensive Supervision Programs to Survive," *Crime and Delinquency* 36 (January 1990): 126–145; and Joan Petersilia and Susan Turner, "Comparing Intensive and Regular Supervision for High-Risk Probationers: Early Results from an Experiment in California," *Crime and Delinquency* 36 (January 1990): 87–111.

73. Joan Petersilia and Susan Turner, *Evaluating Intensive Supervision Probation/Parole: Results of a Nationwide Experiment*, National Institute of Justice (Washington, D.C.: U.S. Department of Justice, May 1993), p. 1.

74. Ibid., pp. 4, 5.

75. See Susan Turner et al., "Evaluating Intensive Supervision Probation/Parole (IPS) for Drug Offenders," *Crime & Delinquency* 38 (October 1992): 539–556.

76. "GAO Finds 'Some Merit' in Intensive Probation," *Criminal Justice Newsletter* 24 (15 July 1993): 4.

77. "Some New Yorkers on Probation."

78. Furman v. Georgia, 408 U.S. 238 (1972).

79. See Gregg v. Georgia, 428 U.S. 153 (1976), *reh'g. denied*, 429 U.S. 895 (1976); and Woodson v. North Carolina, 428 U.S. 280 (1976).

80. "Executions at Highest Pace Since 1962," *St. Petersburg Times* (16 September 1993), p. 6. See also "With Practice, Texas Is the Execution Leader," *New York Times* (5 September 1993), p. 6.

81. "Surveys Show Varying Levels of Support for Death Penalty," *Criminal Justice Newsletter* 24 (15 April 1993): 6. For a discussion of the relationship between religion and attitudes toward the death penalty, see Harold G. Grasmick et al., "Religion, Punitive Justice, and Support for the Death Penalty," *Justice Quarterly* 10 (June 1993): 289–314. See also Samuel Cameron, "The Demand for Capital Punishment," *International Review of Law & Economics* 13 (1993): 47–59.

82. "Cameras Banned, Pens Allowed: San Francisco Judge Refuses TV Stations' Request to Tape Inmate Execution," *American Bar Association Journal* 77 (August 1991): 16. The case is KQED v. Vasquez, 18 Media L. Rep. (N.D.Calif. 1991). For a scholarly discussion of the relationship between television publicity of executions and crime, see William C. Bailey, "Murder, Capital Punishment, and Television: Execution Publicity and Homicide Rates," *American Sociological Review* 55 (October 1990): 628–633.

83. See, for example, Bruce Ledewitz and Ernest van den Haag, "The Morality of Capital Punishment," *Duquesne Law Review* 29 (Summer 1991): 718–631; and James R. Acker, "Dual and Unusual: Competing Views of Death Penalty Adjudication," *Criminal Law Bulletin* 26 (March–April 1990): 123–154.

84. See Robert M. Bohm, ed., *The Death Penalty in America: Current Research* (Cincinnati, Ohio: Anderson, 1991). For a history of capital punishment, along with a discussion of the pros and cons and the legal issues, see Raymond Paternoster, *Capital Punishment in America* (New York: Lexington Books, 1992). See Appendix D for details of the 1994 statute.

85. "An Unusual 'Custody' Dispute," *American Bar Association Journal* 79 (August 1993): 32.

86. "Oklahoma to Return Murderer to New York," *New York Times* (21 October 1993), p. 13. State v. Poe et al., 835 F.Supp. 585 (E.D.Okla. 1993).

87. People v. Proctor, 842 P.2d 1100 (Cal. 1992), *aff'd. sub. nom.*, 114 S.Ct. 2630 (1994); and Tuilaepa v. California, 842 P.2d 1142 (Cal. 1992), *aff'd.*, 114 S.Ct. 2630 (1994). For a discussion of aggravating and mitigating circumstances in capital punishment, see James R. Acker and C. S. Lanier, "Aggravating Circumstances and Capital Punishment: Rhetoric or Real Reforms?" *Criminal Law Bulletin* 29 (November–December 1993): 467–501.

88. Williams v. New York, 337 U.S. 241, 247 (1949), *reh'g. denied*, 337 U.S. 961 (1949), *reh'g. denied*, 338 U.S. 841 (1949).

89. McCleskey v. Kemp, 481 U.S. 279 (1987), *reh'g. denied*, 482 U.S. 920 (1987).

90. For more information on the Baldus study, see David C. Baldus et al., *Equal Justice and the Death Penalty: A Legal and Empirical Analysis* (Boston: Northeastern University Press, 1990). For a discussion of capital punishment and equal protection with regard to race, see Stan R. Gregory, "Capital Punishment and Equal Protection: Constitutional Problems, Race and the Death Penalty," *St. Thomas Law Review* 5 (1992): 257–273.

91. McCleskey v. Zant, 499 U.S. 467 (1991), *reh'g. denied*, 501 U.S. 224 (1991), *and stay denied sub. nom.*, 112 S.Ct. 37 (1991).

92. See "Judges Challenge Rehnquist on Death Row Appeals report," *Criminal Justice Newsletter* 20 (15 November 1989): 5. For a scholarly analysis of the issues, see Vivian Berger, "Justice Delayed or Justice Denied?—A Comment on Recent Proposals to Reform Death Penalty Habeas Corpus," *Columbia Law Review* 90 (1990): 1665–1714.

93. "Report on Habeas Corpus in Capital Cases," *Criminal Law Reporter* 45, no. 25 (27 September 1989): 3240.

94. "The Court's Rush to Kill," *New York Times* (22 April 1992), p. 14.

95. Herrera v. Collins, 113 S.Ct. 853 (1993), *reh'g. denied*, 113 S.Ct. 1628 (1993). See also two other *habeas corpus* cases decided by the Court the same month: Graham v. Collins, 113 S.Ct. 892 (1993), *reh'g. denied*, 113 S.Ct. 1406 (1993) *stay denied, cert. denied*, 113 S.Ct. 2325 (1993); and Lockhart v. Fretwell, 113 S.Ct. 838 (1993). The 30 June 1994 decision written by Blackmun is McFarland v. Scott, 114 S.Ct. 2568 (1994). In another capital punishment case decided in June 1994, the Court held that in a capital case when the prosecution argues that the defendant's future dangerousness is a reason for imposing the death penalty, and a life sentence without the possibility of parole is the only alternative sentence to capital punishment in the case, the defendant has the right to have the jury informed of this fact. This may be done through argument or through court instruction. See Simmons v. South Carolina, 114 S.Ct. 2187 (1994).

96. "Mandatory Minimum Sentences Hit," *American Bar Association Journal* 77 (December 1991): 36, referring to a study by the U.S. Sentencing Commission.

97. "U.S. Appeals Judge's Sentences that Defy Mandatory Guidelines," *New York Times* (29 August 1993), p. 13. The case is United States v. McMurray, 833 F.Supp. 1454 (D.Neb. 1993).

98. See *The Juveniles Taken into Custody Research Program: Estimating the Prevalence of Juvenile Custody by Race and Gender*. Available from the National Council on Crime and Delinquency, 635 Market Street, Suite 640, San Francisco, Calif., 94105, discussed in "Minority Custody Rate Ten Times that of Whites in Some States," *Criminal Justice Newsletter* 24 (16 September 1993): 6.

99. "Vehement Court Voids Black's Death Penalty," *New York Times* (14 December 1989), p. 1. See also *Ex Parte* Brandley, 781 S.W.2d 886 (Tex.Crim.App. 1989).

100. Coramae Richey Mann, *Unequal Justice: A Question of Color* (Bloomington: Indiana University Press, 1993), p. 219. Mann is referring to the work of Harold E. Pepinsky, "Humanizing Social Control," *Humanity and Society* 6, no. 3 (1982): 277–242. See also Pepinsky, *The Geometry of Violence and Democracy* (Bloomington: Indiana University Press, 1982). For recent articles on race and punishment, see the Special Issue, "Race and Punishment," edited by Carl Pope and Todd Clear in *Journal of Research in Crime and Delinquency* 31 (May 1994).

101. State v. Chambers, 307 A.2d 78, 82 (N.J. 1973).

102. People v. Weeks, 372 N.E.2d 163 (Ill.App.4th Dist. 1977), *appeal dismissed sub-nom.*, 439 U.S. 809 (1978).

103. Charles J. Corley et al., "Sex and the Likelihood of Sanction," *Journal of Criminal Law and Criminology* 80 (Summer 1989): 540–556.

104. "Sex Bias is Found Pervading Courts," *New York Times* (2 July 1989), p. 8; "Legal System Called Biased Against Women," *Miami Herald* (11 October 1993), p. 5.

105. See, for example, Darrell Steffensmeier et al., "Gender and Imprisonment Decisions," *Criminology* 31 (August 1993): 411–446.

106. B. Keith Crew, "Sex Differences in Criminal Sentencing: Chivalry or Patriarchy?" *Justice Quarterly* 8 (March 1991): 59–84; quotation is on p. 78.

107. Coker v. Georgia, 433 U.S. 584 (1977), footnotes and citations omitted.

108. Watson v. United States, 439 F.2d 442, 473 (D.C.Cir. 1970).

109. Carmona v. Ward, 576 F.2d 405, 416, 417 (2d Cir. 1978), *cert. denied*, 439 U.S. 1091 (1979).

110. Rummel v. Estelle, 445 U.S. 263 (1980).

111. Solem v. Helm, 463 U.S. 277 (1983), *superseded by statute as stated in In Re Petition of Lauer*, 788 F.2d 135 (8th Cir. 1985).

112. People v. Harmelin, 440 N.W.2d 75 (Mich.App. 1989), *aff'd. sub nom.*, 501 U.S. 957 (1991). For a discussion see Joanne Aylward Pierce, "Constitutional Law—Eighth Amendment Proportionality Analysis of Terms for Years Uncertain," *Suffolk University Law Review* 26 (1992): 210–220.

113. Pulley v. Harris, 465 U.S. 37 (1984).

114. United States v. Spencer, 817 F.Supp. 176 (D.D.C. 1993), *aff'd., remanded*, 25 F. 3d. 1105 (D.C.Cir. 1994).

115. Custis v. United States, 114 S.Ct. 1732 (1994).

116. See People v. Zaring, 10 Cal.Rptr.2d 263 (5th Dist. 1992).

117. Janet F. Ginzberg, "Note: Compulsory Contraception As A Condition of Probation: the Use and Abuse of Norplant," *Brooklyn Law Review* 58 (Fall 1992): 979–1020.

118. Skinner v. Oklahoma, 316 U.S. 535, 541 (1942).

119. See State v. Brown, 326 S.E.2d 410 (1985).

120. See Michael T. McSpadden, "Castration Will Work," *Houston Chronicle* (22 February 1993), p. 13; and James C. Harrington, "Castration Case Highlights Larger Problem for Society," *Texas Lawyer* (6 April 1992), p. 13.

121. "Sterilization Ordered for Child Abuser," *American Bar Association Journal* 79 (May 1993): 32.

122. Sumer v. Shuman, 479 U.S. 948 (1986). See also Skipper v. So. Carolina, 476 U.S. 1 (1986); Baldwin v. Alabama, 472 U.S. 372 (1985); Eddings v. Oklahoma, 455 U.S. 104 (1982); Lockett v. Ohio, 438 U.S. 586 (1978), Blystone v. Pennsylvania, 494 U.S. 299 (1990), and Clemons v. Mississippi, 494 U.S. 738 (1990), *remanded*, 593 So.2d 1004 (Miss. 1992).

123. Tison v. Arizona, 481 U.S. 137 (1987), *reh'g. denied*, 482 U.S. 921 (1987).

124. Enmund v. Florida, 458 U.S. 782 (1982).

125. Thompson v. Oklahoma, 487 U.S. 815 (1988), *remanded*, 762 P.2d 958 (Okla.Crim.App. 1988).

126. Ford v. Wainwright, 477 U. S. 399 (1986).

127. Penry v. Lynaugh, 492 U.S. 302 (1989), cases and citations omitted, *on remand*, 882 F.2d 141 (5th Cir. 1989). For a discussion of this case see "The Supreme Court Deals a Fatal Blow to Mentally Retarded Capital Defendants," *University of Pittsburg Law Review* 51 (1990): 699–725.

128. "Legislation Seeks to Bar Executions of Mentally Retarded; Prosecutors Call the Bill Unnecessary Complication," *The Recorder* (American lawyer Media) (11 March 1993), p. 1.

129. "Convicted Killer of State Trooper Dies in Louisiana Electric Chair," *Miami Herald* (19 May 1990), p. 10.

130. "Louisiana Murderer Is Executed by Injection," *New York Times* (6 March 1993), p. 8; "Legislation Seeks to Bar Executions of Mentally, Retarded."

131. Ford v. Wainwright, 477 U.S. 399 (1986).

132. Washington v. Harper, 494 U.S. 1015 (1990). For a discussion see "Insane Inmate Avoids Death Penalty," *American Bar Association Journal* 79 (January 1993): 32; and Matthew S. Collins, "Involuntarily Medicating Condemned Incompetents for the Purpose of Rendering them Sane and Thereby Subject to Execution," *Washington University Law Quarterly* 70 (1992): 1229–1248.

133. "Child Sex Killer is Executed in First U.S. Hanging Since 1965," *Miami Herald* (6 January 1993), p. 6.

134. See, for example, Graeme Newman, *Just and Painful: A Case for the Corporal Punishment of Criminals* (New York: Macmillan, 1983).

135. "Provision on Death Penalty Is Slowing Anti-Crime Bill," *New York Times* (27 June 1994), p. 7; "Three Strikes a Hot Potato," *American Bar Association Journal* 80 (June 1994): 30

136. See, for example, Graeme Newman, *Just and Painful: A Case for the Corporal Punishment of Crimainals* (New York: Macmillan, 1983).

137. This information on caning comes from the following sources: "Crime & Punishment: The Caning Debate," *Newsweek* (18 April 1994), p. 18; "Justice in Six Lashes? Singapore: An American Faces Cruel Punishment," *Newsweek* (11 April 1994), p. 40; "Overlooked Question in Singapore Caning Debate: Is the Teen-Ager Guilty?" *New York Times* (17 April 1994), p. 6.

Appendix A

Selected Amendments of the U.S. Constitution

Amendment I (1791)

Congress shall make no law respecting an establishment of religion, or prohibiting the free exercise thereof; or abridging the freedom of speech, or of the press; or the right of the people peaceably to assemble, and to petition the Government for a redress of grievances.

Amendment IV (1791)

The right of the people to be secure in their persons, houses, papers, and effects, against unreasonable searches and seizures, shall not be violated, and no Warrants shall issue, but upon probable cause, supported by Oath or affirmation, and particularly describing the place to be searched, and the persons or things to be seized.

Amendment V (1791)

No person shall be held to answer for a capital, or otherwise infamous crime, unless on a presentment or indictment of a Grand Jury, except in cases arising in the land or naval forces, or in the Militia, when in actual service in time of War or public danger; nor shall any person be subject for the same offence to be twice put in jeopardy of life or limb; nor shall be compelled in any criminal case to be a witness against himself, nor be deprived of life, liberty, or property, without due process of law; nor shall private property be taken for public use, without just compensation.

Amendment VI (1791)

In all criminal prosecutions, the accused shall enjoy the right to a speedy and public trial, by an impartial jury of the State and district wherein the crime shall have been committed, which district shall have been previously ascertained by law, and to be informed of the nature and cause of the accusation; to be confronted with the witnesses against him; to have compulsory process for obtaining witnesses in his favor, and to have the Assistance of Counsel for his defence.

Amendment VIII (1791)

Excessive bail shall not be required, nor excessive fines imposed, nor cruel and unusual punishments inflicted.

Amendment XIV (1868)

Section 1.

All persons born or naturalized in the United States, and subject to the jurisdiction thereof, are citizens of the United States and of the State wherein they reside. No State shall make or enforce any law which shall abridge the privileges or immunities of citizens of the United States; nor shall any State deprive any person of life, liberty, or property, without due process of law; nor deny to any person within its jurisdiction the equal protection of the laws.

Section 5.

The Congress shall have power to enforce, by appropriate legislation, the provisions of this article.

Appendix B

How to Read a Case Citation

McKinney v. Anderson, 959 F.2d 853 (9th Cir. 1992), *aff'd., remanded, sub. nom.*, Helling v. McKinney, 113 S.Ct. 2475 (1993), *on remand, remanded*, 5 F.3d 365 (9th Cir. 1993).

Original Citation

[McKinney v. Anderson][1] [959][2] [F.2d][3] [853][4] [9th Cir.][5] [1992][6].

1. Name of case
2. Volume number of reporter in which case is published
3. Name of reporter; see Abbreviations for Commonly Used Reporters.
4. Page in the reporter where the decision begins
5. Court deciding the case
6. Year decided

Additional Case History

[*aff'd., remanded, sub. nom.*][7] [Helling v. McKinney][8] [113][9] [S.Ct.][10] [2475][11] [1993][12] [*on remand, remanded*][13] [5][14] [F.3d][15] [365][16] [9th Cir. 1993][17]

7. Affirmed and remanded (sent back for further proceedings) under a different name
8. The name under which the case was affirmed and remanded
9. Volume number of the reporter in which case is published
10. Abbreviated name of reporter
11. Page number on which the opinion begins
12. The year the Supreme Court decided the case. The name of the court is not included as it is understood that the Supreme Court Reporter (or the United States Reports) report only cases from the U.S. Supreme Court.
13. Additional history—the case on remand

14. Volume number of reporter in which the remanded case is published
15. Abbreviated name of reporter
16. Page number on which the decision begins
17. Court that heard the remanded case and year it was decided

Abbreviations for Commonly Used Reporters for Court Cases

Decisions of the U.S. Supreme Court

S.Ct.: Supreme Court Reporter
U.S.: United States Reports

Decisions from Other Courts: A Selected List

A., A.2d: Atlantic Reporter, Atlantic Reporter Second Series
Cal.Rptr: California Reporter
F.2d: Federal Reporter Second Series; F.3d, Third Series
F.Supp: Federal Supplement
N.Y.S.2d: New York Supplement Second Series
N.W., N.W.2d: North Western Reporter, North Western Reporter Second Series
N.E., N.E.2d: North Eastern Reporter, North Eastern Reporter Second Series
P., P.2d: Pacific Reporter, Pacific Reporter Second Series
S.E., S.E.2d: South Eastern Reporter, South Eastern Reporter Second Series

Definitions

Aff'd.   Affirmed; the appellate court agrees with the decision of the lower court.

Aff'd. sub. nom.   Affirmed under a different name; the case at the appellate level has a different name from that of the trial court level.

Aff'd. per curiam.   Affirmed by the courts. The opinion is written by "the court" instead of by one of the judges; a decision affirmed but no written opinion is issued.

Cert. denied.   Certiorari denied; the Supreme Court, either the state supreme court or the U.S. Supreme Court, refuses to hear and decide the case.

Concurring opinion.   An opinion agreeing with the court's decision, but offering different reasons.

Dissenting opinion.   An opinion disagreeing with the reasoning and result of the majority opinion.

Reh'g. denied.   Rehearing denied, the court's refusal to rehear a case.

Remanded.   The appellate court sending a case back to the lower court for further action.

Rev'd. Reversed, overthrown, set aside, made void. The appellate court reverses the decision of the lower court.

Rev'd. and remanded. Reversed and remanded; the appellate court reverses the decision and sends the case back for further action.

Vacated. Abandoned, set aside, made void. The appellate court sets aside the decision of the lower court.

Appendix C

American Law Institute Model Penal Code* Index of Citations†

Part I. General Provisions

*Official Draft, 1962.
†The Model Penal Code contains numerous sections not covered in this text. This index includes only the sections referenced within this text or its footnotes; it is included here as a reference tool for the reader.

512

Part II. Definition of Specific Crimes

Offenses Against Existence or Stability of the State
Offenses Involving Danger to the Person

Offenses Against Property

Offenses Against the Family

Offenses Against Public Administration

ARTICLE 242. OBSTRUCTING GOVERNMENTAL OPERATIONS; ESCAPES

Offenses Against Public Order and Decency

ARTICLE 250. RIOT, DISORDERLY CONDUCT, AND RELATED OFFENSES

ARTICLE 251. PUBLIC INDECENCY

Appendix D

Violent Crime Control and Law Enforcement Act of 1994

In late August 1994 the U.S. Congress passed a comprehensive crime bill. *Criminal Law*, third edition, was already in press; thus only references to the crime bill could be made within the text. The bill is too long for inclusion here, but this appendix provides a brief statement about the bill, a listing of the Titles and Subtitles of the bill, and the section numbers of those headings. This listing permits readers who desire the full text to identify their searches quickly.

The Violent Crime Control and Law Enforcement Act of 1994, which culminates years of research and politics and passed the Senate by only one vote, will cost the American public an estimated $30 billion. The Act focuses on violent crime and criminals. The Act provides grant money for state and local law enforcement agencies to build more prisons, hire more law enforcement officers, and establish a number of crime prevention programs. Title I is designed to fulfill one of President Clinton's campaign promises: adding 100,000 law enforcement officers. Nearly $8 billion is provided for construction, modification, expansion, or operation of correctional facilities over the next six years.

The Act addresses prison and jail overcrowding by imposing restrictions on courts that order a reduction in the population of such facilities due to overcrowding. Such orders may be given only when an inmate proves that he or she is suffering cruel and unusual punishment (in violation of the Eighth Amendment), and the orders may extend only to eliminating the degree of overcrowding that causes these constitutional violations.

The Act provides for incarceration of illegal aliens; alternatives for the incarceration of juveniles; prison impact statements; drug testing of inmates; crime prevention initiatives; mandatory life sentences for a federal court conviction of a third serious, violent felony (the controversial "three strikes and you are out" provision); establishment of special "drug courts" for processing substance abusers accused of nonviolent drug offenses; and capital punishment for numerous federal crimes associated with murder or drug violations (but only if the offenders are eighteen or older when they commit the crimes).

Some mandatory sentences are relaxed. The age at which juveniles accused of violent crimes may be tried as adults is reduced from fifteen to thirteen. Grant money is available for state and local agencies to develop their own DNA testing capabilities. Several gun control measures are included. A Police Corps is established, providing $100 million over five years for college scholarships of up to $30,000 for students who agree to serve as law enforcement officers for four years upon graduation. Numerous provisions aimed at countering domestic violence as well as protecting all sexual abuse victims are provided as well.

The following Table of Contents for the Act includes the titles and subtitles of the Act, along with the section numbers for each. Space does not permit an analysis of these provisions, but it is clear that many of the provisions are controversial. Some will lead to extensive litigation, as they involve retrenchment of constitutional rights along with other problems.

Violent Crime Control and Law Enforcement Act of 1994: Table of Contents

Subtitle V—Prevention, Diagnosis, and Treatment of Tuberculosis in Correctional Institutions (Sec. 32201).

Subtitle X—Gang Resistance Education and Training (Sec. 32401).

Title IV. Violence Against Women

Subtitle A—Safe Streets for Women (Sec. 40101-40156, including Chapters 1-5 on the following topics, respectively: Federal Penalties for Sex Crimes; Law Enforcement and Prosecution Grants to Reduce Violent Crimes against Women; Safety for Women in Public Transit and Public Parks; New Evidentiary Rules; Assistance to Victims of Sexual Assault).

Subtitle B—Safe Homes for Women (Sec. 40201-40295).

Subtitle C—Civil Rights for Women (Sec. 40301-40304).

Subtitle D—Equal Justice for Women in the Court Act (Sec. 40401-40422).

Subtitle E—Violence against Women Act Improvements (Sec. 40501-40509).

Subtitle F—National Stalker and Domestic Violence Reduction (Sec. 40601-40611).

Subtitle G—Protections for Battered Immigrant Women and Children (Sec. 40701-40703).

Title V. Drug Courts (Sec. 50001-50002).

Title VI. Death Penalty (Sec. 60001-60026).

Title VII. Mandatory Life Imprisonment for Persons Convicted of Certain Felonies (Sec. 70001-70002).

Title VIII. Applicability of Mandatory Minimum Penalties in Certain Cases (Sec. 80001).

Title IX. Drug Control

Subtitle A—Enhanced Penalties and General Provisions (Sec. 90101-90107).

Subtitle B—National Narcotics Leadership Act Amendments (Sec. 90201-90208).

Title X. Drunk Driving Provisions (Sec. 100001-100003).

Title XI. Firearms

Subtitle A—Assault Weapons (Sec. 110101-110106).

Subtitle B—Youth Handgun Safety (Sec. 110201).

Subtitle C—Licensure (Sec. 110301-110307).

Subtitle D—Domestic Violence (Sec. 110401).

Subtitle E—Gun Crime Penalties (Sec. 110501-110519).

Title XII. Terrorism (Sec. 120001-120005).

Title XIII. Criminal Aleins and Immigration Enforcement (Sec. 130001-130010).

Title XIV. Youth Violence (Sec. 140001-140008).

Title XV. Criminal Street Gangs (Sec. 150001-150007).

Title XVI. Child Pornography (Sec. 160001-160003).

Title XVII. Crimes against Children

Subtitle A—Jacob Wetterling Crimes against Children and Sexually Violent Offender Registration Act (Sec. 170101).

Subtitle B—Assaults against Children (Sec. 170201).

Subtitle C—Missing and Exploited Children (Sec. 170301-170303).

Glossary

Abettor. A person who, with the requisite *mens rea*, encourages, promotes, instigates, or stands ready to assist the perpetrator of a crime.

Accessory after the fact. One who, knowing that a felony has been committed, receives, relieves, comforts, or assists the felon to hinder apprehension and conviction.

Accessory before the fact. One who incites or abets a crime but is not actually or constructively present when the crime is committed.

Accomplice. A person who participates in the guilt of a crime but not in the criminal act itself. Such a person assumes criminal liability in terms of his or her degree of participation in the criminal activity.

Actus reus. A criminal act that, if combined with other elements of a crime, may lead to the arrest, trial, and conviction of the accused.

Administrative law. The rules and regulations that come from agencies to which the government has given rule-making power.

Adultery. Consensual sexual intercourse of a married person with someone other than his or her spouse. Some statutes provide that consensual sexual intercourse constitutes adultery by both parties even if only one is married to someone else. Others limit the crime to the married party.

Adversary system. The Anglo-American system for settling disputes in court. It assumes the defendant is innocent until proved guilty. Prosecuting attorneys, representing the state, and defense attorneys, representing the defendant, try to convince a judge or jury of their version of the case.

Affirmative defense. The introduction of new factual allegations which, if true, constitute a defense to the charge (in a criminal case) or the complaint (in a civil case). See also *Defense.*

Aggravating circumstances. Circumstances that are above or beyond those required for the crime but that make the crime more serious. May be used with reference to many crimes, but the concept is critical particularly in capital punishment cases, where it is constitutionally required. See also *Mitigating circumstances.*

Aid and abet. The act of assisting or facilitating the commission of a crime.

A.L.I. rule. The American Law Institute's test of insanity, also called the *substantial capacity test*. It states that a person cannot be held accountable for a criminal act if he or she is unable to appreciate the wrongfulness of that act because of a mental disease or defect. See also *M'Naghten rule* and *Irresistible impulse test.*

Antitrust violations. Violations of state and federal statutes that protect trade and commerce from unlawful restraints, monopolies, price fixing, and price discriminations.

Arson. Any willful or malicious burning or attempt to burn, with or without intent to defraud, a dwelling house, public building, motor vehicle or aircraft, or personal property of another person.

Asportation.   The act of moving things from one place to another. It is a required element of common law larceny.

Assault.   The unlawful attempt or threat to inflict immediate harm or death. See also *Battery*.

Attempt.   A crime that may be defined as an act involving two basic elements: a step toward the commission of a crime and a specific intent to commit that crime.

Attendant circumstances.   This term means that a criminal act cannot be prosecuted as a crime even if the guilty mind is present unless the specified circumstances coexist with the act and guilty mind.

Automatism.   A defense for a defendant who has proof that he or she was unconscious or semiconscious when the crime was committed. Epilepsy, a concussion, or an emotional trauma may be used for this defense.

Bailee.   A person to whom goods are entrusted.

Battered person syndrome.   A defense used by a person who has killed another person who physically or psychologically abused him or her over a period of time. In some jurisdictions, it is not necessary that the battered person be in imminent danger of harm at the time of the killing to be eligible to use the defense. Some jurisdictions reject the defense.

Battery.   The actual unauthorized, harmful touching of another person. The term is used together or interchangeably with *assault*, though each term is different and can be used

without the other. The Model Penal Code defines *assault* to include both assault and battery. See also *Assault*.

Bigamy.   Knowingly and willingly contracting a second marriage when aware that another marriage is undissolved.

Bill of attainder.   An act by the legislature that condemns a person without a judicial trial. A bill of attainder is forbidden by the U.S. Constitution.

Blackmail.   See *Extortion*.

Breach of the peace.   A willfully committed act that disturbs the public tranquillity or order and for which there is no legal justification.

Bribery.   The offering, giving, receiving, or soliciting of anything of value to influence action by public officials.

Buffer.   The people who protect organized crime's criminal group from effective prosecution by corrupting judges, lawyers, politicians, law enforcement officials, gaming establishments, and other national and international businesses.

Burglary.   The unlawful entry of a structure to commit a felony or a theft.

Carjacking.   Auto theft by force or threat of force; a crime that has been increasing in frequency and in violence in recent years.

Case law.   Legally binding judicial interpretations of written laws and of previous court decisions.

Causation.   The idea that a cause-effect relationship must be established between an actor and a harmful consequence for a person to be held accountable for that action.

Child abuse.   The physical or psychological battering of a child by parents, other relatives, acquaintances, or strangers. Abuse may include child stealing or parental kidnapping where parents are divorced.

Circumstantial evidence.   Direct evidence such as eyewitness testimony of facts other than those on which proof is needed but from which deductions or inferences may be drawn concerning the facts in dispute.

Civil law.   In contrast to criminal law, civil law pertains to rules that are concerned with private or civil rights. The wronged person seeks compensation in court rather than criminal punishment through state prosecution.

Clemency.   Mercy, kindness, leniency; a term used to describe the actions of a governor or president when he or she commutes a sentence, for example, from death to life.

Common law.   Contrasted to written law, common law consists of legally binding rules derived from judicial decisions, customs, and traditions. Broadly defined, it refers to the legal system that began in England and was adopted in the United States.

Complicity.   A term used to describe people who participate in the guilt of a crime though not in the criminal act. See *Accomplice*.

Compounding a crime.   An agreement for consideration not to prosecute or inform on another who has committed a felony.

Computer crime.   Crimes committed by use of the computer. Computer criminals have developed programs that scramble or erase computer files and that aid in theft and embezzlement.

Condonation.   The forgiving of a criminal act by a victim. Usually condonation is not a defense, but in some cases a victim of a nonserious crime may negotiate a settlement with the defendant and the court may negate the criminal charge.

Confidence game.   A type of fraud in which a person tricks or swindles money or property from a victim who has confidence in the offender.

Conspiracy.   Broadly defined, conspiracy is an agreement to engage in an unlawful act or to engage in a lawful act by unlawful means. Some jurisdictions specify that the conspiracy must be to commit a *crime*, whereas others specify the type of crime.

Contempt.   The act by public officials or by any other person of willfully disobeying or disregarding a public official. A variety of behaviors may constitute contempt — such as acts that embarrass, hinder, show disrespect, or obstruct the court or legislative process. Civil contempt is an offense against another party; criminal contempt is an offense against the court.

Corporate crime.   A white-collar crime, such as a price-fixing violation, committed by a policy-making corporate executive to benefit the entire corporation. See *White-collar crime*.

Corpus delicti.   The words literally mean "the body of the crime" and refer to the substances that must be found to prove a crime has occurred.

Corroborating evidence.   Additional data to support a charge, especially in rape cases; required because of the lack of witnesses in such cases.

Counterfeiting.   To forge, copy, or imitate without authority and with the intent to defraud. The crime involves an offense against property as well as an obstruction of justice. The object of counterfeiting may be coins, paper money, or anything else of value (such as stamps).

Crime.   An act of omission or intention that violates criminal case or statutory law and is punishable by law.

Criminal facilitation.   Making it easier for another to commit a crime.

Criminal group.   An organized crime

family or gang, characterized by its continuity, structure, defined membership, criminality, violence, and power as its goal.

Criminal law. The statutes that define behavior considered to be a threat to the well-being of society. The accused must be prosecuted by the government.

Criminal protector. A person who conceals offenders after the crime has been committed or assists them in avoiding detection and prosecution.

Criminal solicitation. The asking, inciting, ordering, urgently requesting, or enticing of another person to commit a crime.

Criminal trespass. The entering or remaining unlawfully in or on the premises of another (including land, boats, or other vehicles) under certain circumstances as specified by statute.

Cruel and unusual punishment. Any punishment that has been prohibited by the Eighth Amendment of the U.S. Constitution. Examples are torture, excessively long sentences, and the death penalty for rape without homicide.

Culpability. Being guilty or at fault. There are four criteria that may be used to determine guilt: recklessness, negligence, knowledge, and intention. Different crimes may require different kinds of culpability to prove guilt.

Date rape. A term that describes forced sexual intercourse occurring during a social occasion. The alleged victim may have agreed to some intimacy but not to any of the activities defined in that jurisdiction as providing the elements of rape.

Deadly force. Force intended to inflict great bodily harm or death. It is allowed for self-defense to repel kidnapping, forced sexual intercourse,

threat of death, or threat of serious bodily harm.

Defendant. The person charged with a crime and against whom a criminal proceeding has begun or is pending.

Defense. A response by the defendant in a criminal or civil case. It may consist only of a denial of the factual allegations of the prosecution (in a criminal case) or of the plaintiff (in a civil case). A defense that offers new factual allegations in an effort to negate the charges is an *affirmative defense*.

Defense attorney. The attorney for the defendant in a criminal proceeding, whose main function is to protect the defendant's legal rights.

Determinate sentence. See *Sentence*.

Deterrence. A punishment philosophy that assumes that behavior may be controlled and criminal behavior prevented by discouraging it with punishment of offenders. *General deterrence* strives to discourage criminality by other people by intimidating them with the punishment of an offender. *Specific deterrence* prevents additional crimes by an offender by punishing that offender.

Discretion. Decisions based on one's judgment rather than legal rules. In the criminal justice system it can result in inconsistency but also in actions suitable for individual circumstances.

Disorderly conduct. Minor offenses, such as drunkenness or fighting, that disturb the peace or behavior standards of a community or shock the morality of its population.

Due process. Constitutional principle that a person's life, liberty, or property cannot be deprived without lawful procedures in any criminal action. The courts interpret what due process requires in specific fact patterns.

Duress. In criminal law, a condition in

which an individual is coerced or induced by the wrongful act of another to commit a criminal act. May be used as a defense.

Durham rule.   A test of insanity (also known as the product rule) that states that "an accused is not criminally responsible if his unlawful act was the product of mental disease or mental defect."

Elements of a crime.   All aspects of a criminal act that must be proved beyond a reasonable doubt by the prosecution to substantiate a conviction. This includes the concurrence of an act and a criminal state of mind that produces a harmful result. It may include attendant circumstances, too.

Embezzlement.   Misappropriation or misapplication of money or property entrusted to one's care, custody, or control.

Embracery.   A common law misdemeanor meaning a corrupt attempt to influence a juror by means of promises, money, or other persuasions. Today many jurisdictions include this offense under a separate title such as *corrupt influencing of jurors* or include it within the crime of *obstructing justice*.

Enterprise liability.   Also called *corporate liability*. The theory that under some circumstances corporate officials may be held criminally responsible for the acts of the company's employees.

Entrapment.   A defense that proves a defendant was induced by a government agent to commit a crime that the defendant would not have been inclined to commit without inducement.

Equal protection.   The constitutional principle guaranteeing that the U.S. legal system shall not deny to any person or class of persons the same treatment as other persons or classes of persons in the same or similar situations. Of particular significance are the circumstances of race, ethnicity, religion, and gender.

Escape.   As a crime, the term describes the act of eluding the police or prison authorities whether already under custody or being sought when not previously under custody.

Euthanasia.   A term applied to people who kill someone else, often at that person's request, because of the victim's terminal illness, considerable pain, or debilitating handicap.

Expert testimony.   Opinion evidence given at a trial by a person who possesses technical knowledge or skill relevant to the case and not possessed by the average person.

Ex post facto law.   A law that provides punishment for an act that was not defined as a crime when the act was committed or that increases the penalty for a crime committed prior to the enactment of the statute.

Extortion.   Obtaining property from another by wrongful use of actual or threatened force, fear, or violence, or the corrupt taking of a fee by a public officer, under color of his or her office, when that fee is not due.

False imprisonment.   Under the Model Penal Code, refers to the unlawful and knowing restraint of a person against his or her wishes so as to deny freedom. See also *Kidnapping*.

False pretense.   Representation of some fact or circumstance that is not true and that is meant to mislead the other party.

False swearing.   Untrue statements willfully and knowingly made under oath or equivalent affirmation inside or outside a judicial proceeding. See also *Perjury*.

Felony.   A serious offense such as murder, armed robbery, or rape. Punishments for felonies range from one year's imprisonment to death.

Felony murder. An unlawful killing of a person that occurs while attempting to commit or while committing another felony, such as robbery, rape, or arson.

Fence. The person who receives stolen property from the thief and in turn disposes of it in a profitable manner.

Fighting words. Words that tend to incite violence from the person to whom they are directed. They are more like a slap on the face than a communication of ideas. They are not protected by the First Amendment.

Fine. A sentence that requires the defendant to pay a financial penalty to the state or federal government.

Fleeing felon. A person trying to avoid arrest after committing a felony.

Forcible entry and detainer. The act of forcibly entering another person's property or, on being there peacefully, using force to remain. This act was a common law offense; in many jurisdictions today it is a statutory offense.

Forgery. Making, altering, uttering, or possessing with intent to defraud anything false in the semblance of that which is true.

Fornication. Unlawful sexual intercourse between two unmarried persons.

Fraud. Fraudulent conversion and obtaining of money or property by false pretense.

General deterrence. See *Deterrence*.

Good-time credits. The reduction of a prison term because of an inmate's good behavior during incarceration.

Habeas corpus. Literally "you have the body." A writ filed by an inmate who claims that he or she is being illegally held; a written court order requiring that the person who filed the writ be brought to court to determine the legality of custody and confinement.

Hate crime. Defined in the federal criminal code as crimes "that manifest evidence of prejudice based on race, religion, sexual orientation, or ethnicity, including where appropriate the crimes of murder; non-negligent manslaughter; forcible rape; aggravated assault; simple assault; intimidation; arson; and destruction, damage or vandalism of property."

Hearsay evidence. Evidence offered by testifying witnesses who are referring not to what they have heard, seen, felt, or otherwise experienced, but to what someone else has told them.

Home-invasion robbery. Robbery that occurs when a person enters a dwelling with the purpose of committing a robbery and engages in a robbery of the occupant.

Homicide. An inclusive term that refers to all cases in which human beings by their own acts, omissions, or procurement kill other human beings. Homicide may be *criminal* (murder, manslaughter, or negligent homicide) or *noncriminal* (committed with justification or excuse).

House arrest. A sentence that restricts the offender to his or her home or limits times the offender may leave the home. Some house arrests are monitored electronically.

Incapacitation. A theory of punishment and a goal of sentencing, generally implemented by incarcerating offenders to prevent them from committing any other crimes.

Incest. The act of knowingly marrying, cohabiting as though being married, or having intercourse with a family member. Family includes children, siblings, and parents of blood relation or adoption as well as uncles, aunts, nephews, or nieces of whole-blood relation.

Inchoate crimes.   Crimes that are imperfect or uncompleted and that usually lead to another crime. For example, an attempt to commit rape may lead to rape, but even if it does not, the attempt is a crime.

Inciter.   A person who, though not present when a crime is committed, with *mens rea* encourages or assists another to commit a crime.

Indeterminate sentence.   See *Sentence*.

Infanticide.   Killing an infant soon after its birth.

Infiltrated.   Permeated or moved into.

Inquisitorial system.   A system in which the accused is presumed guilty and must prove his or her innocence.

Insanity.   A state of mind that negates a defendant's responsibility for his or her actions.

Insider information.   Information known to securities officers before it is available to the public. See *Insider trading*.

Insider trading.   The act of trading in the securities market when the trader has information not yet made available to the investing public. See *Insider information*.

Intensive probation supervision (IPS).   Close supervision of probationers by probation officers who have smaller than average case loads.

Intent.   State of mind referring to the willful commission or omission of a criminal act. See also *Mens rea*.

Involuntary manslaughter.   See *Manslaughter*.

Involuntary intoxication.   Intoxication without choice or will, such as that which occurs when someone slips drugs into the food or drink of an unsuspecting person.

Irresistible impulse test.   A test for insanity stating that an accused cannot be found guilty for a criminal act if he or she is unable to control the actions leading to a crime even though the accused may have known the act was wrong. See also *A.L.I. rule*, *M'Naghten rule*.

Jurisdiction.   The lawful exercise of authority, and the geographic area in which authority may be exercised. For instance, city police must operate within the city limits. Courts may hear only cases for which they have jurisdiction (such as civil or criminal cases; misdemeanor or felony cases).

Just deserts.   The philosophy that offenders should receive the punishment they deserve in light of the crimes they committed. See also *retribution*.

Kidnapping.   Restricting the freedom of a victim against his or her will and removing the victim from one place to another. It is false imprisonment with aggravating circumstances, such as ransom, torture, extortion, prostitution, or pornography.

La Cosa Nostra.   Literally "our thing." Reportedly LCN is the name for a syndicate that has replaced the Mafia. See also *Mafia*.

Larceny by trick.   Deceptively obtaining possession of goods from a victim who surrenders possession voluntarily and without knowledge of the deceit involved.

Larceny-theft.   The unlawful taking, carrying, leading, or riding away of property from the possession of another with the intent to steal. Larceny may be categorized as *petit* or *grand*, depending on the value of the stolen property.

Lesser included offenses.   A crime less

serious than the one with which a defendant is being charged. It does not require a separate charge for a guilty verdict because it is implied by the more serious crime.

Libel.   Written communication that tends to harm an individual personally, professionally, or politically. Most libel cases are torts, but some are defined as criminal. Criminal libel requires the malicious publication of durable defamation.

Mafia.   A secret organization with a strict hierarchical structure that allegedly is involved in smuggling, drug trafficking, racketeering, and other illegal activities throughout the world. The influence of the Mafia may be found in legitimate as well as illegitimate business. See also *La Cosa Nostra*.

Mala in se.   Acts such as rape, murder, or robbery that are considered to be inherently wrong.

Mala prohibita.   Acts such as carrying a concealed weapon that are wrong because they are prohibited by law. They are not universally considered criminal.

Malice aforethought.   A requirement to prove one guilty of murder. This element of murder requires that the act be predetermined and intentional without legal justification or excuse. See also *Premeditation*.

Malicious mischief.   The malicious destruction or infliction of damage to the property of another.

Manslaughter.   An unlawful killing without malice. It can be voluntary or involuntary. *Voluntary manslaughter* is a killing that would be murder except that it was committed in the heat of passion for which there is reasonable explanation or excuse. *Involuntary manslaughter* is a criminal homicide that is committed reck-

lessly but unintentionally, as when one is under the influence of alcohol or drugs.

Marital rape.   Forced intercourse of a spouse; not recognized as a crime in all jurisdictions.

Mayhem.   A common law offense sometimes included within the crime of assault and battery. It refers to permanent injury inflicted on a victim with the intent to injure. It may disable or disfigure.

Mens rea.   The guilty intent or evil mind required for criminal liability.

Misdemeanor.   A crime that is less serious than a felony and that is punishable by a fine, probation, or short confinement in a jail.

Misprision of felony.   The act of concealing a felony committed by another but without any involvement in that felony that would constitute an accessory before or after the fact.

Misprision of treason.   The concealment from proper officials of the known treason of another but without sufficient involvement to constitute the elements of a principal in the crime.

Mistake.   A defense stating that a defendant would not have committed a criminal act if he or she had had accurate knowledge of the law or the facts.

Mistrial.   A trial declared invalid for a variety of reasons, such as the inability of a jury to reach a verdict or the death of a juror or counsel.

Mitigating circumstances.   Circumstances that do not justify or excuse a crime but that, because of justice and fairness, make the crime less reprehensible. May be used to reduce a crime to a lesser offense, such as to reduce murder to manslaughter. Mitigating circumstances must be considered before the death penalty is imposed. See also *Aggravating circumstances*.

M'Naghten rule.   Also known as the right-versus-wrong test of insanity, the M'Naghten rule states that an accused cannot be considered guilty of a criminal act if, as a result of a defect of reason caused by disease of the mind, he or she did not *know* the nature and quality of the act or did not know that the act was wrong.

Model Penal Code.   The American Law Institute's systemized statement of criminal law. It is suggested as a model for revision of criminal laws.

Money laundering.   Hiding the existence, illegal use of, or illegal source of income and making that income appear legal by disguising it.

Motive.   The reason for a defendant's actions.

Murder.   An unlawful homicide. In most cases, the element of malice aforethought is required.

Necessity.   Condition in which an act, though criminal in other circumstances, may not be considered criminal because of the compelling force of the circumstances.

Negligence.   A term that refers to acts a normal person would not do or would not fail to do under similar circumstances. It does not require a criminal intent.

Negligent homicide.   A criminal killing that is the result of extreme carelessness.

Norms.   A social group's standards for appropriate behavior.

Obscenity.   Written or visual material that is unprotected by the First Amendment because of its offensive, clear description or depiction of sexual acts; because of its lack of any political, literary, scientific, or artistic value; and because of its tendency to arouse improper sexual reactions in the average person.

Obstruction of justice.   Interference with the orderly processes of civil and criminal courts, such as refusing to produce evidence, intimidating witnesses, and bribing judges. The crime may be committed by judicial and other officials and might constitute official misconduct in office.

Official misconduct in office.   Any willful, unlawful behavior by public officials in the course of their official duties. The misconduct may be a failure to act, a wrongful act, or an improperly performed act that the official has a right to do.

Organized crime.   The highly structured, disciplined, and self-perpetuating associations of people who bind together to make large profits through illegal and legal means while utilizing graft and corruption in the criminal justice arena to protect their activities from criminal prosecution.

Pardon.   The power of a governor or president to exempt the offender from punishment or from further punishment.

Parole.   Release under supervision after part of a prison sentence has been served.

Perjury.   False statements made willfully and knowingly under oath in a judicial proceeding. *Subornation of perjury* is the offense of procuring someone to commit perjury. See also *False swearing*.

Perpetrator.   A person who commits criminal acts with the requisite *mens rea* or who is responsible directly for the crime.

Pinkerton rule.   A co-conspirator may be held accountable for the acts of fellow conspirators even though the requirements of liability for the acts of accomplices are not met.

Plaintiff. In a civil suit, the person who brings the complaint against the defendant; the person claiming harm by the defendant.

Plea bargaining. The process of negotiation between the defense and the prosecution before the trial of a defendant. The process may involve reducing or dropping of some charges or a recommendation for leniency in exchange for a plea of guilty on another charge or charges.

Posttraumatic stress disorder (PTSD). Stress experienced by people returning from war who have such severe nightmares or guilt that they lose their orientation and kill someone, thinking they are back in war. It is argued that victims of this disorder should not be held accountable for their criminal acts because they cannot control their behavior.

Premeditation. A term that may be used synonymously with malice aforethought. It means planning, deliberating, designing, or thinking out in advance an intention to kill another person. See also *Malice aforethought*.

Premenstrual syndrome (PMS). The physiological changes that occur in a woman before menstruation. Examples of symptoms are depression, irritability, and temporary psychosis.

Presumption. An assumption of a fact based on other facts.

Presumptive sentencing. The legislature specifies the normal sentence for each crime, and judges are permitted to deviate only under specified types of circumstances or by giving written reasons or both.

Principal. Under common law, this term described the person who committed the crime, in contrast to the accessory, who assisted in the crime or who encouraged another to commit a crime. Most modern statutes do not make this distinction. Both are treated as principals, and accessories may be convicted even if the principal has not been convicted.

Principal in the first degree. The one who perpetrates the crime either through his or her own acts or by the use of inanimate objects or innocent people.

Principal in the second degree. The one who incites or abets the commission of the crime and is present actually or constructively.

Probation. A sentence that permits the offender to remain in the community, usually under minimum supervision for a specified period of time under specified circumstances.

Procedural law. Law that provides the legal methods and procedures by which substantive law may be enforced.

Prosecutor or prosecuting attorney. A government official whose duty is to initiate and maintain criminal proceedings on behalf of the government against persons accused of committing crimes.

Prostitution. Indiscriminate sexual intercourse for hire. Some statutes specify women as the offenders, but others include men or use a neutral term such as gender. The criminal offense may include not only the prostitute but any persons who solicit or promote the business of prostitution, or who live off of the prostitute's earnings.

Proximate cause. In criminal law, the legal or closest cause of the harm (the act nearest in the order of causation). It must be identified in establishing the guilt of a defendant.

Racketeering. The process of engaging

in a racket such as extortion or conspiracy to obtain an illegal goal by means of threats.

Rape.   Historically, defined as unlawful vaginal intercourse with a woman not the offender's wife; called *forcible rape* if obtained against the will of the woman by the use of threats of force or force; called *statutory rape* if the act were consensual between a man and a woman under the age of consent. More recently, some rape statutes have been rewritten to include male victims, as well as penetration of any body opening (or specified body openings, such as the anus or the vagina) by a foreign object, including but not limited to the male penis. See also *Marital rape*.

Rape shield statutes.   Laws that protect the alleged rape victim from questioning in depositions and in court about evidence of past sexual experiences that are not relevant to the case and that might be prejudicial.

Rape trauma syndrome.   Stress that occurs after forced sex. The symptoms may be as severe as those described in PTSD, which is not limited to war experiences. The syndrome is recognized as a defense in an increasing number of jurisdictions.

Recidivism.   Repeated commission of crimes; the act of a released inmate relapsing to previous behavior or ways.

Rehabilitation.   Punishment philosophy that attempts to reform the offender through education, work, and other appropriate treatment modalities.

Restitution.   Punishment that requires the offender to repay the victim with services or money. This punishment may be instead of or in addition to other punishment, such as fines.

Retribution.   See *Just deserts*.

Revenge.   A reason for punishment.

Today public retaliation through the criminal justice system has replaced the private revenge of earlier days, which tended to get out of control.

RICO.   The Racketeer Influenced Corrupt Organization Act, which Congress passed in 1970 to combat organized crime.

Riot.   See *Unlawful assembly*.

Robbery.   The taking or attempting to take anything of value from the care, custody, or control of a person or persons by force or threat of force or violence or by putting the victim in fear.

Rout.   See *Unlawful assembly*.

Securities.   Stocks, bonds, notes, and other documents that are representative of a share in a company or a debt of a company.

Sedition.   A communication or agreement aimed at stirring up treason or at defaming the government.

Seduction.   The act by a man who uses solicitation, persuasion, promises, bribes, or other methods to entice a woman to have unlawful sexual intercourse with him. Most seduction laws have been repealed, but those that remain generally categorize the crime as a misdemeanor.

Sentence.   The judgment pronounced by the court (trial judge) and imposed upon a defendant who pleads guilty or who is found guilty after a trial. A *determinate sentence* is one in which the legislature has set the type and length of sentence for each crime, leaving the judge little or no discretion. An *indeterminate sentence* leaves the sentence decision up to judges or sets a minimum and maximum term and permits the judge to set the exact sentence in each case.

Sentence disparity.   Inequalities that result when offenders who have committed identical or similar crimes under identical or similar situations receive significantly different sentences.

Sentencing guidelines. Guidelines established by legislatures, judges, or others to be followed by judges in assessing sentences. Some divergence is allowed but usually must be accompanied by a statement of reasons.

Sexual abuse. Sexual mistreatment, which includes child pornography and sexual molestation of children as well as physical sexual abuse of adults.

Social control. Informal ways of regulating small groups and primitive societies without the use of criminal laws.

Sodomy. Generally interpreted as an act involving anal or oral sex with another person of the same or opposite sex or with an animal.

Solicitation. See *Criminal solicitation*.

Specific deterrence. See *Deterrence*.

Statutory law. Law that originates with the legislature in a written enactment. See also *Case law* and *Common law*.

Statutory rape. See *Rape*.

Strict liability. A legal concept that holds defendants responsible for wrongful acts even when they are not guilty of negligence, fault, or bad faith. This concept is used often in tort law to hold an employer liable for the acts of employees.

Subornation of perjury. See *Perjury*.

Substantial capacity test. See *A.L.I. rule*.

Substantive law. Law that defines crimes and their punishments. See also *Procedural law*.

Syndicate. A group of individuals who bind together to carry out some business purpose, which may be legitimate or illegitimate.

Terrorism. Violent acts or the use of the threat of violence to create fear, alarm, dread, or coercion, usually against governments.

Tort. A noncriminal (civil) injury for which one can be sued for damages. Examples include trespassing, slander and libel, automobile accidents, and medical malpractice. Some acts, such as assault and battery, may be crimes as well as torts.

Treason. An attempt to overthrow the government of which one is a member or a betrayal of that government to a foreign power. It was thought to be such a serious offense that it was included within the U.S. Constitution, the only crime specified in that document.

Urban psychosis. A form of post traumatic stress syndrome proposed by some attorneys as a defense to crime; refers to the violent environment (including rap songs and other negative comments about police and others) in which some offenders are reared.

Under color of law. A term referring to a public official's official duties. For a person to be convicted of official misconduct, the person must be a public official or one acting in that capacity. The misconduct must occur during the course of that person's official duties.

Unlawful assembly. The meeting of three or more persons to disturb the public peace with the intention of participating in a forcible and violent execution of an unlawful enterprise or of a lawful enterprise in an unauthorized manner. To constitute unlawful assembly, the group does not have to carry out its purpose; but if it takes steps to carry out the plan, it commits a *rout*. If it carries out the plan, it commits a *riot*.

Vagrancy. Under common law, the term referred to those who wandered about from place to place without any visible means of support, refusing to work even though able to do so, and living off the charity of others. Many statutory vagrancy laws have been declared unconstitutional because of their vagueness and tendency to discriminate against minorities.

Vicarious liability. A term referring to one who is assessed blame for the actions of another person, usually one under his or her supervision. An owner of a bar might be sued because a bartender sold liquor to a minor who caused a serious car accident while drunk as the result of that illegal sale of liquor.

Voluntary intoxication. Intoxication brought on by the free will of the individual. See *Involuntary intoxication*.

Voluntary manslaughter. See *Manslaughter*.

Wharton rule. A rule stating that two people engaging in crimes such as adultery, bigamy, and incest or any other act that requires more than one person for its commission may not be prosecuted for conspiracy to commit those crimes. A third party must be involved for a conspiracy to exist. The Model Penal Code rejects this rule.

White-collar crime. A broad term that includes both the crimes of individuals who act against their company for personal benefit as well as the *corporate crimes* of executives who commit illegal acts to benefit the company.

Case Index

Name Index

Subject Index